# THE ROUGH GUIDE TO
# NORWAY

ROUGH
GUIDES

written and researched by
**Phil Lee**

# Contents

# Introduction to
# Norway

With its rearing mountains and deep, blue-black fjords, Norway remains a wilderness outpost in a tamed and crowded continent. Everything here is on the grand scale with the country boasting some of Europe's harshest and most beautiful land- and seascapes, whose vastness is merely pinpricked by a clutch of likeable cities. From the Skagerrak – the choppy channel that separates the country from Denmark – Norway stretches north in a long and slender band, its wild coastline battered and buffeted by the Atlantic as it rolls up into the Arctic. Behind this rough coast are spectacular mountain ranges, harsh upland plateaux, rippling glaciers, thick forests and mighty fjords of surpassing beauty – an exhilarating landscape begging to be explored by car, boat or bike, on skis or even husky-drawn sled. For many visitors, the sheer size of Norway comes as a real surprise and for many more, with the exception of Oslo, Bergen and the famous fjords, the rest of the country might as well be a blank on the map. Yet it's out of the cities and off the major roads that you'll experience Norway at its most magical: great stretches of serene, postcard-perfect vistas where it is at times possible to travel for hours without spying a single soul.

Perhaps inevitably, the fjords are the apple of the tourist industry's eye – with the infrastructure to prove it – though when well-heeled English and German gentlemen travellers arrived here in the late nineteenth century on the hunt for the Scandinavian exotic, Norwegians were so poor that you could hire a gillie or two for next to nothing. It is this stark contrast – between a severely impoverished past and an astoundingly wealthy present – that, for locals at least, remains a salient characteristic of life up here. Since the country happened upon vast oil and gas reserves under the Norwegian Sea in the 1960s, Norway has managed to assemble one of the most civilized, educated and tolerant societies in the world – one that its population maintains a deep loyalty for and pride in.

**ABOVE** BERGEN **RIGHT** KAYAKING IN THE LOFOTEN ISLANDS

Norway may have a scattering of attractive, cosmopolitan cities, appealing destinations in their own right, but where the country really shines is not in its urban culture, but rather in the low-key, amiable small-town feel that pervades throughout its settlements. This is not to say that Norway suffers from provincialism – Munch, Ibsen, Grieg and Amundsen, to name but four, were all Norwegians of international importance, to say nothing of the many millions of Norwegian descent today successfully making their way somewhere off in the greater world. But one thing is for certain: every Norwegian you ever meet will at some point make their way back to this remarkable country, put on a pair of old hiking shoes and head off on foot for yonder mountain, reminding themselves how lucky they are to have one of the world's most ravishing landscapes right at their back door.

# Where to go

Though for the most part its people live in small towns and villages, Norway's five largest cities are the obvious – and the most popular – initial targets for a visit. They begin with urbane, vivacious **Oslo**, one of the world's most prettily sited capitals, with a flourishing café scene and a clutch of outstanding museums. Beyond Oslo, in roughly descending order of interest, are **Trondheim**, with its superb cathedral and charming, antique centre; the beguiling port of **Bergen**, gateway to the western fjords; gritty, bustling **Stavanger** in the southwest; and northern **Tromsø**. All are likeable, walkable cities worthy of time in themselves, as well as being within comfortable reach of some startlingly handsome scenery. Indeed, each can serve as a starting point for further explorations or as a weekend

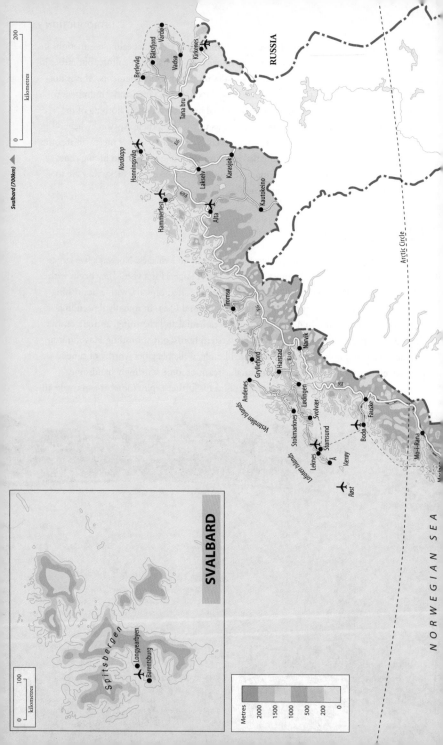

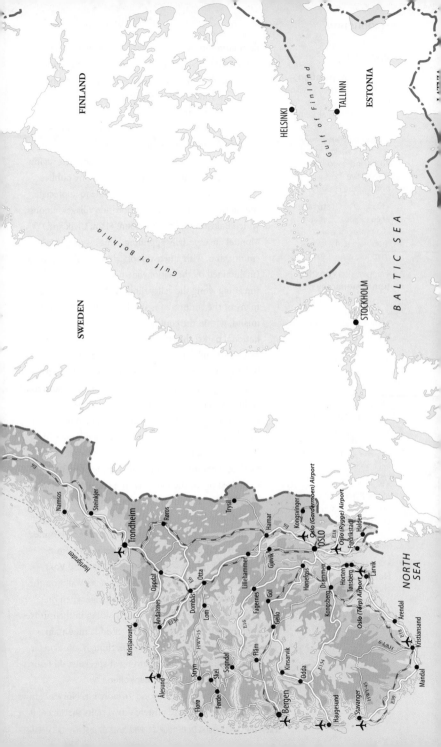

## FACT FILE

• Norway's **population** numbers just over 5 million, of whom 700,000 or so live in Oslo, the capital. Bergen, Norway's second city, clocks up about 265,000 residents, while around 40,000 indigenous Sámi (Lapps) live mostly in the north of the country.

• Norway has a **surface area** of 386,000 square kilometres, of which half is mountain and a further third forest, lake and river.

• Norway is a **constitutional monarchy** and the present king, Harald V, came to the throne in 1991. The parliament – the Storting – sits in Oslo, but many functions are devolved to a complex network of local authorities.

• Forget the seafood – **frozen pizza** can lay claim to being Norway's national dish: Norwegians eat over 20 million of them each year.

• Norway is not a member of the **EU**, but has signed up to the EEA (European Economic Agreement) free-trade deal and the Schengen Agreement.

• The Lutheran **Church of Norway** is the official state church and over eighty percent of the population belong to it, however nominally. Lutheran jokes are legion: one shipwrecked sailor to another "Don't worry: I make 50,000kr a week and I tithe; my Lutheran pastor will find us."

destination in their own right. And wherever you arrive, the trains, buses and ferries of Norway's finely tuned public transport system will take you almost anywhere you want to go – although services are curtailed in winter.

Outside of the cities, the perennial draw remains the **western fjords** – a must, and every bit as scenically stunning as the publicity suggests. Dip into the region from Bergen or **Ålesund**, both accessible by public transport from Oslo, or take more time to appreciate the subtle charms of the tiny, fjordside villages, among which **Balestrand**, **Lofthus**, **Loen**, **Flåm**, **Ulvik** and **Mundal** are especially appealing. This is great hiking country too, with a network of cairned trails and lodges (maintained by the nationwide hiking association DNT) threading along the valleys and over the hills. However, many of the country's finest hikes are to be had further inland, within the confines of a trio of marvellous **national parks**: the **Hardangervidda**, a vast mountain plateau of lunar-like appearance; the **Rondane**, with its bulging mountains; and the **Jotunheimen**, famous for its jagged peaks. Nudging the Skagerrak, the **south coast** is different again. The climate is more hospitable, the landscape gentler and the coast is sprinkled with hundreds of little islands. Every summer, holidaying Norwegians sail down here to explore every nautical nook and cranny, popping into a string of pretty, pint-sized ports, the most inviting being **Arendal** and **Mandal**, the latter the proud possessor of the country's finest sandy beach.

Hiking remains the most popular summer pastime in Norway, but there are alternatives galore, from whitewater rafting – for example at **Sjoa** and **Voss** – sea-kayaking at **Flåm**, and guided glacier walks on the **Jostedalsbreen**. In winter, it's all change when the Norwegians take to cross-country skiing in their droves, shooting off across the Hardangervidda mountain plateau, for example, from **Finse**, though some prefer Alpine skiing and snowboarding at specialist ski resorts like **Geilo** and Oslo's **Holmenkollen**.

Away to the **north**, beyond Trondheim, Norway grows increasingly wild and austere – two traits that make it

## NEW NORWEGIAN CUISINE

Upon tasting a piece of Norwegian flatbread, a Parisian woman in the mid-1800s described it as having "the shape and size of a plate, and the same consistency". With images of dried mutton, potato dumplings, cabbage stew and *lutefisk*, Nordic food has rarely been anything to write home about. That all changed in 2010, when Copenhagen's *Noma* was named the world's top restaurant by a panel of eight hundred chefs and critics, sending the gastronomic world into shock and turning tastebuds towards Scandinavian kitchens.

Even before this time, though, Norway had begun to reinvent its culinary identity, with new foodie movements, celebrity chefs and a series of government initiatives aimed at supporting **local food producers**, preserving farming traditions and championing the rich heritage of Norwegian ingredients. The country is now in the middle of a kitchen renaissance, returning to its long-standing local food traditions; once again, Norwegians are consulting their grandmothers' recipe books.

Given nearly 25,000 kilometres of rugged coastline, 150,000 lakes and some of the world's best angling rivers, it is no surprise that a huge variety of locally caught **fish and seafood** predominate in Norwegian kitchens. Norway's diverse landscape also provides habitat to a range of sheep, elk, reindeer and woodland fowl that graze on some of the greenest, most unpolluted grasses in the world, lending their **meat** a rich, succulent taste. And the country's temperate summers allow plants to ripen at a slower pace than elsewhere, infusing **fruits and vegetables** with a flavour that you can taste the instant they hit your tastebuds – with the yellow cloudberry being a prime example.

perfect for off-the-beaten-track adventurers – as it humps and lumps across the Arctic Circle on the way to the modern, workaday port of **Bodø**. From here, ferries shuttle over to the rugged **Lofoten islands**, which hold some of the most ravishing scenery in the whole of Europe – tiny fishing villages of ochre- and red-painted houses tucked in between the swell of the deep blue sea and the severest of grey-green mountains. Back on the mainland, it's a long haul north from Bodø to the iron-ore town of **Narvik**, and on to **Tromsø**, a delightful little city huddled on an island and with plenty of Arctic charm. These towns are, however, merely the froth of a vast wilderness that extends up to **Nordkapp** (North Cape), one of the northernmost points of mainland Europe, and the spot where the principal tourist trail peters out. Yet Norway continues east for several

**OPPOSITE FROM TOP** LINDESNES FYR; ISFJORD, SVALBARD

hundred kilometres, round to remote **Kirkenes** near the Russian border, while inland stretches an immense and hostile upland plateau, the **Finnmarksvidda**, one of the last haunts of the Sámi reindeer-herders. And finally, a short flight away, there is the wondrous chill of **Svalbard**, rising remote in the Arctic seas, islands of rolling glaciers and ice-glazed mountains where the snowmobile or Zodiac is more useful than a car.

# When to go

In the popular imagination, Norway is commonly regarded as remote and cold – spectacular but climatically inhospitable. There is some truth in this, of course, but when to visit is not, perhaps, as clear-cut a choice as you might imagine with other seasons other than summer offering particular bonuses. There are, for example, advantages to travelling during the long, dark **winters** with their reduced everything: daylight, opening times and transport services. If you are equipped and hardy enough to reach the north, seeing the phenomenal **northern lights** (aurora borealis) is a distinct possibility and later, once the days begin to lighten, the **skiing** – and for that matter the dog-sledding, ice-fishing and snowmobiling – is excellent. There are skiing packages to Norway from abroad, but perhaps more appealing – and certainly less expensive – is the ease with which you can arrange a few days' skiing wherever you happen to be. As the year advances, **Easter** is the time of the colourful Sámi festivals, and **mid-May** can be absolutely delightful if your visit coincides with the brief Norwegian **spring**, though this is difficult to gauge. Springtime is particularly beguiling in the fjords, with a thousand cascading waterfalls fed by the melting snow, and wild flowers in abundance everywhere. **Autumn** can be exquisite too, with **September** often bathed in the soft sunshine of an Indian summer, but – especially in the far north – it is frequently cold, often bitterly so, from late September to mid- to late May. Nevertheless, most people travel during the **summer** season, when bus, ferry and train connections are at their most frequent. This is the time of the **midnight sun**: the further north you go, the longer the day becomes, until at Nordkapp the sun is continually visible from mid-May to the end of July (see box below). Something worth noting, however, is that the summer season in Norway is relatively short, stretching roughly from the beginning of June to the end of August. Come in September and you'll find that many tourist offices, museums and other sights have cut back their hours and buses, ferries and trains have already switched to reduced schedules.

## THE MIDNIGHT SUN

The **midnight sun** is visible at the following places on the following dates, though climbing the nearest hill can – trees and clouds permitting – extend this by a day or two either way:
**Bodø** June 2 to July 10
**Hammerfest** May 14 to July 28
**Longyearbyen** April 19 to Aug 23
**Nordkapp** May 12 to July 29
**Tromsø** May 20 to July 21

# Author picks

Our author and his accomplices have combed Norway to prepare this new edition. Here are some of their personal favourites:

**Mountain roads** Not for the faint-hearted, or for the poor-of-steering, Norway's mountain roads boast some of the most imposing scenery imaginable – the Sognefjellsveg (p.237) and the Trollstigen (p.252) are two of the best.

**Stave churches** If there is one architectural symbol of Norway that stands out, it's the stave church: ornate and delicate outside; dark, pine-scented and mysterious within. Borgund is the most elegiac (p.174), Urnes (p.236) the wildest and Eidsborg the most idiosyncratic (p.181).

**Historic hotels** Finding a lovely country hotel in Norway is rarely difficult, but three of the best are the expansive *Hotel Alexandra* in Loen (p.244), the antique and remote *Hotel Union* in Øye (p.246) and the stylish, fin-de-siècle *Edvardas Hus* on Tranøy (p.299).

**Great hikes** Norway offers the adventurous hiker some wonderful experiences: the trek up from Lofthus to the lunar-like Hardangervidda plateau (p.215), the jaunt along the Besseggen ridge in the Jotunheimen Nasjonalpark (p.165) and the remote, fjord-and-mountain hike from Vindstad to Bunes (p.330) are three such favourites.

**Prettiest villages** Not all of Norway's villages match the beauty of their setting but tiny Mundal (p.233), with its pocket of fjordside houses, Ulvik (p.218), set 'twixt fjord and mountain, and quainter than quaint Å i Lofoten (p.331), certainly do.

**Skiing** Blanketed in snow for several months a year, skiing in Norway – be it downhill, cross-country or Telemark – is more a way of life than a sport. Join in, whether it's on the outskirts of Oslo (p.93), in small-town Lillehammer (p.155), or even up the Lofoten coast setting off from Kabelvåg (p.322).

> Our author recommendations don't end here. We've flagged up our favourite places – a perfectly sited hotel, an atmospheric café, a special restaurant – throughout the Guide, highlighted with the ★ symbol.

**FROM TOP** THE TROLLSTIGEN; BORGUND STAVE CHURCH; CROSS-COUNTRY SKIING

# 24

# things not to miss

It's not possible to see everything Norway has to offer in one trip – and we don't suggest you try. What follows is a selective take on the country's highlights, including outstanding scenery, picturesque fjordland villages and thrilling wildlife safaris. All highlights are colour-coded by chapter and have a page reference to take you straight into the Guide, where you can find out more.

1

### 1 GEIRANGERFJORD
Page 246

Shadowed by rearing mountains, the S-shaped Geirangerfjord is one of Norway's most stunningly beautiful fjords.

### 2 CROSS-COUNTRY SKIING
Page 44

Norway's meadows, moors and mountains boast thousands of kilometres of powdered runs just waiting for adventuresome skiers. You might choose to start at Lillehammer (see p.155).

### 3 VIGELANDSPARKEN
Page 78

Before his death in 1943, Gustav Vigeland populated Oslo's favourite park with his fantastical, phantasmagorical sculptures.

### 4 WILDLIFE SAFARIS IN SVALBARD
Page 375

From polar-bear spotting to birdwatching to husky drives, the vast, glaciated landscapes of this gorgeous Arctic archipelago offer a spectacular range of wildlife safaris.

### 5 THE NORSK FISKEVAERSMUSEUM, Å
Page 331

Hanging on for dear life between the mountains and the sea, the tiny village of Å has preserved many of its nineteenth-century buildings within the Norwegian Fishing Village Museum.

### 6 THE OSLOFJORD
Page 105

The islands of the Oslofjord are great for swimming, sunbathing and walking – and they are just a short ferry ride from the city centre.

### 7 VÆRØY'S SEA-BIRD COLONIES
Page 333

This remote Lofoten island is renowned for its profuse birdlife, which includes puffins, cormorants, kittiwakes, guillemots and even rare sea eagles.

### 8 HJØRUNDFJORD
Page 245

Wild and windswept, the deep, dark waters and icy peaks of this distant fjord make it one of Norway's most elegiac.

### 9 BERGEN
Page 189

Norway's second city is an eminently appealing place with a clutch of fine old buildings, great restaurants and top-notch art galleries.

### 10 ÅLESUND
Page 255

Nudging out into the ocean, beguiling Ålesund boasts a wonderful coastal setting and a platoon of handsome Art Nouveau buildings.

### 11 THE FLÅMSBANA
Page 223

A ride on the Flåm railway from high up in the mountains to the fjords way down below is one of the most dramatic train journeys in the world.

### 12 WHALE-WATCHING, ANDENES
Page 310

Pilots, minkes, humpbacks and sperm whales show themselves in all their glory during summertime excursions off the Vesterålen coast.

### 13 NIDAROS DOMKIRKE, TRONDHEIM
Page 270

Trondheim's vaunted Gothic and neo-Gothic *domkirke* (cathedral) is the largest medieval building in Scandinavia – and one of northern Europe's finest religious structures.

### 14 THE JOSTEDALSBREEN GLACIER
Page 240

Take a guided hike out on to this mighty ice plateau as it grinds and groans, slips and slithers its way across the mountains behind the Nordfjord.

### 15 URNES STAVE CHURCH
Page 236

Perhaps the finest of Norway's stave churches, Urnes is distinguished by the frenzied intricacy of its woodcarving.

### 16 THE HURTIGRUTEN
Page 30

See Norway in all its scenic splendour on the Hurtigruten coastal boat, which sails north all the way from Bergen to Kirkenes.

### 17 STAY IN A LIGHTHOUSE
Pages 128

Glued to a storm-battered islet, Ryvingen Fyr, near Mandal (see p.130), is one of several lighthouses that make for fabulous places to stay.

### 18 THE OSEBERG LONGSHIP
Page 86

Of the handful of Viking longships that have survived, the *Oseberg* is the best preserved – and was unearthed complete with a rich treasure-trove of burial goods.

# Itineraries

These three itineraries will give you a taste of Norway's astounding variety. Our Grand Tour mixes urban charm with stunning scenery while the western fjords will help you plan a route through these majestic rifts in the landscape. Real adventure junkies, however, will want to head north to the Arctic wilds for some of the most exhilarating thrills anywhere on Earth.

## GRAND TOUR

Spend two weeks – though three would be ideal – following the country's invigorating, surf-battered coast, experiencing its laidback cities and wild landscapes en route.

❶ **Oslo** Allow yourself a few days in the Norwegian capital, taking in its parks, museums, seafood restaurants and bars. **See p.59**

❷ **Stavanger** Stroll through the atmospheric old town, visit the canning museum, boat out to the dramatic Lysefjord and then climb up to Pulpit Rock. **See p.133**

❸ **Bergen** This lovely old port is celebrated for its handsome coastal setting and fine wooden architecture. Time your stay to coincide with a festival – Nattjazz, for instance. **See p.189**

❹ **Bergen to Trondheim by boat** No Norwegian holiday would be complete without a sea cruise – sit back and enjoy the views from the Hurtigruten. **See p.30**

❺ **Trondheim** Trondheim features a magnificent cathedral, a charming old city centre and is a great springboard for points north. **See p.270**

❻ **Lofoten** With its rearing peaks and turbulent ocean, this archipelago is Norway at its most beautiful. **See p.315**

❼ **Tromsø** Home to lively restaurants and simmering bars, this "Paris of the north" is the perfect spot to spend a few days gearing up for an excursion into the depths of the Arctic hinterlands. **See p.342**

❽ **Nordkapp** The northern end of mainland Europe, this jagged promontory pokes a knobbly finger out into the Arctic Sea. **See p.366**

## THE WESTERN FJORDS

Starting from Bergen (see pp.189–208), this fjord itinerary will take about ten days – fourteen if you add a hike or two – at a comfortable pace by car, and a little longer by public transport.

❶ **Lofthus** Snuggling the Sørfjord, this lovely little village sits amid fruit orchards – and is within a day's hike of the Hardangervidda mountain plateau. **See p.215**

❷ **Trolltunga** Hike up to this remarkable overhang – the "Troll's Tongue" – for a truly incredible view. **See p.214**

❸ **Balestrand** Loveable village with an exquisite setting, its huddle of houses pressing up against the mountains. **See p.231**

❹ **Solvorn** From this quaint hamlet, which ambles up from the Lustrafjord, you can visit the remarkable Urnes stave church. **See p.236**

❺ **Mundal, Fjærlandsfjord** Isolated until the 1980s, the Fjærlandsfjord is gloriously wild. From Mundal you can hike up into the hills to long-abandoned mountain farms. **See p.233**

**ABOVE** WALRUSES

**⑥ Jostedalsbreen glacier** A guided walk on this groaning, creaking glacier, one of the largest in Europe, is a must. **See p.240**

**⑦ Cruise the Geirangerfjord** Hemmed in by mountains, this fjord is truly spectacular, and the boat cruise along it a real treat. **See p.250**

**⑧ Ålesund** Draped around its pretty, little harbour, this delightful town boasts a confetti of Art Nouveau buildings. **See p.255**

## ARCTIC NORWAY

The more northerly stretches of Norway's beguiling coast beckon with gorgeous indigo light, a distinctly warm camaraderie and limitless outdoor activities – perfect for a couple of weeks' heart-pounding adventure.

**❶ Maelstrom in Saltstraumen** Experience the world's strongest tidal whirlpool, which sends some 400 million tonnes of water through the coastline's narrow fjords, sometimes producing an uncanny yelping sound. **See p.296**

**❷ Cross-country skiing in Kabelvåg** Spend a day or two skiing across the powdered marshes

and soaring mountains of this up-and-coming destination. **See p.322**

**❸ Climbing in Svolvær** Hike up from Svolvær to the Svolværgeita (the "Svolvær Goat"), a nerve-jangling, two-pronged pinnacle that rises high above town. **See p.320**

**❹ Whale-watching in Vesterålen** Pilots, minke and humpback congregate here amid the Vesterålen's nutrient-rich waters, which are perfect for whale-watching excursions. **See p.310**

**❺ Dog-sledding outside Karasjok** Harness, rig, and prep your pack of snow-white Siberian huskies and head off on the Arctic's Formula 1 – a day-long sledding safari. **See p.358**

**❻ Sleep in an igloo, Kirkenes** Jump into an expedition-strength sleeping bag and drift off to sleep in a room made out of blocks of snow and ice. **See p.373**

**❼ Explore the ends of the Earth on Svalbard** Ride the fjords in a rugged Zodiac or snowmobile out to an abandoned satellite-station-turned-guesthouse, the perfect base for snowy wilderness exploration. **See p.375**

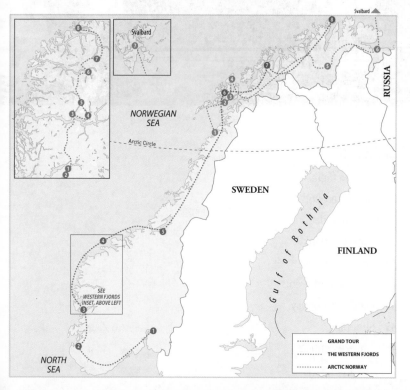

FJORDLAND FERRY

# Basics

# Getting there

**There is a reasonably good range of inexpensive flights from London direct to Norway, though the UK's regional airports offer surprisingly little. Oslo Gardermoen airport is the main point of arrival. Flights are almost invariably cheaper than the long and arduous journey from the UK to Norway by train or car. There are currently no ferry services direct from the UK to Norway, but this situation may change and it's worth checking out if you're considering taking your car.**

From **Ireland**, there is less choice than from the UK, but there are regular flights to Oslo Gardermoen airport. For visitors travelling from **North America**, the main decision is whether to fly direct to Oslo – though the options are limited – or via another European city, probably London. **Australians**, **New Zealanders** and **South Africans** have to fly via another country – there are no nonstop, direct flights. Finally, getting to Norway **from the rest of Scandinavia** (Denmark, Sweden and Finland) is quick, easy and relatively inexpensive, whether you travel by plane, bus or train.

## Flights from the UK

From the UK, there's a healthy choice of **direct, nonstop flights** from London to Oslo as well as a scattering of flights there from the UK's **regional airports**. Norway's main international airport is Oslo Gardermoen, 45km north of the city, but several budget airlines use the deceptively named Oslo (Torp) airport, which is actually just outside Sandefjord, 110km from Oslo, and Oslo (Rygge) airport, 60km south of the city near the little town of Moss.

There are also a handful of nonstop, direct flights from the UK to other Norwegian cities, including Stavanger, Bergen and Trondheim, but for the likes of Tromsø you'll have to change planes. Scandinavian Airlines (SAS), Norwegian (aka Norwegian Airlines) and Widerøe have the largest number of routes.

**Prices** vary enormously, but Norwegian mostly offers the least expensive tickets with a return from London Gatwick or Manchester to Oslo costing from as little as £50, though £150 is more typical. Norwegian have also brought fares right down for flights from London to Longyearbyen, on Svalbard; this summer-only service via Oslo (June–Aug) can cost as little as £220 return, which is really rather remarkable. Generally speaking, prices are at their peak in the high season – from mid-June to late August. **Flying times** are insignificant: Aberdeen to Stavanger takes just one hour, London to Oslo a little over two.

## Flights from Ireland

**Flying from Ireland** to Norway, there's not much choice, but Ryanair (Ⓦ ryanair.com) has flights from Dublin to Oslo (Rygge) and Norwegian (Ⓦ norwegian .com) flies between Dublin and Oslo Gardermoen. As sample fares, Norwegian flights from Dublin to Oslo can cost as little as €50, but €140 is a more usual figure with a **flying time** of just over two hours.

## Flights from the US and Canada

From the US, the main carrier is Norwegian (Ⓦ norwegian.com), who fly direct/nonstop from New York to Bergen and Oslo Gardermoen; and from Boston, Florida, Los Angeles and San Francisco to Oslo Gardermoen. **Return fares** are competitively priced, ranging from US$200–525

---

**AIRLINES AND ROUTES FROM THE UK**

The following airlines currently offer direct, nonstop flights from the **UK to Norway**. Note that some of these routes only operate during the summertime.

**bmi** (Ⓦ bmiregional.com). Aberdeen to Oslo Gardermoen; Newcastle to Stavanger.
**British Airways** (Ⓦ britishairways.com). London Heathrow to Oslo Gardermoen.
**Eastern Airways** (Ⓦ easternairways.com). Aberdeen to Bergen and Stavanger; Newcastle to Stavanger.
**Norwegian** (Ⓦ norwegian.com). Edinburgh to Oslo Gardermoen; London Gatwick to Ålesund, Bergen, Oslo Gardermoen, Stavanger and

Trondheim; Manchester to Oslo Gardermoen and Stavanger.
**Ryanair** (Ⓦ ryanair.com). Edinburgh, Manchester and London Stansted to Oslo (Rygge); Liverpool, Manchester and London Stansted to Oslo (Torp); London Stansted to Oslo Gardermoen.
**Scandinavian Airlines** (SAS; Ⓦ flysas.com). London Heathrow to Oslo Gardermoen.
**Widerøe** (Ⓦ wideroe.no). Aberdeen to Bergen and Stavanger.

**A BETTER KIND OF TRAVEL**

At Rough Guides we are passionately committed to travel. We believe it helps us understand the world we live in and the people we share it with – and of course tourism is vital to many developing economies. But the scale of modern tourism has also damaged some places irreparably, and climate change is accelerated by most forms of transport, especially flying. All Rough Guides' flights are carbon-offset, and every year we donate money to a variety of environmental charities.

one-way from New York to Oslo and US$290–720 from Los Angeles.

**From Canada**, the best deals are usually offered by Air Canada (W aircanada.com), which flies nonstop to London Heathrow, with onward connections to Norway. From Toronto to Oslo, expect to pay around Can$2000 in high season and Can$1500 in low season, while typical fares from Vancouver are around Can$2200 in high season and, likewise, Can$1500 in low season.

The **flying time** on a direct, nonstop flight from the east coast of North America to Norway is just over seven hours.

## Flights from Australia and New Zealand

There are no direct/nonstop flights **from Australia or New Zealand** to Norway. Most itineraries will involve two changes, one in the Far East – Singapore, Bangkok or Kuala Lumpur – and then another in the gateway city of the airline you're flying with – most commonly Copenhagen, Amsterdam or London. You can get tickets to Oslo from Sydney, Melbourne or Perth for Aus$1500–2500; from Auckland expect to pay NZ$2000–3000.

## Flights from South Africa

There are no direct/nonstop flights **from South Africa** to Norway, but several airlines will get you to Oslo with one stop via a European hub city. For example, KLM (W klm.com) fly from Cape Town to Amsterdam with onward connections to Oslo for a return fare of between ZAR9500 and ZAR12,500.

## Flights from the rest of Scandinavia

**From the rest of Scandinavia**, particularly Copenhagen and Stockholm, there are frequent daily nonstop flights to Norway's main airports, principally Oslo Gardermoen, Bergen and Trondheim. These three airports also serve as hubs for a battalion of smaller Norwegian airports. The two main carriers are SAS (W sas.com) and Norwegian (W norwegian.com), while Widerøe (W wideroe.no) chips in with a trio of routes to Norway from Copenhagen and one from Gothenburg. **Prices** are very reasonable with Norwegian, for example, charging around 600kr for the flight from Copenhagen to Oslo, 400kr from Stockholm; note, however, that prices vary considerably depending on demand. **Flying times** are insignificant: Copenhagen to Oslo takes just over one hour, Stockholm to Oslo an hour.

## By train from the UK

**Eurostar** (W eurostar.com) services running through the Channel Tunnel to Brussels put Norway within reasonable striking distance of the UK by **train**, but the whole journey from London to Oslo, which is usually routed via Brussels and Copenhagen, still takes about 22 hours and costs about £300 one-way (£350 return), though special deals and concessionary rates can reduce these fares considerably.

### Rail passes

If you're visiting Norway as part of a longer European trip, it may be worth considering a **pan-European rail pass**. There are lots to choose from and both **Rail Europe** (W raileurope.com) and **Eurail** (W eurail.com), two umbrella companies for national and international passes, operate comprehensive websites detailing all the options with prices. Note in particular that some passes have to be bought before leaving home, others can only be bought in specific countries and some can only be purchased by non-Europeans. Note also that rail pass holders are sometimes entitled to discounts on some internal ferry and bus journeys within Norway. For train travel within Norway and Norway-only train passes, see p.28.

## Driving from the UK

To reach Norway by **car or motorbike** from the UK, the best bet is to use **Eurotunnel's** (W eurotunnel .com) shuttle train through the Channel Tunnel.

Note that the Eurotunnel only carries cars (including occupants) and motorbikes, not cyclists and foot passengers. From the Eurotunnel exit in Calais, it's a somewhat epic journey of around 1600km or so to Oslo.

## By ferry from the UK

There are currently no **car ferries** from the UK to either Norway or its immediate neighbour, Denmark. It's possible that car ferries may resume, however – check Ⓦ directferries.co.uk for the latest news.

## By train, bus and ferry from the rest of Scandinavia

### By train

There are regular **trains** to **Oslo** from both Stockholm (2–3 daily; 6hr) and Copenhagen (2 daily; 8hr). There are also regular services from Stockholm to **Narvik** (1–2 daily; 21hr), operated by the Swedish company SJ (Ⓦ sj.se). For online tickets, go to Ⓦ raileurope.com.

### By bus

Several **bus companies** provide services into Norway from other parts of Scandinavia. These include **Eurolines** (Ⓦ eurolines.co.uk) buses from London to Oslo, which pass through several Danish and Swedish towns, notably Copenhagen, Malmö and Gothenburg; the Swedish operating arm of **Nettbuss** (Ⓦ nettbuss.se), which has services to Oslo from Stockholm, Copenhagen, Malmö and Gothenburg among others; and **Swebuss** (Ⓦ swebuss.se), which operates an express bus from Stockholm to Oslo. In the far north, **Eskelisen Lapin Linjat** (Ⓦ eskelisen.fi) runs a number of bus services from Finland to Norwegian destinations, including Tromsø, Karasjok, Vadsø and Nordkapp. As a sample, **one-way fare**, the Swebuss express bus from Stockholm to Oslo takes 8hr and costs in the region of 400kr.

### By car ferry

A number of **car ferries** shuttle across the Skagerrak **from Denmark** to Norway and there's a car ferry from Sweden too. **Prices** vary enormously – but reckon on about 1900kr for two people with car from Hirtshals to Stavanger, half that from Hirtshals to Kristiansand.

**Copenhagen to**: Oslo (1 daily; 17hr; Ⓦ dfdsseaways.no).

**Frederikshavn (Denmark) to**: Oslo (1 daily; 9hr; Ⓦ stenaline.no).

**Hirtshals (Denmark) to**: Kristiansand (2–3 daily; 2hr 15min–3hr 30min; Ⓦ colorline.com and Ⓦ fjord line.com); Langesund, in between Sandefjord and Kragerø (1 daily; 4hr 30min; Ⓦ fjordline.com); Larvik (1–2 daily; 4hr; Ⓦ colorline.com); Stavanger/Bergen (7 weekly; 11hr/17hr; Ⓦ fjordline.com).

**Strömstad (Sweden) to**: Sandefjord (4–6 daily; 2hr 30min; Ⓦ colorline.com and Ⓦ fjordline.com).

## Tours and organized holidays

**Tourism** in Norway is a multi-million-dollar industry that has spawned a small army of tour operators. Some provide generic bus tours of parts of the country, but there are many more specialist companies too, featuring everything from skiing and walking through to whale-watching and cycling. Many of the better companies offer a choice of escorted and independent tours. Additional, domestic tour operators are detailed throughout the Guide.

### TOUR AND HOLIDAY OPERATORS

**Anglers' World Holidays** UK ☎ 01246 221 717, Ⓦ anglersworld.tv. Sea- and river-fishing holidays in Norway.

**Brekke Tours & Travel** US ☎ 1 800 437 5302, Ⓦ brekketours.com. A well-established company offering a host of sightseeing and cultural tours of Scandinavia in general and Norway in particular.

**Den Norske Turistforening** Ⓦ turistforeningen.no. The Norwegian Trekking Association manages all aspects of hiking in Norway (see box, p.43). They also organize a range of all-inclusive tours, both skiing and hiking.

**Discover the World** UK ☎ 01737 214 250, Ⓦ discover-the-world .co.uk. Specialist adventure tours including whale-watching in Norway, wildlife in Spitsbergen and dog-sledding in Lapland. Independent, tailor-made tours too.

**Exodus** UK ☎ 0203 811 7281, Ⓦ exodus.co.uk. Large, activity-holiday specialist offering cross-country skiing and all sorts of other winter sports plus whale-watching, hiking and Spitsbergen excursions.

**Fjord Tours** Norway ☎ 55 55 76 60, Ⓦ fjordtours.com. One of the best nonspecialist tour operators in Norway, Bergen-based Fjord Tours is the main organizer of the much-vaunted Norway in a Nutshell excursion (see box, p.210). They also offer an imaginative range of other fjordland excursions (see box, p.204) and manage the Fjord Pass discount scheme. There are no tour guides on any of their excursions, which suits most independent travellers just fine, and almost all use public transport – bus, train and ferry. Fjord Tours also offer adventure packages – cycling on the Rallarvegen (see box, p.224) or winter skiing for example – and, if you're travelling by car, they will book accommodation on your behalf and advise on itineraries.

**Headwater** UK ☎ 01606 369 406, Ⓦ headwater.com. Limited but well-chosen selection of winter fun holidays in Geilo and Venabu, where punters choose anything from skiing to reindeer safaris.

**Hurtigruten** ☎ 0203 131 5321, ⓦ hurtigruten.co.uk. The Hurtigruten coastal voyage is Norway's most celebrated sea cruise (see p.30). Also cruises to Svalbard.

**Inntravel** UK ☎ 01653 617 001, ⓦ inntravel.co.uk. Outdoor holidays in Norway including skiing, walking, dog-sledding, fjord cruises, and whale- and reindeer-watching.

**North South Travel** UK ☎ 01245 608 291, ⓦ northsouthtravel .co.uk. Friendly, competitive travel agency, offering discounted fares worldwide. Profits are used to support projects in the developing world, especially the promotion of sustainable tourism.

**Saddle Skedaddle** UK ☎ 0191 265 1110, ⓦ skedaddle.co.uk. Highly recommended company organizing (at least) one guided cycling tour of Norway each year, usually to the Lofoten islands. Also self-guided cycling tours.

**ScanAm World Tours** US ☎ 1 800 545 2204, ⓦ scandinaviantravel.com. Scandinavian specialist offering an extensive programme of group and individual tours and cruises within Norway.

**Scantours** US ☎ 1 800 223 7226 ⓦ scantours.net. Huge range of packages and tailor-made holidays to every Scandinavian nook and cranny.

# Getting around

**Norway's public transport system – a huge mesh of trains, buses, car ferries and passenger express ferries – is comprehensive and reliable. In the winter (especially in the north) services can be cut back severely, but no part of the country is unreachable for long.**

Bear in mind, however, that Norwegian villages and towns usually spread over a large distance, so don't be surprised if you end up walking a kilometre or two from the bus stop, ferry terminal or train station to get where you want to go. It's this sprawling nature of the country's towns and, more especially, the remoteness of many of the sights, that encourages visitors to **rent a car**. This is an expensive business, but costs can be reduced if you rent locally for a day or two rather than for the whole trip, though in high season spare vehicles can get very thin on the ground.

## By plane

**Internal flights** can prove a surprisingly inexpensive way of hopping around Norway and are especially useful if you're short on time and want to reach the far north: Tromsø to Kirkenes, for instance, takes the best part of two days by bus or car, but it's just an hour by plane. Several companies combine to operate an extensive network of internal flights with the three big players being **Norwegian** (ⓦ norwegian.com), **SAS** (ⓦ sas.no) and **Widerøe** (ⓦ wideroe.no). For example, a one-way Widerøe fare from Oslo to Trondheim costs from about 900kr, while the cost from Oslo to Kirkenes is 1200kr. In terms of **concessionary fares**, all the airlines offer discounts of some sort to seniors (67+ years) and the young (2–25 years); infants under 2 years travel free. In the summer time (late June to late August), Widerøe also offers an **Experience Norway** ticket, which is valid for two weeks' unlimited travel: Norway is divided into three zones with flights in one zone only costing 3390kr, two zones 3990kr and three zones (the whole of the country) 4590kr; an extra week costs 2000kr.

## By train

With the exception of the Narvik line into Sweden, operated by SJ (see p.302), all Norwegian **trains** are run by Norges Statsbaner (NSB; ☎ 815 00 888, ⓦ www.nsb.no). Apart from a sprinkling of branch lines, NSB services operate on **three main domestic routes**, which link Oslo to Stavanger in the southwest, to Bergen in the west and to Trondheim and on to Bodø in the north. The nature of the country has made several of these routes engineering feats of some magnitude, worth the trip in their own right – the tiny **Flåm line** (see box, p.223) and the sweeping **Rauma line** (see box, p.166) from Dombås to Åndalsnes are exciting examples.

NSB have two main types of train – **Lokaltog** (local) and **Regiontog** (regional). There is one standard class on both, but certain regional trains have "**Komfort**" carriages (read slightly more spacious), for which you pay a supplement of 90kr per person. Most and eventually all Regiontog have (or will have) free **wi-fi**. It's also worth noting that on many long-distance intercity trains and on all overnight and international services, an **advance seat reservation** is compulsory. In high season, it's wise to reserve a seat on main routes anyway, as trains can be jam-packed. **NSB timetables** are available online and free individual route timetables are available at every train station. In the case of the more scenic routes, there are also (purple-prose) leaflets describing the sights as you go.

### Fares and discounts

**Fully flexible, standard-fare prices** are bearable, with the popular Oslo–Bergen run, for example, costing around 860kr one-way, while the price to travel Oslo–Trondheim is 940kr – a little less than twice that for a return. The Trondheim journey takes between seven and eight hours, Bergen six and a half to seven and a half hours. NSB also offers a variety of **discount fares**. The main discount ticket scheme is the **Minipris** (mini-price), under which you can cut up to sixty percent off the price of long-distance journeys. In general, the further you travel, the more economic they become. The drawbacks are that Minipris tickets must be purchased at least one day in advance, are not available at peak periods and on certain trains, and are neither refundable nor exchangeable. For overnight trains, two-berth **sleepers** (*sove*) are reasonably priced at 900kr, an especially good bargain if you consider you'll save a night's hotel accommodation.

In terms of **concessionary fares** on standard-price tickets, there are group and family reductions; children under 4 years travel free; 4–15-year-olds pay half-fare, and so do senior citizens (67+). Pan-European **Interrail** and **Eurail passes** can include the Norwegian railway system (see p.26) and there's also a **Norway Eurail Pass** (for non-Europeans only), which entitles the holder to between three and eight days unlimited rail travel within one month. Prices for three days are 1750kr (1420kr for 4–25-year-olds), while eight days cost 3071kr (2500kr). The rules and regulations regarding these passes are convoluted – consult the websites of two umbrella companies, **Eurail** (Ⓦ eurail.com) and **Rail Europe** (Ⓦ raileurope.com). Note that some passes have to be bought before leaving home.

## By bus

Both supplementing and on occasion duplicating the train network, **buses** reach almost every corner of the country. In southern Norway, up as far as Trondheim, the principal long-distance carriers are **Nor-Way Bussekspress** (Ⓦ nor-way.no) and **Nettbuss** (Ⓦ nettbuss.no), whose services operate in conjunction with a dense, sometimes baffling, network of local buses, some of which only run in the summertime. In the north, beyond Trondheim, the bus network is more fragmented with a variety of operators, whose services are listed on an overarching website, Ⓦ rutebok.no. There's also a national public transport helpline, ❶ 177. **Bus tickets** are usually bought on board, but on both Nor-Way Bussekspress and Nettbuss there are generally significant discounts for advance purchase. Bus travel is almost invariably less expensive than the train – and prices are bearable, especially as all tolls and ferry costs are included in the price of a ticket. For instance, the nine-hour Nor-Way Bussekspress trip from Oslo to Haugesund costs 700kr (560kr in advance), while the fourteen-hour journey from Bergen to Trondheim costs 880kr (no advance discount).

As far as **concessionary fares** are concerned, children under 4 travel free and both youngsters (under 16) and seniors (over 67) are entitled to discounts of up to fifty percent. Rail-pass holders and students are sometimes eligible for a fifty-percent reduction on the full adult rate too – ask and you may receive.

## By ferry

Using a **ferry** is one of the highlights of any visit to Norway – and, indeed, among the western fjords and around the Lofotens they are all but impossible to avoid. The majority are roll-on, roll-off **car ferries**; these represent an economical means of transport, with **prices** (*ferjetakster*) fixed on a nationwide sliding scale: short journeys (10–20min) cost foot passengers 27–37kr, whereas a car and driver will pay 60–110kr. The maximum tariff on this national scale (for sea journeys of up to 15km) is currently 65kr for foot passengers, 205kr for car and driver. The latest rates are listed on Ⓦ vegvesen.no, though they can be difficult to locate amid the shrubbery of other information. **Ferry procedures** are

---

## USEFUL WEBSITES FOR PUBLIC TRANSPORT

Ⓦ **nor-way.no** Timetables and booking for one of southern Norway's largest long-distance bus companies, Nor-Way Bussekspress.

Ⓦ **nettbuss.no** Timetables and booking for the platoon of long-distance express buses provided by Nettbuss.

Ⓦ **www.nsb.no** Norges Statsbaner (Norwegian State Railways) timetables and booking.

Ⓦ **rutebok.no** National route planner website covering every sort of public transport from one end of the country to the other.

Note that details of local and regional public transport companies are provided throughout the Guide.

straightforward: foot passengers walk on and pay the conductor, car drivers pay when the conductor appears at the car window either on the jetty or on board – although some busier routes have a drive-by ticket office. One or two of the longer car ferry routes – in particular Bodø–Moskenes – take advance reservations, but the rest operate on a **first-come, first-served** basis. In the off season, there's no real need to arrive more than twenty minutes before departure – with the possible exception of the Lofoten island ferries – but in the summer allow two hours to be safe. There are **concessionary rates** on standard fares on all ferry routes, with infants up to the age of 4 travelling free, and children (4–15) and senior citizens (over 67) getting a fifty-percent discount.

### Hurtigbåt passenger express boats

Norway's **Hurtigbåt** passenger express boats are catamarans that make up in speed what they lack in enjoyment: unlike the ordinary ferries, the landscape whizzes by and in choppy seas the ride can be disconcertingly bumpy. Nonetheless, they are a convenient time-saving option: it takes just four hours on the Hurtigbåt service from Bergen to Balestrand, for instance, and the same from Narvik to Svolvær. There are Hurtigbåt services all along the west coast, with a particular concentration in and around Bergen; the majority operate all year. There's no fixed tariff table, so **rates** vary

considerably, though Hurtigbåt boats are significantly more expensive per kilometre than car ferries – Bergen–Flåm, for instance, costs 800kr for the five-and-a-half-hour journey, 580kr for the four-hour trip from Bergen to Balestrand. There are **concessionary rates** on standard fares on all Hurtigbåt routes, with infants up to the age of 4 travelling free, and children (4–15) and senior citizens (over 67) getting a fifty-percent discount. Advance reservations can also attract discounts.

### The Hurtigruten

Norway's most celebrated ferry journey is the long and beautiful haul up the coast from Bergen to Kirkenes on the **Hurtigruten coastal boat** (literally, "rapid route"; ⓦ hurtigruten.co.uk). To many, the Hurtigruten remains the quintessential Norwegian experience, and it's certainly the best way to observe the drama of the country's extraordinary coastline. Eleven ships combine to provide one daily service in each direction, and the boats stop off at over thirty ports on the way. The whole round-trip lasts twelve days and prices vary enormously depending on when you go and what level of comfort you require: the start-off "Basic" package can cost as little as 11,000kr per person in winter, though 14,300kr is more typical, 17,600–22,000kr in summer; prices include a berth in a two- or three-berth cabin, breakfast, lunch and dinner. There is a restaurant and a 24-hour cafeteria supplying coffee and snacks on all Hurtigruten boats;

---

## HURTIGRUTEN SAILING SCHEDULE

The **Hurtigruten** schedule fluctuates according to the season: the summer timetable runs from June to August, the spring from April to May, the autumn from September to October and the winter from November to March. **Southbound**, the service sticks to pretty much the same route throughout the year, but **northbound** the route varies to include Geiranger in the summertime. Below is a list of summer **departure times** from principal ports.

### NORTHBOUND (JUNE TO AUGUST)

| | |
|---|---|
| Bergen 8pm | Stamsund 7.30pm |
| Florø 2.15am | Svolvær 10pm |
| Ålesund 9.30am | Harstad 8am |
| Geiranger 1.30pm | Tromsø 6.30pm |
| Ålesund 7pm | Hammerfest 6am |
| Trondheim noon | Honningsvåg 2.45pm (arrives 11.15am) |
| Bodø 3pm | Arrive Kirkenes 9am |

### SOUTHBOUND (JUNE TO AUGUST)

| | |
|---|---|
| Kirkenes 12.30pm | Stamsund 10.30pm |
| Honningsvåg 5.45am (arrives 5.30am) | Bodø 4.15am |
| Hammerfest 12.45pm | Trondheim 10am |
| Tromsø 1.30am | Ålesund 1am |
| Harstad 8.30am | Florø 8.15am |
| Svolvær 8.30pm | Arrives Bergen 2.30pm |

the restaurants are very popular, so reserve a table as soon as you board.

A **short or medium-sized hop** along the coast on a portion of the Hurtigruten route is also possible – indeed, it's an excellent idea. **Port-to-port fares** are not particularly cheap, especially in comparison with the bus, but they are affordable, especially on the shorter trips where you do not have to have a cabin. For example, a one-way fare for two people with a car from Bodø to Stamsund (4hr 30min) costs in the region of 850–1050kr. By comparison, the one-way fare for two people with or without a car from Trondheim to Bodø (26hr) ranges from 1500–3000kr, including a (compulsory) cabin.

**Bookings** can be made online or at the local tourist office: in the Hurtigruten ports, the tourist office should be willing to telephone the captain of the nearest ship to make a reservation on your behalf. Most – but not all – of the Hurtigruten boats carry **cars**.

# By car

Norway's **main roads** are excellent, especially when you consider the rigours of the climate, and nowadays, with most of the more hazardous sections either ironed out or tunnelled through, driving is comparatively straightforward. Nonetheless, you still have to exercise some caution on some of the higher sections and in the longer (fume-filled) tunnels. Once you leave the main roads for the narrow **mountain byroads**, however, you'll be in for some nail-biting experiences – and that's in the summertime. In winter the Norwegians close many roads and concentrate their efforts on keeping the main highways open, but obviously blizzards and ice can make driving difficult to dangerous anywhere, even with winter tyres (which are compulsory), studs and chains. At any time of the year, the more adventurous the drive, the better equipped you need to be, especially in the sparsely inhabited north: on remote drives you should pack provisions, have proper hiking gear, check the car thoroughly before departure, carry a spare can of petrol and take a mobile phone.

Norway's main highways carry an **E prefix** – E6, E18, etc. The E roads are the nearest thing Norway has to motorways, but only rarely are they dual carriageways – and indeed they are often interrupted by roundabouts and even traffic lights. All the country's other significant roads (**riksvei**, or **rv**) are assigned a number and, as a general rule, the lower the number, the busier the road. In our guide, we've used the E prefix, but designated other roads as **Highways** (Hwy), followed by the number. In an

**TOP 5 DRIVES**
**Filefjell** See p.174
**Haukelifjell** See p.183 & p.211
**Sognefjellsveg** See p.237
**Ørnevegen** See p.247 & p.252
**Trollstigen** See p.252

effort to boost tourism, around twenty routes or roads have been designated **Nasjonale Turistveger** (National Tourist Routes; ⓦ nasjonaleturistveger.no) with more to follow. Each is equipped with strategically positioned visitor centres and viewpoints.

## Toll-roads

**Tolls** are imposed on certain roads to pay for construction work such as bridges, tunnels and motorway improvements. Once the costs are covered the toll is normally removed. The older projects levy a fee of around 15–30kr, but the tolls for the newer works may run to well over 100kr per vehicle. There's a toll on entering the country's larger cities (15–30kr), but whether this is an environmental measure or a means of boosting city coffers is a moot point.

There are **automatic toll stations** (*automatisk bomstasjon*) on every toll-road. Here, signs indicate the amount of the toll to be levied and cameras read the **electronic tag** – officially the "AutoPASS On-Board Unit (OBU)" – that has, by law, to be attached to the windscreen of every Norwegian vehicle. Drivers do not need to stop, but the owner of the vehicle is billed in due course (usually within a week). All Norwegian car rental vehicles have one of these tags and the car rental companies are billed like everyone else – but predictably they pass on the charge to their customers (and that's why you can never wrap up the car rental bill completely when you return your vehicle). If you are taking your **own vehicle** to Norway, you can purchase a tag at or near your point of entry, but it is much easier to set up an online credit-card **Visitors' payment account**, in which the cameras read your number plate and invoice you accordingly. For further details, consult ⓦ autopass.no.

Entirely separate from the state-run system are the modest tolls of 20–40kr levied on privately maintained country/mountain roads; drivers are expected to deposit their money in an easy-to-spot roadside **honesty box**.

## Fuel

**Fuel** is readily available, even in the north of Norway, though here the settlements are so widely separated that you'll need to keep your tank pretty full; if you're using the byroads extensively,

## OPENING AND CLOSING DATES OF MAJOR MOUNTAIN PASSES

Obviously enough, there's no preordained date for the opening of **mountain roads** in the springtime – it depends on the weather, and the threat of an avalanche is often much more of a limitation than actual snowfalls. The dates below should therefore be treated with caution; if in doubt, seek advice from the local tourist office. If you do head along a mountain road that's closed, sooner or later you'll come to a barrier and have to turn round.

**E6**: Dovrefjell (Oslo–Trondheim). Usually open all year.
**E69**: Skarsvåg–Nordkapp. Closed late October to April.
**E134**: Haukelifjell (Oslo–Bergen/Stavanger). Usually open all year.
**Highway 7**: Hardangervidda (Oslo–Bergen). Usually open all year.
**Highway 51**: Valdresflya. Closed December to early May.
**Highway 55**: Sognefjellet. Closed November to early May.
**Highway 63**: Grotli–Geiranger–Åndalsnes (Trollstigen). Closed early October to mid-May.

remember to carry an extra can. At the time of writing, fuel prices were 13–15kr a litre, and there are four main grades, all unleaded (*blyfri*): 95 octane, 98 octane, super 98 octane and diesel.

### Documentation

All EU/EEA **driving licences** are honoured in Norway, but other nationals will need – or are recommended to have – an **International Driver's Licence** (available at minimal cost from your home motoring organization). No form of provisional licence is accepted. If you're bringing your own car, you must have vehicle registration papers, adequate insurance, a first-aid kit, and a warning triangle. Extra insurance coverage for unforeseen legal costs is also well worth having, as is an appropriate **breakdown policy** from a motoring organization. In Britain, for example, the AA charges members and non-members about £170 for a month's Europe-wide breakdown cover,

## NORWAY: DISTANCE CHART (IN KILOMETRES)

| | Ålesund | Bergen | Bodø | Hamar | Hammerfest | Kirkenes | Kristiansand |
|---|---|---|---|---|---|---|---|
| **Ålesund** | 0 | 378 | 1010 | 441 | 1844 | 2218 | 811 |
| **Bergen** | 378 | 0 | 1380 | 471 | 2214 | 2588 | 492 |
| **Bodø** | 1010 | 1380 | 0 | 1108 | 962 | 1392 | 1534 |
| **Hamar** | 441 | 471 | 1108 | 0 | 1942 | 2316 | 443 |
| **Hammerfest** | 1844 | 2214 | 962 | 1942 | 0 | 494 | 2368 |
| **Kirkenes** | 2218 | 2588 | 1392 | 2316 | 494 | 0 | 2742 |
| **Kristiansand** | 811 | 492 | 1534 | 443 | 2368 | 2742 | 0 |
| **Lillehammer** | 382 | 439 | 1065 | 59 | 1899 | 2273 | 471 |
| **Narvik** | 1191 | 1561 | 304 | 1279 | 652 | 1027 | 1715 |
| **Nordkapp** | 1913 | 2283 | 1059 | 2011 | 181 | 517 | 2437 |
| **Oslo** | 533 | 478 | 1217 | 123 | 2051 | 2425 | 320 |
| **Røros** | 430 | 637 | 936 | 289 | 1810 | 2185 | 753 |
| **Stavanger** | 621 | 170 | 1560 | 575 | 2394 | 2768 | 245 |
| **Tromsø** | 1519 | 1844 | 562 | 1606 | 549 | 944 | 2054 |
| **Trondheim** | 287 | 657 | 723 | 385 | 1567 | 1931 | 811 |

Ferry crossings not included in distances quoted.

with all the appropriate documentation, including green card, provided.

## Rules of the road

Norway has strict **rules of the road**: you drive on the right, with dipped headlights required at all times; seat belts are compulsory for drivers and front-seat passengers, and for back-seat passengers too, if fitted; and winter tyres are compulsory in winter. There's a **speed limit** of 30kph in many residential areas, 50kph in built-up areas, 80kph on open roads and 80kph, 90kph or sometimes 100kph on motorways. Speed cameras monitor hundreds of kilometres of road – watch out for the **Automatisk Trafikkontroll** warning signs – and they are far from popular with the locals: there are all sorts of folkloric (and largely apocryphal) tales of men in masks appearing at night with chain saws to chop them down. **Speeding fines** are so heavy that local drivers stick religiously within the speed limit. If you're filmed breaking the limit in a rental car, expect your credit card to be stung by the car rental company to the tune of at least 600kr and a maximum of 7800kr (yes, that's right). If you're stopped for speeding, large spot fines are payable within the same price range and, if you are way over

the limit (say 60kph in a 30kph zone) you could well end up in jail; rarely is any leniency shown to unwitting foreigners. **Drunk driving** is also severely frowned upon. You can be asked to take a breath test on a routine traffic-check; if you're over the limit, you will have your licence confiscated and may face a stretch in prison. It is also an offence to drive while using a hand-held mobile/cell phone.

**On-street parking** restrictions are rigorously enforced and clearly signed with a white "P" on a blue background; below the "P" are the hours during which parking restrictions apply – Monday to Friday first and Saturday in brackets; below this are any particular limits – most commonly denoting the maximum (*maks*) number of hours (*timer*) – and then there's *mot avgift*, which means there's a fee to pay at the meter.

## Breakdown

If you **break down** in a rental car, you'll get roadside assistance from the particular repair company the car rental firm has contracted. This is a free service, though some car rental companies charge you if you need help changing a tyre in the expectation that you should be able to do it

| Lillehammer | Narvik | Nordkapp | Oslo | Røros | Stavanger | Tromsø | Trondheim |
|---|---|---|---|---|---|---|---|
| 382 | 1191 | 1913 | 533 | 430 | 621 | 1519 | 287 |
| 439 | 1561 | 2283 | 478 | 637 | 170 | 1844 | 657 |
| 1065 | 304 | 1059 | 1217 | 936 | 1560 | 562 | 723 |
| 59 | 1279 | 2011 | 123 | 289 | 575 | 1606 | 385 |
| 1899 | 652 | 181 | 2051 | 1810 | 2394 | 549 | 1567 |
| 2273 | 1027 | 517 | 2425 | 2185 | 2768 | 944 | 1931 |
| 471 | 1715 | 2437 | 320 | 753 | 245 | 2054 | 811 |
| 0 | 1246 | 1968 | 167 | 282 | 587 | 1562 | 342 |
| 1246 | 0 | 721 | 1398 | 1123 | 1741 | 251 | 904 |
| 1968 | 721 | 0 | 2120 | 1869 | 2463 | 609 | 1626 |
| 167 | 1398 | 2120 | 0 | 423 | 452 | 1733 | 494 |
| 282 | 1123 | 1869 | 423 | 0 | 740 | 1352 | 166 |
| 587 | 1741 | 2463 | 452 | 740 | 0 | 1852 | 837 |
| 1562 | 251 | 609 | 1733 | 1352 | 1852 | 0 | 1205 |
| 342 | 904 | 1626 | 494 | 166 | 837 | 1205 | 0 |

yourself. The same principles work with your own vehicle's breakdown policy. Two major vehicle **breakdown companies** in Norway are Norges Automobil-Forbund (NAF; 24hr; ☎08 505) and Viking Redningstjeneste (24hr; ☎06000). There are emergency telephones along some motorways, and breakdown trucks patrol all major mountain passes between mid-June and mid-August.

### Car rental

All the major international **car rental** companies have outlets in Norway, especially at the country's airports. To rent a car, you'll need to be 21 or over (and have been driving for at least a year), and you'll need a credit card. Rental **charges** are fairly high, beginning at around 4300kr per week for unlimited mileage in the smallest vehicle, but include collision damage waiver and vehicle (but not personal) insurance. To cut costs, watch for special local deals – a Friday to Monday weekend rental might, for example, cost you as little as 800kr. If you rent from a local company rather than one of the big names, you should proceed with care. In particular, check the policy for the excess applied to claims and ensure that it includes collision damage waiver (applicable if an accident is your fault). There are lots of these local car rental companies in Norway, listed in the *Yellow Pages* under *Bilutleie*. Bear in mind, too, that **one-way car-rental drop-off charges** are almost always wallet-searing: if you pick up a car in Oslo and drop it off in Bodø, it will cost you 6000kr – or nearer 8000kr in Tromsø.

### By bike

Despite the difficulty of much of the terrain, **cycling** is popular in Norway in the summertime. Cycle lanes and tracks as such are few and far between, and are mainly confined to the larger towns, but there's precious little traffic on most of the minor roads and cycling along them can be a delight. Furthermore, whenever a road is improved or rerouted, the old highway is often redesigned as a cycle/walking route. At almost every place you're likely to stay in, you can anticipate that someone will **rent bikes** – whether the tourist office, a sports shop, hostel, hotel or campsite. Costs are pretty uniform: reckon on paying between 120kr and 200kr a day for a seven-speed bike, plus a refundable deposit of up to 1000kr; mountain bikes are about thirty percent more.

A few tourist offices have maps of recommended **cycling routes** but this is a rarity. It is, nonetheless, important to check your itinerary thoroughly, especially in the more mountainous areas. Cyclists aren't allowed through the longer tunnels for their own protection (the fumes can be life-threatening), so discuss your plans with whoever you hire the bike from. With regard to **bike carriage**, bikes mostly go free on car ferries and attract a nominal charge on passenger express boats, but buses vary: sometimes they take them free, sometimes they charge and sometimes they do not take them at all. Nor-Way Bussekspress (see p.29) accepts bikes only when there is space and charges a child fare, while taking a bike on an NSB train (see p.28) costs half the price of your ticket up to a maximum of 200kr. In both cases, advance reservations are advised.

If you're planning a **cycling holiday**, your first port of call should be the Norwegian Tourist Board's website (Ⓦvisitnorway.com), where you can get general cycling advice, information on roads and tunnels inaccessible to cyclists and a list of companies offering all-inclusive cycling tours. Obviously enough, tour costs vary enormously, but as a baseline reckon on about 6500kr per week all-inclusive.

### CYCLING INFORMATION

**Syklist Velkommen** Ⓦcyclingnorway.no. The website of "Cyclists Welcome" lists ideas for a dozen routes around the country from 100km to 400km, plus useful practical information about road conditions, repair facilities and places of interest en route.

# Accommodation

**Inevitably, accommodation is one of the major expenses you will incur on a trip to Norway – indeed, if you're after a degree of comfort, it's going to be the costliest item by far. There are, however, budget alternatives, principally guesthouses (*pensjonater*), bed & breakfasts, campsites and cabins, and last but certainly not least, a good range of HI-registered hostels. Also bear in mind that many hotels offer myriad special deals as well as substantial weekend discounts of 25–40 percent.**

Almost everywhere, you can **reserve ahead** easily enough on websites, by email or phone as English is nearly always understood or spoken. Most tourist offices also operate an on-the-spot service for same-night accommodation for free or at minimal charge.

## Hotels

Almost universally, Norwegian **hotels** are of a high standard: neat, clean and efficient. Special bargains and impromptu weekend deals also make many of them, by European standards at least, reasonably economical. Another plus is that the price of a hotel room usually includes a **buffet breakfast** – in mid- to top-range hotels especially, these can be sumptuous banquets. The only negatives are the size of the rooms in the larger cities, especially Oslo, where they tend to be small, and their sameness: Norway abounds in mundanely modern, concrete-and-glass, sky-rise chain hotels, though thankfully most of the country's more distinctive hotels are gathered together under the **De Historiske Hoteller** banner (see box below). For a comprehensive list of hotels – along with special bargains and an online booking facility – consult the tourist board's principal website, Ⓦvisitnorway.com.

Predictably, **prices** are sensitive to demand – a double room that costs 1000kr when a hotel is slack, soon hits the 2000kr mark if there's a rush on. Generally speaking, however, 1500kr should cover the cost of two people in a double room at most hotels most of the time, nearer to 1200kr at the weekend, slightly more in Oslo. The stated price will include breakfast unless stated otherwise.

### Hotel loyalty schemes

One way to cut costs is to sign up for one of Norway's **hotel loyalty schemes**, though this does bring a certain sameness to any itinerary as schemes are tied to specific hotel chains. All the major chains offer a loyalty/discount scheme of some sort, including **Scandic** (Scandic Friends; Ⓦscandichotels.com), which has a varied portfolio of around forty Norwegian hotels, and **Thon** (Thon Discovery; Ⓦthonhotels.com), which owns seventy-four Norwegian hotels. The principles behind both schemes ate straightforward – you accumulate points whenever you stay at a Thon or Scandic hotel and points can be exchanged for discounts on further stays; members are also entitled to a number of minor benefits – free gym access and so forth.

## Pensions, guesthouses and inns

For something a little less anonymous than the average hotel, **pensions** (*pensjonater*) are your best bet – small, sometimes intimate guesthouses, which can usually be found in the larger cities and more touristy towns. Rooms go for in the region of 650–800kr single, 700–900kr double, and breakfast is generally extra. Broadly comparable in price and character is a *gjestgiveri* or *gjestehus*, a **guesthouse** or **inn**, though some of these offer superb lodgings in historic premises with prices to match. Facilities in all of these establishments are usually adequate and homely without being overwhelmingly comfortable; at the least expensive places you'll share a bathroom with others. Some pensions and guesthouses also have kitchens available for the use of guests, which means you're very likely to meet other residents – a real boon (perhaps) if you're travelling alone.

## Hostels

For many budget travellers, as well as hikers, climbers and skiers, the country's **HI hostels**, run by the Norwegian hostelling association, **Norske Vandrerhjem** (❶22 15 21 85, ⓦhihostels.no), are the accommodation mainstay. There are around fifty in total, with handy concentrations in the western fjords, the central hiking and skiing regions and in Oslo. Norske Vandrerhjem maintains an excellent website, which details hostel locations, opening dates, prices, facilities and telephone numbers, and has a bookings facility; advance **reservations** are strongly recommended. The hostels themselves are almost invariably excellent – the only quibble, at the risk of being churlish, is that those occupying schools (during the summer holidays) tend to be rather drab and institutional.

**Prices** for a single **dorm bed** per night range from 150kr to 300kr, which almost always includes breakfast, often a lavish buffet at the better hostels. Almost all hostels have at least a few regular **double and family rooms** as well with a price range of 500–700kr a double including breakfast; these are among the least expensive rooms you'll find in Norway. There's usually a choice of en-suite or shared facilities for both rooms and dorms with the en suite costing 70–100kr more per person. Bed-sheet rental will push you a further 50kr, towels 20kr.

If you're not a **member** of Hostelling International (HI) you can still use the hostels, though there's a surcharge of around 10 percent – so, considering the low cost of annual membership (150kr), it's better to join up either before you go to Norway or at the first hostel you stay at. Some hostels are only open from mid-June to mid-August and some close between 11am and 4pm. There's sometimes an 11pm or midnight curfew, though this isn't a huge drawback in a country where carousing is so expensive.

---

**TOP 5 HI HOSTELS**

**Oslo Vandrerhjem Haraldsheim**
See p.96
**Preikestolen Vandrerhjem** See p.142
**Kongsberg Vandrerhjem** See p.180
**Åndalsnes Vandrerhjem** See p.254
**Stamsund Vandrerhjem** See p.327

---

Many hostels serve a hot evening **meal** at around 130–160kr. Hostel meals are nearly always excellent value, though of variable quality, ranging from the bland and filling to the delicious. Most, though not all, hostels have small **kitchens**, but often no pots, pans, cutlery or crockery, so self-caterers should take their own. Inexpensive **packed lunches** are often available as well, which can be particularly useful if you are heading off into the great outdoors.

## Bed and breakfast

There's no strong tradition of **B&Bs** as such, but the website of **Bed & Breakfast Norway** (ⓦbbnorway .com) brings together a disparate bunch of places from farms and cabins to family houses with a spare room or two. Prices are generally competitive – reckon on 900–1300kr for a double – though you should check if bedding is included and whether the room is en suite or with shared facilities. Norway also has a reasonably strong presence on **Airbnb** (ⓦairbnb.co.uk).

## Camping

**Camping** is a popular pastime in Norway, and there are literally hundreds of sites to choose from – anything from a field with a few tent pitches to extensive complexes with all mod cons. The Norwegian tourist authorities detail several hundred campsites online at ⓦwww.camping.no, classifying them on a one- to five-star grading depending on the facilities offered (and not on the aesthetics and/ or the location). Most sites are situated with the motorist (rather than the cyclist or walker) in mind, and a good few occupy key locations beside the main roads, though in summer these prime sites can be inundated by seasonal workers. The vast majority of campsites have at least a few cabins or chalets, called *hytter* (see opposite).

Most campsites are two- and three-star establishments, where charges are usually per tent, plus a small fee per person and then for vehicles; on average expect to pay around 200–350kr for two people using a tent and with a car, though four- and five-star sites average around twenty percent more. During peak season it can be a good idea to **reserve ahead** if you have a car and a large tent or trailer; contact details are listed online and, in some cases, in this Guide. The **Camping Key Europe Card** (ⓦcampingkey europe.com) brings faster registration at many Norwegian campsites and often entitles the bearer to special/discounted camping rates.

## WILD CAMPING

**Wild camping** in Norway is a tradition enshrined in law. You can camp anywhere in open areas as long as you are at least 150m away from any houses or cabins, though certain restrictions apply in a limited number of circumstances; for example in sea-bird sanctuaries. As a common courtesy, you are also expected to ask the landowner/farmer for **permission** to use their land if feasible – and it's rarely refused. **Fires** are not permitted in woodland areas or in fields between April 15 and September 15, and camper vans are not allowed (ever) to overnight in lay-bys. A good sleeping bag is essential, since even in summer it can get very cold, and, in the north at least, mosquito repellent is absolutely vital.

It is valid for one year, costs 250kr and can be purchased from participating campsites or online.

## Cabins

The Norwegian countryside is dotted with hundreds of timber **cabins/chalets** (called *hytter*), ranging from simple wooden huts through to comfortable lodges. They are usually two- or four-bedded affairs, with full kitchen facilities and often a bathroom, even TV, but not necessarily **bed linen**. Some hostels have them on their grounds, there are nearly always at least a handful at every campsite, and in the Lofoten islands they are the most popular form of accommodation, occupying refurbished fishermen's huts called *rorbuer* (or their modern replicas). **Costs** vary enormously, depending on location, size and amenities, and there are significant seasonal variations, too. However, a four-bed *hytter* will rarely cost more than 850kr per night – a more usual average would be about 650kr. If you're travelling in a group, they are easily the cheapest way to see the countryside – and in some comfort. Hundreds of *hytter* are also rented out as holiday cottages by the week.

## Mountain huts

One great option for hikers is the **mountain hut** (again called *hytter*). These are strategically positioned on every major hiking route and, although some are privately run, the majority are operated by **Den Norske Turistforening** (DNT; ⓦdnt.no; see pp.42–43) and its affiliated regional organizations. There are three types of mountain hut/lodge – staffed, self-service and unstaffed. **Staffed** mountain lodges, found mostly in the southern part of the country, provide meals and lodging and are often quite large, accommodating a hundred guests or more. They are characteristically clean, friendly and well run, usually by DNT staff. **Self-service** huts, with twenty to forty beds, are also concentrated in the mountains of southern

Norway and offer lodging with bedding, a shop selling groceries and a well-equipped kitchen. **Unstaffed** huts, often with fewer than twenty beds, are mostly in the north. They provide bedding, stoves for heating and cooking and all kitchen equipment, but you must bring and prepare your own food. **Reservations** are accepted at staffed lodges for stays of more than two nights, though the lodges are primarily for guests in transit. Otherwise, beds are provided on a first-come, first-served basis. During high season, lodges occasionally get full. If beds are not available, you are given a mattress and blankets for sleeping in a common area. DNT members over 50 years of age are always guaranteed a bed. No one is ever turned away.

You don't have to be a DNT member to use these huts, but **annual membership** only costs 640kr (less with concessions) and you'll soon recoup your outlay through reduced hut charges. For members staying in staffed huts, a bunk in a dormitory costs 180kr (non-members 240kr), a family, three-berth room costs 305kr per person (395kr); meals start at 125kr (165kr) for breakfast, 310kr (385kr) for a three-course dinner. At unstaffed huts, where you leave the money for your stay in a box provided, an overnight stay costs 245kr (355kr).

## Lighthouses

The **Norsk Fyrhistorisk Forening** (Norwegian Lighthouse Association; ⓦfyr.no; details: ⓦlighthouses ofnorway.com) is an umbrella organization that has taken the lead in preserving and conserving the country's **lighthouses**. Norway's coastal waters are notoriously treacherous and in the second half of the nineteenth century scores of lighthouses were built from one end of the country to the other. Initially, they were manned, but mechanization proceeded from the 1950s onwards and the old lighthousemens' quarters risked falling into decay. The Norsk Fyrhistorisk Forening is keen for new uses to be found for these quarters and already around sixty are open to the public for overnight stays or day-trips –

## TOP 5 ADVENTURE PLACES TO STAY
**Ryvingen Fyr** See p.130
**Turtagrø Hotel** See p.238
**Juvet Landscape Hotel** See p.253
**Kirkenes Snowhotel** See p.373
**Isfjord Radio** See p.380

and more will follow. Some of these sixty lighthouses can be reached by road, but others can only be reached by boat and, with one or two lavish exceptions, the **accommodation** on offer – where it is on offer – is fairly frugal and inexpensive, with doubles averaging around 600kr. The reward is the scenery – almost by definition these lighthouses occupy some of the wildest locations imaginable.

## Farm holidays

In Norway, **rural tourism** is increasingly popular with several hundred farms (and similar) providing accommodation, local food, hunting and fishing from one end of the country to the other. The national trade organization coordinating all this is **Hanen** (Ⓦhanen.no), whose portal website details everything that's on offer – and many of the locations are also described on Norway's official tourist website, Ⓦvisitnorway.com. Costs do vary enormously, but for a night's bed and breakfast on a farm you can expect to pay around 450kr per person.

# Food and drink

**At its best, Norwegian food can be excellent: fish is plentiful and carnivores can have a field day trying meats like reindeer and elk or even, conscience permitting, seal and whale. Admittedly it's not inexpensive, and those on a tight budget may have problems varying their diet, but by exercising a little prudence in the face of the average menu (which is almost always in Norwegian and English), you can keep costs down to reasonable levels.**

**Vegetarians**, however, will have slim pickings (except in Oslo), and **drinkers** will have to dig very deep into their pockets to maintain much of an intake. Indeed, most drinkers end up visiting the supermarkets and state off-licences (Vinmonopolet) so that they can sup and sip away at home (in true Norwegian style) before setting out for the evening.

## Food

There are scores of great places to eat in Norway, but because of the cost many travellers exist almost entirely on a mixture of picnic food and self-catering, with the odd café meal thrown in to boost morale. Frankly, this isn't really necessary (except on the tightest of budgets), as there are a number of ways to eat out inexpensively. To begin with, a good self-service **buffet breakfast**, served in almost every hostel and hotel, goes some way to solving the problem, while special **lunch deals** will get you a tasty hot meal for 150kr or so. Finally, alongside the regular restaurants – which are indeed expensive with mains from 250kr and up – there's the usual array of budget pizzerias, cafeterias, hot-food stands and café-bars in most towns.

### Breakfast, picnics and snacks

More often than not, **breakfast** (*frokost*) in Norway is a substantial self-service affair of bread, crackers, cheese, eggs, preserves, cold meat and fresh and pickled fish, washed down with tea or ground coffee. It's usually first-rate at HI hostels, and often memorable in hotels, filling you up for the day and almost universally included in the price of the room – where it isn't, we have indicated in the Guide.

For **picnic food**, bread, cheese, yoghurt and local fruit are all relatively good value, but other staple foodstuffs – rice, pasta, meat, cereals and vegetables – can be way above the European average. Anything tinned is particularly dear (with the exception of fish), but coffee and tea are quite reasonably priced. **Supermarkets** are ten-a-penny.

As ever, **fast food** offers the best chance of a hot, cheap takeaway snack. The indigenous Norwegian stuff, served up from a thousand and one street kiosks and stalls – **gatekjøkken** – consists mainly of rubbery hot dogs (*varm pølse*), while pizza slices and chicken pieces and chips are much in evidence too. A better choice, if a shade more expensive, is simply to get a sandwich, a **smørbrød** (pronounced "smurrbrur"), normally a slice of bread heaped with a variety of garnishes. You'll see them groaning with meat or shrimps, salad and mayonnaise in the windows of bakeries and cafés, or in the newer, trendier sandwich bars in the cities.

A standard cup of **coffee** is bitter and strong and served black with cream on the side, but lots of places – especially city coffee shops – have moved up a notch, serving mochas, cappuccinos and so forth. **Tea** is just as popular, but the local preference is for lemon tea or a variety of flavoured infusions; if you want milk, ask for it. All the familiar **soft drinks** are available, too.

## Lunch

For the best deals, you're often going to have to eat your main meal of the day at lunchtime, when **kafeterias** (often self-service restaurants) lay on daily specials, the *dagens rett*. This is a fish or meat dish served with potatoes and a vegetable or salad, often including a drink, sometimes bread, and occasionally coffee, too; it should go for 180–220kr. You'll find *kafeterias* hidden above shops and offices and adjoining hotels in larger towns, where they might be called *kaffistovas*. Most close at around 6pm, and many don't open at all on Sunday. As a general rule, the food these places serve is plain (though there are exceptions), but the same cannot be said of the much more up-to-date **café-bars** which abound in all of Norway's larger towns and cities. These affordable establishments offer much tastier (and sometimes more adventurous) meals like pasta dishes, salads and vegetarian options with main courses in the region of 180–220kr. They are also open longer – usually till late at night. **Restaurants** are worth investigating at lunchtimes too, as it's then that many of them cut their prices to pull in extra trade.

## Dinner

They may now share the gastronomic laurels with the nation's café-bars (see above), but there are first-rate **restaurants** in every Norwegian city and most towns, though the villages can lose out if the catering of the local hotel(s) doesn't cut the mustard. Apart from exotica such as reindeer and elk, the one real speciality is the **seafood**, simply prepared and wonderfully fresh – whatever you do, don't go home without treating yourself at least once. Main courses begin at around 240kr, starters and desserts at around 120kr. Smoked salmon comes highly recommended, as does catfish, halibut and monkfish. The best deals are often at lunchtime, though some restaurants don't open till the evening. In the western fjords, look out also for the help-yourself, all-you-can-eat **buffets** available in many of the larger hotels from around 6pm; go early to get the best choice and expect to pay around 600kr to be confronted by mounds of pickled herring, salmon (*laks*), cold cuts of meat, a feast of breads and crackers, and usually a few hot dishes too – meatballs, soup and scrambled eggs. In the towns, and especially in Oslo, there is also a sprinkling of **non-Scandinavian restaurants**, mostly Italian with a good helping of Chinese and Indian places. Other cuisines pop up too – Japanese, Moroccan and Persian to name but three.

Most restaurants have bilingual menus (in Norwegian and English), but we have also provided a **menu reader** (see pp.428–430).

## Vegetarians

**Vegetarians** are in for a hard time. Apart from a handful of specialist restaurants in the big cities, there's little option other than to make do with salads, look out for egg dishes in *kafeterias* and supplement your diet from supermarkets. If you are a **vegan** the problem is greater: when the Norwegians are not eating meat and fish, they are attacking a fantastic selection of milks, cheeses and yoghurts. At least you'll know what's in every dish you eat, since

---

### STOKFISK, KLIPPFISK AND LUTEFISK

The Vikings were able to sail long distances without starving to death because they had learnt how to dry white fish (mostly cod) in the open air. This dried fish, **stokfisk**, remained edible for years and was eaten either raw or after soaking in water – chewy and smelly no doubt, but very nutritious. In time, *stokfisk* became the staple diet of western Norway and remained so until the early twentieth century, with every fishing port festooned with massive wooden A-frames holding hundreds of drying white fish, headless and paired for size. Only in the 1690s did the Dutch introduce the idea of salting and drying white fish, again usually cod, to the Norwegians. The fish was decapitated, cleaned and split, then heavily salted and left for several weeks before being dried by being left outside on rocky drying grounds; *klipper* in Norwegian, hence **klippfisk** – or **bacalao** in Spanish. The Norwegians never really took to eating *klippfisk*, but their merchants made fortunes exporting it to Spain, Portugal, Africa and the Caribbean. The Norwegians did, however, take to eating **lutefisk**, in which either *stokfisk* or *klippfisk* is soaked in cold water and, at certain stages, lye, to create a jelly-like substance that many Norwegians regard as a real delicacy, though it is very much an acquired taste. The American storyteller and humourist Garrison Keillor would have none of it, suggesting in *Pontoon: A Lake Wobegon Novel* that "Most lutefisk is not edible by normal people." Most will find it hard to disagree.

everyone speaks English. If you're self-catering, look for **health food shops** (*helsekost*), which can be found in some of the larger towns and cities.

## Alcoholic drinks

One of the less savoury sights in Norway – and more common in the north – is the fall-over **drunk**: you can spot one at any time of the day or night zigzagging along the street, a strangely disconcerting counter to the usual stereotype of the Norwegian as a healthy, hearty figure in a wholesome woolly jumper. For reasons that remain obscure – or at least culturally complex – many Norwegians can't just have a drink or two, but have to get absolutely wasted. The majority of their compatriots deplore such behaviour and have consequently imposed what amounts to alcoholic **rationing**: thus, although booze is readily available in the bars and restaurants, it's taxed up to the eyeballs and the distribution of wines, strong ales and spirits is strictly controlled and is in the hands of a state-run monopoly, Vinmonopolet (see opposite). Whether this paternalistic type of control makes matters better or worse is a moot point, but the majority of Norwegians support it.

You can get a drink at most outdoor cafés, in restaurants and obviously at bars, pubs and cocktail bars, but only in the towns and cities is there any kind of "European" bar life. Wherever you go for a drink, the least expensive brand of beer should cost around 90kr for a half litre, though craft beers, which have become increasingly popular in the last decade, can rush you up to 180kr per half litre; wine starts at 40kr per glass.

### What to drink

If you decide to splash out on a few **drinks**, you'll find the most widely available Norwegian **beers** are almost universally lager-like and uninspiring; the two big-name brewers are **Ringnes**, owned by Carlsberg, and Hansa Borg, which produces Hansa beers and Heineken (under licence). More positively, Norway now has around fifty **microbreweries** producing some outstanding brews with two notable star-turns being the **Ægir** microbrewery, at the Flåmsbrygga in Flåm (see p.226), and **Inderøy Gårdsbryggeri** (🔵 igb.no), out in the sticks near Steinkjer (see p.285), whose beers are sold at *Olympen* in Oslo (see p.101), *Cardinal* in Stavanger (see p.139), and *Ramp Pub* in Trondheim (see p.282). Also out in the sticks is the **Espedalen Mountain Brewery**, whose beers are, apparently, flavoured with a small amount of gunpowder.

There has also been a minor boom in farmhouse **cider-making** across the western fjords: Ulvik, for example, has several producers. As regards **wine**, there's no domestic production to speak of and most **spirits** are imported too, with the principal exception being **aquavit** (*akevitt*), a bitter concoction served ice-cold in little glasses and, at forty percent proof or more, is real head-banging material; it's more palatable with beer chasers. **Linie aquavit**, made in Norway from potatoes, is one of the more popular brands.

### Where to buy alcohol

**Weaker beers** (below 4.75 percent ABV) are sold in supermarkets and shops all over Norway, though generally (for all but the weakest) not after 8pm on weekdays and 6pm on Saturday. Stronger beers, along with **wines and spirits**, can only be purchased from state-run **Vinmonopolet** stores (🔵 vinmonopolet.no). There's generally one branch in each medium-sized town and many more in each of Norway's cities. Characteristically, these stores are open Monday to Friday 10am–4/6pm and Saturday 10am–1/3pm, but they all close on public holidays. At Vinmonopolet stores, wine is quite a bargain, from 80kr a bottle, and there's generally a wide choice.

# The media

**British and American newspapers and magazines can be hard to find in Norway. The most likely outlets are the Narvesen kiosks at train stations and airports. Most hotels have cable or satellite TV access.**

## Newspapers and magazines

**British newspapers** – from tabloid through to broadsheet – are a rare sight in Norway, though you should have more luck with the more popular **English-language magazines** in both Oslo and Bergen. Internationally distributed **US newspapers** – principally the *Wall Street Journal*, *USA Today* and the *International Herald Tribune* – are commonly available in all of Norway's main cities at larger Narvesen kiosks.

As for the **Norwegian press**, state advertising, loans and subsidized production costs sustain a wealth of smaller papers that would bite the dust elsewhere. Most are closely linked with political parties, although the bigger city-based titles tend to be independent. The most popular newspapers in Oslo are the independent *Verdens Gang* (Ⓦ vg.no) and the independent-conservative *Aftenposten* (Ⓦ aftenposten.no); in Bergen it's the liberal *Bergens Tidende* (Ⓦ bt.no). One reliable and independent source of Norwegian news in English is online at Ⓦ norwaynews.no.

## TV and radio

Norway's **television** network has expanded over the last few years in line with the rest of Europe. Alongside the national channels, NRK1, NRK2, NRK3 and TV2, there are satellite channels like TV Norge and TV3; you can also pick up Swedish TV in many parts of the country. Many of the programmes are English-language imports with Norwegian subtitles, so there's invariably something on that you'll understand, though much of it is pretty average stuff. The big global cable and satellite channels are routinely accessible in hotel rooms.

Local tourist **radio**, giving details of events and festivals, is broadcast during the summer months; watch for signposts by the roadside and tune in. Shortwave frequencies and schedules for the BBC World Service (Ⓦ bbc.co.uk), Radio Canada (Ⓦ rcinet.ca) and Voice of America (Ⓦ voanews.com) are listed on their respective websites.

# Festivals and events

**Almost every town in Norway has some sort of summer shindig. There are winter celebrations too, though for the most part at least, these are worth attending if you are already in the area rather than meriting a special trip. Festivals fall broadly into two types, one focusing on celebrations of historical or folkloric events, the other based around music, whether jazz, pop or classical.**

As you might expect, most tourist-oriented events take place in summer and, as always, national and local tourist offices can supply details of exact dates, which tend to vary from year to year. Below we have listed the more important festivals, some of which are also mentioned in the Guide.

### JANUARY

**Nordlysfestivalen** (Northern Lights Festival), Tromsø. Late Jan. Ⓦ nordlysfestivalen.no. This week-long festival of classical and contemporary music coincides with the return of the sun, hence its name.

### MARCH/APRIL

**Birkebeinerrennet** Lillehammer. Mid-March. Ⓦ birkebeiner.no. Famous 54km cross-country-ski race from Rena to Lillehammer, which celebrates the dramatic events of 1206, when the young prince Håkon Håkonsson was rushed over the mountains to safety. The race follows what is thought to have been the original route.

**Easter Festivals** Finnmarksvidda. Easter. Ⓦ festivalerkarasjok .no. Finnmark's largest festival, held in the town of Karasjok, is something of a Sámi New Year. Sámis prepare by fashioning new *gáktis* (Sámi dress), polishing their silver and cooking large meals, while during the festival there are snowmobile, reindeer and cross-country-skiing races, lassoing contests, art exhibitions and concerts.

### MAY

**Nasjonaldagen/Grunnlovsdagen** (National Day/Constitution Day). Nationwide. May 17. Many processions and much flag-waving with cheering crowds celebrating the signing of the Norwegian constitution on May 17, 1814.

**Festspillene i Bergen** (Bergen International Festival), Bergen. Late May until early June. Ⓦ fib.no. Much-praised festival of contemporary music that puts a real spring in Bergen's summer step. Venues across the city. See p.208.

### JUNE

**Norwegian Wood** Oslo. Mid-June. Ⓦ norwegianwood.no. Three-day, open-air rock festival, arguably Norway's best. Showcases big-name international artists as well as up-and-coming local bands.

**Ekstremsportveko** (Extreme Sport Week). Voss. Late June. Ⓦ ekstremsportveko.com. Every reckless sport imaginable and then some – from paragliding and base jumping through to rafting and bungee jumping.

**Midnight Sun Marathon** Tromsø. Late June. Ⓦ msm.no. Taking advantage of 24hr daylight, this "night-time" run attracts hundreds of athletes. You can opt for shorter distances too.

### JULY

**Kongsberg Jazz Festival** Kongsberg. Four days in early July. Ⓦ kongsbergjazz.no. Large-scale jazz festival, one of the country's biggest, where the emphasis is on Norwegian musicians.

**Molde Jazz** Molde. Mid-July. Ⓦ moldejazz.no. Held over a six-day period in the middle of the month, this is one of the best festivals of its type, attracting big international names.

**Bukta** Tromsø. Late July. Ⓦ bukta.no. Large and ambitious open-air concert spread over three days. Big names, like Iggy Pop, and up and coming.

**Olsokdagene** (St Olav Festival), Stiklestad. Late July. Ⓦ stiklestad .no. St Olav, Norway's first Christian king, was killed at the battle of Stiklestad in 1030 (see p.284). Historical pageants and plays honouring him are staged on the King's feast day (July 29) as well as during the days just before and just after.

## AUGUST

**Rauma Rock** Åndalsnes. Early Aug. ⓦ raumarock.com. Three-day knees-up showcasing the talents of a wide range of local and international acts from the likes of the Far Relatives to the Raga Rockers and the Stage Dolls.

**Øyafestivalen** Oslo. Mid-Aug. ⓦ oyafestivalen.com. Four-day rock concert that attracts large crowds and famous names – Massive Attack were here in 2016, for example. Held in the Tøyenparken.

**Oslo Jazzfestival** Oslo. Mid-Aug. ⓦ oslojazz.com. A week-long event attracting a veritable raft of big international names.

**Parkenfestivalen** Two days in late August. ⓦ parkenfestivalen.no. Bodø's prime rock concert held over two days.

**Norwegian International Film Festival** Haugesund. One week in late August. ⓦ filmfestivalen.no. Norway's most prestigious film festival, with a wide selection of the latest releases from across Scandinavia.

## SEPTEMBER

**Ultima** Oslo. Ten days in early to mid-Sept. ⓦ ultima.no. Much-vaunted festival showcasing the talents of contemporary, mainly classical musicians from Scandinavia and beyond. Various venues.

**Bergen Internasjonale Filmfestival (BIFF)** Bergen. Late Sept. ⓦ biff.no. Week-long international film festival, one of the best of its type in the country. Various venues across the city centre.

## OCTOBER

**UKA** Trondheim. Three and a half weeks in Oct. ⓦ uka.no. Prestigious cultural festival, one of Norway's largest, featuring a battery of international and domestic artists in everything from classical music to rock, theatre to wrestling, juggling and crime writing.

# Outdoors Norway

**Most Norwegians have a deep and abiding love of the great outdoors. They enjoy many kinds of sports – from dog-sledding and downhill skiing in winter, through to mountaineering, angling and whitewater rafting in the summer – but the two most popular activities are hiking and cross-country skiing.**

## Hiking

Norway boasts some of the most beautiful mountain landscapes in the world, its soaring peaks accentuated by icy glaciers, rocky spires and deep green fjords. Great chunks of this wild terrain have been incorporated into a string of **national parks**; there are 44 in total, with 37 on the mainland and seven in Svalbard. These parks, especially the more accessible, are magnets for **hikers** in search of everything from easy rambles to full-scale expeditions along clearly marked trails, served by an excellent network of mountain cabins, which provide the most congenial of accommodation (see p.37).

The short **hiking season**, loosely defined by the opening and closing of the mountain lodges, runs from early July (mid-June in some areas) through to late September. This coincides with mild weather – daytime mountain temperatures of between 20°C

---

### HIKING: TOP 5 NATIONAL PARKS

Each of Norway's national parks has its particular charms, but here are a Top 5 selected with **hikers** in mind. For a list of all of Norway's national parks, go to ⓦ miljodirektoratet.no.

**Dovrefjell-Sunndalsfjella Nasjonalpark** Reached via the E6 and the Dombås–Trondheim railway, the eastern reaches of this large park are rugged and severe, but as you hike west the terrain gets even wilder as the serrated alpine peaks of the Romsdal come into view. See p.168.

**Hardangervidda Nasjonalpark** Europe's largest mountain plateau stretches east from the Hardangerfjord to Finse in the north and Rjukan in the east, its bare, almost lunar-like rocks and myriad lakes make for some spectacular hiking. The Hardangervidda begins about 130km east of Bergen. See p.217.

**Jotunheimen Nasjonalpark** Norway's most famous hiking area has a heady concentration of towering, ice-tipped peaks, more than two hundred rising above 1900m, including

northern Europe's two highest. The park is near the east end of the Sognefjord, about 300km from Oslo. See p.163.

**Nordre Isfjorden Nasjonalpark, Svalbard** One of the archipelago's largest protected areas, the coastal tundra stretches across the Isfjorden north of Barentsburg. It comprises wetlands, lake and pond complexes, and is great for light day-hikes and wildlife-spotting; wildlife includes eider ducks, pink-footed geese, ringed seals, arctic fox and the Svalbard rock ptarmigan. See p.380.

**Rondane Nasjonalpark** The Rondane comprises both a high alpine zone, with ten peaks exceeding the 2000-metre mark, and a much gentler upland area punctuated by rounded, treeless hills. It is on the E6 between Oslo and Trondheim and is especially popular with families. See p.161.

## DNT

**Den Norske Turistforening** (The Norwegian Trekking Association; ⓦdnt.no) manages all aspects of hiking in Norway. It organizes all-inclusive tours and, in conjunction with a small army of local hiking associations, takes care of trails and waymarking. It also operates several hundred mountain lodges (see p.37). DNT has outlets in all of Norway's largest cities, including Oslo, Bergen, Stavanger and Trondheim, which stock hiking maps and give advice on equipment. They also sell DNT **membership**, which confers, among much else, substantial discounts at its mountain huts (see p.37), though you can also join at any staffed DNT lodge. Neither is **annual membership** expensive at 640kr (330kr for 19–26-year-olds; 200kr for 13–18 years, 67-plus 495kr, under 12 120kr.

and 25°C – which is ideal for hiking. And, of course, it's daylight for most of the time – beyond the Arctic Circle, all the time – so you're unlikely to be searching for a mountain lodge after dark.

### Hiking trails and maps

Norway's **hiking trails** are typically marked at regular intervals by cairns (piles of stones). Most junctions are marked by signposts, some of which are small and hard to spot. There are also red "T" symbols painted on rocks, which are especially useful when visibility is poor. Although waymarking is good, you'll always need a **hiking map**. The classic map range, with red and white covers and covering every part of the country, is the **Statens Kartverk M711 Norge 1:50,000 series**, though in recent years many of these maps have been updated and upgraded with red or blue covers and made waterproof and tear-resistant; many of the new maps in the series are also co-productions between Statens Kartverk (the Norwegian Mapping Authority) and a commercial publisher. To complicate matters, Statens Kartverk was tied in with the Nordeca group in 2011 and Nordeca (ⓦforhandler.nordeca.com) has now produced top-quality, GPS-compatible maps – **Turkart** – for all the key hiking areas at three scales – 1:25,000, 1:50,000 and 1:100,000 and at the current price of 200kr. These are the **best hiking maps** on the market, and are on sale at DNT outlets, many tourist offices and some bookshops; you would, however, be well advised to buy before you go – Stanfords (ⓦstanfords.co.uk), in London, is as good a source as any.

### Guided glacier hiking

**Guided glacier hikes** can be terrific – and the widest selection is available in the western fjords on the **Jostedalsbreen** glacier (see box, p.241). Glaciers are in constant, if generally imperceptible motion, and are therefore potentially dangerous. People, often tourists, die on them nearly every year. Never hike on a glacier without a guide, never walk beneath one and always heed local instructions.

## Skiing

Norway has a strong claim to be regarded as the home of **skiing**: a 4000-year-old rock carving found in northern Norway is the oldest-known illustration of a person on skis; the first recorded ski competition was held in Norway in 1767; and Norwegians were the first to introduce skis to North America. Furthermore, one of the oldest cross-country ski races in the world, the 54km **Birkebeinerrennet**, is held annually in late March, attracting several thousand skiers to partici-pate in the dash between Rena and Lillehammer. The race follows the route taken by Norwegian mountain-men in 1206 when they rescued the two-year-old Prince Håkon. The rescuers wore birch-bark leggings known as Birkebeiners, hence the name of the race.

Although you may be tempted to go on a **ski package** via a tour operator (see p.27) remember that in most places you should find it easy (and comparatively inexpensive) to go **skiing indepen-dently**. Even in Oslo, there are downhill and cross-country ski runs within the city boundaries as well as convenient places from which to rent equipment. As a halfway house between independ-ence and the package tour, **DNT**, the Norwegian Trekking Association (ⓦdnt.no), arranges a limited range of guided skiing excursions – see their website for details.

In terms of **preparation**, lessons on a dry slope are useful in so far as they develop confidence and balance, but cross-country skiing needs stamina and upper body as well as leg strength.

### Downhill skiing and snowboarding

**Downhill skiing** and **snowboarding** conditions in Norway are usually excellent from mid-November through to late April, though daylight hours are at a premium around the winter solstice. Otherwise, Norway scores well in comparison with the better-known skiing regions of southern Europe: temperatures tend to be a good bit colder and the country has, in general terms at least, a more

---

## OUTDOOR SPORTS AND WHERE TO DO THEM

Norway's vast wild spaces provide an almost infinite variety of **outdoor sports**. A comprehensive list of **what to do and where** could fill pages, but here are a few pointers to get you started.

**Climbing** Henningsvær (see p.325); Kjeragbolten, Lysefjord (see p.141); Narvik (see p.301).

**Cycling** The Rallarvegen from Finse to Flåm (see p.224).

**Dog-sledding** Alta (see p.353); Karasjok (see p.358); Tromsø (see p.347).

**Extreme sports** Narvik (see p.301); Rjukan (see p.177); Voss (see p.221).

**Guided glacier hikes** Folgefonna (see p.213); Svartisen (see p.289); Seiland (see p.362); Hardangerjøkulen (see p.223); Jostedalsbreen glacier (see p.237).

**Hiking** See national parks box, p.42.

**Kayaking (fjord and sea)** Flåm (see p.227); Oslo (see p.93); Odda (see p.214); Ålesund (see p.258); Kabelvåg (see p.322); Tromsø (see p.347).

**Skiing (downhill and cross-country)** Geilo (see p.175); Lillehammer (see p.155); Oslo (see p.93); Voss (see p.221).

**Summer skiing** Fonna Glacier Ski Resort (see p.213).

**Whitewater rafting** Sjoa (see p.160); Voss (see p.221).

---

consistent snowfall; Norway's resorts tend to be less crowded, have smaller class sizes, shorter lift queues, and are at a lower altitude. Three main centres for downhill skiing are Voss (see p.221), Lillehammer (see p.155) and Geilo (see p.175).

### Cross-country skiing

**Cross-country skiing** is a major facet of winter life in Norway. Approximately half the population are active in the sport, and many Norwegians still use skis to get to work or school. Wherever you are in wintertime Norway, you're never far from a **cross-country ski route** and at major ski resorts sets of parallel ski tracks called *loipe* are cut in the snow by machines with the cross-country skier in mind: they provide good gliding conditions and help keep the skis parallel; some *loipe* are floodlit.

Cross-country skis can be **waxed** or **waxless**. Waxless skis have a rough tread in the middle called "fishscales", which grips adequately at temperatures around zero. Waxed skis work better at low temperatures and on new snow. Grip wax is rubbed onto the middle third of the ski's length, but a sticky substance called *klister* is used instead in icy conditions. All skis benefit from hard glide wax applied to the front and back thirds of the base.

All the main skiing centres, including Oslo's Holmenkollen (see p.89 & p.93), have designated cross-country skiing areas with at least some floodlighting.

### Telemarking

In the Telemark region of southern Norway a technique has been developed to enable skiers to descend steep slopes on free-heel touring skis. This technique, known as **telemarking**, provides a stable and effective turning platform in powder snow. Essentially the skier traverses a slope in an upright position, but goes down on a right knee to execute a right turn and vice versa.

### Summer skiing

**Summer skiing** on Norway's mountains and glaciers – both alpine and cross-country – is very popular. Lots of places offer this, but one of the largest and most convenient spots is the **Fonna Glacier Ski Resort** (Ⓦ folgefonn.no; see p.213), not far from Bergen, which has ski rental, a ski school, a café and a ski lift to the slopes.

## Fishing

Norway's myriad rivers and lakes offer some of Europe's finest **freshwater fishing**. Common species include trout, char, pike and perch, not to mention the salmon that once brought English aristocrats here by the buggy load. In the south of the country, freshwater fishing is at its best from June to September, in July and August in the north. **Seawater fishing** is more the preserve of professionals, but (amateur) sea-angling off the Lofoten islands is a popular pastime.

Sea- and freshwater fishing are both tightly controlled. The first does not require a national **licence**, but is subject to national and local restrictions regarding the size of the fish you can land and so forth. The second, freshwater fishing, needs both a local licence, which costs anything from 50kr to 400kr per day, and a national licence if you're after salmon, sea trout and char – while, that is, these fish are in fresh water. National licences are available at any post office and online (Ⓦ inatur.no or Ⓦ fefo.no for

Finnmark) for 625kr and local licences (*fiskekort*) are sold at sports shops, a few tourist offices, some hotels and many campsites. If you take your own fishing tackle, you must have it disinfected before use.

A number of **tour companies** specialize in Norwegian fishing trips and holidays (see p.27), but if you're just after a day or two's fishing, it's easy enough to get fixed up locally – start off by asking at the nearest tourist office.

## Fjord and sea-kayaking

**Fjord and sea-kayaking** are popular in Norway with a small army of tour operators concentrated in the western fjords. Local tourist offices have the details of what's on offer, and there's more information on Innovation Norway's official website (Ⓦvisitnorway .com); but one place to aim for is Flåm, which is home to the sea-kayaking specialists, **Njord Flåm** (Ⓦnjord.as). There's also Oslo Kayak Tours (Ⓦoslo kayaktours.no) in Oslo (see p.93).

## Whitewater rafting

Norway has literally dozens of top-notch **whitewater-rafting** runs. Two of the best places are Voss (see p.221) and Sjoa (see p.160). For details of **tour operators** offering rafting trips, consult **Innovation Norway**'s official website (Ⓦvisitnorway.com).

## Extreme sports

Norway's fierce landscapes offer all sorts of opportunities for **extreme and adventure sports**, from bungee jumping to paragliding. Voss has led the way – it even has its own week-long extreme sports festival (see p.221) – but Narvik (see p.301) and Rjukan (see p.177) are closing in fast.

# Shopping

**As you might expect, Norway has a flourishing retail sector and all the large towns and cities are jammed with department stores and international chains. There are a handful of obvious Norwegian goods – cheese, knitted pullovers and dried fish (*klippfisk*; see box, p.39) are three that spring to mind – but it's the Norwegian flair for design that is the country's most striking feature, especially as reflected in its fine art and interior design. You will, however, have to dig deep to bring any of it home – Norway is not a land of bargains. If you're visiting the far north, please resist the temptation to bring back reindeer antlers – they really are naff.**

## CLOTHING AND SHOE SIZES

### WOMEN'S CLOTHING

| | | | | | | | | |
|---|---|---|---|---|---|---|---|---|
| American | 4 | 6 | 8 | 10 | 12 | 14 | 16 | 18 |
| British | 6 | 8 | 10 | 12 | 14 | 16 | 18 | 20 |
| Continental | 34 | 36 | 38 | 40 | 42 | 44 | 46 | 48 |

### WOMEN'S SHOES

| | | | | | | | |
|---|---|---|---|---|---|---|---|
| American | 5 | 6 | 7 | 8 | 9 | 10 | 11 |
| British | 3 | 4 | 5 | 6 | 7 | 8 | 9 |
| Continental | 36 | 37 | 38 | 39 | 40 | 41 | 42 |

### MEN'S SHIRTS

| | | | | | | | | |
|---|---|---|---|---|---|---|---|---|
| American | 14 | 15 | 15.5 | 16 | 16.5 | 17 | 17.5 | 18 |
| British | 14 | 15 | 15.5 | 16 | 16.5 | 17 | 17.5 | 18 |
| Continental | 36 | 38 | 39 | 41 | 42 | 43 | 44 | 45 |

### MEN'S SHOES

| | | | | | | | | | |
|---|---|---|---|---|---|---|---|---|---|
| American | 7 | 7.5 | 8 | 8.5 | 9.5 | 10 | 10.5 | 11 | 11.5 |
| British | 6 | 7 | 7.5 | 8 | 9 | 9.5 | 10 | 11 | 12 |
| Continental | 39 | 40 | 41 | 42 | 43 | 44 | 44 | 45 | 46 |

### MEN'S SUITS

| | | | | | | | | |
|---|---|---|---|---|---|---|---|---|
| American | 34 | 36 | 38 | 40 | 42 | 44 | 46 | 48 |
| British | 34 | 36 | 38 | 40 | 42 | 44 | 46 | 48 |
| Continental | 44 | 46 | 48 | 50 | 52 | 54 | 56 | 58 |

## NORWEGIAN SWEATERS

No single item is more emblematic of Scandinavian tradition, workmanship and attention to detail than the Norwegian **wool sweater**. These beautiful items, many of which are handcrafted, have defined the Scandi look at home and abroad for centuries. Knitting has a strong tradition in Norway, and the stitching techniques used in the wool sweaters of today had already been put in place by the ninth century, when the garments were the simple colours of natural wool. The best-known traditional design – the bespeckled black, grey and white **lusekofte sweater** – dates from the nineteenth century and hails from the Setesdal region. This sweater, traditionally worn by men, translates as "lice jacket" on account of the black and white diagonal check pattern.

Today, a number of shops in Oslo sell everything from poor-quality, machine-made discount sweaters to hand-knitted delights; the best ones are the hand-made items from the **Dale of Norway** brand (see p.103; ⓦ daleofnorway.com), the best-known name in the country. Other respected brands include Devold (ⓦ devold.com), Norway's oldest knitwear producer, and Nordstrikk (ⓦ nordstrikk.no), a company based near Ålesund whose products employ a combination of durable Norwegian and soft, nimble Australian wools.

Taking advantage of their decision not to join the EU, the Norwegians run a **tax-free shopping scheme** for tourists. If you spend more than 315kr at any of the three thousand outlets in the tax-free shopping scheme, you'll get a tax refund cheque voucher for the amount of VAT you paid. On departure at an airport, ferry terminal or frontier crossing, present the goods, the voucher and your passport and – provided you haven't used the item and are within 30 days of purchase – you'll get a 15–25 percent refund, depending on the item. There isn't a reclaim point at every exit from the country, however – pick up a leaflet at any participating shop to find out where they are – and note that many of the smaller reclaim points keep normal shop hours, closing for the weekend at 2/3pm on Saturday. The downside is the shops themselves: the bulk are dedicated to selling souvenir goods you can well manage without.

# Travel essentials

## Addresses

Norwegian addresses are always written with the number after the street name. In multi-floored buildings, the ground floor is always counted as the first floor, the first the second and so on.

## Alphabet

The letters Æ, Ø and Å come at the end of the Norwegian alphabet, after Z (and in that order). Note that for convenience – rather than linguistic accuracy – we have alphabetized Æ as ae, Ø as O and Å as A throughout this guide.

## Border crossings

With regard to **border crossings**, there is (usually) little formality at either the Norway–Sweden or Norway–Finland borders, but the northern border with **Russia near Kirkenes** is a different story. Border patrols (on either side) won't be overjoyed at the prospect of you nosing around. If you want to visit Russia from Norway, it's best to sort out the paperwork – visas and so forth – before you leave home.

## Climate

The Gulf Stream keeps all of **coastal Norway** temperate throughout the year. **Inland**, the **climate is more extreme** – bitterly cold in winter and hot in summer, when temperatures can soar to surprising heights. January and February are normally the coldest months in all regions, July and August the warmest. **Rain** is a regular occurrence throughout the year, particularly on the west coast, though there are significant local variations in precipitation (see box opposite).

## Costs

Norway has a reputation as one of the most expensive European holiday destinations, and in some ways (but only some) this is entirely justified. Most of what you're likely to need – from a cup of coffee to a bottle of beer – is very costly, but on the other hand certain major items are reasonably priced, most notably **accommodation** which, compared with other North European countries, can be surprisingly inexpensive especially when special deals kick in, as they often do. Norway's (usually) first-rate youth hostels, almost all of which have family, double and dormitory rooms, are particularly good value. **Getting around** is reasonably good news too, as the relatively high cost of normal bus, boat and train tickets can be offset by a number of passes and there are myriad discounts and deals. Furthermore, **concessions** are almost universally available at attractions and on public transport, with infants (under 4) going everywhere free, plus children (up to 15 years) and seniors (over 67) paying – on average at least – half the standard rate. **Food** is, however, a different matter. With few exceptions – such as tinned fish – it's expensive, while the cost of alcohol is enough to make even a heavy drinker contemplate abstinence.

Travelling by bicycle, eating picnics bought from supermarkets and cooking your own food at campsites, it's possible to keep **average costs** down to 400kr a day per person. Moving up a notch, if you picnic at lunch, stick to less expensive cafés and restaurants, and stay in cheap hotels or hostels, you could get by on around 850kr a day. Staying in three-star hotels and eating out in medium-range restaurants, you should reckon on about 1500kr a day, the main variable being the cost of your room. On 2800kr a day and upwards, you'll be limited only by time, though if you're planning to stay in a five-star hotel and have a big night out, this still won't be enough. As always, if you're **travelling alone** you'll spend more on accommodation than you would in a group of two or more: many hotels do have single rooms, but they're often no less expensive than a double, though at least most youth hostels buck this trend.

## Crime and personal safety

Norway is one of the least troublesome corners of Europe, so there's little reason why you should ever come into contact with the Norwegian police. You will find that most public places are well lit and secure, most people genuinely friendly and helpful, and street crime and hassle relatively rare even late at night. It would be foolish, however, to assume that problems don't exist. Oslo in particular has its share of **petty crime**, fuelled – as elsewhere – by drug addicts and alcoholics after easy money. But keep tabs on your possessions and use the same common sense you would use at home and you should have little reason to visit the police. If you do, you'll find them courteous, concerned, and usually able to speak English. If you have something stolen, make sure you get a copy of the police report or its number, which is essential if you are to make a claim against your insurance.

As for offences *you* might commit, drinking alcohol in public places is not permitted, and being drunk on the streets can get you arrested. Drinking and driving is treated especially rigorously. Drug

## AVERAGE DAILY TEMPERATURES AND MONTHLY RAINFALL

| | Jan | Feb | Mar | Apr | May | June | July | Aug | Sept | Oct | Nov | Dec |
|---|---|---|---|---|---|---|---|---|---|---|---|---|
| **OSLO** | | | | | | | | | | | | |
| °C | -3 | -3 | 2 | 5 | 12 | 16 | 18 | 16 | 12 | 7 | 2 | -3 |
| °F | 27 | 27 | 36 | 41 | 54 | 61 | 64 | 61 | 54 | 45 | 36 | 27 |
| Rainfall (mm) | 49 | 36 | 47 | 41 | 53 | 65 | 81 | 89 | 90 | 84 | 73 | 55 |
| **BERGEN** | | | | | | | | | | | | |
| °C | 2 | 2 | 4 | 6 | 11 | 14 | 15 | 15 | 12 | 9 | 5 | 3 |
| °F | 36 | 36 | 39 | 43 | 52 | 57 | 59 | 59 | 54 | 48 | 41 | 37 |
| Rainfall (mm) | 190 | 152 | 170 | 114 | 106 | 132 | 148 | 190 | 283 | 271 | 259 | 235 |
| **TRONDHEIM** | | | | | | | | | | | | |
| °C | -3 | -3 | -1 | 4 | 8 | 12 | 15 | 14 | 10 | 5 | 1 | -2 |
| °F | 27 | 28 | 31 | 38 | 46 | 53 | 59 | 56 | 49 | 41 | 34 | 29 |
| Rainfall (mm) | 63 | 52 | 54 | 49 | 53 | 68 | 84 | 87 | 113 | 104 | 71 | 84 |
| **TROMSØ** | | | | | | | | | | | | |
| °C | -4 | -4 | -3 | 1 | 5 | 9 | 12 | 11 | 7 | 3 | -1 | -3 |
| °F | 25 | 25 | 27 | 34 | 41 | 48 | 54 | 52 | 45 | 37 | 30 | 27 |
| Rainfall (mm) | 95 | 87 | 72 | 64 | 48 | 59 | 77 | 82 | 102 | 131 | 108 | 106 |

## EMERGENCY NUMBERS

**Ambulance ☎ 113**
**Fire ☎ 110**
**Police ☎ 112**

offences, too, are met with the same attitudes that prevail throughout most of Europe.

## Customs (duty-free)

**Duty-free limits** at points of entry into Norway are complicated with a variety of pick and mix options. For example, you can choose 1 litre of spirits, 1.5 litres of wine, 2 litres of beer and 200 cigarettes; a second option is 1 litre of spirits, 3 litres of wine and 2 litres of beer – but no cigarettes. Don't miss your plane while you're trying to work it all out. For further details, go to ⓦ toll.no.

## Electricity

The current is 220 volts AC, with standard European-style two-pin **plugs**. British equipment needs only a plug adaptor; American apparatus requires a transformer and an adaptor.

## Entry requirements

Citizens of the EU/EEA, US, Canada, Australia and New Zealand need only a valid **passport** to enter Norway for up to ninety days. At time of writing, the UK seemed poised to leave the EU, but was unlikely to leave (or be disbarred from) the EEA. All other nationals should consult the relevant embassy or consulate about visa requirements. For longer stays, including periods of paid employment in Norway, there are different rules for different nationals with EU/EEA citizens having greater ease of access than non-EU/EEA citizens. For further information, contact the relevant embassy in your country of origin, referring first to ⓦ udi.no.

### NORWEGIAN EMBASSIES AND CONSULATES ABROAD

**Australia** ⓦ norway.org.au
**Canada** ⓦ emb-norway.ca
**Ireland** ⓦ norway.ie
**New Zealand** ⓦ norway.org.au
**South Africa** ⓦ norway.org.za
**UK** ⓦ norway.org.uk
**US** ⓦ norway.org
For a full list of Norwegian consulates and embassies, consult ⓦ norway.info.

## Health

Under **reciprocal health-care arrangements**, all citizens of the EU and EEA (European Economic Area) are entitled to discounted medical treatment within Norway's public health-care system. At time of writing, it is unclear what reciprocal health-care arrangements will survive the UK's exit from the EU; for the latest developments, go to ⓦ ehic .org.uk. Non-EU/EEA nationals are not entitled to discounted treatment and should, therefore, take out their own medical insurance to cover them while travelling in Norway. That said, some non-EU/EEA countries, for example Australia, do have limited mutual agreements – check the details before you depart. EU/EEA citizens will want to consider private health insurance (see opposite) too, in order to cover the cost of the discounted treatment as well as items not within the EU/EEA's scheme, such as dental treatment and repatriation on medical grounds. Note also that the more worthwhile policies promise to sort matters out before you pay (rather than after) in the case of major expense; if you do have to pay upfront, get and keep the receipts.

Health care in Norway is of a very high standard and widely available: even the remotest communities are within relatively easy – or well-organized – reach of medical attention. Rarely will **English speakers** encounter language problems – if the doctor or nurse can't speak English themselves (which is unlikely) there will almost certainly be someone at hand who can. Your local pharmacy, tourist office or hotel should be able to provide the address of an English-speaking doctor or dentist. For **medical emergencies**, call ☎ 113.

If you're seeking treatment under EU/EEA **reciprocal public health agreements**, double-check that the doctor/dentist who is seeing you is working within (and seeing you as) a patient of the relevant public health-care system. This being the case, you'll receive reduced-cost/government-subsidized treatment just as the locals do; any fees must be paid upfront, or at least at the end of your treatment, and are non-refundable. Sometimes you will be asked to produce documentation to prove you are eligible for EU/EEA health care, sometimes no one bothers, but technically at least you should have your passport and your **European Health Insurance Card** (**EHIC**) to hand. If, on the other hand, you have a travel insurance policy covering medical expenses, you can seek treatment in either the public or private health sectors, the main issue being whether – at least in major cases – you

## MOSQUITOES

These pesky blighters thrive in the myriad lakes and lochs of northern Norway, though they can be a handful (or mouthful) in the south too. They are especially bothersome if you are camping. An antihistamine cream such as Phenergan is the best antidote, although this can be difficult to find – in which case, preventative sticks like Autan or Citronella are the best bet.

have to pay the costs upfront and then wait for reimbursement or not.

## Insurance

Prior to travelling, you'd do well to take out an insurance policy to cover against theft, loss and illness or injury. Before paying for a new policy, however, it's worth checking whether you already have some degree of cover: for instance, EU/EEA health-care privileges apply in Norway (see opposite), some all-risks home insurance policies may cover your possessions when overseas, and many private medical schemes include cover when abroad.

After exhausting the possibilities above, you might want to contact a travel insurance company. A typical **travel insurance policy** usually provides cover for loss of baggage, tickets and – up to a certain limit – cash, as well as cancellation or curtailment of your journey and medical costs. Most of them exclude so-called dangerous sports – climbing, horseriding, rafting, windsurfing and so forth – unless an extra premium is paid. Many policies can be chopped and changed to exclude coverage you don't need – for example, sickness and accident benefits can often be excluded or included at will. If you do take medical coverage, ascertain whether benefits will be paid as treatment proceeds or only after you return home, and whether the policy has a

24-hour medical emergency number. When securing baggage cover, make sure that the per-article limit will cover your most valuable possessions. If you need to make a claim, keep receipts for medicines and medical treatment. In the event you have anything stolen, you should obtain a crime report statement or number.

## Internet

Almost all of the country's hotels, B&Bs and hostels provide **internet access/wi-fi** for their guests either free or at minimal charge. Most cafés, restaurants and bars offer internet access too, as does every library, though here services are usually free but time-limited. Internet access in the open-air/public spaces is, however, much more sporadic.

## Left luggage

There are coin-operated lockers in most train and bus stations and at all major ferry terminals.

## LGBT travellers

In 1981, Norway was one of the first countries in the world to pass a law making discrimination against homosexuals and lesbians illegal. Twelve years later, it followed this up by becoming only the second country to pass legislation giving lesbian and gay couples the same rights as married couples, while retaining a bar on church weddings and the right to adopt children. Further legislation in 2002 and 2003 relaxed the restrictions on gay adoption, and same-sex marriages became legal in 2009. All this progressiveness, however, has more to do with respect for the rights and freedoms of the individual than a positive attitude to homosexuality – Norway remains, in essence at least, very much a (heterosexual) family-oriented society. Nevertheless, the general attitude to homosexuals is so tolerant that few feel the need to disguise their sexuality.

### ROUGH GUIDES TRAVEL INSURANCE

Rough Guides has teamed up with WorldNomads.com to offer great travel insurance deals. Policies are available to residents of over 150 countries, with cover for a wide range of adventure sports, 24hr emergency assistance, high levels of medical and evacuation cover and a stream of travel safety information. Roughguides.com users can take advantage of their policies online 24/7, from anywhere in the world – even if you're already travelling. And since plans often change when you're on the road, you can extend your policy and even claim online. Roughguides.com users who buy travel insurance with WorldNomads.com can also leave a positive footprint and donate to a community development project. For more information go to ⓦ roughguides.com/travel-insurance.

The age of consent for both homosexuals and heterosexuals is sixteen.

It's commonplace for bars and pubs to have a mixture of gays and heterosexuals in their clientele. There is something of a separate scene in Bergen, Trondheim and especially Oslo (see p.105), but it's pretty low-key stuff – and the same applies to the weekly gay and lesbian nights held in some small-town nightclubs. The main gay events are the Gay Pride celebrations in Oslo (June; @oslo pride.no), Bergen (June; @bergenpride.no) and Trondheim (September; @trondheimpride.no). **Landsforeningen for Lesbisk og Homofil frigjøing** (LLH; @llh.no), Norway's strong and effective gay and lesbian organization, has its national office in Oslo (see p.105).

# Mail

Norway has an efficient **postal system** (Posten Norge; @posten.no), but it is one that has moved away from traditional post offices (there are now only thirty in the whole of the country) to locations in retail stores and shops, of which there are about 1500. **Postage** varies according to weight, size and urgency. Currently, a standard-size letter or postcard under 20g that is sent "Priority" class costs 11kr within Norway, 14kr within Europe, and 18kr to everywhere else. Mail to the US should take about a week, post to places within Europe usually takes two to three days. **Stamps** are widely available from post offices, tourist offices and many hotels.

# Maps

The **maps** in this book should be adequate for most general purposes, especially as they can be readily supplemented by the local maps supplied for free by most tourist offices. Drivers, cyclists and hikers will, however, require something more detailed. Buying before you go helps in planning, and often saves a bit of money too – standard maps in a Norwegian bookshop will cost you around 200kr. For **Scandinavia** as a whole, the AA (@theaa.com) produces a good-quality **road map** at 1:1,000,000. For **Norway**, Hallwag's *Norge/Norwegen* road map (@swisstravelcenter.com) is excellent. It has two scales – one for the south (1:800,000) and one for the north (1:900,000) – an index and a handy distance calculator on the back. Michelin (@via michelin.com) also publishes a widely available *Norway* map (1:1,250,000), but although this is very accurate and useful for route planning, the index is very scanty; Cappelen Damm's (@cappelendamm

.no) *Hele Norge* (1:1,000,000) map has the advantage of being updated every year, includes an exhaustive index and marks the country's designated, scenic tourist routes (*Turistveger*), but at this scale is hard to drive by, especially in the more crowded parts of the country. The best and most detailed **book of Norwegian road maps** is the *Stort bilatlas Norge* (1:325,000) produced by Cappelen Damm (@cappelendamm.no). It has a comprehensive index, is updated every year or two, and includes 75 good-quality city and town maps; it is, however, expensive (350kr), hard to get hold of outside of Norway, and – even at this scale – much too cluttered for clarity in the country's most populated areas. Your best bet is to use it in conjunction with the Hallwag map (see above). Cappelen also produce excellent **city maps** covering Bergen, Oslo, Trondheim and so on; they are at a variety of scales (1:4000 to 1:10,000) and are on sale locally at any good bookshop.

**Cycling maps**, with route suggestions, are usually on sale at tourist offices in the more popular cycling areas. **Hiking maps** are covered under "Hiking trails and maps" (see p.43).

# Money

Norway has its own currency, the **kroner**; one krone (literally "crown"; abbreviated to **kr** or NOK) is divided into 100 **øre**. Coins in circulation are 1kr, 5kr, 10kr and 20kr; notes are for 50kr, 100kr, 200kr, 500kr and 1000kr (though note that smaller retailers often look askance at this last, largest note). At the time of writing the rate of exchange for 1kr is £0.09, €0.11, US$0.12, Can$0.16, Aus$0.16, NZ$0.17, ZAR1.71. For the most up-to-date rates, check the currency converter website @oanda.com. As means of comparison – and to show the effects of the fall in the price of oil – in 2012 the exchange rates were 1kr equals £0.11, €0.13, US$0.17, Can$0.17, Aus$0.16, NZ$0.20, ZAR1.34.

**ATMs** ('Mini-Banks') are liberally distributed around every city, town and large village in Norway, and accept a host of debit cards without charging a transaction fee. Credit cards can be used in ATMs too, but in this case transactions are treated as loans, with interest accruing daily from the date of withdrawal. All major **credit/debit cards**, including American Express, Visa and MasterCard, are widely accepted. Typically, Norwegian ATMs give instructions in a variety of languages. You can change **foreign currency** into kroner at most banks, which are ubiquitous; banking hours vary, but are generally Monday to Friday 8am to 3.30pm.

**NORWAY'S PUBLIC HOLIDAYS**

**New Year's Day**
**Maundy Thursday** The Thursday before Easter.
**Good Friday**
**Easter Monday**
**Labour Day** May 1
**Ascension Day** Forty days after Easter.
**National (or Constitution) Day** May 17
**Whit Monday** The seventh Monday after Easter.
**Christmas Day**
**Boxing Day** The day after Christmas Day.

Note that when a public holiday falls on a Sunday, then the next day becomes a public holiday.

## Opening hours and public holidays

**Business hours** (i.e. office hours) normally run from Monday to Friday 9.30/10am to 4.30/5pm. Normal **shopping hours** are Monday through Friday 10am to 5pm, with late opening on Thursdays till 6pm, 7pm or 8pm, plus Saturdays 10am to 1pm, 2pm or 3pm. Most supermarkets stay open much longer – from 9am until 8pm in the week and from 9am to 6pm on Saturdays, but close on Sundays. In addition, many kiosks-cum-newsstands open from 8/9am or so till 9pm or 10pm every day of the week (including Sun), but much more so in the cities and towns than in the villages. Many fuel stations sell a basic range of groceries and stay open till 11pm daily. Vinmonopolet, the state-run liquor chain, has outlets in almost every town and large village, but they operate limited opening hours; each store fixes its own schedule, but generally they're open Monday to Friday 10am–4/6pm and Saturday 10am–1/3pm. Norway has literally hundreds of **museums**. The more important ones are open all year, but many close for winter from October or November to April, May or even mid-June. Opening hours are usually 9.30/10am–5pm every day, including Saturday and Sunday, but some limit their hours at the weekend and many more close on Mondays.

**National public holidays** (see box above) are keenly observed across Norway and, although much of the tourist industry carries on regardless, almost every museum and gallery in the land is closed. Otherwise most businesses and shops close, and the public transport system operates a skeleton or Sunday service. Some of these public holidays are also **official flag-flying days**, but there are additional flag days as well – for example on Queen Sonja's birthday (July 4).

## Phones

Given the sheer size of the country and its stretches of wilderness, it's amazing just how much of Norway has **mobile phone** (**cell phone**) coverage – it's around 80 percent and counting. Norway is on the mobile phone (cell phone) network at GSM900/1800, the band common to the rest of Europe, Australia and New Zealand. Mobile/cell phones bought in North America need to be of sufficient specification to adjust to this GSM band. If you intend to use your phone in Norway, note that call charges can be excruciating – particularly irritating is the supplementary charge you often have to pay on incoming calls – so check with your supplier. You might also consider buying a **Norwegian SIM card**, though this can get

**INTERNATIONAL CALLS**

**PHONING HOME FROM NORWAY**

To make an international phone call from within Norway, dial the appropriate international access code as below, then the number you require, omitting the initial zero where there is one.

| | |
|---|---|
| **Australia** ☎0061 | **South Africa** ☎0027 |
| **Canada** ☎001 | **UK** ☎0044 |
| **New Zealand** ☎0064 | **US** ☎001 |
| **Republic of Ireland** ☎00353 | |

**PHONING NORWAY FROM ABROAD**

To call a number in Norway, dial the local international access code, then ☎47, followed by the number you require, omitting the initial zero where there is one. There are **no area codes** in Norway and the vast majority of Norwegian telephone numbers have eight digits; where this isn't the case, it's probably a premium-rated line, except those numbers beginning ☎800, which are toll-free.

complicated: many mobiles/cells will not permit you to swap SIM cards and the connection instructions for the replacement SIM card can be in Norwegian only. If you overcome these problems, there are myriad deals on offer beginning at about 100kr per SIM card; these can be bought at larger 7-Eleven and Narvesen kiosks. **Text messages/ SMS**, on the other hand, are normally charged at ordinary or at least bearable rates – and with your existing SIM card in place; WhatsApp, among other similar services, is of course free wherever you can get a connection – but 3G/4G coverage is not nearly as good as phone coverage.

## Smoking

**Smoking** is prohibited in all public buildings, including train and bus stations, as well as in restaurants, clubs, bars and cafés. Nonetheless, one in four Norwegians still puffs away.

## Time

Norway is on **Central European Time** (**CET**) – one hour ahead of Greenwich Mean Time, six hours ahead of US Eastern Standard Time, nine hours ahead of US Pacific Standard Time, nine hours behind Australian Eastern Standard Time and eleven hours behind New Zealand. There are, however, minor variations during the changeover periods involved in **daylight saving**. Norway operates daylight saving time, moving clocks forward one hour in the spring and one hour back in the autumn.

## Tipping

Cafés and restaurants often add a service charge to their bills and this is – or at least should be – clearly indicated. Otherwise, few Norwegians **tip** at cafés, restaurants or bars and, given the country's high prices, you'll probably be disinclined as well, though restaurant waiters and taxi drivers may be disappointed not to get a tip of 10 percent. Rounding your bill up by a few kroner to make a round number is, on the other hand, pretty standard and considered polite.

## Tourist information

The **Norwegian Tourist Board** operates an all-encompassing website, covering everything from hotels and campsites to forthcoming events. It also publishes a wide range of glossy, free booklets of both a general and specific nature, which for the most part at least are available at all the larger tourist offices throughout the country. Inside Norway, every town and most of the larger villages have their own **tourist office**; we've given their addresses, opening hours, websites and telephone numbers throughout the Guide. Staff almost invariably speak good to fluent English and dispense, among much else, free local maps, local brochures and public transport timetables; many will also help arrange last-minute/in-person accommodation. In addition, Norway is spectacularly well represented on the internet in terms of everything from activity holidays through to bus timetables; we've listed a few general websites below – many more are in the Guide.

### USEFUL WEBSITES

ⓦ **nfl.no** The website of the Norwegian Film Institute covers the country's cinematic comings and goings in admirable depth.

ⓦ **norwaynews.no** Excellent and detailed coverage of all that happens in Norway.

ⓦ **regjeringen.no** Government site which, despite its plain presentation, has everything you ever wanted to know about Norway's various ministries and what they are up to.

ⓦ **visitnorway.com** The official site of the Norwegian Tourist Board has links to all things Norwegian, as well as its own good sections on outdoor activities and events.

## Travelling with children

In general terms at least, Norwegian society is sympathetic to its **children** and the tourist industry follows suit. Extra beds in hotel rooms are usually easy to arrange, baby-changing stations are commonplace, and high-chairs for young children are usually at hand in cafés, if not so much in restaurants. Furthermore, **concessionary rates** are the rule, from public transport through to museums, and pharmacists carry all the kiddie stuff you would expect – nappies, baby food, and so forth – but this being Norway they cost a lot, so try to bring the gubbins with you. As far as **breastfeeding** in public is concerned, the *Journal of Human Lactation* states that in Norway "There is no problem with breastfeeding almost anywhere at any time. A mother might get an ugly glance once in a while, but restaurants, shopping centres, and even government offices allow breastfeeding without any discussion". As for things to do, Norway's many adventure activities can be ideal for kids, from kayaking to fishing, horseriding to skiing. Big-city Oslo has perhaps more **child-friendly attractions** than anywhere else (see box, p.104).

# Travellers with disabilities

There are decent facilities for **travellers with disabilities** across the whole country. An increasing number of hotels, hostels and campsites are equipped for disabled visitors, and are credited as such in the tourist literature by means of the standard wheelchair-in-a-box icon. Furthermore, on most main routes the trains have special carriages with wheelchair space, hydraulic lifts and disabled toilets; domestic flights either cater for or provide assistance to disabled customers; and the latest ships on all ferry routes have lifts and cabins designed for disabled people.

In the cities and larger towns, many restaurants and most museums and public places are wheelchair-accessible, and although facilities are not so advanced in the countryside, things are improving. Drivers will find that most motorway service stations are wheelchair-accessible and that, if you have a UK-registered vehicle, the disabled car parking badge is honoured. Note also that several of the larger car rental companies have modified vehicles available. On a less positive note, city pavements can be uneven and difficult to negotiate and, inevitably, winter snow and ice can make things much, much worse.

Getting to Norway should be relatively straight-forward too. Most airlines and shipping companies provide assistance to disabled travellers, while some also have specific facilities, such as DFDS Scandinavian Seaways ferries' specially adapted cabins.

# Oslo and the Oslofjord

DEN NORSKE OPERAHUSET

# 1

# Oslo and the Oslofjord

Quite simply, Oslo is one of Europe's most amenable capitals, a vibrant, self-confident city with a relaxed and easy-going air, its handsome centre set between the rippling waters of the Oslofjord and the green, forested hills of the interior. Yet Oslo's confidence is new-found: for much of its history, the city was something of a poor relation to the other Scandinavian capitals, Stockholm and Copenhagen especially, and it remained dourly provincial until well into the 1950s. Since then, however, Oslo has transformed itself, forging ahead to become an enterprising and cosmopolitan commercial hub with a population approaching 700,000. Oslo is also the only major metropolis in a country brimming with small towns and villages – its nearest rival, Bergen, is less than half its size. This gives the city a powerful voice in the political, cultural and economic life of the nation and it's pulled in all of Norway's big companies, as a rash of concrete and glass tower blocks testifies.

Fortunately, these monoliths rarely interrupt the stately Neoclassical lines of the late nineteenth-century **city centre**, Oslo's most appealing district, which boasts a lively restaurant and bar scene as well as a clutch of excellent museums. Indeed, Oslo's biggest single draw is its **museums**, which cover a hugely varied and stimulating range of topics: the fabulous Viking Ship Museum, the National Gallery, which showcases the paintings of Edvard Munch, the magnificent sculpture park devoted to the stirring bronze and granite works of Gustav Vigeland, and the moving historical documents of the Resistance Museum, are, to name just four, enough to keep even the most jaded visitor enthralled for days. There's also a first-rate **outdoor scene**, with Oslo rustling up a good range of parks, pavement cafés, street entertainers and festivals, especially in summer when virtually the whole population seems to live outdoors – and visiting is a particular delight. Winter is also a good time to be here, when Oslo's position amid hills and forests makes it a thriving, convenient and (surprisingly) affordable **ski centre**.

Although Oslo's centre is itself compact, its outer districts spread over a vast 454 square kilometres, encompassing huge chunks of woodland, beach and water. Almost universally, the city's inhabitants have a deep and abiding affinity for these wide-open spaces and, as a result, the waters of the **Oslofjord** to the south and the forested hills of the **Nordmarka** to the north are tremendously popular for everything from boating and swimming to hiking and skiing. On all but the shortest of stays, there's ample opportunity to join in – the open forest and **cross-country ski** routes of the Nordmarka and the **island beaches** just offshore in the Oslofjord are both easily reached by metro or ferry.

# Highlights

**❶ Nasjonalgalleriet** Norway's most ambitious collection of fine art, the National Gallery has a bit of everything, from Dahl to Kittelsen and Tidemand to Krohg, but the key paintings are by Edvard Munch. **See p.66**

**❷ Ibsenmuseet** See exactly where Norway's greatest dramatist, Henrik Ibsen, spent his last years and breathed his last breath. **See p.71**

**❸ Vigelandsparken** Take a stroll round the fantastical creations of Gustav Vigeland in this wonderful open-air sculpture park. **See p.78**

**❹ Vikingskipshuset** The world-famous Viking Ship Museum exhibits a trio of Viking longships preserved in the subsoil since they were interred in the Viking period. **See p.84**

**❺ Hovedøya** You can swim, walk through woods or laze on the beach on this charming Oslofjord island, just a short ferry ride from the city centre. **See p.88**

**❻ Stratos** Oslo has some great places to drink, but this laidback, infinitely groovy rooftop bar is hard to beat. **See p.101**

HIGHLIGHTS ARE MARKED ON THE MAP ON PP.60–61

**1**

Oslo curves round the innermost shore of the **Oslofjord**, whose tapered waters extend for some 100km from the Skagerrak, the choppy channel separating Norway and Sweden from Denmark. As Norwegian fjords go, the Oslofjord is not especially beautiful – the rocky shores are generally low and unprepossessing – but scores of pretty little islets diversify the seascape. Many of these wooded bumps accommodate summer chalets, but several have been protected from development and one of them – **Hovedøya** – makes for a lovely excursion. By comparison, the towns that trail along the shores of the Oslofjord are for the most part of little immediate appeal, being mostly for workaday industrial settlements. The exceptions include, on the eastern shore, **Fredrikstad**, home to a delightful and superbly well-preserved seventeenth-century fortress, and on the western shore, the Viking burial mounds of **Borre** and, at a pinch, the holiday resort of **Tønsberg**.

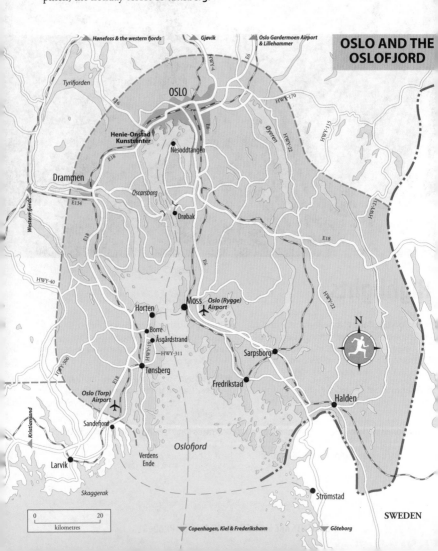

# Oslo

1

If **OSLO** is your first taste of Norway, you'll be struck by the light – soft and brilliantly clear in the summer and broodingly gloomy in winter. The grand, late nineteenth- and early twentieth-century buildings of **central Oslo** suit the light well – and look reassuringly sturdy just as once they gave a sense of security to an emergent nation. Consequently, much of the centre remains easy and pleasant to walk around, a humming, good-natured place whose breezy streets and squares combine these appealing remnants of the city's earlier days with a clutch of good museums. Highlights include the **Ibsenmuseet** (Ibsen Museum), the **Nasjonalgalleriet** (National Gallery) and the **Hjemmefrontmuseum** (Resistance Museum) – plus dozens of lively bars, cafés and restaurants. Edging the centre is the **harbour**, at its prettiest immediately behind the **Rådhus**, though the waterfront's proudest building, the glossy new **Operahuset**, is further to the east on the next cove along.

Oslo's showpiece museums – most memorably the remarkable **Vikingskipshuset** (Viking Ship Museum) – are on the **Bygdøy peninsula**, which is readily reached by ferry from the jetty behind the Rådhus (City Hall) as are the rusticated **islands** that confetti the inner waters of the Oslofjord with wooded **Hovedøya** being the cream of the scenic crop. Back on the mainland, **east Oslo** is the least prepossessing part of town, a gritty sprawl housing the poorest of the city's inhabitants, though the reinvigorated district of **Grünerløkka** is now home to a slew of fashionable bars and clubs. The main sight on the east side of town is the **Munchmuseet** (Munch Museum), which owns a superb collection of the artist's work, though the museum will be moving to the harbourfront beside the Operahuset by 2020.

**Northwest Oslo** is far more prosperous, with big old houses lining the avenues immediately to the west of the Slottsparken. Beyond is the **Frognerparken**, a chunk of parkland where the wondrous open-air sculptures of Gustav Vigeland are displayed in the **Vigelandsparken**. Further west still, beyond the city limits in suburban Høvikodden, the **Henie-Onstad Kunstsenter** displays more prestigious modern art, enhanced by the museum's splendid setting on a headland overlooking the Oslofjord.

The city's enormous reach becomes apparent to the north of the centre in the **Nordmarka**, a massive wilderness that stretches far inland patterned by hiking trails and cross-country ski routes. Two **T-bane** (Tunnelbanen) lines provide ready access, weaving their way up into the rocky hills that herald the region. The more westerly of these two T-bane lines rolls past **Holmenkollen**, a ski resort where the ski jump makes a crooked finger on Oslo's skyline, before terminating at **Frognerseteren**. Here the station is still within the municipal boundaries, but the surrounding forested hills and lakes feel anything but urban. The more easterly T-bane offers less wilderness, but it does end up close to **Sognsvannet**, a pretty little lake set amid the woods and an ideal place for an easy stroll and a picnic.

---

### SAVING MONEY: THE OSLO PASS

The useful and money-saving **Oslo Pass** gives **free admission** to almost every museum in the city, unlimited **free travel** in zones 1 and 2 of the municipal transport system (see p.93) and free parking in municipal car parks (but not private ones). It also provides some **discounts** in shops, hotels and restaurants, but nevertheless in winter, when opening hours for many sights and museums are reduced, you may have to work hard to make the card pay for itself. Valid for 24, 48 or 72 hours, it costs 335kr, 490kr or 620kr respectively, with children aged 4 to 15 years and seniors (over 67 years) charged 170kr, 250kr or 310kr. It's available at the Oslo Visitor Centre (see p.92) and at many hotels and hostels. The card is valid for a set number of hours (rather than days) starting from the moment it is first used, at which time it should either be presented and stamped or franked in an automatic machine, though you can always fill in the date and time yourself. A booklet detailing every advantage the Oslo Pass brings is issued when you purchase one.

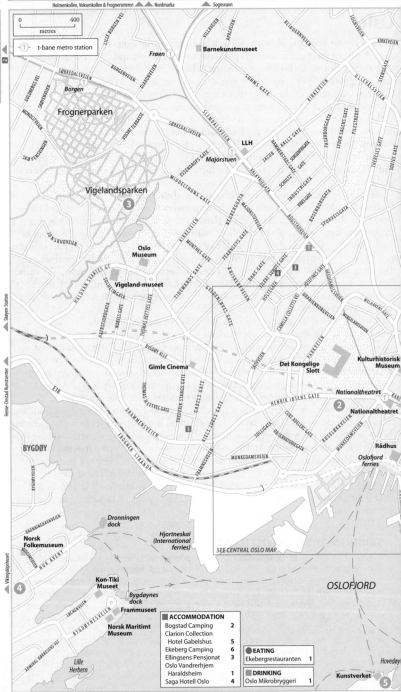

Holmenkollen, Voksenkollen & Frognerseteren ▲▲ Nordmarka ▲ Sognsvann

0 ——— 400
metres

Ⓣ t-bane metro station

Barnekunstmuseet

Frøen Ⓣ

Borgen

Frognerparken

Vigelandsparken

LLH

Majorstuen

Oslo Museum

Vigeland-museet

Skøyen Station

Henie-Onstad Kunstsenter

Gimle Cinema

Det Kongelige Slott

Kulturhistorisk Museum

Nationaltheatret

Nationaltheatret

Rådhus

BYGDØY

Oslofjord ferries

Vikingskiphuset

Dronningen dock

Hjortneskai (International ferries)

SEE CENTRAL OSLO MAP

Norsk Folkemuseum

Kon-Tiki Museet

Bygdøynes dock

Frammuseet

Norsk Maritimt Museum

Lille Herbern

OSLOFJORD

Hovedøy

Kunstverket

Gressholmen ▼

**ACCOMMODATION**
Bogstad Camping 2
Clarion Collection
 Hotel Gabelshus 5
Ekeberg Camping 6
Ellingsens Pensjonat 3
Oslo Vandrerhjem
 Haraldsheim 1
Saga Hotell Oslo 4

●**EATING**
Ekebergrestauranten 1

■**DRINKING**
Oslo Mikrobryggeri 1

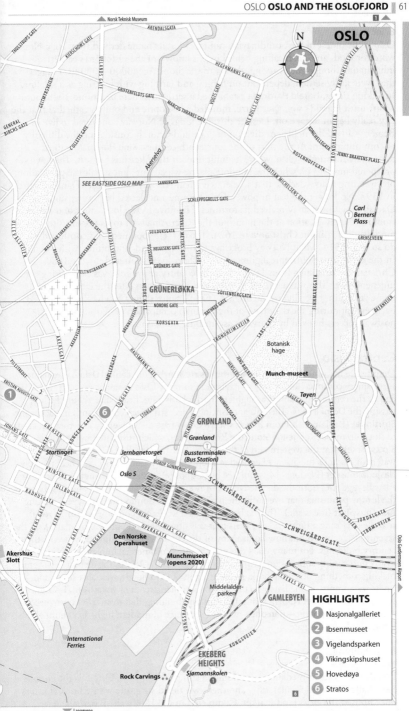

**OSLO**

Norsk Teknisk Museum

SEE EASTSIDE OSLO MAP

GRÜNERLØKKA

Carl Berners Plass

Botanisk hage

Munch-museet

Tøyen

GRØNLAND

Grønland

Jernbanetorget

Bussterminalen (Bus Station)

Stortinget

Oslo S

Den Norske Operahuset

Munchmuseet (opens 2020)

Akershus Slott

Middelalderparken

GAMLEBYEN

International Ferries

EKEBERG HEIGHTS

Rock Carvings

Sjømannskolen

Langøyene

Oslo Gardermoen Airport

**HIGHLIGHTS**

1 Nasjonalgalleriet
2 Ibsenmuseet
3 Vigelandsparken
4 Vikingskipshuset
5 Hovedøya
6 Stratos

**1**

## Brief history

Oslo is the oldest of the Scandinavian capital cities, its name derived from *Ås*, a Norse word for God, and *Lo*, meaning field. Little is known of the Oslofjord's earliest inhabitants, though rock carvings dating to the Stone Age (3000–2000 BC) suggest they were fairly settled, dependent on fishing and farming with hunting as a sideline. In Viking times, **Harald Hardrada** established a settlement here in around 1048, but it wasn't until Harald's son, **Olav Kyrre**, founded a bishopric and built a cathedral that the city really began to take off. Despite this, the kings of Norway continued to live in Bergen – an oddly inefficient division of State and Church considering the difficulty of communication. At the start of the fourteenth century, **King Håkon V** rectified matters by moving to Oslo, where he built himself the Akershus fortress. The town prospered until 1349, when the bubonic plague wiped out almost half the population, precipitating a slow decline that accelerated when Norway came under Danish control in 1397. No longer the seat of power, Oslo became a neglected backwater until the Danish king **Christian IV** revived its fortunes. He moved Oslo lock, stock and barrel from its marshy location at the mouth of the River Alna west to its present site, modestly renaming it **Christiania** in 1624. The new city boomed, and continued to do so after 1814, when Norway broke away from Denmark and united with Sweden. In the event, this political realignment was a short-lived affair and, by the 1880s, Christiania – **Kristiania** from 1877 – and the country as a whole was clamouring for independence. This was achieved in 1905 and twenty years later the city changed its name yet again, reverting to the original "Oslo". Since then, Oslo has hardly looked back, except during the dark days of the German occupation of World War II, its postwar success buoyed by Norway's astonishing oil boom.

## Central Oslo

Despite the mammoth proportions of the Oslo conurbation, **central Oslo** has remained surprisingly compact, and is easy to navigate. From the Oslo S train station, at the eastern end of the centre, the main thoroughfare, **Karl Johans gate**, heads directly up the hill, passing the **Domkirke** (Cathedral) and cutting a pedestrianized course until it reaches the **Stortinget** (Parliament). From here it sweeps down past the **University** and then proceeds to slope up to **Det Kongelige Slott** (the Royal Palace), which is situated in parkland – the **Slottsparken** – at the western end of the centre. South of the Royal Palace, on the waterfront, stands the glassy **Aker Brygge** shopping and leisure complex, where the new **Nasjonalmuseet** (National Museum; see box opposite) is under construction. Across from Aker Brygge rises both the distinctive twin-towered **Rådhus** (City Hall) and, just beyond, the lumpy peninsula that overlooks the harbour and accommodates the severe-looking **Akershus Slott** (the castle). The castle, Stortinget and Oslo S combine to form a rough triangle enclosing a tight grid of streets that was originally laid out by Christian IV in the seventeenth century, but now holds many of the city's most imposing early twentieth-century buildings. For many years this was the city's commercial hub, and although Oslo's burgeoning suburbs undermined its position in the 1960s, the district is currently making something of a comeback, reinventing itself with hotels, specialist shops and smart restaurants. Immediately to the east, on another stretch of waterfront, is Oslo's sweeping **Operahuset** (Opera House), a stunning building that forms the centrepiece of a major redevelopment – **Barcode** – where a sequence of modern high-rises shunt along Dronning Eufemias gate.

### Basarhallene

Corner Karl Johans gate and Dronningens gate

Presiding over its immediate surroundings a stone's throw from Oslo S is the curious **Basarhallene**, a semicircular, one- and then two-tiered structure whose brick cloisters once housed the city's food market. Completed in the 1850s, the Basarhallene was

## THE NEW NASJONALMUSEET AND MUNCHMUSEET

Under construction down on the Aker Brygge, and scheduled to be finished by 2020, is Norway's ambitious new **Nasjonalmuseet** (National Museum; ⓦ nasjonalmuseet.no). In preparation, three of Oslo's existing museums are being closed down as their collections are moved into the new museum. The **Kunstindustrimuseet** (Museum of Applied Art), on St Olav's gate, and the **Museet for Samtidskunst** (Contemporary Art Museum), on Bankplassen, have already closed, while the **Nasjonalgalleriet** (National Gallery), on Universitetsgata, will cease operations in 2019. Incidentally, the **Arkitekturmuseet** (Museum of Architecture; see p.75) is counted as the fourth section of the Nasjonalmuseet, but will remain unmoved and unchanged. There's movement elsewhere too, with the relocation of the existing **Munchmuseet** (see p.81) to a prime location down on the waterfront close to the Operahuset; the new Munchmuseet is currently under construction and is scheduled to open in 2020.

designed by Christian Heinrich Grosch (1801–65), a prolific architect responsible for a platoon of Oslo buildings – including several at Oslo University – and no fewer than eighty churches from one end of Norway to the other. Today, the market is long gone and has been replaced with shops and cafés, several of which have pleasant garden terraces to the rear.

## Domkirke

Stortorvet, off Karl Johans gate • Mon–Thurs, Sat & Sun 10am–4pm, Fri 4–6pm • Free • ☎ 23 62 90 10, ⓦ oslodomkirke.no

The Basarhallene arches round the back of the **Domkirke** (Cathedral), an attractive albeit rather chunky structure, which mostly dates from the late seventeenth century, though its heavyweight tower was remodelled in 1850. From the outside, the cathedral may appear a little plain and dour, but the elegantly restored **interior** is a delightful surprise, its homely, low-ceilinged nave and transepts awash with maroon, green and gold paintwork. At the central crossing, the flashy Baroque pulpit, where cherubs frolic, faces a royal box that would look more at home at the opera. The high altar is Baroque too, its relief of the Last Supper featuring a very Nordic-looking sacrificial lamb. To either side are stained-glass windows created in 1910 by Emanuel Vigeland (1875–1948), the younger brother of Gustav (see p.78). The brightly coloured **ceiling paintings** are also modern, with a representation of God the Father taking precedence in the Holy Trinity above the high altar, while Jesus is the pre-eminent figure in the north transept, the Holy Spirit in the south. Down below, the **crypt** is sometimes used for temporary exhibitions of religious fine and applied art.

## Stortorvet

The front doors of the Domkirke face out onto **Stortorvet**, once the main city square, but no longer of much account, its modest flower market overseen by a nineteenth-century **statue** of a distinctly chubby **Christian IV** (1577–1648). He deserves better: one of the few Dano-Norwegian kings to take a real interest in Norway, Christian was a hard-working diligent ruler and, although his reign was ultimately scarred by military failure, he remained popular in Norway until the end of his days – quite a tribute considering he ruled for almost six decades.

## Stortingsbygningen

Karl Johans gate • Guided tours: mid-May to mid-June Sat 2 daily; 45min • Free • ☎ 23 31 31 80, ⓦ stortinget.no

Home to the **Stortinget** (Parliament – literally "Great Council"), the **Stortingsbygningen** is an imposing chunk of neo-Romanesque architecture, whose stolid, sandy-coloured brickwork, dating from the 1860s, exudes bourgeois certainty. The building had a long gestation; to begin with it took years for the

1

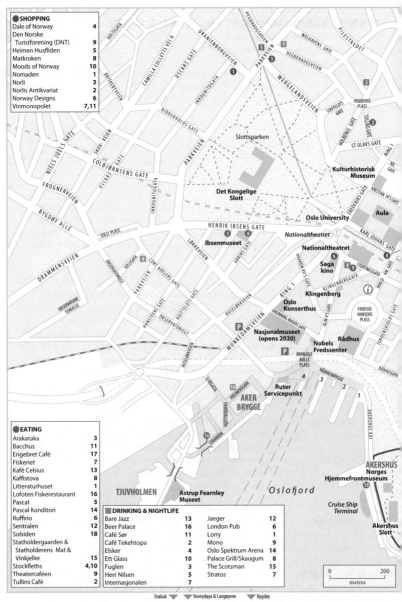

**● SHOPPING**

| | |
|---|---|
| Dale of Norway | 4 |
| Den Norske Turistforening (DNT) | 9 |
| Heimen Husfliden | 5 |
| Matkroken | 8 |
| Moods of Norway | 10 |
| Nomaden | 1 |
| Norli | 3 |
| Norlis Antikvariat | 2 |
| Norway Designs | 6 |
| Vinmonopolet | 7,11 |

**● EATING**

| | |
|---|---|
| Arakataka | 3 |
| Bacchus | 11 |
| Engebret Café | 17 |
| Fiskeriet | 7 |
| Kafé Celsius | 13 |
| Kaffistova | 8 |
| Litteraturhuset | 1 |
| Lofoten Fiskerestaurant | 16 |
| Pascal | 5 |
| Pascal Konditori | 14 |
| Ruffino | 6 |
| Sentralen | 12 |
| Solsiden | 18 |
| Statholdergaarden & Statholderens Mat & Vinkjeller | 15 |
| Stockfleths | 4,10 |
| Theatercaféen | 9 |
| Tullins Café | 2 |

**■ DRINKING & NIGHTLIFE**

| | | | |
|---|---|---|---|
| Bare Jazz | 13 | Jaeger | 12 |
| Beer Palace | 16 | London Pub | 6 |
| Café Sør | 11 | Lorry | 1 |
| Café Tekehtopa | 2 | Mono | 9 |
| Elsker | 4 | Oslo Spektrum Arena | 14 |
| Ett Glass | 10 | Palace Grill/Skaugum | 8 |
| Fuglen | 3 | The Scotsman | 15 |
| Herr Nilsen | 5 | Stratos | 7 |
| Internasjonalen | 7 | | |

Drøbak ▼   ▼ Hoveydøya & Langøyene   ▼ Bygdøy

parliamentarians to actually agree to the construction of a parliament building at all and then, after they had run a competition, they argued about which design was the best until the present structure – by the Swede Emil Langlet – just pipped the vote. Nowadays, the parliament is open for infrequent guided tours and although the interior is notably unexciting, the parliamentary chamber is of some mild interest for its informality – it looks like a ballroom.

**ACCOMMODATION**

| | |
|---|---|
| Clarion Collection Hotel Folketeateret | 7 |
| Cochs Pensjonat | 1 |
| Comfort Hotel Xpress Youngstorget | 4 |
| Continental | 8 |
| Grand | 9 |
| Hotell Bondeheimen | 6 |
| Perminalen | 10 |
| Scandic Edderkoppen | 3 |
| Scandic Holberg | 2 |
| Thon Hotel Oslo Panorama | 11 |
| Thon Hotel Rosenkrantz | 5 |

Ⓣ t-bane metro station

**CENTRAL OSLO**

▽ DFDS Seaways & Stena ferries to Denmark

Ekebergparken & Rock Carvings ▽

## Eidsvoll plass

In front of the Parliament building, a narrow and particularly pleasant park-piazza – **Eidsvoll plass** – runs west, filling out the space between Karl Johans gate and Stortingsgata. In summer, the park brims with promenading city folk, who dodge between the jewellery hawkers, ice-cream kiosks and street performers; in winter there are dinky little open-air and floodlit **ice-skating rinks**, where skates can be rented at minimal cost.

**1**

## Nationaltheatret

Johanne Dybwads plass 1, Stortingsgata • Tickets ☎ 815 00 811, ⓦ nationaltheatret.no

Lurking at the western end of Eidsvoll plass is the Neoclassical **Nationaltheatret** (National Theatre), built in 1899 and fronted by statues of Henrik Ibsen and Bjørnstjerne Bjørnson. The **Ibsen statue** went up during the great man's lifetime, which pleased him no end. Inside the theatre, the 800-seater red-and-gold main hall has been restored to its turn-of-the-twentieth-century glory and can be savoured during a performance – though these are usually in Norwegian.

The Nationaltheatret is also a useful **transport interchange**. A pair of tunnels round the back – one for points west, the other east – give access to NSB trains, the T-bane and the Flytoget, the airport express train. In addition, many city buses and trams stop behind the Nationaltheatret, on Stortingsgata.

## The University Aula

Karl Johans gate • Only open for special events & concerts • Free • ☎ 22 85 50 50, ⓦ uio.no

Across from the Nationaltheatret stand three of the **University**'s main buildings, grand nineteenth-century structures whose classical columns, pilasters and imperial pediments fit perfectly with this monumental part of the city centre. The middle of the trio is the **Aula**, where the imposing, deeply recessed entrance leads to a hall decorated with **murals by Edvard Munch**. The controversial result of a competition held by the university authorities in 1909, the murals weren't actually unveiled until 1916, after years of heated debate. Munch had just emerged (cured) from a winter in a Copenhagen psychiatric clinic when he started on the murals, and they reflect a new mood in his work – confident and in tune with the natural world they trumpet. All three main pieces feature a recognizably Norwegian landscape, harsh and bleak and painted in ice-cold blues and yellowy whites. *History* focuses on an old, bearded man telling stories to a young boy, and *Alma Mater* has a woman nourishing her children, but it is *The Sun* which takes the breath away, a searing globe of fire balanced on the horizon to shoot its laser-like rays out across a rocky landscape. If you can't manage to get in to see them, there are photos of all the Aula's Munch paintings on the UiO website.

## Nasjonalgalleriet

Universitetsgata 13 • Tues, Wed & Fri 10am–6pm, Thurs 10am–7pm, Sat & Sun 11am–5pm • 100kr • ☎ 21 98 20 00, ⓦ nasjonalmuseet.no/en/

The **Nasjonalgalleriet** (National Gallery), Norway's largest and most prestigious art gallery, occupies a whopping nineteenth-century building a couple of minutes' walk from Karl Johans gate – although from 2019 onwards the collection will be moved to the new Nasjonalmuseet (see box, p.63). The collection may be short on internationally famous painters – apart from a fine body of work by **Edvard Munch** – but there's generous compensation in the oodles of Norwegian art, including work by all the leading practitioners up until 1950. The only irritation is the way the museum is organized: the main body of the collection is displayed on the **first floor**, which is convenient enough, but the room-by-room thematic divisions are unnecessarily complicated with one result being that the work of individual artists can be displayed across several different rooms. The **free plan** available at reception helps illuminate matters and explains the colour coding of the galleries. The text below mentions many of the key paintings, but note that there isn't enough room to display the whole of the collection at any one time, so exhibits are regularly rotated.

### Johan Christian Dahl and Thomas Fearnley

Near the top of the main staircase, rooms 13 and 12 feature the work of the country's most important nineteenth-century landscape painters, **Johan Christian Dahl** (1788–1857) and his pupil **Thomas Fearnley** (1802–42). The Romantic Naturalism of their finely detailed canvases expressed Norway's growing sense of nationhood after the break-up of the Dano–Norwegian union in 1814. In a clear rejection of Danish lowland civil-servant culture, Dahl and Fearnley asserted the beauty (and moral virtue) of Norway's wild landscapes, which had previously been seen as uncouth and barbaric. This reassessment was clearly influenced by the ideas of the Swiss-born philosopher Jean-Jacques Rousseau (1712–78), who believed that the peoples of mountain regions possessed an intrinsic nobility precisely because they were remote from the corrupting influences of (lowland) civilization. Dahl, who was a professor at the Academy of Art in Dresden for many years, wrote to a friend in 1841:

*Like a true Poet, a Painter must not be led by the prevailing, often corrupt Taste, but attempt to create … a landscape [that] … exposes the characteristics of this Country and its Nature – often idyllic, often historical, melancholic – what they have been and are.*

As for the **paintings** themselves, Dahl's large 1842 canvas *Stalheim* is typical of his work, a mountain landscape rendered in soft and dappled hues, dotted with tiny figures and a sleepy village, while his *Larvik havn i Måneskinn* (Larvik harbour in Moonlight) is pure romance, but a handsome painting all the same. Dahl's *Hjelle in Valdres* (1851) adopts the same approach as his *Stalheim*, although here the artifice behind the Naturalism is easier to detect. Dahl had completed another painting of Hjelle the year before; returning to the subject, he widened the valley and heightened the mountains, sprinkling them with snow. Fearnley often lived and worked abroad, but he always returned to Norwegian themes, painting no fewer than five versions of the moody *Labrofossen ved Kongsberg* (The Labro Waterfall at Kongsberg); his 1837 version is displayed in Room 12.

### Adolph Tidemand and Hans Frederik Gude

A third Norwegian artist to look out for is **Adolph Tidemand** (1814–76), if not so much for the quality of his painting as for its content. Born in Mandal on the south coast, Tidemand went to art college in Denmark and lived in Düsseldorf, but was firmly attached to his homeland, making a series of long research trips to study rural Norwegian folk customs and costumes. Tidemand's drawings were so precise that they are still used as a reference by students of traditional Norwegian dress, but his paintings are absurdly Romantic, reflecting the bourgeois nationalism that swept Norway in the middle of the nineteenth century. The museum displays a whole batch of Tidemand's paintings, but his most famous work is the *Bridal Voyage on the Hardanger Fjord* (Room 14), in which **Hans Frederik Gude** (1825–1903) painted the landscape and Tidemand filled in the figures. Gude was a great friend of Tidemand, sharing his Romantic nationalism as they chewed the cud as fellow lecturers at the art academy in Düsseldorf.

### Gerhard Munthe, Erik Werenskiold and Christian Krohg

In the 1880s, Norwegian landscape painting took on a mystical and spiritual dimension. Influenced by French painters such as Théodore Rousseau, Norwegian artists abandoned the Naturalism of an earlier generation for more symbolic representations. **Gerhard Munthe** (1849–1929), for one, dipped into lyrical renditions of the Norwegian countryside, and his cosy, folksy scenes were echoed in the paintings of **Erik Werenskiold** (1855–1938), who is well represented by *Peasant Burial* in Room 16. Of a similar ilk was the work of the novelist, journalist and artist **Christian Krohg** (1852–1925), whose highly stylized paintings of the poor and destitute pricked many a middle-class conscience. It was, however, his sympathetic paintings of prostitutes that created the real brouhaha, as exemplified by his tongue-in-cheek *Albertine at the Police Doctor's Surgery*, again in Room 16.

### Theodor Kittelsen

Also during the late nineteenth century, **Theodor Kittelsen** (1857–1914) defined the appearance of the country's trolls, sprites and sirens in his illustrations for Asbjørnsen and Moe's *Norwegian Folk Tales*, published in 1883. Four of Kittelsen's original paintings are in the possession of the gallery and, although they are regularly moved around and sometimes not displayed at all, they are simply splendid, especially the one of a princess delousing a troll, a time-consuming job if ever there was one. Kittelsen's other work is perhaps less striking, but the gallery does own a self-portrait, a landscape or two, and a platoon of his sketches.

### Harald Sohlberg and Halfdan Egedius

In Room 18, you encounter the works of **Harald Sohlberg** (1869–1935), who clarified the rather hazy vision of many of his Norwegian contemporaries, painting a series of sharply observed Røros streetscapes and expanding into more elemental themes with such stunning works as *En blomstereng nordpå* (A Northern Flower Meadow) and *Sommernatt* (Summer Night). These paintings are comparable with those of **Halfdan Egedius** (1877–99), as in *Opptrekkende uvaer* (The Approaching Storm), again in Room 18, though Egedius also touched on darker, gloomier themes as in his unsettling *Dansende jenter* (Girls Dancing).

### Edvard Munch

The Nasjonalgalleriet's star turn is its **Munch collection**, with representative works from the 1880s up to 1916 gathered together in Room 19. His early work is very much in the Naturalist tradition of his mentor Christian Krohg, though by 1885 Munch was already pushing back the boundaries in *The Sick Child*, a heart-wrenching evocation of his sister Sophie's death from tuberculosis. Other works displaying this same sense of pain include *The Dance of Life*, *Madonna* and *The Scream*, a seminal canvas of 1893 whose swirling lines and rhythmic colours were to inspire the Expressionists. Munch painted several versions of

---

## ARTISTIC TURBULENCE: EDVARD MUNCH

Born in 1863, **Edvard Munch** had a melancholy **childhood** in what was then Christiania (Oslo). His early years were overshadowed by the early deaths of both his mother and a sister from tuberculosis, as well as the fierce Christian piety of his father, but by his mid-twenties Munch was in open revolt against his family, persevering in his ambition to become a painter and living it up in what was then considered a rakish, bohemian set. After a number of early works, including several self-portraits, attracted some interest – and a scholarship – he went on to study in **Paris**, a city he returned to again and again, and where he fell (fleetingly) under the sway of the Impressionists in general and Gauguin in particular, responding to the French painter's simplified forms and non-naturalistic colours. In 1892, Munch moved on to **Berlin**, where his style developed and he produced some of his best and most famous work, though his first exhibition there was considered so outrageous it was closed after only a week. His painting was, a critic opined, "an insult to art": his recurrent themes, notably jealousy, sickness, alienation and the awakening of sexual desire, all of which he had extrapolated from his childhood, were simply too much for his audience. Nevertheless, despite the initial criticism, Munch's work was subsequently exhibited in many of the leading galleries of the day.

Thereafter, Munch wandered Europe, painting and exhibiting prolifically, but meanwhile overwork, drink and problematic love affairs were fuelling an instability that culminated, in 1908, in a **nervous breakdown**. Munch spent six months in a Copenhagen clinic, after which his health improved greatly – and his paintings lost the hysterical edge characteristic of his most celebrated work. Nonetheless, he never dismissed the importance of his mental frailness, writing, for example, "I would not cast off my illness, for there is much in my art that I owe to it." Munch **returned to Norway** in 1909 and was based there until his death in 1944. He wasn't, however, a popular figure in his homeland despite – or perhaps because of – his high international profile and he was regularly criticized in the press for all manner of alleged faults, from miserliness to artistic arrogance. Neither was his posthumous reputation enhanced by the **state funeral** organized for him by the occupying Germans, his coffin paraded up Karl Johans gate in a cortege of guns, eagles and swastikas. To be fair, Munch had certainly not wanted a fascist funeral and neither was he sympathetic to the Germans, who he feared would end up confiscating his paintings and burning them as "degenerate" art – as they nearly did.

*The Scream*, but this is the original, so it is hard to exaggerate the embarrassment felt by the museum when, in 1994, someone climbed in through the window and stole it – and, even worse, a similar theft happened at the Munchmuseet ten years later (see box, p.81). The painting was eventually recovered, but the thief was never caught. Consider Munch's words as you view it:

*I was walking along a road with two friends. The sun set. I felt a tinge of melancholy. Suddenly the sky became blood red. I stopped and leaned against a railing feeling exhausted, and I looked at the flaming clouds that hung like blood and a sword over the blue-black fjord and the city. My friends walked on. I stood there trembling with fright. And I felt a loud unending scream piercing nature.*

The gallery's sample of Munch paintings serves as an excellent introduction to the artist and, if your curiosity is wetted, you can see more of his work on display at the Munch Museum (see p.81).

### Norwegian paintings from 1910 to 1950

Munch aside, the general flow of Norwegian art was reinvigorated in the 1910s by a new band of artists who had trained in Paris under Matisse, whose emancipation of colour from Naturalist constraints inspired his Norwegian students. The canvases of this group are exhibited in the **yellow section** (Rooms 21–24) and although the paintings here are frequently rotated, there's usually something from **Henrik Sørensen** (1882–1962), the group's outstanding figure. Sørensen summed up the Frenchman's influence on him thirty years later: "From Matisse, I learned more in fifteen minutes than from all the other teachers I have listened to" – and it was these lessons that inspired Sørensen's surging, earthy landscapes of the lowlands of eastern Norway. **Axel Revold** (1887–1962) was trained by Matisse too, but also assimilated Cubist influences as in *The Fishing Fleet leaves the Harbour*, while **Erling Enger** (1899–1990) maintained a gently lyrical, slightly whimsical approach to the landscape and its seasons. Revold spent a few months teaching **Arne Ekeland** (1908–94), though this later artist was much more influenced by German Expressionism and Cubism, which suited his leftist, class-conscious politics perfectly. Ekeland's various World War II paintings are bleak and powerful in equal measure – as evidenced by the fractured, mosaic-like composition of *The Last Shots*.

### International art

Finally, in several of its galleries the museum exhibits an enjoyable sample of work by the **Impressionists** and **Post-Impressionists**, with assorted bursts of colour from Manet, Monet, Degas and Cézanne, as well as a distant, piercing Van Gogh self-portrait. There is also a light scattering of early twentieth-century paintings by the likes of Picasso and Braque, but it must be said that for a national gallery there are few works of international significance, reflecting Norway's past poverty and its lack of an earlier royal or aristocratic collection to build upon.

## Kulturhistorisk Museum

Frederiks gate 2 · Mid-May to mid-Sept Tues–Sun 10am–5pm; mid-Sept to mid-May Tues–Sun 11am–4pm · 80kr · ☎ 22 85 19 00, ⓦ khm.uio.no

Just north of Karl Johans gate, Oslo's **Kulturhistorisk Museum** (Cultural History Museum) occupies a handsome neo-Romanesque structure of imposing proportions. The capacious interior holds the university's hotchpotch historical and ethnographical collections, among which the undoubted highlight is the **Viking and early medieval section**, on the ground floor in the rooms to the left of the entrance.

### Viking and early medieval section

The museum's **Viking and early medieval section** features several magnificent portals from twelfth- and thirteenth-century **stave churches** (see box, p.174), alive with dragons and beasts emerging from swirling, intricately carved backgrounds, plus weapons, coins,

**1**

drinking horns, runic stones, religious bric-a-brac and bits of clothing. The special highlight is, however, a superb **vaulted chancel ceiling** dating from the late thirteenth century and retrieved from the stave church in Ål, near Geilo. The room's brightly coloured wooden planks are painted in tempera – a technique in which each pigment was mixed with glue, egg white and ground chalk – and feature a complicated biblical iconography, beginning at the apex with the Creation and Adam and Eve, followed, as you work your way down, by depictions of Christ's childhood and ultimately his death and resurrection. An English-language booklet gives the full lowdown, but it's the dynamic forcefulness of these naive paintings, as well as the individuality of some of the detail, that really impresses – look out, in particular, for the nasty-looking Judas at the Last Supper, and the pair of amenable donkeys peeping into Christ's manger.

### Viking Age exhibition

The rest of the ground floor is taken up by a pretty average **Viking Age exhibition** geared towards school parties. The tiny dioramas are downright silly, and detract from the exhibits, which attempt to illustrate various aspects of early Norwegian society, from religious beliefs through to military hardware, trade and craft. More positively, there is a good sample of Viking decorative art, including several pieces illustrating the intensely flamboyant, ninth-century Oseberg and Borre styles and continuing into the Jellinge style, where greater emphasis was placed on line and composition. There's also a **skattkammeret** (treasure room) of precious objects – finger rings, crucifixes, pendants, brooches, buckles and suchlike – illustrating the sustained virtuosity of Norse goldsmiths and silversmiths.

### Etnografiske utstillingene (Ethnographic exhibition)

On the floor above, the beginning of the **etnografiske utstillingene** has an enjoyable collection of ancient Egyptian artefacts, but is mostly devoted to the Arctic peoples with an illuminating section on the Sámi, who inhabit the northern reaches of Scandinavia. Moving on, the top floors contain a diverse collection of African and Asiatic art and culture, from Samurai suits to African masks, and host temporary exhibitions on ethnographers and ethnography.

## Det Kongelige Slott and Slottsparken

Slottsplassen • English-language guided tours of the palace: mid-June to late Aug 3 daily; 1hr • 135kr • Tickets in advance from any Narvesen store or on the day at the entrance, if there are any tickets left – demand often exceeds supply • Tickets: ☎ 815 33 133, Ⓦ kongehuset.no

Stuck on the hill at the west end of Karl Johans gate, **Det Kongelige Slott** (Royal Palace) is a monument to Norwegian openness. Built between 1825 and 1848, when the

---

### JEAN-BAPTISTE BERNADOTTE AND THE ROYAL PALACE

The toings and froings of Scandinavian royalty can be befuddling, but few accessions were as unusual as that of **Karl XIV Johan** (1763–1844), king of Norway and Sweden. Previously, Karl Johan had been the Napoleonic Marshal Jean-Baptiste Bernadotte, a distinguished military commander who had endured a turbulent relationship with his boss, **Napoleon**, who sacked and reinstated him a couple of times before finally stripping him of his rank for alleged lack of military ardour at the battle of Wagram, outside Vienna, in 1809. In a huff, Bernadotte stomped off back to Paris, where – much to his surprise – he was informed that the **Swedish court** had elected him as the heir to their king, the childless Charles XIII. This was not, however, a quixotic gesture by the Swedes, but rather a desire to ensure that their next king was a good soldier able to protect them from their enemies, especially Russia. In the event, it worked out rather well: Bernadotte successfully steered the Swedes through the tail end of the Napoleonic Wars, firstly as Crown Prince to a decrepit King Charles XIII from 1810 and then, on Charles's death, as the Swedish king, adding Norway to his future kingdom in 1818. Not content, seemingly, with the terms of his motto, "The people's love is my reward", Karl Johan had the whopping **Kongelige Slott** built for his further contentment, only to die before it was completed.

1

monarchs of other European nations were nervously counting their friends, it now stands almost entirely without railings and walls, its grounds – the **Slottsparken** – freely open to the public, who can get up close to a snappy **changing of the guard**, which takes place outside the palace daily at 1.30pm. Directly in front of the palace is an equestrian statue of king **Karl XIV Johan**, inscribed with his motto (see box below). In the summertime, there are hour-long **guided tours** of parts of the palace, though you really have to be a fan of Norway's royal family to find these of much interest.

## Ibsenmuseet

Henrik Ibsens gate 26 • Mid-May to mid-Sept daily 11am–6pm; mid-Sept to mid-May daily 11am–4pm, Thurs till 6pm; apartment tour hourly • 100kr; tour no extra charge • ☎ 40 02 36 30, ⓦ www.ibsenmuseet.no

The grand, nineteenth-century mansions bordering the southern perimeter of the Slottsparken once housed Oslo's social elite. It was here, in a fourth-floor apartment at Arbins gate 1, on the corner of what is now Henrik Ibsens gate, that Norway's most celebrated playwright, **Henrik Ibsen** (see box below), spent the last ten years of his life,

---

### HENRIK IBSEN

**Henrik Johan Ibsen** (1828–1906), Norway's most famous and influential playwright, is generally regarded as one of the greatest dramatists of all time, and certainly his central themes have powerful modern resonances. In essence, these concern the alienation of the individual from an ethically bankrupt society, loss of religious faith and the yearning of women to transcend the confines of their roles as wives and mothers. Ibsen's central characters often speak evasively, mirroring the repression of their society and their own sense of confusion and guilt, with venomous exchanges – a major characteristic of the playwright's dialogue – appearing whenever the underlying tensions break through. Ibsen's protagonists do things that are less than heroic, often incompetent, even malicious. Nevertheless, they aspire to **dåd** – acting with heroism – arguably a throwback to the old Norse sagas. These themes run right through Ibsen's plays, the first of which, *Catalina* (1850), was written while he was employed as an apothecary's assistant at Grimstad on the south coast (see p.123).

The alienation the plays reveal was undoubtedly spawned by Ibsen's troubled **childhood**: his father had gone bankrupt in 1836, and the disgrace – and poverty – weighed heavily on the whole family. More humiliation followed at Grimstad, where the shy, young Ibsen worked for a pittance and was obliged to share a bed with his boss and two maids, which resulted in one of them bearing a child in 1846. Ibsen escaped small-town Norway in 1850, settling first in Oslo and then Bergen. But he remained deeply dissatisfied with Norwegian society, which he repeatedly decried as illiberal and small-minded. In 1864, he **left the country** and spent the next 27 years living in Germany and Italy. It was during his exile that Ibsen established his literary reputation – at first with the rhyming couplets of **Peer Gynt**, featuring the antics of the eponymous hero, a shambolic opportunist in the mould of Don Quixote, and then by a vicious attack on provincial values in *Pillars of Society*. It was, however, *A Doll's House* (1879) that really put him on the map, its controversial protagonist, Nora, making unwise financial decisions before walking out not only on her patronizing husband, Torvald, but also on her loving children – all in her desire to control her own destiny. *Ghosts* followed two years later, and its exploration of moral contamination through the metaphor of syphilis created an even greater furore, which Ibsen rebutted in his next work, *An Enemy of the People* (1882). Afterwards, Ibsen changed tack (if not theme), firstly with *The Wild Duck* (1884), a mournful tale of the effects of compulsive truth-telling, and then *Hedda Gabler* (1890), where the heroine is denied the ability to make or influence decisions, and so becomes perverse, manipulative and ultimately self-destructive.

Ibsen **returned to Oslo** in 1891. He was treated as a hero, and ironically – considering the length of his exile and his comments on his compatriots – as a symbol of Norwegian virtuosity. Indeed, the daily strolls he took from his apartment to the *Grand Hotel* on Karl Johans gate became something of a tourist attraction – not that Ibsen, who was notoriously grumpy, often wanted to talk to anyone. Ibsen was incapacitated by a stroke in 1901 and died from the effects of another five years later.

**1**

strolling down to the *Grand* (see p.95) every day to hold court. Admirers did their best to hobnob with the great man as he took his daily walk, but Ibsen was unenthusiastic about being a tourist attraction in his own lifetime and mostly ignored all comers – no one could ever accuse him of being overly sociable. Ibsen's old apartment is now incorporated within the **Ibsenmuseet** (Ibsen Museum), which begins with a well-considered introduction to Ibsen and his plays, exploring, over two small floors, the themes that underpinned his work and his uneasy relationship with his home country. Beyond, **Ibsen's apartment** has been restored to its appearance in 1895, including many of the original furnishings, but it can only be visited on a guided tour. Both Ibsen and his wife died here: Ibsen breathed his last as he lay paralysed in bed, but his wife, unwilling to expire in an undignified pose, dressed herself to die sitting upright in a chair in the library. Ibsen was argumentative to the end – famously, his final words were "To the contrary" in reply to his poor old maid, who had tried to cheer him up by suggesting he was looking better.

## The Rådhus

Fridtjof Nansens plass • Daily 9am–4pm • Free • ☎ 23 46 12 00, ⊕ rft.oslo.kommune.no

Rearing high above the harbourfront, and twenty years in the making, Oslo's **Rådhus** (City Hall) finally opened in 1950 to celebrate the city's nine-hundredth anniversary. Designed by Arnstein Arneberg and Manus Poulsson, this firmly Modernist, twin-towered building of dark-brown brick was intended to be a grandiose statement of civic pride – and a statement of intentions as to where the city wanted to go.

Initially, few locals had a good word for what they saw as an ugly and strikingly un-Norwegian addition to the city, but with the passing of time the obloquy has fallen on more recent additions to the skyline – principally Oslo S – and the Rådhus has become one of the city's more popular buildings. At first, the ornamentation was equally contentious. Many leading Norwegian painters and sculptors contributed to the decoration, which was designed to celebrate all things Norwegian, but the pagan themes chosen for much of the work gave many of the country's Protestants the hump.

The **main approach** to the Rådhus is on its landward side via a wide ramp, whose **side galleries** are adorned by garish **wood panels** illustrating pagan Nordic myths with several featuring the Tree of the World, Yggdrasil or Yggdrask (see p.407).

### The interior

Inside, the principal hall – the **Rådhushallen** – is decorated with vast, stylized and very secular murals. On the north wall, Per Krohg's *From the Fishing Nets in the West to the Forests of the East* invokes the figures of polar explorer Fridtjof Nansen (on the left) and dramatist Bjørnstjerne Bjørnson (on the right) to symbolize, respectively, the nation's spirit of adventure and its intellectual development. On the south wall is the equally vivid *Work, Administration and Celebration*, which took Henrik Sørensen a decade to complete. The self-congratulatory nationalism of these two murals is hardly attractive, but the effect is partly offset by the forceful fresco in honour of the Norwegian Resistance of World War II, which runs along the east wall.

### The rear

Outside, at the back of the Rådhus, a line of six realistic **bronzes** represents the trades – builders, bricklayers and so on – who worked on the building. Behind them, four massive, granite female sculptures surround a fountain whose plinth sports four more figures, and beyond is the busy central **harbour**, with the bumpy Akershus peninsula on the left and the islands of the Oslofjord filling out the backdrop. This is a delightful spot, one of the city's happiest moments, and from here you can either catch a ferry to the museums of the Bygdøy peninsula (see p.82) or the Oslofjord islands (see p.88) – or stroll over to the Nobels Fredssenter.

## Nobels Fredssenter

Rådhusplassen • Mid-May to Aug daily 10am–6pm; Sept to mid-May Tues–Sun 10am–6pm • 100kr • ☎ 48 30 10 00, ⓦ nobelpeacecenter.org

The **Nobels Fredssenter** (Nobel Peace Centre) was founded to celebrate and publicize the Nobel Peace Prize. Born in Sweden, **Alfred Nobel** (1833–96) invented dynamite in his thirties and went on to become extraordinarily rich with factories in over twenty countries. In his will, Nobel established a fund to reward good works in five categories – physics, chemistry, medicine, literature and peace. The awards were to be made annually, based on the recommendations of several Swedish institutions, with the exception of the Peace Prize, the recipient of which was to be selected by a committee of five, itself appointed by the Norwegian parliament.

Inside, the Peace Centre's **ground floor** features a series of temporary displays designed to get visitors into thinking about conflict and peace, poverty and wealth, refugees and asylum. **Upstairs**, there are more temporary exhibitions; a small display on the life of Alfred Nobel; "wall papers" (broadly, information sheets) on all things to do with peace; and the so-called "**Nobel Field**", where each of the past holders of the Peace Prize is represented by a celebratory plaque attached to a light bulb on a wispy stalk. With the overhead lights dimmed right down, the stalks make a sort of miniature electrical forest, which really looks both effective and very engaging. As for the winners of the Peace Prize themselves, there are many outstanding individuals – Martin Luther King, Desmond Tutu, Nelson Mandela and Willy Brandt to name but four – but some real surprises too, notably Theodore Roosevelt, who was part of the American invasion of Cuba in the 1890s, and the USA's **Henry Kissinger**, who was widely blamed for destabilizing Cambodia in the 1970s, his award prompting a leading comedian of the day to announce that political satire was dead. Indeed, despite its current exemplary image, the Nobel Prizes are in fact steeped in controversy: the writer and playwright Johan August Strindberg (1849–1912) was the pre-eminent literary figure in Sweden for several decades, but he was much too radical for the tastes of the prize givers and in 1911, after he had again failed to get one, the Swedish trades union movement organized a whip-round and gave him a "Nobel Prize" themselves.

## Aker Brygge and Tjuvholmen

Behind the Peace Centre, the new Nasjonalmuseet is under construction (see box, p.63), while the adjacent **Mellomstasjonen** (Sat noon–4pm; free), itself a former tram station, provides some background to this prestige project. Metres way, the old Aker shipyard has been turned into the swish **Aker Brygge** shopping-cum-office complex, a gleaming concoction of walkways, circular staircases and glass lifts, all decked out with neon and plastic; the bars and restaurants here are some of the most popular in town. At the far end of Aker Brygge, a brace of footbridges span a slip of water to reach the first of two newly created artificial islands, together known as **Tjuvholmen** (literally "Thief Island"). Depressingly, it's apartment-block mania here, though the developers did squeeze in an ultrasmart hotel, *The Thief*, and the Astrup Fearnley art museum.

## Astrup Fearnley Museet

Strandpromenaden 2, Tjuvholmen • Tues–Fri noon–5pm, Thurs till 7pm, Sat & Sun 11am–5pm • 120kr • ☎ 22 93 60 60, ⓦ afmuseet.no

There's more than a sniff of money shaking hands with contemporary art in the glistening new premises inhabited by the **Astrup Fearnley Museet** (Astrup Fearnley Museum), just beyond the far end of Aker Brygge. The museum occupies two new buildings: designed by Renzo Piano it meant to impress with features including the fjordside setting and delightful footbridge access through to the arching, sail-shaped roofs with their glassy connecting spans. One of the buildings is devoted to a prestigious programme of temporary exhibitions, the other showcases a rotating selection from the extravagantly well-endowed permanent collection – the beneficiary of two Norwegian shipping-family trusts. The **permanent collection** covers most major postwar Norwegian artists (see box, p.74) and also boasts an eclectic assortment of

**1**

## MODERN ART IN NORWAY

Norway has a well-organized, high-profile body of **professional artists** whose long-established commitment to encouraging artistic activity throughout the country has brought them respect, as well as state subsidies. In the 1960s, abstract and conceptual artists ruled the roost, but at the end of the 1970s there was a renewed interest in older art styles, particularly Expressionism, Surrealism and Cubism, plus a new emphasis on technique and materials. To a large degree these opposing impulses fused, or at least overlapped, but by the late 1980s several definable movements had emerged. One of the more popular trends was for artists to use beautiful colours to portray disquieting visions, a dissonance favoured by the likes of **Knut Rose** (1936–2002) and **Bjørn Carlsen** (b.1945), whose ghoulish *Searching in a Dead Zebra* has been highly influential. Other artists, the most distinguished of whom is **Tore Hansen** (1949–2013), have developed a naive style. Their paintings, apparently clumsily drawn without thought for composition, are frequently reminiscent of Norwegian folk art, and constitute a highly personal response often drawn from the artist's subconscious experiences.

Both of these trends embody a sincerity of expression that defines the bulk of contemporary Norwegian art. Whereas the prevailing mood in international art circles encourages detached irony, Norway's artists characteristically adhere to the view that their role is to interpret, or at least express, the poignant and personal for their audience. An important exception is **Bjørn Ransve** (b.1944), who creates sophisticated paintings in constantly changing styles, but always focused on the relationship between art and reality. Another exception is the small group of artists, such as **Bjørn Sigurd Tufta** (b.1956) and **Sverre Wyller** (b.1953), who have returned to non-figurative Modernism to create works that explore the possibilities of the material, while the content plays no decisive role.

An interest in materials has sparked a variety of experiments among the country's artists, whose **installations** incorporate everyday utensils, natural objects and pictorial art. These installations have developed their own momentum (some would say banality), pushing back the traditional limits of the visual arts in their use of many different media including photography, video, textiles and furniture. One notable practitioner has been **Ida Ekblad** (b.1980), who paints, performs and sculpts using scrap. Leading an opposing faction is the painter **Odd Nerdrum** (b.1944), who has long spearheaded the figurative rebellion against the Modernists, though some artists straddle the divide, such as **Astrid Løvaas** (b.1957) and **Kirsten Wagle** (b.1956), who work together to produce flower motifs in textiles. The most influential Norwegian sculptor of recent years has been Bergen's **Bård Breivik** (1948–2016), who explored the dialogue between nature and humankind. With similarly ambitious intent are the much-lauded installations of **Jørgen Craig Lello** (b.1978) and the Swede **Tobias Arnell** (b.1978), who claim to "utilize logically broken trains of thought, false statements and fictional scenarios in their examination of how the world is interpreted and understood". Good luck to them, then.

foreign works by such celebrated figures as Francis Bacon, Damien Hirst, David Hockney, Jeff Koons and Anselm Kiefer. Indeed, it's Hirst who sets the scene in the first gallery with his famous *Mother & Child Divided* – the pickled and bisected cows of 1993. Just in case you were tempted to dismiss any of the exhibits as being dire or incomprehensible, labels provide full-on "artesque" descriptions and explanations.

### Rådhusgata and the Posthallen

**Rådhusgata** runs southeast from the Rådhus, cutting off the humpy spur of land that is dominated by the Akershus Slott (castle; see opposite). At the foot of Øvre Slottsgate, it bisects an elegant cobbled square, **Christiania torv**, where attractively designed modern buildings jostle for space with older structures, including the courtyard complex holding the *Kafé Celsius* (see p.98) and Oslo's old town hall, the pint-sized **Gamle Rådhus**, which was badly damaged by fire in 1996 and now holds a restaurant.

Beyond the square, Rådhusgata continues by crossing what was once the commercial heart of the city, a role it shared with neighbouring Tollbugata and Prinsens gate. It was here that Oslo's late nineteenth-century business elite built a string of imposing, heavy-duty buildings, usually of roughly dressed stone in a sort of Romanesque Revival meets Second Empire style. There are lots of examples, but pride of architectural place goes to the old postal sorting office, the **Posthallen**, a slightly later building at Dronningens gate 15. Erected between 1914 and 1924, and part of a large complex that occupies the bulk of a city block in between Tollbugata, Dronningens gate and Prinsens gate, the Posthallen is a transitional structure, part Art Nouveau, part Art Deco, which is framed by a pair of imposing clocktowers and encloses a large courtyard. The Posthallen is now divided up between apartments and offices, but you can wander into the courtyard for a gander.

## Bankplassen

With its fountain and cobbles, **Bankplassen**, one block south of Rådhusgata, is the prettiest square in this part of Oslo. It holds an especially fine example of the proud commercial buildings of yesteryear in the former **Norges Bank headquarters**, a redoubtable Art Nouveau-meets-Romanesque edifice completed in 1907. For the last few years, this edifice has housed the Museet for Samtidskunst (Contemporary Art Museum), but this closed in 2017 as part of the creation of the new Nasjonalmuseet (see box, p.63).

## Arkitekturmuseet

Bankplassen 3 • Tues–Fri 11am–5pm, Thurs till 7pm, Sat & Sun noon–5pm • 50kr • ☎ 21 98 20 00, ⓦ nasjonalmuseet.no

The enjoyable **Arkitekturmuseet** (Architecture Museum), one part of the Nasjonalmuseet (see box, p.63), is an absorbing affair in which keynote architectural displays are laid out in both the original building – a stolid edifice from 1830 – and an immaculate modern pavilion at the back. The temporary exhibitions, of which there are normally two at any one time, usually focus on Norwegian architects – and Norwegian design – as does the permanent exhibition in the pavilion, where there is enough room to display models and photos of important buildings constructed in every part of the country from 1831 onwards. Some of these structures are singularly impressive, though the write-ups can verge on the pretentious: the town of Halden (see p.109) has a new prison, but to describe its design as encouraging "freer movements between various activities" can't but help raise a smile.

## Akershus complex

Myntgata gate: Oct–April Mon–Fri 7am–6pm, Sat & Sun 8am–6pm; May–Sept daily 8am–9pm • Free • ☎ 23 09 39 17, ⓦ forsvarsbygg.no

Though very much part of central Oslo by location, the thumb of land that holds the sprawling fortifications of the **Akershus complex** is quite separate from the city centre in feel. The original **Slott** (castle) was built on a rocky knoll overlooking the harbour in around 1300 and was already the battered veteran of several unsuccessful sieges when **Christian IV** (1596–1648) took matters in hand. The king had a passion for building cities and took a keen interest in Norway – during his reign he visited the country around thirty times, more than all the other kings of the Dano-Norwegian union put together. So, when old Oslo was badly damaged by fire in 1624, he took his opportunity and simply ordered the town to be moved round the bay and rebuilt in its present position, modestly renaming it Christiania, a name which stuck until 1877. As the centrepiece of the new settlement, he transformed the medieval Akershus castle into a Renaissance residence and around it he constructed a new fortress – the **Akershus Festning** – whose thick earth-and-stone walls and protruding bastions were designed to resist artillery bombardment. Refashioned and enlarged on several later occasions – and now bisected by Kongens gate – parts of the fortress have remained in military use until the present day. There are several **entrances** to the Akershus complex, but the most appealing is at the west end of **Myntgata**.

**1**

### Besøkssenteret

May–Aug Mon–Fri 10am–5pm, Sat & Sun 11am–5pm; Sept–April Mon–Fri 11am–4pm, Sat & Sun noon–5pm • Free • ☎ 23 09 39 17, ⓦforsvarsbygg.no

From the west end of Myntgata, a footpath leads up to a narrow **side-gate** in the perimeter wall. Just beyond the gate is the **Besøkssenteret** (Visitor Centre), which explores the history of the castle, especially its use as a prison, a role it performed until 1950. There are several interesting displays on notable prisoners, including **Christian Jensen Lofthus** (1750–97), a farmers' leader from the south coast who petitioned the government over excessive taxation and corruption in the civil service. He managed to meet the Crown Prince, who seemed to be sympathetic, but was subsequently arrested and imprisoned – and the armed revolt that broke out in his support was suppressed; Lofthus died in prison here in the Akershus.

Back outside the Besøkssenteret, follow the signed **footpath** that twists its way up to the castle and the Resistance Museum, from where there are grand views over the harbour.

### Norges Hjemmefrontmuseum

June–Aug Mon–Sat 10am–5pm, Sun 11am–5pm; Sept–May Mon–Fri 10am–5pm, Sat & Sun 11am–4pm • 50kr • ☎ 23 09 31 38, ⓦforsvaretsmuseer.no

The **Norges Hjemmefrontmuseum** (Norwegian Resistance Museum) occupies a distinctive brick building just outside the castle entrance, an apt location given that the Gestapo had the habit of executing captured Resistance fighters a few metres away – after torturing them inside the castle first. Labelled in English and Norwegian, the displays detail the history of World War II in Norway, from defeat and occupation through resistance to final victory. There are tales of extraordinary heroism here – notably the determined resistance of hundreds of the country's **teachers** to Nazi instructions – plus a section dealing with Norway's **Jews**, who numbered 1800 in 1939; the Germans captured 760, of whom 24 survived. There's also the moving story of a certain **Petter Moen**, who was arrested by the Germans and imprisoned in the Akershus, where he kept a diary by using a nail to pick out letters on toilet paper; the diary survived, but he didn't. Other acts of resistance included the sabotaging of German attempts to produce heavy water for an atomic bomb deep in southern Norway, at Rjukan (see p.176), and there's also an impressively honest account of Norwegian **collaboration**: fascism struck a chord with the country's petit bourgeois, and hundreds of volunteers joined the Wehrmacht. The most notorious collaborator was **Vidkun Quisling**, who was executed by firing squad for his treachery in 1945. When the German army invaded in April 1940, Quisling assumed he would govern the country and made a radio announcement proclaiming his seizure of power, though in the event the Germans soon sidelined him, opting for military control instead.

### Akershus Slott

May–Aug Mon–Sat 10am–4pm, Sun noon–4pm; Sept–April Sat & Sun noon–5pm • 70kr • ☎ 23 09 35 53, ⓦforsvarsbygg.no

Beyond the Resistance Museum, the severe stone walls and twin spires of the largely medieval **Akershus Slott** (Akershus Castle) perch on a rocky ridge high above the zigzag fortifications added by Christian IV. The castle is approached through two narrow tunnel-gateways, which lead to a cobbled courtyard at the heart of the fortress. So far so good, but thereafter the interior is a bit of a disappointment as you are arrowed round a string of sparsely furnished rooms linked by bare-brick passageways. Nevertheless, there are one or two items of interest, primarily the **royal crypt**, holding the sarcophagi of Norway's current dynasty – not that there have been many of them, just two in fact, Håkon VII (1872–1957) and Olav V (1903–91) – and the **royal chapel**. Among the castle's assorted halls, the pick are the **Romerikssalen**, worth a few moments for its Baroque fireplace and Flemish tapestries, and the grand neo-Gothic **Olavshallen**.

Near the end of a visit, it's a real surprise to stumble across the well-preserved office of **Henrik Wergeland** (1808–45), who worked in the castle as a royal archivist for the last four years of his life. Wergeland was one of the most prominent Norwegian poets and dramatists of his day and also an ardent campaigner for greater Norwegian independence. He was, therefore, roundly mocked for accepting the archivist's job – and pension – from the regime he had disparaged and ended up a bitter man: he kept a (fang-less) adder in his office to disconcert the unwary visitor, a not-so-playful reminder of one of his last works, *Vinaegers Fjeldeventyr*, in which the cruellest critic of a poet is so poisonous that a snake dies after it has bit him – and hence the plastic snake in the office today.

### The castle walkway

Back in the castle courtyard, walk through the nearest of the tunnel-gateways and then turn left along the **walkway** running down the side of the castle with the walls pressing in on one side and views out over the harbour on the other. At the foot of the castle, the path swings across a narrow promontory and soon reaches the **footbridge** over Kongens gate. Cross the footbridge for the Forsvarsmuseet (see below), or keep straight for the string of ochre-coloured barrack blocks that lead back to Myntgata.

### Forsvarsmuseet

May–Aug daily 10am–5pm; Sept–April Tues–Sun 10am–4pm • Free • ☎ 23 09 35 82, ⓦ forsvaretsmuseer.no

The **Forsvarsmuseet** (Armed Forces Museum), on the far side of the army parade ground from the castle, tracks Norwegian military history from the early Middle Ages to postwar UN peace-keeping. The first floor sets a hectic pace, beginning with a surprisingly cursory look at the Vikings before ploughing on as far as the German invasion of 1940. There's a mildly interesting section on the country's early use of ski troops, but otherwise it's hard to get enthralled by the innumerable wars fought between the Scandinavian countries for obscure dynastic reasons. By contrast, the section on **World War II** is much more detailed and the photographs chosen to illustrate the invasion and occupation are first-rate.

## Den Norske Operahuset

Kirsten Flagstads plass 1 • Mon–Fri 10am–7pm, Sat 11am–6pm, Sun noon–6pm • Free • ☎ 21 42 21 21, ⓦ operaen.no

**Den Norske Operahuset** (Opera House) is one of the city's proudest buildings. Completed in 2008, and home to the city's opera and ballet companies, it's a glassy, cuboid structure with exterior ramps that look like extended ski slopes – all to a loquacious design by the Norwegian company, Snøhetta. It's meant to impress, with no expense spared either outside or inside, and since its opening Norwegians have visited in their thousands. The Operahuset is a key part of an ambitious, long-term project to transform this part of the city's waterfront. A new library is under construction across the street from the Operahuset; the Munchmuseet (see p.81) will be moved to a second glossy and glassy building that will rise on the next pier along from the Operahuset in 2020; and – less positively – a string of predictable, modern high-rises stretches southeast from the Operahuset, shunting up along Dronning Eufemias gate in a development known as the **Barcode**.

## Ekebergparken

Tram #18 or #19 from outside Oslo S to the Ekebergparken stop

Readily accessible by tram, **Ekebergparken** (Ekeberg Park) occupies the wooded heights just to the southeast of the city centre. Locals have been coming up here to admire the harbour view for decades – hence the couple of teahouses and the splendid *Ekebergrestauranten* (see p.99) – and they can now enjoy a delightful **open-air sculpture park**, whose thirty-or-so pieces are spread out through the woods. As you enter the park from beside the tram stop, you will find a **map** showing the location of each sculpture. Some of the sculptures are older, traditional pieces – there's a Rodin and a Gustav Vigeland – but most are modern, with British sculptors well-represented by the likes of Sarah Lucas (b.1962) and Richard Hudson (b.1954).

**1**

The park is to the immediate east of the tram stop and the conspicuous building to the west is the former **Sjømannskolen** (Merchant Marine Academy), now an academy. To the rear of the academy, a narrow drive – Karlsborgveien – leads downhill into a little dell. Here, a few metres down on the left-hand side, you'll spot a group of faded **rock carvings** depicting elk, deer, birds and matchstick people, around 6000 years old and the earliest evidence of habitation along the Oslofjord.

## Northwest Oslo: Frognerparken and Vigelandsparken

To the northwest of the city centre, the green expanse of **Frognerparken** (Frogner Park) incorporates one of Oslo's most celebrated and popular cultural targets, the remarkable open-air **Vigelandsparken**, where a small army of bronze, granite and cast-iron statues forms what amounts to a grand processional highway. The statues were the inspiration of just one man, **Gustav Vigeland** (1869–1943), a modern Norwegian sculptor of world renown, who spent several decades of his life working on this project before presenting it to the city in return for favours received by way of a studio and apartment during the years 1921–30. Such is the visual appeal of Vigeland's masterpiece that it's hard to resist walking straight into the Vigelandsparken, but actually it's best to start by visiting the neighbouring **Vigeland-museet** (Vigeland Museum), which is crammed with plaster casts of Vigeland's statues and is where you get a real sense of the man and his sculptural mission. Frognerparken is also home to Frogner Manor, which now accommodates the mildly diverting **Oslo Museum**.

### Vigelandsparken

Kirkeveien • Daylight hours • Free • Tram #12 to the Vigelandsparken stop – one stop from the Frogner Plass tram stop (for the Vigeland-museet; see below)

A country boy, raised on a farm just outside Mandal, on the south coast, **Gustav Vigeland** began his career as a woodcarver but later, when studying in Paris, he fell under the influence of Rodin, and switched to stone, iron and bronze. He started work on the **Vigelandsparken** (Vigeland Park) in 1924, and was still working on it when he died almost twenty years later. It's a literally fantastic concoction, medieval in spirit and complexity, and it was here that Vigeland had the chance to let his imagination run riot. Indeed, when the place was unveiled, many city folk were simply overwhelmed – and no wonder. From the monumental **wrought-iron gates** on Kirkeveien, the central path takes you to the **footbridge** over the river and a world of frowning, fighting and posturing bronze figures – the local favourite is *Sinnataggen* (The Angry Child), whose hand has been rubbed smooth by a thousand visitors. Beyond, the **central fountain** is an enormous bowl representing the burden of life, supported by straining, sinewy bronze Goliaths. The water tumbles down into a pool flanked by **Tree Groups** – sculpted figures in a series of Art Nouveau clumps of trees that portray the cycle of life: the young woman who glides/ dives through one set of trees is perhaps the most arresting piece, representing puberty.

Yet it is the 20m-high **obelisk** up on the stepped embankment just beyond the central fountain that really takes the breath away. It's a deeply humanistic work, a writhing mass of sculpture that depicts the struggle of life as Vigeland saw it: a vision of humanity playing, fighting, teaching, loving, eating and sleeping – and clambering on and over each other to reach the top. The granite sculptures grouped around the obelisk are exquisite too, especially the toddlers, little pot-bellied figures who tumble over muscled adults, both old and in their prime.

### Vigeland-museet

Nobels gate 32 • May–Aug Tues–Sun 10am–5pm; Sept–April Tues–Sun noon–4pm • 60kr • ☎ 23 49 37 00, ⓦ vigeland.museum.no • Tram #12 to the Frogner Plass stop – one stop from the Vigelandsparken tram stop

The distinctive, dark-red-brick **Vigeland-museet** (Vigeland Museum), on the southern edge of the Vigelandsparken, was Gustav Vigeland's studio and home during the

1920s. It was built for him by the city, who let him live here rent-free on condition that the building – and its contents – passed back to public ownership on his death. The museum holds a comprehensive range of Vigeland sculptures, beginning with the busts he made of many of his contemporaries, but it's the **plaster casts** of the statues in the Vigelandsparken that grab the attention – arranged in the same order as they appear outside. Well-written explanatory cards help explain Vigeland's themes and purposes. Intriguingly, there are also discarded or unused sculptures, preparatory pieces and incidental photographs of the workforce. Vigeland seems to have become obsessed with his creation during his last years, and you get the feeling that given half a chance he would have had himself cast and exhibited. As it is, his ashes were placed in the museum tower (no public access).

## Oslo Museum

Frognerveien 67 • May–Aug Tues–Sun 10am–5pm; Sept–April Tues–Sun noon–4pm • Free • ☎ 23 28 41 70, ⓦ oslomuseum.no • Tram #12 to the Frogner Plass stop – one stop from the Vigelandsparken tram stop

From the Vigeland-museet, it's a couple of minutes' walk over to the **Oslo Museum**, which is housed in the expansive, eighteenth-century **Frogner Manor**. The buildings are actually rather more distinctive than the museum: a central courtyard is bounded on one side by the half-timbered Manor House, complete with its dinky little tower, and by antique agricultural buildings on the other three – and if the weather is good the courtyard is a pleasant spot for a cup of tea. The museum is in one of the old agricultural buildings – the renovated barn – and holds a sequence of displays spread over two floors. The upper floor is devoted to temporary exhibitions – a recent one explored the evolution of Norway's dialects, while the lower floor features a permanent display on the history of the city. It's not perhaps as dry as it sounds, but still it's the photos of old Oslo and its people that really catch the eye.

# Eastside Oslo

Long the home of Oslo's working class, **east Oslo** has never been as prosperous as the western half of the city and although the tenements of yesteryear are long gone, it's still a patchy area that stretches east from Akersgata/Ullevålsveien. The obvious attraction hereabouts is the **Munchmuseet** (see p.81) – though this will be moving very soon (see box, p.63) – but it's here you'll also find three of Oslo's most distinctive neighbourhoods: **Grünerløkka**, a funky district crowded with great cafés, bars, restaurants and clubs; neighbouring **Vulkan**, an excellent example of urban renewal that's turned a run-down industrial area into one of the most agreeable parts of the city; and poor old **Grønland**, a seedy, down-at-heel neighbourhood in the vicinity of Oslo S that is perhaps best avoided. Specific sights are thin on the ground – it's the general feel of Grünerløkka and Vulkan that are their main appeal – but the **DogA Norsk Design og Arkitektursenter** is of some passing interest.

## Grünerløkka

Trams #11, #12 & #13 run along Thorvald Meyers gate back and forth to the city centre

Formerly a run-down working-class district, **Grünerløkka** has recently been reinvigorated in a boho sort of way, its regeneration turning it into one of the most fashionable parts of the city, particularly among artists and students. The main drag, **Thorvald Meyers gate**, is dotted with retro cafés, shops, bars and restaurants plus a couple of pocket-sized city parks – people come here from all over the city to eat (see p.99) and drink (see p.101). Of the several entrances to the area, the prettiest is across the pedestrianized **Ankerbrua** (Anker bridge), which spans the **River Akerselva** to link Markveien with Torggata. The bridge sports four large, folkloric sculptures by Norwegian sculptor Per Ung (1933–2013), including Peer Gynt and his reindeer and Kari Trestakk and her helpful bull.

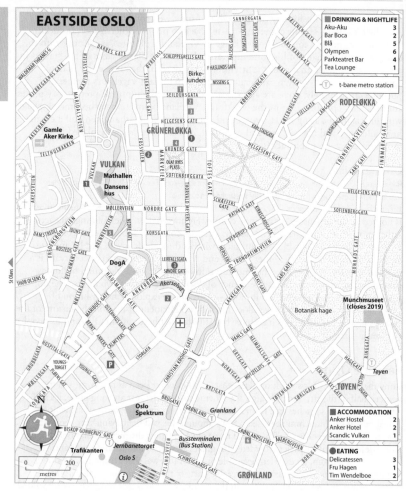

## DogA: Norsk Design og Arkitektursenter

Hausmanns gate 16 • Mon, Tues & Fri 10am–5pm, Wed & Thurs 10am–8pm, Sat & Sun noon–5pm • Free • ☎ 23 29 28 70, ⊛ doga.no

Housed in a former electricity station, the **DogA Norsk Design og Arkitektursenter** (Norwegian Design and Architecture Centre) shunts up against the south bank of the River Akerselva, a short walk from the Ankerbrua. There's no permanent collection here, but rather temporary displays that trumpet contemporary Norwegian design. One popular theme is climate – and the various efforts the Norwegians are making to combat global warming, from insulation to wind farms.

## Vulkan

From DogA, it's a shortish walk north along Hausmanns gate and then Maridalsveien to **Vulkan**, a revived neighbourhood that extends along a dell on the west side of the River Akerselva immediately to the north of Møllerveien. The neighbourhood takes its name from the iron foundry that once hogged the riverbank here, but was closed in the late 1950s to leave a postindustrial eyesore.

The redevelopment now complete, Vulkan holds a platoon of bright apartment blocks, a capacious food hall – the **Mathallen** – and the city's premier contemporary dance school, the **Dansens Hus** (ⓦdansenshus.com).

## Telthusbakken

Branching off Maridalsveien close to Vulkan, **Telthusbakken** is a narrow lane where a string of old and brightly coloured timber houses have survived in fine fettle – and very fetching they are too. The lane emerges on Akersveien, next to the Gamle Aker Kirke.

## Gamle Aker Kirke

Akersbakken 26 • Usually mid-June to mid-Aug Mon, Tues, Thurs & Fri noon–4pm • Free • ☎ 23 62 91 20, ⓦ gamleakerkirke.no

The **Gamle Aker Kirke** (Old Aker Church) is a sturdy stone building still in use as a Lutheran parish church. It dates from around 1100, which makes it the oldest stone church in Scandinavia, although most of what you see today is the result of a heavy-handed nineteenth-century refurbishment. Curiously, the grassy hillock beneath the church is riddled with the workings of an old **silver mine**, which pumped up Oslo's economy in Viking times. Flooding closed the mines in the twelfth century, but legend had it that would-be prospectors were driven away by a gang of dragons – and on old city maps the silver workings are marked as "Dragehullene" (dragon holes).

## Damstredet

Proceeding south from the Gamle Aker Kirke along Akersveien, it's a brief stroll to **Damstredet**, a steep cobbled lane that rolls down to Fredensborgveien flanked by early nineteenth-century clapboard houses built at all kinds of odd angles. These are some of the few wooden buildings to have survived Oslo's developers and they make the street a picturesque affair, a well-kept reminder of how the city once looked. From the bottom of Damstredet, you can stroll south along Fredensborgveien to regain the city centre in around fifteen minutes.

## The Munchmuseet

Tøyengata 53 • Daily: mid-June to late Sept 10am–5pm; late Sept to mid-June 10am–4pm • 100kr • ☎ 23 49 35 00, ⓦ munchmuseet.no •
T-bane to Tøyen station, from where it's an easy 5min walk – just follow the signs

In his will, **Edvard Munch** (1863–1944; see box, p.68) donated all the works in his possession to Oslo city council, a mighty bequest of several thousand paintings, prints, drawings, engravings and photographs, which took nearly twenty years to catalogue and organize before being displayed in this purpose-built gallery, the **Munchmuseet** (Munch Museum). The gallery is, however, simply not large enough to display the whole collection at any one time, so the paintings are frequently rotated, which means that you can't be certain what will be displayed and when, though the key paintings mentioned below are usually on view. There are two other negatives: the museum hosts an ambitious programme of temporary exhibitions, which often further reduces the number of Munch paintings on display, and – given that the new Munch Museum is

### HOW EMBARRASSING: ART THEFT AT THE MUNCHMUSEET

In August 2004, two armed **robbers** marched into the **Munchmuseet** and, in full view of dozens of bemused visitors, lifted two Munch paintings – the *Madonna* and *The Scream*, his most famous work (though fortunately Munch painted four versions). As if this wasn't bad enough, further humiliations followed: it turned out that the paintings were not alarmed and neither were they especially secure, only being attached to the wall by a cord. There were red faces all round, but the police finally came to the rescue by recovering the paintings two years later in circumstances that they have consistently refused to reveal, though several of the thieves were convicted, imprisoned and fined – unlike the comparable theft of a Munch from the Nasjonalgalleriet in 1994 (see p.69), when the thieves were never apprehended.

under construction for completion in 2020 (see box, p.63), this museum is starting to feel somewhat jaded and faded. At the start of the museum, a short **film** on Munch's life and times sets the scene.

### Early and 1890s paintings

The landscapes and domestic scenes of Munch's **early paintings**, such as *Tête à Tête* and *At the Coffee Table*, reveal the perceptive if deeply pessimistic realism from which Munch's later work sprang. Even more riveting are the great works of the **1890s**, which form the core of the collection. Considered Munch's finest achievements, several of these key paintings are grouped together in the so-called *Frieze of Life*, whose preoccupations were love, anxiety and death. Among the wonderful paintings from this period come *Dagny Juel*, a portrait of the Berlin socialite Ducha Przybyszewska, with whom both Munch and Strindberg were infatuated; the searing representations of *Despair* and *Anxiety*; the chilling *Red Virginia Creeper*, a house being consumed by the plant; the deeply unsettling *Eye in Eye*; and, of course, *The Scream* – of which the museum holds several versions.

### Later paintings

Munch's style was never static and a batch of his **later paintings**, produced after he had recovered from his breakdown and withdrawn to the tranquillity of the Oslofjord, reflect a renewed interest in nature and physical work – *Workers On Their Way Home* (1913) is a prime example. His technique was also changeable: in works like the *Death of Marat II* (1907) he began to use streaks of colour to represent points of light. Later still, paintings such as *Garden in Kragerø* and *Model by the Wicker Chair*, with skin tones of pink, green and blue, begin to reveal a happier, if rather idealized, attitude to his surroundings, though this is most evident in works like *Spring Ploughing*, painted in 1916. But for Munch, the unsettling and the perturbing were never far away and so he returned to the themes of the 1890s again and again as in the *Dance of Life*, first painted in 1900 with another version appearing twenty-five years later.

### Self-portraits

Throughout his life, Munch had a penchant for **self-portraits** and these provide a graphic illustration of the artist's state of mind at various points in his life. There's a palpable sadness in his *Self-Portrait with Wine Bottle* (1906), along with obvious allusions to his heavy drinking, while the telling perturbation of *In Distress* (1919) and *The Night Wanderer* (1923) indicates that he remained a tormented, troubled man even in his later years. One of his last works, *Self-Portrait by the Window* (1940), shows a glum figure on the borderline between life and death, the strong red of his face and green of his clothing contrasting with the ice-white scene visible through the window.

### Lithographs and woodcuts

Munch's **lithographs and woodcuts**, of which the museum owns several hundred, are a dark catalogue of swirls and fogs, technically brilliant pieces of work and often developments of his paintings rather than just simple copies. In them, he pioneered a new medium of expression, experimenting with colour schemes and a huge variety of materials, which enhance the works' rawness: many of his wood blocks, for example, show a heavy, distinct grain, while there are colours like rust and blue drawn from the Norwegian landscape. The hand-coloured lithographs tend to be, by comparison, more sensuous with many focusing on the theme of love (taking the form of a woman) bringing death.

## Bygdøy peninsula

Easy to reach by passenger ferry or bus, the leafy and well-heeled **Bygdøy peninsula**, just across the Oslofjord from the city centre, holds no fewer than **five museums**, which together make for an absorbing cultural and historical excursion. It's possible to cram all of them into a day's sightseeing, but it's better to spread a visit over a couple of mornings or afternoons – or stick to the three most interesting, the **Norsk Folkemuseum**, the **Vikingskipshuset** and the **Frammuseet**. Incidentally, plans are afoot to build a brand-new Viking Age museum here on the Bygdøy, but this won't happen (if it ever does) for a few years yet.

| **ARRIVAL AND DEPARTURE** | **BYGDØY PENINSULA** |

**By ferry** The most enjoyable way to reach the Bygdøy is by passenger ferry from Pier 3, behind the Rådhus on the Rådhusbrygge (daily every 20–30min: May–Sept 9am–6pm; early Oct 10am–5.30pm). All these ferries perform a one-way loop, calling first at the Dronningen dock (10min from Rådhusbrygge) and then the Bygdøynes dock (15min from Rådhusbrygge) before returning to the Rådhusbrygge; note, therefore, that there is no ferry service from Bygdøynes to Dronningen. The two most popular attractions – the Vikingskipshuset and the Norsk Folkemuseum – are within easy walking distance of the first ferry stop, the Dronningen dock; the other three are a stone's throw from Bygdøynes.

If you decide to walk between the two groups of museums, allow about 15min: the route is well signposted but dull.
**Ferry tickets** The Bygdøy ferry is part of the city's public transport system – and Oslo passes (see p.59) are accepted – but if you're paying separately it's 60kr return from the automatic ticket machines on the pier, 60kr each way if you pay on board.
**By bus** The alternative to the ferry is bus #30 (every 10–20min), which runs all year from Jernbanetorget and the Nationaltheatret to the Norsk Folkemuseum (in about 20min) and the Vikingskipshuset before proceeding onto Bygdøynes for the other three museums in another 5min (25min).

## Norsk Folkemuseum

Museumsveien 10 • Mid-May to mid-Sept daily 10am–6pm; mid-Sept to mid-May Mon–Fri 11am–3pm, Sat & Sun 11am–4pm • 125kr • ☎ 22 12 37 00, ⓦ norskfolkemuseum.no • The museum is about 700m up from the Dronningen dock – just follow the signs

The **Norsk Folkemuseum** (Norwegian Folk Museum) combines indoor collections on folk art, furniture, dress and customs with an extensive open-air display of reassembled buildings, mostly wooden barns, stables, storehouses and dwellings from the seventeenth to the nineteenth centuries. Look out also for the imaginative temporary exhibitions, for which the museum has a well-deserved reputation. Pick up a free **map** of the museum at the entrance. The complex of buildings round the courtyard just beyond the entry turnstiles holds the museum's **indoor collections**, both permanent and temporary.

### The indoor collection: Folk art

The permanent **folk art** section on the ground floor of the leading exhibition building is delightful, exhibiting samples of handsome carved and painted furniture from the sixteenth century onwards. It's here you'll also spot the occasional fancily carved **mangle board**, the significance of which is not at first apparent: these were given by boys to girls as **love gifts** – though quite how a mangle board could be construed as romantic requires a leap of the imagination – and, if the attraction was mutual, the girls gave the boys mittens or gloves. In rural Norway, it was considered improper for courting couples to be seen together during the day, but acceptable (or at least tolerated) at night – and to assist the process parents usually moved girls of marrying age into one of the farm's outhouses, where tokens could be swapped without embarrassment. In this section also are examples of the **woven coverlets** that were once the pride and joy of many a Norwegian family. Using skills distantly inherited from Flemish weavers, the Norwegians took to pictorial coverlets in a big way, their main modification being the elimination of perspective in the attempt to cover the seams. Of ceremonial significance, these items were brought out on all major occasions – weddings and festivals in particular. The coverlets began as fairly crude affairs at the start of the seventeenth century, but achieved greater precision and detail throughout the eighteenth century, after which the art went into a slow decline. Most coverlets were decorated with religious and folkloric motifs and two of the most popular were the arrival of the Magi, and the Wise and Foolish Virgins, a suitably didactic subject – so it was thought – for any newlyweds.

**1**

Folk dress

On the next floor up from the folk art, the **folk dress** section is excellent too. Rural custom specified the correct dress for every sort of social gathering with variations in colour and design dependent on the area. Interestingly, Norway's age-old isolation meant that some items of dress imported and adopted in medieval times stayed in vogue for several centuries – the short **tunic** being a case in point. The most striking items are the **bridal headdresses**, at their most elaborate in the *bringesylv*, for which silver jewellery and other precious ornaments were attached to a red bib. Neither was the bridegroom ignored: in many areas, custom dictated they wore a *brudgomsduk*, a richly embroidered square of linen cloth fastened to the shirt.

Church art

Near the folk art and folk dress is a small section devoted to the **Norwegian Church**. This begins with a modest display on the **clergy**, whose assembled portraits show the comings and goings of beards and wigs as fashion accessories. The portraits are a preamble to a substantial collection of **church art**, mostly wooden altarpieces, furniture and statues. There's some exquisite carving here with one of the finest items being a Buskerud birchwood altarpiece from 1697, in which a swirling undergrowth of acanthus leaves frames the story of Jesus from the Last Supper to the Resurrection.

Open-air collection

The **open-air collection** consists of more than 150 reassembled and/or reconstructed buildings. Arranged geographically, they provide a marvellous sample of Norwegian rural architecture, somewhat marred by inadequate explanations. That said, it's still worth tracking down the **stave church** (see box, p.174), particularly if you don't plan to travel elsewhere in Norway. Dating from the early thirteenth century but extensively restored in the 1880s, when it was moved here from Gol, near Geilo, the church is a good example of its type, with steep, shingle-covered roofs, dragon finials, an outside gallery and fancily carved doorposts. The interior is cramped and gloomy, the nave preceding a tiny chancel painted with a floral design and sporting a striking, if faded, *Last Supper* above and behind the altar. Elsewhere, the cluster of buildings from **Setesdal** in southern Norway holds some especially well-preserved dwellings and storehouses from the seventeenth century, while the **Numedal** section contains one of the museum's oldest buildings, a late thirteenth-century **house from Rauland** (number 21), whose doorposts are embellished with Romanesque vine decoration.

Many of the buildings are open for viewing and in the summertime **costumed guides** roam the site to both explain the vagaries of Norwegian rural life and demonstrate traditional skills, from spinning and carving to dancing and horn blowing.

## Vikingskipshuset

Huk Aveny 35 • Daily: May–Sept 9am–6pm; Oct–April 10am–4pm • 80kr • ☎ 22 13 52 80, ⓦ khm.uio.no

The **Vikingskipshuset** (Viking Ship Museum) occupies a large, cross-shaped hall specially constructed to house a trio of ninth-century Viking longships, with viewing platforms to enable you to see inside the hulls. The museum's star exhibits are the Oseberg and Gokstad longships, named after the places on the west side of the Oslofjord where they were discovered in 1904 and 1880 respectively. All three oak vessels were retrieved from ritual **burial mounds**, each embalmed in a subsoil of clay, which accounts for their excellent state of preservation. The size of a Viking burial mound denoted the dead person's rank and wealth, while the possessions buried with the body were designed to make the afterlife as comfortable as possible. Implicit was the assumption that a chieftain in this world would be a chieftain in the next, a belief that would give Christianity, with its alternative, less fatalistic vision, an immediate appeal to those at the bottom of the Viking pile – slaves, for example, were frequently killed and buried with

**1**

## ANNE STINE AND HELGE INGSTAD – OR HOW THE NORSE BEAT CHRISTOPHER COLUMBUS

Often unnoticed, a modest **monument** beside the entrance to the Vikingskipshuset honours **Helge Marcus Ingstad** (1899–2001) and his wife **Anne Stine** (1918–1997), explorer-archeologists who spent years looking for Norse settlements on the North Atlantic seaboard. Their efforts were inspired by two medieval Icelandic sagas, which detailed the establishment of the colony of **Vinland** somewhere along the American coast in about 1000 AD. Many academics were sceptical, but Ingstad and Stine were proved right when, in 1960, they discovered the remnants of a **Norse village** at L'Anse aux Meadows in Canada's Newfoundland. These remains comprised the foundations of eight turf and timber buildings and a ragbag of archeological finds, including a cloak pin, a stone anvil, nails, pieces of bog iron and an oil lamp. Ingstad and Stine concluded that these were left behind by a group of about one hundred sailors, carpenters and blacksmiths who probably remained at the site for just one or maybe two years – several hundred years before Columbus reached the Americas.

their master or mistress. Quite how the Vikings saw the **transfer to the afterlife** taking place is less certain. The evidence is contradictory: sometimes the Vikings stuck the anchor on board the burial longship in preparation for the spiritual journey, but at other times the vessels were moored to large stones before burial. Neither was longship burial the only type of Viking funeral – far from it. The Vikings buried their dead in mounds and on level ground, with and without grave goods, in large and small coffins, both with and without boats – and they practised cremation too.

### Oseberg longship

The first vessel you see as you enter the museum is the **Oseberg longship**, which is, at 22m long and 5m wide, representative of the type of vessel the Vikings used to navigate fjords and coastal waters. The longship has an ornately carved prow and stern, both of which rise high above the hull, where thirty oar-holes indicate the size of the crew. It is thought to be the burial longship of a Viking chieftain's wife and much of the treasure buried with it was retrieved and is now displayed just behind. The **grave goods** reveal an attention to detail and a level of domestic sophistication not traditionally associated with the Vikings. There are marvellous decorative items like the fierce-looking animal-head posts and exuberantly carved ceremonial pieces, including a sled and a cart, plus a host of smaller, more mundane household items such as shoes, rattles, agricultural tools and cooking pots.

### The Gokstad and Tune longships

Mixed in among the treasure from the Oseberg longship are finds from the **Gokstad longship**, most memorably an ornate bridle and two dragon-head bedposts, though the Gokstad burial chamber was ransacked by grave robbers long ago and precious little has survived. The Gokstad longship itself is slightly longer and wider than the Oseberg vessel and is quite a bit sturdier too. Its seaworthiness was demonstrated in 1893 when a replica sailed across the Atlantic to the US. The third vessel, the **Tune longship**, is the smallest of the nautical trio and only fragments survive; these are displayed unrestored, much as they were discovered in 1867 on the eastern side of the Oslofjord.

## Frammuseet

Bygdøynesveien • Daily: May & Sept 10am–5pm; June–Aug 9am–6pm; Oct–April 10am–4pm • 100kr • ☎ 23 28 29 50, ⓦ frammuseum.no

Just up from the Bygdøynes dock stands the **Frammuseet** (Fram Museum), whose twin triangular display halls are devoted to polar exploration in general and the assorted endeavours of the Norwegian explorer **Roald Amundsen** (1872–1928) in particular. Beyond the entrance, the **first hall** exhibits the **Fram**, the ship that carried Amundsen to within striking distance of the South Pole in 1911. Designed by Colin Archer, a Norwegian shipbuilder of Scots ancestry, and launched in 1892, the *Fram*'s design was unique, its sides made smooth to prevent ice from getting a firm grip on the hull, while inside a veritable maze of beams, braces and stanchions held it all together. Living quarters inside the ship were necessarily cramped – as visitors can observe as they wander through the bowels of the vessel, clambering up and down its steep and narrow stairways. It may have been cramped, but – in true Edwardian style – Amundsen still found space for a piano.

### The Fram's walkway-galleries (middle level)

The walls of the **three walkway-galleries** surrounding the *Fram* are lined with display cases devoted to many aspects of polar exploration. The star turn is the **Race to the Pole** on the **middle level**, which includes original footage of **Amundsen**'s dash to the South Pole in 1911 and potted biographies of his men – and a singular bunch they were too. Famously, Amundsen reached the South Pole ahead of his British rival, the ill-starred **Captain Scott**, and a further section compares the two expeditions. Scott's main mistake was to rely on Siberian ponies and motorized sledges to transport his tackle. The sledges broke down and the animals were useless in Antarctic conditions, so Scott and his team ended up pulling the sledges themselves – a miscalculation that cost Scott and several of his men their lives. Much more flexible than Scott, Amundsen brought a team of huskies and had his men trained in what was then the new technique of skiing behind dog sledges.

### The Fram's walkway-galleries (top level)

The **top level** walkway-gallery looks at life on the *Fram* during the long voyage south and provides access to the ship's deck. Here also is a feature on one of Norway's most remarkable men, **Fridtjof Nansen** (1861–1930), an all-rounder who clocked up an extraordinary range of achievements. In 1895, Nansen made an unsuccessful attempt to reach the North Pole having previously hiked across Greenland. He then proceeded to publish six volumes of scientific observations on the Arctic before championing the cause of an independent Norway – and the break-up of the Norway–Sweden union. Later, he became a leading figure in the League of Nations, running their High Commission for Refugees and organizing the vital supplies that saved millions of Russians from starvation during the famine of 1921–22. He was awarded the Nobel Peace Prize in 1922.

### The Gjøa

An underground passageway links the museum's first hall with its second, where you'll find the **Gjøa**, the one-time sealing ship in which Amundsen made the first complete sailing of the **Northwest Passage** in 1906. The fulfilment of a nautical mission that had preoccupied sailors for several centuries, this was by any measure a remarkable achievement and it took three years to complete, with Amundsen and his crew surviving two icebound winters deep in the Arctic. The *Gjøa* is much smaller than the *Fram* – and neither is it in such pristine condition, so you are not allowed go on board.

### The Gjøa's walkway-galleries

The two **walkway-galleries** flanking the *Gjøa* have three particularly interesting sections – one on Amundsen's sailing of the Northwest Passage; another on the nature and location of the Magnetic North; and a third on the British explorer Ernest Shackleton (1874–1922).

## Kon-Tiki Museet

Bygdøynesveien • Daily: March–May, Sept & Oct 10am–5pm; June–Aug 9.30am–6pm; Nov–Feb 10am–4pm • 100kr • ☎ 22 13 52 80, ⓦ kon-tiki.no

The **Kon-Tiki Museet** (Kon-Tiki Museum) displays the eponymous balsawood raft on which, in 1947, the Norwegian **Thor Heyerdahl** (1914–2002) made his famous journey across the Pacific from Peru to Polynesia. Heyerdahl wanted to prove the trip could be done: he was convinced that the first Polynesian settlers had sailed from pre-Inca Peru,

1

and rejected prevailing opinions that South American balsa rafts were unseaworthy. Looking at the flimsy raft, you could be forgiven for agreeing with Heyerdahl's doubters – and for wondering how the crew didn't murder each other after a day, never mind several weeks in such a confined space, especially as – horror upon horror – one of them brought his guitar. The whole saga is outlined here in the museum, and if you're especially interested, the story is also told in his book *The Kon-Tiki Expedition*.

Heyerdahl went on to attempt several other voyages, sailing across the Atlantic in a papyrus boat, **Ra II**, in 1970, to prove that there could have been contact between Egypt and South America. *Ra II* is also displayed here and the exploit is recorded in another of Heyerdahl's books, *The Ra Expeditions*. Preoccupied with transoceanic contact between prehistoric peoples, Heyerdahl also organized two major archeological expeditions to **Easter Island**, one in 1955–56 and again in 1986–88. Heyerdahl was keen to demonstrate that there had been contact between the islanders and the mainland of South America, but later genetic analysis has proved conclusively that the islanders' forebears came from Polynesia. Perhaps more importantly, Heyerdahl undertook invaluable work in restoring the island's giant statues – the Moai – and the museum gives the lowdown.

## Norsk Maritimt Museum

Bygdøynesveien • Mid-May to mid-Sept daily 10am–5pm; mid-Sept to mid-May Tues–Sun 10am–4pm • 100kr • ☎ 24 11 41 50, ⓦ marmuseum.no

Across from the Kon-Tiki Museet, the **Norsk Maritimt Museum** (Norwegian Maritime Museum) occupies two buildings, the larger of which is a modern brick structure holding a varied collection of all things nautical. The best place to start is in the basement, where there are regular showings of a dramatic, twenty-minute film on the Norwegian coast as seen from the air. Above this, the ground floor – perhaps the most interesting floor – has a collection of old sailing boats and ships' figureheads plus a selection of naturalistic maritime paintings from the late nineteenth and early twentieth centuries. The two larger floors up above feature a hotchpotch of marine items, including pinpoint-accurate ship models; a peculiar-looking fog cannon dating to 1900; a section on shipwrecks; a short film of a dramatic sailing round Cape Horn in 1929; old passenger-ferry cabins and even part of the deck of an old sailing ship from 1893.

The museum's second and much smaller building, the **Båthallen** (Boat Hall), holds an extensive collection of small and medium-sized wooden boats from all over Norway, mostly inshore sailing and fishing craft from the nineteenth century, though, frankly, non-sailors may find it all of limited interest.

# The islands of the inner Oslofjord

Necklacing the **inner Oslofjord**, the archipelago of low-lying, lightly forested **islands** to the south of the city centre has become the capital's summer playground. On sunny, summer days, the city's youth troop off to the less populated islands to party in earnest – with a bit of **beach** life added to the stew – though the prettiest island, **Hovedøya**, with its pocket-sized beaches and wooded walks, avoids the high jinks.

| ARRIVAL AND DEPARTURE | THE ISLANDS OF THE INNER OSLOFJORD |
|---|---|
| **By ferry** Passenger ferries to the islands of the inner Oslofjord leave from Pier 4, behind the Rådhus on the Rådhusbrygge. The islands are in Zone 1 of the public transport network – so | a single ticket costs 32kr beforehand, 50kr on board (it's free with the Oslo Pass). There are automatic ticket machines on the quayside. |

## Hovedøya

Ferries B1, B2 and B3: Late March to Sept daily every 30min–1hr; 10min; Oct to late March daily, hourly; 10min • ⓦ ruter.no

Conveniently, **Hovedøya**, the nearest island to the city centre, is both the most interesting and the prettiest, its rocky, rolling hills decorated with woods and pastures. There are several specific attractions too, beginning with the **Kunstverket** (June to mid-Aug Fri–Sun 1–5pm; free; ⓦkunstverket.no), a little art gallery housed in an old building just up from the jetty, where there are displays of contemporary art. There are also the substantial ruins of a **Cistercian monastery** (open access; free), built by English monks in the twelfth century, and incidental **military remains**, reminders of the time when the island was garrisoned and armed to protect Oslo's harbour. Maps of the island are displayed here and there – there's one at the jetty – and these help with orientation, but on an islet of this size – it's just ten minutes' walk from one end to the other – getting lost is pretty much impossible. There are plenty of **footpaths** to wander, you can swim at the shingle **beaches** on the south shore, and there's a seasonal **café** opposite the monastery ruins. Camping, however, is not permitted as Hovedøya is a protected area, which is also why there are no summer homes.

## Langøyene

Ferry B4: Mid-May to Sept every 30min to hourly; 30min • ⓦ ruter.no

After Hovedøya, the pick of the other islands is **Langøyene**, a pint-sized, H-shaped islet, just ten minutes' walk or so from one side to the other, where a central meadow is flanked on either side by low, lightly wooded rocky hills. There are no houses on the island and no roads to speak of, but there is a long and narrow sandy(ish) **beach**, plus a rudimentary café. Most visitors, however, bring their own supplies, especially those who camp here – there's no campsite as such but **wilderness camping** is permitted and quite a few visitors do just that.

# The Nordmarka

Crisscrossed by **hiking trails** and **cross-country ski routes**, the forested hills and lakes that comprise the **Nordmarka** occupy a tract of land that extends deep inland from central Oslo, but is still within the city limits for some 30km. A network of byroads, as well as two T-bane lines (#1 and #5), provides dozens of access points to this wilderness, which is extremely popular with the capital's outdoor-minded citizens. **Den Norske Turistforening (DNT)**, the Norwegian hiking organization, maintains a handful of staffed and unstaffed huts here – and its Oslo branch has detailed **maps** and sells DNT membership (see p.93).

## Holmenkollen Skimuseet and ski jump

Kongeveien 5 • **Skimuseet** Daily: June–Aug 9am–8pm; May & Sept 10am–5pm; Oct–April 10am–4pm • 130kr • ☎ 22 92 32 00, ⓦ holmenkollen.com • **Ski Simulator** Daily: June–Aug 9am–8pm; Sept 9am–5pm; Oct–April 10am–4pm • 75kr • ☎ 90 01 20 46, ⓦ skisimulator.no • T-bane #1 to Holmenkollen; the Skimuseet and ski jump are about 1km from the T-bane station

**Holmenkollen** is one of Norway's busiest ski resorts, its popularity bolstered by its international **ski jump**, a gargantuan affair that dwarfs its surroundings. A mountain of metal steps leads up to the top of the ski jump from where the view down is, for most people, horrifyingly steep. It seems impossible that the tiny bowl at the bottom could pull the skier up in time – or that anyone could possibly want to jump off in the first place. When competition skiers aren't hurling themselves off it, the ski jump can be visited as part of the **Skimuseet** (Ski Museum), whose various exhibits explore the history of skiing at some length, and there's a **Ski Simulator** here as well.

## Frognerseteren and Ullevålseter lodges

**Frognerseteren** Mon–Sat 11am–10pm, Sun 11am–9pm • ☎ 22 92 40 40, ⓦ frognerseteren.no • **Ullevålseter** Tues–Sun 9am–5pm • ☎ 22 14 35 58, ⓦ ullevalseter.no

**Frognerseteren**, a few stops on from Holmenkollen and a 30min ride from the city centre, is the terminus of T-bane #1. From the station, it's just a couple of hundred metres to Frognerseteren's large and good-looking wooden **lodge**, where the views from the terrace out over Oslo and the Oslofjord are much more enjoyable than the food. From the T-bane terminus, there's also a choice of **signposted trails** across the surrounding countryside.

**1**

Forest footpaths link Frognerseteren with **Sognsvannet** to the east (see below), an arduous and not especially rewarding trek over the hills of about 5km. Locals mostly shun this route in summer, but it's really popular in winter with parents teaching their children to cross-country ski. A better alternative, especially in summer, is the longer but more interesting hike to Sognsvannet via **Ullevålseter**, where the lodge has a very good café serving excellent home-made apple cake. The whole route is about 9km long, and takes about three hours to complete.

## Sognsvannet

T-bane #5 to the Sognsvann terminus (15min from central Oslo), from where it's a 5min walk straight ahead down the slope to the lake

The T-bane trip to the **Sognsvann terminus** is not quite as pleasant a journey as the T-bane trip to Frognerseteren (see p.89) – the landscape is flatter and you never really leave the city behind – but Sognsvann is but a brief walk from **Sognsvannet**, an attractive lake flanked by forested hills and encircled by an easy 4km-long hiking trail. The lake is iced over until the end of March or early April, but thereafter it's a perfect spot for a picnic or a swim, though Norwegian assurances about the warmth of the water should be treated with caution (or mirth). Forest footpaths link Sognsvannet with Frognerseteren.

# Henie-Onstad Kunstsenter

Sonja Henies vei 31, Høvikodden • Tues–Thurs 11am–7pm, Fri–Sun 11am–5pm • 100kr • ☎ 67 80 48 80, ⓦ hok.no • Bus #151 from either Oslo bus station or Nationaltheatret (every 15–30min; 25min); ask to be let off at the Høvikodden bus stop – or else you'll go whistling past; from the bus stop, it's a 10min walk to the Art Centre – just follow the signs. By car, the Art Centre is close to – and signposted from – the E18 road to Drammen

Overlooking the Oslofjord, some 15km west of the city centre in Høvikodden, the **Henie-Onstad Kunstsenter** (Henie-Onstad Art Centre) is one of Norway's most prestigious modern art centres. There's no false modesty here – it's all about art as an expression of wealth – and the low-slung, modernistic building is a glossy affair located on a handsomely landscaped, wooded headland. The gallery was founded in the 1960s by ice-skater-cum-movie-star **Sonja Henie** (1910–69) and her third husband, the shipowner and art collector Niels Onstad. Henie won three Olympic gold medals (1928, 1932 and 1936) and went on to appear in a string of lightweight Hollywood musicals. Many of her accumulated cups and medals are displayed in a room of their own, and they once prompted a critic to remark: "Sonja, you'll never go broke. All you have to do is hock your trophies." Despite her successes, Henie was not universally admired – far from it, not least because of her links with the Nazi elite both before and during World War II.

The wealthy couple accumulated an extensive collection of **twentieth-century paintings and sculpture**. Matisse, Miró and Picasso, postwar French abstract painters, Expressionists and modern Norwegians all feature, but these now compete for gallery space with **temporary exhibitions** of contemporary art, making it impossible to predict what part of the permanent collection will be on display at any one time. After the museum, be sure to spend a little time wandering the surrounding **Skulpturparken** (Sculpture Park), where you'll see work by the likes of Henry Moore and Arnold Haukeland; plans of the park are available at reception.

## ARRIVAL AND DEPARTURE                                                                    OSLO

Central Oslo lies at the heart of an outstanding public transport system, which makes arriving and departing convenient and straightforward. The principal arrival hub is **Oslo Sentralstasjon** (normally shortened to **Oslo S**), a sprawling, notably ugly complex that includes the main train and bus stations as well as city tram, metro and bus stops; it lies at the eastern end of the main thoroughfare, Karl Johans gate. The other, if less comprehensive, transport hub is **Nationaltheatret**, at the west end of Karl Johans gate, which is handier for most city-centre sights and Oslo's main harbour.

## BY PLANE
### OSLO GARDERMOEN AIRPORT

Oslo Gardermoen airport (@ osl.no) is about 45km north of the city centre, just off the E6 motorway. It's a lavish affair designed in true pan-Scandinavian style, with high ceilings and acres of lightly varnished pine. Departures is on the upper level, Arrivals on the lower, where there are also currency exchange facilities/ATMs, car rental offices (see p.92) and a visitor information desk. There are three ways to get from the airport to the centre of Oslo by public transport: express train, local train and airport bus.

**By Flytoget express train** The fastest and most expensive way (with the exception of taxis) to get to central Oslo from the airport is on the FlyToget (Airport Express train; daily every 10–20min 5am–11.30pm; 180kr one-way, 360kr return; @ flytoget.no), which takes about 20min to reach Oslo S with most trains continuing on to Nationaltheatret.

**By NSB train** Several NSB (Norwegian Railway; @ nsb.no) regional trains – including the hourly train from Lillehammer – stop at the airport before proceeding on to Oslo S and usually Nationaltheatret (around 30min; 95kr each way). Note also that there are NSB trains north from Gardermoen to a number of destinations, including Trondheim; long-distance services often require a reservation. You can find details and make reservations at the train ticket office in Arrivals.

**By Flybussen bus** Departing from platform 11 outside Arrivals, Flybussen go to the main downtown bus station, Oslo Bussterminalen, which is part of the Oslo S complex (Mon–Fri 5.20am–1am, Sat & Sun 5.30am–1am; every 20–30min; 180kr one-way, 275kr return; @ flybussen.no); the journey takes about 50min, traffic depending. These same buses then continue on to the *Radisson Blu Scandinavia Hotel* on Holbergs gate with a couple of stops in between – one is outside the *Hotel Bondeheimen* (see p.95). For Gardermoen departures, the Flybussen follows the same route in the opposite direction.

**By Nor-way Bussekspress** Operated by Nor-way Bussekspress (@ norway.no), Flybussekspressen run from the airport to the small towns surrounding Oslo at regular intervals and at reasonable rates; the same company also runs several long-distance buses from the airport, including a service to Trondheim.

**By taxi** The taxi fare from Gardermoen to the city centre is a wallet-singeing 800kr. There's a taxi rank immediately outside Arrivals.

### TORP SANDEFJORD (OSLO TORP) AIRPORT

Torp Sandefjord (@ torp.no) – or Oslo Torp – is Oslo's second international airport, located just outside the town of Sandefjord, about 110km southwest of Oslo.

**By bus** The Torp-Ekspressen bus (@ torpekspressen.no) links Torp airport with Oslo's main downtown bus station, Oslo Bussterminalen. The bus schedule, both to and from Torp, usually connects with flight arrivals and departures. The bus journey takes around 2hr and costs 240kr one-way, 440kr return; tickets from the driver.

**By train** Shuttle buses from Torp airport go to the nearest train station, Torp, just 5min away. From Torp train station, there is a frequent service to Oslo S (hourly; 1hr 40min; 249kr one-way).

### MOSS AIRPORT, RYGGE (OSLO RYGGE AIRPORT)

Oslo's third international airport, Moss Airport, Rygge – or Oslo Rygge (@ en.ryg.no) – is located about 10km southeast of Moss, a small town about 60km south of Oslo on the east side of the Oslofjord.

**By bus** The Rygge-Ekspressen bus (@ ryggeekspressen.no) links the airport with Oslo's downtown Bussterminalen. The bus schedule usually connects with flight arrivals and departures; tickets from the driver. A one-way fare is 170kr, return 300kr; the journey time is about 45min.

**By train** Shuttle buses take about 10min to run from the airport to the nearest train station, Rygge, from where there is a frequent service to Oslo S (hourly; 50min; 164kr each way).

## BY TRAIN

**Oslo S** Operated by NSB (Norwegian State Railways; @ nsb.no), both international and domestic trains use Oslo Sentralstasjon, known as Oslo S, which is beside Jernbanetorget, the square at the eastern end of the main drag, Karl Johans gate. There are money exchange facilities here, an army of shops and just outside – in the distinctive Trafikanten clocktower marked Ruter – is the city's main public transport information office (see p.93); Oslo's tourist office (see p.92) is next door to Oslo S in a recycled former train station, the Østbanehallen. Note that reservations are compulsory on most long-distance trains and that most trains heading north from Oslo S stop at Oslo Gardermoen airport.

Destinations Åndalsnes (4 daily, change at Dombås; 5hr 30min); Bergen (3–4 daily; 6hr 50min); Dombås (4 daily; 4hr); Fredrikstad (hourly; 1hr); Geilo (3–4 daily; 3hr 30min); Halden (hourly; 1hr 30min); Hamar (hourly; 1hr 30min); Kongsberg (hourly; 1hr 15min); Kristiansand (4–5 daily; 4hr 40min); Lillehammer (hourly; 2hr); Myrdal (3–4 daily; 4hr 30min); Røros (4–6 daily, change at Hamar; 5hr); Sandefjord (hourly; 1hr 40min); Stavanger (4 daily; 8hr); Tønsberg (hourly; 1hr 20min); Trondheim (3 daily; 6hr 40min); Voss (3–4 daily; 5hr 30min).

**Nationaltheatret station** On their way to and from Oslo S, many domestic trains pass through the Nationaltheatret station, at the west end of Karl Johans gate, which is slightly more convenient for the city centre.

1

## BY BUS

**Oslo Bussterminalen** Part of the whopping Oslo S complex, Oslo's central Bussterminalen (bus terminal) is a short, signposted walk northeast from the train station on Schweigårdsgate. International and domestic long-distance buses arrive at and depart from here, as do the Flybussen (for Oslo Gardermoen airport); the Torp-Ekspressen (for Oslo Torp airport); and the Rygge-Ekspressen (for Oslo Rygge airport). Nor-Way Bussekspress (ⓦnor-way.no) and Nettbus (under various designations, including TIMEkspressen; ⓦnettbuss.no) are the largest domestic carriers. Among several other bus companies using the bus station, Swebus (ⓦswebus.se) operates a number of useful, international buses to Sweden and Denmark, including those to Copenhagen, Gothenburg and Stockholm.

Destinations (Nor-Way Bussekspress) Bergen (1–2 daily; 9hr 30min); Haugesund (1–3 daily; 8hr 45min); Kongsberg (1–3 daily; 1hr 20min); Kristiansand (6 daily; 5hr); Lillehammer (1–2 daily; 2hr 30min); Otta (1–2 daily; 5hr); Rjukan (4 daily, change at Notodden; 3hr 30min); Sogndal (2 daily; 7hr 30min); Stavanger (1–2 daily; 9hr); Trondheim (1–2 daily; 8hr 30min).

## BY CAR FERRY

For details of fares and schedules of ferries see the information in Basics (see p.27).

**DFDS Seaways** DFDS Seaways (ⓦdfdsseaways.co.uk) operates car ferries between Copenhagen and Oslo. Ferries dock at the Vippetangen quay, a 15min walk (1200m) from Oslo S – or catch bus #60 marked "Jernbanetorget" (Mon–Fri 6.30am to midnight, Sat from 8.30am, Sun from 9am; every 20–30min; 8min).

**Stena Line** Stena Line (ⓦstenaline.co.uk) runs car ferries from Fredrikshavn, in Denmark, to Oslo. They also dock at the Vippetangen quay (see DFDS above).

**Color Line** On Color Line (ⓦcolorline.co.uk), car ferries from Kiel berth at the Hjortneskaia, some 3km west of the city centre. A special connecting bus runs from the quay to Jernbanetorget and then Oslo Bussterminalen.

## BY CAR

**Ring roads** Oslo's ring roads encircle and tunnel under the city; if you follow the signs for "Ring 1" you'll be delivered right into the centre and emerge (eventually) at the multi-storey Sentrum P-hus car park (see below).

**Automatic toll points** Driving into Oslo, you'll have to proceed through one of the automatic toll points that surround the city. The toll for ordinary cars is 32kr – but note there is no toll when you leave the city. All number plates are read electronically and an invoice is sent to either the car rental company concerned or the registered owner of the vehicle; you can also speed the process by paying online within three days (ⓦfjellinjen.no).

**Parking** You won't need your car to sightsee in Oslo, so you'd do best to use a designated car park. There are half a dozen multistorey car parks in the centre, though some of them operate restricted hours: both the Sentrum P-hus at CJ Hambros Plass 1, two blocks north of Karl Johans gate, and Aker Brygge P-hus, Sjøgata 4, are open 24hr.

**Parking fees** Car park charges begin at about 32kr for 30min during the daytime (Mon–Sat 7am–7pm), up to a maximum of around 320kr for 24hr; Sunday and overnight rates are heavily discounted. Alternatively, you can park at on-street metered spaces around the city. Identified by blue "P" signs, these metered spaces are operated by the municipality, and are usually free of charge from Monday to Friday between 6pm and 9am and over the weekend after 3pm on Saturday. There is usually a maximum 2hr stay in pay periods. Charges vary considerably: a prime on-street parking spot (if you can get one) costs 70kr for 2hr, half that further out. The municipality also owns a scattering of parking lots – similar rules apply. Oslo Pass (see p.59) holders get free parking in all municipal parking spaces, but have to abide by the posted regulations.

**Car rental** Car rental companies are legion. Options include Bislet Bilutleie, Pilestredet 70 (☎22 60 00 00, ⓦeng.bislet .no); Europcar, Dronning Mauds gate 10 (☎22 83 12 42) and at Gardermoen airport (☎64 81 05 60, ⓦeuropcar.com); and Sixt, at Gardermoen airport (☎66 69 99 00, ⓦsixt.no). See also under "Bilutleie" in the *Yellow Pages*.

## INFORMATION

**City tourist office** The Oslo Visitor Centre is at Jernbanetorget 1, in the Østbanehallen, a converted former railway station next to Oslo S train station (June–Aug Mon–Sat 8am–8pm & Sun 9am–6pm; Sept–May daily 9am–6pm; ☎81 53 05 55, ⓦvisitoslo.com). Oslo Visitor Centre has a full range of information about Oslo and its environs. They issue free and very handy city maps marked with tram and principal bus routes and supply free copies of both the very thorough *Oslo Guide* and the listings brochure *What's On in Oslo*. They also sell public transport tickets, concert tickets and the Oslo Pass (see box, p.59); do currency exchange; and can make accommodation reservations both in person or online.

**Youth information centre** Unginfo (Use-it) is located at Møllergata 3, a brief walk from Oslo S (Mon–Fri 11am–5pm & Sat noon–5pm; ☎24 14 98 20, ⓦuse-it.no). Oslo's Youth Information Centre provides help and support to young people (26 years old and below) in everything from accommodation to healthcare and employment. They also do a helpful sideline in youth tourism, producing an annual *Free Map for Young Travellers*, which provides tips and hints and gives a roundup of their favourite bars and clubs etc – and marks them on a map. They carry all manner of fliers for gigs and concerts as well, plus there's lots more information on their website.

**Hiking information office** Den Norske Turistforening (DNT) is situated at Storgata 3 (Mon–Fri 10am–5pm, Thurs 10am–6pm, Sat 10am–3pm; ☎ 22 82 28 00, ⓦ dntoslo.no). The Norwegian hiking organization's city-centre office stocks a full range of Norwegian hiking maps, books and equipment. They also sell DNT membership (640kr per annum), which confers substantial discounts at DNT huts.

## ACTIVITIES

Surrounded by forest and fjord, Oslo is very much an outdoor city, offering a wide range of sports and outdoor pursuits. In summer, locals take to the hills to **hike** the network of trails that lattice the forests and lakes of the Nordmarka – and Oslo's DNT office have the details (see above) – where many also try their hand at a little freshwater **fishing**, while others head out to the offshore islets of the Oslofjord to kayak, sunbathe and **swim**. In winter, the cross-country **ski** routes of the Nordmarka are especially popular, as is downhill skiing. Indeed skiing is such an integral part of winter life here that the T-bane carriages all have ski racks. Every winter, from November to March, a floodlit **skating rink**, Narvisen, is created in front of the Stortinget, beside Karl Johans gate. Admission is free and you can rent skates on the spot at reasonable rates. The tourist office also has the details of all sorts of other winter fun in the Nordmarka – from **tobogganing** and **horse-drawn sleigh rides** to guided **winter walks**.

### KAYAKING

The sheltered waters of the Oslofjord are ideal for kayaking and the excellent and extremely efficient Oslo Kayak Tours, Drammensveien 164 (☎ 95 36 82 49, ⓦ oslokayaktours .no), offers several good choices, including three- and four-hour trips (850kr/1050kr per person). Some tours leave from near the Operahuset (see p.77), others from the quiet bay nudging out from the Sjølyst Marina, to the west of the city at the northern tip of the Bygdøy peninsula – and near a confetti of islets and skerries. Kayak experience is not necessary and tours can be adapted to customers' requirements. Advance reservations are essential.

### SKIING

**Information** Both cross-country and downhill enthusiasts might begin by either calling in at the tourist office (see opposite) or contacting Skiforeningen (Ski Association;

☎ 22 92 32 00, ⓦ skiforeningen.no). They both have lots of information on Oslo's floodlit trails, cross-country routes, downhill and slalom slopes, ski schools (including one for children) and excursions to the nearest mountain resorts.

**Equipment rental** Most Norwegians have their own skiing gear, but equipment rental is available – among several suppliers – from Oslo Ski Centre, out in the Nordmarka at Trollvannsveien 2 (☎ 22 09 91 98, ⓦ oslo -skisenter.no) or at Oslo Vinterpark.

**Oslo Vinterpark** Oslo's largest and best downhill ski area is Oslo Vinterpark (ⓦ oslovinterpark.no), where there are eighteen ski slopes and eleven ski lifts. Its facilities include a ski school and ski equipment rental and, snow permitting, the park is open from December to April. It's also easy to reach by public transport – take T-bane #1 to Voksenkollen station and catch the shuttle bus.

## GETTING AROUND

Oslo's safe and efficient public transport system, Ruter (☎ 177, ⓦ ruter.no), consists of buses, trams, a small underground rail system – the Tunnelbanen, or T-bane – and local ferries.

**Information** Ruter's main information office is at the foot of Trafikanten, the distinctive, transparent clocktower in front of Oslo S, on the Jernbanetorget (Mon–Fri 7am–8pm, Sat & Sun 9am–6pm). The office sells tickets and passes, has racks of free timetables and gives away a useful visitor's transit map, the *Besøkskart* – though tram and principal bus routes are marked on the city map given away at the tourist office (see opposite). Route plans for the buses and trams are also posted at most stops. There's a second, smaller information office (a *servicepunkt*) on the harbour-front at the start of Aker Brygge (June–Aug Mon–Fri 7am–7pm, Sat 9.30am–6pm, Sun 9.30am–3.30pm; Sept–May Mon–Fri 7am–7pm, Sat 9.30am–6pm).

**Tickets** The Oslo conurbation is divided into zones and the more zones you cross, the higher the fare. However, central Oslo and its immediate surroundings, including the islands of the inner Oslofjord (see p.88), are all in Zone 1, where flat-fare tickets cost 32kr if purchased before the journey, 50kr if purchased from a bus or tram driver or on a ferry; note that transport to the airport is priced separately. There are automatic ticket machines at all T-bane stations, most tram stops and some bus stops. Zone 1 tickets are valid for unlimited travel within the aforesaid zone for 1hr including transfers; seniors (67 years and above) and children 4–15 years old travel half-price, babies and toddlers free. All tickets and passes must be stamped or electronically read when they are first used: buses, trams and T-bane stations all have automatic stamping machines, but on ferries there's usually a conductor.

**Passes** There are several ways to cut costs. Perhaps the easiest is to buy an Oslo Pass (see box, p.59), which is valid on the whole network, but not on trains or buses to the

**1**

airport. If you're not into museums, however, a straight travel pass might be a better buy. A Zone 1 unlimited 24hr pass (*Dagskort*) costs 90kr, while a seven-day pass costs 240kr. Passes and tickets can be bought at the automatic ticket machines (see p.93), as well as from either of the Ruter offices, which also sell discounted electronic travel cards – *Reisekortet* – for frequent travellers.

### BY BUS

Many city bus services originate at – or pass through – Jernbanetorget, the square in front of Oslo S, while most suburban services depart from the Bussterminalen nearby. A second common port of call is Nationaltheatret, which is further to the west near the harbour. Most buses stop running at around midnight, though thereafter night buses (*nattbussen*) take over on a handful of major routes.

### BY TRAM

The city's trams run on six routes through the city, criss-crossing the centre from east to west, and sometimes duplicating the bus routes. They are a bit slower than the buses, but are a rather more enjoyable and relaxing way of getting about. Major stops include Jernbanetorget, Nationaltheatret and Aker Brygge. Most operate regularly – every 10–20min (daily 6am–midnight).

### BY T-BANE

The Tunnelbanen – T-bane – has five lines, which converge to share a common slice of track crossing the city centre from Majorstuen in the west to Tøyen in the east, with Nationaltheatret, Stortinget, Jernbanetorget/Oslo S and Grønland stations in between. From this central section, lines run west (*Vest*) and east (*Øst*) out into the suburbs. The system mainly serves commuters, but you may find it useful for hopping around the centre and for trips out into the forested hills of the Nordmarka. Outside the central section, trains travel above ground. The system runs from around 6am until 12.30am.

### BY PASSENGER FERRY

**To Bygdøy** For visitors, the most popular ferries (April–Sept) are those departing from Pier #3, immediately behind the Rådhus, bound for the museums of the Bygdøy peninsula (see pp.82–88).

**To the islands of the inner Oslofjord** There are all-year passenger ferry services to a number of Oslofjord islets, including Hovedøya, and a late May to Sept service to Langøyene. These depart from Pier #4, immediately behind the Rådhus.

### BY TAXI

**Fares** Taxi fares are expensive but regulated, with the tariff varying according to the time of day – night-times are about 25 percent more expensive than daytime – though on many longer routes there is a fixed tariff. As a sample fare, central Oslo to Gardermoen airport costs about 800kr in the daytime.

**Taxi ranks** There are taxi ranks dotted all over the city centre and outside all the big hotels. You can also telephone Oslo Taxi on ☎ 02323 or Norgestaxi on ☎ 08000.

### BY BIKE

**Renting a bicycle** is a pleasant way to get around Oslo, particularly as the city has a reasonable range of cycle tracks and many roads have cycle lanes.

**Bike rental** There is a municipal bike rental scheme (April–Nov; ⓦ oslobysykkel.no) in which bikes are released like supermarket trolleys from racks all over the city. Visitors can join the scheme at the tourist office by paying 349kr (plus 200kr for the appropriate smartcard), though note there are substantial discounts if you do this online. Bikes can be used for up to 3hr before they have to be dropped off (or swapped) at one of the bike racks; otherwise cyclists get penalized. A map showing you the location of the racks and cycle lanes is provided by the tourist office, and is also available on the website.

## ACCOMMODATION

Oslo has the range of **hotels** you would expect of a capital city, though surprisingly few of them are independents – most are chain hotels with Thon and Scandic being the two big players. The city also has a light smattering of **B&Bs** and **guesthouses** plus several **(youth) hostels**.

**Where to stay** To appreciate the full flavour of the city, you're best off staying on the western reaches of Karl Johans gate/Stortingsgata or immediately to the north on or close to Rozenkrantz gate – though noise can be a problem here in the summertime when Oslo's youth take to the streets in numbers, peaceable but loud: be sure to choose a room away from the street unless you are a heavy sleeper. A second pleasant – and rather quieter – area is among the late nineteenth-century buildings on and around Bankplassen. There is also a clutch of hotels in

the immediate vicinity of Oslo S, but this is a glum district that's best avoided.

**How to get a good deal** Accommodation prices are firmly pegged to demand and consequently they vary enormously, but nevertheless there are often good deals to be had in the summertime when many of the country's business folk are on holiday. As ever, advance online booking can save you substantial sums, but the tourist office (see p.92) does provide a same-day and in-person accommodation booking service, and they often get discounted rates too.

1

## HOTELS

At all but the busiest of times, you should be able to get a fairly small and simple, en-suite double room in a hotel in central Oslo for about 900kr. You hit the comfort zone at about 1200kr, and luxury from around 2000kr. However, special offers and summer and weekend deals often make the smarter hotels more affordable than this, with discounts of 30–40 percent commonplace. Also, most room rates are tempered by the inclusion of a self-service buffet breakfast, that tends to range from good to excellent.

## CENTRAL OSLO

**Clarion Collection Hotel Folketeateret** Storgata 21 ☎ 22 00 57 00, ⊛ choicehotels.com; map pp.64–65. In the delightful Art Deco passageway connecting Youngstorget with Storgata, this deluxe hotel has 160 slick, modern bedrooms and a rooftop terrace bar. Some of the hotel's original features have been kept, but most have been swept away in the super-duper decorative rush. **1300kr**

**Comfort Hotel Xpress Youngstorget** Møllergata 26 ☎ 22 03 11 00, ⊛ nordicchoicehotels.com; map pp.64–65. Opened in 2011, and aimed firmly at the youth/clubbing market, this chain hotel in a seven-storey block does its best to create a cool/relaxed vibe, beginning with the striking Pop Art decor in the foyer. There are few formalities at reception – you check in at the electronic kiosks – and the 175 guest rooms beyond, which feel a blend of modernism and spartan, are similarly high-tech. **650kr**

★ **Continental** Stortingsgata 24–26 ☎ 22 82 40 00, ⊛ hotelcontinental.no; map pp.64–65. The classiest hotel in town is a family-owned place with swish public areas that ooze an easy comfort – all pastel shades, flowers, and even some Munch paintings (or at least near-perfect copies of them). The bedrooms beyond are extremely comfortable and decorated in a fetching, modern style with delicate patterned wallpaper setting the tone. The hotel is also ideally located, a stone's throw from Karl Johans gate, though the rooms overlooking the street can be a tad noisy. Wonderful, banquet-like breakfasts too. **2100kr**

**Grand** Karl Johans gate 31 ☎ 23 21 20 00, ⊛ grand.no; map pp.64–65. Once Norway's most prestigious hotel, the Grand has long been famous as the one-time haunt of Ibsen and his admirers. At the time of writing, the hotel was undergoing an extensive renovation, which had already turned the foyer into a glitzy modern affair with few concessions to what went before. Quite what will happen to the hotel's 300-odd guest rooms is hard to predict, but they certainly did vary enormously: the ones at the front, complete with balconies overlooking Karl Johans gate and all sorts of period touches, were a delight, the ones at the back much more mundane. Expect the room rate to hike up when the work is completed. **1800kr**

**Hotell Bondeheimen** Rosenkrantz gate 8 ☎ 23 21 41 00, ⊛ bondeheimen.com; map pp.64–65. One of Oslo's older hotels, dating from 1913, the Bondeheimen is handily placed just 2min walk north of Karl Johans gate. Both the public areas and the bedrooms are decorated in modern, pan-Scandinavian style, with polished pine everywhere. The buffet breakfast, served in the Kaffistova (see p.98), is substantial, and there's free coffee and tea in the evenings. The rooms towards the back are much quieter than those at the front. **1100kr**

**Perminalen** Øvre Slottsgate 2 ☎ 24 00 55 00, ⊛ perminalen.no; map pp.64–65. This hostel-like hotel has two things going for it – a central location and budget prices: a bed in a four- or six-berth room costs just 425kr, a single 685kr. At these rates, it's hardly surprising that the guest rooms are positively frugal, though at least all the doubles and singles are en suite. It's popular with the Norwegian military. Doubles **960kr**

**Scandic Edderkoppen** St Olavs plass 1 ☎ 23 15 56 00, ⊛ scandichotels.com; map pp.64–65. Overlooking one of the city's more pleasant, semi-pedestrianized squares, this Scandic hotel occupies a straightforward, fairly brutal modern block, but the interior has been pleasantly remodelled in a bright and stylish manner. The rooms vary considerably – by and large you get precisely what you pay for. **950kr**

**Scandic Holberg** Holbergs plass 1 ☎ 23 15 72 00, ⊛ scandichotels.com; map pp.64–65. This grand nineteenth-century building has been thoroughly refurbished both inside and out, but still retains fragments of its historic atmosphere. The public rooms, with their slender pillars and skylight, are appealing, while the bedrooms are spick, span and modern, though one or two of them might be considered a tad small. It overlooks Holbergs plass, a pint-sized square about 500m from the Slottsparken. **900kr**

★ **Thon Hotel Oslo Panorama** Rådhusgata 7B ☎ 23 31 08 00, ⊛ thonhotels.com; map pp.64–65. In an agreeable part of town, a 10min walk from Oslo S and the Operahuset, this is one of Oslo's more affordable chain hotels. Unusually, the street facade comprises an old building, but the foyer beyond is modern – as are the spacious guest rooms, which occupy an imaginatively converted 1960s tower block. A key selling point is the wide views over the city centre from the upper (not lower) floors. Most rooms have mini-balconies, many have simple self-catering facilities and the breakfasts are excellent. **1000kr**

**Thon Hotel Rosenkrantz** Rosenkrantz gate 1 ☎ 23 31 55 00, ⊛ thonhotels.com; map pp.64–65. After the sombre-looking, red-brick facade, the bright and cheerful interior of this 151-room hotel comes as a bit of a surprise – it's hardly tasteful perhaps, but it is good fun. Many of the rooms have balconies and some have basic self-catering facilities. There are great breakfasts and the location is handy, a brief stroll from Karl Johans gate. **1400kr**

**1**

### WESTSIDE

**Clarion Collection Hotel Gabelshus** Gabels gate 16 ☎ 23 27 65 00, ⓦ choicehotels.com; map pp.60–61. In a good-looking, ivy-covered building dating from 1912, this attractive, medium-sized hotel stands in a smart residential area a couple of kilometres west of the city centre, off Drammensveien. The public areas are kitted out with antique furnishings, while the bedrooms are smart, very modern and very well appointed. Tram #13 from the centre to the Skillebekk stop. **1300kr**

**★Saga Hotell Oslo** Eilert Sundts gate 39 ☎ 22 55 44 90, ⓦ sagahoteloslo.no; map pp.60–61. West of the centre, in a pleasant and quiet residential area, this 47-room hotel occupies a tastefully updated late nineteenth-century, three-storey building. The decor is mostly charcoal, black and grey and all the guest rooms are well appointed. Tram #19 stops at Rosenborg, the nearest tram stop, a 5min walk away. **1200kr**

### EASTSIDE

**Anker Hotel** Storgata 55 ☎ 22 99 75 00, ⓦ anker-hotel.no; map p.80. This large budget hotel occupies a high-rise block beside the Akerselva River at the east end of Storgata. The clientele is mainly Norwegian, and the facilities are adequate, if somewhat frugal, though all the rooms are en suite. Very handy for Grünerløkka, the trendiest part of the city, and just 15min walk from Oslo S, or 5min by tram; the same block also houses the *Anker Hostel* (see opposite). **1000kr**

**Scandic Vulkan** Maridalsveien 13 ☎ 21 05 71 00, ⓦ scandichotels.com; map pp.80. Out from the centre, near Grünerløkka in the thriving district of Vulkan (see p.80), the attractive, glassy facade of this chain hotel mitigates against the clumsiness of the rest of the building – a clumpy deck of no distinction. The rooms are kitted out in the full flush of Scandic style – wooden floors and big windows – and are pleasant and enjoyable. Its out-from-the-centre location keeps prices down; bus #34 or #54. **900kr**

### HOSTELS, B&BS AND GUESTHOUSES

Oslo has two extremely popular hostels and one of them is a member of the HI-affiliated Norske Vandrerhjem (Norwegian Hostelling Association; ⓦ hihostels.no). The city also possesses a handful of guesthouses, or *pensjonater*, which offer basic but generally adequate accommodation, either with or without en-suite facilities, though breakfast is not included in the price, and at some places you may need to supply your own sleeping bag.

### CENTRAL OSLO

**Cochs Pensjonat** Parkveien 25 ☎ 23 33 24 00, ⓦ cochspensjonat.no; map pp.60–61. Friendly and engaging guesthouse occupying the upper floors of an old apartment block, in a handy location behind the Slottsparken. There are 89 rooms of various dimensions and each is decorated in frugal modern style – wood laminate floors and so on. The least expensive rooms are those with shared facilities; you'll have to pay more for an en-suite room (single 650kr; double 850kr) or for those with a kitchenette (single 690kr; double 900kr). Breakfasts (42kr extra) are served just along the street at *Espresso House*, Parkveien 27. Singles **530kr**, doubles **720kr**

### WESTSIDE

**Ellingsens Pensjonat** Holtegata 25 ☎ 22 60 03 59, ⓦ ellingsenspensjonat.no; map pp.60–61. Competitively priced accommodation in a large, well-equipped and attractively decorated late nineteenth-century house on the west side of the city centre, just beyond the Slottsparken. Rooms are spacious – those with en suite cost more (990kr). Guests have access to a small garden. **800kr**

### EASTSIDE

**Anker Hostel** Storgata 55 ☎ 22 99 72 00, ⓦ anker hostel.no; map p.80. In the same large modern block as the *Anker Hotel* (see opposite), this all-year hostel has 50 rooms – and 250 beds. The rooms are plain and simple, but perfectly adequate. Bed linen and towels are for rent, or bring your own; sleeping bags are not allowed. The least expensive dorm beds are in four- or six-bedded rooms but there are also en-suite singles and en-suite doubles. The hostel is 15min walk from Oslo S or 5min by tram. Dorms **260kr**, singles **640kr**, doubles **700kr**

**★Oslo Vandrerhjem Haraldsheim** Haraldsheimveien 4, Grefsen ☎ 22 22 29 65, ⓦ haraldsheim.no; map pp.60–61. This excellent HI hostel, 4km northeast of the centre, has public areas that are comfortable and attractively furnished in brisk, modern style and frugal but clean bedrooms. There are 315 beds in 88 rooms, most of which are four-bedded, and a majority have their own showers and toilet. The hostel also has self-catering facilities and washing machines. The only downside can be parties of noisy school kids. It's a very popular spot, so advance reservations are pretty much essential throughout summer. To get there, take tram #17 from Jernbanetorget, outside Oslo S train station, and get off at the Sinsenkrysset stop, from where it's a signed 5min walk. By road, the hostel is close to – and signed from – Ring 3. There's a range of accommodation options, with dorms, singles and doubles – expect to pay more for en-suite facilities (dorms 280kr; singles 510kr; doubles 690kr). Open all year except Christmas week. Dorms **255kr**, singles **455kr**, doubles **610kr**

### CAMPING AND CABINS

The peripheries of Oslo are dotted with campsites – a dozen or so are within a 50km radius and the nearest is just

1

3km away. Most sites also offer cabins (*hytter*), which can be a good option if you're out of luck with rooms in town – but be sure to ring ahead to check availability.

**Bogstad Camping** Ankerveien 117 ☏ 22 51 08 00, ⓦ bogstadcamping.no; map pp.60–61. Massive, lakeside campsite on the edge of the Nordmarka, about 9km north of the city centre, with a good range of facilities, including self-catering, plus access to the Nordmarka's walking trails and ski slopes. They have fifty or so cabins – from simple to deluxe, en suite and with shared facilities – with prices starting at 1000kr/night to accommodate up to four adults.

To get there, take bus #32 from Oslo S or the Nationaltheatret; the journey takes about 35min. Open all year. Camping **290kr**, cabins **1000kr**

**Ekeberg Camping** Ekebergveien 65 ☏ 22 19 85 68, ⓦ www.ekebergcamping.no; map pp.60–61. Sprawling campsite on a field but edged by woods just 3km southeast of the city centre – and on the east side of the Ekebergparken. Has self-catering facilities, rudimentary shower and toilet blocks and an on-site shop. Take bus #34 from Oslo S – it's a 10min journey. June–Aug. **300kr**

## EATING

At the top end of the market, Oslo possesses several dozen fine **restaurants**, the most distinctive of which feature Norwegian cuisine and ingredients, especially fresh North Atlantic fish, but also more unusual dishes of elk, caribou and salted-and-dried cod – for centuries Norway's staple food. There is a reasonable selection of less expensive, non-Scandinavian restaurants too – everything from Italian to Vietnamese. More affordable – and more casual – are the city's **cafés and café-bars**. These run the gamut from homely places offering traditional Norwegian stand-bys to student haunts and ultra-trendy joints. Nearly all serve inexpensive lunches, and many offer excellent, competitively priced evening meals as well, though some cafés close at around 5 or 6pm as do the city's many **coffee houses**, where coffee is, as you might expect, the main deal alongside maybe a light snack. Finally, those carefully counting the kroner will find it easy to buy bread, fruit, snacks and sandwiches from stalls, **supermarkets** and kiosks across the city centre, while fast-food joints offering hamburgers and *warme pølser* (hot dogs) are legion. **Smoking** is forbidden inside every Norwegian bar, café and restaurant – hence the smoky huddles outside.

### CAFÉS, CAFÉ-BARS AND COFFEE HOUSES
#### CENTRAL OSLO

★ **Bacchus** Dronningsgate 27 ☏ 22 33 34 30, ⓦ bacchus spiseri.no ; map pp.64–65. In the Basarhallene (see p.62), near Oslo S, this charming café, with its antique decor and ricketty-racketty furniture, does a tasty line in salads at around 170kr and an even tastier line in home-made cakes. There's a small garden terrace to the rear in the shadow of the cathedral and has a first-rate selection of wines. Mon–Sat 11am–11pm.

**Fiskeriet** Youngstorget 2B ☏ 22 42 45 40, ⓦ fiskeriet .com; map pp.64–65. Casual, fresh-fish bar that shares its premises with a fishmonger. Take away or eat in perched on a stool – everything from fresh prawns and fish cakes through to herring and cod, all at affordable prices – from 150kr and up. Mon–Fri 11am–7.30pm, Sat noon–7.30pm.

**Kafé Celsius** Rådhusgata 19 ☏ 22 42 45 39, ⓦ kafecelsius.no; map pp.64–65. Smashing café-bar occupying imaginatively refurbished old premises just off the cobbled square at the junction of Rådhusgata and Øvre Slottsgate. Especially attractive courtyard seating – for either a drink or a light meal: a chicken salad, for instance, costs 190kr. Mon–Fri 11am–11pm, Sat noon–11pm, Sun 11am–11pm.

**Kaffistova** Rosenkrantz gate 8 ☏ 23 21 42 10, ⓦ kaffistova.com; map pp.64–65. Part of the *Hotell Bondeheimen* (see p.95), this neat and trim, self-service cafeteria serves tasty, traditional Norwegian cooking in substantial portions and at very fair prices – reckon on

160kr for a main course. Meatballs, gravy and potatoes are the house speciality. There's usually a vegetarian option, too. Mon–Fri 11am–9pm, Sat & Sun 11am–7pm.

★ **Litteraturhuset** Wergelandsveien 29 ☏ 22 95 55 30, ⓦ litteraturhuset.no; map pp.64–65. Opposite the tail end of the Slottsparken, this amenable café-bar-cum-bookshop spreads a wide net with poetry readings, public debates and book signings as well as a café and outside terrace. Light meals here – the salads are good – will cost you around 180kr (kitchen closes Mon–Sat at 10pm, Sun at 6pm). Café-bar: Mon–Thurs 10am–midnight, Fri & Sat 10am–2am, Sun noon–8pm.

★ **Pascal Konditori** Tollbugata 11 ☏ 22 42 11 19, ⓦ pascal.no; map pp.64–65. Lovely little café-patisserie comprising two rooms – one pleasantly modern, the other, in the original bakery, decorated with antique ceramic tiles of cherubs and fruit. Mouth-watering pastries, great coffee and delicious, freshly prepared lunches – the salads (180kr) are delicious and the fish soup first-rate. Also at Henrik Ibsen's gate (see opposite). Mon–Fri 9.30am–5pm, Sat 10am–5pm.

★ **Stockfleths** Lille Grensen, off Karl Johans gate; and C.J. Hambros plass; ⓦ stockfleths.as; map pp.64–65. With good reason, many locals swear by the coffee served at this medium-sized (ten-location) chain, which often wins awards for its brews. Lille Grensen: Mon–Fri 7am–7pm, Sat 10am–6pm, Sun 11am–5pm. C.J. Hambros plass: Mon–Fri 7am–7pm, Sat 10am–5pm.

**Tullins Café** Tullins gate 2 ☏ 22 20 46 16, ⓦ tullins.no; map pp.64–65. The building may be glum – it's a dull modern high-rise – but this ground-floor café-bar is painted in attractive modern style and furnished with an idiosyncratic mix of bygones. A wide-ranging, notably inexpensive menu covers everything from salads and burgers to pizzas, pastas and Indian dishes – reckon on 150kr per main course. There's (comparatively) inexpensive beer here too as the place morphs into a late-night bar. Mon–Thurs 10am–2am, Fri 10am–3am, Sat 11am–3.30am, Sun noon–1am.

### EASTSIDE

**Delicatessen** Søndre gate 8, Grünerløkka ☎ 22 46 72 00, ⓦ delicatessen.no; map p.80. Lovely, boho café-bar with large, push-back windows and a fine line in authentic tapas (70–150kr) as well as the freshest of salads (150kr). Be prepared to wait for a table at the weekend. Mon & Tues 11am–10pm, Wed–Fri 11am–11pm, Sat noon–11.30pm & Sun noon–10pm.

**Fru Hagen** Thorvald Meyers gate 40, Grünerløkka ☎ 45 49 19 04, ⓦ fruhagen.no; map p.80. Long-standing, colourful joint that still manages to be trendy, serving tasty snacks and meals from an inventive menu with a Mediterranean slant. Main courses around 180kr. The kitchen closes at 9pm, after which the drinking gets going in earnest – the cocktails are a treat. Very popular so go early to be sure of a seat. Mon & Tues 11am–11pm, Wed & Thurs 11am–midnight, Fri & Sat 11am–3am, Sun noon–11pm.

**Tim Wendelboe** Grünersgate 1, corner Fossveien, Grünerløkka ☎ 40 00 40 62, ⓦ timwendelboe.no; map p.80. One room, one outside bench, bare-brick walls, one counter and one noisy coffee grinder are the modest-looking accoutrements to Wendelboe's coffee-making business – but make no mistake, he is a coffee star (who now supplies *Noma* in Copenhagen). Take away or drink inside and smell the beans. Mon–Fri 8.30am–6pm, Sat & Sun 11am–5pm.

## RESTAURANTS

Dining out at one of Oslo's restaurants can make a sizeable dent in your wallet unless you exercise some restraint. In most places, a main course will set you back between 250kr and 350kr – not terribly steep until you add on a couple of beers or a bottle of wine. Advance reservations are a good idea almost everywhere, especially at the weekend, and note that many restaurants have summer holidays, usually in July.

### CENTRAL OSLO

**Arakataka** Mariboes gate 7 ☎ 23 32 83 00, ⓦ arakataka.no; map pp.64–65. This smart, modern restaurant serves excellent food, mostly fish and meat, at reasonable prices with à la carte mains averaging 190kr. Highly recommended, and a good place to sample that old

Norwegian favourite, salted cod (*bacalao*), when it is on the menu. A side-street location, a 10min walk north of the Domkirke on the way to Grünerløkka. Mon–Sat 4–10pm, Sun 4–9pm.

★ **Ekebergrestauranten** Kongsveien 15 ☎ 23 24 23 00, ⓦ ekebergrestauranten.com; map pp.60–61. On the Ekeberg heights, just to the southeast of the centre, this combined café, lounge-bar and restaurant occupies a splendid Art Deco building dating from the 1920s. There are panoramic views over the Oslofjord from inside as well as from the spacious terrace-veranda. The food is international meets Norway with the likes of sea-trout served with new cabbage, petit pois and bacon. Mains average 280kr at the restaurant, less in the café and at lunchtimes. To get there by public transport, take tram #18 or #19 from outside Oslo S and get off at the Ekebergparken stop; from here, it's a 5min walk up through the woods and past the assorted sculptures of the open-air Ekebergparken (see p.77). Restaurant: Mon–Sat 11am–midnight, Sun noon–10pm; bar: Mon–Sat 11am–1am, Sun noon–10pm.

**Engebret Café** Bankplassen 1 ☎ 22 82 25 25, ⓦ engebret-cafe.no; map pp.64–65. On one of Oslo's prettiest squares, this comparatively formal restaurant occupies a fetching old building with oodles of wood panelling and vintage oil paintings on the walls. It specializes in Norwegian delicacies such as reindeer and fish, including *bacalao*, with main courses in the region of 330kr, less at lunchtime; try the halibut in a beetroot sauce. Attracts an older clientele. In summer, there's outside seating on the square. Mon–Fri 11.30am–11pm, Sat 5–11pm.

★ **Lofoten Fiskerestaurant** Stranden 75, Aker Brygge ☎ 22 83 08 08, ⓦ lofoten-fiskerestaurant.no; map pp.64–65. This smart, modern restaurant offers an excellent selection of fish and shellfish, all immaculately prepared and served. It's beside the harbour towards the far end of the Aker Brygge complex, which makes it popular with locals and tourists alike. Mains kick off at around 300kr, but some of the more unusual fish – including the wonderfully textured catfish (*steinbit*) – cost a little more. Mon–Sat 11am–11pm, Sun noon–10pm.

**Pascal** Henrik Ibsens gate 36 ☎ 22 55 00 20, ⓦ pascal .no; map pp.64–65. An offshoot of the *Pascal Konditori* on Tollbugata (see opposite), this bright and breezy restaurant-cum-café offers tasty salads, cakes and pasties plus more substantial meals from around 200kr. Mon–Fri 8am–7pm, Sat 10am–7pm, Sun noon–5pm.

**Ruffino** Arbins gate 1 ☎ 22 55 32 80, ⓦ ruffino.no; map pp.64–65. Located on the corner of Henrik Ibsens gate, *Ruffino* is a bright, modern and cheerful, first-rate Italian restaurant with a well-chosen menu featuring fresh pastas (150kr) and a handful of meat and fish dishes (280–300kr). Exemplary service; delicious, unpretentious food; and no pizzas. Mon–Sat 4–11pm.

1

★ **Sentralen** Øvre Slottsgate 3 ☎ 22 33 33 22, ⓦ sentralen.no; map pp.64–65. Part of a larger "culture house" complex located within the former HQ of a savings bank, *Sentralen* has one of the city's most popular restaurants, an informal, almost canteen-like affair with bare-brick walls and long benches. The imaginative, competitively priced menu features such delights as blackened cod with mussels and cabbage (190kr) and smoked beef tartare (160kr). The restaurant adjoins a separate area where they specialize in pizza – just half a dozen different sorts at 175kr – which is served from the afternoon into the evening (daily 3pm–9.30pm). Restaurant: daily 11am–midnight.

★ **Solsiden** Akershusstranda 13 ☎ 22 33 36 30, ⓦ solsiden.no; map pp.64–65. Tucked in below the Akershus castle, right on the harbourside in an attractively kitted out container-like structure, this lively and relaxed restaurant specializes in seafood, which is reckoned to be as good as anywhere in Oslo. The signature dish is a mountain bouquet of shellfish (it has its own lobster tank), but there's lots more; try, for example, the turbot in a mustard purée. Mains are 250–350kr. May–early Sept Mon–Sat 5–10pm, Sun 5–9pm.

**Statholdergaarden & Statholderens Mat & Vinkjeller** Rådhusgata 11 ☎ 22 41 88 00, ⓦ statholdergaarden.no; map pp.64–65. Distinctive, top-of-the-range restaurant in lovely period rooms dating back to the eighteenth century. The house speciality is a four-course set menu for 1100kr. No one could say they don't think about the menu, with dishes such as lamb served with orange pickled tomato, spinach, cauliflower purée, lentils and bay leaves. Downstairs in the cellar is the companion *Statholderens Mat & Vinkjeller* (same phone), a more informal affair where they do à la carte (mains around 340kr) and a ten-course set menu with a theme – fish and shellfish, Tuscan food and so on. Statholdergaarden: Mon–Sat 6pm–midnight (kitchen till 9.30pm); Statholderens: Tues–Sat 4pm–midnight (kitchen till 9.30pm).

★ **Theatercaféen** Hotel Continental, Stortingsgata 24–26 ☎ 22 82 40 50, ⓦ theatercafeen.com; map pp.64–65. This handsome restaurant, with its long mirrors, vaulted ceiling and marble pillars, has been pulling in the city's movers and shakers for decades. The imaginative menu features such delights as halibut in a cream and crab sauce with beet and pickled onions. Mains cost around 330kr, a three-course set menu 600kr, though you can slum it with a hamburger (240kr). Mon–Sat 11am–11pm, Sun 3–10pm; closed most of July.

## DRINKING AND NIGHTLIFE

Central Oslo boasts a vibrant **bar scene**, boisterous but generally good-natured and at its most frenetic on summer weekends, when the city is crowded with visitors from all over Norway. There's an infinitely groovy string of bars out of the centre too, in the Grünerløkka district. With the city's bars staying open till the wee hours, Oslo's **nightclubs** struggle to make themselves heard – indeed there's often little distinction between the two – though there is still a reasonably good and varied scene. **Live music** is not Oslo's forte, and few would say Norway's domestic rock and pop is particularly inspiring, but **jazz** fans are well served, with a couple of first-rate venues in the city centre.

### BARS

Bar-hopping in Oslo is an enjoyable affair. The more mainstream (meat-market) bars are in the centre along and around Karl Johans gate, while the sharper, more alternative spots are concentrated on and around Youngstorget and, further out, in the Grünerløkka district to the northeast. The west side of the city has its chic spots too, mostly along and around Hegdehaugsveien and Bogstadveien. Most city bars stay open until around 1am on weekdays, often 3–4am at the weekend, and almost all of them are open daily. Drinks are uniformly expensive, so if you're after a big night out, it's a good idea to follow Norwegian custom and have a few warm-up drinks at home before you set out (*vorspiel* in Norwegian). A number of bars feature live music, blurring the lines between the bars listed here and the dedicated live venues (see opposite).

### CENTRAL OSLO

**Beer Palace** Holmensgata 3, Aker Brygge ☎ 22 83 71 55, ⓦ beerpalace.no; map pp.64–65. One of the old shipyard buildings down on the Aker Brygge has been turned into this large, cellar-like, split-level bar where there is – as you might expect from the name – a wide range of domestic and international beer, mostly bottled. It is heaving at the weekend. Daily 1pm–3am.

**Café Sør** Torggata 11 ☎ 41 46 30 47, ⓦ cafesor.no; map pp.64–65. This groovy daytime café, with its funky music and modern art on the walls, turns into a late-night bar with a good line in cocktails. Mon–Thurs 10am–12.30am, Fri & Sat 10am–3am, Sun 11am–12.30am.

**Café Tekehtopa** St Olavs plass 2 ☎ 47 97 80 89, ⓦ tekehtopa.no; map pp.64–65. *Tekehtopa* is *Apoteket* (pharmacy) spelt backwards – a nice little verbal play as this laidback café-bar occupies a former pharmacy, complete with the original wooden fittings. There's an agreeable atmosphere here, lots of students and a wide range of beers on draught and in bottles. The food is so-so. Mon–Fri 11am–midnight, Sat noon–midnight, Sun noon–10pm.

**Ett Glass** Karl Johans gate 33, entrance just up Rosenkrantz gate ☎ 23 16 17 10, ⓦ ettglass.no; map pp.64–65. Dark and intimate, split-level café-bar with an inexpensive menu, featuring burgers and more (served till 10pm), and a good line in drinks. Guest DJs on Sat nights. Popular with a mixed clientele, but notably gay-friendly. Mon, Tues & Sun 11am–1am, Wed–Sat 11am–3am.

★**Fuglen** Universitetsgata 2 ☎ 22 20 08 80, ⓦ fuglen .com; map pp.64–65. During the day, *Fuglen*, with its vintage furniture and boho vibe, serves some of the best coffee in town to a discerning crew, some of whom switch over to cocktails early or late as the fancy takes them. It's located beside a busy road and is rammed at the weekend. Mon & Tues 7.30am–10pm, Wed & Thurs 7.30am–1am, Fri 7.30am–3.30am, Sat 11am–3.30am, Sun 11am–10pm.

★**Internasjonalen** Youngstorget 2 ☎ 22 42 08 19, ⓦ internasjonalen.no; map pp.64–65. On the ground floor of the 1930s tower block overlooking Youngstorget, this super-cool bar specializes in cocktails served up in stylish retro surroundings: Pop Art meets Eastern Europe. Live bands too. Mon 10am–1am, Tues–Sat 10am–3am, Sun 4pm–1am.

**London Pub** C.J. Hambros plass 5 ☎ 22 70 87 00, ⓦ londonpub.no; map pp.64–65. Something of a LGBT institution, this is the best – and certainly the busiest – gay bar in town with a pool table, jukeboxes, guest DJs and karaoke nights. Daily 3pm–3.30am.

**Lorry** Parkveien 12, cnr Hegdehaugsveien ☎ 22 69 69 04, ⓦ lorry.no; map pp.64–65. Popular and enjoyable bar with a cranky mix of fixtures and fittings from maquettes to stuffed animals. There's a wide choice of beers – well over a hundred – and outdoor seating in the summer. Also serves food. Mon–Sat 11am–3.30am, Sun noon–1.30am.

**Palace Grill/Skaugum** Solligata 2 ☎ 23 13 11 40, ⓦ palacegrill.no; map pp.64–65. A real rabbit warren of a place, this popular New Age-meets-alternative café-bar has a roots, rock and jazz soundtrack, and serves filling food too (Mon–Sat). There's also a heaving outside bar, *Skaugum*, in the yard behind and beside the *Palace*. Palace Grill Bar: Mon–Sat 3pm–3am, Sun 3pm–1am. Skaugum: May–Sept Tues–Sat 6pm–3am; Oct–April Fri & Sat 10pm–3am.

**The Scotsman** Karl Johans gate 17 ☎ 22 47 44 77, ⓦ scotsman.no; map pp.64–65. Traditional pub with a dark interior and a good range of brews, both on draught and in bottles, as well as a popular pavement terrace. The big draw is, perhaps, its clientele – sometimes calm shoppers breaking for a tipple, other times raucous and/or bizarre. Mon & Tues 11am–1am, Wed–Sat 11am–3am, Sun noon–1am.

★**Stratos** Youngstorget 2A ☎ 21 04 64 00, ⓦ stratos .as; map pp.64–65. At the top of the large and distinctive Art Deco tower dominating Youngstorget, this outstanding rooftop bar offers great views and great cocktails from

amid its decorative brickwork. Accessible by lift. Late June to mid-Aug Tues–Sat 3pm–3am, Sun 8pm–3am.

## WESTSIDE

**Oslo Mikrobryggeri** Bogstadveien 6, entrance on Holtegata ☎ 22 56 97 76, ⓦ omb.no; map pp.60–61. Dark, almost gloomy, bar with loud music and a dartboard plus a tasty range of ales, the pick of which are brewed on the premises. Mon–Fri & Sun 3pm–1am, Sat noon–1am.

## EASTSIDE

**Aku–Aku** Thorvald Meyers gate 32, Grünerløkka ☎ 41 76 69 66; map p.80. Bizarre-meets-idiosyncratic bar with a Polynesian theme – hence the wooden masks – and volcanic cocktails. Attracts a humdinger of a crowd, especially when there's a live (Polynesian) show. Mon–Thurs 6pm–1am, Fri & Sat 3pm–3am, Sun 3pm–1am.

**Bar Boca** Thorvald Meyers gate 30, Grünerløkka ☎ 22 04 13 77; map p.80. Tiny 1950s retro-style bar serving some of the best cocktails in town. The bartenders take their work very seriously, and you need to get there early to avoid the crush. Live jazz once or twice weekly. Mon–Thurs 2pm–1am, Fri & Sat 2pm–3am, Sun noon–1am.

**Olympen** Grønlandsleiret 15, Grønland ☎ 24 10 19 99, ⓦ www.olympen.no; map p.80. A rare survivor, this old beer hall, dating from the 1890s, has kept many of its antique furnishings and fittings, from the chandeliers down to the oil paintings and the wooden benches. It sells a good range of specialist beers at reasonable prices – and has food too. Familiarly known as "Lompa" (sausage wrap), rather than its grand official name. In the seedy Grønland district near Oslo S. Mon–Thurs 11am–midnight, Fri 11am–3am, Sat noon–3am, Sun noon–midnight.

**Parkteatret Bar** Olaf Ryes plass 11, Grünerløkka ☎ 22 35 63 00, ⓦ parkteatret.no; map p.80. Choose a brew from the extensive beer menu at this boho bar, which occupies the foyer of a disused cinema – hence the old cinema seats. Sandwiches are supplied by an excellent local deli, and Scandinavian indie rock is pumped up round the clock. There are regular live acts. Mon–Thurs & Sun 11am–1am, Fri & Sat 11am–3am.

**Tea Lounge** Thorvald Meyers gate 33C, Grünerløkka ☎ 22 37 07 05, ⓦ tealounge.no; map p.80. Super-cool, lounge-type café-bar with velvety red couches and big windows. As you might guess from the name, tea is a big deal here – all sorts are on offer, served to a soft house backtrack. Cocktails and spirits too. Sun–Wed 11am–1am, Thurs–Sat noon–3am.

## CLUBS AND LIVE MUSIC

At the city's nightclubs, nothing much gets going before 11pm with venues generally closing around 3.30am. Most clubs focus on DJ events and special party or theme nights, but some also host a variety of live music, ranging from local home-grown talent to big-name bands. Some clubs charge an entrance fee, but many don't, depending on what's on and who is performing. At the smarter places there's an informal dress code – go scruffy and you will be turned away. Oslo has a strong jazz tradition, as evidenced by its jazz festival (see box opposite); otherwise, check out *Bare Jazz* or *Herr Nilsen* for regular jazz acts (see below). For entertainment listings, it's worth checking out *What's On Oslo*, a free, monthly English-language brochure produced by Oslo tourist office. The tourist office website (Ⓦvisitoslo.com) is also good for upcoming events as is that of Unginfo (Ⓦuse-it.no), the city's youth information shop (see p.92). For tickets, contact the venue direct or try Ticketmaster (Ⓦticketmaster.no), who use some Narvesen kiosks as outlets – details on the website.

**CENTRAL OSLO**

**Bare Jazz** Grensen 8 ☎22 33 20 80, Ⓦbarejazz.no; map. pp.64–65. Split-level joint with a superb selection of jazz CDs for sale on the ground floor and a jazz café up above with frequent live sounds, both home-grown and imported. There's a courtyard café too. Mon & Tues 10am–6pm, Wed–Sat 10am–midnight.

**Elsker** Kristian's IV gate 9 ☎45 21 41 33, Ⓦelsker-oslo .no; map pp.64–65. Relaxed, stylish and easygoing bar and club that is a favourite with Oslo's LGBT community. DJ sounds on Friday and Saturday nights. Wed–Sat 6pm–3am.

★**Herr Nilsen** C.J. Hambros plass 5 ☎22 33 54 05, Ⓦherrnilsen.no; map pp.64–65. Small and intimate jazz club whose brick walls are decorated with jazz memorabilia. There's live jazz – sometimes traditional and bebop – most nights. In a handy, central location too. Daily 2pm–3am.

**Jaeger** Grensen 9 Ⓦjaegeroslo.no; map pp.64–65. Two dancefloors, a great sound system, top DJs and a downtown location make this one of the city's most popular clubs at night – and it doubles up as a café-bar during the day. Mon–Thurs & Sun 2pm–3am, Fri & Sat noon–3am; club from 11pm.

**Mono** Pløens gate 4 ☎22 41 41 66, Ⓦwww.cafemono .no; map pp.64–65. Darkly lit bar, with retro fixtures and fittings, which attracts a largely student crowd. Showcases a wide range of pop/rock music with elements of folk, country, electronica and jazz. Features live acts every week. A good place to check out up-and-coming (sometimes going nowhere) Norwegian bands. Pløens gate is off Youngstorget, a short walk from Oslo S. Mon–Sat 4pm–3am.

**Oslo Spektrum Arena** Sonja Henies plass 2, Box office: ☎815 11 211, Ⓦoslospektrum.no; map pp.64–65. Major venue, close to Olso S, showcasing big international acts, as well as smaller-fry local bands.

**EASTSIDE**

★**Blå** Brenneriveien 9C ☎40 00 42 77, Ⓦblaaoslo.no; map p.80. Creative, cultural nightspot in Grünerløkka with a New Age feel, featuring – beyond the frenetic graffiti – everything from live jazz, rock and cabaret through to poetry readings. Also features some of the best DJs in town, keeping the crowd moving until 3.30am at the weekend. In summer, there's a riverside terrace too. Usually daily from 10pm, though depends on events – check the website.

## ENTERTAINMENT

### CLASSICAL MUSIC AND OPERA

Classical music enthusiasts can enjoy an ambitious concert programme. In the summertime, in addition to the Konserthus (see below), there are also classical concerts at a variety of other venues, including the Domkirke; for details of the summer programme, contact the tourist office (see p.92). In September, the ten-day Ultima Contemporary Music Festival (Ⓦultima.no) gathers together Scandinavian and international talent in an impressive programme of concerts featuring everything from modern contemporary music to opera, ballet, classical and folk. The performances take place in a number of venues throughout the city; for full details check Ultima's website or, again, contact Oslo tourist office.

**Oslo Konserthus** Munkedamsveien 14 ☎23 11 31 11, Ⓦoslokonserthus.no. Opened in 1977, Oslo's main concert hall has two auditoria – one large and one small – and offers a wide-ranging programme. The city's principal orchestra, the Oslo Filharmonien (Ⓦofo.no), is based here and, as you might expect, its programme often includes works by Norwegian and other Scandinavian composers.

**Operahuset** Kirsten Flagstads plass. Box office: ☎21 42 21 21, Ⓦoperaen.no. Oslo's spanking-new Operahuset (Opera House) is home to Den Norske Opera & Ballett (same website), Norway's prolific opera and ballet company, which offers a popular repertoire – Mozart, R. Strauss and the Italians – but also undertakes a number of contemporary works each year. The Operahuset is on the waterfront near Oslo S.

### CINEMA

The ease with which most Norwegians tackle other languages is best demonstrated at the cinema, where films are shown in their original language with Norwegian subtitles. Given that American (and British) films are the most popular, this has obvious advantages for visiting English-speakers. Oslo has its share of mainstream multi-screens, as well as a good art-house cinema. Prices are

## OSLO'S MUSIC FESTIVALS

From rappers to rock, big-name bands and artists often include Oslo on their tours with many of them appearing at Oslo Spektrum (see opposite). The most prestigious **annual event** is **Norwegian Wood** (Ⓦnorwegianwood.no), a three-day, open-air rock festival held in the city in June. Previous years have attracted the likes of Iggy Pop, Patti Smith, Israel Nash and Van Morrison, and the festival continues to pull in major international artists, supported by a variety of Norwegian acts; tickets sell out well in advance – so book early.

Oslo also hosts the **Øyafestivalen** (Ⓦoyafestivalen.com), a five-day event held in various venues across the city in August that showcases a wide range of artists, mostly Scandinavian but with a string of imports too – Massive Attack appeared in 2016, for instance. A club night traditionally kicks the whole thing off in style. Finally, also in August, Oslo's week-long **Jazz Festival** (Ⓦoslojazz.no) attracts internationally renowned artists as well as showcasing local talent, who perform at a variety of venues, both inside and outside. **Tickets** for all three festivals are available either direct or from Ticketmaster (☎815 33 133, Ⓦticketmaster.no).

surprisingly reasonable with tickets averaging 100–130kr.
**Filmens Hus** Dronningens gate 16, corner Tollbugata ☎22 47 45 00, Ⓦnfi.no. Home to the Norwegian Film Institute, this standout art-house cinema offers a varied and extremely enjoyable programme mixing mainstream and alternative/avant-garde films.

**Gimle** Bygdøy Allé 39 ☎820 50 001, Ⓦoslokino.no. A sympathetically revamped old cinema with some of the most comfortable seats in town. There's a varied programme, though films are mostly mainstream. One screen only.

**Saga kino** Stortingsgata 28, corner Olav V's gate

☎99 43 20 00, Ⓦnfkino.no. Mainstream cinema with six screens metres from the Nationaltheatret.

### THEATRE

Nearly all of Oslo's theatre productions are in Norwegian, making them of limited interest to (most) tourists, though there are occasional English-language performances by touring theatre companies.

**Nationaltheatret** Stortingsgata ☎815 00 811, Ⓦnationaltheatret.no. Oslo's principal theatre has a lively programme of classics and modern works and also hosts the prestigious, annual Ibsen Festival.

## SHOPPING

Make no mistake, **shopping** in Oslo is expensive and, like so much else in western Europe, it's the big multinational chains that ring the changes. The city's most individual offering is its **bookshops**, but for many travellers the key search is for the nearest **supermarket** to stock up for picnics and so forth. Fortunately, there are lots of small supermarkets in the city centre – Rimi, Matkroken and Kiwi are three of the larger chains – and all of them sell at least a small selection of fresh fruit and vegetables.

### CLOTHING AND DESIGN

**Dale of Norway** Karl Johansgate 45 ☎97 48 12 07, Ⓦdale.no; map pp.64–65. The flagship store to Norway's most famous clothing brand, where you can pick up everything from classic, colourful handknit sweaters to mittens and hats – some in strikingly modern interpretations of traditional knitwear patterns. Dale's sweaters are always pricey, but you'll only ever have to buy one or two in your life. Mon–Fri 10am–8pm, Sat 10am–6pm.

**Heimen Husfliden** Rosenkrantz gate 8 ☎23 21 42 00, Ⓦheimenhusfliden.no; map pp.64–65. Norwegian handicrafts are not cheap – you wouldn't expect them to be – but this long-established shop does have the city's most extensive range of traditional Norwegian clothing – the pullovers are perhaps the most appealing items. Mon–Fri 10am–6pm, Sat 10am–4pm.

**Moods of Norway** Akersgata 18 ☎46 62 77 96, Ⓦmoodsofnorway.com; map pp.64–65. This small

Norwegian chain has created quite a stir with its offbeat T-shirts and design logo – the good, old Norwegian tractor in all sorts of weird and wonderful colours. Concentrates on clothing for the young and young at heart. Mon–Fri 10am–7pm, Sat 10am–6pm.

**Norway Designs** Stortingsgata 28 ☎23 11 45 10, Ⓦnorwaydesigns.no; map pp.64–65. From ties to cutlery, this large shop sells a wide range of high-spec Scandinavian goods. The clocks and watches are especially stylish. Mon–Fri 10am–6pm, Thurs till 7pm, Sat 10am–4pm.

### FOOD AND DRINK

**Matkroken** Akersgata 45 ☎22 42 01 94; map pp.64–65. Small but central, standard-issue supermarket near the corner of Grensen. It has a better than average selection of fruit and vegetables. Mon–Fri 7am–9pm, Sat 9am–8pm.

**1**

## OSLO WITH CHILDREN

There's no shortage of things to do with young (pre-teen) children in Oslo, beginning with the enchanting, open-air **Vigelandsparken** (see p.78) and, if the weather is good, the **beaches** of the Oslofjord islands (see p.88). In wintertime, ice-skating, tobogganing and horse-drawn sleigh rides (see p.93) are almost bound to appeal.

Few children will want to be dragged round Oslo's main museums, except perhaps for the **Frammuseet** (see p.86), but there are a couple of museums geared up for youngsters (see below). Another bit of good news is that **discounts** for children are commonplace. Almost all sites and attractions let babies and toddlers in free, and charge half of the adult tariff for children between 4 and 16 years of age. It's the same on public transport, and hotels are usually very obliging too, adding camp beds of some description to their rooms with the minimum of fuss and expense.

### NORSK TEKNISK MUSEUM

One of the most popular museums for children in Oslo is the **Norsk Teknisk Museum**, out to the north of the city centre at Kjelsåsveien 143 (Science & Technology Museum; late June to late Aug daily 11am–6pm; late Aug to late June Tues–Fri 9am–4pm, Sat & Sun 11am–6pm; adults 150kr, children (4–16 years) 100kr; ☎22 79 60 00, ⓦteknisk museum.no). This is an interactive museum *par excellence*, equipped with working models and a galaxy of things to push and touch, as well as a café and picnic area. To get there, take bus #54 from Jernbanetorget, outside Oslo S.

### BARNEKUNSTMUSEET

The **Internasjonale Barnekunstmuseet**, at Lille Frøens vei 4 (International Museum of Children's Art; mid-Jan to late June & mid-Sept to Dec Tues–Thurs 9.30am–2pm, Sat & Sun 11am–4pm; late June to late Aug Tues–Thurs 11am–4pm, Sat & Sun 11am–4pm; closed late Aug to mid-Sept; 75kr, children 40kr; ☎22 69 17 77, ⓦbarnekunst.no), holds an international collection of children's art, including drawings, paintings, sculpture and handicrafts. There are also children's workshops and special events where painting, music and dance are frequent activities – call ahead for details or check the website. To reach the museum, take the T-bane to Frøen station, though plans are afoot to expand the museum and move it to the city centre.

**Vinmonopolet** Oslo S; Rosenkrantz gate 11; ⓦvinmonopolet.no; map pp.64–65. In Oslo, there are lots of branches of Vinmonopolet, the state-run liquor and wine store, and the Oslo S outlet is one of the largest. There's another downtown branch at Rosenkrantz gate. For a complete list of stores, with opening hours, check the website. Oslo S branch Mon–Thurs 10am–6pm, Fri 9am–6pm & Sat 9am–3pm; Rosenkrantz gate branch Mon–Fri 10am–6pm, Sat 9am–3pm.

### MAP AND BOOKSHOPS

**Den Norske Turistforening (DNT)** Storgata 3 ☎22 82 28 00, ⓦdntoslo.no; map pp.64–65. The Norwegian hiking organization's city-centre office stocks a full range of Norwegian hiking maps and accompanying paraphernalia. Mon–Fri 10am–5pm, Thurs till 6pm, Sat 10am–3pm.

**Nomaden** Uranienborgveien 4 ☎23 13 14 15, ⓦnomaden.no; map pp.64–65. Located just behind the Slottsparken, this medium-sized bookshop sells the city's best selection of Norwegian road maps, both national and regional, as well as travel guides to scores of countries and incidental outdoors equipment. Sells Norwegian hiking maps too. Mon–Fri 10am–6pm, Sat 10am–5pm.

**Norli** Universitetsgata 20–24 ☎22 00 43 00, ⓦnorli .no; map pp.64–65. This particular branch of Norli, a bookshop chain, has a competent range of English fiction as well as a separate – and especially interesting – section devoted to English translations of Norwegian writers. Mon–Fri 9am–7pm, Sat 10am–5pm.

**Norlis Antikvariat** Universitetsgata 18 ☎22 20 01 40, ⓦantikvariat.no; map pp.64–65. Oslo does a good line in secondhand bookshops and Norlis is perhaps the best among them. Most of their stock is Norwegian, but there is a good smattering of English titles too. It's located opposite the National Gallery. Mon 10am–5pm, Tues–Fri 9am–5pm, Thurs till 6pm.

## DIRECTORY

**Dentist** Emergency, municipal dentist on the third floor of the Galleriet shopping centre, in the same complex as the main bus station, Schweigaardsgate 6 (☎22 67 30 00). Otherwise, see under "Tannleger" in the *Yellow Pages*.

**1**

**Embassies and consulates** Canada, Wergelandveien 7 (☎ 22 99 53 00); Ireland, Haakon VII's gate 1 (☎ 22 01 72 00); Netherlands, Oscars gate 29 (☎ 23 33 36 00); Poland, Olav Kyrres plass 1 (☎ 24 11 08 50); South Africa, Drammensveien 88C (☎ 23 27 32 20); UK, Thomas Heftyes gate 8 (☎ 23 13 27 00); US, Henrik Ibsens gate 48 (☎ 21 30 89 96). For others, look under "Ambassadeur og Legasjoner" in the *Yellow Pages*. There is no Australian or New Zealand consulate or embassy.

**Emergencies** ☎ 112. For emergency medical treatment, go to Oslo Legevakt, the A&E department of the nearest hospital, which is located at the north end of Storgata, beside the river.

**LGBT Oslo** There's not too much of a scene as such, primarily because Oslo's gays and lesbians are mostly content to share pubs and clubs with heteros. That said, gay men do congregate at the *London Pub* (see p.101), lesbians favour *Elsker* (see p.102) and both head for

*Ett Glass* (see p.100). The main LGBT event is Gay Pride (ⓦ oslopride.no), held over ten days in June with parties, parades, political meetings and a film festival. Norway's national gay and lesbian organization is LLH (Landsforeningen for lesbisk og homofil frigjøring; ⓦ foreningenfri.no); their Oslo office is at Tollbugata 24 (Mon–Fri 10am–3pm; ☎ 23 10 39 39).

**Left luggage** Coin-operated lockers (24hr) at Oslo S.

**Lost property** (*Hittegods*) Trams, buses and T-bane at the Nationaltheatret station (☎ 22 08 53 61); NSB railways at Oslo S (☎ 815 68 340).

**Pharmacy** Oslo has scores of pharmacies (*Apotek*), including the 24hr Vitusapotek, in front of Oslo S at Jernbanetorget 4B (ⓘ 23 35 81 00).

**Police** In an emergency, phone ☎ 112.

**Post offices** The central post office is at Tollbugata 17 at Kirkegaten (Mon–Fri 8am–5pm, Sat 9am–11am; ⓦ posten.no).

# Around Oslo: the Oslofjord

Around 100km from top to bottom, the narrow straits and podgy basins of the **Oslofjord** link the capital with the open sea. This waterway has long been Norway's busiest, an islet-studded channel whose sheltered waters were once crowded with steamers shuttling passengers out along the Norwegian coast. The young **Roald Dahl**, who spent his summer holidays here in the 1920s, loved these waters, writing in his autobiography, *Boy*: "Unless you have sailed down the Oslofjord … on a tranquil summer's day, you cannot imagine the sensation of absolute peace and beauty that surrounds you." Even now, though the steamers are long gone, the Oslofjord makes for delightful sailing, and in good weather you can spy dozens of tiny craft scuttling round its nooks and crannies. The **ferry ride** from Oslo to **Drøbak**, a pretty village on the fjord's east shore, provides a pleasant introduction to these nautical pleasures, though, at risk of stating the obvious, it's not quite the same as having your own boat.

Ferry rides – and Drøbak – apart, the shores of the Oslofjord are dotted with humdrum industrial towns that are far from irresistible if your time is limited. But with more time, there are several places that warrant a stop, beginning on the Oslofjord's **eastern shore** with the town of **Fredrikstad** – or rather the old part of Fredrikstad, which comprises an immaculately preserved fortress whose late seventeenth-century gridiron streets and earthen bastions snuggle up to a narrow river. The fortress was built to defend the country from the Swedes, as was the imposing hilltop stronghold that rears up above **Halden**, an otherwise innocuous town further along the eastern shore, hard by the Swedish border. On the Oslofjord's **western shore**, the pickings are slighter, but there is cluster of Viking burial mounds at **Borre**, just outside the ferry port of **Horten**, from where a **car ferry** scuttles across the Oslofjord to Moss (see p.106). Beyond Horten lies the breezy town and port of **Tønsberg**, which gives ready access to the shredded archipelago that pokes a rural finger out into the Skagerrak.

## ARRIVAL AND DEPARTURE | AROUND OSLO: THE OSLOFJORD

**By train** There's a regular train service from Oslo S serving both sides of the Oslofjord. On the east side, the train stops at Fredrikstad and Halden, but not Drøbak, which is best reached from Oslo by ferry (see p.106). On the western side, trains run to Tønsberg, but not Borre or Horten.

**By car and ferry** Motorways leave Oslo to strip along both sides of the Oslofjord – the E6 in the east, the E18 to the west. To cross the Oslofjord, you can either use the 7km tunnel that runs west from Drøbak, or catch the car ferry linking Horten and Moss (weekdays every 30min, weekends every 45min: Mon–Fri 5.30am–midnight, Sat & Sun 7am–midnight; 30min; driver & car 140kr; ⓦ basto-fosen.no); Moss is about 60km south of Oslo.

# Drøbak

The first place of any real interest on the Oslofjord's **eastern shore** is **DRØBAK**, a pocket-sized port that slopes along the shoreline about 35km from the capital. It's at its prettiest round the **harbour**, where a cluster of cheery clapboard houses lead towards a handsome timber **church** dating from the early eighteenth century.

## Drøbak's Tregaarden's Julehus

Havnebakken 6 • March–Oct Mon–Fri 10am–5pm, Sat 10am–3pm, plus June–Oct Sun noon–4pm; Nov Mon–Fri 10am–7pm, Sat 10am–3pm & Sun noon–4pm; 1–23 Dec Mon–Fri 10am–8pm, Sat 10am–4pm & Sun noon–4pm; Dec 24 9am–noon • ☎ 64 93 41 78, ⓦ julehus.no

Among Norwegians at least, Drøbak is famous for its specialist Christmas shop, the **Tregaarden's Julehus**, which sells all sorts of Yuletide trinkets and baubles – and incorporates a post office, where you can get cards and letters franked with a special Christmas stamp. The shop's popularity is such that many Norwegian kids believe that Father Christmas lives here; he doesn't, of course, because his reindeer prefer Lapland.

## Oscarsborg island

Fort & museum: daily noon–4pm • Free • ☎ 64 90 41 61, ⓦ oscarsborgfestning.no • Passenger ferries to Oscarsborg run from both Drøbak harbour (hourly; 10min; 100kr return) & Oslo's Aker Brygge (see below)

During the German invasion of 1940, Drøbak witnessed a rare Norwegian success when the cruiser *Blucher* was sunk by artillery as it steamed towards Oslo. The gunners, who were stationed just offshore on the tiny island-fortress of **Oscarsborg**, had no way of realizing just how important this was: the delay to the German flotilla gave the Norwegian king, Håkon VII, just enough time to escape the capital and avoid capture. Few commented upon it at the time, but the gun that did the damage was made in Germany by Krupp, a rich irony if ever there was one.

Dating from the middle of the nineteenth century, Oscarsborg was one of a series of forts built to defend the seaward approaches to Oslo, but the only action it ever saw was during 1940. Today, the military are long gone, but **footpaths** trail round the islet offering gentle views over the Oslofjord and you can wander round the **fortress**, whose thick, semicircular stone walls are in excellent condition; there's a small military **museum** and a hotel (see below) on the island too.

### ARRIVAL AND DEPARTURE                                                      DRØBAK

**By passenger ferry** The most enjoyable way to get from Oslo to Drøbak is by passenger ferry from beside Oslo's Aker Brygge Pier 4 (late April to mid-June & late Aug to Sept Sat & Sun 1 daily; mid-June to late Aug 1 daily; 1hr; 72kr each way; ☎ 177, ⓦ ruter.no). As it nears Drøbak, the boat also docks at Oscarsborg. The boat's timetable often makes it possible to complete the return trip on the same day, though this isn't crucial as you can always return on the bus.
**By bus** There's a fast and frequent bus service between Oslo's bus station and Drøbak (every 30min; 50min; ☎ 177, ⓦ ruter.no). In Drøbak, buses from Oslo stop on Storgata, just to the south of the harbour.

### ACCOMMODATION AND EATING

**Oscarsborg Hotel & Resort** Oscarsborg ☎ 64 90 40 00, ⓦ oscarsborghotel.no. Opinions vary as to the quality of this resort-hotel, which sits on Oscarsborg island, a brief walk from the fortress. It's perhaps best suited as a conference centre as the 89 modern rooms, which are spilt between two former barracks, can seem somewhat severe; the best have fjord views. To get to Oscarsborg, you'll need to catch a passenger ferry from either Oslo's Aker Brygge (see above) or Drøbak (see above). **1300kr**
**Skipperstuen** Havnebakken 11 ☎ 64 93 07 03, ⓦ skipperstuen.no. In the wooden house on the knoll

next to the harbour, this likeable café-restaurant offers a wide-ranging menu from local seafood to Spanish-style tapas. At lunchtimes, main courses average 170kr. Mon–Sat noon–9pm, Sun 1–7pm.

**1**

## Fredrikstad

An ideal day-trip from the capital, **FREDRIKSTAD**, about 90km from Oslo, is a modest little town of 80,000 people that fills out a thumb of land just across the river from a superbly preserved seventeenth-century **fortress**, now known as **Gamlebyen** (Old Town). The fortress may be inordinately pretty, but it does reflect Norway's long subordination to the interests of Denmark, whose kings ruled the country from 1387 to 1814. One major problem was the bitter rivalry between the Swedish and Danish monarchies, which prompted a seemingly endless and particularly pointless sequence of wars lasting from the early sixteenth century until 1720. Most Norwegians may have preferred to keep at a safe distance from this dynastic squabbling, but as part of Denmark they were inevitably involved, especially as the eastern approaches to Oslo (then Christiania), along the Oslofjord, were vulnerable to attack from Sweden. To thwart the Swedes, a string of Danish kings installed defences along the Oslofjord, no one more so than king **Frederik II**, who had a fortified town built here at the mouth of the River Glomma in 1567 – and modestly named it after himself. In the event, Frederik II's fort only lasted three years before it was burnt to the ground, though it didn't take long for a replacement to be constructed – and for the whole process to be repeated again.

The Gamlebyen remained in military use until well into the twentieth century, which partly accounts for its excellent state of preservation, and it was also unaffected by the development of **modern Fredrikstad**, a timber town built at a safe distance on the other (west) side of the River Glomma. Fredrikstad's other claim to fame is as the place where the last woman to be executed in Norway met her untimely end: the year was 1876 and the woman was a certain Sophie Johannesdatter, who had allegedly poisoned her husband.

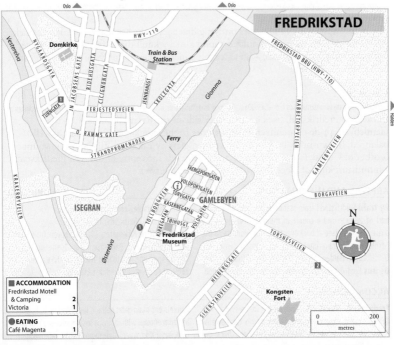

**1**

## Gamlebyen

From Fredrikstad's bus and train station, in the modern town, it's a 5min walk via Jernbanegata, to the Gamlebyferga (passenger ferry) over to the Gamlebyen's gated back wall (every 5–15min; 5min; free) • ☎ 69 30 60 00, ⓦ fredrikstad.kommune.no

In the late seventeenth century, Fredrikstad's **Gamlebyen** began to take on its present shape when its fortifications were strengthened: the central gridiron of cobbled streets was encircled on three sides by zigzag bastions, which allowed the defenders to fire into any attacking force from several angles, and, in their turn, these bastions were protected by a moat, concentric earthen banks and outlying redoubts. Armed with 130 cannons, Fredrikstad was by 1685 the strongest fortress in all of Norway and in the eighteenth century the pastel-painted timber and stone houses that you see today were built for the garrison and its officers. Exploring the Gamlebyen, which is just three blocks deep and six blocks wide, is a delightful way to spend an hour or two and, although it's the general appearance of the place that appeals rather than any specific sight, the main square, **Torvgaten**, does hold an unfortunate **statue of Frederik II**, who appears to have a serious problem with his pantaloons.

### Fredrikstad Museum

Tøihusgaten 41 • Late June to late Aug daily noon–4pm; early May to late June Sat & Sun noon–3pm • 60kr • ☎ 69 11 56 50, ⓦ ostfoldmuseene.no

In the last few years, the Gamlebyen has picked up a scattering of modest attractions, but the one with the most general appeal is perhaps the unassuming **Fredrikstad Museum**, which gives the historical background to the fortress supported by a bobble of archeological finds. The museum also holds temporary art displays, often featuring the work of local artists.

### Kongsten fort

Wilhelm Blakstads gate • Late June to late Aug daily noon–4pm; early May to late June Sat & Sun noon–3pm • 60kr • ☎ 69 11 56 50, ⓦ ostfoldmuseene.no • A 10min walk from the Gamlebyen: go straight ahead from the main gate, take the first right along Heibergsgate and it's clearly visible on the left

The most impressive of the town's outlying defences is the **Kongsten Fort**. Here, thick stone and earthen walls are moulded round a rocky knoll that offers wide views over the surrounding countryside – an agreeably quiet vantage point from where you can take in the lie of the land.

## Domkirke

Nygaardsgata • Late June to mid-Aug Tues–Fri 9.30am–1.30pm; mid-Aug to late June Tues–Fri 11am–2pm • Free • ⓦ fredrikstad.kirken.no

In modern Fredrikstad, back on the other side of the River Glomma from the Gamlebyen, pride of architectural place goes to the **Domkirke** (Cathedral), a well-balanced, brown-brick building with stained glass by Emanuel Vigeland, the younger brother of Gustav (see p.78). Beyond the church is the centre of modern Fredrikstad, a humdrum kind of place that nudges up along the river.

### ARRIVAL AND INFORMATION

### FREDRIKSTAD

**By train** Fredrikstad's train station is located in the new part of town – and a couple of minutes' walk from the passenger ferry (see above) over the River Glomma to the Gamlebyen. For train timetable details, consult ⓦ nsb.no.
Destinations Halden (hourly; 30min); Oslo S (hourly; 1hr).
**By bus** Fredrikstad bus station adjoins the train station.

For bus timetables, consult ⓦ rutebok.no.
Destinations Oslo (hourly; 1hr 20min).
**Tourist office** Kirkegaten 31, Gamlebyen (mid-June to late Aug Mon–Fri 9am–5pm, Sat 10am–4pm & Sun 11am–4pm; late Aug to mid-June Mon–Fri 9am–4.30pm; ☎ 69 30 46 00, ⓦ visitfredrikstadhvaler.no).

### ACCOMMODATION

**Fredrikstad Motell & Camping** Torsnesveien 16 ☎ 99 22 19 99, ⓦ www.fredrikstadmotel.no. This bargain-basement place is about 400m straight ahead from the

Gamlebyen's main gate; nothing fancy and no frills, but neat and trim enough with cabins, a small motel and tent pitches. Camping 200kr, motel-style rooms 550kr, cabins 850kr

**1**

**Victoria** Turngata 3 ☎ 69 38 58 00, ⓦ hotelvictoria.no. Fredrikstad may have several somewhat plusher chain hotels, but this family-owned place is a tad more distinctive and it has a pleasant location overlooking the park next to the Domkirke. The rooms are perhaps a little staid, but they are comfortable enough and competitively priced. **695kr**

## EATING

**Café Magenta** Toldbodgaten 104 ☎ 69 32 00 12, ⓦ cafemagenta.no. Popular and fashionable Gamlebyen café-bar offering a tasty range of light snacks and meals at affordable prices – the home-made soup is especially good. Great coffee too, plus a lip-smacking chocolate cake. Eat and drink either inside or outside. Regular live music, usually on Wednesday and Friday nights. Daily 11am–2am.

# Halden

Workaday **HALDEN**, hard by the Swedish border about 40km from Fredrikstad, once had a dreadful reputation for the quality of its environment, its fjord and rivers polluted by its wood-processing mills. Things are much better today and the town's economy is more diverse with a new high-security prison and a clutch of IT companies adding some zip, but still Halden's most striking feature is its setting, its centre bisected by the River Tista and hemmed in by steep forested hills. The closest of these hills is crowned by Halden's major attraction, the commanding **Fredriksten Festning** (fortress). Work began on the fortress in 1661 at the instigation of Frederik III during a lull in the fighting between Sweden and Denmark. The stakes were high: the Swedes were determined to annihilate the Dano-Norwegian monarchy and had only just failed in their attempt to capture Oslo and Copenhagen. Consequently, Frederik was keen to build a fortress of immense strength to secure his northerly possessions. He called in Dutch engineers to design it and, after a decade, the result was a labyrinthine citadel whose thick perimeter walls, heavily protected gates, bastions and outlying forts were perfectly designed to suit the contours of the two steep, parallel ridges on which they were built. And so it proved – the Swedes besieged Fredriksten on several occasions without success, though the town itself suffered badly. In 1716, with the Swedes threatening yet again, the Norwegians razed the town to the ground, a scorched-earth policy that later prompted some nationalistic poppycock from the writer Bjørnstjerne Bjørnson: "We chose to burn our nation, ere we let it fall."

## Fredriksten Festning

**Fortress** Dawn–dusk • Free • **Museums** June–Aug daily 11am–5pm • 60kr • **Guided tours** June–Aug 3 daily, 1hr • 80kr • ☎ 69 19 09 80, ⓦ visithalden.com • Allow at least an hour for a visit

Ingenious and impregnable, **Fredriksten Festning** (Fredriksten Fortress) rises up on the south side of the River Tista, its forested slopes climbed by several steep footpaths. The most enjoyable is **Peder Colbjørnsens gate**, which runs up from Torget to one of the lower gatehouses. Beyond, a jumble of fortifications and old buildings ramble over the ridge in various states of repair. Most of the buildings are labelled and several hold modest **museums** with the most diverting being the **Krigshistorisk Museum** (War History Museum), in the old prison in the eastern curtain wall, which traces the evolution of the fortress and its involvement in several wars. Elsewhere, the stronghold's brewery has survived as have the bakery ovens and several distinctly spooky connecting tunnels.

On the far (eastern) side of the fortress, where the terrain is nowhere near as steep, you'll find a **monument** to the **Swedish king Karl XII**, who was killed by a bullet in the temple as he besieged the fort in 1718. An inveterate warmonger, Karl had exhausted the loyalty of his troops, and whether the bullet came from the fortress or one of his own men has been a matter of considerable Scandinavian speculation.

## ARRIVAL AND INFORMATION
**HALDEN**

**By train** Halden train station abuts the south bank of the River Tista, a short walk from the main square, Torget. For train timetables, consult ⓦ nsb.no.

**Destinations** Fredrikstad (hourly; 30min); Oslo S (hourly; 1hr 30min).
**By bus** The bus station is situated close to the train

**1**

station on Jernbanegata.
**Tourist office** Halden's main tourist office, Kongens Brygge 3 (Mon–Fri 9am–3.30pm; ☎ 69 19 09 80, ⓦ visit halden.com), is right in the centre of the city at the top of the harbour – and midway between the train station and the fortress.

## ACCOMMODATION AND EATING

**Fredriksten Hotell** Generalveien 25 ☎ 69 02 10 10, ⓦ fredrikstenhotell.no. The pick of Halden's hotels, this slick, modern place has been shoehorned into an old, barracks-like building on the hill to the south of the fortress. The guest rooms, many of which have wide views, are well-equipped and well-appointed. **1300kr**
**Restaurant Curtisen** Indre Festning 2 ☎ 95 99 81 84,
ⓦ curtisen-halden.no. In an attractive old building inside the fortress, this is the smartest restaurant in Halden by a mile, offering a well-considered menu with the emphasis on local ingredients: try, for example, the roasted veal in a mustard-tarragon sauce. A three-course set meal costs 650kr. Tues–Sat 6–11pm.

# Åsgårdstrand

Strung along the Oslofjord's **western shore**, about 90km from central Oslo, the seaside village of **ÅSGÅRDSTRAND** was where **Edvard Munch** spent many of his summers. Munch avoided the mountains of Norway whenever he could, sticking firmly to the country's flattest parts on account of his agoraphobia – and the lightly forested shoreline here at Åsgårdstrand suited him just fine.

## Munchs Hus

Edvards Munchs gate 25 • May & Sept Sat & Sun 11am–4pm; June–Aug Tues–Sun 11am–5pm • 70kr • ☎ 40 91 59 00, ⓦ munchshus.no
Perhaps surprisingly, the old, ochre-painted fisherman's **cottage** Munch purchased in 1897 has survived and – renamed the **Munchs Hus** (Munch House) – it has been returned to its appearance when the artist lived and painted here; the adjoining studio is actually a replacement of the original, but it fits in well. There are no Munch paintings on display, but there are a few Munch prints and bits and bobs of period furniture.

## Borre's Viking burial mounds

Birkelyveien, Borre • Midgard Historisk Senter: May–Aug daily 11am–4pm; Sept to April Sun 11am–4pm • 70kr • ☎ 33 07 18 50, ⓦ midgardsenteret.no • From Åsgårdstrand, take Hwy-311 west and then Hwy-325 north
The scattered hamlet of **BORRE**, just along the coast from Åsgårdstrand, boasts the **Borrehaugene**, one of the largest ensembles of extant **Viking burial mounds** in all of Scandinavia. There are seven large and twenty-one small mounds in total, with the best-preserved being clustered together in the woods by the water's edge, a five-minute walk from the car park. These grassy bumps date from the seventh to the tenth century, when Borre was a royal burial ground and one of the wealthiest districts in southern Norway. The mounds are interesting in themselves but the setting is perhaps even better – in springtime wild flowers carpet the ground under the trees, making this a perfect spot for a picnic. The area has been designated a national park and a visitor centre, the **Midgard Historisk Senter** (Midgard Historical Centre) stands beside the car park, though there's precious little actually in it – replica Viking Hall or not – so save yourself the entrance fee.

# Tønsberg and around

The last town of any size on the Oslofjord's western shore, **TØNSBERG**, about 100km from Oslo and 16km from Borre, was founded by Harald Hårfagre in the ninth century, and rose to prominence in the Middle Ages as a major ecclesiastical and trading centre: its sheltered sound made a safe harbour; the plain behind it was ideal for settlement; and the town's palace and castle assured the patronage of successive monarchs. All of which sounds exciting, and you might expect Tønsberg to be one of the country's more important historical attractions, but sadly precious little survives from the town's medieval heyday. On the other hand, the waterfront makes for a pleasant stroll, zeroing in on the handsome set of renovated, nineteenth-century warehouses that comprise the **Tønsberg Brygge**, where the narrow lanes are dotted with bars and restaurants.

## Slottsfjellet

Nedre Slottsgate • Castle open access; tower June–Aug daily 11am–4pm • Free

Of Tønsberg's medieval castle, the **Slottsfjellet**, only the foundations have survived, fragmentary ruins perched on a steep, wooded hill immediately to the north of the centre – though it's easy to appreciate the castle's strategic and defensive virtues. The Swedes burned it down in 1503 and the place was never rebuilt. Today's watchtower, the clumpy **Slottsfjelltårnet**, was plonked on top in the nineteenth century.

## Verdens Ende

The low-lying **islands and skerries** that nudge out into the Skagerrak to the south of Tønsberg are a popular holiday destination. By and large, people come here for the peace and quiet, with a bit of fishing and swimming thrown in, and the whole coast is dotted with summer homes. To the outsider, this is not especially stimulating, but there is one obvious target, **Verdens Ende** – "World's End" – about thirty minutes' drive (26km) from Tønsberg, right at the southernmost tip of the southernmost island, **Tjöme**. In this blustery spot, rickety jetties straggle across a cove whose shimmering waters are interrupted by bare, sea-smoothed rocks and miniature islets. It would be nice to think a wandering Viking gave the place its name, but in fact it was a romantic gesture by a visiting Victorian.

### ARRIVAL AND INFORMATION　　　　　　　　　　　　　　TØNSBERG AND AROUND

**By train** From Tønsberg's train station, it's a 5–10min walk south to the main square, Torvet, and just a couple of hundred metres more – along Rådhusgaten – to the waterfront Tønsberg Brygge. For train timetables, consult ⓦnsb.no.
Destinations Oslo (hourly; 1hr 20min); Sandefjord (hourly; 20min).

**By bus** The bus station is adjacent to the train station.
Destinations Oslo (every 2hr; 1hr 40min); Sandefjord (hourly; 45min).
**Tourist office** Tønsberg tourist office is a few metres from the train and bus stations at Tollbodgaten 22 (late June to mid-Aug Mon–Fri 9.30am–4.30pm, plus July Sat 10am–2pm; ☏33 34 81 00, ⓦvisitvestfold.com).

### ACCOMMODATION AND EATING

**Quality Hotel Tønsberg** Ollebukta 3 ☏33 00 41 00, ⓦnordicchoicehotels.com. Right on the waterfront, this is the most stylish of Tønsberg's several central hotels, handsomely built in the shape of a ship's bow and as such a striking addition to the town's skyline. Part conference centre – and even including a concert hall – the hotel has three hundred comfortable rooms with all mod cons, and most have harbour views. **1600kr**
**Restaurant Havariet** Nedre Langgate 30E ☏33 35 83 90, ⓦhavariet.no. The pick of the several waterfront

options, this popular and informal spot in a replica warehouse offers a wide-ranging menu with seafood and salads to the fore. Salads average 170kr. Mon–Sat 11am–11pm, Sun noon–11pm.
**Thon Hotel Brygga** Nedre Langgate 40 ☏33 34 49 00, ⓦthonhotels.no. Routine chain hotel with 68 spick-and-span modern rooms in a somewhat glum-looking building that has been constructed in the general style of an old warehouse. Good breakfasts and great harbourfront location. **1200kr**

# The South

THE COAST NEAR STAVANGER

# The South

Arcing out into the Skagerrak between the Oslofjord and Stavanger, Norway's south coast may have little of the imposing grandeur of other, wilder parts of the country, but its eastern half, running down to Kristiansand, is undeniably lovely. Speckled with islands and backed by forests, fells and lakes, it's this part of the coast that attracts Norwegians in droves, equipped not so much with bucket and spade as with boat and navigational aids – for these waters, with their narrow inlets, islands and skerries, make for particularly enjoyable sailing.

The first part of the south coast, down to Kristiansand, is within easy striking distance of Denmark and as such has always been important for Norway's international trade. Consequently, several of the region's larger towns, **Larvik** and **Porsgrunn** for instance, are little more than humdrum, industrial centres, but aesthetic help is at hand in a string of smaller ports/resorts with **Risør**, **Lillesand** and **Grimstad** being the prime examples. This trio have dodged (nearly) all the industry to become pretty, pocket-sized resorts, their white-painted clapboard houses giving an appropriately nautical, almost jaunty, air. Larger **Arendal** does something to bridge the gap between the resorts and the industrial towns and does so very nicely. There's also amenable **Sandefjord**, which may well provide you with your first taste of Norway as it has its own international airport – Torp Sandefjord (sometimes Oslo Torp).

Anchoring the south coast is Norway's fifth largest city, **Kristiansand**, a bustling port and lively resort with enough sights, restaurants, bars and beaches to while away a night, maybe two. Beyond Kristiansand lies **Mandal**, an especially fetching holiday spot with a great beach, but thereafter the coast becomes harsher and less absorbing, and there's precious little to detain you before **Stavanger**, an oil town and port with a clutch of historical sights and a full set of first-rate restaurants. Bergen may lay claim to being the "Gateway to the Fjords", but actually Stavanger is closer with the splendid **Lysefjord** and its famous **Preikestolen** rock leading the scenic charge.

Right along the south coast, **accommodation** of one sort or another is legion, with all the larger towns having at least a couple of hotels, but if you're after a bit of social bounce bear in mind the **season** is short, running from the middle of June to August; outside this period many attractions are closed and local boat trips curtailed.

## GETTING AROUND

**By train** There are regular NSB trains (⦿ nsb.no) from Oslo to Kristiansand and ultimately Stavanger, but the train line runs inland for most of its journey, only occasionally dipping down to the coast, which makes for a disappointing ride with the sea mostly shielded from view. Note also that several mainline train stations are some way inland, meaning you'll need to take another connecting journey by local bus (⦿ akt.no or ⦿ rutebok.no) to get to the smaller seaside resorts. Kristiansand, on the other hand, has its own mainline bus and train stations.

**By bus** Long-distance express buses (⦿ rutebok.no) connect Oslo with Kristiansand, and Kristiansand with Stavanger. As with the train, long-distance buses almost invariably take inland routes, dropping passengers at rural

Ibsen sharpens his claws in Grimstad p.123
Cruising the Blindleia p.124
Staying in a lighthouse p.128

Antony Gormley in Stavanger p.135
The Kystvegen: Stavanger to Bergen p.140

GAMLE STAVANGER

# Highlights

❶ **M/B Øya** Take a delightful three-hour cruise along the coast between Lillesand and Kristiansand on this dinky little ferryboat. **See p.124**

❷ **Stay in a lighthouse** A string of coastal lighthouses offer simple lodgings in wild locations. One of the most enticing is Ryvingen, out in the Skagerrak, southeast of Mandal. **See p.128**

❸ **Mandal** One of the prettiest ports on the south coast, Mandal boasts the country's finest beach, a long and wide sandy expanse flanked by forested dunes. **See p.129**

❹ **Gamle Stavanger** The most appealing part of Stavanger, comprising a network of lovely old clapboard houses with picket fences and immaculate gardens. **See p.135**

❺ **Kjeragbolten** Not for the faint-hearted, this rock is snagged between cliffs high above the Lysefjord – walk on it if you dare. **See p.141**

❻ **Preikestolen** A geological oddity near Stavanger, this great hunk of rock offers staggering views down to the Lysefjord on three of its sides. **See p.142**

**HIGHLIGHTS ARE MARKED ON THE MAP ON P.116**

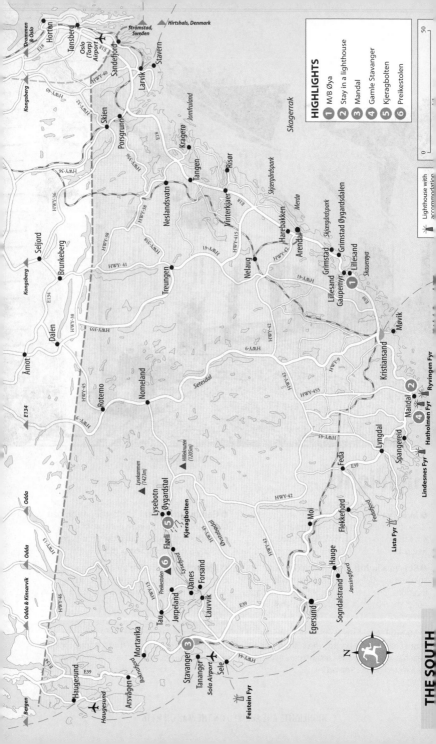

**THE SOUTH**

**HIGHLIGHTS**

1. M/B Øya
2. Stay in a lighthouse
3. Mandal
4. Gamle Stavanger
5. Kjeragbolten
6. Preikestolen

Lighthouse with accommodation

0   50

bus stops from where connecting local buses (⊛akt.no) run to the smaller resorts – Risør is a case in point.
**By car** Like the train line, the main road– the E18/E39

– sticks stubbornly inland for most of the 320km from Oslo to Kristiansand (E18) and again for the 240km on to Stavanger (E39).

# Sandefjord to Lillesand

The fretted **shoreline** that stretches the 200km southwest from Tønsberg (see p.110) to Lillesand is home to a series of small resorts that are especially popular with weekenders from Oslo. The most interesting is **Grimstad**, with its Ibsen connections; the liveliest is **Arendal**; and the prettiest are **Lillesand** and **Risør**. These four as well as many of their neighbours offer **boat trips** out to the myriad islets that dot this coast, with visitors bent on a spot of swimming and beach – or at least rock – combing. Local farmers once owned these islands and islets, but many are now in public ownership and zealously protected from any development. Some of the resorts hereabouts also offer longer cruises along the coast during the summer, one of the most enticing being the delightful three-hour trip from Lillesand to Kristiansand (see box, p.124).

2

| **GETTING AROUND** | **SANDEFJORD TO LILLESAND** |

**By train** A train line runs just inland from the coast, but it's not a particularly useful service – of the places described here only Arendal and Sandefjord have their own train stations.
**By bus** There is a fast and frequent bus service from Oslo

to Kristiansand along the E18. To get from the E18 to the coastal resorts, you usually have to change to a local bus at a motorway intersection; sometimes the buses connect, sometimes they don't – check before you set out (⊛akt.no or ⊛rutebok.no).

## Sandefjord

An amiable, low-key kind of place, **SANDEFJORD**, some 120km from Oslo, is best known as an international ferry port and as the site of Torp Sandefjord (sometimes Oslo Torp) airport. It's at its most attractive along its wide and open waterfront, which culminates in a spectacular water fountain – the **Hvalfangstmonumentet** (Whalers' Monument) – where, amid the billowing spray, a slender rowing boat and its crew ride the tail fluke of a whale. This is perhaps as good as it gets, but the town does rustle up a quartet of other lesser attractions.

### Kurbadet

Thor Dahls gate 7 • ⊛sandefjordkurbad.no • A 2min walk from the Hvalfangstmonumentet – to the right as you face inland
Sandefjord's former thermal baths, the **Kurbadet**, are housed in a distinctive wooden complex built in a Viking-inspired dragon style during the late nineteenth century; the baths closed at the beginning of World War II and have come close to being demolished on several occasions, but they have managed to hang on and are now in use as a cultural centre.

### Hvalfangstmuseet

Museumsgata 39 • June–Aug daily 11am–5pm; May & Sept Tues–Sun 11am–5pm; Oct–April Tues–Sat 11am–4pm, Sun noon–4pm • 70kr • ☎94 79 33 41, ⊛hvalfangstmuseet.no
The town's best museum, the **Hvalfangstmuseet** (Whaling Museum), trumpets the town's whalers – just like the Hvalfangstmonumentet. The local whaling industry built up a head of steam at the end of the nineteenth century, peaking in the early 1950s, when as many as three thousand local men were dependent on the industry for their livelihood. The museum's forte is its large collection of photographs of whalers at work, rest and play – a tough existence by any standard. If all this whets your interest, then pop down to the old whaling vessel, the *Southern Actor*, moored down on the harbourfront (see p.118).

### The Southern Actor

Brygga 1 • July daily noon–5pm; June & Aug Sat & Sun noon–5pm • 20kr, but free with Hvalfangstmuseet ticket • ☎ 94 79 33 41, ⓦ hvalfangstmuseet.no

Built in the 1950s and brought here in the 1980s, the **Southern Actor** has been restored to its original appearance, down to the harpoon at its bow and spy mast up above. Considering the turbulence of the waters it once negotiated, the ship lies surprisingly low in the water, but there's no mistaking its strength.

### Gokstadhaugen

Helgerødveien • Open access • Free

It's just a couple of kilometres northeast from the town centre along Hwy-303 to the **Gokstadhaugen**, the grassy mound which marks the spot where the **Gokstad Viking longship** was unearthed in 1880. The vessel is now on display in Oslo (see p.86), but information plaques displayed here add some context.

**ARRIVAL AND INFORMATION**            **SANDEFJORD**

**By plane** Torp Sandefjord international airport (or Oslo Torp; ⓦ torp.no) is located about 10km northeast of Sandefjord. Airport shuttle buses run to the nearest train station, also called Torp, just 5min away; Torp station is just one stop along the line from Sandefjord station (hourly; 5min). Public transport also runs from Torp airport to Oslo (see p.91).
**By train** Sandefjord train station (ⓦ nsb.no) is about 900m from the waterfront, straight down Jernbanealleen.
Destinations Oslo S (hourly; 1hr 40min); Tønsberg (hourly; 20min).

**By bus** Sandefjord bus station is on Møllers gate, a 4min walk from the train station.
Destination Oslo (every 1–3hr; 1hr 50min).
**By ferry** Regular Color Line car ferries (ⓦ colorline.com) link Sandefjord with Strömstad in Sweden. The ferry dock is at the foot of the town, close to the Hvalfangsmonumentet.
**Tourist office** Sandefjord tourist office is in the Kurbadet (see p.117), at Thor Dahls gate 7 (July & Aug Mon–Fri 9am–5pm, Sat & Sun noon–5pm; Sept–June Mon–Fri 9am–4pm; ☎ 33 46 05 90, ⓦ visitsandefjord.com).

**ACCOMMODATION**

**Clarion Collection Hotel Atlantic** Jernbanealleen 33 ☎ 33 42 80 00, ⓦ nordicchoicehotels.no. In a really rather grand nineteenth-century building, the public rooms of this substantial hotel are certainly idiosyncratic – from the bright striped wallpaper to the whalers' mementoes and cabin-like breakfast room. The guest rooms beyond are standard-issue chain, but just fine. In the town centre, between the train station and the waterfront. **1200kr**
**Hotel Kong Carl** Torggata 9 ☎ 33 46 31 17, ⓦ kongcarl .no. This is Sandefjord's most distinctive hotel, located in

an old timber building right in the centre of town. The 32 guest rooms vary considerably, from the "historical" rooms (an extra 300kr), which have a 1950s vibe, to the more prosaic "budget" rooms. **1240kr**
**Scandic Park Hotel** Strandpromenaden 9 ☎ 33 44 74 00, ⓦ scandichotels.com. This large, chain hotel in a big, modern tower block just back from the waterfront is one of Sandefjord's more appealing places to stay. The rooms lack distinction, but they are proficiently modern. **1200kr**

**EATING**

**Brygga 11, Geir Skeie** Brygga 11 ☎ 95 55 91 91, ⓦ brygga11.no. In a pleasant building down on the harbourfront, this excellent restaurant – which is named after its personality chef – is the best place to eat in town. Seafood is the big deal here – from fish burgers (180kr) to the catch of the day (from 275kr). Reservations advised. Tues–Fri 5–10.30pm, Sat 1–10.30pm.

**La Scala** Brygga 5 ☎ 33 46 15 90, ⓦ la-scala.no. Glued to a pontoon that nudges out into the harbour, *La Scala* occupies glassy – and classy – modern premises with lovely views out over the water. The menu is wide ranging (perhaps too much so), the presentation nouvelle cuisine, and the steaks are perhaps the biggest hit. Mains from 200kr. Daily 11am–11pm.

## Kragerø

Pocket-sized **KRAGERØ**, about 90km from Sandefjord, is one of the busiest resorts on the coast, its cramped lanes and alleys sloping up from the harbour, which is no more than a narrow slip of water spanned by a dinky little bridge. Kragerø was founded as a timber port in the seventeenth century and later boomed as a shipbuilding centre, its past importance recalled by a clutch of handsome old houses. Later, the port became a fashionable watering hole for the bourgeoisie and it was here that **Edvard Munch** produced some of his jollier paintings. Today, Kragerø makes a good living as a supply depot for the summer cottages that inhabit the surrounding coves and islets.

## Kittelsenhuset

Theodor Kittelsens vei 5, off Storgata • Mid-June to mid-Aug daily 11am–5pm • 70kr • ☎ 47 47 34 23, ⓦ telemarkmuseum.no/museum /kittelsenhuset

A middling painter but superb illustrator, **Theodor Kittelsen** (1857–1914) defined the popular appearance of the country's folkloric creatures – from trolls through to sirens – in his illustrations for Asbjørnsen and Moe's *Norwegian Folk Tales*, published in 1883. A native of Kragerø, the adult Kittelsen spent many of his summers here and his family home, in the centre of town just west of the harbour, is now the bright and breezy **Kittelsenhuset**. This lively little museum celebrates the artist's life and times with a smattering of his paintings and a few family knick-knacks.

## Jomfruland

Ferries from Kragerø harbour: 3–5 daily; 30min • 65kr each way • ☎ 40 00 58 58, ⓦ fjordbat.no

The most popular jaunt out from Kragerø is the ferry to **Jomfruland**, a slender and low-lying island stuck out in the Skagerrak beyond the offshore skerries. The island, which is just 7.5km long and never more than 900m wide, is very different from its rocky neighbours, its fertile soils supporting deciduous woodland and providing good pastureland. The flatness of the terrain, plus the abundant bird life, attracts scores of **walkers**, who wander the island's network of footpaths. For many, the **beach** is the main target, rough and pebbly on the island's sea-facing side, more shingle and sand on the other with the best bit generally reckoned to be **Øitangen** in the north. The ferry docks about halfway along the island, an easy stroll from either end.

## Skjærgårdspark

Contact the Kragerø tourist office (see below) for information and advice on boats

Many of the myriad islands that guard the seaward approaches to Kragerø are protected within the **Skjærgårdspark**, and have public access moorings, as well as picnic and bathing facilities. One or two of them can be reached by water taxi, but mostly you'll have to rent a boat.

### ARRIVAL AND INFORMATION                                           KRAGERØ

**By train** The nearest train station is at Neslandsvatn, on the Oslo–Kristiansand line. There is a connecting bus service from Neslandsvatn to Kragerø (1hr), but note that buses do not meet all the trains – check with NSB (ⓦ nsb.no) before you set out.
Destinations Neslandsvatn to: Kristiansand (2–4 daily; 1hr 50min); Oslo (2–4 daily; 3hr).

**By bus** Long-distance buses between Oslo and Kristiansand stop at Tangen, from where there is a connecting local bus service down to the coast at Kragerø; the journey from Tangen takes 25min. Kragerø bus station is a stone's throw from the northern tip of the harbour. Local bus timetables on ⓦ akt.no.
Destinations Oslo, change at Tangen (every 1–2hr; 3hr 30min); Kristiansand, change at Tangen (every 1–2hr; 2hr 30min).

**Tourist office** A hop and a skip from the northern tip of the harbour, Kragerø tourist office is at Torvgata 1 (June–Aug daily 10am–6pm; ☎ 35 98 23 88, ⓦ visitkragero.no).

### ACCOMMODATION AND EATING

**Tollboden Restaurant** P. A. Heuchs gate 4 ☎ 35 98 90 90, ⓦ tollboden.com. Popular, waterfront café-restaurant with a large open-air terrace. Spreads a wide gastronomic net from pizzas through to seafood. Pizzas begin at 170kr; main courses – both meat and fish – are around 300kr. June–Aug daily noon–10pm; Sept–May Fri 5–10pm & Sat noon–10pm.

**Victoria Hotel** P.A. Heuchs gate 31 ☎ 35 98 75 25, ⓦ kragero-hotel-booking.no. This agreeable hotel occupies a good-looking, brightly-painted harbourside building right in the centre of town. Each of the hotel's guest rooms are decorated in browns and creams and the best have balconies overlooking the harbour. They also offer massage sessions and bike rental. **1500kr**

2

# Risør

Attractive **RISØR**, about 50km from Kragerø, is a good-looking town, its genial array of old, white timber houses spreading back from a wide and deep harbour. Risør started out as a small fishing village, but the Dutch fleet began dropping by for timber in the 1570s and the port boomed until, by the 1880s, one hundred sailing vessels – and one thousand seamen – called the place home. A fire destroyed much of the town in 1861 but it was quickly rebuilt, and most of the wooden houses that survive date from this period. Risør's marine economy collapsed in the 1920s and today it looks like a rather conservative little town, but – surprise, surprise – in 2007 its citizens elected Knut Henning Thygesen, a member of the Red Party, a fusion of the Workers' Communist Party (AKP) and the Red Electoral Alliance (RV), as their mayor. Red or not, few would say Risør hops, but it is something of a centre for arts and crafts and it does rustle up several summer festivals, including a week-long chamber music shindig in late June (ⓦkammermusikkfest.no).

## ARRIVAL AND INFORMATION                                                      RISØR

**By bus** Express buses between Oslo and Kristiansand mostly stop at Vinterkjaer, from where there is a connecting local bus service down to the coast at Risør; the journey from Vinterkjaer takes 15min. Risør bus station is on Krags gate, about 400m west of the harbour. For timetables, go to ⓦakt.no.

**Destinations** Kristiansand, change at Vinterkjaer (every 2–3hr; 2hr 30min); Oslo, change at Vinterkjaer (every 2–3hr; 4hr 30min).
**Tourist office** Risør tourist office is down by the harbour at Torvet 1 (June–Aug Mon–Fri 10am–4pm; ☎37 15 22 70).

## ACCOMMODATION AND EATING

**Kast Loss** Strandgata 23 ☎37 15 07 77, ⓦstrandgt.no /kastloss. Bijou restaurant down by the water's edge – just south of the harbour – where they serve delicious seafood in the full flourish of nouvelle style. It's pricey, at about 300kr for a main course, though the pizzas are cheaper. Mon–Fri 6pm–10pm, Sat & Sun noon–10pm.

**Det Lille Hotel** Storgata 5 ☎37 15 14 95, ⓦdetlille hotel.no. Among the town's several hotels and guesthouses, the most distinctive is this small hotel whose twelve deluxe suites are decorated in a pleasing rendition of period style. The suites are distributed between two old buildings, one in the centre, one by the harbour. **1700kr**

**Risør Hotell** Tangengata 16 ☎37 14 80 00, ⓦrisor hotel.no. Just south along the seafront from the harbour, this tastefully decorated, family-run hotel occupies a handsome jiggle of older buildings. Many of its guest rooms have charming sea views and the hotel has its own passenger boat that will shuttle you out to the bony, offshore islet of Stangholmen, where the clumpy lighthouse stands glued to the rocks. The hotel has a smart restaurant – and very good it is too, with seafood to the fore; mains from 220kr. Mon–Sat 5–9pm. **1500kr**

# Arendal

The bustling town of **ARENDAL**, about 50km from Risør, is one of the most appealing places on the coast, its sheltered harbour curling right into the centre, which is further crimped and cramped by the forested hills that push in from behind. The town's heyday was in the eighteenth century when its shipyards churned out dozens of the sleek wooden sailing ships that then dominated international trade. The shipyards faded away in the late nineteenth century, but there's an attractive reminder of the boom times in the striking medley of old timber buildings that make up the oldest part of town, **Tyholmen**, which rolls over the steep and bumpy promontory just to the southwest of the modern centre. To explore Tyholmen's every nook and cranny, sign up for one of the tourist office's guided walking tours.

## Gamle Rådhus
Rådhusgaten 10

Tyholmen's architectural highlight is the **Gamle Rådhus** (Old Town Hall), Norway's tallest wooden house, a handsome, four-storey structure, whose classical symmetries overlook the Tyholmen waterfront. The house was built as a private residence in 1815, but the Danish merchant who owned the place died twelve years later and his widow sold it to the council, who turned it into the town hall, a role it performed until 2004 when it was converted into offices.

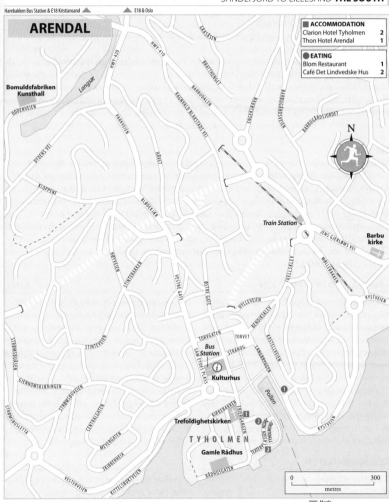

## Trefoldighetskirken

Friergangen • Tues–Thurs noon–4pm • Free • ☎ 37 01 35 80, ⓦ arendal.kirken.no

Overlooking the town centre at the northern edge of Tyholmen, the massive – and massively ugly – red-brick **Trefoldighetskirken** (Church of the Trinity) was meant to celebrate the town's economic success as well as its godliness. Instead, it almost ended up in farce and fiasco: Arendal hit the financial skids in 1886 and, although the church had been finished, there was no money left to equip the interior – and the altar was only installed twenty years later.

## Kulturhus and Pollen

The town centre's most conspicuous building is the boxy, modern **Kulturhus**, on Sam Eydes plass (ⓦ arendalkulturhus.no), which hosts conferences, public meetings and concerts to suit (almost) every musical taste. From here, it's a couple of minutes' walk east to **Pollen**, the short, rectangular inner harbour, which is flanked by pavement cafés and bars.

## Bomuldsfabriken Kunsthall

Oddenveien 5 • Tues–Sun noon–4pm • Free • ☎ 37 01 31 43, ⓦ bomuldsfabriken.no • Signposted from Hwy-42 to the northwest of the town centre on the way to the E18

The region's largest contemporary arts gallery, the **Bomuldsfabriken Kunsthall** is housed within a sympathetically converted former textile factory about 2km north of the town centre. The gallery hosts half a dozen exhibitions of contemporary art every year with Norwegian work to the fore, though Swedes and Danes get regular outings here too. One recent exhibition featured the talented **Sverre Malling** (b.1977), whose precise and intricate work is magic realism at its unsettling best.

## Merdø

Passenger ferries to Merdø leave from Pollen • Late June to mid-Aug daily every 30min to hourly; rest of year sporadic service – details from the tourist office; 30min • 50kr • **Merdøgaard Museum** Late June to mid-Aug guided tours only, on the hour, every hour, daily noon–4pm • 50kr

Among the scattering of islands lying just offshore from Arendal, one of the most appealing is **Merdø**, a flattish, lightly wooded islet, whose safe anchorages, orchards and fresh water made it a popular haven for sailing ships right up until the end of the nineteenth century. About 1km long and a few hundred metres wide, footpaths network the island and there are a couple of small sandy beaches as well as a summertime café. The islet is also home to the **Merdøgaard Museum**, which comprises a small coastal farm as it was in around 1800.

## ARRIVAL AND INFORMATION                                      ARENDAL

**By train** At the end of its own branch line (beginning at Nelaug station), Arendal train station is on the north side of town, a 10min walk from Torvet, the main square: go to the roundabout close to the station and then either proceed up and over the steep hill (Iuellsklev and then Bendiksklev), or (more easily) stroll through the tunnel. Torvet is metres from the inner harbour, Pollen.

Destinations Nelaug (4 daily; 45min); Kristiansand, change at Nelaug (4 daily; 2hr); Oslo, change at Nelaug (4 daily; 4hr); Stavanger, change at Nelaug (4 daily; 5hr).

**By bus** Long-distance express buses between Oslo and Kristiansand mostly stop at Harebakken, beside the E18,

where you change once, often twice, for the connecting local bus/buses down to Arendal; the journey from Harebakken to Arendal takes 10min. Local buses link Arendal bus station with neighbouring points along the coast; for bus timetables, consult either ⓦ akt.no or ⓦ rutebok.no. Arendal bus station is in the centre of town beside the Kulturhus on Vestre gate.

Destinations Grimstad (hourly; 30min); Oslo (1 daily; 4hr); Kristiansand (hourly; 1hr 30min); Lillesand (hourly; 1hr).

**Tourist office** Arendal tourist office is in the Kulturhus complex, downtown at Sam Eydes plass 1 (July to mid-Aug Mon–Fri 9am–4pm & Sat 11am–4pm; rest of year Mon–Fri 9am–3pm; ☎ 37 00 55 44, ⓦ arendal.com).

## ACCOMMODATION

**Clarion Hotel Tyholmen** Teaterplassen 2 ☎ 37 07 68 00, ⓦ nordicchoicehotels.com. This smashing hotel occupies a matching pair of warehouse-style buildings right on the Tyholmen quayside: full marks to the architects, who designed the second, newer block to blend in seamlessly with its older neighbour. The guest rooms are resolutely modern, with blues and whites throughout, and most have sea views. **1500kr**

**Thon Hotel Arendal** Friergangen 1 ☎ 37 05 21 50, ⓦ thonhotels.com. This straightforward, modern chain hotel is in the centre just off the west side of Pollen. Browns and creams predominate and there are wooden floors throughout. **1500kr**

## EATING

In the summertime, Arendal hums at night with a clutter of busy cafés, bars and restaurants lining up along and around **Pollen**, which is very much the amiable centre of things.

**Blom Restaurant** Langbryggen 9 ☎ 37 00 14 14, ⓦ blom restaurant.no. Smart, modern restaurant with an outside terrace overlooking Pollen. An inventive menu features the likes of grilled reindeer with pear cooked in cassis, creamed celeriac and rosemary sauce (325kr). Daily 4–10pm.

**Café Det Lindvedske Hus** Nedre Tyholmsvei 7B

☎ 95 70 68 95. Upstairs in an old building just to the south of Pollen, the grooviest place in town is a laidback, artsy sort of place serving light meals – pastas, salads and so forth. Mains start at around 90kr and the kitchen closes at 9pm, whereupon it's over to the drinking. Mon–Thurs 11am–11pm, Fri & Sat 11am–1am, Sun noon–9pm.

# Grimstad

Famous for its Ibsen connections, good-looking **GRIMSTAD**, about 20km from Arendal, is a brisk huddle of white timber houses with orange- and black-tiled roofs that stack up behind the harbour. Nowadays scores of yachts are moored here, but at the beginning of the nineteenth century the town had no fewer than forty shipyards and carried on a lucrative import-export trade with France – hence the arrival of a young **Henrik Ibsen** (see box below).

## Ibsen-museet

Henrik Ibsens gate 14 • Mid-June to mid-Aug daily 11am–4pm; rest of year by arrangement with Grimstad tourist office on ☎ 37 25 01 68 • 90kr • ☎ 37 04 04 90, ⊕ gbm.no

The small house where Ibsen lived and worked as a pharmacist is now the **Ibsen-museet**, located just up from the harbour in the centre of town. The alley that serves as the entrance to the museum as well as much of the ground floor beyond has been returned to an approximation of its appearance when Ibsen lived here, complete with creaking wooden floors and narrow-beamed ceilings. Upstairs, there's a detailed display on Ibsen the dramatist plus an assortment of original letters and documents and, best of all, a glass cabinet of Ibsen memorabilia: his glasses and their case, an inkstand, a ruler and even a piece of the great man's hair.

## ARRIVAL AND INFORMATION                                    GRIMSTAD

**By bus** Local buses link Grimstad with neighbouring points along the coast; for timetable details consult ⊕ akt.no or ⊕ rutebok.no. For places further afield, principally Oslo, long-distance buses drop and pick up passengers about 2km from town, just off the motorway at Grimstad Øygardsdalen; connecting buses onto Grimstad are, however, few and far between – check before you depart. In Grimstad, buses pull into the centre of the village, beside the harbour.

**Destinations** Arendal (hourly; 30min); Kristiansand (hourly; 1hr); Lillesand (every 1–3hr; 35min with one change); Oslo from Grimstad Øygardsdalen (every 2–3hr; 4hr 15min).

**Tourist office** Grimstad tourist office is down by the harbour in the centre of town at Storgata 1A (late June to late Aug Mon–Fri 9am–6pm, Sat & Sun 10am–4pm; rest of year Mon–Fri 8.30am–4pm; ☎ 37 25 01 68, ⊕ visit grimstad.com).

## ACCOMMODATION AND EATING

**Apotekergården** Skolegata 3 ☎ 37 04 50 25, ⊕ apotekergaarden.no. The liveliest place in town, this informal restaurant-pub has a wide-ranging menu, featuring everything from pizzas and burgers to meat and fish dishes; pizzas from 150kr, meat and fish mains around 240kr. There's a summer terrace too. Mon–Thurs 4pm–midnight, Fri 4pm–2am, Sat noon–2am &

Sun 1pm–midnight.

**Scandic Grimstad Hotell** Kirkegata 3 ☎ 37 25 25 25, ⊕ scandichotels.com. The best hotel in town, occupying an old and cleverly converted clapboard complex among the narrow lanes near the Ibsen Museum. One hundred briskly modern guest-rooms decorated in pastel shades. **1400kr**

---

## IBSEN SHARPENS HIS CLAWS IN GRIMSTAD

**Henrik Ibsen** (1828–1906) left his home in Skien at the tender age of sixteen, moving down along the coast to **Grimstad**, where he worked as an apprentice pharmacist for the next six years. The ill-judged financial dealings of Ibsen's father had impoverished the family, and Henrik's already jaundiced view of Norway's provincial bourgeoisie was confirmed here in the port, whose worthies Ibsen mocked in poems like *Resignation* and *The Corpse's Ball*. It was here too that Ibsen picked up first-hand news of the Paris Revolution of 1848, an event that radicalized him and inspired his paean to the insurrectionists of Budapest, *To Hungary*, written in 1849. Nonetheless, Ibsen's stay on the south coast is more usually recalled as providing the setting for some of his better-known plays, especially his *Pillars of Society*.

**2**

## CRUISING THE BLINDLEIA

Lillesand's nautical highlight is the three-hour cruise aboard **M/B Øya** (July to early Aug Mon–Sat daily at 10am; 290kr one-way, 460kr return; ☎95 93 58 55, ⊛blindleia.no), a dinky little passenger ferry which wiggles its way south to Kristiansand (see below) in part along a narrow channel separating the mainland from the offshore islets. Sheltered from the full force of the ocean, this channel – the **Blindleia** – was once a major trade route, but today it's trafficked by every sort of pleasure craft imaginable, from replica three-mast sailing ships and vintage tugboats to the sleekest of yachts. Other, faster, boats make the trip too, but the M/B Øya is the most charming.

If the sailing schedule of the M/B Øya does not suit, contact Lillesand tourist office for details of a wide variety of **local boat trips**, from fishing trips and cruises along the coast to the summertime **badeboot** (bathing boat), which shuttles across to Hestholm bay on the island of **Skauerøya**, where swimmers don't seem to notice just how cold the Skagerrak actually is.

## Lillesand

Bright and cheery **LILLESAND**, just 20km from Grimstad, is one of the most popular holiday spots on the coast, the white clapboard houses of its tiny centre draped prettily round the harbour. One or two of the buildings, notably the **Rådhus** of 1734, are especially fetching, but it's the general appearance of the place that appeals, best appreciated from the terrace of one of the town's waterfront café-bars. Like many of its coastal neighbours, Lillesand's boom times were in the days of sail, when the village had nine shipyards and its own fishing fleet, but the local economy hit the skids in the early twentieth century when steel ships replaced timber – and hundreds of locals emigrated to the US.

### ARRIVAL AND INFORMATION

LILLESAND

**By bus** Local buses link Lillesand with neighbouring points along the coast; for timetable details consult ⊛rutebok.no or ⊛akt.no. Long-distance buses drop and pick up passengers about 1km north of Lillesand, just off the E18 motorway at Lillesand Gaupemyr. In Lillesand, buses pull into the centre of the village just north of the harbour. Destinations Arendal (hourly; 50min); Grimstad (every 1–3hr; 35min with one change); Kristiansand (every 30min; 40min); Oslo from Lillesand Gaupemyr (every 2–3hr; 4hr 30min).

**Tourist office** Lillesand tourist office is in the centre at Havnegata 10 (late June & early Aug Mon–Sat 10am–6pm & Sun noon–4pm; July daily 10am–6pm; ☎37 26 17 50, ⊛lillesand.kommune.no).

### ACCOMMODATION AND EATING

**Kafe Strandhaven** Strandgata 10 ☎99 04 16 04, ⊛kafestrandhaven.com. Appealing café with a cosy, retro vibe and an attractive garden running down towards the waterfront. Serves a mix of snacks and light meals, from burgers to cakes. Mon–Thurs & Sat 10.30am–5pm, Fri 10.30am–1am, Sun noon–5pm.

★**Lillesand Hotel Norge** Strandgata 3 ☎37 27 01 44, ⊛hotelnorge.no. Lillesand's one first-rate hotel occupies a grand old wooden building metres from the harbour. Refurbished in attractive vintage style, the interior holds some charming stained-glass windows and its guest rooms are named after some of the famous people who have stayed here – the novelist Knut Hamsun for starters. **1800kr**

**Tingsaker Familiecamping** Bergstø ☎37 27 04 21, ⊛tingsakercamping.no. Well-equipped and very popular seashore campsite with self-catering facilities, canoe rental, a pool and cabins with en-suite facilities, two bedrooms and a mini-veranda; electrics hook-up 35kr. About 1km northeast of the centre – to get there, take Storgata and keep going. May to mid-Sept. Camping **340kr**, cabins **990kr**

## Kristiansand

With a population of 87,000, **KRISTIANSAND**, some 30km from Lillesand, is Norway's fifth-largest city and a part-time holiday resort – altogether a genial, energetic place which thrives on its ferry connections with Denmark, busy marinas, passable **sandy beaches** and, last but not least, its offshore oil industry. In summer, the seafront and adjoining streets are a frenetic bustle of bars, fast-food joints and flirting holidaymakers, and even in winter Norwegians come here to live it up.

Like many other Scandinavian towns, Kristiansand was founded by – and named after – **Christian IV**, who saw an opportunity to strengthen his coastal defences here. Building started in 1641, and the town has retained the spacious quadrant plan that characterizes all of Christian's projects. There are few specific sights as such, but the place is well worth a quick gander, especially when everyone else has gone to the beach and left the central pedestrianized streets relatively empty. The main historic attraction, however, is a few kilometres out of town at the **Kristiansand Kanonmuseum**, the forbidding remains of a large coastal gun battery built during the German occupation of World War II.

**2**

## Domkirke

Kirkegata at Gyldenløves gate • Late June to July Mon–Fri 11am–2pm; rest of year, no fixed opening times • Free • ☏ 38 19 69 00, ⓦ kristiansanddomkirke.no

Neat and trim, the gridiron streets that make up Kristiansand's compact centre hold one architectural highlight, the **Domkirke** (Cathedral), an imposing neo-Gothic edifice dating from the 1880s, whose spire pokes high into the sky beside a wide and airy square. The interior of the cathedral is sombre-serious, but there is one notable decorative feature, the large **painting** above the main altar showing a post-Resurrection scene – the breaking of bread at Emmaus – by Eilif Peterssen (1852–1928), a prominent portrait-painter and illustrator.

## Sørlandets Kunstmuseum

Skippergaten 24B • Tues–Sat 11am–4pm, Thurs 11am–8pm, Sun noon–4pm • 60kr • ☏ 38 07 49 00, ⓦ skmu.no

The pick of the town's several museums is the **Sørlandets Kunstmuseum** (Sørlandet Art Museum), whose well-appointed premises are used for a lively programme of

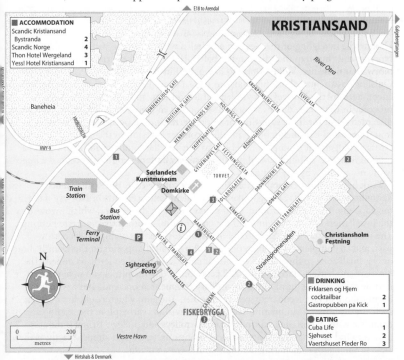

temporary exhibitions with contemporary art to the fore. The museum's permanent collection is modest, but it does hold examples of the work of many of Norway's leading nineteenth-century painters, including two works by Johan Dahl (see p.66), a Munch, and Christian Krohg's earthy *Admonition*. There are also several paintings by Amaldus Nielsen (1838–1932), a largely forgotten Norwegian Romanticist whose smooth and glossy landscapes are best exemplified by the beatific *Morgen i Ny-Hellesund*.

## Christiansholm Festning

Strandpromenaden • Mid-May to mid-Sept daily 9am–9pm • Free • ☎ 38 07 51 50

As a point of interest, the main rival to Kristiansand's cathedral is the **Christiansholm Festning** (Christiansholm Fortress), a squat fortress whose sturdy circular tower and zigzagging earth-and-stone ramparts overlook the marina in the east harbour. Built in 1672, the tower's walls are 5m thick, a defensive precaution that proved unnecessary since it never saw action. These days it houses various arts and crafts displays.

## Galgebergtangen

If you fancy a **swim**, one option is to head off to **Galgebergtangen** (Gallows' Point), an attractive rocky cove with a small sandy beach, 2km east of the town centre. To get there, go over the bridge at the end of Dronningens gate, take the first major right at the lights – Kuholmsveien – and follow the signs.

## Kristiansand Kanonmuseum

Krooddveien, Møvik • Mid-Feb to mid-May & mid-Sept to mid-Nov Sun noon–4pm; mid-May to mid-June & mid-Aug to mid-Sept Mon–Wed 11am–3pm, Thurs–Sun 11am–5pm; mid-June to mid-Aug daily 11am–6pm • 80kr • ☎ 38 08 50 90, ⓦ kanonmuseet.no • About 11km from the city centre: take Hwy-456 out of Kristiansand, then Hwy-457 for the last 3km

Despite the inveigling of the German admiralty, who feared the British would occupy Norway and thus trap their fleet in the Baltic, **Hitler** was lukewarm about invading Norway until he met **Vidkun Quisling** (see p.399) in Berlin in late 1939. Hitler took Quisling's assurances about his ability to stage a coup d'état at face value, no doubt encouraged by the Norwegian's virulent anti-Semitism, and was thereafter keen to proceed. In the event, the invasion went smoothly enough – even if Quisling was soon discarded – but for the rest of the war Hitler overestimated both Norway's strategic importance and the likelihood of an Allied counter-invasion in the north. These two errors of judgement prompted him both to garrison the country with nigh on half a million men and to build several hundred **artillery batteries** round the coast – a huge waste of resources by any standard.

Work began on the coastal battery that is now conserved as the **Kristiansand Kanonmuseum** in 1941, using – like all equivalent emplacements in Norway – the forced labour of POWs. Around 1400 men worked on the project, which involved the installation of four big guns and the construction of protective concrete housings. The idea was to make the Skagerrak impassable for enemy warships at its narrowest part, and so complementary batteries were also installed opposite on the Danish shore; only a small zone in the middle was out of range, and this the Germans mined. The Kristiansand battery once covered 220 acres, but today the principal remains hog a narrow ridge, with a massive, empty **artillery casement** at one end, and a whopping **38cm-calibre gun** in a concrete well at the other. The gun, which could fire a 500kg shell almost 55km, is in pristine condition, and visitors can explore the loading area, complete with the original ramrods, wedges, trolleys and pulleys. Below is the underground command post and soldiers' living quarters, again almost exactly as they were in the 1940s – including the odd bit of German graffiti.

## ARRIVAL AND DEPARTURE

Note the distinction between Kristiansund (see p.262) in the north and Kristiansand in the south: to make things easier, on timetables and in brochures they are often written as Kristiansund N and Kristiansand S.

**By train** Kristiansand train station is beside Vestre Strandgate, on the edge of the central town grid.
Destinations Arendal (4 daily; 2hr, change at Nelaug); Egersund (4–6 daily; 2hr); Kongsberg (4 daily; 3hr 20min); Oslo (4 daily; 4hr 40min); Stavanger (4 daily; 3hr).

**By bus** Local and long-distance buses pull into Kristiansand bus station on Vestre Strandgate, near the ferry terminal and the train station. There is a fast and frequent bus service between Kristiansand and Oslo, but only Nor-Way Bussekspress (Ⓦ nor-way.no) currently operates an express bus service from Kristiansand to Flekkefjord and Stavanger; bus timetables are on Ⓦ akt.no and Ⓦ rutebok.no.
Destinations Flekkefjord (3–4 daily; 1hr 50min); Mandal (every 30min to 1hr; 45min); Oslo (3 daily; 5hr);

Stavanger (3 daily; 4hr).

**By car** The main car parks are along Vestre Strandgate and, although spaces can be hard to find at the height of the season, they remain your best bet as on-street parking in the rest of the town centre is strictly limited. Moving on from Kristiansand, the most obvious, as well as the most pleasant, journey is west to Stavanger (see p.133), about 230km away – allow three to four hours; it's certainly a lot better than the dreary 240km haul north up Setesdal along Hwy-9 to the E134.

**By boat** In July and early August, the best maritime option hereabouts is the 3hr cruise to Lillesand on the M/B Øya (see box, p.124). Boats depart from Quay 6, down on the waterfront.

## GETTING AROUND

**By foot** The best way to explore the town centre is on foot – it only takes about 10min to walk from one side to the other.
**By bike** For outlying attractions, you might want to rent a bike

at Kristiansand Sykkelsenter, about 800m northwest beyond the train station, just off Hwy-9 at Grim Torv 3 (Mon–Fri 9am–5pm, Sat 9am–3pm; ☎ 38 02 68 35, Ⓦ sykkelsenter.no).

## INFORMATION

**Tourist office** Kristiansand tourist office is handily located at Rådhusgaten 18 (mid-June to mid-Aug Mon–Fri

8am–6pm, Sat 10am–6pm; mid-Aug to mid-June Mon–Fri 8am–3.30pm; ☎ 38 07 50 00, Ⓦ visitkrs.no).

## ACCOMMODATION

Kristiansand has a scattering of chain **hotels** and a **guesthouse** or two, but nevertheless vacant rooms can get thin on the ground in high season, when you should reserve ahead.

**Scandic Kristiansand Bystranda** Østre Strandgate 74 ☎ 21 61 50 11, Ⓦ scandichotels.com. The enterprising Scandic group has a small army of hotels in Norway and this is one of the most popular, inhabiting a large modern block down by the marina. The rooms come in several different sizes, but all are well turned out in calm pastel shades with unfussy furnishings and fittings. **1300kr**
**Scandic Norge** Dronningens gate 5 ☎ 38 17 40 00, Ⓦ scandichotels.com. No prizes for architectural charm, but this large chain hotel is right in the centre of town and its guest rooms are decorated in a bright and cheerful modern style. Has its own spa too. **1300kr**

**Thon Hotel Wergeland** Kirkegata 15 ☎ 38 17 20 40, Ⓦ thonhotels.com. Neat and trim chain hotel in the centre of the city with just thirty rooms kitted out in browns and creams. Nothing too startling perhaps, but perfectly adequate – and there are free waffles in the lobby as well. **1300kr**
**Yess! Hotel Kristiansand** Tordenskjoldsgate 12 ☎ 38 70 15 70, Ⓦ yesshotel.no. In a modern block, in the centre of town about 300m from the train station, this budget hotel provides frugal, modern and very clean rooms at bargain prices. The beds are noticeably comfortable and cheered by blown-up nature photos. All rooms are en suite and the family rooms are equipped with bunk beds. **1000kr**

## EATING

There are lots of **cafés** and **restaurants** in the centre of Kristiansand, with a particular concentration in the **Fiskebrygga**, a huddle of mostly modern timber houses set around a small harbour just off the southern end of Vestre Strandgate. Standards are, however, very variable, so it pays to be selective.

**Cuba Life** Tollbodgaten 6 ☎ 95 94 09 95, Ⓦ nordiccoffee culture.com. Laidback, pocket-sized coffee-serious café, where the roaster – never mind the beans – is a matter of earnest debate. But, make no mistake, the coffee is great

and the premises cosy and familiar. Mon–Fri 8am–4pm, Sat 8am–6pm, Sun 10am–4pm.
★ **Sjøhuset** Østre Strandgate 12A ☎ 38 02 62 60, Ⓦ sjohuset.no. In an old converted warehouse down by

the harbour at the east end of Markensgate, this excellent restaurant serves superb fish dishes at around 340kr – less if you stick to the bar menu. Nautical fittings and wooden beams set the scene and there's an attractive outside terrace with sea views too. Sept–April Mon–Sat 3–11pm; May–Aug Mon–Sat 3–11pm, Sun noon–11pm.

**Vaertshuset Pieder Ro** Gravane 10 ☏ 38 10 07 88, ⓦ pieder-ro.no. Many locals swear this is the best seafood restaurant in town – and it certainly does have a lively atmosphere. It occupies an ersatz traditional timber building down in the Fiskebrygga complex, and it's so popular that reservations are advisable at all times. Main courses from 250kr, a little less at lunchtimes. Mon–Sat 11am–11pm, Sun 1–11pm.

## 2 DRINKING AND NIGHTLIFE

Kristiansand has a reasonably lively **nightlife** based around a handful of downtown bars and clubs, which stay open till the wee hours.

**Frklarsen og Hjem cocktailbar** Markens gate 5 at Kongens gate ☏ 38 07 14 13. It's something of a surprise that this resolutely alternative café-bar has survived for so long – but here it is in all its retro-New Age glory. Cocktails from 8pm and weekly live acts. Mon–Wed 11am–11.30pm, Thurs–Sat 11am–2am, Sun noon–11.30pm.

**Gastropubben pa Kick** Dronningens gate 8 ☏ 38 02 83 30, ⓦ gastropuben.no. In the heart of downtown, this lively and very popular bar and restaurant offers an outstanding range of draft ales amidst its wood panelling and bare-brick walls. As if that wasn't enough, they also offer a tasty menu featuring local ingredients – try, for example, the halibut with avocado cream and potato salad (295kr). Mon–Sat 3pm–1am, kitchen till 10pm; Sun 3pm–midnight, kitchen till 8pm.

# Mandal to Egersund

To the west of Kristiansand lies a sparsely inhabited region, where the rough uplands and long valleys of the interior roll down to a shoreline pierced by a necklace of inlets and fjords. The highlight is undoubtedly **Mandal**, a fetching seaside resort with probably the best sandy **beach** in the whole of Norway, but thereafter it's a struggle to find much inspiration. The best you'll do is the old harbour towns of **Flekkefjord** and **Egersund**, though most visitors press on to Stavanger.

The **E39** weaves its way west for 240km from Kristiansand to Stavanger, staying a few kilometres inland for the most part and offering only the odd sight of the coast. The **train line** follows pretty much the same route – though it does, unlike the E39, bypass Flekkefjord – until it reaches **Egersund**, where it returns to the coast for the final 80km, slicing across long flat plains with the sea on one side and distant hills away to the east.

---

### STAYING IN A LIGHTHOUSE

The rocks and reefs of the **southwest coast** between Mandal and Stavanger prompted the construction of a string of **lighthouses** and now, with the lighthouse keepers long gone, several of them offer simple, hostel-like **accommodation**. Lighthouse lodging is inexpensive, though you're almost always responsible for your own food, water and bed linen – and getting there by boat can be both difficult and pricey: most people arrive on their own boats, so there is rarely a ferry schedule as such, though the local tourist office should be able to tell you who will sail there and at what cost. Arranging accommodation can be difficult too, especially if you don't speak Norwegian, though again the local tourist office will help. The number of lighthouses offering accommodation seems to change from year to year, but there's an up-to-date list on the Nordsjøvegen website (ⓦ www .northsearoad.co.uk) and the rather more detailed ⓦ lighthousesofnorway.com.

#### LIGHTHOUSES OFFERING ACCOMMODATION

**Hatholmen Fyr** (see opposite) Glued to a rocky islet in the Skaggerak, due south of Mandal.
**Lindesnes Fyr** (see p.130) Readily accessible lighthouse on a steep and rocky headland about 40km west of Mandal via the E39 and Hwy-460.
**Ryvingen Fyr** (see p.130). Stuck way out in the Skagerrak southeast of Mandal, this is a fabulously wild place to spend the night.

# Mandal

Appealing **MANDAL**, just 45km from Kristiansand, is Norway's southernmost town, its centre spread out along the north bank of the Mandalselva River as it approaches the ocean. This old timber port had its salad days in the eighteenth century, when local pines and oaks were much sought after by the Dutch to support their canal houses and build their trading fleet, but although the timber boom fizzled out long ago, Mandal has preserved its quaint **old centre**, with its platoon of white clapboard buildings. The town also holds an enjoyable **museum** and has a long, sandy **beach** – hardly the Mediterranean, but still very popular.

**2**

## Vest-Agder Museum

Store Elvegate 5 • Late June to mid-Aug Mon–Fri 11am–5pm, Sat & Sun noon–5pm • 70kr • ☎ 95 15 55 92, ⓦ vestagdermuseet.no

Occupying an antique merchant's house overlooking the river, Mandal's rambling **Vest-Agder Museum** holds a varied collection, from agricultural implements to seafaring tackle, as well as a small but enjoyable collection of nautical paintings. Outside in the garden there's also a statue of the Viking chieftain Egil Skallagrimsson by the town's most famous son, **Gustav Vigeland** (see p.78). The central character of *Egil's Saga*, Skallagrimsson is a complex figure, sometimes wise and deliberate, at other times rash and violent. Vigeland has him putting on a horse's head, presumably a reference to his family's reputation as shape-shifters: it was this ability to change form that the Skallagrimssons shared with several Norse gods, including Odin himself.

## Sjøsanden and Furulenden

Mandal's popularity as a holiday spot is down to its fine beach, **Sjøsanden**. An 800m stretch of golden sand, backed by pine trees and framed by rocky headlands, it's touted as Norway's best beach – and although this isn't saying an awful lot, it's still a pleasant spot to unwind for a few hours. The beach is about 1km from the town centre: walk along the harbour to the end of the road and keep going through the woods on the signed footpath.

You can also explore **Furulenden**, a tiny wooded peninsula directly to the west of the beach, where a network of paths winds through the trees and rocks to reveal sand and shingle coves; pick up a map at the tourist office.

## ARRIVAL AND INFORMATION

MANDAL

**By bus** Buses to Mandal pull in at the bus station by the bridge on the north bank of the Mandalselva River. From the bus station, it's a brief walk west along the riverbank to the old town centre. For bus timetables, consult ⓦ akt.no.
Destinations Kristiansand (hourly; 50min).

**Tourist office** Mandal tourist office is on the south side of the river, over the bridge from the old centre in the sleek Buen Kulturhus, Havnegata 2 (June–Aug daily 10am–7pm; Sept–May Mon–Fri 9am–4pm; ☎ 38 27 83 00, ⓦ lindesnesregionen.com).

## ACCOMMODATION

**Kjøbmandsgaarden Hotel** Store Elvegate 57 ☎ 38 26 12 76, ⓦ kjobmandsgaarden.no. Handy and affordable hotel, which occupies an old timber house in a street of antique buildings not far from the bus station. All the dozen or so rooms here are spick-and-span and the decor is bright and cheerful, albeit a little staid. **1000kr**

**Sjøsanden Feriesenter** Sjøsandveien 1 ☎ 38 26 10 94, ⓦ sjosanden.no. You can camp very close to the western end of the Sjøsanden beach at this holiday centre – though note that the access road to the camp detours round the back of the woods, which back onto the beach; it's well signposted. The complex includes a water slide and that good old Norwegian favourite, minigolf. They also offer simple motel-style accommodation (mid-June to mid-Aug) and rent

out two-bedroom cabins that can sleep up to six people. Camping **280kr**, motel **850kr**, cabins **1350kr**

## LIGHTHOUSES

**Hatholmen Fyr** Hatholmen ☎ 95 94 75 82, ⓔ mandal kystlag@gmail.com. Out in the Skaggerak, about 15min by boat from Mandal, the stumpy Hatholmen lighthouse perches on a rocky headland with a trio of white-painted houses in its lee. All told, there are twenty beds here, available from late June to late August, as well as self-catering facilities, an outside toilet and a cold shower – and they do mean cold. Take your own food, water and bed linen. The return boat trip from Mandal costs about 250kr; the tourist office will make all the necessary arrangements or call ☎ 90 28 27 62. Per person per night 200kr

**Ryvingen Fyr** Ryvingen ☎ 97 77 93 50, ⓦ www
.ryvingensvenner.no. There's been a lighthouse way out in
the Skagerrak on the rocky islet of Ryvingen since 1867, though
the first version was far from universally popular – a bunch of
fishermen wrote to the local newspaper complaining that the
light was so bright it scared the fish. The present lighthouse,
a sturdy red-and-white structure, is glued to a large shank of
rock with the churning ocean down below. Nearby, the old
lighthouse keeper's quarters have been pleasantly modernized

and eight cheerfully bright rooms (nineteen beds) are available
for rent from late June to late Aug. Guests are responsible for
their own food, water and bed linen; there is an outside toilet,
but no shower facilities. From Mandal, the boat takes about
45min to get to the lighthouse – less if it leaves from the nearby
port of Tregde – and although there's no set schedule, several
boat owners will make the journey for a round-trip price of
about 600kr. Ring Knut Joseland (☎ 90 17 44 21) or ask the
tourist office to help you make the necessary arrangements.
Per person per night 400kr

### EATING AND DRINKING

**Hr.Redaktor** Store Elvegate 23A ☎ 38 27 15 30,
ⓦ red.no. In the centre of town, this groovy restaurant-
cum-bar has a lively and inventive menu – fried redfish
with tomato fennel and olive compote being a good
example (320kr). The kitchen closes at 10pm, after which
the place morphs into a busy bar. Fri 1pm–2am & Sat
11am–2.30am.

**Marna Café** Store Elvegate 47B ☎ 38 26 27 00,
ⓦ marnacafe.no. Located right in the centre, this combined
restaurant and bar is the liveliest place in town, offering a
wide-ranging menu from salads and tapas (95kr) through
to steak and tasty home-made burgers (190kr). They host
occasional live bands too. Mon–Thurs 11am–11pm, Fri &
Sat 11am–2.30am, Sun noon–10pm.

## Spangereid and Lindesnes

Some 12km west of Mandal on the E39, **Hwy-460** branches south to snake its way the
15km to **Spangereid** at the start of **Lindesnes** (literally "where the land curves round"),
a chubby promontory that juts out into the Skagerrak. Formidable seamen they may
have been, but the Vikings feared the promontory's treacherous waters to such an
extent that they cut a canal across its base at Spangereid to avoid the vagaries of the
open sea. In honour of this nautical achievement, a new canal was cut here in 2007.

### Lindesnes Fyr

Lindesnes • April to mid-May & Sept to mid-Oct Wed–Sun 10am–5pm; mid-May to Aug daily 10am–5pm; mid-Oct to March Sat & Sun
11am–4pm • 75kr • ☎ 38 25 54 20, ⓦ lindesnesfyr.no

At Norway's most southerly point, 10km south of Spangereid, a sturdy red-and-white
lighthouse – **Lindesnes Fyr** – perches on a knobbly, lichen-stained headland. There has
been a lighthouse here since the seventeenth century, but today's structure and its
assorted outhouses mostly date from 1915. The history of the lighthouse and its
keepers is explored in a modest **museum**, the **tower** is open to the public and there's a
surprisingly fancy **café** here too. The most dramatic time to visit is during bad weather:
the headland is exposed to extraordinarily ferocious storms, when the warm westerly
currents of the Skagerrak meet cold easterly winds.

### ACCOMMODATION                                    SPANGEREID AND LINDESNES

**Lindesnes Fyr** Lindesnes ☎ 38 25 54 20, ⓦ lindesnesfyr
.no. The old lighthouse keeper's cottage has been modernized
to hold an apartment for up to six guests – a sleeping couch

for two in the living room and a bedroom on the first floor for
a maximum of four people. There's also a shower, toilet and
kitchen – and superb views out to sea. 1200kr

## Flekkefjord

With a population of just 9000, **FLEKKEFJORD**, 65km from Mandal, is an unassuming
sort of place, its compact centre straddling the banks of a short (500m) channel that
connects the Lafjord and the Grisefjord. Flekkefjord prospered in the sixteenth century
on the back of its trade with the Dutch, who purchased the town's timber for their
houses and its granite for their dykes and harbours. Later, in the 1750s, the herring

**2**

industry was the main money-spinner, along with shipbuilding and tanning, but the Flekkefjord economy had pretty much collapsed by the end of the nineteenth century when sailing ships gave way to steam.

The oldest and prettiest part of Flekkefjord – known as **Hollenderbyen** after the town's Dutch connections – is on the west side of the channel, and only takes a few minutes to explore, though you can extend this pleasantly enough by visiting the nearby nineteenth-century period rooms of the **Vest-Agder-museet Flekkefjord** at Dr Krafts gate 15 (Flekkefjord Museum; late June to late Aug Mon–Fri 11am–5pm, Sat & Sun noon–5pm; 50kr; ⓦvestagdermuseet.no).

### ARRIVAL AND INFORMATION                                    FLEKKEFJORD

**By bus** In Flekkefjord, buses pull in on Jernbaneveien, just south of the main drag and about 250m east of the central waterway. The main long-distance bus is Nor-Way Busekspressen's Sør-Vest ekspressen (ⓦnor-way.no). Destinations Egersund (1 daily with 1 change; 1hr 30min); Kristiansand (3 daily; 2hr); Stavanger (3 daily; 2hr).

**Tourist office** Flekkefjord tourist office is on the west side of the main channel, beside Hwy-44 at Kirkegata 33 (mid-June to mid-Aug Mon–Fri 10am–6pm, Sat 10am–4pm, plus Sun in July 11am–4pm; rest of year Mon–Fri 9am–4pm; ☎38 32 80 81, ⓦflekkefjord.no).

### ACCOMMODATION

**Grand Hotell** Anders Beergata 9 ☎38 32 53 00, ⓦwww.grand-hotell.no. There's no pressing reason to overnight in Flekkefjord, but if you do decide to stay, the best bet is this medium-sized hotel, where the guest rooms are ok, but not quite as appealing as the handsome, nineteenth-century exterior, with its turrets and arcaded gallery, might suggest. It's located on the west side of the central waterway, one block north of the main road (Hwy-44). **1300kr**

## Jøssingfjord (Highway 44)

At Flekkefjord, the **E39** turns inland, threading its way over the hills and down the dales en route to Stavanger, 130km away. Alternatively, the marginally more appealing, albeit slightly longer, **Highway 44** takes a more southerly route via Egersund (see opposite) – allow three hours for the 160km-long drive. For most of its course, Hwy-44 runs just inland from the sea, but there are occasional glimpses of the ocean, most memorably when – about 30km from Flekkefjord – the road negotiates the deep and narrow **Jøssingford**. At the northern tip of the fjord, just off Hwy-44, is **Helleren** where a couple of early nineteenth-century wooden houses oversee the fjord from within a deep cleft at the base of a cliff. It's a dramatic setting and living here was always hard: the inhabitants eked out an existence by cultivating oats, barley and potatoes on modest plots and sallied off down the fjord to fish. In the 1840s, when cultivable land was at a premium across Norway, three families lived here, but by 1900 it was down to just three adults and the place was deserted by 1920. Had they lasted out till World War II, they probably would have been half frightened to death when, in February 1940, a British destroyer, HMS *Cossack*, chased a German supply ship, the *Altmar*, into the Jøssingfjord. The British freed the 300 Allied POWs the *Altmar* was transporting back to Germany, a rare British success at this time in the war. This naval skirmish prompted those Norwegians who were opposed to the Germans – the vast majority – to call themselves "Jossings" throughout hostilities.

## Sogndalstrand

From the Jøssingfjord, it's a few kilometres more – and a brief detour south off Hwy-44 – to **SOGNDALSTRAND**, a lovely old sailing port, whose narrow main street with its old and handsome timber houses meanders down towards a pretty little harbour. If you want to break your journey hereabouts, this is a good place to do it – and there's an attractive hotel here too.

## ACCOMMODATION

**Sogndalstrand Kulturhotell** Strandgata 22 ☎ 51 47 72 55, 🖰 sogndalstrand-kulturhotell.no. Fascinating and appealing hotel, which occupies a string of old timber buildings that dawdles along the village's main street as it runs parallel to the seashore. Has 29 cosy and intimate guest rooms with oodles of period charm. There's a very good restaurant here also, where they feature local ingredients – try the salmon; reservations for dinner are required. Easter– Aug Mon–Sat noon–4pm & 7–10pm, Sun noon–4pm; Sept–Easter Mon–Sat noon–4pm & 7–10pm. <u>**1600kr**</u>

# Egersund

**2**

A minor manufacturing centre and oil industry hub, **EGERSUND**, around 30km from Sogndalstrand, spreads over a jigsaw of bays and lakes at the end of a deep and sheltered ocean inlet. Egersund has one of Norway's finest natural harbours and nudging up against it is the town's prettiest district, where **Strandgata**, once the town's commercial hub, rustles up an attractive ensemble of old timber houses. Anchoring the north end of Strandgata is the town's oldest **church**, a good-looking cruciform structure dating from the seventeenth century, but of earlier origin. Its location is far from random: before the nineteenth century, the church sat on a short and narrow promontory that poked out into the harbour; it appears that pagan ceremonies took place here – so the construction of the church was to hammer home the Christian nail.

## ARRIVAL AND DEPARTURE

**By train** Egersund train station is on the north edge of town, just over 1km from Strandgata.
Destinations Kristiansand (4 daily; 2hr); Stavanger (4–6 daily; 1hr).

**By bus** The bus station is about 400m from the north end of Strandgata, just over the bridge to the left of the roundabout. The most useful service is the bus to Flekkefjord (1 daily with 1 change; 1hr 30min; 🖰 akt.no).

## ACCOMMODATION

**Grand Hotell Egersund** Johan Feyers gate 3 ☎ 51 49 60 60, 🖰 grand-egersund.no. Easily the best place to stay in town, this comfortable hotel has two different sections – one in the original, nineteenth-century building, with its splendid timber facade, and another in a workaday modern extension. All the guest rooms are, however, bright and modern. Handily located, one block from Strandgata. <u>**1200kr**</u>

# Stavanger

**STAVANGER** is something of a survivor. Many Norwegian coastal towns have fallen foul of the precarious fortunes of fishing, but not Stavanger, which has diversified and is now the possessor of a dynamic economy, its population swelling to over 210,000. It was the herring fishery that first put money into the town, crowding its nineteenth-century wharves with coopers and smiths, net makers and menders. Then, when the fishing failed, the town moved into shipbuilding and now it makes its money through oil – Stavanger builds rigs for Norway's offshore oilfields and refines it as well – backed up by a profitable sideline in tourism as witnessed by the mammoth cruise ships that regularly pull into its harbour.

Much of central Stavanger is noticeably modern, a jingle and a jangle of mini- and not-so-mini tower blocks that spreads over the hilly ground abutting the main harbour and the decorative, central lake, **Breiavatnet**, the most obvious downtown landmark. None of this may sound terribly enticing, but in fact Stavanger is an excellent place to start a visit to Norway: all the town's amenities are within easy walking distance of each other; it has excellent train, bus and ferry connections; and it possesses an especially attractive harbour, an enjoyable museum, and several excellent restaurants. The town is also – and this comes as a surprise to many first-time visitors – nearer to the fjords than Bergen, the self-proclaimed "Gateway to the Fjords": within easy reach of Stavanger are the **Lysefjord** (see p.140) and the dramatic **Preikestolen** rock formation (see p.142).

## Domkirke

Domkirkeplassen • June–Aug daily 9am–6pm; Sept–May Mon–Thurs 9am–4pm, Fri 9am–6pm & Sat 11am–4pm • 30kr • ☎ 51 84 04 00, ⓦ kirken.stavanger.no

The principal relic of medieval Stavanger is the **Domkirke** (Cathedral), whose pointed-hat towers signal a Romanesque church dating from the early twelfth century, though it has been modified on several subsequent occasions. Inside, the squat pillars, dog-tooth arches and rough stonework of the narrow, three-aisled **nave** are the

Stavanger Konserthus                                Tau & Bergen

0                  400

metres

N

Cruise Ship Terminal

Norsk Oljemuseum

Norsk Hermetikmuséet

Vågen

GAMLE STAVANGER

Fjord Sightseeing Boats

SKAGEN

Fiskepiren Hurtigbåt & Car Ferry Terminal

Valbergtårnet

SF Kino Kulturhus

Stavanger Sjøfartsmuseum

Fish Market

Straensenteret

TORGET

A. Kielland Statue

Domkirkeplassen

Domkirke

Vitusapotek

Breiavatnet

Renseriet

Train & Bus Station

Stavanger Turistforening (DNT)

### EATING
| | |
|---|---|
| Fisketorget | 4 |
| Nero | 1 |
| Sjøhuset Skagen | 3 |
| Thai Cuisine | 2 |

### SHOPPING
| | |
|---|---|
| Vinmonopolet | 1 |

### DRINKING & NIGHTLIFE
| | |
|---|---|
| Bøker og Børst | 2 |
| Café Sting | 3 |
| Cardinal | 5 |
| Hall Toll | 1 |
| Hansen Hjørnet | 4 |
| Taket Nattklubb | 6 |

### ACCOMMODATION
| | |
|---|---|
| Best Western Havly Hotel | 1 |
| Clarion Collection Hotel Skagen Brygge | 2 |
| Darby's Inn Bed and Breakfast | 7 |
| Myhregaarden Hotel | 3 |
| Radisson Blu Atlantic Hotel | 5 |
| Stavanger Bed and Breakfast | 6 |
| Stavanger Camping Mosvangen | 8 |
| Stavanger Vandrerhjem Mosvangen | 9 |
| Stavanger Vandrerhjem St Svithun | 10 |
| Thon Hotel Maritim | 4 |

**STAVANGER**

Airport & Tananger

---

**ANTONY GORMLEY IN STAVANGER**

In a well-conceived attempt to add character to the city, **Stavanger** engaged the contemporary British sculptor **Antony Gormley** to do something special – and the result is his *Broken Column*, whose aim is to illustrate the many facets of the city and, for that matter, life (and death) itself by means of 23 sculptures. Each and every sculpture is a blank-faced human figure made of cast iron and 195cm high, the same height as – and apparently modelled on – Gormley himself, with some partly sunk into the ground. This sinking is, as you might expect from Gormley, not at random: each location has a predetermined height quota and the last one in the series, which is stuck out on a rock in the harbour, is mostly (149cm) under water. One of the sculptures is beside the Domkirke, a second is beside Torget's covered fish market. Work began on *Broken Column* in 1999 and the project was completed four years later.

---

Romanesque heart of the church, but the **choir** beyond, with its flowing tracery and pointed windows, is Gothic, the work of English masons who were brought here in the 1270s. This was far from unusual: the Norwegians had little experience of building in stone, so whenever they decided to build a stone church they imported skilled craftsmen, mainly from England and Germany. The ornate seventeenth-century **pulpit** is the most distinctive feature of the nave along with several conspicuous **memorial tablets** that hang on its walls – sombre-serious family portraits surrounded by a jumble of richly carved cherubs, angels and biblical scenes.

## Torget

From the top of **Torget**, the main square, there is a fine view of Stavanger's principal harbour, **Vågen**, a tapering finger of water that buzzes with cruise ships, yachts, ferryboats and catamarans. Sharing the view is a **statue** of the author **Alexander Kielland** (1849–1906), one of the city's most famous sons, looking decidedly pleased with himself in his top hat and cape. Born into a rich merchant family, Kielland was a popular figure hereabouts, praised for his novels and plays and for his (relatively) generous treatment of the workers in his factory. He also set about building a political career, becoming burgomaster of Stavanger in 1891, but it was food – not his political rivals – that did for him: Kielland loved food and, to all intents and purposes, ate himself to death.

## Stavanger Sjøfartsmuseum

Strandkaien 22 • Mid-May to mid-Sept Mon–Wed & Fri–Sun 10am–4pm, Thurs 10am–7pm; mid-Sept to mid-May Tues, Wed & Fri 11am–3pm, Thurs 11am–7pm, Sat & Sun 11am–4pm • 90kr • ☎ 51 84 27 00, ⊕ museumstavanger.no

The mildly diverting **Sjøfartsmuseum** (Stavanger Maritime Museum) occupies two former warehouses facing the west side of the harbour, metres from Torget. The museum's interior is jam-packed with all things nautical, from replica offices and stores, through to archeological finds, paintings of ships, model boats and, perhaps best of the lot, scores of old photos drawn from a huge permanent collection.

## Gamle Stavanger

On the western side of the main harbour is the city's star turn, **Gamle Stavanger** (Old Stavanger). Though very different in appearance from the modern structures back in the centre, the buildings here were also the product of a boom. From 1810 until around 1870, herring turned up just offshore in their millions, and Stavanger took advantage of this slice of luck. The town flourished and expanded, with the number of merchants and shipowners increasing dramatically. Huge profits were

**2**

made from the exported fish, which were salted and later, as the technology improved, canned. Today, some of the wooden stores and warehouses flanking the western quayside hint at their nineteenth-century pedigree, but it's the succession of narrow, cobbled lanes behind them – along and around **Øvre Strandgate** – that shows Gamle Stavanger to best advantage. Formerly home to local seafarers, craftsmen and cannery workers, the area has been maintained as a residential quarter, mercifully free of tourist tat: the long rows of white-painted, clapboard houses are immaculately maintained, complete with picket fences and tiny terraced gardens. There's little architectural pretension, but here and there flashes of fancy wooden scrollwork must once have had the curtains twitching among the staunchly Lutheran population.

## Norsk Hermetikkmuseet

Øvre Strandgate 88 • Mid-May to mid-Sept daily 10am–4pm; mid-Sept to mid- May Tues–Fri 11am–3pm, Sat & Sun 11am–4pm • 90kr • ✆ 40 72 84 70, ⊚ museumstavanger.no

In the heart of Gamle Stavanger, the **Norsk Hermetikkmuseet** (Norwegian Canning Museum) occupies an old **sardine-canning factory** and gives a glimpse of the industry that saved Stavanger from collapse at the end of the nineteenth century. When the herring vanished from local waters in the 1870s, the canning factories switched to imported fish, thereby keeping the local economy afloat. They remained Stavanger's main source of employment until as late as 1960: in the 1920s there were seventy canneries here, and the last one only closed down in 1983.

A visit to an old canning factory may not seem too enticing, but the museum is actually very good. Downstairs the assorted drying racks, canning trays, smokers and other paraphernalia set the scene, but the highlight is upstairs in the museum's collection of **sardine tin labels**, called *iddis* in these parts from the local pronunciation of *etikett*, the Norwegian for label. A couple of hundred labels have survived, in part because they were avidly collected by the town's children, though this harmless hobby seems to have worried the town's adults no end – "Label thefts – an unfortunate collection craze", ran a 1915 headline in the *Stavanger Aftenblad* newspaper. The variety of label design is extraordinary – anything and everything from representations of the Norwegian royal family to surrealistic fish with human qualities. Spare a thought also for a Scottish seaman by the name of William Anderson: it was his bearded face, copied from a photograph, that beamed out from millions of Skippers' sardine tins, a celebrity status so frowned upon by shipowners that Anderson couldn't find work, though fortunately the story ended happily: Anderson wrote to the cannery concerned to complain and they put him on the payroll for the remainder of his working life.

The museum **smokes its own sardines** on the first Sunday of every month and every Tuesday and Thursday from June to August – and deliciously tasty they are too.

## Skagen

After years in the doldrums, **Skagen**, the bumpy promontory on the east side of the main harbour, is on the up, its old, bright-white wooden houses now holding some of the city's best bars and cafés, especially along **Øvre Holmegate**, where white is abandoned for a New Age-meets-hippy mix of yellow, green and red facades. Skagen's mazy street plan is the legacy of the original Viking settlement, but there is nothing else to recall them and the only sight as such is the spiky **Valbergtårnet** (Valberg tower), a nineteenth-century fire-watch sitting atop Skagen's highest point and offering sweeping views of the city and its industry. The only mild fly in the architectural ointment is the **Kulturhus**, at the centre of Skagen, whose clumsy modernity does its surroundings poor service.

# Norsk Oljemuseum

Kjeringholmen • June–Aug daily 10am–7pm; Sept–May Mon–Sat 10am–4pm, Sun 10am–6pm • 120kr • ☎ 51 93 93 00, Ⓦ norskolje.museum.no

The intricate workings of the offshore oil industry are explored in depth at the excellent **Norsk Oljemuseum** (Norwegian Petroleum Museum), located in a sleek modern building beside the waterfront on the far side of Skagen. The first tentative searches for oil beneath the North Sea began in the early 1960s and the first strike was made in 1969. Production started two years later and has continued ever since with Norway making an enormous fortune from its vast oil and gas reserves – easily enough to transform what had once been one of Europe's poorer countries to one of the richest. The museum is not especially large, but it is a little confusing unless you pick up a free plan at reception.

There are introductory displays on North Sea geology, explaining how the oil was created, and on how much money Norway is making (or occasionally losing) from its oil and gas, but you're soon into the offshore section with scale models of oil rigs, explanations as to how oil wells are sunk, and a few mechanical bits and pieces – drill bits, diving bells and so forth. There's also a small section on the **Alexander Kielland disaster** of 1980, when the eponymous oil rig collapsed in heavy seas, killing 123 oil workers, Norway's worst offshore disaster by a mile. The museum has a mini-cinema, showing a film about the industry, plus several hands-on exhibits, notably a mock-up of a drilling platform. Embedded in the museum are nuggets of social commentary: women were only allowed to work offshore from the late 1970s and soon after their arrival the oil companies had to bring in more toiletries for the men, who suddenly started to shower (more). A further section is devoted to the divers who work on the seabed, their endeavours illustrated with a remarkable film on the laying and repairing of a stretch of underwater pipeline.

Incidentally, the open-air playground outside the museum is – as it looks – made up from discarded oil industry tackle.

## ARRIVAL AND DEPARTURE                                    STAVANGER

**By plane** Stavanger's international airport is 14km southwest of the city centre at Sola. A Flybussen (every 15–30min; 30–40min depending on traffic; 120kr one-way, 180kr return; Ⓦ flybussen.no) links the airport with the city centre, stopping at several downtown hotels, including the *Radisson Blu Atlantic*, as well as the Fiskepiren ferry terminal and the combined bus and train station.

**By train** Stavanger's train station (Ⓦ nsb.no) is handily located in the centre on the south side of lake Breiavatnet.
Destinations Arendal (4 daily; 5hr, change at Nelaug); Egersund (4–6 daily; 1hr); Kristiansand (4 daily; 3hr); Oslo (4 daily; 8hr).

**By bus** Stavanger bus terminal is adjacent to the train station. Among several bus companies, Nor-Way Bussekspressen (Ⓦ nor-way.no) operates several particularly useful long-distance routes. Local and long-distance bus timetables are on Ⓦ rutebok.no.
Destinations Bergen (every 1–2hr; 5hr–5hr 30min); Flekkefjord (3 daily; 2hr); Haugesund (every 1–2hr; 2hr); Kristiansand (3 daily; 4hr).

**By international ferry** There are no international car ferries into Stavanger itself, but Fjordline (Ⓦ fjordline .com) operates a car ferry service between Hirstals in

Denmark, Tananger (about 13km west of Stavanger), and Bergen.

**By domestic ferry** Most domestic ferries from the islands and fjords around Stavanger, including both Hurtigbåt passenger express boats and car ferries, dock at the Fiskepiren terminal, a shortish walk to the northeast of lake Breiavatnet – and about 800m from the train and bus stations. Note that at time of writing the Hurtigbåt passenger express boat from Stavanger to Haugesund and Bergen was not in operation, though this may change.

**Public transport information** There's a Kolumbus Kundesenter at the bus station (information centre; Mon–Fri 7am–7pm, Sat 10am–3pm; ☎ 177, Ⓦ kolumbus.no) and another at the Fiskepiren terminal (Mon–Fri 7am–6pm). Both provide comprehensive details of buses, boats and trains in the city and its environs.

**By car** Stavanger is small enough to be easily negotiated by car and although on-street parking is a little difficult, there are several handy car parks, including a large one just a few metres to the west of the Fiskepiren ferry terminal. Car rental is available from several companies, including Europcar, at the airport (☎ 51 65 10 90) and in the city centre at Olav V's gate 13 (☎ 51 53 82 00).

**2**

## GETTING AROUND

**By bike** Stavanger is readily explored on foot – all the key attractions are close together in the centre – but the tourist office does rent out bikes (300kr/day, plus 200kr refundable deposit) and issues free cycling maps.
**By taxi** Stavanger Taxi ☏ 51 90 90 90.

## INFORMATION

**Tourist office** Stavanger tourist office, Domkirkeplassen 3 (June–Aug daily 9am–8pm; Sept–May Mon–Fri 9am–4pm, Sat 9am–2pm; ☏ 51 85 92 00, ⍵ regionstavanger.com), publishes a useful and free guide to the Stavanger region and issues free city maps. They will also make bookings on guided tours and excursions to Lysefjord and Preikestolen (see p.142). Some trips depart from the Fiskepiren terminal, others from Skagenkaien, beside the main harbour, Vågen.

## ACTIVITIES

**Hiking and skiing** The DNT-affiliated Stavanger Turistforening in the underpass at the top of Olav V's gate (Mon–Wed & Fri 10am–4pm, Thurs 10am–7pm, Sat 10am–4pm; ☏ 51 84 02 00, ⍵ stf.no) will advise on local hiking routes and sells a comprehensive range of hiking maps. They maintain around 900km of hiking trails and run more than thirty cabins in the mountains east of Stavanger, as well as organizing ski schools at winter weekends. They also offer general advice about local conditions, weather and so on, and you can obtain DNT membership here too.

## ACCOMMODATION

There's no shortage of accommodation in Stavanger. A string of **hotels** is dotted around the town's compact centre or you can opt for a no-frills guesthouse, an HI **hostel** and a **campsite**.

### HOTELS AND B&BS

**Best Western Havly Hotel** Valberggata 1 ☏ 51 93 90 00, ⍵ havly-hotell.no. Neat and trim, medium-sized, independet hotel occupying a rather bunker-like modern building squeezed into a narrow side street off Skagenkaien. Forty-two spick-and-span modern rooms. **1600kr**

**Clarion Collection Hotel Skagen Brygge** Skagenkaien 30 ☏ 51 85 00 00, ⍵ nordicchoicehotels .com. A pleasing quayside hotel, built in the style of an old warehouse but with lots of glass and great views over the harbour (unless a cruise ship moors outside). The rooms are modern and unfussily decorated, the buffet breakfast very good and mid-afternoon nibbles are free. The only quibble concerns the noise from outside: if you are a light sleeper, either take potluck (summer weekends are noisiest) or a room at the back. **1200kr**

**★ Darby's Inn Bed and Breakfast** Oscarsgate 18 ☏ 47 62 52 48, ⍵ darbysbb.com. In a beautifully maintained, timber mansion dating from the 1890s, this immaculate B&B has a handful of rooms decorated in sumptuous country-house style. Great breakfasts too, and a quiet back street location a shortish walk to the west of the central lake, Breiavatnet. **1180kr**

**Myhregaarden Hotel** Nygata 24 ☏ 51 86 80 00, ⍵ myhregaardenhotel.no. Housed in part of a large and really rather grand, late nineteenth-century building, this modern hotel has a handy location and 53 boutique-style guest rooms with the comfiest of beds. The decor is bright if a tad spartan and the attic rooms are especially pleasant. **1200kr**

**★ Radisson Blu Atlantic Hotel** Olav V's gate 3 ☏ 51 76 10 00, ⍵ radissonblu.com. There was a time when this was *the* place to stay in Stavanger, hosting every celebrity who ever set foot in the city from Paul Gascoigne to Fats Domino. The hotel looks a tad staid now – and it certainly occupies a big bruiser of a modern block – but the wood panelling of the public areas has a comforting charm and the guest rooms are large and spacious with most offering attractive views over the central lake. **1000kr**

**Stavanger Bed and Breakfast** Vikedalsgaten 1A ☏ 51 56 25 00, ⍵ stavangerbedandbreakfast.no. This friendly, hostel-like B&B has over twenty simple and straightforward modern rooms, most of which have showers and sinks (but shared toilets). Every evening, guests gather in the dining room for the complimentary coffee and waffles – and a very sociable affair it is too. The B&B is in a residential area just 10min walk from the train station. A real snip, even if some of the inter-room walls are paper-thin. **890kr**

**Thon Hotel Maritim** Kongsgata 32 ☏ 51 85 05 00, ⍵ thonhotels.com. No points for architectural style – this chain hotel occupies a glum-looking modern block – but the interior has been nicely remodelled. It's in a quiet, central location, and the upper floors overlook the city's dinky little central lake, Breiavatnet. **1300kr**

### HOSTELS AND CAMPING

**Stavanger Camping Mosvangen** Henrik Ibsens gate 21 ☏ 51 53 29 71, ⍵ stavangercamping.no. On the south side of lake Mosvatnet, just 3km from the centre – and not far from the nearest HI hostel (see below) – this large and well-equipped campsite has space for tents and caravans as well as a selection of cabins for up to six people. May to mid-Sept. Camping **290kr**, cabin **500kr**

**Stavanger Vandrerhjem Mosvangen** Henrik Ibsens gate 19 ☏ 51 54 36 36, ⍵ hihostels.no. This no-frills, chalet-meets-barracks HI hostel stands on the south side of Mosvatnet lake, a 3km walk from the centre. The hostel has self-catering and laundry facilities, and the twenty en-suite rooms hold between one and four bunk beds each; advance reservations are advised. The nearest you'll get by public transport is on bus #4 from the bus station – get off at the start of Ullandhaugsveien (or at least ask the driver to drop you off) on the southeast side of the lake. Mid-June to late Aug. Dorms 200kr, doubles 545kr

**Stavanger Vandrerhjem St Svithun** Gerd-Ragna Bloch, Thorsens gate 8 ☎ 51 51 26 00, ⓦ hihostels.no. In a modern block attached to the university hospital, this all-year HI hostel has self-catering facilities, a laundry and a café. Most of the rooms are en-suite singles or doubles, but there are six-bunk dorms with shared facilities. The hostel is located about 2km south of the train/bus station – a 20min walk or take bus #4 or #11 and ask to be dropped. Dorms 295kr, doubles 900kr

## EATING

The centre of Stavanger's **restaurant** scene is down by the harbour, where a gaggle of places line up along Skagen and neighbouring Skagenkaien, though there is another concentration of more boho places along Øvre Holmegate, a short walk away. Culinary standards vary enormously, so it pays to be a little picky.

**Fisketorget** Strandkaien ☎ 51 52 73 50, ⓦ fisketorget -stavanger.no. Well, you won't escape the tourists if you eat at this café-restaurant, which occupies a good-looking and conspicuous glassy structure at the head of the harbour – and shares its premises with a fishmonger. But, there again, the *Fisketorget* has the widest selection of seafood in town from monkfish through to Arctic char with mains from around 250kr. Mon–Sat 11am–10pm.

**Nero** Øvre Holmegate 8 ☎ 51 55 21 19, ⓦ restaurant -nero.no. Well-turned-out Italian restaurant where they make good use of local ingredients – from rhubarb to cheese and seafood. The menu is creative and imaginative – and a three-course set meal costs 600kr. Tues–Sat 6pm–1am.

**Sjøhuset Skagen** Skagenkaien 13 ☎ 51 89 51 80, ⓦ sjohusetskagen.no. Good-quality seafood restaurant in an attractive and brightly painted old harbourside building with an interior which is partly antique, part reproduction. Main courses average 250kr – the oven-baked pollock is particularly tasty. Mon–Sat 11.30am–11pm, Sun 1–9pm.

**Thai Cuisine** Kirkegata 41 ☎ 51 86 07 88, ⓦ thaicuisine .no. Sociable and very popular restaurant in trim modern premises that serves the best Thai food in Stavanger. The menu, which covers all the classics and then some, has main courses from around 260kr. Mon–Fri 11am–11pm, Sat noon–11pm & Sun 2–11pm.

## DRINKING AND NIGHTLIFE

Stavanger is lively at night, particularly at weekends when a rum assortment of oil workers, sailors, fishermen, executives, tourists and office workers gathers in the **bars** on or near the harbour to live (or rather drink) it up. Most places stay open until 2am or later, with rowdy – but usually amiable – boozers lurching from one bar to the next.

★ **Bøker og Børst** Øvre Holmegate 32 ☎ 51 86 04 76, ⓦ bokerogborst.no. Charming café-bar where the decor really does set the tone – from the vintage posters and Oriental bric-a-brac through to the jam-packed bookshelves that seem to fill out every spare corner. There's a pavement terrace at the front and a mini-courtyard at the back plus an oh-so-relaxing soundtrack. The drinks – both soft and alcoholic – are the main event, but they do sell snacks and there are live gigs here too. Daily 9/10am–2am.

**Café Sting** Valberget 3 ☎ 94 84 67 89, ⓦ cafesting.no. At the top of Skagen, next to the Valbergtårnet tower, this laidback café-bar attracts a youthful, vaguely arty crew. The food is filling and inexpensive, there's a pleasant albeit small pavement terrace, and the place doubles as an art gallery and live music venue, hosting anything from indie to rock. Mon–Wed 11am–midnight, Thurs–Sat 11am–1am, Sun 1pm–midnight.

**Cardinal** Skagen 21 ☎ 98 20 42 01, ⓦ cardinal.no. One of the best pubs in town with a dark and antique interior, a long wooden bar and a first-rate range of ales, both in bottle and

on draught. Rammed at the weekend – quite rightly so. Sun–Thurs 3pm–1.30am, Fri & Sat noon–1.30am.

**Hall Toll** Skansegata 2 ☎ 51 51 72 32, ⓦ hall-toll.no. Down at the far end of the harbour, in the capacious former toll house, this restaurant-cum-bar and club is one of the busiest places in town. The restaurant is pretty average, but the bar does a good line in cocktails and beers, as does the club. Bar: Mon–Sat 5pm–1.30am; club: Fri & Sat 10pm–3am.

**Hansen Hjørnet** Skagen 18 ☎ 51 89 52 80, ⓦ hansen hjornet.com. When the sun is out, this harbourside café-bar has the prettiest outside terrace in town – decorated with flowers and protected by a windbreak – though you my struggle to find an empty chair. Mon–Sat 11am–midnight, Sun 1–11pm.

**Taket Nattklubb** Nedre Strandgate 13 ☎ 51 84 37 01, ⓦ herlige-stavanger.no. The best club in town, strong on house music with great cocktails too; don't be surprised if you have to queue. It's located a few metres west of Torget. Wed–Sun midnight–3.30am.

---

### THE KYSTVEGEN: STAVANGER TO BERGEN

With great ingenuity, Norway's road builders have cobbled together the **E39** coastal road, the **Kystvegen** (Ⓦ kystvegen.no), which traverses the west coast from Stavanger to Bergen and ultimately Trondheim with eight ferry trips breaking up the journey. The first part of the trek, the 210km (5hr) haul up from Stavanger to Bergen, includes two ferry trips and sees the highway slipping across a string of islands, which provide a pleasant introduction to the scenic charms of western Norway – and hint at the sterner beauty of the fjords beyond. Perhaps surprisingly, this region is primarily agricultural: the intricacies of the shoreline, together with the prevailing westerlies, make the seas so treacherous that locals mostly stuck to the land, eking out a precarious existence from the thin soils that had accumulated on the leeward sides of many of the islands.

---

### ENTERTAINMENT

**SF Kino Stavanger** Kulturhus, Sølvberggata 2 Ⓣ51 51 07 00, Ⓦsfkino.no. Stavanger has several cinemas and this one, inside the Kulturhus, is one of the handiest. Shows the latest blockbusters, both international and Scandinavian.

**Stavanger Konserthus** Sandvigå 1 Ⓣ51 53 70 00 (box office), Ⓦstavanger-konserthus.no. The city's concert hall hosts regular performances by visiting artists, from pop to classical and theatre, and is home to the Stavanger Symphony Orchestra (Ⓦsso.no). It's located north of the centre, on the waterfront just beyond the main cruise-ship terminal.

### SHOPPING

**Vinmonopolet** Lars Hertevigs gate 6. State-run liquor and wine outlet in the Straensenteret shopping centre, just west of Torget. Mon–Fri 10am–6pm, Sat 10am–3pm.

### DIRECTORY

**Left luggage** Coin-operated lockers at the Fiskepiren terminal (Mon–Fri 6.30am–11.15pm, Sat 6.30am–8pm, Sun 8am–10pm); at the train station (Sun–Fri 6am–11pm, Sat 6am–6pm); and at the bus station (daily 7am–10pm).

**Pharmacy** Among many, there is a Vitusapotek at Olav V's gate 11 (Mon–Fri 8.30am–11pm, Sat 9am–11pm, Sun & hols 11am–9pm).

**Post office** The main post office is on Lars Hertevigs gate, just a few metres from Haakon VII's gate (Mon–Fri 9am–6pm & Sat 10am–3pm).

# Around Stavanger: Lysefjord and Preikestolen

Stavanger sits on the east side of a long promontory that pokes a knobbly head north towards the **Boknafjord**, whose wide waters form a deep indentation in the coast and lap against a confetti of islets and islands. To the east of Stavanger, longer, narrower fjords drill far inland, the most diverting being the blue-black **Lysefjord**, famous for its precipitous cliffs and an especially striking rock formation, the **Preikestolen**. This distinctive 25m-square table of rock boasts a sheer 600m drop to the Lysefjord down below on three of its sides and is a popular tourist destination – indeed the popularity of both the Lysefjord and the Preikestolen has spawned a battery of Stavanger tour operators offering a mixed bag of cruises and hikes.

Getting to the trail-head for Preikestolen by ferry and bus is comparatively straightforward, but cruising the Lysefjord by ferry requires a little forethought – best with the help of Stavanger tourist office (see p.138), who sell the boat tickets. Note also that no matter what the publicity hype says, you do not get a decent view of **Preikestolen** from the waters of the Lysefjord.

## The Lysefjord: Stavanger to Lysebotn

Heading out from the Fiskepiren dock in Stavanger, **Lysefjord car ferries** (see opposite) chop through raggle-taggle islands before turning into the **Lysefjord** between **Oanes**, on its northern shore, and **Forsand** to the south. Before long the ferry passes the base of Preikestolen (see p.142), though from this angle the rock hardly makes any impression at all, and then proceeds to nudge on up the fjord with mighty cliffs to either side. Sometimes the ferry pauses at **Flørli**, one of several request stops, where a scattering of houses hugs the shore in sight of the old power station – the new one is actually inside the mountain. A remarkably long wooden stairway leads up the mountainside here and, even more remarkably, the occasional visitor gets off the boat to clamber up it.

### Lysebotn

**Lysebotn**, at the far end of the Lysefjord, is the neatest of villages, a tiny little place built to house hydroelectric workers in the middle of the twentieth century. It's also extremely popular with base-jumpers, who hunker down here before heading off into the mountains nearby, and is home to a pleasant **hostel** (see below).

## Lysebotn to Stavanger via Øygardstøl and Kjerag

Leaving the Lysefjord behind, the narrow road up from **Lysebotn** (closed for much of the year; opens in June, weather depending) offers spectacular views as it wiggles and wriggles its way up the mountainside. Eventually, after 7km, just above the last hairpin, the road reaches **Øygardstøl**, where the roadside café has panoramic views back down towards the fjord. Øygardstøl is also the starting point for the **hiking trail** that leads west along the south side of the Lysefjord to **Kjerag**, an 11000m-high mountain whose most famous feature is the **Kjeragbolten**, a much-photographed boulder wedged between two cliff faces high above the ground. It's a tough route, so allow seven hours for the round trip – and steel your nerves for the dizzying drops down to the fjord below.

Beyond Øygardstøl, the road crosses a beautiful mountain plateau, a barren, treeless expanse of boulder and loch whose wide vistas are intercepted by the occasional cabin. Eventually, the road meets Hwy-45, which slices west between the bulging mountains of **Øvstabødal** on its way back to Stavanger.

### ARRIVAL AND TOURS

### THE LYSEFJORD

There are no roads along the length of the Lysefjord, so although the fjord can be reached by car at three points – one at the west end, one at the east and one in the middle – you'll need to take a **boat trip** to appreciate its full dimensions.

**By car ferry** A car ferry-cum-Hurtigbåt express boat runs from the Fiskepiren terminal in Stavanger to Lysebotn, at the far end of the Lysefjord; advance booking is essential if you are taking your own vehicle (1–3 daily except Sat; 1hr 40min; passengers 90kr, car and driver 370kr; ⓦ kolumbus .no) and can be made at Stavanger tourist office (see p.138). From Lysebotn, drivers can head off into the mountains and/ or return to Stavanger, whereas foot passengers are often obliged to hang around Lysebotn and then come back along the same route, which can be a bit of a drag: check to see if there are connecting/onward buses from Lysebotn before you embark.

**By express boat** The fastest trips along the Lysefjord are by Hurtigbåt passenger express boat (May, June & Sept 2 daily; July & Aug 3 daily; Oct–April Wed–Sun 1 daily; 3hr; 480kr; ⓣ 51 89 52 70, ⓦ rodne.no), but these round-trip excursions, which depart from Stavanger's Skagenkaien,

only go halfway up along the Lysefjord and the views from the boat are not nearly as good as they are from the car ferry. **By tourist ferry** Among several operators, Norled (ⓣ 51 86 87 00, ⓦ norled.no) offers ferry cruises from Stavanger's Skagenkaien to the Lysefjord and back, but again they only go halfway up the Lysefjord (June–Aug 1 daily; 2hr 30min; 420kr).

**Cruise and hiking tours** Among many options, Rodne's (ⓣ 51 89 52 70, ⓦ rodne.no) "Kjerag Cruise & Hike" excursion (late June to late Aug Sat & Sun 1 daily; 12hr; 1400kr) includes the ferry trip from Stavanger's Skagenkaien to Lysebotn, at the far end of the Lysefjord, followed by the dramatic hairpin bus ride up to Øygardstøl, the trail head for the (unguided) 3hr 30min hike to Kjerag mountain; later in the day, the bus departs Øygardstøl for the return journey to Stavanger. You can undertake this excursion the other way round too.

### ACCOMMODATION

**Lysefjorden Vandrerhjem** Lysebotn ⓣ 94 82 66 02, ⓦ hihostels.no. Housed in a pleasant, cabin-like modern building, this well-equipped hostel has a café, self-catering facilities, a common room and an outdoor area. There are 49 beds in 22 rooms, each with shower and toilet. Late May to Aug. Dorms **320kr**, doubles **970kr**

## Preikestolen

**Preikestolen** (Pulpit Rock), Lysefjord's most celebrated vantage point, offers superlative views, though on sunny summer days you'll be sharing them with lots of others. How much you enjoy it depends on your vertigo: the bold/foolhardy dangle the odd limb over the abyss, the more cautious stay away from the edge – and there are no fences or barriers. It's a **four-hour hike** there and back to Preikestolen along a clearly marked trail that begins at the car park at the end of the road, which is where you'll also find a hostel and a mountain lodge (see below). The first half of the hike is steep in parts and paved with uneven stones, while the second half – over bedrock – is a good bit easier. The change in elevation is 350m and you should take food and water; the hike is not feasible in winter unless you really know what you are doing.

### Alternative hikes from the Preikestolen car park

The DNT-affiliated Stavanger Turistforening (see p.138) have details of hikes around Preikestolen, and sell an excellent English-language hiking guide to the area

From the Preikestolen car park, a short sharp hike leads down to **Refsvatn**, a small lake encircled by a footpath which takes three hours to negotiate, passing birch and pine woods, marshes, narrow ridges and bare stretches of rock. The path also threads through **Torsnes**, an isolated farm that was inhabited until 1962. The lake footpath connects with a rough path that careers down to the **Refsa quay** down on the Lysefjord.

### ARRIVAL AND DEPARTURE
PREIKESTOLEN

**By ferry and car** To get to Preikestolen by car, take the ferry east from Stavanger's Fiskepiren terminal to Tau (every 40min–1hr; 40min; passengers 52kr, car and driver 155kr; ⓦ norled.no) and then drive south along Hwy-13 until, after about 14km, you reach the signed side-road leading to Preikestolen. Parking costs 160kr.

**By ferry and bus** During the summer, connecting buses link the Stavanger–Tau ferry with the Preikestolen car park (mid-March to mid-May 4 daily; mid-May to mid-Sept every 40min to 1hr; 35min). A return bus ticket costs 175kr – the ferry is extra (see above). Timetables are available from Stavanger tourist office or online at ⓦ pulpitrock.no.

### ACCOMMODATION

**Preikestolen Vandrerhjem** Preikestolveien ☎ 51 74 20 74, ⓦ hihostels.no. Right by the Preikestolen car park, this first-rate HI hostel perches high on the hillside with great views over the surrounding mountains. Built on the site of an old mountain farm, it comprises a small complex of turf-roofed lodges, each of which has a spick-and-span pine interior. There are self-catering facilities, and a café serving breakfasts, lunches and simple evening meals; reservations are advised as the place is popular with school groups. Offers a mix of dorm beds and two- to four-bunk rooms with shared facilities. Mid-April to Sept. Dorms **300kr**, doubles **760kr**

**Preikestolenfjellstue** Preikestolveien ☎ 51 74 20 74, ⓦ preikestolenfjellstue.no. Operated by the Stavanger branch of DNT, the Norwegian hiking association, this large and comfortable mountain lodge is a handsome wood and glass structure that blends in well with its environs. It's well equipped too, with a restaurant and spacious common areas. The rooms, all of which are en suite, are priced according to the view – those offering panoramic views are the most expensive, about 200kr more than those looking out into the forest. It's located close to the Preikestolen car park, and there are substantial discounts (20 percent) for YHA and DNT members. March–Dec. **1320kr**

# Haugesund

There's no overpowering reason to break your journey between Stavanger and Bergen, but **HAUGESUND**, a lively industrial town 85km north of Stavanger, via the E39 and the Mortavika–Arsvågen ferry, has its moments. Now a major player in the North Sea oil industry, Haugesund once thrived on its herring fisheries, whose whopping profits funded the large and imposing, early twentieth-century stone buildings that dot **Smedasundet** as it runs alongside the harbour. Indeed, strolling the harbour is a pleasant way to spend an hour or so and afterwards you can take a peek at the tumbling water fountains of **Torggata**, just up from the harbour, which lead up to the town's prettiest church, **Vår Frelsers Kirke** (no fixed opening hours; ☎52 80 95 00), a slender brick affair of 1901 whose neo-Gothic design is enlivened by some *Jugendstil* flourishes. Otherwise, specific sights are thin on the ground, though Haugesund does do well for festivals, including the **Sildajazz Festival** (ⓦsildajazz.no) and the first-rate **Norwegian International Film Festival** (ⓦfilmfestivalen.no), both of which are held in August. The town's other claim to fame is as the hometown of the baker Edward Mortenson, who emigrated to the US, where he (almost certainly) fathered Norma Jean, otherwise **Marilyn Monroe (1926–62).**

**2**

# Haraldshaugen

The first ruler of a united Norway, **Harald Hårfagre** (Harald Fair Hair; c.880–930), is thought to have been buried up along the coast just 2km north of Haugesund – and a grand granite obelisk, the **Haraldshaugen**, now marks his presumed resting place, in workaday suburban surroundings just off Hwy-47. Hårfagre defeated a coalition of local chieftains at the battle of Hafrsfjord just south of Stavanger in about 885, thereby cementing his control of the fjordland, an achievement that apparently released him from a ten-year vow not to cut his hair. In a nationalist flush, the Norwegians erected the Haraldshaugen monument to celebrate Hårfagre in 1872, but very little is known about Hårfagre's rule or the extent of his real power. The most detailed evidence comes from the sagas, which insist that Harald "kept a sharp eye on the landed men and rich farmers", so much so that many fled west to settle in Iceland and the Faroes, though this does not entirely match with the facts – the move west began earlier.

## ARRIVAL AND INFORMATION

HAUGESUND

**By plane** Haugesund's pocket-sized international airport is some 14km southwest of the centre. From the airport, there is a regular Flybussen service to Haugesund (30min; 90kr one-way, 140kr return; ⓦflybussen.no), with departure times linked to flight arrivals.

**By bus** Long-distance buses pull into Haugesund bus station, beside Hwy-47 and an inconvenient 15min walk from the harbourfront. The taxi fare from the station to the harbour is about 80kr. Nor-Way Bussekspress (ⓦnor-way .no) currently operates two useful long-distance services, the Kystbussen (#400) up and down the west coast and the Haukeliekspressen (#180) to points east and Oslo.

Destinations Bergen (every 1–2hr; 3hr 15min); Oslo

(3 daily; 9hr); Stavanger (every 1–2hr; 2hr).

**By car** Haugesund is 15km west of the main coastal road, the E39. Moving on from Haugesund, drivers can either continue north on the E39 to Bergen (see box, p.140), or branch off northeast along the E134 towards either Odda (see p.213) and the Hardangerfjord (see p.211) or Oslo via the wild and woolly Haukelifjell mountain pass.

**Tourist office** Haugesund tourist office is in a lemon-painted building one block from the main harbour at Strandgata 171 (May–Aug Mon–Fri 9am–5pm, Sat & Sun 10am–3pm; Sept–April Mon–Fri 10am–4.30pm; ☎52 01 08 30, ⓦvisithaugesund.no).

## ACCOMMODATION

**Clarion Collection Hotel** Amanda Smedasundet 93 ☎52 80 82 00, ⓦnordicchoicehotels.com. On the main harbourfront, this medium-sized hotel occupies a good-looking, early twentieth-century stone building; the rooms are large and comfortable, and have benefited from a recent upgrade. An evening buffet meal is included in the

price on weekdays. There's a sauna, steam room and bike rental too. **1400kr**

**Scandic Haugesund** Kirkegata 166 ☎21 61 41 00, ⓦscandichotels.com. Smart, standard-issue chain hotel in an ultramodern block a short walk back from the harbourfront. Good breakfasts and gym facilities. **1000kr**

## EATING AND DRINKING

**Lothes Mat & Vinhus** Skippergata 4 ☎52 71 22 01, ⓦlothesmat.no. The pick of the town's several restaurants, located in a cosy huddle of old timber buildings just up from the harbourfront. The wide-ranging menu features a whole raft of Norwegian favourites, with main courses

costing in the region of 300kr. When the kitchen closes at night, the place morphs into a bar. Restaurant: Tues–Sat 6–10pm; bar: Mon–Thurs 11am–11pm, Fri & Sat 11am–1am, Sun 2–9pm.

# Central Norway

*DALEN HOTEL*

# Central Norway

Preoccupied by the fjords and the long road to Nordkapp, few tourists are tempted to explore central Norway. The Norwegians know better. This great chunk of land, trapped between Sweden and the western fjords, boasts some of the country's finest scenery, with the forested dales that trail north and west from Oslo heralding the region's mountain passes and rearing peaks. And among much else, it's here, within shouting distance of the country's principal train line and the E6 – long the main line of communication between Oslo, Trondheim and the north – that you'll find three of Norway's prime hiking areas. These comprise a trio of mountain ranges, each partly contained within a national park – from south to north, Jotunheimen, Rondane and the Dovrefjell-Sunndalsfjella.

**3**

There are **four main highways** running from Oslo and its environs to the western fjords. Whichever one you choose, allow a little time to appreciate the scenery and to muse on the ingenuity of Norway's road builders – and the difficulty of communication before they went to work: until well into the 1970s, a trip to Oslo from many a fjordland village could take at least a couple of days. Among these four major highways, the **E6** is the busiest, first running up to **Lake Mjøsa**, where you skip past the amenable little town of **Hamar** and ski-crazy **Lillehammer**, which is also home to one of the best of Norway's many open-air folk museums. Beyond is the **Gudbrandsdal valley**, where among a string of pint-sized towns, you'll find **Ringebu stave church**, the burial mounds of **Hundorp**, and **Sjoa**, a centre for whitewater rafting. The valley is also within easy striking distance of a battery of **national parks**, most notably Jotunheimen, Rondane and Dovrefjell-Sunndalsfjella. Of the three, **Jotunheimen** is the harshest and most stunning, with its string of icy, jagged peaks; the **Dovrefjell-Sunndalsfjella** is more varied with severe mountains in the west and open moors and rounded ridges in the east; while **Rondane**, a high alpine zone, has more accessible mountains and low vegetation. Each of the parks is equipped with well-maintained walking trails and DNT huts, two of which – **Rondvassbu** and **Gjendesheim** – are ideal for hiking expeditions deep into Rondane and Jotunheimen respectively. For Dovrefjell-Sunndalsfjella, the easiest place to start is **Kongsvoll**, on both the E6 and the train line. The E6 also passes reasonably near to the intriguing old copper-town of **Røros** and is the starting point for Hwy-15 and the E136, two magnificent roads that thread through the mountains to the fjords (see Chapter 4).

Alternatively, the **E16** is the most direct route to the fjords, a 350km yomp up the Valdres valley and over the Filefjell mountain pass to **Lærdal**, firmly in fjord country and at the start of the series of long **tunnels** that enable the E16 to fast-track west to Flåm (see p.226) and ultimately Bergen. The long lakes and wooded hills of the **Valdres valley** make for a delightful drive and on the way you'll shoot past several

# Highlights

**❶ Whitewater rafting, Sjoa** Brave some of
Norway's most exciting whitewater-rafting on
the River Sjoa. **See p.160**

**❷ Lake Gjende** A boat trip along one of
Norway's most beautiful lakes provides a scenic
introduction to the mighty Jotunheimen
mountains. **See p.163**

**❸ Hike the Besseggen ridge** Norway at its
wildest: sample the magnificent scenery of
the Jotunheimen Nasjonalpark on this classic
walk, one of the country's most celebrated. **See
box, p.165**

**❹ Kongsvold Fjeldstue** This lovely hotel
occupies a tastefully restored complex of old

timber buildings, and is convenient for
exploring the Dovrefjell-Sunndalsfjella National
Park. **See p.169**

**❺ Borgund stave church** One of the best
preserved and most harmonious of Norway's
remaining stave churches: admire the intricacy
of its construction and the intimacy of its
decoration. **See p.174**

**❻ Kongsberg** This amenable little town is
home to Norway's most imposing Baroque
church. **See p.178**

**❼ Dalen Hotel** Immaculately restored 1890s
hotel in a quiet country town halfway between
Oslo and the western fjords. **See p.182**

**HIGHLIGHTS ARE MARKED ON THE MAP ON PP.148–149**

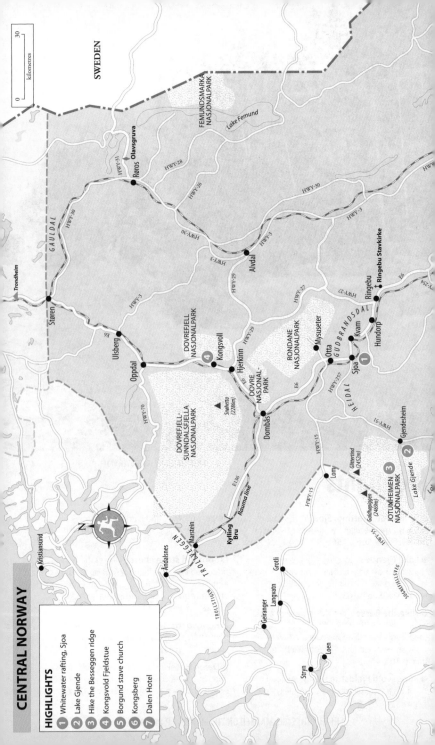

# CENTRAL NORWAY

## HIGHLIGHTS

1. Whitewater rafting, Sjoa
2. Lake Gjende
3. Hike the Besseggen ridge
4. Kongsvold Fjeldstue
5. Borgund stave church
6. Kongsberg
7. Dalen Hotel

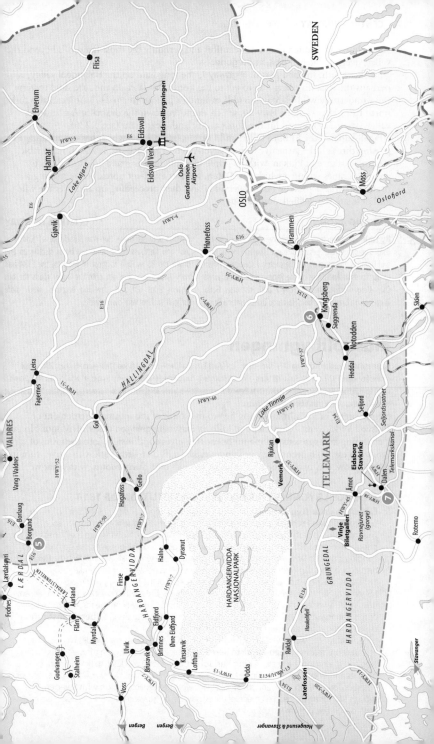

**stave churches**, though the most beautiful and certainly the most famous is beyond the valley, over the Filefjell pass, at **Borgund**.

Further south, the first part of **Highway 7**, the long haul up the **Hallingdal valley**, is perhaps the least diverting way to get to the fjords, but later on the road does traverse the wonderfully wild Hardangervidda mountain plateau (see p.217). You can also fork north from Hwy-7 along **Hwy-50**, which thunders down the dramatic Aurlandsdal valley (see p.227) bound for the fjords at Aurland, near Flåm (see p.226).

Finally, there's the **E134** to Odda and Lofthus (see p.215), which has the advantage of passing through the attractive former silver-town of **Kongsberg**, is within reasonable striking distance of **Rjukan**, with its prime wartime museum and adventure sports, and also comes within a whisker of **Dalen**, with its excellent hotel, before making a dramatic defile across the Hardangervidda and then proceeding up and over the wild and desolate **Haukelifjell mountain pass**.

## GETTING AROUND                                                            CENTRAL NORWAY

**By train** Two main train-lines traverse central Norway: the Oslo–Trondheim line passes through Hamar, Lillehammer and Dombås, the junction for the superbly scenic run down to the fjords at Åndalsnes on the Rauma branch line, while Oslo–Bergen trains shadow Hwy-7 until just after Geilo. There's also a branch line from Hamar to Trondheim via Røros.

**By bus** Between them, Nor-Way Bussekspress (ⓦ nor-way .no) and Nettbuss (ⓦ nettbuss.no) buses shuttle up and down the E6 as well as most of the E16, the E134 and Hwy-7, but once you get onto the minor roads the bus system thins out and travelling becomes much more difficult without your own vehicle.

# Eidsvollbygningen

House and visitor centre: May–Aug daily 10am–5pm; Sept–April Tues–Fri 10am–3pm, Sat & Sun 11am–4pm • House: 125kr; visitor centre: free • ☎ 63 92 22 10, ⓦ eidsvoll1814.no • Eidsvollbygningen is 2km off the E6 – just follow the signs; it's also about 1.5km (20min walk) from Eidsvoll Verk train station: trains run to Eidsvoll Verk from Oslo S (every 30min; 30min) and Hamar (every 30min; 1hr; change at Eidsvoll). You can check train timetables on ⓦ nsb.no

Sitting pretty in a semirural setting just to the south of the industrial settlement of Eidsvoll Verk, about 70km north of Oslo, is **Eidsvollbygningen** (Eidsvoll Manor House), a charming and spacious old manor house that gives a real insight into the tastes of Norway's early nineteenth-century upper class. In its own little park with a river running down below, this two-storey timber house has just over thirty rooms, with what were

---

### EIDSVOLLBYGNINGEN AND THE CONSTITUTION OF 1814

Eidsvoll Verk's **Carsten Ankers** (1747–1824) was a close friend and ally of the Danish crown prince **Christian Frederik**, a connection that has given the village national importance. Towards the end of the Napoleonic Wars, the Russians and the British insisted the Danes be punished for their alliance with the French, and proposed taking Norway from Denmark and handing it over to Sweden. In an attempt to forestall these territorial shenanigans, the Danes dispatched Christian Frederik to Norway, where he set up home in Carsten Ankers' house in 1813, and proceeded to lobby for local support. In April of the following year more than a hundred of Norway's leading citizens gathered here near **Eidsvoll** to decide whether to accept union with Sweden or go for independence with Christian Frederik on the throne. The majority of this National Assembly chose independence, and set about drafting a **liberal constitution** based on those of France and the United States.

Predictably, the Swedes would have none of this. Four years earlier, the Swedes had picked one of Napoleon's marshals, **Jean-Baptiste Bernadotte** (see p.70), to succeed their previous king who had died without an heir. As **King Karl Johan**, Bernadotte was keen to flex his military muscles and, irritated by the putative National Assembly, he invaded Norway in July 1814. Frederik was soon forced to abdicate and the Norwegians were pressed into **union with Sweden**, though Karl Johan did head off much of the opposition by guaranteeing the Norwegians a new constitution and parliament, the Stortinget.

once the owners' living areas on the first floor, beneath the servants' quarters and above the basement kitchens. The main entrance hall is in the Neoclassical style much favoured by the Dano-Norwegian elite, its columns a suitably formal introduction to the spacious suites that lie beyond. The library is well stocked, and there's a billiard room and a smoking room, as well as a string of elegant dining rooms and bedrooms. Oriental knick-knacks and English furniture appear throughout, and the occasional mural depicts Greek mythological figures. There's also an obsession with symmetry: doors were camouflaged and false windows created to avoid breaking up the architectural regularity whenever it was threatened. The house was owned by the **Ankers family**, who made their money from the local ironworks – hence the splendid cast-iron stoves.

It's a delightful ensemble, but the house owes much of its present appearance – perhaps even its survival – to its historical significance (see box opposite) rather than its aesthetics. One of the family, Carsten Ankers, converted the upper storey of his home into premises for the **National Assembly**, comprising a handful of administrative offices plus the Room for the Constitutional Committee, where the original wooden benches have survived along with various landscape paintings. There's a rusticated modesty to it all which is really rather lovely, and a painting of Venus has been put back in the room after years of being shunted up and down the adjoining corridors: after prolonged discussion, it had originally been removed because the representatives considered it an erotic distraction. For more on the evolution of democracy in general and the Norwegian Constitution in particular, drop by the **visitor centre** just down from the house near the river.

# Hamar

Easy-going **HAMAR** is a pleasant if undemanding town of 30,000 inhabitants that sits about halfway along the eastern shore of **Lake Mjøsa** around 130km from Oslo. There was an important settlement here in medieval times, but today's town was founded – almost refounded – as a lakeside trading centre in the 1840s and consequently its centre rustles up a scattering of substantial **nineteenth-century buildings**, including a large and really rather imposing train station. It's easy to unwind here in Hamar, which is at its prettiest in the little **park** in between Strandgata and the railway embankment that separates the town centre from the lakeshore. In the summertime, Hamar is a good place to join the *Skibladner*, a vintage paddle steamer that shuttles across Lake Mjøsa (see box, p.153); but the main sight is the **Hedmarksmuseet**, which incorporates the ruins of a medieval cathedral and an open-air museum of relocated old buildings.

## Hedmarksmuseet

Domkirkeodden, Strandvegen • Late May to late June Tues–Sun 10am–4pm; late June to mid-Aug daily 10am–5pm; late Aug Tues–Sun 10am–4pm • 110kr • ☏ 62 54 27 00, ⊕ hedmarksmuseet.no • The most scenic approach to the museum is along the lakeshore footpath that stretches 2km north from the train station

Unlikely though it may seem today, Hamar was once the seat of an important medieval bishopric, and the battered remains of its Romanesque-Gothic **Domkirke** (Cathedral), now protected by a glass and steel superstructure – the Hamardomen – are stuck out on the Domkirkeodden (Cathedral Point), a low, leafy headland about 2km west of the centre. The cathedral is thought to have been built by the "English pope" Nicholas Breakspear, who spent a couple of years in Norway as the papal legate before becoming Adrian IV in 1154, but the building, along with the surrounding episcopal complex, was ransacked during the Reformation, and local road-builders subsequently helped themselves to the stone. The cathedral ruins are part of the rambling **Hedmarksmuseet** (Hedmark Museum), which also contains an archeological section, the remains of the bishop's palace, a display of vintage photographs of Hamar and its surroundings, and

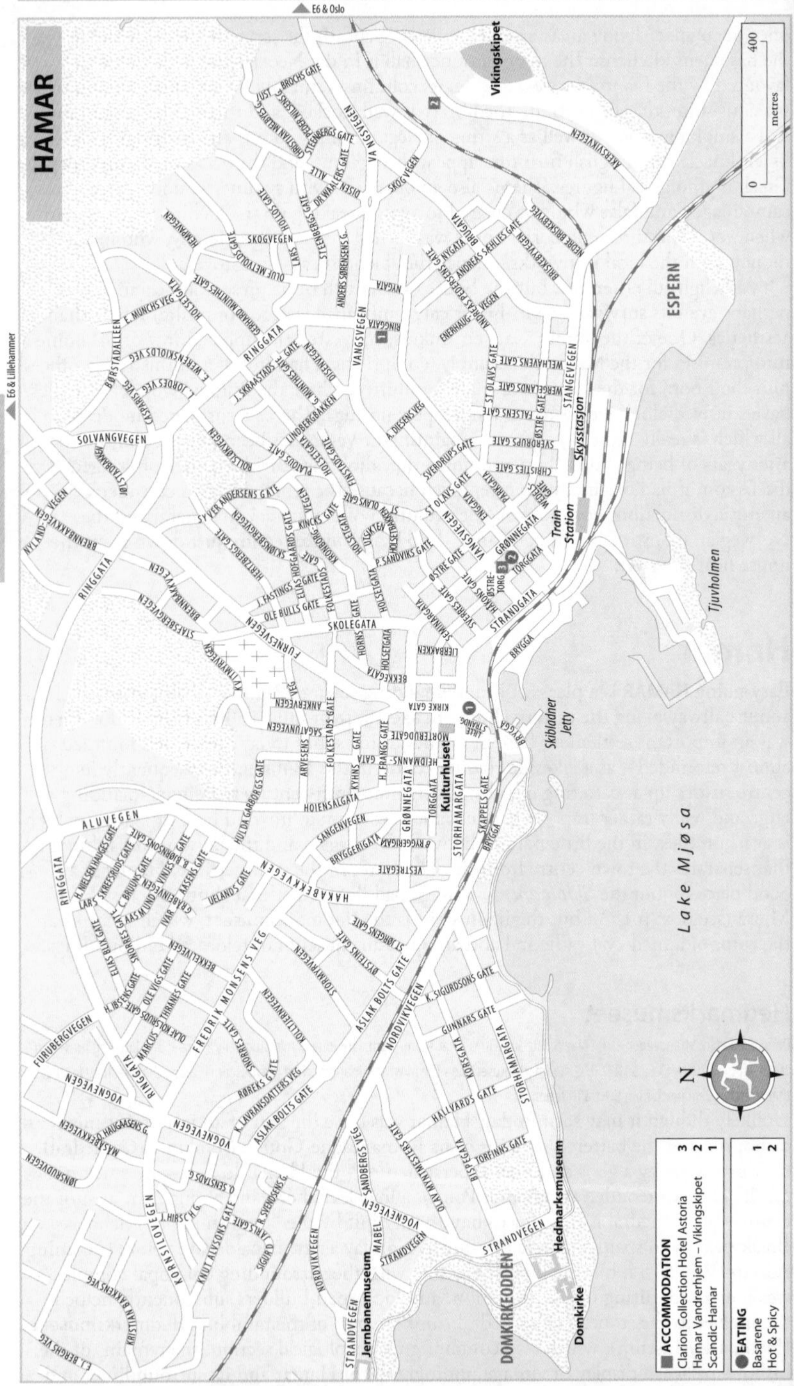
HAMAR
E6 & Oslo
E6 & Lillehammer
0
400
metres
Vikingskipet
ESPERN
Skysstasjon
Train Station
Tjuvholmen
Skibladner Jetty
Lake Mjøsa
Kulturhuset
Hedmarksmuseum
Domkirke
DOMKIRKEODDEN
Jernbanemuseum
ACCOMMODATION
Clarion Collection Hotel Astoria 3
Hamar Vandrerhjem – Vikingskipet 2
Scandic Hamar 1
EATING
Basarene 1
Hot & Spicy 2
RINGGATA
VANGSVEGEN
STRANDGATA
GRØNNEGATA
TORGGATA
SKOLEGATA
FURNESVEGEN
ALUVEGEN
HAKABEKKVEGEN
ASLAK BOLTS GATE
NORDVIKVEGEN
STORHAMARGATA
STRANDVEGEN
VOGNEVEGEN
FREDRIK MONSENS VEG
SOLVANGVEGEN
SKOGVEGEN
STANGEVEGEN
AKERSVIKVEGEN
BRYGGA
ST OLAVS GATE
KIRKE GATA
N

## DS SKIBLADNER

Hamar is as good a place as any to pick up the vintage **paddle steamer**, the DS *Skibladner* (☎61 14 40 80, ⓦskibladner.no), which shuttles up and down **Lake Mjøsa** during the summer offering wide views over rolling forested hills to east and west. Travellers heading north may find the trip to Lillehammer tempting at first sight, but the lake is not particularly scenic, and after four hours on the boat you may well feel like jumping overboard. The best bet is to take the shorter ride to Eidsvoll instead.

Sailings run from late June to mid-August. On Tuesdays, Thursdays and Saturdays the boat makes the return trip across the lake from Hamar to **Gjøvik** and on up to **Lillehammer** (7hr 30min); on Wednesdays, Fridays and Sundays it chugs south to **Eidsvoll** and back (6hr); there's no Monday service. Sailing times are available direct or at any local tourist office. **Tickets** are bought on board with the one-way fare from Hamar to Lillehammer costing 250kr, 210kr to Eidsvoll; return fares cost 150kr extra. In Hamar, the *Skibladner* jetty is handily located about 600m to the west of the train station along the lakeshore; in Lillehammer, it's on the west side of the lake, across the bridge from the town centre, beside the E6.

**3**

an open-air museum. The latter holds around sixty buildings collected from across the region and, although it's not as comprehensive as the one in Lillehammer (see p.155), it does contain several particularly fine buildings, the oldest of which are clustered in the Hedmarkstunet section.

## ARRIVAL AND DEPARTURE · HAMAR

**By train** Hamar train station is near the lakeshore at the southeast corner of the downtown grid. It's on the main train-line north between Oslo and Trondheim and is also the starting point of a branch line that leads to Røros (see p.169) – and ultimately Trondheim – a fine ride over hills and through huge forests. Timetables on ⓦnsb.no.
Destinations Lillehammer (hourly; 45min); Oslo (hourly; 1hr 30min); Oslo Gardermoen (hourly; 1hr); Røros (3–4

daily; 3hr 30min); Trondheim (3–4 daily; 5hr 25min).
**By bus** Local buses pull into Hamar Skysstasjon, a couple of minutes' walk to the east of the train station. Long-distance buses mostly stop on the edge of town at the Nydal Statoil exchange – take a taxi.
Destinations Oslo (1–2 daily; 1hr 40min); Oslo Gardermoen (1–2 daily; 1hr); Otta (1–2 daily; 3hr 20min); Trondheim (1–2 daily; 7hr).

## ACCOMMODATION

**Clarion Collection Hotel Astoria** Torggata 23 ☎62 70 70 00, ⓦnordicchoicehotels.com. Plumb in the centre of town, with its best rooms overlooking the main square, this medium-sized and noticeably friendly chain hotel is decorated in bright and cheerful colours. There are substantial breakfasts. 1100kr
**Hamar Vandrerhjem – Vikingskipet** Åkersvikvegen 24 ☎62 52 60 60, ⓦhihostels.no. Hamar's all-year HI hostel occupies a modern two-storey motel-style timber building about 1km east along the lakeshore from the train station. It's in the middle of nowhere, just across from the massive skating arena, the Vikingskipet, built for the 1994 Winter Olympics in

the shape of an upturned Viking longship. There's a café, a laundry and self-catering facilities. All the rooms are en suite. Dorms 410kr, doubles 880kr
**Scandic Hamar** Vangsvegen 121 ☎21 61 40 00, ⓦscandichotels.com. Located in a large modern block on the northeast edge of the town centre, this chain hotel may not be especially prepossessing from the outside, but the interior has been kitted out in a bright and well-conceived modern/minimalist style as have the spacious bedrooms, some of which – on the top floors – have wide views over town. The breakfasts here are first-rate too. 1000kr

## EATING

**Basarene** Storhamargata 2 ☎91 90 00 90, ⓦbasarene .no. In an attractive, low-slung, multi-arched older building, this large and popular restaurant-bar offers a short but well-chosen menu featuring the likes of pan-fried monkfish with tomato salsa (335kr). Also does a sideline in bar food – pizzas, burgers etc – and brews its own beers, which are best enjoyed on the lakeside terrace at the back. Tues–Sat

11am–3.30pm & 4.30–10pm, Sun noon–7pm.
**Hot & Spicy** Torggata 21, cnr Enggata ☎62 52 02 60, ⓦhotandspicy.no. Handily located in the centre of town, this cheerfully decorated Chinese/Thai restaurant is an informal, family-run place, where the service is fast and efficient and main courses are priced 150–190kr. Mon 5–9pm, Wed–Sat 3–11pm, Sun 2–10pm.

# Lillehammer and around

**LILLEHAMMER** (literally "Little Hammer"), 60km north of Hamar and 190km from Oslo, is Lake Mjøsa's largest settlement and, in winter, its most worthwhile destination. The town is one of Norway's top ski centres (see box opposite), its semirural lakeside setting and extensive cross-country ski trails contributing to its selection as host of the **1994 Olympic Winter Games**. The Lillehammer area is a popular summer holiday spot too. As soon as the weather picks up, hundreds of Norwegians hunker down in their second homes in the hills that flank the town, popping into the centre for a drink or a meal. Cycling, walking, fishing and canoeing are popular pastimes at this time of year, but however appealing the area may be to Norwegians, the countryside hereabouts has little of the wonderful wildness of other parts of Norway, and unless you're someone's guest or bring your own family, you'll probably feel rather out on a limb.

Lillehammer's compact **centre** does look a tad humdrum – especially as many of the shopkeepers seem to insist on putting plastic trolls outside their premises – but nevertheless the town is a convenient place to break your journey on the way to either Trondheim or the western fjords and there are three worthwhile attractions: the **Kunstmuseum** (Art Museum); **Maihaugen** open-air museum; and **Aulestad**, the country home of Norwegian author Bjørnstjerne Bjørnson, about thirty minutes' drive away. It's also one of the ports of call of the antique **DS Skibladner** paddle steamer as it shuttles up and down Lake Mjøsa (see box, p.153). **Orientation** couldn't be easier: pretty much everything that's happening is focused on the pedestrianized part of **Storgata**, which runs north from Bankgata to the tumbling River Mesnaelva, a five-minute stroll away; **Kirkegata**, another useful street, runs one block parallel to the west of Storgata (down the hill).

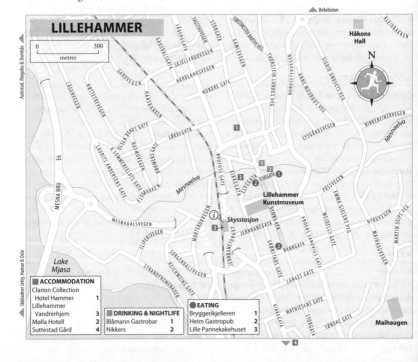

LILLEHAMMER

■ **ACCOMMODATION**
| Clarion Collection | |
| Hotel Hammer | 1 |
| Lillehammer | |
| Vandrerhjem | 3 |
| Mølla Hotell | 2 |
| Suttestad Gård | 4 |

■ **DRINKING & NIGHTLIFE**
| Blåmann Gastrobar | 1 |
| Nikkers | 2 |

● **EATING**
| Bryggerikjelleren | 1 |
| Heim Gastropub | 2 |
| Lille Pannekakehuset | 3 |

**LILLEHAMMER: WINTER ACTIVITIES**

In preparation for the 1994 Winter Olympics, the Norwegian government spent a massive two billion kroner on the town's **sporting facilities**, which are now among the best in the country. Spread along the hillsides above and near the town, they include several dozen downhill **ski trails** catering for everyone from beginner to expert, floodlit slopes for night skiing, ski-jumping towers and multiple chairlifts. There is also an **ice hockey** arena and a special stadium – the **Birkebeiner** – where cross-country skiers can hone their skills before setting off into the mountains, which are crisscrossed by 350km of trails. As you would expect, most Norwegians arriving here in winter come fully equipped, but it's possible to rent or buy equipment locally – the tourist office (see p.156) will advise, but note that advance booking is strongly recommended. A further possibility in both summer and winter is to have a go on the **bobsleigh and luge track** in Hunderfossen, about 15km north of Lillehammer along the E6 (☎61 05 42 00, ⊛olympiaparken.no); it's not for the faint-hearted (unsurprisingly), but there are various ways of negotiating the track with the least expensive costing just 250kr per person; reservations are required.

**3**

## Lillehammer Kunstmuseum

Stortorget 2, Kirkegata • Late June to mid-Aug daily 11am–5pm; mid-Aug to late June Tues–Sun 11am–4pm • 100kr; extra admission charge for temporary exhibitions • ☎ 61 05 44 60, ⊛ lillehammerartmuseum.com

Lillehammer's top-quality **Kunstmuseum** (Art Museum) is housed in two adjacent buildings – one a municipal structure from the 1960s, the other a newer, flashier building. The gallery is renowned for its temporary exhibitions, but the small permanent collection is also very worthwhile, comprising a representative sample of the works of most major Norwegian painters, from Johan Dahl and Christian Krohg to Munch and Erik Werenskiold. In particular, look out for the striking landscapes painted by one of the less familiar Norwegian artists, **Axel Revold** (1887–1962). A student of Matisse and an admirer of Cézanne, Revold spent years working abroad before returning home and applying the techniques he had learned to his favourite subject, northern Norway: his beautifully composed and brightly coloured *Nordland* is typical. Revold also dabbled in the bizarre, as in the bold Expressionism of *A Sailor's Dream*.

## Maihaugen

Maihaugvegen; Maihaugen is about 1.5km southeast of the town centre • June–Aug daily 10am–5pm; Sept– May Tues–Sun 11am–4pm • Frequent guided tours in summertime • 130kr, June–Aug 170kr; tours free • ☎ 61 28 89 00, ⊛ maihaugen.no • From Storgata, walk up Bankgata, turn right onto Maihaugenvegen, and keep going, following the signs (20min)

The much-vaunted **Maihaugen open-air folk museum**, on the southeast edge of town, is the largest of its type in northern Europe. Incredibly, the bulk of the collection represents the lifetime's work of one man, a magpie-ish dentist by the name of **Anders Sandvig** (1862–1950), who only ended up in Lillehammer by accident: he contracted tuberculosis and moved there from Oslo to recuperate in the clear mountain air. Since Sandvig's death, the collection has gradually been increased and Maihaugen now holds almost two hundred relocated buildings, brought here from all over the region and including several real treasures such as a charming seventeenth-century **presbytery** (*prestegårdshagen*) and a thirteenth-century **stave church** from Garmo. The museum has also attempted to widen its range, one recent addition being a **1970s house**.

During the summertime, **costumed guides** give the lowdown on traditional rural life and there's often the chance to have a go at domestic activities such as spinning, baking, weaving and pottery – good, wholesome fun. You can spend time too in the main **museum** building, which features temporary exhibitions on folkloric themes. Allow a good half-day for a visit and you might also want to take advantage of the English-language **guided tours** when they are scheduled.

## Maihaugen's farms

Maihaugen's key exhibits are two **farms**, one from **Bjørnstad**, the other **Øygarden**, both of which date from the late seventeenth century. Complete with their various outhouses and living areas, the two comprise 36 buildings, each with a specific function, such as food store, sheep-shed, hay barn, stable and bathhouse. This set-up may have worked, and it certainly looks quaint, but it was, in fact, forced upon farmers by their tried-and-tested method of construction, **laft**. Based on the use of pine logs notched together at right angles, the technique strictly limited the dimensions of every building, as the usable part of the pine tree was rarely more than 8m long. Indeed, it seems likely that many farmers would have preferred to keep their winter supplies in the main farmhouse rather than in a separate store, as implied by a draconian medieval law that stated, "When a man discovers another in his storehouse ... then he may kill the man if he so wishes."

# Aulestad

**3**

Aulestadvegen 6, 18km north of Lillehammer • Late May to Aug daily 10am–5pm; Sept to early Oct Sat & Sun 11am–4pm • 130kr • ☎ 95 45 12 07, ⓦ aulestad.no • By car, head north from Lillehammer on the E6 & turn onto Hwy-255 after about 4km; to get back onto the E6 heading north, follow Hwy-255 from the house, then turn onto Hwy-254, which brings you out on the E6 halfway between Lillehammer and Ringebu (see p.158)

Perched on a leafy knoll in the hamlet of **Follebu**, 18km north of Lillehammer, is **Aulestad**, a good-looking if somewhat sombre-looking villa that was home to **Bjørnstjerne Bjørnson** (see box below) from 1875 onwards. The house, which has been restored to its late nineteenth-century appearance, was gifted to the nation on the death of Bjørnstjerne's widow Karoline in 1934, and is jam-packed with family mementoes. A short film gives further details on the man and his times.

### ARRIVAL AND INFORMATION

**LILLEHAMMER AND AROUND**

**By train** The Skysstasjon, on Jernbanetorget, at the foot of Jernbanegata, incorporates the train station and the bus terminal. From here, it's just a couple of minutes' walk to the main drag, Storgata – just walk up the hill. Train timetables on ⓦ nsb.no.

Destinations Hamar (hourly; 45min); Oslo (hourly; 2hr); Oslo Gardermoen (hourly; 1hr 40min); Trondheim (3–4 daily; 4hr 30min).

**By bus** The bus station is in the Skysstasjon, in the same complex as the train station.

Destinations Bergen (1 daily; 9hr); Flåm (1 daily; 6hr); Oslo (1–2 daily; 2hr 30min); Oslo Gardermoen (1–2 daily;

2hr); Otta (1–2 daily; 2hr 30min); Sjoa (1–3 daily; 2hr); Stryn (1–2 daily; 6hr); Trondheim (1–2 daily; 6hr); Voss (1 daily; 7hr).

**By car** The E6 cuts along the lakeshore about 500m below – and to the west of – the town centre. Lillehammer's one-way system is befuddling, but once you have reached the city centre, on-street parking is (usually) easy to find.

**Tourist office** Lillehammer tourist office is in the Skysstasjon, on Jernbanetorget (mid-June to mid-Aug Mon–Fri 8am–6pm, Sat & Sun 10am–4pm; mid-Aug to mid-June Mon–Fri 8am–4pm, Sat 10am–2pm; ☎ 61 28 98 00, ⓦ lillehammer.com).

### ACCOMMODATION

**Clarion Collection Hotel Hammer** Storgata 108 ☎ 61 26 73 73, ⓦ nordicchoicehotels.com. Gallant and largely successful attempt by this large chain to create a hotel with a cosy, traditional feel – from the open fireplaces of the

---

### BJØRNSTJERNE BJØRNSON

**Bjørnstjerne Bjørnson** (1832–1910) was a major figure in the bourgeois literary and cultural revival that swept Norway at the end of the nineteenth century. Bjørnson made his name with the peasant tales of *Synnøve Solbakken* in 1857 and thereafter he churned out a veritable flood of novels, stories, poems and plays, many of which romanticized Norwegian country folk and, unusually for the time, were written in Norwegian, rather than the traditional Danish. He also championed all sorts of progressive causes, from Norwegian independence through to equality of the sexes and crofters' rights, albeit from a liberal (as distinct from leftist) viewpoint. Nowadays, however, his main claim to fame is as author of the poem that became the **national anthem**, *Ja, vi elsker dette landet* (Yes, we love this country).

public areas through to the retro, high-gabled facade. The rooms are well equipped and comfortable and set round a courtyard with the quieter ones to the rear. Just west of the centre, about 5min walk from the train station. Rates include an evening buffet meal. **1200kr**

**Lillehammer Vandrerhjem** Jernbanetorget 2 ☎61 26 00 24, ⓦhihostels.no. Spick-and-span, all-year HI hostel in the same block as the train station. It has a good range of facilities, from a self-catering kitchen and a daytime café through to free parking and common rooms. The guest rooms – eighty-odd bunk beds divided into thirty rooms – are fairly spartan, but they are perfectly adequate and all are en suite. Dorms **340kr**, doubles **890kr**

**Mølla Hotell** Elvegata 12 ☎61 05 70 80, ⓦmollahotell .no. This is Lillehammer's most distinctive hotel, occupying a centrally located, intelligently recycled nineteenth-century mill – a tall hunk of a building painted (perhaps rather unfortunately) in mustard yellow. The guest rooms are reassuringly comfortable and decorated in soft pastel shades. **1350kr**

**Suttestad Gård** Suttestådveien 17 ☎46 85 56 33, ⓦlillehammer.com. Large former farmhouse with five modern guest rooms, most of which are en suite and have pleasant views down towards the lake. *Suttestad Gård* is 1.5km south of the train station: take Kirkegata and Suttestådveien is a turning on the right. **800kr**

## EATING

In downtown Lillehammer, much of the **gastronomic** action – as well as the drinking – is focused towards the west end of pedestrianized **Storgata**, often to the sound of the River Mesna as it tumbles through town heading for Lake Mjøsa.

**Bryggerikjelleren** Elvegata 19 ☎61 27 06 60, ⓦbblillehammer.no. Smart and stylish restaurant-cum-bar in attractively decorated cellar premises. The big deal here are the steaks – well-cooked and well-prepared at around 360kr. A popular spot, so advance reservations are a good idea. Mon–Sat 6pm–midnight, Sun 3–10pm.

**Heim Gastropub** Storgata 84 ☎61 10 00 82, ⓦheim lillehammer.no. Bustling gastropub with a dark and

intimate interior. The excellent range of beers matched by an inviting menu, featuring such delights as bangers and mash (165kr) and *moules frites* (179kr). Mon–Fri 3pm–midnight, Sat noon–3am.

**Lille Pannekakehuset** Storgata 46 ☎91 99 30 52. Amenable downtown café with a small pavement terrace and a cosy interior. Tasty waffles and even better pancakes served every which way, from 80kr. Mon–Fri 10am–6pm, Sat 10am–4pm.

## DRINKING AND NIGHTLIFE

**Blåmann Gastrobar** Lilletorvet 1 ☎61 26 22 03, ⓦblaamann.com. One of the better spots in town, this large and popular bar and restaurant, just off the pedestrianized part of Storgata, has a leafy terrace suspended over the cascading river below. The food is average, but the drinks are good. Daily noon–11pm, Sun till 9pm.

**Nikkers** Elvegata 18 ☎61 24 74 30, ⓦnikkers.no. Spread over two premises on short and sweet Elvegata, *Nikkers* has a pretty routine restaurant in one building and a sports bar in the other, with nine large screens plus the gubbins for shuffleboard, darts and chess. There's a top-floor nightclub too, on Fridays and Saturdays. Bar: Mon–Wed 11am–11pm, Thurs–Sat 11am–3am, Sun 1–10pm.

# The Gudbrandsdal

Heading north from Lillehammer, the E6 and the railway leave the shores of Lake Mjøsa to run along the **Gudbrandsdal**, an appealing 160km-long river valley, which was for centuries the main route between Oslo and Trondheim. Enclosed by mountain ranges, the valley has a comparatively dry and mild climate, and its fertile soils have nourished a string of farming villages since Viking times. Even today, despite the thunderings of the E6, the Gudbrandsdal remains predominantly – and distinctly – rural and it holds several appealing attractions, particularly the cluster of old buildings and Viking burial mounds at Dale-Gudbrands gard in **Hundorp**.

## ARRIVAL AND DEPARTURE               THE GUDBRANDSDAL

**By train and bus** All the larger towns in the valley are accessible by train and bus, and at the smaller places where the trains don't stop the buses will. Long-distance express buses along the Gudbrandsdal currently include Nor-Way

Bussekspress's (ⓦnor-way.no) Lavprisekspressen (late June to late Aug 1 daily) and Nettbuss's (ⓦnettbuss.no) NX146 (2 daily).

## Ringebu stavkirke

Ringebu • Daily: late May to June & early to late Aug 9am–5pm; July 8am–6pm • 50kr, 80kr including Weidemannsamlingen (see below) •
ⓣ 61 28 27 00 • The church is 1km off the E6

Some 60km north of Lillehammer, the E6 swings past the turning to **Ringebu stavkirke** (Ringebu stave church), whose distinctive maroon spire stands on a hill a couple of kilometres south of Ringebu village. Dating from the thirteenth century, the original church was modified and enlarged in the 1630s, reflecting both an increase in the local population and the new religious practices introduced after the Reformation. At this time, the nave was broadened, the chancel replaced and an over-large tower and spire plonked on top. Today, the exterior is somewhat glum, but the western entrance portal sports some superb, if badly weathered, zoomorphic carvings from the original church. Inside, the highlights are mainly eighteenth-century Baroque – from the florid pulpit and altar panel through to a memorial to the Irgens family, complete with trumpeting cherubs and intricate ruffs.

## Weidemannsamlingen

Late May to mid-Aug Tues–Sun 10am–5pm • 50kr, 80kr including stave church

The old **vicarage** behind the church now holds the **Weidemannsamlingen** (Weidemann Exhibition), featuring forty-or-so paintings by the prolific **Jakob Weidemann** (1923–2001), one of Norway's most talented modern artists. Many of Weidemann's works were inspired by the Norwegian landscape, but he eschewed realism for deeply coloured abstract canvases of great emotional intensity. Curiously, it was Weidemann's eyesight – or rather the loss of it – which seems to have propelled him into abstraction: a member of the Resistance during World War II, he was blinded by an explosion and although he regained sight in his left eye, the experience left him keen to experiment with bold flashes of colour in a lyrical style that has had many Scandinavian admirers.

## Hundorp

The southern peripheries of the straggling village of **HUNDORP**, about 11km from Ringebu, hold **Dale-Gudbrands gard** (see opposite), comprising a neat little quadrangle of old timber buildings situated beside the E6 and serving as a combined educational and conference centre. The site has been settled since prehistoric times, its most famous occupant being the eponymous Viking warrior **Dalegudbrand**, who became a bitter enemy of St Olav after his enforced baptism in 1021. Evidence of Hundorp's long history is easy to spot as there are half a dozen small but distinct **Viking burial mounds**, as well as a rough circle of **standing stones** close to the conference centre. The stones, which date from around 700 AD, mark the spot where freemen gathered in the *allting* to discuss issues of local importance – such meetings were nearly always held in the open air. The most powerful local chieftain presided over the *allting* with the assistance of a "law speaker", who was able to recite existing law and memorize new decisions. Theoretically at least, it was one man, one vote, but in practice the more powerful landowners usually had their own way with the assembled freemen showing their consent by brandishing their weapons and/or banging on their shields. A **display board** in the gard's courtyard provides a general map of Hundorp, showing what is where, but it's rather hard to follow and the best bet is to take the grassy **track** that leads left from the farm entrance to the standing stones and the nearest burial mound. Thereafter, just follow your nose.

**ARRIVAL AND DEPARTURE**        **HUNDORP**

**By bus** There's no train station at Hundorp, but buses stop in front of the conference centre beside the E6. Timetables on ⓦ rutebok.no.

Destinations Kvam (1–4 daily; 30min); Lillehammer (1–4 daily; 1hr); Otta (1–4 daily; 1hr 30min).

## ACCOMMODATION

**Dale-Gudbrands gard** Hundorpgjeilen 12, Hundorp ☎ 91 15 89 38, ⓦ dalegudbrands-gard.no. The huddle of old timber houses that make up this conference centre holds twelve guest rooms, each of which is kitted out in a neat and trim modern style. The rooms may be a little uninspiring, but it's a lovely setting and a great place to unwind. **1450kr**

★ **Sygard Grytting** Sør-Fron ☎ 61 29 85 88, ⓦ grytting.com or ⓦ gryttingweb.wpengine.com. This ancient farmstead, overlooking the E6 about 6km north of the Hundorp conference centre, provides some of the region's most distinctive lodgings. Nestling among the orchards, the eighteenth-century farm buildings are in an

almost perfect state of preservation, a beautiful ensemble with the assorted barns, outhouses and the main house facing onto a tiny courtyard. An even older building, dating from the fourteenth century, houses dormitory accommodation – and was once used to shelter pilgrims on the long haul north to Trondheim cathedral. Most of the double rooms are in the main farmhouse, which has been superbly renovated to provide extremely comfortable lodgings amid antique furnishings, faded oil paintings and open fires. Breakfast is splendid too – the bread is baked on the premises – and dinner is available by prior arrangement (at 7pm; 560kr). July to mid-Aug. Dorms (without breakfast) **300kr**, doubles (with breakfast) **1260kr**

# Kvam

**KVAM**, about 20km north of Hundorp along the E6, is a modest chipboard-producing town that witnessed some of the worst fighting of World War II. Once the Germans had occupied Norway's main towns in the spring of 1940, they set about extending their control of the main roads and railways, marching up the Gudbrandsdal at the double. At Kvam, they were opposed by a scratch force of Norwegian and British soldiers, who delayed their progress for two weeks (April 14–30, 1940) despite being poorly equipped – the captain in charge of the British antitank guns had to borrow a bicycle to patrol his defences – and these desperate days are now recalled at Kvam's War Museum.

## Gudbrandsdal Krigsminnesamling

Teigajordet • Late June to mid-Aug Tues–Sun 10am–5pm • 50kr • ☎ 61 29 40 33, ⓦ gudbrandsdalsmusea.no

The World War II battle for the Gudbrandsdal is commemorated at the **Gudbrandsdal Krigsminnesamling** (Gudbrandsdal War Museum), beside the E6 in the centre of Kvam. A series of excellent multilingual displays runs through the campaign, supported by a substantial collection of military mementoes and lots of fascinating photographs. There are also informative sections on the rise of Fascism and the Norwegian Resistance, plus a modest display on the role played by the villagers of neighbouring Otta in the Kalmar War between Sweden and Denmark/Norway in 1611–13. Across the main street from the museum, in the **church graveyard**, is a Cross of Sacrifice, honouring the 54 British soldiers who died here in Kvam while trying to halt the German advance.

## ARRIVAL AND DEPARTURE                                                    KVAM

**By train** Kvam train station, a request stop, is about 200m south of the museum. Train timetables on ⓦ nsb.no. Destinations Lillehammer (2–3 daily except Sat & Sun; 1hr 10min); Otta (2–3 daily except Sat & Sun; 15min).

**By bus** Long-distance buses travel through Kvam on the E6; there's a request stop a few metres from the museum. Destinations Lillehammer (1–3 daily; 1hr 40min); Otta (1–3 daily; 20min); Sjoa (1–3 daily; 10min).

# Sjoa and the Heidal valley

**SJOA**, 9km further up the valley from Kvam, is a scattered hamlet whose assorted timber chalets sit among the woods at the junction of the E6 and Hwy-257. The latter cuts west along the **Heidal valley**, where the **River Sjoa** boasts some of the country's most exciting **whitewater rafting** (see p.160). Beyond the Heidal valley, Hwy-257 continues west to meet Hwy-51, the main access road to the east side of the Jotunheimen National Park at Gjendesheim (see p.163).

### ARRIVAL AND DEPARTURE

### SJOA AND THE HEIDAL VALLEY

**By bus** There's no longer a train station at Sjoa, but buses (ⓦ rutebok.no) stop just off the E6, near the Hwy-257 intersection – and a 1.5km walk from *Sjoa*

*Vandrerhjem* (see below).

Destinations Lillehammer (1–3 daily; 1hr 50min); Otta (1–3 daily; 10min); Kvam (1–3 daily; 10min).

### ACTIVITIES

**Whitewater rafting** If you want to get to grips with the Sjoa River's gorges and rapids, contact the local specialists, Heidal Rafting (ⓣ 61 23 60 37, ⓦ heidalrafting.no). An all-inclusive, one-day rafting excursion costs around 1090kr,

790kr for half a day. The season lasts from May to October and reservations are recommended, though there's a reasonably good chance of being able to sign up at the last minute. Heidal Rafting is based at the HI hostel, *Sjoa Vandrerhjem*.

### ACCOMMODATION AND EATING

**Sjoa Vandrerhjem** Åmotsvegen 79 ⓣ 61 23 62 00, ⓦ hihostels.no. Perched on a wooded hillside high above the river, the main building of this HI hostel is a charming log farmhouse dating from 1747 and, although visitors sleep in more modern quarters, this is where you eat. Breakfasts are banquet-like, and dinners (by prior arrangement only) are reasonably priced if rather less spectacular (two-course set

menu for 135kr). The hostel offers two types of accommodation: a no-frills dormitory block at the bottom of the slope and a handful of spacious and comfortable chalets up above. All the doubles are en suite. Reservations are advisable for the chalets at weekends. The hostel is just off Hwy-257, about 1500m west of the E6. Mid-May to mid-Sept. Dorms **340kr**, doubles **975kr**

# Otta

**OTTA**, just 11km beyond Sjoa, is an unassuming and unexciting little town at the confluence of the rivers Otta and Lågen. It may be a bit dull, but Otta does make a handy base for hiking in the nearby Rondane National Park (see opposite), especially if you're reliant on public transport – though staying in one of the park's mountain lodges is much to be preferred. The town is also within easy driving distance (100km or so) of the Jotunheimen (see p.163). In Otta itself, everything you need is within easy reach: the E6 sweeps along the east bank of the Lågen, passing within 300m of the town centre, while Hwy-15 bisects the town from east to west with the few gridiron streets that pass for the centre lying a few metres to the south.

### ARRIVAL AND INFORMATION

### OTTA

**By train** Otta's train station is part of the Otta Skysstasjon, just off the E6 and on the north side of Hwy-15. Timetables on ⓦ nsb.no.
Destinations Oslo (2–4 daily; 3hr 30min); Oslo Gardermoen (2–4 daily; 3hr); Trondheim (2–4 daily; 3hr).

**By bus** The bus terminal is also located inside the Skysstasjon. Timetables on ⓦ rutebok.no.
Destinations Kvam (1–3 daily; 20min); Lillehammer (1–3 daily; 2hr); Lom (3–5 daily; 1hr); Sjoa (1–3 daily; 10min); Stryn (2–4 daily; 3hr); Trondheim (1–3 daily; 4hr).
**Tourist office** Otta tourist office is inside the Skysstasjon

---

### PILLARGURI AND PILLARGURITOPPEN

A **statue** outside Otta's Skysstasjon commemorates a certain **Pillarguri**, whose alertness made her an overnight sensation. During the Kalmar War of 1611–13, one of many wars between Sweden and Denmark, a band of Scottish mercenaries hired by the king of Sweden landed near Åndalsnes (see p.253), intent on crossing Norway to join the Swedish army. The Norwegians – Danish subjects at that time – were fearful of the Scots, and when Pillarguri spotted them nearing Otta she dashed to the top of the nearest hill and blew her birch-bark horn to sound the alarm. The locals hastily arranged an ambush at one of the narrowest points of the trail and all but wiped the Scots out – a rare victory for peasants over professionals. One of Pillarguri's rewards was to have a hill named after her, and today the stiff hike along the footpath up the forested slopes to the summit, **Pillarguritoppen** (853m), across the River Otta south of the town centre, is a popular outing; free trail maps are available at the tourist office (see above).

## OTTA TO THE WESTERN FJORDS

Running west from Otta, **Highway 15** sweeps along wide river valleys en route to Lom (see p.239), where there's a choice of wonderful routes on into the western fjords, including the stirring **Sognefjellsveg** (see p.237) over the mountains to Sogndal (see p.234). Several **long-distance buses** currently link Otta with the western fjords, including Nor-Way Bussekspress's Fjordekspressen (1 daily; ⓦ nor-way.no) running to Lom, Langvatn, Stryn and Bergen and **Nettbuss's NX146** (2 daily; ⓦ nettbuss.no), which follows the same route as far as Stryn, but then veers off to Måloy.

(Mon–Fri 8am–4pm; ☏ 61 24 14 44, ⓦ nasjonalparkriket .no). They can provide local bus timetables, book accommodation and reserve Lake Gjende boat tickets (see p.165); they also sell local hiking maps.

### ACCOMMODATION AND EATING

**Aasaaren Nedre Bed & Breakfast** Ottadalsvegen 621 ☏ 45 20 80 57, ⓦ aasaaren.info. Out in the countryside, beside the river 5km west of Otta along Hwy-15, this immaculately maintained old farmhouse offers a handful of lovely guest rooms – all with the whiff of timber. There's an outside hot tub, which must be booked in advance, and toilet facilities are also in a separate building in the garden. There's also tasty country breakfasts. 490kr

**Pillarguri Café** Storgata 7 ☏ 61 23 01 04, ⓦ pillarguri cafe.no. Otta's selection of places to eat is constrained and this is the best you'll do – a cosyish café-cum-restaurant and bar serving burgers (190kr), pizzas plus standard Norwegian dishes; a reindeer dish costs 290kr. It's bang in the centre of town, just south of Hwy-15. Mon–Thurs 8am–8pm, Fri 8am–10pm, Sat 8am–2am, Sun 2–8pm. Kitchen: Mon–Thurs 11am–7pm, Fri & Sat 11am–9pm & Sun 2–7pm.

**Thon Hotell Otta** Ola Dahls gate 7 ☏ 61 21 08 00, ⓦ thonhotels.com. In a pretty gruesome-looking modern block just a few minutes' walk west of the Skysstasjon, this chain hotel offers neat and trim modern rooms that fill up fast in the summer. 1400kr

# Rondane Nasjonalpark

Spreading north and east of Otta, **Rondane Nasjonalpark** was established in 1962 as Norway's first national park and is now one of the country's most popular hiking areas, its 963 square kilometres, much of which is in the high alpine zone, appealing to walkers of all abilities. The soil is poor, so vegetation is sparse – lichens, especially reindeer moss, predominate – but the views across this bare landscape are serenely beautiful, and a handful of lakes and rivers plus patches of dwarf birch forest provide some variety. Within the Rondane, the most obvious target is **Rondvatnet** lake, a lazy blue flash of water surrounded by wild mountain peaks. To the west of the lake are the wild cirques and jagged peaks of Storsmeden (2017m), Sagtinden (2018m) and Veslesmeden (2015m), while to the east of the lake rise Rondslottet (2178m), Vinjeronden (2044m) and Storronden (2138m). Further east still, Høgronden (2115m) dominates the landscape. The mountains in the vicinity of the lake, ten of which exceed the 2000m mark, are mostly accessible to any reasonably fit and eager walker, thanks to a network of trails and hiking huts/lodges – and you can vary your starting point by catching the **passenger boat** (see p.162) that weaves along Lake Rondvatnet in the summer season. Note that parts of the park are out of bounds during the reindeer calving season, from early May to the middle of June: the Rondane is home to several hundred **wild reindeer**, the sole remaining strain of the original Euro-Asiatic tundra reindeer that once roamed much of Scandinavia. The reindeer have been hunted hereabouts for several thousand years, hence the park's scattering of reindeer-trapping sites.

## Hikes in the Rondane

There are scores of **hikes** to choose from in the Rondane, but one popular choice is the haul up from **Rondvassbu Turisthytte** (mountain lodge; see p.163) to the top of

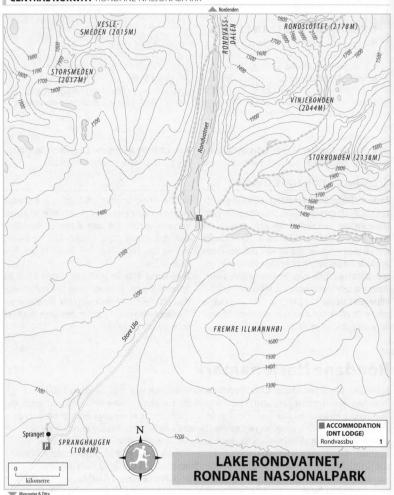

Lake Rondvatnet, Rondane Nasjonalpark

**Storronden** (2138m), the first peak to the right of Rondvatnet. This makes a fine excursion for the beginner, since, except for a short steep and exposed section just below the summit, there is no really difficult terrain to negotiate and the trail is clearly signed; the round trip takes about five hours – three up and two down. Neighbouring peaks involve more arduous mountain hiking, with the finest views over the range generally reckoned to be from **Vinjeronden** and nearby **Rondslottet**, which are both to the north of Storronden.

## Boat trips on Lake Rondvatnet

Early July to early Sept 2–3 daily; 15min each way • 120kr one-way • ☎ 61 23 18 66

The dinky **Rondejenta passenger boat** sallies forth from Rondvassbu bound for **Nordenden** at the northern end of the lake during the hiking season. It's a delightful excursion and from Nordenden it takes about two and a half hours to walk back to Rondvassbu along the lake's steep western shore.

## ARRIVAL AND INFORMATION

**By car** Access to the Rondane is by a series of narrow roads that thread their way either into or to the peripheries of the park from pretty much every point of the compass. From Otta, the main access route is the byroad leading first to the sprawling chalet settlement of Mysusæter (15km) and then the Spranget car park (20km), right on the edge of the national park itself. From the car park, it's a level walk northeast (1hr 30min) along the service road to the southern tip of Lake Rondvatnet, where the *Rondvassbu* lodge (see below) is located. There's also a designated, 75km-long scenic route – Nasjonale Turistveger (ⓦ nasjonaleturistveger. no) – along the eastern perimeter of the park: take Hwy-27

### RONDANE NASJONALPARK

north into the hills from near Hundorp (see p.158) to Folldal and then Hwy-29 west to Hjerkinn (see p.166) on the E6.

**By bus** Local buses link Otta Skysstasjon with Mysusæter and Spranget during the high season (late June to late Aug 3 daily; 25min to Mysusæter/35min to Spranget; ⓦ rutebok.no).

**By taxi** Taxis can be picked up at Otta Skysstasjon; reckon on 500kr for the trip to Spranget.

**Tourist office** Otta tourist office, in the Skysstasjon (see p.160), sells a wide range of maps of Rondane Nasjonalpark, will advise on hikes and has local bus timetables.

## ACCOMMODATION

**Rondvassbu Turisthytte** ⓘ 61 23 18 66, ⓦ rondvassbu .dnt.no. One of the more accessible of the Rondane's several huts and lodges, this large and popular DNT lodge has more than a hundred beds and offers filling meals. For all but the briefest of hikes, it's best to arrive at the lodge the day before so that you can start first thing the next morning – either on foot or by boat. The lodge is staffed

mid-June to early October, when you are also advised to make an advance reservation, and is open but unstaffed at certain periods during the rest of the year. There is a range of prices, with the smaller rooms (1–3 bunks) costing 305kr per person with non-members surcharged an extra 90kr. Dorm beds (DNT members) **180kr**

**3**

# Jotunheimen Nasjonalpark

Norway's most celebrated hiking area, **Jotunheimen Nasjonalpark** ("Home of the Giants" National Park), lives up to its name: pointed summits and undulating glaciers dominate the skyline, soaring high above river valleys and lake-studded plateaus. Covering no less than 1152 square kilometres, the park offers an amazing concentration of high peaks, more than two hundred of which rise above 1900m, including Norway's (and northern Europe's) two highest mountains, **Galdhøpiggen** (2469m) and **Glittertind** (2452m). Here also is Norway's highest waterfall, **Vettisfossen**, boasting a 275-metre drop and located a short walk from the *Vetti* lodge on the west side of the park. A network of **footpaths** and **mountain lodges** lattices the Jotunheimen, which is flanked in the west by Hwy-55 (see p.237) and to the east by Hwy-51. Be warned, however, that the weather is very unpredictable and at high altitudes the winds can be bitingly cold – take care and always come well equipped.

## Gjendesheim and Lake Gjende

**Gjendesheim**, just off Hwy-51 some 80km from Otta, has long been a popular base for exploring the Jotunheimen, but it is still no more than a ferry dock and a couple of buildings – including an excellent DNT lodge – at the tip of **Lake Gjende**. Some 18km long and 146m deep, the lake is one of Norway's most beautiful, its glacially fed waters tinted green by myriad clay particles; it was also here that Ibsen had his Peer Gynt tumble into the water from the back of a reindeer. Every summer, the lake is a hive of activity with hikers stalking off into the mountains and up onto the Besseggen ridge (see box, p.165) or hopping into the **passenger boats** (see p.165) that whisk along the lake.

## ARRIVAL AND DEPARTURE

**By car** There are no public/tarmac roads into Jotunheimen, but two well-maintained roads do trim the extremities – the Sognefjellsveg (Hwy-55; see p.237) to the west

### JOTUNHEIMEN NASJONALPARK

and Hwy-51 to the east; the latter passes within 2km of Gjendesheim.

**By bus** There are no direct buses from Otta to Gjendesheim,

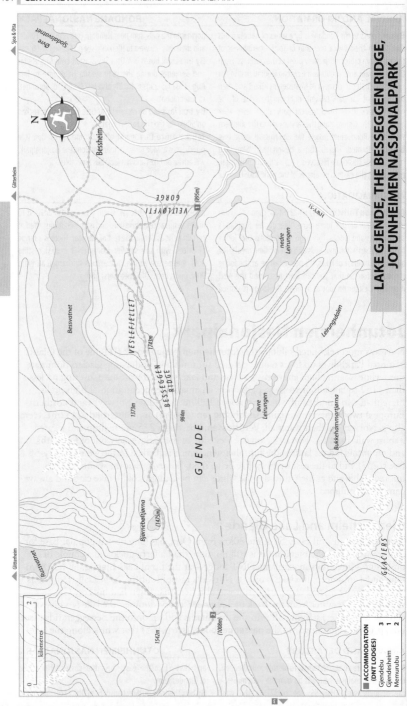

LAKE GJENDE, THE BESSEGGEN RIDGE, JOTUNHEIMEN NASJONALPARK

Sjoa & Otta

Øvre Sjodalsvatnet

Glitterheim

Bessheim

VELTLØYFTI GORGE

995m

nedre Leirungen

HGV.51

Bessvatnet

VESLEFJELLET

1743m

BESSEGGEN RIDGE

1373m

984m

GJENDE

øvre Leirungen

Leirungsdalen

Bukkehammartjønna

Bjørnbøltjørna

(1425m)

GLACIERS

Glitterheim

Russvatnet

1542m

(1008m)

N

kilometres

0                    2

ACCOMMODATION
(DNT LODGES)
Gjendebu          3
Gjendesheim      1
Memurubu         2

## HIKING THE BESSEGGEN RIDGE

**Start** Memurubu (1008m).
**Finish** Gjendesheim (995m).
**Distance** 15km.
**Time** 6hr.
**Highest point** Besseggen ridge (1743m).
**Maps** There is an excellent Nordeca Turkart map of the eastern Jotunheimen at 1:50,000 and another in the same series of the Jotunheimen as a whole at 1:100,000.
**Transport** Buses are detailed in 'Arrival and departure' (see p.163 & below) and boat schedules for the Lake Gjende boat are outlined in 'Getting around' (see below).
**Accommodation** *Gjendesheim*, full-service DNT hut (see below); *Memurubu*, full-service private hut (see p.166).

### THE HIKE

The day-long hike across the Jotunheimen's Besseggen ridge high above Lake Gjende is one of Norway's most popular excursions. Starting at the **Memurubu** jetty, the first part of the hike involves a stiff haul up to the base of the **Besseggen ridge** (2hr 30min), which is a good spot to take a break and enjoy the views over the surrounding wilderness before tackling the ridge itself. Thereafter, the thirty-minute scramble up to the peak of the ridge is very steep, with ledges that are, on occasion, chest high; you need to be moderately fit to negotiate them. In places, the ridge narrows to 50m with a sheer drop to either side, but you can avoid straying close to the edge by following the DNT waymark "T"s. The views are superlative, but the drops disconcerting – and a head for heights is essential. Beyond the peak of the ridge, the trail is less dramatic as you cross a couple of plateaus and clamber up the slopes in between before reaching the **Veltløyfti gorge**. Here, a slippery scramble with steep drops requires care, though the trail is well marked and the final destination, **Gjendesheim**, is clearly visible.

   If you hike in the opposite direction to the route described here, you can return by boat to Gjendesheim in the evening, but you'll have to calculate your speed accurately to meet the boat at Memurubu – and that isn't easy. Whichever direction you take, be sure to confirm boat departure times before you set out, and check weather conditions too, as snow and ice can linger well into July.

3

you have to change at Randen (late June to late Aug 3 daily; 1hr 30min–2hr; ⊕ rutebok.no). In addition, Nor-Way Bussekspress (⊕ nor-way.no) provides a good bus service on their Valdresekspressen from Oslo to Fagernes (4–8 daily), where you change for Gjendesheim (late June to late Aug 3 daily; 1hr 20min). For buses along the Sognefjellsveg, see p.238.
**By foot/skis** Hikers, mountaineers and skiers usually enter the Jotunheimen from the west, from the Sognefjellsveg (see p.237).

### GETTING AROUND

**By boat** Starting from Gjendesheim, boats (early June to early Oct 2–6 daily to Memurubu, 2 daily to Gjendebu; ☎ 91 30 67 44, ⊕ gjende.no) travel the length of Lake Gjende, connecting with mountain trails and dropping by *Memurubu* (20min) and *Gjendebu* lodges (45min). A one-way fare from Gjendesheim to Memurubu costs 140kr, Gjendebu 200kr; returns are twice that unless you make the round trip on the same day, in which case fares are 160kr and 220kr respectively. Naturally, you get to see a slice of the Jotunheimen and avoid a hike by riding the boat and sleeping at the lodges – a prudent choice in bad weather.

### ACCOMMODATION

**Gjendebu** ☎ 61 23 89 44, ⊕ gjendebu.com. At the west end of Lake Gjende, this DNT lodge, at an elevation of nigh on 1000m, is staffed and serviced (with 120 beds) from mid-June to mid-September and is unstaffed (with 34 beds, and no doubles) for the rest of the year. Mid-Sept to mid-June dorms DNT members <u>240kr</u>, non-members <u>350kr</u>; mid-June to mid-Sept dorms DNT members <u>180kr</u>, non-members <u>240kr</u>; doubles DNT members <u>610kr</u>, non-members <u>790kr</u>

**Gjendesheim** ☎ 61 23 89 10, ⊕ gjendesheim.dnt.no. At the eastern tip of long and slender Lake Gjende, this staffed DNT lodge, one of the organization's most famous, has 180 bunk beds in different permutations from one-bunk to four-bunk rooms with shared facilities in one building, dorm beds in the other. Open in both the summer and the winter seasons (late Feb to April & mid-June to early Oct). Summer: dorms DNT members <u>180kr</u>, non-members

240kr; doubles DNT members 610kr, non-members 790kr
**Memurubu** ☎61 23 89 99, ⍵memurubu.no. In a
relatively sheltered location, halfway along the lake's north
shore, this privately owned lodge mostly dates from a
recent rebuild following fire damage, though its origins

are as a mountain farm. All the two- to four-bunk rooms
are en suite and the rate includes breakfast and dinner; the
dorm rate is just for the bed – breakfast (125kr) and dinner
(325kr) cost extra. Mid-June to mid-Sept. Dorms 260kr,
doubles with all meals 1720kr

# Dombås

Straddling an important crossroads, **DOMBÅS**, 45km north of Otta and 200km from
Trondheim, manages to be almost entirely without interest, its indeterminate ramble
of modern buildings trailing along the E6 where it intersects with the E136. More
positively, Dombås train station is the starting point of the dramatic Rauma train line
(see box below) down to the western fjords at Åndalsnes (see p.253) and the town has
one minor claim to fame: it was here that an American air attaché, the unfortunate
Robert Losey, was killed by the bombs of the Luftwaffe in April 1940, making him the
first US military fatality of World War II.

## ARRIVAL AND DEPARTURE
DOMBÅS

**By train** Dombås train station (⍵nsb.no) is about 800m
from the E6/E136 junction.
Destinations Åndalsnes (3–4 daily; 1hr 20min); Hjerkinn
(3–4 daily; 20min; request stop only); Kongsvoll (3–4
daily; 30min; request stop only); Oslo (3–4 daily; 4hr);
Trondheim (3–4 daily; 2hr 40min).

**By bus** Dombås bus station is situated a brief walk from
the train station.
Destinations Lillehammer (1–2 daily; 3hr); Oslo (1–2
daily; 5hr 40min); Oslo Gardermoen (1–2 daily; 5hr); Otta
(1–2 daily; 1hr); Trondheim (2 daily; 3hr).

## ACCOMMODATION

**Dombås Vandrerhjem** Skitrekkveien ☎61 24 09 60,
⍵hihostels.no. Chalet-style hostel way up on the hillside
above the E6, with just thirteen rooms, all en suite, plus
self-catering facilities and a café-restaurant. To get there,

drive north out of Dombås along the E6 for around 1km and
follow the signs up the hill (a further 500m). Open all year.
Dorms 325kr, doubles 895kr

# Hjerkinn

The outpost of **HJERKINN**, stuck out on bare and desolate moorland about 30km from
Dombås, comprises a light scattering of houses, which are battened down against winter's
wind and snow. Hjerkinn may be small, but it does possess an excellent place to stay, the
**Hjerkinn Fjellstue**, and is a good place to sign up for a **musk-oxen safari** – the hairy beasts

---

### THE E136 AND THE RAUMA BRANCH LINE TO ÅNDALSNES

**Dombås** is where the **E136** (no express buses) and the **Rauma train line** (3–4 trains daily;
⍵nsb.no) spear west for the thrilling 110km rattle down to Åndalsnes. The journey begins
innocuously enough with road and rail slipping along a ridge high above a wide, grassy valley,
but soon the landscape gets wilder as both nip into the hills. After 65km, they reach **Kylling
bru**, an ambitious stone railway bridge, 56m high and 76m long, which spans the River
Rauma. Pressing on, it's a further 20km to the shadowy hamlet of **Marstein** with the grey,
cold mass of the **Trollveggen** ("Troll's Wall") rising straight ahead. The Trollveggen, at around
1100m, incorporates the highest vertical overhanging mountain wall in Europe and as such is
a favourite with experienced mountaineers, though it wasn't actually scaled until 1967.
Somehow, the E136 and the railway then manage to squeeze through the mountains and
soon they slide down to Åndalsnes (see p.253), the fjord glistening beyond.

THE BESSEGGEN RIDGE (P.165) >

## MUSK OXEN

On the first part of any hike west from Kongsvoll into the **Dovrefjell-Sunndalsfjella Nasjonalpark**, you're quite likely to spot **musk oxen**, the descendants of animals imported from Greenland in the late 1940s. These hefty beasts have lived in the Arctic for thousands of years, protected from the cold by two coats of hair and using their hooves to dig through the snow to reach the roots, lichens and mosses on which they depend. So far so good, but their habit of herding together with the adults surrounding the young when faced with danger proved disastrous when they were hunted by rifle. By the mid-1940s, the future of the Greenland herd looked decidedly grim, so some were transferred to Norway to help preserve the species, and here in their new home they have prospered in a modest sort of way and now number about five hundred. Conventional wisdom is that they will ignore you if you ignore them and keep at a distance of at least 200m. They are, however, not afraid of humans and will charge if irritated – retreat as quickly and quietly as possible if one starts snorting and scraping. If you want to observe them more closely, invest in a **musk-oxen safari** (see below). Incidentally, there's no truth in the rumour, promulgated by the mockumentary film *Trolljegeren* ("Troll Hunter"; 2010) that the musk oxen serve as a handy larder for local trolls – or is there?

**3**

(see box above) wander the neighbouring **Dovrefjell-Sunndalsfjella Nasjonalpark** (see opposite). Incidentally, if you're heading for Røros (see p.169), you can branch off here along Hwy-29 – a long-winded (145km) drive that takes about two hours.

### ARRIVAL AND DEPARTURE                                                          HJERKINN

**By train** Hjerkinn train station overlooks the E6/Hwy-29 junction. Note that trains only stop here by prior arrangement with the conductor. Timetables on ⊚ nsb.no.

Destinations Dombås (3–4 daily; 20min); Kongsvoll (3–4 daily; 10min; request stop only); Oslo (3–4 daily; 4hr 30min); Trondheim (3–4 daily; 2hr 20min).

### ACTIVITIES

**Musk-oxen safaris** Several companies in the Dombås/Hjerkinn area offer musk-oxen safaris but perhaps the best are coordinated by the local hostel – the *Hjerkinnhus Vandrerhjem* (☎ 46 42 01 02, ⊚ hjerkinnhus.no), which is located beside the short (700m) side road linking the train station with the E6. The once-daily guided tours require

a reasonable level of fitness – you hike for anywhere between 7km and 15km – last about five hours and cost 350kr per person; the season runs from late June to mid-August. Advance reservations are required. You'll need warm, waterproof clothes and proper hiking boots.

### ACCOMMODATION

**Hjerkinn Fjellstue** Hjerkinn ☎ 61 21 51 00, ⊚ hjerkinn.no. This engaging hotel is set on a hill overlooking the moors beside Hwy-29, about 2km east of Hjerkinn train station. Family owned, it comprises two expansive wooden buildings featuring big open fires and solid pine furniture, but the speciality is horseriding,

which is available for guests at extra cost. The restaurant is good too and dinner is served at 7pm (310kr) – try the reindeer culled from local herds. The hotel also has a small campground and an old pilgrims' hut (*pilegrims-stua*) with five beds (May–Sept; 350kr per person). Early June to Sept. **1400kr**

# Kongsvoll and the Dovrefjell-Sunndalsfjella Nasjonalpark

North of Hjerkinn, the E6 slices across barren uplands before descending into a shallow ravine, the **Drivdal**, where tiny **KONGSVOLL train station** looks positively Ruritanian, its windows and doors painted blue and mustard yellow. There isn't a village here at all, but the station is just 500m north along the E6 from the delightful *Kongsvold Fjeldstue*, which provides some especially charming accommodation and can serve as a great base for hikes into the neighbouring **Dovrefjell-Sunndalsfjella Nasjonalpark**.

## Dovrefjell-Sunndalsfjella Nasjonalpark

Running west towards the coast from the E6, **Dovrefjell-Sunndalsfjella Nasjonalpark** comprises a great slab of wilderness, 1693 square kilometres in extent, its mountains becoming increasingly steep and serrated as they approach the jagged spires backing onto Åndalsnes. **Hiking trails** and **huts** are scattered across the park with Kongsvoll (see below) making an ideal starting point: it's possible to hike all the way from Kongsvoll to the coast, but this takes all of nine or ten days. A more feasible expedition for most visitors is the two-hour circular walk up to the mountain plateau, or a two-day, round-trip hike to one of the four ice-tipped peaks of mighty **Snøhetta**, at 2286m. There's accommodation five hours' walk west from Kongsvoll at the unstaffed **Reinheim hut** (all year). On the way, you may spot the **musk oxen** for which this park is famous (see box opposite). Further hiking details and maps are available at the *Kongsvold Fjeldstue*.

### ARRIVAL AND DEPARTURE                    KONGSVOLL AND DOVREFJELL-SUNNDALSFJELLA

**By train** Kongsvoll train station is about 50m from the E6 – and 500m north of *Kongsvold Fjeldstue* (see below). Be aware that trains only stop here by prior arrangement with the conductor. Kongsvoll is 160km from Trondheim.

**Destinations** Hjerkinn (3–4 daily; 10min; request stop only); Dombås (3–4 daily; 30min); Oslo (3–4 daily; 4hr 30min); Trondheim (3–4 daily; 2hr).

### ACCOMMODATION AND EATING

★ **Kongsvold Fjeldstue** Kongsvoll ☎ 90 08 48 02, ⓦ kongsvold.no. As at Hjerkinn, an inn has stood here at Kongsvoll since medieval times and the present complex, a huddle of tastefully restored timber buildings with sun-bleached reindeer antlers tacked onto the outside walls, dates back to the eighteenth century. Once a farm as well as an inn, its agricultural days are recalled by several outbuildings: there are the little turf-roofed storehouses (*stabbur*), the lodgings for farmhands (*karstuggu*) and the barn (*låve*), on top of which is a bell that was rung to summon the hands from the fields. The main building retains many of its original features and also holds an eclectic sample of antiques. The bedrooms, dotted round the compound, are of the same high standard (en suite 350kr extra) – and the old vagabonds' hut (*fantstuggu*), built outside the white picket fence that once defined the physical limits of social respectability, contains the cosiest family rooms imaginable. Dinner is served in the restaurant (daily at 7pm), with mains averaging 260kr, and the complex also includes a café. Located just off the E6 and 500m south of the train station. Closed Jan & Feb. **1500kr**

# Røros and around

**RØROS**, glued to a treeless mountain plateau some 150km northeast of Hjerkinn, is a blustery place even on a summer's afternoon, when it's full of day-tripping tourists surveying the old part of town, which is little changed since its days as a **copper-mining centre**. Mining was the basis of life here from the seventeenth century onwards and although the mining company finally went bust in 1977, its assorted industrial remains were never bulldozed, making Røros a unique and remarkable survivor of the resource towns that once littered Norway's more isolated regions. Copper mining was dirty and dangerous work and even if the locals supplemented their incomes with a little farming and hunting, life for the average villager can't have been anything but hard.

Remarkably, Røros' **wooden houses**, some of them three hundred years old, have escaped the fires which have devastated so many of Norway's timber-built towns, and as a consequence the town is on UNESCO's World Heritage list. Firm regulations now protect this rare townscape and changes to its grass-roofed cottages are strictly regulated. Film companies regularly use the town as a backdrop for their productions: as early as 1971, it featured as a Soviet labour camp in the film version of Alexander Solzhenitsyn's **One Day in the life of Ivan Denisovich**, a choice of location that gives something of the flavour of the place.

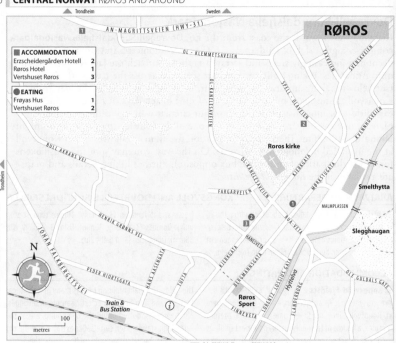

Røros makes for a pleasant **overnight stay**, which is just as well given its solitary location, and is a good base for both **hiking** and **cross-country skiing** across the surrounding uplands.

## Røros kirke

Kjerkgata • Early June to mid-Aug Mon–Sat 10am–4pm, Sun 12.30–2.30pm; mid-Aug to mid-Sept Mon–Sat 11am–1pm; mid-Sept to May Sat 11am–1pm • 50kr, including English-language guided tour (1–2 daily most days; times from the tourist office) • ☎ 72 41 00 00, ⓦ www.roros.no

In the town centre, **Røros kirke** (Røros church) is the most obvious target for a stroll, its heavy-duty tower reflecting the wealth of the early mine-owners. Built in 1784, and once the only stone building in Røros, the church is a massive structure designed – like the church at Kongsberg (see p.178) – to overawe rather than inspire. The most notable feature of the interior, which looks more like a theatre than a place of worship, is the two-tiered gallery running around the nave. Mine labourers were accommodated in the gallery's lower level, while "undesirables" were compelled to sit above, and even had to enter via a separate, external staircase. Down below, the nave exhibited even finer distinctions: you moved a pew closer to the front as you climbed the social ladder and mine managers vied for the curtained boxes, each of which had a well-publicized annual rent. The monarch (or royal representative) had a private box commanding views from the back and the pulpit was placed directly over the altar to sanctify the priest.

## Slegghaugan

Immediately below the church, on either side of the river, lies the oldest part of Røros, a huddle of sturdy cross-timbered smelters' cottages, storehouses and workshops squatting in the shadow of the **slegghaugan** (slagheaps) – more tourist attraction than eyesore, and providing fine views over the town and beyond.

## Smelthytta

Malmplassen • Daily: late June to mid-Aug 10am–6pm; mid-Aug to mid-Sept 10am–4pm; mid-Sept to May 11am–3pm • 100kr •
☎ 72 40 61 70, Ⓦ rorosmuseet.no

Next to the river are the rambling main works, the **Smelthytta** (literally "melting hut"),
which has been tidily restored and turned into a museum. A large three-storey affair,
the museum's most interesting section, housed in the cavernous hall that once
contained the smelter, explains the intricacies of copper production. Dioramas
illuminate every part of the process, and there are production charts, samples of ore
and a potted history of the company – pick up the comprehensive English-language
leaflet available free at reception. All that said, there's actually not that much to look
at – the building was gutted by fire in 1975 – and so the museum is perhaps for
genuine mining enthusiasts only.

## Malmplassen and around

The Smelthytta faces on to **Malmplassen** ("ore-place"), the wide earthen square
where the ore drivers arrived from across the mountains to have their cartloads of
ore weighed on the outdoor scales. In the square also, hung in a rickety little tower,
is the **smelters' bell**, which used to be rung at the start of each shift. Malmplassen is
near the top of **Bergmannsgata** which, together with parallel **Kjerkgata**, forms the
heart of today's Røros. Conspicuously, the smaller artisans' dwellings, some of
which have become art and craft shops, are set near the works, away from the rather
more spacious dwellings once occupied by the owners and overseers, which cluster
round the church.

## Olavsgruva copper mine

Hwy-31 • Guided tours (1hr): early June 2 daily; late June to mid-Aug 5 daily; mid-Aug to mid-Sept 2 daily; mid-Sept to May 1 weekly •
120kr • Ⓦ rorosmuseet.no • Reservations at Røros tourist office (see below)

Some 13km east of Røros off Hwy-31, one of the old copper mines, the **Olavsgruva**,
has been kept open as a museum, and there are guided tours of its workings throughout
the summer. The temperature down the mine is a constant 5°C, so remember to take
something warm to wear – you'll need sturdy shoes too.

### ARRIVAL AND INFORMATION

### RØROS AND AROUND

**By train** Røros train station is at the foot of the
town centre beside Johan Falkbergetsvei. Timetables
on Ⓦ nsb.no.

Destinations Hamar (3–6 daily; 3hr 30min); Oslo (3 daily;
5hr); Trondheim (3 daily; 2hr 30min).

**By bus** Røros bus station is next to the train station and
there are direct local buses to several local destinations,
including Trondheim (1–2 daily; 3hr). Timetables on
Ⓦ rutebok.no.

**By car** There are three main routes to Røros from the E6:
from south to north they are Hwys-29/3/30 from Hjerkinn
(150km; see p.166); Hwy-3/30 from Ulsberg (130km); and

Hwy-30 from Støren (100km). The last route is the most
scenic – though there's not much in it. Røros is 155km from
Trondheim via Støren.

**Tourist office** Røros tourist office, at Peder Hiortsgata 2
(mid-June to mid-Aug daily 10am–5pm, Sun till 4pm; rest
of year Mon–Fri 9am–3.30pm, Sat 10am–4pm; ☎ 72 41
00 00, Ⓦ www.roros.no), is located a couple of minutes'
walk from the train and bus stations. They supply a
comprehensive booklet on Røros and the surrounding
region, provide hiking and cycling information and have
bus and train timetables.

### ACTIVITIES

The sparse uplands that encircle Røros are good for **hiking**, with one of the more popular routes being the 5hr trek
east to the self-service DNT hut at **Marenvollen**. There are a trio of **wilderness cycling trails** too – the tourist
office (see above) has maps and several places rent out bikes, including Røros Sports (see p.172). In winter, the
uplands are popular with **cross-country skiers** – the tourist office has a leaflet mapping out several possible
routes – and there is **reindeer sledding** with **Rørosrein** (see p.172).

**Rørosrein** Hagaveien 17 ☎91 91 50 61, ⓦrorosrein .no. Small and enterprising family-run company specializing in all things reindeer – feeding, walking, lassoing and, best of the lot, winter sledding pulled by, you guessed it, reindeer. Advance reservations are required; sledding from 650kr.

**Equipment and rentals** Røros Sport at Bergmannsgata 13 (Mon–Fri 9am–5pm, Sat 9am–3pm; ☎72 41 12 18, ⓦgsport.no) is a conveniently located sports shop selling a wide range of activity equipment. It also does a good sideline in bike and mountain-bike rental. Advance reservations advised.

## ACCOMMODATION

★**Erzscheidergården Hotell** Spell-Olaveien 6 ☎72 41 11 94, ⓦerzscheidergaarden.no. The best place to stay in town, this small, family-run hotel has some especially charming rooms in its main wooden building. Some rooms also have fine views over Røros, and there's an attractive subterranean breakfast area as well as a cosy lounge. 1500kr

**Røros Hotel** An-Magrittsveien 6 ☎72 40 80 00, ⓦroros hotell.no. Big, modern, independent hotel located on the northern edge of the centre, 1.3km from the train station.

The *Røros* has made something of a bid for the conference and package-tourist trade, which partly explains its indoor pool and sauna. 1300kr

**Vertshuset Røros** Kjerkgata 34 ☎72 41 93 50, ⓦvertshusetroros.no. This appealing guesthouse has been dovetailed into an old timber building of 1914 and an adjacent former textile factory. There are about thirty guest rooms, half with their own kitchenette, and (at about 1900kr) a handful of self-catering apartments. 1500kr

## EATING

**Frøyas Hus** Mørkstugata 4 ☎72 41 10 11, ⓦfroyashus.no. This nifty little place, tucked away in an old wooden building in the oldest part of town, houses the cosiest of cafés, an informal affair with tables inside and a flowery courtyard beyond. Snacks and light meals from 60–120kr. Try the home-cured ham. Daily 10am–5pm.

**Vertshuset Røros** Kjerkgata 34 ☎72 41 93 50,

ⓦvertshusetroros.no. The unfussy homeliness of this hotel restaurant makes it a good spot to enjoy an evening meal – choose from traditional Norwegian dishes like *kjøttkaker i brun saus* (meatballs in brown sauce) or breast of veal with cabbage and carrot. À la carte or a three-course set meal for 525kr. Advance reservations are advised. Snacks and light meals daily from noon–10pm. Dinner daily 5–10pm.

# The E16: Oslo to the western fjords

The **E16** is the fastest (if not quite the shortest) route from Oslo to the western fjords, a quick and handsome 350km (6hr) gallop up from the capital to both the fjord car ferry near Sogndal (see p.234) and the colossal 24.5km tunnel leading to Flåm (see p.226). En route, it shoots past several **stave churches**, the most remarkable of them being **Borgund stavkirke**, and you can break your journey pleasantly enough about halfway along at the modest little town of **Fagernes**.

## GETTING AROUND

**THE E16: OSLO TO THE WESTERN FJORDS**

**By bus** Nor-Way Bussekspress's (ⓦnor-way.no) Valdreseks-pressen (4–8 daily) runs from Oslo to Hønefoss and Fagernes bus station, where you change onto the same company's Øst-VestXpressen (1 daily) to and from Lillehammer and for

points in the western fjords, including Flåm, Voss and ultimately Bergen. At Fagernes in the summertime, you can also change for the bus to Gjendesheim and its lodge in the Jotunheimen (see p.163).

## Hønefoss

The humdrum, former paper-mill town of **HØNEFOSS**, 60km from Oslo beside the E16, lies at the confluence of two serpentine rivers. Of only minor importance today, the town hit the international headlines in June 1935 when the exiled **Leon Trotsky** (1879–1940) arrived here from France at the invitation of a local politician and journalist, Konrad Knudsen. Trotsky and his wife, Natalia Sedova, were speedily installed in Knudsen's villa just outside town, but Trotsky was hardly enthusiastic, proclaiming "Norway is at least much better than Madagascar". In the event, their exile in Norway was short-lived: Stalin put pressure on the Norwegians to eject his bitter enemy and the Trotskys were plonked on a freighter bound for Mexico, their next – and final – place of exile, in December 1936.

# Fagernes

Clipping along the E16 from Hønefoss, it's about 130km up through wide, wooded dales to **FAGERNES**, an amenable little town whose modern centre is sandwiched between a lake and a river. A handy pit-stop, it possesses a couple of hotels and is just short of Hwy-51, which branches north from the E16 to run along the eastern edge of the Jotunheimen Nasjonalpark, passing near Gjendesheim and its lodge (see p.163) before finally joining Hwy-15 west of Otta (see p.160) and east of Lom (see p.239).

## ARRIVAL AND DEPARTURE                                          FAGERNES

**By bus** Buses to and from Fagernes pull into the Skysstasjon, bang in the centre of town on Jernbanegvegen, between the E6 and the lake.
Destinations Bergen (1 daily; 6hr 30min); Borgund

stavkirke (June–Aug 1–3 daily; 2hr); Flåm (1 daily; 4hr); Gjendesheim (late June to late Aug 3 daily; 1hr 20min); Hønefoss (4–8 daily; 1hr); Oslo (4–8 daily; 3hr); Sogndal (1 daily; 3hr, change at Håbakken); Voss (1 daily; 5hr).

## ACCOMMODATION

**Thon Hotel Fagernes** Jernbanegvegen 26 ☎61 35 80 00, ⓦthonhotels.com. Dominating the lakeshore, right in the centre of town opposite the Skysstasjon, this large chain hotel is built in the style of a lodge. Though the

1960s look and feel of its capacious public areas – down to the gold-embossed wallpaper – may not be to everyone's taste, the 138 bedrooms are mostly large and well appointed, and some have pleasant fjord views. **1300kr**

# Fagernes to Lomen

Beyond Fagernes, the **E16** sweeps up the valley at the heart of the **Valdres district** with forested hills rising on either side of a string of lakes. It's lovely scenery, with none of the harshness of the mountains further west, where farmers have tilled the land and fished the lakes for many centuries as witnessed by the four **stave churches** dotted along – or at least near – this section of the E16. You'd have to be something of an ecclesiastical fanatic to want to see them all – especially as the wonderful Borgund stave church beckons nearby (see p.174) – but **Lomen stavekirke** will do very nicely.

## Lomen stavkirke

Lomen • July to mid-Aug daily 11am–5pm • 50kr • ☎61 34 50 00, ⓦvaldres.no

Dating from the late twelfth century, and in regular use until 1914, **Lomen stavkirke** (Lomen stave church) occupies a pretty, rural setting just above the E16 about 30km west of Fagernes. The church's interior has a charmingly folksy atmosphere and boasts the finely decorated woodwork and cleverly interlaced joists that characterize stave churches. There's also an unusual medieval chest inscribed with a spell-casting runic inscription.

# Vang i Valdres

Around 25km west of the Lomen stave church, standing beside the road in the hamlet of **VANG I VALDRES**, is the curious **Vangsteinen** (Vang stone), a two-metre-high hunk of slate inscribed with runes and decorated with a lion-like animal, foliage and a tangle of braided ribbons. The carving dates from around 1000, a time when the Norwegians were abandoning paganism in favour of Christianity – though you would never guess it from the design on the stone. Curiously, the church behind the stone is a replacement for Vang stave church, which was sold, lock, stock and barrel to a Prussian royal and re-erected in Poland in the 1840s; apparently, it still stands there today.

## Filefjell and the Lærdal valley

Beyond Vang i Valdres, it's just 11km to **ØYE**, where the E16 begins its long climb up and over the **Filefjell mountain pass** amid a bare and treeless landscape dotted with lakes and sprinkled with mountain cabins. On the far side of the mountains, the E16 slips along the **Lærdal valley** bound for tiny **Borgund** and its famous stave church (see below). For almost all of its long history, the church stood beside the main road, but not any longer: in 2003, a new set of tunnels bypassed the church as well as one of the most beautiful portions of the **old E16 (now Highway 630)**, the twisting, 10km-long route through the rocky ravine trimming the River Lærdal. This ravine loop, now signed as a "**Historic Route**", has Borgund stave church at its east end and is an enjoyable detour that only takes about half an hour. From Borgund stave church, it's about 30km to the eastern end of the massive **Lærdalstunnelen** (see p.229), which links the Lærdal valley with Aurland, Flåm (see p.226) and points west to Bergen. The tunnel is part of the E16, but you can instead branch off here for the short trip north along Hwy-5 to Lærdalsøyri (see p.229) and the Fodnes–Mannheller car ferry (for Sogndal; see p.234).

### Borgund stavkirke

Borgund • Daily: May to mid-June & late Aug to Sept 10am–5pm; mid-June to late Aug 8am–8pm • 90kr • ☎ 57 66 81 09, ⓦ stavechurch.com • The church is 2km off the E16 – just follow the signs

The wooded slopes of the Lærdal valley shelter the stepped roofs and angular gables of **Borgund stavkirke**, one of the best-preserved stave churches in Norway. The church was built beside what was once one of the major pack-roads between east and west Norway until bubonic plague wiped out most of the local population in the fourteenth century, leaving Borgund pretty much high and dry. Much of the church's medieval appearance has been preserved, its tiered exterior protected by shingles and decorated with finials

### STAVE CHURCHES: NORWAY'S PRIDE AND JOY

The majority of Norway's **thirty surviving stave churches** (ⓦ stavechurch.com) are inland in the south and centre of the country, but taken together they represent the nation's most distinctive architectural legacy. The **key feature** of their design is that their timbers are placed vertically into the ground – in contrast to the log-bonding technique used by the Norwegians for everything else. Thus, a stave wall consists of vertical planks slotted into sills above and below, with the sills connected to upright posts – or **staves**, hence the name – at each corner. The general design seems to have been worked out in the twelfth century and common features include external wooden galleries, shingles and finials. There are, however, variations: in some churches, the nave and chancel form a single rectangle, in others the chancel is narrower than, and tacked onto, the nave. In virtually all the stave churches, the **door frames** (where they survive) are decorated from top to bottom with surging, intricate carvings that clearly hark back to Viking design, most memorably fantastical long-limbed dragons entwined in vine tendrils.

The **origins** of stave churches have attracted an inordinate amount of academic debate. Some scholars argue that they were originally pagan temples, converted to Christian use by the addition of a chancel, while others are convinced that they were inspired by Russian churches. Pagan or not, each part of the stave church acquired a symbolic Christian significance with, for example, the corner posts representing the four Gospels, the ground beams God's apostles upon whom (literally in this case) the church was built.

In the nineteenth century, they also acquired symbolic importance as reminders of the time when Norway was independent. Many had fallen into a dreadful state of repair and were clumsily renovated – or even remodelled – by enthusiastic medievalists with a nationalist agenda. Undoing this repair work has been a major operation, and one that continues today. For most visitors, seeing one or two will suffice – and three of the finest are those at **Heddal** (see p.180), **Borgund** (see above) and **Urnes** (see p.236).

in the shape of dragons and Christian crosses, the whole ensemble culminating in a slender ridge turret. A rickety wooden gallery runs round the outside of the church, and the doors sport an intense swirl of carved animals and foliage. Inside, the dark, pine-scented nave is framed by the upright wooden posts that define this type of church. The **visitor centre**, just 100m away, fills in some of the historical and architectural background.

# Highway 7: Hønefoss to the western fjords

The E16's nearest rival, the slower but slightly shorter and equally pretty **Highway 7**, branches off the E16 at **Hønefoss**, about 60km from Oslo. The road begins by clipping across lowlands before weaving its way up the **Hallingdal valley** and then slicing across the wild wastes of the Hardangervidda plateau en route to the fjords at Eidfjord (see p.216) near Hardangerfjord, a distance of 260km. If you need to break your journey, workaday **Geilo** is your best bet. Alternatively, 150km from Hønefoss at **Hagafoss**, you can pick up **Highway 50**, which splits off Hwy-7 to descend the dales to reach, after a further 100km, the Aurlandsfjord just round the coast from Flåm (see p.226). For most of its length, Hwy-7 is shadowed by the **Oslo–Bergen railway**, though they do part company near Geilo when the train swings north for its spectacular traverse of the mountains, barrelling its way over to Finse, Myrdal – where you change for the scenic branch line down to Flåm (see p.226) and points to Bergen.

**3**

### GETTING AROUND                           HIGHWAY 7: HØNEFOSS TO THE WESTERN FJORDS

**By train** The Oslo to Bergen train line stays close to Hwy-7 as far as Geilo, where it forks northbound for Myrdal (see p.222) and Voss (see p.220).

**By bus** Buses play second fiddle to the train on Hwy-7,

but Nettbuss's #NX170 (ⓦ nettbuss.no) from Oslo to Sogndal does travel along Hwy-7 as far as Gol, where you can change for Geilo.

## Geilo

With mountains and hills to either side, sprawling **GEILO**, 170km from Hønefoss, is one of the largest winter ski resorts in Norway, its assorted chalets and second homes spreading out along Hwy-7. Nevertheless, despite its open aspect, Geilo struggles to make much of an impression outside of its skiing offerings, though it is at least a convenient pit-stop if you are heading onto the fjords.

### ARRIVAL AND INFORMATION                                                    GEILO

**By train** Geilo train station is handily located in the town centre just to the north of Hwy-7. Timetables on ⓦ nsb.no. Destinations Bergen (3–4 daily; 3hr); Finse (3–4 daily; 40min); Myrdal (3–4 daily; 1hr 10min); Oslo (3–4 daily; 3hr 30min).

**By bus** The bus station is a stone's throw from the train station. Timetables on ⓦ rutebok.no.

Destinations Oslo (1–2 daily; 4hr with one change, usually at Gol); Eidfjord (1–2 daily; 1hr 45min).

**Tourist office** Geilo tourist office, Vesleslåttvegen 13 (late June to mid-Aug daily 9am–5pm, Sat till 4pm; mid-Aug to late June Mon–Sat 9am–4pm; ☎ 32 09 59 00, ⓦ geilo.no). The office is located about 300m southwest of the train station – follow the signs.

### ACCOMMODATION

**Dr Holms Hotel** Timrehaugveien 2 ☎ 32 09 57 00, ⓦ drholms.no. Dating back to the early twentieth century, this sprawling hotel started out as a spa for the pale and wan of Oslo – and is named after its founder, a specialist in respiratory diseases. The original building has been added to over the years, but it's all

been sympathetically done and the hotel has the look of a rather grand country villa. There are 125 guest rooms, some antique, others very modern. It's in a handy location too – just above, and to the northeast of, the train station. Prices rise during the ski season, otherwise **1500kr**

**Geilo Vandrerhjem** Lienvegen 139 ☎ 32 08 70 60, ⓦ hihostels.no. This large and really rather frugal hostel, part of a larger tourist complex, occupies two modern structures built in the style of mountain lodges. Has a café and self-catering facilities and sits beside Hwy-7, about 2km east of the train and bus stations. Dorms **290kr**, doubles **685kr**

# Rjukan

Deep in the wild, **RJUKAN**, 120km south of Geilo and 100km northwest of Kongsberg, spreads out along the bottom of the Vestfjorddalen valley, its oldest buildings dating from its foundation as a saltpetre (fertilizer) manufacturing centre at the start of the twentieth century. Saltpetre needs power and Rjukan had plenty of that in the form of the water that tumbles down into the valley from the harsh mountains up above – and this was harnessed to create a reliable source of electricity. Saltpetre production has moved elsewhere, but Rjukan still produces hydroelectricity in abundance and in essence it remains a company settlement, its six thousand inhabitants sharing a neat and trim town centre that was originally assembled by the Norsk Hydro power company. That said, Rjukan has also diversified into tourism: the power station at **Vemork** has become an industrial museum of some repute and the town has taken full advantage of its proximity to the **cross-country skiing and hiking trails** of the Hardangervidda mountain plateau (see p.217) with **adventure sports** – ice-climbing and bungee jumping for example – an added speciality. The problem of getting up from the valley bottom to the Hardangervidda was solved in the 1920s by the **Krossobanen cable car** – and, to help counteract Rjukan's valley-bottom gloom, the city council has recently paid for the **mirror project** in which three large solar-powered mirrors perched high above town bounce light down to the depths below.

## Norsk Industriarbeidermuseum

Vemork • May to mid-June & mid-Aug to Sept daily 10am–4pm; mid-June to mid-Aug daily 10am–6pm; Oct–April Tues–Fri noon–3pm, Sat & Sun 11am–4pm • 90kr • ☎ 35 09 90 00, ⓦ visitvemork.com • Visitors have to park on the far side of the suspension bridge & walk the last 700m (15min); there is a minibus service in summer (late June to mid-Aug; 30kr)

Rjukan's key sight is the **Norsk Industriarbeidermuseum** (Norwegian Industrial Workers' Museum), housed in the former **Vemork hydroelectric station**, some 7km to the west of Rjukan. When it was opened in 1911, Vemork had the greatest generating capacity in the world – its ten turbines provided a combined output of 108 megawatts – and it remains a fine example of industrial architecture pretending to be something else: with its high gables and symmetrical windows it looks more like a country mansion. Inside, the museum explores the effects of industrialization on what was then a profoundly rural region, has displays on hydroelectric power and the development of the trade unions, and features a gallery of propagandist paintings about workers and the class struggle by Arne Ekeland (1908–94).

Yet, most foreigners come to the museum because of the plant's role in – and excellent displays on – **World War II**, when it was the site chosen by the Germans for the manufacture of **heavy water**, which is necessary for regulating nuclear reactions in the creation of a nuclear bomb. Aware of Vemork's importance, the Americans bombed it on several occasions and the **Norwegian Resistance** mounted a string of guerrilla attacks; as a result, the Nazis decided to move the heavy water they had made to Germany. The only way they could do this was by train, and part of the journey was across **Lake Tinnsjø** just east of Rjukan – ingeniously the ferry was fitted with a set of railway tracks. This was the scene of one of the most spectacular escapades of the war, when the Norwegian Resistance sunk ferry and train on January 20, 1944. All the heavy water was lost, but so were the fourteen Norwegian passengers – a story recounted in the 1965 film *The Heroes of Telemark*, in which **Kirk Douglas** played the cinematic stereotype of the Norwegian: an earnest man with an honest face, wearing a big pullover.

# Krossobanen cable car

Kraftledningsveien 1 • Daily: late June to mid-Oct 9am–8pm; mid-Oct to late June 10am–4pm • 65kr each way • ☎ 35 09 00 27,
ⓦ krossobanen.no

Easy access to the Hardangervidda is provided by Rjukan's **Krossobanen cable car**,
which carries passengers up to the plateau from a station at the west end of town, about
2km from the bus station. Built in 1928, the Krossobanen was the first cable car to be
built in northern Europe and Norsk Hydro stumped up the money, curiously enough
because they wanted their workers to be able to see the sun in winter.

# Gaustabanen

Hwy-651 • Late June to mid-Oct daily 10am–5pm • 350kr return, single 250kr • ☎ 45 50 22 22, ⓦ gaustabanen.no • The terminal is
14km southeast of Rjukan – along the main road, Hwy-37, and then up a difficult mountain road (Hwy-651); it's much easier to catch the
shuttle bus from the town centre (40kr return)

Built for the military in the 1950s, Rjukan's **funicular railway**, the **Gaustabanen**,
goes 860m into the heart of Mount Gausta, where you change for the 1km-long
journey up to the top of the mountain. By means of this railway, Norwegian
soldiers could maintain their mountain-top radio-listening gear with the greatest of
ease and, now that the army has gone, it's open to tourists – and the views from the
top are stupendous.

**3**

## ARRIVAL AND INFORMATION RJUKAN

**By car** The most scenic way to reach Rjukan is from
Kongsberg to the southeast via Hwys-40/37 (95km). There
are also two side roads to Rjukan from the E134: Hwy-37
(65km) from a point just west of Heddal stave church (see
p.180); and another also along Hwy-37 (66km) from the
Åmot crossroads (see p.181).

**By bus** Buses to Rjukan pull in at the bus station on the
south side of the river, over the bridge and about 400m
from the town centre.

**Destinations** Kongsberg (4–6 daily; 2hr 30min; change at
Notodden); Oslo (4–6 daily; 4hr; change at Notodden).
**Tourist office** Rjukan tourist office is right in the centre
of town at Torget 2 (Mon–Fri 9am–6pm, Sat & Sun
10am–4pm; ☎ 35 08 05 50, ⓦ visitrjukan.com). They can
provide local bus timetables, sell maps and can give advice
on hiking the Hardangervidda as well as other outdoor
pursuits, from ice-climbing to bungee jumping.

## ACTIVITIES

**Adventure sports** Rjukan's Telemark-Opplevelser
(☎ 99 51 31 40, ⓦ telemark-opplevelser.no) offers a wide
range of adventure sports including bungee jumping
(790kr) from the suspension bridge leading to the
Industriarbeidermuseum in Vemork. They also offer guided
ice-climbing tours (half-day 850kr) and ice-climbing
courses for beginners (half-day 800kr). There are well over
a hundred ice-climbing routes in the vicinity of Rjukan;
the best ice-climbs are on frozen waterfalls of which

there are a hatful near Rjukan.
**Hiking** From the upper terminal of the Krossobanen
(see above), it's a superb 3hr (8km) hike north across
the Hardangervidda to the self-service *Helberghytta*
DNT hut.
**Cross-country skiing** There are over 80km of groomed
cross-country ski trails beginning at the *Gaustablikk
Høyfjellshotell* (see below). They range from a beginner's
easy 2km-long trail to a mountain haul of 23km.

## ACCOMMODATION AND EATING

**Gaustablikk Høyfjellshotell** Kvitåvatnvegen 372
☎ 35 09 14 22, ⓦ gaustablikk.no. Several of the
mountain roads in the vicinity of Rjukan are dotted with
lodges and this is one of the best of them, a substantial
affair with smashing wilderness views and ninety neat
and trim modern rooms. It's situated up in the mountains
to the southeast of Rjukan along a seemingly interminable
mountain road. **1600kr**

**Rjukan Admini** Sølvvoldveien 3 ☎ 90 89 49 09,
ⓦ rjukanadmini.com. Dating from 1908, this attractive

and capacious wooden villa, built for one of the leading
lights of Rjukan, offers fifteen guest rooms decorated in
a fairly formal version of country-house style with pastel
shades to the fore. Handily located just off Hwy-37 on the
west side of the centre. **1400kr**

**Rjukan Hytteby** Brogata 9 ☎ 35 09 01 22, ⓦ rjukan
-hytteby.no. Downtown Rjukan is short of good
accommodation, but this enjoyable and distinctive place
helps fill the gap, occupying a batch of modern cottage-
cabins built in the style of the original workers' houses

of the 1910s. As an added bonus, the complex's straight-forward café-restaurant (daily 11am–11pm) sells filling basics like burgers, pizza, and fish and chips at affordable prices (mains average 160kr). The cabins string along the south side of the river about 800m east of the centre. **1200kr**

# Kongsberg

Stuck up in the hills some 90km from Oslo, **KONGSBERG** is a pretty little place with plenty of green spaces: the **River Lågen** tumbles and rumbles through its centre and merely wandering around the town is an enjoyable a way as any of spending an hour or two. Specific sights are thin on the ground, but the town does have a particularly splendid church, **Kongsberg kirke**, and an appealing set of **statues** on the town **bridge**, at the foot of Storgata. These commemorate various local activities, notably foolhardy attempts to locate new finds of silver – one of which involved the use of divining rods – for Kongsberg's history has been pretty much defined by its **silver mines**. A local story claims that the silver responsible for Kongsberg's existence was discovered by two goatherds, who stumbled across a vein of the metal laid bare by the scratchings of an irritable ox. True or not, Christian IV (1577–1648), with his eye on the main chance, was quick to exploit the find, sponsoring the development of mining here – the town's name means "King's Mountain" – at the start of a **silver rush** that boosted his coffers no end. In the event, it turned out that Kongsberg was the only place in the world where silver could be found in its pure form, and there was enough of it to sustain the town for a couple of centuries. By the 1750s, it was

**KONGSBERG**

REINS GATE
KONGENS GATE
Bus Station
Train Station
0 — 200 metres
D'YRNYRGATA
STIKSBRIDGATA
TRELETRUKGATA
HERMANN FOSSGT.
SKOLEGT.
AUGUSTS GATE
STORGATA
DRAMMENSVEIEN
NUMEDALSVEIEN
Lågen
17 MAIGT.
CHRISTIAN
TINIUS OLSENSGT.
KARSCHESGATA
N
NYBRUA
STASJONSBAKKEN
Norsk Bergverksmuseum
VINJESGATE
**2** Footbridge
MYNTBRUA (E134)
GLITREGATA
KIRKETORGET
**Bandstand**
Kongsberg kirke
HYTTEGATA
Rådhus
BERGMANNSVEIEN
CHR. IV GT.
MYNTGATA
GOMSRUDVEIEN
KIRKEGATA
**2**
GAMLEBRUA

| ACCOMMODATION | |
|---|---|
| Kongsberg Vandrerhjem | 2 |
| Quality Hotel Grand | 1 |

| ● EATING | |
|---|---|
| Opsahlgården | 2 |
| Skragata mat og Vinhus | 1 |

E134, Notodden & Saggrenda

Larvik

the largest town in Norway, with half its eight thousand inhabitants employed in and around the three-hundred-odd mine shafts that dotted the area. The silver works closed in 1805, but by this time Kongsberg was also the site of a royal mint, which still employs people to this day.

## Kongsberg kirke

Kirketorget • Jan–May & Sept–Dec Tues–Thurs 10am–noon; June–Aug Mon–Fri 11am–3pm • 40kr • ☎ 32 86 60 30, ⓦ kongsberg.kirken.no

To appreciate the full economic and political clout of the mine owners, it's necessary to visit the church they funded – **Kongsberg kirke** (Kongsberg church), the largest and arguably most beautiful Baroque church in Norway. It dates from 1761, when the mines were at the peak of their prosperity, its ruddy-brown brickwork and copper-green spire shadowing a large square, whose other three sides are flanked by period wooden buildings. The church **interior** is a grand affair too, with its enormous and showy mock-marble western wall incorporating the altar, pulpit and organ. Unusually, the **pulpit** is actually above the altar to hammer home the point that the priest was expressing God's will. And it wasn't just the will of God: the mine owners looked on the priest as a sort of ex officio member of the board, who could be relied upon to extol the virtues of hard work, sobriety and punctuality. The owners also prescribed the church's **seating arrangements**, which were rigidly and hierarchically defined. Facing the pulpit are the King's Box and boxes for the silver-works' managers, while other officials sat in the glass enclosures. The pews on the ground floor were reserved for their womenfolk, while the sweeping balcony was divided into three tiers to accommodate the Kongsberg petite bourgeoisie, the workers and, squeezing in at the top and back, the lumpenproletariat.

## Norsk Bergverksmuseum

Hyttegata 3 • Mid-May to Aug daily 10am–5pm; Sept to mid-May Tues–Sun noon–4pm • 90kr • ☎ 91 91 32 00, ⓦ norsk-bergverksmuseum.no

Mining enthusiasts will enjoy the **Norsk Bergverksmuseum** (Norwegian Mining Museum), housed in the old smelting works near the river. It shares its premises with a tiny ski museum, but the main attractions are its silver collection, including examples of the silver coins minted here in town, and its gems and precious stones. Kongsberg's mint – Det Norske Myntverket – was established in 1686, but it was removed from state control and privatized in 2004.

## Sølvgruvene silver mine

Malmveien, Saggrenda • Tours (1hr 30min): mid-May to Aug 3–4 tours daily; Sept Sat & Sun 2 tours daily; consult tourist office (see p.180) for times • 160kr • ☎ 91 91 32 00, ⓦ norsk-bergverksmuseum.no • Signed off the E134 south of Kongsberg on the road to Notodden

One set of Kongsberg's silver mines, the **Sølvgruvene**, in the hamlet of **Saggrenda**, about 8km west of Kongsberg, is open for tours and makes for a good excursion, especially if you have pre-teen children in tow. The entertaining tour includes a ride on a **miniature train** into the shafts through dark tunnels – take a sweater, as it's cold underground. After you've finished the tour, you can explore the old ochre-painted workers' compound – the **Sakkerhusene** – just 350m or so down the hill from the mine. The compound has been carefully restored and contains a **café** as well as some rather half-hearted displays on the history of the mines.

### ARRIVAL AND INFORMATION

**By train** Kongsberg's branch-line train station is on the north side of town, a 5min walk from the centre. Timetables on ⓦ nsb.no.

**Destinations** Kristiansand (every 2hr; 3hr 30min); Oslo (every 1–2hr; 1hr 20min); Oslo Gardermoen airport (every 1–2hr; 1hr 40min).

**By bus** The bus station is a few metres from the train station.

Destinations Åmot (2–4 daily; 2hr 45min); Haugesund (2–4 daily; 7hr 30min); Oslo (2–4 daily; 1hr 15min); Seljord (2–4 daily; 1hr 45min);

**Tourist office** Kongsberg tourist office is metres from Kongsberg kirke at Kirketorget 4 (late June to mid-Aug Mon–Fri 9am–5pm, Sat 10am–2pm; mid-Aug to late June Mon–Fri 9am–4pm; ☎ 32 29 90 50, ⓦ www .kongsberg.no).

## ACCOMMODATION

**Kongsberg Vandrerhjem** Vinjesgate 1 ☎ 32 73 20 24, ⓦ hihostels.no. This all-year, well-kept HI hostel occupies an attractive timber lodge close to the town centre, and has both dorms and en-suite doubles, a well-equipped self-catering kitchen, laundry and café serving breakfast, lunch and dinner. To get there, drivers need to follow the signs on the E134, whereas train and bus users should walk south from the station along Storgata, cross the bridge, walk round the back of the church on the right-hand side, then head down the lane beside the bandstand and cross over the footbridge – a 15min walk in all. Dorms 350kr, doubles 970kr

**Quality Hotel Grand** Christian Augusts gate 2 ☎ 32 77 28 00, ⓦ nordicchoicehotels.no. Easily the most appealing hotel in downtown Kongsberg, the *Grand* occupies a large modern block down near the river. From the outside, the hotel is undistinguished, but the interior, which is decorated in crisp modern style, is well maintained and the 175 guest rooms are well appointed and comfortable; the best, on the higher floors, offer wide views over the churning, tumbling River Lågen. 1400kr

## EATING

**Opsahlgården** Kirkegata 10 ☎ 32 76 45 00, ⓦ opsahlgarden.no. Arguably the pick of the town's several restaurants, this smart and cosy little place does a particularly good line in seafood with main courses averaging 280kr. It's located near the church. Mon–Sat 5–10pm.

**Skragata mat og Vinhus** Nymoens skrågate 2, entrance Christian Augusts gate ☎ 32 72 28 22, ⓦ skragata.no. Smart, modern restaurant where the menu is a canny mix of French and Norwegian dishes – the reindeer is particularly tasty. Set menus and à la carte with mains around 280kr. Mon–Sat 5–10pm.

# The E134: Kongsberg to the western fjords

The **E134** is the most southerly of the main roads linking Oslo and its environs with the western fjords, stretching the 400km from Drammen to Haugesund, passing near Odda on the way. From Oslo, the first part of the E134 is unremarkable, but beyond the attractive town of **Kongsberg** (see p.178), the road weaves and wends its way across **Telemark** (ⓦ visittelemark.no), a profoundly rural county that occupies a great forested chunk of southern Norway. In a country where the fjords are the apple of the tourist industry's eye, Telemark is often neglected, but it can be stunningly beautiful, its deep valleys, blue-black lochs and bulging wooded hills intercepted by tiny villages in a manner that resembles the Swiss Alps. The key targets here are **Heddal stave church** and **Dalen**, the site of the region's most enjoyable hotel (see p.182). Beyond Telemark, the E134 nudges its way over the southern reaches of the wonderful **Hardangervidda plateau** (see p.217) to cross one of Norway's highest mountain passes, the storm-blasted **Haukelifjell**, a suitably dramatic introduction to the western fjords (see p.209).

**GETTING AROUND**          **THE E134: KONGSBERG TO THE WESTERN FJORDS**

**By bus** Nor-Way Bussekspress's (ⓦ nor-way.no) Haukelieks-pressen (2–4 daily) runs from Oslo to Kongsberg and then proceeds along the E134 to Notodden, Seljord, Åmot and ultimately Haugesund. However, bus stops are not necessarily handy for either the centre of the nearest village or its sights, which can be a pain if it's raining.

## Heddal stavkirke

Heddalsvegen, just off the E134 • Late May to mid-Sept daily 10am–5pm, but Sun from 12.30pm when there is a service; museum same times • 70kr; museum included in price of church • ☎ 92 20 44 35, ⓦ heddalstavkirke.no

Some 30km west of Kongsberg, and 5km beyond the workaday industrial town of Notodden, is **HEDDAL**, whose delightful **stave church** stands beside the road fronted by the neatest of cemeteries. The largest surviving stave church in Norway, it boasts a pretty tumble of shingle-clad roofs, each of which was restored to something like its medieval appearance in 1955, rectifying a heavy-handed nineteenth-century remodelling. The crosses atop the church's gables alternate with dragon-head gargoyles, a mix of Christian and pagan symbolism typical of many stave churches (see box, p.174). Inside, masks surmount the masts of the nave and there's some attractive seventeenth-century wall decoration in light blues, browns and whites; but pride of place goes to the ancient **bishop's chair** in the chancel. Dating from around 1250, the chair carries a relief retelling the saga of Sigurd the Dragonslayer, a pagan story that Christians turned to their advantage by recasting the Viking as Jesus and the dragon as the Devil. Across from the church, there's a **café** and a modest **museum** illustrating further aspects of the church's history.

# Seljord

Heading west, the E134 rattles up the valley before making a dramatic defile over the mountains en route to **SELJORD**, a small but straggly industrial town at the head of **Seljordsvatnet lake**, about 55km from Heddal. Modest it may be, but Seljord seems to have attracted more than its fair share of "Believe It or Not" stories: a **monster** is supposed to lurk in the depths of the lake; elves are alleged to gather here for some of their soirees; and the **medieval stone church**, with its whitewashed walls and dinky little spire, was, so the story goes, built by a goblin. Beside the church are two more curiosities: the nearer is a large **granite slab** carved with a picture of the Norwegian pastor **Magnus Brostrup Landstad** (1802–80), shown mounted on his horse with an open hymnbook in his hand. Landstad, who was briefly a minister here in Seljord, made his name among the Norwegian nationalists of his day by collecting traditional country ballads and by creating the *Landstad Hymnbook*, which discarded the Danish of its predecessors for Norwegian; it was in use until 1985. A few metres away, stuck in the ground, is the **570-kilogram stone**, which was lifted for the first and last time by a Telemark strongman, one **Nils Langedal** (1722–1800), who, according to local legend, was reared on mare's milk.

# To Dalen from the E134

To the west of Seljord, there are **two roads** leading south from the E134 to Dalen (see p.182) – Hwy-45 and, further to the west from the **Åmot crossroads**, Hwy-38. Both are around 20km long, but **Highway 38** has the more imperious scenery as it inches its way along the edge of the **Ravnejuvet** (Raven Gorge), a severe gash in the landscape whose sheer dark walls are no less than 350m high. According to the local tourist brochure, the gorge's unusual air currents mean you can throw a banknote over the edge and it will come back to you – but most people experiment with ordinary bits of paper instead. The second road, the more subdued **Highway 45**, threads its way over forested hills before nipping through a series of alpine-like valleys, where old farmsteads hug the hillsides flanked by bright-green pastureland. This is fine scenery indeed and it's here you'll find Eidsborg stavkirke.

### Eidsborg stavkirke

Vest-Telemark Museum, Hwy-45 • Late June to Aug daily 10am–5pm • 80kr, including museum • ☏ 35 06 90 90, ⓦ visittelemark.no

Situated just 13km southwest of the E134 along Hwy-45 is **Eidsborg stavkirke** (Eidsborg stave church), whose tightly packed roofs, decorative finials and cedar shingles date back to the thirteenth century. The church, which is now the prize exhibit among the old timber buildings of the **Vest-Telemark Museum** (West Telemark Museum), remains one of the best preserved in the country (albeit with several renovations), and its interior sports some fascinating, if faded, watercolour friezes of biblical scenes. Given its remote location, it's not surprising that the church has attracted more than its fair share of legend, one of the most charming of which relates to the adjacent graveyard: digging graves was so difficult in this rocky plot of land that a local magistrate offered mercy to a pair of condemned women if they could rectify matters; they solved the problem by carrying sand here in their aprons and were promptly pardoned. The church is dedicated to St Nicholas of Bari (aka Santa Claus) and, in an echo of a pagan past, a wooden image of the saint was carried round the lake below the church three times once every year and then ceremonially washed, right up until the 1850s.

## Dalen

Trailing along the valley between steep forested hills, the sleepy little town of **DALEN** is a pleasant place in a pleasant setting, its string of modern houses somewhat reminiscent of small-town USA. Dalen's four hundred inhabitants mostly work in the hydro and timber industries, but a fair few of them are reliant on the town's star turn, the *Dalen Hotel* (see below), right at the end of town facing the lake. In the 1890s, the opening of the Telemarkskanal (see box below) made Dalen an important transit point and it was then that a group of businessmen decided to build the hotel as the region's showpiece – as it remains today.

### ARRIVAL AND INFORMATION

DALEN

**By car** Heading west from Seljord on the E134, it's 30km to Hwy-45, the first of the two turnings for Dalen, and 16km more to the Åmot crossroads at the start of the second turning, Hwy-38.

**By bus** In the summertime, there are local buses between Dalen and Åmot on the E134 (late June to mid-Aug Mon–Fri & Sun 3 daily, Sat 1 daily; 40min; ⓦvkt.no). These local buses connect with the Haukeliekspressen (ⓦnor-way.no), which pauses in Åmot on its way between Oslo and Haugesund (2–4 daily).

**Tourist office** Dalen tourist office is a few metres from the *Dalen Hotel* at Hotellvegen 5 (mid-June to mid-Aug Mon–Fri 10am–6pm, Sat & Sun 10am–4pm; mid-Aug to mid-June Mon–Fri 10am–3.30pm; ☏35 07 56 56, ⓦvisittelemark.com).

### ACCOMMODATION AND EATING

**Dalen Bed & Breakfast** ☏35 07 70 80, ⓦwww .dalenbb.com. If your budget won't stretch as far as the *Dalen Hotel*, then this all-year B&B, which occupies an attractive and modern chalet-like house just a few metres away, is a good alternative; there are thirteen guest rooms here and most are en suite (250kr extra). **990kr**

★ **Dalen Hotel** ☏35 07 90 00, ⓦdalenhotel.no. Dating back to the 1890s, this lavish hotel was once one of the most fashionable spots in the country, but it hit the skids after World War II when the development of the road system began to undermine its importance. Luckily it was picked up and expertly restored in the 1990s. The hotel's main facade is an imposing affair, whose twin towers are topped by finials in a permutation of Viking style. Inside, pride of place goes to the galleried hall with its huge stained-glass ceiling, open fireplace and carved woodwork. The 42 very comfortable guest rooms, which are in the hotel's two wings, have been returned to an approximation of their original appearance too, and the pick of the rooms have balconies overlooking the hotel gardens, which stretch down to the lake. The hotel dining room is also very grand with its acres of wood panelling and the food – traditional Norwegian – is top-notch with main courses averaging 300kr. **2100kr**

---

### THE TELEMARKSKANAL

Dalen is the western terminus of the **passenger ferry** that winds its way northwest along the **Telemarkskanal** from **Skien** (late May to early Sept 1 daily; 1000kr one-way; ☏35 90 00 20, ⓦvisittelemark.no), a journey that takes nine hours. Extending for 105km, the canal links a string of lakes and rivers by means of eighteen locks that negotiate a difference in water levels of 72m. Completed in 1892, the canal was once an important trade route into the interior, but today it's mainly used by pleasure craft; it's also possible to make shorter excursions out by boat and back by bus – see the website for details. In Dalen, the jetty is 750m beyond the *Dalen Hotel*.

## Vinje Biletgalleri

Late June to early Aug Tues–Sun noon–5pm • 50kr • ☎ 35 06 90 90, ⓦ vest-telemark.museum.no

From the **Åmot crossroads**, it's about 16km along the E134 to the signed (1.3km-long) turning to the **Vinje Biletgalleri**, which exhibits the paintings of two artists with local connections – **Harald Kihle** (1905–1997) and the more talented **Henrik Sørensen** (1882–1962). The gallery itself is a handsome, granite structure in a deeply rural location – an apt spot to admire Sørensen's lyrical, Matisse-influenced landscapes.

## Haukelifjell and Røldal

Pushing on west from the Vinje Biletgalleri, the **E134** zigzags across hill and dale before beginning its long climb up to the bare and bleak wastes of the Hardangervidda mountain plateau (see p.217) via the wild and storm-buffeted **Haukelifjell**, one of Europe's highest mountain passes. The road cuts a nervous course across the plateau, diving into a series of tunnels before slipping down into the hamlet of **RØLDAL**, a remote little place nestled in the greenest of valleys – 250km from Åmot.

### Røldal stavkirke

Røldal • Daily: June & mid- to late Aug 10am–4pm; July & early Aug 9.30am–6.30pm • 50kr • ☎ 48 10 92 84, ⓦ roldalstavkyrkje.no

Within shouting distance of the E134, **Røldal stavkirke** (stave church) is a trim, rusticated affair dating from the thirteenth century – and the only stave church still in religious use today. In medieval times, it was a major place of pilgrimage on account of the crucifix with healing powers that still hangs above the altar – and it was then that the elaborate wall paintings were added.

## Røldal to Odda

After Røldal, the **E134** makes another stirring climb to reach its first junction with **Highway 13**, the scenic but extremely long-winded road south to Stavanger (see p.133). From this crossroads, the combined E134/Hwy-13 forges on across the southwest edge of the Hardangervidda en route to another crossroads, where you either keep going on the E134 to Haugesund (see p.142), 130km away, or stay on Hwy-13 as it drops down a severe, boulder-strewn river valley, passing, in 5km, the **Latefossen waterfall**, where two huge torrents empty into the river with a deafening roar. Beyond lie Odda (see p.213) and Lofthus (see p.215).

**3**

# Bergen and the western fjords

VIEW ACROSS THE FJÆRLANDSFJORD FROM MUNDAL

# Bergen and the western fjords

If there's one familiar and enticing image of Norway it's the fjords, giant clefts in the landscape running from the coast deep into the interior. Rugged yet serene, these huge, wedge-shaped inlets are visually stunning. Indeed, the entire fjord region elicits inordinate amounts of purple prose from tourist-office handouts, and for once it's rarely overstated – especially around early May, when the fjords are undeniably beautiful, after the brief Norwegian spring has brought colour to the landscape.

Visiting the fjords in **winter**, when all is unerringly quiet, has its charms too, the blue-black waters of the fjords contrasting with the blinding white of the snow that blankets the hills, valleys and mountains. In **summer**, the wilds are filled with hikers and the waters patrolled by a steady flotilla of bright-white ferries, but don't let that put you off: the tourists are rarely in such numbers as to be intrusive, and even in the most popular districts, a brief walk off the beaten track will bring solitude in abundance.

The fjords run all the way up the coast from Stavanger to the Russian border, but are most easily – and impressively – seen on the west coast near **Bergen**, the self-proclaimed "Gateway to the Fjords". Norway's second-largest city, Bergen is a welcoming place with a fascinating old warehouse quarter, a relic of the days when it was the northernmost port of the Hanseatic trade alliance. It's also – as its tag suggests – a handy springboard for the nearby fjords, beginning with the gentle charms of the **Hardangerfjord** and the Flåmsdal valley, where the inspiring **Flåmsbana** mountain railway trundles down to the Aurlandsfjord, a small arm of the mighty **Sognefjord**. Dotted with pretty village resorts, the Sognefjord is the longest and deepest of the country's fjords and is perhaps the most beguiling, rather more so than the **Nordfjord**, lying parallel to the north. Between the Sognefjord and Nordfjord lies the growling and groaning **Jostedalsbreen glacier**, mainland Europe's largest ice-sheet, while east of the Nordfjord is the narrow, S-shaped **Geirangerfjord**, a rugged gash in the landscape that is perhaps the most beautiful of all the fjords. Further north still, the scenery becomes even more extreme, reaching pinnacles of isolation in the splendid **Trollstigen** mountain highway, a stunning prelude to both the unassuming town of **Åndalsnes** and the charming port of **Ålesund**, with its attractive Art Nouveau buildings.

URNES STAVE CHURCH

# Highlights

**❶ Bergen's Fløibanen** There are wonderful views over the city at the top of what must be Europe's quaintest funicular railway. **See p.195**

**❷ Troldhaugen** Visit the delightful fjordside home and studio of Edvard Grieg, Norway's foremost composer. **See p.201**

**❸ Hardangervidda** A mountain plateau of striking beauty, the Hardangervidda offers some of the country's finest hiking. **See p.217**

**❹ The Flåmsbana** The exhilarating Flåm railway careers down the mountainside with the fjords waiting down below. **See p.223**

**❺ Balestrand** The relaxing charms of small-town Balestrand make it a fine base for further Sognefjord explorations. **See p.231**

**❻ Urnes stave church** The oldest stave church in Norway is renowned for its exquisite, almost frenzied, Viking woodcarvings. **See p.236**

**❼ The Sognesfjellsveg** View the sharp, ice-tipped peaks of the Jotunheimen, Norway's most imposing mountain range, from the Sognefjellsveg mountain road. **See p.237**

**❽ Kjenndalsbreen** Inspect the mighty Jostedalsbreen glacier at close quarters on the Kjenndalsbreen, "nodule". **See p.243**

**❾ Ålesund** A beguiling ferry and fishing port, whose streets are flanked by handsome Art Nouveau buildings. **See p.255**

**HIGHLIGHTS ARE MARKED ON THE MAP ON P.188**

# Bergen and around

As it has been raining ever since she arrived in the city, a tourist stops a young boy and asks if it always rains here. "I don't know," he replies, "I'm only thirteen." The joke isn't brilliant, but it does contain a grain of truth. Of all the things to contend with in **BERGEN**, the weather is the most predictable: it rains on average 260 days a year, often relentlessly even in summer, and its forested surroundings are often shrouded in mist. Yet, despite its dampness, Bergen is one of Norway's most enjoyable cities, boasting a spectacular setting, amid seven hills and sheltered to the north, south and west by a series of straggling islands. There's plenty to see in town too, from sturdy old stone buildings and terraces of tiny wooden houses to a veritable raft of **museums** and **art galleries**, while just outside the city limits are Edvard Grieg's home, **Troldhaugen**, as well as the charming open-air **Gamle Bergen** (Old Bergen) museum.

More than anything else, though, it's the general flavour of the place that appeals. Although Bergen has become a major port and something of an industrial centre in recent years, its population rising to around 270,000, it remains a laidback, easy-going town with a firmly nautical air. Fish and fishing may no longer be Bergen's economic lynchpins, but the bustling main harbour, **Vågen**, is still very much the focus of attention. If you stay more than a day or two – perhaps using Bergen as a base for visiting the nearer fjords – you'll soon discover that the city also has the region's best choice of **restaurants** and a decent nightlife.

## Brief history

Founded in 1070 by **King Olav Kyrre** ("the Peaceful"), a Norwegian survivor from the Battle of Stamford Bridge in 1066, Bergen was the largest and most important town in medieval Norway and a regular residence of the country's monarchs. In the fourteenth century the town also became an ecclesiastical centre, supporting no fewer than thirty churches and monasteries, and a member of the **Hanseatic League**, as by this time the town had become a prosperous port linked to other European cities by a vigorous trading life, with **fish** being the main commodity. The League was, however, controlled by German merchants and, after Hansa and local interests started to diverge, the Germans came to dominate the region's economy, reducing the locals to a state of dependency. Neither could the people of Bergen expect help from their kings and queens: rather, in return for easily collected taxes from the Hansa merchants, Norway's

**4**

---

### BERGEN ORIENTATION

Very little of medieval Bergen has survived, although parts of the fortress, the **Bergenhus Festning** – which commands the entrance to the harbour – date from the thirteenth century. The rest of the city centre divides into several distinct parts, the most historically interesting being the harbourside **Bryggen**, which accommodates an attractive ensemble of stone and timber eighteenth- and nineteenth-century merchants' trading houses. The Bryggen ends at the head of the harbour, where Bergen's main square, the **Torget**, features an open-air fish market. East of here, stretching up towards the train station, is one of Bergen's older areas, a mainly nineteenth-century quarter that's at its prettiest along and around **Lille Øvregaten**. This quarter's main thoroughfare, **Kong Oscars gate**, has been roughly treated by the developers, but it does lead to the city's most endearing museum, the **Lepramuseet** (Leprosy Museum). A stone's throw away, the modern concrete blocks surrounding the central **lake**, Lille Lungegårdsvann, form the cultural focus of the city, holding Bergen's art galleries and main concert hall, while the chief commercial area is a few metres to the northwest along the wide and airy **Torgalmenningen**. The steep hill to the south of the central lake is hogged by – and topped off with – the **university**.

Most of the main sights and museums are concentrated in these areas, but no tour of the city is complete without a stroll out along the **Nordnes peninsula**, where fine timber houses pepper the bumpy terrain and the old USF sardine factory now contains a lively and very fashionable arts complex and café.

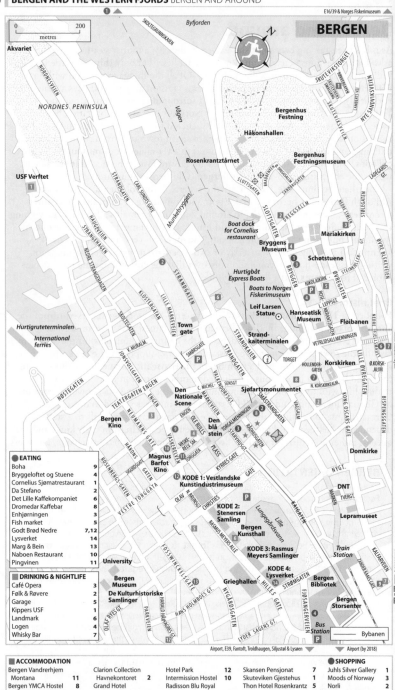

**BERGEN**

medieval monarchs compelled west-coast fishermen to sell their catch to the merchants – at prices the merchants set themselves. As a result, the German trading station that flourished on the Bryggen, Bergen's main wharf, became wealthy and hated in equal measure, a self-regulating colony with its own laws and an administration that was profoundly indifferent to local sentiment.

In the 1550s, with Hansa power finally evaporating, a local lord – one **Kristoffer Valkendorf** – reasserted Norwegian control, but not out of the goodness of his heart. Valkendorf and his cronies simply took over the monopolies that had enriched their German predecessors, and continued to operate this iniquitous "truck" system, which so pauperized the region's fishermen, right up to the late nineteenth century. Bergen's merchants benefited from Norway's neutrality in World War I, developing their trade and expanding their fleets, but it was only after World War II that the town got into its stride, transforming itself from a fish-dependent backwater to the lively city of today.

## Torget

Torget's fish market: May–Sept daily 7am–8pm; Oct–April Mon–Sat 7am–5pm • Free

In 1890, Lilian Leland, author of *Traveling Alone: A Woman's Journey Around the World*, complained of Bergen that "Everything is fishy. You eat fish and drink fish and smell fish and breathe fish." Those days are long gone, but now that Bergen is every inch a go-ahead, modern city, tourists in search of all things piscine flock to **Torget**'s open-air **fish market**. It's not a patch on the days when scores of fishing vessels crowded the quayside to empty their bulging holds, but the stalls still display mounds of prawns and crab-claws, dried cod, herring and a score of other varieties of marine life on slabs, in tanks, under the knife, and in packets. Fruit, vegetables and flowers – as well as souvenirs – have a place in today's market too, and there's easily enough variety to assemble an excellent picnic lunch, so load up or eat up. At the end of the jetty behind Torget, also take a peek at the **statue** of Leif Andreas Larsen, aka Shetlands Larsen, one of Norway's most renowned World War II heroes (see p.283), now presiding over a semicircular, stone war memorial.

## Bryggen

Spearing down the north side of Vågen, **Bryggen** is the obvious historical and cultural target after Torget and the site of the original settlement. The whole area between the Bryggen and Øvregaten just to the rear (see p.193) was once known as Tyskebryggen, or "German Quay", after the **Hanseatic** merchants who operated their trading station here, but the name was unceremoniously dumped after World War II. The **medieval buildings** of the Bryggen were destroyed by fire in 1702, to be replaced by another set of wooden warehouses. In turn, many of these were later demolished to make way for the brick-and-stone warehouses that characterize most of the Bryggen today, though at least these were built in a style modelled on – and sympathetic to – the Hansa period, their distinctive gable ends facing out to the waterfront. Nevertheless, a significant number of early eighteenth-century **timber buildings** have survived, though the first you'll come to, the **Hanseatic Museum** (see p.192), at the north end of Torget, has brick-and-stone neighbours.

A few metres on from here is the **main block** of old timber buildings, now housing souvenir shops, restaurants and bars. Despite the crowds of tourists, it's well worth nosing around here, wandering down the passageways wherever you can. Interestingly, these eighteenth-century timber buildings carefully follow the original building line: the governing body of the Hansa trading station stipulated the exact depth and width of each merchant's building, and the width of the passage separating them – a regularity that's actually best observed from Øvregaten. The planning regulations didn't end there: trade had to be carried out in the front section of the building, with storage rooms to the rear; above were the merchant's office, bedroom and dining room. Up above those, on the top floor, were the living quarters of the employees, grouped into rooms by rank – junior merchants, journeymen/clerks and foremen, wharf hands and, last (and least), errand boys. Every activity in this rigidly hierarchical, all-male society was tightly controlled – employees were forbidden to fraternize with the locals and stiff fines were imposed for hundreds of "offences" including swearing, waking up the master and singing at work.

### Hanseatisk Museum

Bryggen • Daily: June–Aug 9am–6pm; early Sept 9am–5pm; mid-Sept to May 11am–3pm • 100kr, including Schøtstuene; 150kr including Schøtstuene (see opposite) & Norges Fiskerimuseum (see opposite) • ☎ 53 00 61 10, ⓦ museumvest.no

The **Hanseatisk Museum** (Hanseatic Museum) may not be entirely authentic or original, but it's still a fine illustration of an early eighteenth-century merchants' dwelling, kitted out in late Hansa style. As per standard Hansa format, it was a real rabbit-warren of a place in which the trading area occupied the ground floor and the junior staff the top, with the merchants in between. There was, predictably enough, a considerable difference in the comfort afforded to the juniors as distinct from the merchants, but everyone hunkered down in the panelled bunk beds that survive to this day. Also of particular interest is the building's **painted woodwork**, with broad, bold and colourful floral designs in many of the working areas and more formal, Italianate scenes in the merchants' quarters – though the exact provenance of these designs has been the subject of much debate. Dotted throughout the museum is an idiosyncratic assortment of bygones, including the possessions of contemporary families, a medley of indeterminate portraits, several fine pieces of furniture, and an ancient and much-used fish press.

### Bryggens Museum

Dreggsalmeningen • Mid-May to Aug daily 10am–4pm; Sept to mid-May Mon–Fri 11am–3pm, Sat noon–3pm, Sun noon–4pm • 80kr • ☎ 55 30 80 30, ⓦ bymuseet.no

Just off the Bryggen, beside the *Radisson Blu Royal Hotel*, stands the lumpily modern **Bryggens Museum**. Visits begin in the basement, which exhibits all manner of things dug up in the archeological excavations that investigated the Bryggen in the 1950s. A wide range of items was unearthed, from domestic implements like combs and pots through to shoes, buckles and trade goods plus several runic sticks – perhaps surprisingly, Norwegians were laboriously carving runes (see p.385) onto their sticks well into medieval times. The museum displays these finds thematically, both to illustrate the city's early history and provide the backcloth to a set of twelfth-century foundations at the back of the basement, left in situ where they were discovered. The museum's two upper floors are given over to modest temporary exhibitions exploring other aspects of Bergen's past and present.

### Mariakirken

Dreggsalmeningen • June to mid-Sept Mon–Fri 9am–4pm; mid-Sept to May Tues & Thurs 1–3pm • 50kr • ☎ 55 59 32 70

Behind the Bryggens Museum, the perky twin towers of the **Mariakirken** (St Mary's Church) are the most distinctive feature of what is Bergen's oldest extant building, a Romanesque-Gothic church dating from the twelfth century. Still in use as a place of worship, Mariakirken is now firmly Norwegian, but from 1408 to 1706 it was the church of the Hansa merchants, who purchased it lock, stock and barrel. The merchants installed the church's ostentatious Baroque pulpit and its gaudy North German altarpiece, a fifteenth-century triptych, whose exquisite framing is really rather wasted on the sentimental carvings of saints and apostles it surrounds. The walls of the Mariakirken are hung with old commemorative paintings, an insipid lot for the most part with the exception of a finely detailed portrait of *Pastor Lammer, His Wife and Six Children*, looking suitably serious in their Sunday best. The painting is by Lambert von Haven, a seventeenth-century Dutch artist, who went on to greater things at the royal court in Copenhagen; it hangs above the side door on the right-hand side of the nave.

### Schøtstuene

Øvregaten 50 • June–Aug daily 10am–6pm; early Sept daily 10am–5pm; mid-Sept to May Sun 11am–3pm • 100kr, including Hanseatisk Museum; 150kr including Hanseatisk Museum (see opposite) & Norges Fiskerimuseum (see below) • ☎ 53 00 61 10, ⓦ museumvest.no

The **Schøtstuene**, at the back of the Mariakirken, comprises the old Hanseatic assembly rooms, where the merchants would meet to lay down the law or just relax – it was the only building in the whole trading post allowed heating and so it was here that they held their feasts, ceremonies and celebrations. As you explore the comfortable and commodious rooms, it's hard not to conclude that the merchants cared not a jot for their employees shivering away nearby – though, to be fair, their bunk beds weren't much fun either.

### Øvregaten

The Schøtstuene is on **Øvregaten**, an attractive cobbled street that has marked the boundary of the Bryggen for the last eight hundred years and was once, despite the fulminations of the Hansa merchants, the haunt of the city's prostitutes, whose activities were largely tolerated by the Norwegians until Erik Rosenkrantz got on the case (see p.194). From Øvregaten, it's still possible to discern the layout of the old Bryggen **trading station**, a warren of narrow passages separating warped and crooked buildings surmounted by their hat-like, high-pitched roofs. On the upper levels, the eighteenth-century loading bays, staircases and higgledy-piggledy living quarters are still much in evidence, while the overhanging eaves of the passageways were designed to shelter trade goods.

## Norges Fiskerimuseum

Sandviksboder 23 • Mid-June to Aug daily 9am–6pm; Sept to mid-Oct & May to mid-June daily 11am–3pm; mid-Oct to April Sat & Sun 11am–3pm • 90kr, 150kr including Schøtstuene (see above) & Hanseatisk Museum (see opposite) • ☎ 53 00 61 60, ⓦ fiskerimuseum .museumvest.no • Ferry from the Hanseatisk Museum (mid-May to mid-Sept every 40min; 60kr each way)

Amid a cluster of old timber warehouses to the north of the city centre, the new and slightly self-conscious **Norges Fiskerimuseum** (Norwegian Fisheries Museum) covers its subject in detail – from displays on the lives of the fishermen and an underwater panorama through to the processing of the catch. The best bit is, perhaps, the twenty-minute boat trip there from outside the Hanseatisk Museum.

## Bergenhus Festning

Overlooking the mouth of the harbour, **Bergenhus Festning** (Bergen Fortress) is a large and roughly star-shaped fortification now used mostly as a park. The fort's thick stone-and-earth walls date from the nineteenth century, but they enclose the remnants of earlier strongholds – or rather their copies: the Bergenhus was wrecked when an ammunition ship exploded just below the walls in 1944, killing 160 people and wounding 5000 more. The explosion happened on Hitler's birthday, so initially the Germans were convinced it was an act of sabotage, but in fact it was just a dreadful accident.

## WITCHERY IN BERGEN: ANNE PEDERSDATTER

In 1590, **Anne Pedersdatter** was burnt as a witch in Bergen and, remarkably enough, the court proceedings have survived. They reveal a strong-willed and sharp-tongued woman, who antagonized many of her neighbours, whose chosen course of revenge was to accuse her of being a **witch**. As far as the judge was concerned, the crucial bit of evidence came from Anne's maid, who claimed she had been used as a horse to transport her mistress to a Sabbat (Witches' Sabbath). Clearly, Anne's maid either had a grudge or was suborned, but no matter, and, despite the objections of Bergen's bishop, Anne went to the flames. She was not alone: 300 "witches" were executed in Norway in the sixteenth and seventeenth centuries – 250 of them women – in a cruel mix of misogyny and superstition that was then common across most of Europe.

### Rosenkrantztårnet

Bergenhus • Mid-May to mid-Sept daily 9am–4pm; mid-Sept to mid-May Sun noon–3pm • 80kr • ☎ 55 30 80 30, ⓦ bymuseet.no

Of the two main medieval replicas in the Bergenhus, the more diverting is the forbidding **Rosenkrantztårnet** (Rosenkrantz Tower), whose spiral staircases, medieval rooms and low rough corridors make an enjoyable gambol. It's also possible to walk out onto the rooftop battlements, from where there is a wide view over the harbour. The tower is named after **Erik Rosenkrantz** (1519–75), governor of Bergen in the 1560s, who turned his draughty medieval quarters into a grand fortified residence, equipping his own chamber with fine large windows and a handsome Renaissance chimneypiece, both of which have survived in good condition. This same room also has a copy of Rosenkrantz's gravestone, a somewhat ill-balanced but still strikingly realistic work depicting his wife in a long flowing dress and him in a suit of armour with a codpiece so tight it would bring tears to most men's eyes. Also within the tower are several other small but intriguing exhibits, principally one on the sophisticated penal codes instituted by King Magnus Lagabøter ("Lawmender"; 1238–80) and another on Anne Pedersdatter (see box above). As for Rosenkrantz himself, he was known principally as the architect of a new law under which anyone found guilty of an illegitimate sexual affair had to confess to a priest before being fined. The law applied initially to men and women in equal measure, but by the 1590s women bore the brunt of any punishment – surprise, surprise. In Bergen, for example, women who could not pay the fine had to stand naked at the entrance to a church before being thrown out of town, whereas the men just got exiled.

### Håkonshallen

Bergenhus • Daily: mid-May to mid-Sept 10am–4pm; mid-Sept to mid-May noon–3pm • 80kr • ☎ 55 30 80 30, ⓦ bymuseet.no

In the Bergenhus, metres from the Rosenkrantztårnet, is the entrance to a large cobbled courtyard, which is itself flanked by nineteenth-century officers' quarters and the **Håkonshallen**, a careful reconstruction of the Gothic ceremonial hall built for King Håkon Håkonsson in the middle of the thirteenth century. After Norway lost its independence, the capacious hall became surplus to requirements and no one knew quite what to do with it for several centuries; but it was revamped in 1910 and rebuilt after the 1944 explosion and is now in use once again for public ceremonies.

### Bergenhus Festningsmuseum

Øvre Dreggsalmeningen • Tues–Sun 11am–5pm • Free • ☎ 55 54 63 87, ⓦ forsvarsmuseer.no

Often neglected, the **Bergenhus Festningsmuseum** (Bergenhus Fortress Museum) is one of the city's better museums, its first floor holding several well-composed displays exploring the effects of World War II on Bergen. There's a detailed account of the German naval attack on Bergen in 1940 and on the development of the Resistance thereafter. The Resistance was particularly strong in Bergen, partly because the city had long-standing seafaring links with Great Britain and partly because it had suffered grievously from U-boat attacks on Norwegian shipping in World War I. Unfortunately, the Germans proved adept at tracking down their enemies, and time and again they broke the back of the main Resistance groups, though they were flummoxed by the explosion that levelled much of the Bergenhus in 1944 (see p.193). The museum's second floor is far less interesting, being given over to a detailed exploration of the history of the Bergenhus fortress; the ground floor is for temporary displays.

## Lille Øvregaten

Running east from the lower Fløibanen terminal, **Lille Øvregaten** is lined by an appealing mix of expansive nineteenth-century villas and dinky timber houses, mostly bright-white clapboard, but some deep red, ochre and light blue too. There are more old timber houses up above, and these are, if anything, even quainter, pressing in against the steep cobbled lanes that steer and veer around hunks of stone which were, at the time, simply too bothersome to move: to explore the area, take the first left up the hillside from Lille Øvregaten and follow your nose.

## Domkirke

Domkirkeplassen • July & Aug Mon–Fri 10am–4pm • Free • ☎ 55 59 71 75, ⊛ bergendomkirke.no

Lille Øvregaten curves round to the **Domkirke** (Cathedral), a heavy-duty edifice whose stern exterior, with its whopping clocktower, has been restored and rebuilt several times since its original construction in the twelfth century. The interior doesn't set the pulse racing, though there's a noticeable penchant for fancy wooden staircases – two leading to the organ and one to the pulpit – which can't help but seem a little flippant given the dourness of their surroundings.

## Lepramuseet

Kong Oscars gate 59 • Mid-May to Aug daily 11am–3pm • 80kr • ☎ 48 16 26 78, ⊛ bymuseet.no

Telling the intriguing tale of Norway's fight against leprosy, the **Lepramuseet** (Leprosy Museum) is housed in the charming, eighteenth-century buildings of **St Jørgens Hospital** (St George's Hospital), whose assorted dwellings are ranged around a paved courtyard. The disease first appeared in Scandinavia in Viking times and became especially prevalent in the coastal districts of western Norway, with around three percent of the population classified as lepers in the early nineteenth century. St George's specialized in the care of lepers, assuming a more proactive role from 1830, when a series of Norwegian medics tried to find a cure. The most successful of them was **Armauer**

---

### THE FLØIBANEN FUNICULAR RAILWAY

Dating back to the 1910s, the distinctly Ruritanian lower terminus of the **Fløibanen funicular railway** is a delightful introduction to one of Bergen's major attractions, whose trains shuttle passengers up to the top of **Mount Fløyen** – "The Vane" – at 320m above sea level. When the weather is fine, you get a bird's-eye view of the city and its surroundings from the plateau-summit, and here also is a large and popular café-restaurant. Afterwards, you can walk back down to the city in about 45 minutes, or push on into the woods along several well-marked, colour-coded footpaths (pick up free trail maps at the lower terminal). The shortest and perhaps the most enjoyable is the 1.6km-loop trail to Skomakerdiket lake and back.

#### PRACTICALITIES

The lower terminal is on Vetrlidsallmenningen (☎ 55 33 68 00, ⊛ floyen.no). Departures every 15–30min: Mon–Fri 7.30am–11pm, Sat & Sun 8am–11pm; return fare 90kr, one-way 45kr. Note that when a cruise ship is in port, the queues are long – come back later.

**Hansen**, who in 1873 was the first person to identify the leprosy bacillus. The last lepers left St Jørgens in 1946 and the hospital has been left untouched, the small rooms off the central gallery revealing the patients' humble living quarters. Also on display are a few medical implements and a number of gruesome sketches and paintings of sufferers alongside their desperate life stories. Dating from 1702, the adjoining hospital **chapel** is delightfully homely, its rickety, creaking timbers holding a domineering pulpit topped off by half a dozen folksy cherubs and an altarpiece decorated with yet more cherubs and some dainty scrollwork. The two altar paintings are crude but appropriate – *Jesus and the Ten Lepers* and *The Canaanite's Daughter Healed*.

## Lille Lungegårdsvann

Bergen's attractively landscaped central lake, **Lille Lungegårdsvann**, is a focus for festivals and parades, and its southern side is flanked by no fewer than five **art galleries** – KODE 1, 2, 3 and 4 and the Bergen Kunsthal. Taken together, they hold an excellent collection of Norwegian art, though the finest work is on display at **KODE 3: the Rasmus Meyers Samlinger** and **KODE 4: Lysverket**. KODE 4 in particular has benefited from the largesse of Oslo-born **Rolf Stenersen** (1899–1978), who gifted much of his substantial art collection to his adopted city of Bergen in the 1970s. Stenersen was something of a Renaissance man – one-time Olympic athlete, financier and chum of Munch – who seems to have had a successful stab at almost everything, even writing some highly acclaimed short stories in the 1930s.

Also on the southern side of the lake, behind the galleries on Nygårdsgaten, is the **Grieghallen** concert hall, a large modern edifice that serves as a principal venue for the annual Bergen International Festival (see p.208).

### KODE 4: Lysverket

Rasmus Meyers Allé 9 • Mid-May to Aug daily 11am–5pm; Sept to mid-May Tues–Fri 11am–4pm, Sat & Sun 11am–5pm • Joint ticket for KODEs 1, 2, 3 & 4 is 100kr • ☎ 53 00 97 04, ⓦ kodebergen.no

The easternmost of the lakeside galleries is **Lysverket**, which occupies a distinctive and very appealing Art Deco/Functionalist building – complete with its own mini-rotunda – that started out as offices for a power company. The gallery spreads over **three floors** and is divided up both thematically and chronologically, which can be a tad confusing, and there's some rotation of the paintings on display too.

#### The ground floor

The ground floor is largely devoted to **temporary exhibitions**, though there is also a separate, semipermanent section on **Nikolai Astrup** (1880–1928), who is generally regarded as the last of the Norwegian Romantics – or at least neo-Romantics: sometimes Astrup's paintings portray a benign and strongly coloured rural idyll, at other times – as in *Kollen* – the Norwegian landscape appears dangerous and malevolent.

#### The first floor

The first floor holds a good sample of the work of **Johan Christian Dahl** (1788–1857), one of Norway's finest landscape painters. Several of Dahl's early sketches are exhibited here, but these are crude affairs executed before he hit his artistic stride, whereas his *Bergen Harbour* and *Nordic Landscape with a River* reveal Dahl at his most accomplished. On this floor also are several examples of the work of **Adolph Tidemand** (1814–76) and **Hans Gude** (1825–1903), both of whom specialized in rural scenes populated by idealized versions of Norwegian country folk, and of the influential **Christian Krohg** (1852–1925), whose striking Realism is seen to fine advantage in his *Fight for Survival*, which rails against urban poverty. A final section on this floor holds the museum's modest selection of **old masters**, mostly Dutch and Italian paintings, plus an engaging miscellany of medieval Greek and Russian **icons**.

The top floor

The top floor is dedicated to the twentieth century and it's here you'll find a selection of watercolours and oils by the versatile Norwegian **Jakob Weidemann** (1923–2001), whose work was much influenced by French Cubists during the 1940s, though he is now associated with the shimmering, pastel-painted abstracts he churned out in the 1960s. There's also a delightful *Four Sisters* by **Alf Rolfsen** (1895–1979), the disturbing magic realism of **Bjarne Lund** (1896–1931), and a searing *Sisters of Liberty* by **Arne Ekeland** (1908–94). A self-taught painter from Eidsvoll, near Oslo, Ekeland was a committed leftist whose paintings either protest the oppression of the working class or portray a vision of a Socialist utopia – though some do both at the same time. A final section on the same floor displays a small selection of twentieth-century international works, most notably from Miró, Picasso, Braque, Ernst and the Bauhaus painter, Paul Klee.

## KODE 3: Rasmus Meyers Samlinger

Rasmus Meyers Allé 7 • Mid-May to Aug daily 10am–5pm; Sept to mid-May Tues–Fri 11am–4pm, Sat & Sun 11am–5pm • Joint ticket for KODEs 1, 2, 3 & 4 is 100kr • ☎ 53 00 97 04, ⓦ kodebergen.no

Housed in a substantial and distinctive building with a pagoda-like roof, **KODE 3: Rasmus Meyers Samlinger** (Rasmus Meyer Collection) boasts a superb survey of Norwegian art from 1815 to 1945, gifted to the city by one of its old merchant families – the Meyers – and now displayed broadly chronologically on two easily absorbed and well-organized floors. On the **ground floor**, a string of rooms concentrates on **Norwegian Romanticism**, with Dahl, Gude, Thomas Fearnley and Tidemand much in evidence – Dahl's *Nigardsbreen* landscape is a typical work as is Tidemand's *The Youngest Son's Farewell*. There are a couple of period rooms on this floor too, most memorably the Rococo excesses of the **Blumenthal room**, whose fancy stuccowork and allegorical wall and ceiling paintings were knocked up in the 1750s for a Bergen merchant by an itinerant Danish artist, one Mathias Blumenthal.

First floor

The **first floor** displays examples of the decorative medievalism of **Gerhard Munthe** (1849–1929) and the finely executed canvases of **Axel Revold** (1887–1962), a one-time pupil of Matisse – his *Mediterranean Fishermen* being a case in point. Look out also for the work of the talented **Henrik Sørensen** (1882–1962) and of **Erik Werenskiold** (1855–1938), who is perhaps best remembered for his colourful illustrations of the folk stories collected by Asbjørnsen and Moe in rural Norway. The stories had already been published several times when Werenskiold and his accomplice Theodor Kittelsen (1857–1914) got working on them, but it was they who effectively defined the appearance of the country's various folkloric figures – from trolls upwards – in the popular imagination.

Munch

KODE 3's star turn, however, is its sizeable sample of the work of **Edvard Munch** (1863–1944) – if you missed out in Oslo (see p.68 & p.81), then this is the place to make amends. There are examples from all Munch's major periods, with the disturbing – and disturbed – works of the 1890s inevitably stealing the spotlight: among several, there is the searing and unsettling *Jealousy*, the fractured *Woman in Three Stages*, the piercing *At the Deathbed* and the ghoulish *Evening on Karl Johan*. The last was painted in 1892, just two years after Munch's relaxed and cheerful *Spring Day on Karl Johan*, a measure of the man's mental collapse.

## Bergen Kunsthall

Rasmus Meyers Allé 5 • Tues & Wed, Fri–Sun 11am–5pm, Thurs 11am–8pm • 50kr • ☎ 94 01 50 50, ⓦ kunsthall.no

The **Bergen Kunsthall** (Bergen Fine Art Society) has developed into the city's most imaginative contemporary arts venue with up to three separate exhibitions at any one time. It's all very hit and miss – banal at worst, stunning at best – but no one could say the exhibitions were predictable. Norwegian artists predominate, but there is a leavening of international stuff too.

### KODE 2: Stenersens Samling

Rasmus Meyers Allé 3 • Mid-May to Aug daily 11am–5pm; Sept to mid-May Tues–Fri 11am–4pm, Sat & Sun 11am–5pm • Joint ticket for KODEs 1, 2, 3 & 4 is 100kr • ☎ 53 00 97 04, ⓦ kodebergen.no

In a glum concrete block, **KODE 2: Stenersens Samling** (Stenersen Collection) specializes in temporary exhibitions of contemporary art, mostly international but with a strong Norwegian showing. The gallery occupies one medium-sized, split-level floor above the ground-floor shop and coffee bar.

### KODE 1: Vestlandske Kunstindustrimuseum

Nordahl Bruns gate 9 • Mid-May to Aug daily 11am–5pm; Sept to mid-May Tues–Fri 11am–4pm, Sat & Sun 11am–5pm • Joint ticket for KODEs 1, 2, 3 & 4 100kr • ☎ 55 33 66 33, ⓦ kodebergen.no

The varied set-piece collections of **KODE 1: Vestlandske Kunstindustrimuseum** (West Norway Decorative Art Museum) are displayed in the Permanenten building, a whopping Neoclassical-meets-mock-Gothic structure built as a cultural centre in the 1890s. The museum's permanent collection features silver, furniture, glass, porcelain and textiles plus an extensive range of Chinese arts and crafts gifted to Bergen by Johan Munthe (1864–1935), who was Bergen-born, but a long-time resident in China, where he served as an officer in the Chinese army. KODE 1 also offers a varied and imaginative programme of temporary exhibitions focused on contemporary craft and design.

## Torgalmenningen and the Sjøfartsmonumentet

The broad sweep of pedestrianized **Torgalmenningen** is a suitably handsome setting for the commercial heart of modern Bergen, lined with arcaded shops and department stores and decorated at its Torget end by the splendid **Sjøfartsmonumentet** (Seafarers' Monument), a vigorous, large-scale granite and bronze composition celebrating the city's seafaring traditions. Unveiled in 1950, it sports twelve sculptures on its lower section with two sets of reliefs up above. Its southeast side – nearest the Galleriet shopping centre – bears the inscription **Tiende Århundre** (Tenth Century), the theme being the Vikings' semi-legendary voyages to Vinland (North America). The reliefs depict a Viking longship with its sails hoisted and a meeting between the Norsemen and indigenous Americans; down below there is a Norwegian chieftain with a spear, a *skald* (Norse bard) wearing sheepskin clothing, and a *berserker* (warrior) with a shield on his back. On the monument's southwest side, inscribed **Attende Århundre** (Eighteenth Century), the theme is the rediscovery of Greenland by Bergen seamen, with reliefs of the Norwegian missionary Hans Egede preaching to the Inuit and a ship being launched while a huge sea serpent writhes in the water beneath it. The northwest side of the monument is dedicated to Bergen's mercantile success in the **Nittende Århundre** (Nineteenth Century). There are sculptures of a wealthy ship-owner with a top hat, a rookie merchant seaman and a pilot; the reliefs above show whaling and a scene from a shipyard. The fourth side, facing towards Torget, and inscribed **Tjuende Århundre** (Twentieth Century), has the theme of carrying oil and the sculptures depict a young deckhand, a first mate with binoculars and a ship's engineer with a spanner – respectively symbolizing daring, watchfulness and loyalty. One relief up above has a ship with the rising sun behind it (symbolizing hope) and the other depicts the Resurrection in which the drowned souls on the left are resurrected to eternal life by an angel.

---

**THE ULRIKSBANEN: A BIRD'S-EYE VIEW**

Providing panoramic views over Bergen and its surroundings, the **Ulriksbanen cable car** (April to mid-Oct daily 9am–9pm; mid to late Oct & Jan–March Tues–Sun 10am–5pm; weather/wind permitting; 100kr single, 160kr return; ☎ 53 64 36 43, ⊛ ulriken643.no) whisks passengers up to the top of **Mount Ulriken**, which at 643 metres is the highest of the seven hills around town. There's a café at the top and you can hike (or ski) off into the surrounding hills, but most people come here for the view. The cable car's lower terminal is behind the Haukeland Sykehus (hospital) about 6km east of the centre. In the summer, the special Ulriken Express bus shuttles between Torget, in the centre, and the lower terminal (May–Sept hourly); at other times of the year, take city bus #2 or #3 (Mon–Fri every 10–20min, Sat & Sun every 20–30min) from Småstrandgaten.

---

## Ole Bulls plass

Pedestrianized **Ole Bulls plass** is the town's main meeting point with locals gathering here for all sorts of reasons, from first dates to commemorations, at **Den blå stein** (The Blue Stone), a 3m-long rectangular hunk of stone jacked up on a cross-lying block by the sculptor Asbjørn Andersen in 1993. Ole Bulls plass also sports a rock pool and fountain, above which stands a jaunty statue of local lad **Ole Bull**, the nineteenth-century virtuoso violinist and heart-throb – his island villa just outside Bergen is a popular day-trip (see p.202). Ole Bulls plass stretches up to the municipal **theatre**, Den Nationale Scene, a curious Art Nouveau building from 1909 that hogs the brow of a hill guarded by a singularly fearsome, saucer-eyed statue of Henrik Ibsen.

## Bergen University: De Kulturhistoriske Samlinger

Håkon Sheteligsplass 10 • June–Aug Tues–Fri 10am–4pm, Sat & Sun 11am–4pm; Sept–May Tues–Fri 10am–3pm, Sat & Sun 11am–4pm • 60kr • ☎ 55 58 31 40, ⊛ uib.no

Bergen University sprawls over the hill at the south end of Christies gate, its campus zeroing in on the several collections of the **Bergen Museum**. Pride of place here goes to **De Kulturhistoriske Samlinger** (Cultural History Museum), whose large and rambling collection includes excellent sections on stave churches, medieval woodcarvings, folk art – most memorably several charming coverlets – and St Olav, the patron saint of Norway. In the foyer, look out also for the **Eggjasteinen** (Eggja Stone), dated to between the seventh and ninth centuries and inscribed with one of the longest runes to have survived. Life must have been pretty gloomy – one verse reads: "Over my relatives the wild one cast a corpse wave".

## Nordnes peninsula

On the south side of Vågen, the hilly **Nordnes peninsula** pokes out into the fjord, its narrow streets and alleys negotiating an assortment of ridges and rises. Nordnes is at its prettiest on **Skottegaten** and **Nedre Strangehagen**, where an attractive mix of old timber houses and nineteenth-century stone villas ramble along the peninsula's southern flank. Nearby, reached via a cutting through a steep bluff, is the old, waterside United Sardine Factories, imaginatively converted into an arts complex, the **USF Verftet** (see p.208). From here, it takes about ten minutes to get to the **aquarium**, the peninsula's main tourist attraction.

### Akvariet

Nordnesbakken 4 • Daily: May–Aug 9am–6pm; Sept–April 10am–4pm • May–Aug 250kr; Sept–April 200kr • ☎ 55 55 71 71, ⊛ akvariet.no • A 20min walk from Ole Bulls plass or city bus #11

Perched on the western tip of the Nordnes peninsula, and set amid a pleasant park, Bergen's **Akvariet** (Aquarium) has all the marine gubbins you might expect from penguin and seal hidey-holes – and feeding times – to numerous indoor and outdoor tanks packed with North Sea fish of every conceivable species.

# Out from the centre

The lochs, fjords and rocky wooded hills surrounding central Bergen have channelled the city's **suburbs** into long ribbons, which trail off in every direction. These urban outskirts are not in themselves particularly enticing – even if they are extraordinarily handsome when viewed from either **Mount Fløyen** (see box, p.195) or **Mount Ulriken** (see box opposite) – but tucked away among them, to the south of the centre, are three prime attractions: **Troldhaugen**, Edvard Grieg's former home; Ole Bull's fanciful villa on the island of **Lysøen**; and the composer Harald Sæverud's former home at **Siljustøl**. The fourth attraction hereabouts, **Fantoft stave church**, is not really in the same league, but it is a popular target. All four sights are accessible by **public transport** with varying degrees of ease and there are organized excursions too – the tourist office has details and sells tickets (see p.204).

## Troldhaugen

Troldhaugveien • Daily: May–Sept 9am–6pm; Oct–April 10am–4pm • 100kr • ☎ 55 92 29 92, ⓦ griegmuseum.no • Bybanen to Hop station (every 10–20min; 23min; 36kr), from where it's a dull 30min walk to Troldhaugen: double back from the station towards Bergen and you'll spot the sign; by car take the E39 south from the centre and follow the signs

**Troldhaugen** (Hill of the Trolls), about 8km south of the city centre off Hwy-580, was the lakeside home of **Edvard Grieg** (see box below) for the last 22 years of his life – though "home" is something of an exaggeration, as he spent several months every year touring the concert halls of Europe. Norway's only composer of world renown,

### THE MODEST MAN: EDVARD GRIEG

The composer of some of the most popular works in the standard orchestral repertoire, **Edvard Grieg** (1843–1907) was born in Bergen, the son of a saltfish merchant. It was, considering the region's historical dependence on the product, an appropriate background for a man whose romantic compositions have come to epitomize western Norway, or at least an idealized version of it: certainly, Grieg was quite happy to accept the connection, and as late as 1903 he modestly commented that "I am sure my music has the taste of codfish in it." In part this was sincere, but the composer had an overt political agenda too. Norway had not been independent since 1380, and, after centuries of Danish and Swedish rule, its population lacked political and cultural self-confidence – a situation the Norwegian nationalists of the day, including Ibsen and Grieg, were determined to change. Such was their success that they played a key preparatory role in the build-up to the dissolution of the union with Sweden, and the creation of an independent Norway in 1905.

**Musically**, it was Grieg's mother, a one-time professional pianist, who egged him on, and at the tender age of 15 he was packed off to the Leipzig Conservatory to study music, much to the delight of his mentor, **Ole Bull** (see p.202). In 1863, Grieg was on the move again, transferring to Copenhagen for another three-year study stint and ultimately returning to Norway an accomplished performer and composer in 1866. The following year he married the Norwegian soprano **Nina Hagerup** (1845–1935), helped to found a musical academy in Oslo and produced the first of ten collections of folk-based *Lyric Pieces* for piano. In 1868, Grieg completed his best-known work, the *Piano Concerto in A minor*, and, in 1869, his *25 Norwegian Folk Songs and Dances*. Thereafter, the composer's output remained mainly songs and solo piano pieces with a strong folkloric influence, even incorporating snatches of traditional songs.

During the 1870s Grieg collaborated with a number of Norwegian writers, including **Bjørnstjerne Bjørnson** and **Henrik Ibsen**, one of the results being his much acclaimed *Peer Gynt* suites, and, in 1884, he composed the *Holberg Suite*, written to commemorate the Dano-Norwegian philosopher and playwright, Ludvig Holberg. It is these orchestral suites, along with the piano concerto, for which he is best remembered today. In 1885, now well-heeled and well-known, Grieg and his family moved into **Troldhaugen**, the house that had been built for them near Bergen. By that time, Grieg had established a pattern of composing during the spring and summer, and undertaking extended performance tours around Europe with his wife during the autumn and winter. This gruelling schedule continued until – and contributed to – his death in Bergen in 1907.

**4**

> ## RECITALS AT TROLDHAUGEN
>
> Troldhaugen offers a top-ranking programme of **Grieg concerts**, held in the Troldsalen, throughout the summer both at lunchtimes (mid-May to Sept 1 daily; 30min; 160kr) and in the evening (mid-June to mid-Aug 2 weekly; 1hr 30min; 250kr). For evening performances, free buses leave from near the tourist office one hour before the concert begins. Tickets can be bought online (Ⓦ griegmuseum.no) or from the tourist office, but are snapped up quickly.

Grieg has a good share of commemorative monuments in Bergen – a statue in the city park and the Grieghallen concert hall to name but two – but it's here that you get a sense of the man, an immensely likeable and much-loved figure of leftish opinions and disarming modesty: "I make no pretensions of being in the class with Bach, Mozart and Beethoven," he once wrote, "Their works are eternal, while I wrote for my day and generation."

It's best to begin a visit at the **museum**, where Grieg's life and times are chronicled and a short film provides further musical insights. From here, it's a brief walk to the **house**, a pleasant and unassuming villa built in 1885, and still pretty much as Grieg left it, with a jumble of photos and period furniture. Grieg didn't, in fact, compose much in the house, but preferred to walk down to a small **hut** he had built just along the shore – the hut has survived, though today you can't actually go in. Also at Troldhaugen is a modern concert hall, the **Troldsalen**, where there are recitals of Grieg's works in the summer (see box above). Finally, the ashes of Grieg and his wife – the singer Nina Hagerup – are inside a curious **tomb** blasted into a rock face overlooking the lake, and sealed with twin memorial stones; it's only a couple of minutes' walk down from the main footpath, but few people venture out to this lovely, melancholic spot.

### Lysøen

Lysøen • Villa: mid-May to Aug daily 11am–4pm • 60kr • ☎ 56 30 90 77, Ⓦ lysoen.no • To get there on public transport, take the Bybanen to Lagunen station (every 10–20min; 30min; 36kr), then bus #62 (Mon–Fri 5 daily, Sat 2 daily, no Sun service; 25min; Ⓦ rutebok.no) to Buena Kai (quay); from here, passenger ferries run to Lysøen (hourly on the hour when the villa is open; last ferry back at 4.30pm; 10min; 60kr return; Ⓦ lysoen.no). By car, head south out of Bergen on the E39, then take Hwy-580 to Lagunen followed by Hwy-546 to Fana; at Fana, Hwy-546 turns sharp right, but you keep straight over the Fanafjell and then follow the signs; allow 40min • There are also guided tours here from Bergen (see p.205)

Some 27km south of Bergen, the leafy, hilly little island of **Lysøen** holds the eccentrically ornate summer **villa** of the violinist **Ole Bull** (1810–80), which, like Grieg's home, has been turned into a museum packed with biographical bits and pieces. With its onion dome and frilly trelliswork, Bull's villa was supposed to break with what the musician felt to be the dour architectural traditions of Norway, but whether it works or not is difficult to say – for one thing, the arabesque columns and scrollwork of the capacious music-hall-cum-main-room look muddled rather than inventive – though the whole ensemble still manages to be charming. Bull may have chosen to build in a foreign style, but he was a prominent member of that group of nineteenth-century artists and writers, the **Norwegian Romanticists**, who were determined to revive the country's traditions – his special contribution being the promulgation of its **folk music**. He toured America and Europe for several decades, his popularity as a sort of nineteenth-century Mantovani dented neither by his fervent utopian socialism, nor by some of his eccentric remarks: asked who taught him to play the violin, he replied "The mountains of Norway". Then again, people were inclined to overlook his faults because of his engaging manner and stunning good looks – smelling salts were kept on hand during his concerts to revive swooning women, and were much in use. The hourly **guided tour** of the house is amusingly anecdotal and afterwards the island's wooded footpaths, laid out by Bull himself, make for some energetic walks. Maps of the island are given away free at the house, from where it's a stiff, steep but short walk over the hill to **Lysevågen**, a sheltered cove where you can go for a dip.

## Siljustøl Museum

Siljustølveien 50, Rådal • Late June to mid-Aug Sun noon–4pm • 60kr • ☎ 55 92 29 92, ⓦ siljustolmuseum.no • There are no good public transport links between Bergen and the museum. By car, drive south out of Bergen on the E39, forking off onto Hwy-580; proceed and then turn left onto Hwy-546 at the island, followed by a first right as per the signs; allow 30min

Bergen's own **Harald Sæverud** (1897–1992) was a classical composer of some European standing, whose oeuvre included a hatful of symphonies and concertos. Among Norwegians he was, however, more popular for the anti-Nazi music he wrote during the German occupation of World War II and his gallows humour. After his death, his old home and studio at **Siljustøl**, about 14km south of Bergen, were turned into the **Siljustøl Museum**, where you can nose around his life and musical times. Sæverud's music is showcased in a series of **summer concerts** (tickets from Bergen tourist office) and the house, a large wood and stone structure dating from the 1930s, is surrounded by wooded parkland, crisscrossed by footpaths.

## Fantoft stavkirke

Fantoftvegen • Mid-May to mid-Sept daily 10.30am–6pm • 55kr • ☎ 55 28 07 10, ⓦ fantoftstavkirke.com • Bybanen to Paradis (every 10–20min; 21min; 36kr), then a 25min walk: from the station walk east along Sandbrekkevegen and then veer left up Birkelundsbakken & watch for the signs. By car take the E39 south from the centre, turn onto Hwy-582 and follow the signs

**Fantoft stavkirke** (Fantoft stave church), about 8km south of downtown Bergen, was actually moved here from a tiny village on the Sognefjord in the 1880s. The first owner, a government official, had the structure revamped in the style of Borgund stave church (see p.174), complete with dragon finials, high-pitched roofs and an outside gallery, though in fact it's unlikely that the original church looked much like Borgund at all. This is, however, somewhat irrelevant as the Fantoft church was burnt to the ground in 1992 by a supposed Satanist. Extraordinarily, the then owner didn't surrender, but had a replica of the destroyed church built instead and it stands today, a finely carved affair with disconcertingly fresh timbers, set among beech and pine trees.

**4**

---

### ARRIVAL AND DEPARTURE | BERGEN AND AROUND

#### BY PLANE

**Bergen airport** is at Flesland, about 15km south of the city centre, and Flybussen connect the two (every 15–30min; 30–45min depending on traffic; 100kr oneway, 170kr return; ⓦ flybussen.no). In the city centre, these Flybussen pull in at several stops, including the bus and train stations, before terminating at the harbourfront *Radisson Blu Royal Hotel*, on the Bryggen. Taxis from the airport to the city centre cost in the region of 400kr. Note that the Bybanen (Light Railway; see p.204), which begins in the city centre, will be extended to the airport by 2018.

#### BY TRAIN

**Bergen train station** (ⓦ www.nsb.no) is located on Strømgaten, from where it's a 5–10min walk to Bergen's main harbour, Vågen.

Destinations Finse (3–4 daily; 2hr 20min); Myrdal (3–4 daily; 2hr); Oslo (3–4 daily; 6hr 30min); Voss (5 daily; 1hr 20min).

#### BY BUS

**Bergen bus station** is attached to the Bergen Storsenter shopping mall, on Strømgaten, metres from the train station and a 5–10min walk from Bergen's main harbour. Local timetables on ⓦ skyss.no; local and long distance on ⓦ rutebok.no.

Destinations Ålesund (1 daily; 10hr with one change); Flåm (2–4 daily; 3hr); Florø (every 3hr; 5hr with one change); Gudvangen (2–4 daily; 2hr 35min); Haugesund (every 1–2hr; 3hr 15min); Lom (1 daily; 8hr 30min); Norheimsund (every 1–2hr; 1hr 25min); Odda (1 daily; 3hr); Oslo (1–2 daily; 9hr 30min); Sogndal (2–4 daily; 4hr 30min); Stavanger (every 1–2hr; 5hr–5hr 30min); Stryn (1 daily; 6hr 15min); Voss (2–4 daily; 1hr 50min).

#### BY HURTIGBÅT PASSENGER EXPRESS BOAT

Hurtigbåt boats line up on the south side of the head of the harbour at the Strandkaiterminalen. Note that at time of writing the Hurtigbåt service linking Bergen with Stavanger and Haugesund was not in operation, though this may change.

Destinations Norled (ⓦ norled.no) currently provides a particularly useful Hurtigbåt service from Bergen to the Sognefjord at Vik (1–2 daily; 3hr 30min), Balestrand (1–2 daily; 4hr), Flåm (1–2 daily; 5hr 30min), and Sogndal (1–2 daily; 5hr). There are also Hurtigbåt boats between Bergen and Florø (1–2 daily; 3hr 30min) and Rosendal (1–2 daily; 2hr).

#### BY HURTIGRUTEN

Bergen is the home port of the Hurtigruten coastal boat (ⓦ hurtigruten.co.uk), which docks at the

Hurtigruteterminalen, on the south side of the city centre, off Nøstegaten, about 900m due south of the main harbour. Destinations Florø (1 daily; 6hr); Ålesund (1 daily; 13hr); Geiranger (June–Aug only 1 daily; 16hr 30min).

### INTERNATIONAL CAR FERRY

Fjord Line (ⓦ fjordline.com) international car ferries from Stavanger and Hirsthals in Denmark berth at the dock next to the Hurtigruteterminalen, off Nøstegaten, about 900m due south of the main harbour.

### BY CAR

**Driving** If you're driving into Bergen, note that a toll (19kr) is charged on all vehicles entering the city centre, but you don't have to stop – it's levied electronically with cameras reading your vehicle's toll tag. There's no charge for driving out of the city. In an attempt to keep the city centre relatively free of traffic, there's a confusing and none-too-successful one-way system in operation, supplemented by rigorously enforced on-street parking restrictions.

**Parking** Outside peak periods, on-street parking is free but difficult to find, whereas during peak periods (Mon–Fri 8am–5pm, Sat 8am–10am) it's both hard to find and metered for a maximum of 2hr at 30kr/hr. Your best bet, therefore, is to make straight for one of the central car parks: the largest is the 24hr Bygarasjen, a short walk from the city centre, behind the Storsenter shopping mall and bus station. Charges here are heavily discounted – it costs just 150kr for 24hr. The 24hr Rosenkrantz P-Hus, on Rosenkrantzgaten, is much handier for the harbourfront, but charges are higher: 24hr costs 225kr.

## GETTING AROUND

Most of Bergen's leading attractions are located in the city centre, which is compact enough to be readily explored **on foot**. For outlying sights and accommodation, however, you may well need to use the city's **public transport network**, whose buses and one-line Bybanen (Light Rail) are coordinated by Skyss (ⓦ skyss.no).

**By bus** Bergen's buses reach into every corner of the city and its environs. The hub of the network is the bus stops that line up along Olav Kyrres gate between the terminus of the Bybanen (Light Rail) and Småstrandgaten. Flat-fare tickets for travel within the city limits cost 36kr; they are available from the driver.

**By Bybanen** Beginning in the city centre at the junction of Olav Kyrres gate and Starvhusgate, Bergen's one-line Bybanen stretches south into the suburbs, stopping at the train/bus station before proceeding onto Lagunen, a distance of 12km, with an extension of the line to the airport under construction and planned for completion by 2018. Flat-fare tickets cost 36kr and there are trains every 10–20min; tickets are available from the automatic machines at every station.

**By passenger ferry** Two passenger ferries offer useful short cuts across the harbour. The first chugs out from the jetty on the south side of Torget to the Nordnes peninsula, docking not far from the Akvariet (late May to Aug daily 10am–6pm; 70kr return, 45kr one-way). The second, the Beffenfergen (Mon–Fri 7.30am–4pm & May–Aug Sat 11am–4pm; every 15min; 25kr each way; ⓦ beffenfergen.no), links the Dreggekaien, the jetty opposite the *Clarion Collection Havnekontoret*, with Munkebryggen, off Carl Sundts gate. From mid-May to mid-September, the Beffenfergen also sallies out from the harbour to the Fisheries Museum (see p.193).

**Car rental** All the major international car rental companies have offices in town and/or at the airport, including Hertz, at the airport (☎ 55 22 60 75); and Europcar, also at the airport (☎ 55 22 79 30).

## INFORMATION

**Tourist office** The tourist office is at Strandkaien 3, off Torget (May & Sept daily 9am–8pm; June–Aug daily 8.30am–10pm; Oct–April Mon–Sat 9am–4pm; ☎ 55 55 20 00, ⓦ visitbergen .com). Handily located beside the head of the harbour, the tourist office supplies free copies of the detailed *Bergen Guide*, sells the Bergen Card (see box, p.192), provides listings leaflets, changes foreign currency, stocks oodles of free information about the whole of the western fjords and operates a last-minute, in-person accommodation service. In high season, expect long queues. They also have loads of

information on – and will sell tickets for – a veritable battalion of fjordland excursions. Favourites include trips to Troldhaugen (mid-May to Sept 1 daily; 250kr; ⓦ griegmuseum.no) and both "Norway in a Nutshell" (see box, p.210) and the comparable "Hardanger in a Nutshell" (1400kr; ⓦ fjordtours.com).

**DNT (Hiking)** The DNT-affiliated Bergen og Hordaland Turlag, Tverrgate 4–6 (Mon–Wed & Fri 10am–4pm, Thurs 10am–6pm, Sat 10am–2pm; ☎ 55 33 58 10, ⓦ bergen oghordalandturlag.no), will advise on hiking trails in the region, sells hiking maps and arranges guided walks.

## GUIDED TOURS AND ACTIVITIES

**Guided tours** of Bergen and its surroundings are big business and the tourist office (see above) has a flood of details. The most trumpeted is the "Norway in a Nutshell" excursion (see box, p.210), but the excellent, Bergen-based Fjord Tours (ⓦ fjordtours.com) also offers, among much else, "Sognefjord in a Nutshell" (May–Sept; 1540kr return from Bergen), "Hardanger in a Nutshell" (May–Sept; 1380kr return from Bergen), and a trip to Hardanger and Rosendal (May–Sept; 1510kr return from Bergen). All these tours use public transport – bus, train and ferry – and can be modified and extended to taste with, for example, overnight stays and fjordland hikes included (though add-ons cost extra). Also of interest are the guided tours from Bergen to Ole Bull's villa on Lysøen (July 1 weekly; 350kr; ⓦ visit bergen.com; for more on the villa, see p.202).

**Activities** Fjord Tours also offer adventure tours – cycling on the Rallarvegen (see box, p.224) or winter skiing for example – while Norled (ⓦ norled.no) does a first-rate round-trip from Bergen to the Folgefonna ski resort (see p.213), where you undertake a 5hr guided glacier hike (mid-June to mid-Aug; 1350kr). For paragliding and sea-kayaking, check out the varied programme of Gudvangen-based Nordic Ventures (ⓦ nordicventures.com), while Bergen Base Camp, on the Bryggen at Holmedalsgården 3 (ⓦ bergenbasecamp.no), offers a number of guided cycling trips, the most popular being to the top of Mt Ulriken (May–Sept; 1090kr). The most accessible hiking trails are on Mt Fløyen, reached by the funicular (see p.195).

## ACCOMMODATION

Bergen has a wide range of accommodation, but even so vacant rooms can get tight in the height of the season, when advance reservations are a good idea. At the budget end of the market, Bergen has three **hostels** as well as a good choice of **guesthouses** while, moving up the economic tree, there is a platoon of centrally located **hotels**, from mid-range to deluxe. It's actually the deluxe end of the market that has seen most expansion in the last few years; at the time of writing another boutique hotel was under construction – *Zander K*, beside the train station on Zander Kaes gate.

### HOTELS

★**Clarion Collection Havnekontoret** Slottsgaten 1 ☎ 55 60 11 00, ⓦ nordicchoicehotels.com. Prestigious development in which Bergen's former harbour office has been imaginatively converted into a deluxe hotel. The public areas are spacious and although the emphasis is on the modern, the original 1920s entrance, featuring a vaulted ceiling and intricate murals, has been preserved. The best of the guest rooms, where browns and creams predominate, have harbour views. There are even wider views from the tower on top of the hotel, but guests need to get the key from reception. Rates include an evening buffet meal. <u>2000kr</u>

**Clarion Hotel Admiral** Carl Sundts gate 9 ☎ 55 23 64 00, ⓦ nordicchoicehotels.com. This mid-range chain hotel has several bonus points: the public areas are slick and polished; it backs right onto the harbour, but at a safe distance from the main tourist scrum; and it occupies a large and comely building that dates back to 1906. The guest rooms are fairly routine, but the pick look out over the harbour and have mini-balconies, which is a real plus. <u>1500kr</u>

**Grand Hotel Terminus** Zander Kaaes gate 6 ☎ 55 21 25 00, ⓦ grandterminus.no. There was a time when tweed-jacketed, salmon-hunting gentlemen from Britain headed straight for the *Grand* as soon as they arrived in Bergen – and not just because the hotel is next door to the train station. Those ritzy days are long gone, but the hotel, which opened in 1928, does make the most of its public areas, where quasi-baronial flourishes, notably the extensive wood panelling, chandeliers and stained glass, survive in good condition. Breakfasts are very good too, but the bedrooms vary considerably and some are rather poky: if you can, have a look before you commit. Interestingly, Roald Amundsen spent his last night on land here at the *Grand* on Sunday 17 June, 1928: the next day he set out by flying boat on his ill-fated expedition to save a group of Italians who had become stranded in the Arctic; he never made it. <u>1800kr</u>

★**Hotel Park** Harald Hårfagres gate 35 ☎ 55 54 44 00, ⓦ hotelpark.no. This excellent hotel occupies two handsome, late nineteenth-century townhouses on the edge of the city centre near the university. The charming and attractively modern interior is painted in soft pastel colours and the public areas are dotted with antiques. The bedrooms are smart, neat and appealing. It's very popular, so reservations are advised. <u>1300kr</u>

**Radisson Blu Royal Hotel** Bryggen ☎ 55 54 30 00, ⓦ radissonblu.com. Full marks here to the architects, who have built a smart hotel behind a brick facade that mirrors the style of the old timber buildings that surround it. It has all facilities – pool, health club and so forth – plus attractively appointed rooms in a great Bryggen location. <u>1800kr</u>

**Thon Hotel Rosenkrantz** Rosenkrantzgaten 7 ☎ 55 30 14 00, ⓦ thonhotels.com. Proficient, mid-range chain hotel in an excellent location – in a pleasant, old(ish) building just behind the Bryggen. The rooms are neat, trim and modern, but it's worth avoiding the ones that face the interior courtyard, insisting instead on a room overlooking the Bryggen and, on the top floors, the harbour; there's no extra charge. Excellent buffet breakfast too. <u>1500kr</u>

### GUESTHOUSES

★**Skansen Pensjonat** Vetrlidsallmenningen 29 ☎ 55 31 90 80, ⓦ skansen-pensjonat.no. This pleasant little guesthouse occupies a nineteenth-century stone house of elegant proportions just above – and up the hairpins from – the terminus of the Fløibanen funicular railway, near Torget: it's a great location in one of the most beguiling parts of town. The pension has eight guest rooms, most of which have shared facilities, and all are very homely. A snip at <u>900kr</u>

4

**Skuteviken Gjestehus** Skutevikens smalgang 11 ☎ 93 46 71 63, ⓦ skutevikenguesthouse.com. Set amid one of the oldest parts of town, a huddle of narrow, cobbled lanes and bright-white clapboard houses, this excellent guesthouse offers five tastefully renovated apartments, all wood floors, attractive modern bathrooms and neat modern furniture. Each apartment has a living room, kitchenette, bathroom and bedroom. Parking nearby on Skutevikstorget. A good deal at <u>1100kr</u>

★ **To Sostre Gjestehus** Nedre Stølen 4C ☎ 93 06 60 46, ⓦ tosostre.no. This delightful, family-run guesthouse – "The Two Sisters" – is really rather special, a lovingly renovated old timber house with three tastefully decorated, en-suite rooms (and four apartments) in a modern rendition of period style – the Attic Room is just fantastically cosy. On a narrow cobbled lane among a small pocket of wooden houses close to the Bryggen. <u>1000kr</u>

### HOSTELS

**Bergen Vandrerhjem Montana** Johan Blyttsvei 30, Landås ☎ 55 20 80 70, ⓦ montana.no. This large and comfortable HI hostel occupies lodge-like premises in the hills overlooking the city. Great views and good breakfasts, plus self-catering facilities, a café, and a laundry. Has dorm accommodation, family rooms and doubles – almost all of which are en suite. The hostel is 6km east of the centre, 15min on local bus #12 from the bus station (every 10–20min) – ask the driver to put you off and it's a 200m walk from the bus stop. Popular with school parties, who are (usually) housed in a separate wing. Open all year. Dorms (in 4/5-bunk rooms) <u>310kr</u>, doubles (en suite) <u>905kr</u>

**Bergen YMCA Hostel** Nedre Korskirkealmenning 4 ☎ 55 60 60 55, ⓦ bergenhostel.com. Comparatively neat and trim hostel right in the centre of the city, a short walk from Torget. Has room for a couple of hundred guests, but fills up fast in summer. There are dorms and doubles (all double rooms are en suite). Facilities include self-catering, common rooms and a roof terrace. Winter (Oct–March) discounts of fifteen percent. Open all year. Dorms <u>205kr</u>, doubles <u>980kr</u>

**Intermission Hostel** Kalfarveien 8 ☎ 55 30 04 00, ⓦ intermissionhostel.no. Christian-run, private hostel in a two-storey, oldish wooden building, a 5min walk from the train station – just beyond one of the old city gates. There's a self-catering kitchen, laundry and limited parking plus 39 beds in one dormitory (for both sexes). Breakfast costs 35kr. Mid-June to mid-Aug. Dorm beds <u>190kr</u>

### EATING

Bergen has an excellent range of **restaurants**, the pick of which focus on seafood – the city's main gastronomic asset. The pricier tourist haunts are concentrated on the Bryggen, but these should not be dismissed out of hand – several are very good indeed. Other, marginally less expensive restaurants are dotted across the city centre with another cluster on and around Engen. Many locals, however, choose to eat more economically and informally at the city's many **café-bars** and these are also spread across the city centre – as are the city's best **cafés** and **coffee houses**.

### MARKETS

**Fish market** Torget. For picnics, the assorted, open-air stalls of the fish market offer everything from dressed crab, prawn rolls and smoked-salmon sandwiches to pickled herring and canned caviar. May–Sept daily 7am–8pm; Oct–April Mon–Sat 7am–5pm.

### CAFÉS AND COFFEE HOUSES

**Da Stefano** Strandgaten 96 ☎ 55 24 24 44, ⓦ da stefano.no. Informal neighbourhood café, where they specialize in pizzas – both eat in and takeaway, slices or whole (whole pizza 160–210kr). The vegetarian and *stagioni* pizzas are particularly tasty. Mon–Sat 10am–11.30pm, Sun noon–9pm.

**Dromedar Kaffebar** Torgallmenningen 8 ☎ 73 50 25 02, ⓦ dromedar.no. Neat café where the coffee – in all shapes and sizes – is especially good. Efficient, friendly service and a handy central location too. One of a small Norwegian chain. Mon–Fri 8am–9pm, Sat 9am–6pm, Sun 11.30am–5pm.

**Godt Brød** Nedre Korskirkealmenning 12 ☎ 55 32 80 00; Vestre Torggata 2 ☎ 55 56 33 10, ⓦ godtbrod.no. The Nedre Korskirkealmenning branch of this medium-sized Norwegian chain is an eco-bakery and café (in that order), with a wide range of breads plus coffee and made-to-order sandwiches; at the Vestre Torrgate branch the order is reversed – it's a café first and then a bakery. Nedre Korskirkealmenning & Vestre Torrgate branches Mon–Fri 7.30am–6pm, Sat 8am–5pm, Sun 9am–5pm.

★ **Det Lille Kaffekompaniet** Nedre Fjellsmau 2 ☎ 55 31 67 20. Many locals swear by the coffee here, reckoning it to be the best north of the Alps. Great selection of teas too, plus delicious cakes and funky premises – just one medium-sized room in an old building, up two flights of steps from the Fløibanen funicular terminal. Mon–Fri 10am–10pm, Sat & Sun 10am–6pm.

### CAFÉ-BARS AND RESTAURANTS

**Boha** Vaskerelven 6 ☎ 55 31 31 60, ⓦ boha.no. Smooth and polished restaurant kitted out in attractive modern style and offering a small(ish) but extremely well-chosen menu. Main courses – for example pan-fried skate with leek compote – hover around 290kr. Mon–Thurs 4–10pm, Fri 4–11pm, Sat 5–11pm.

**Bryggeloftet og Stuene** Bryggen 11 ☎ 55 30 20 70, Ⓦ bryggeloftet.no. A tourist favourite, this restaurant may be a little old-fashioned – the decor is too folksy for its own good – but they do serve a first-rate range of seafood: delicious, plainly served meals usually with a good wallop of potatoes. Elk, reindeer and other Nordic beasts too, plus occasional diversions into that old Norwegian favourite, *lutefisk*. Main courses around 280kr. Mon–Sat 11am–11.30pm, Sun 1–11.30pm.

**Cornelius Sjømatrestaurant** Katlavika 14, Bjørøyhamn ☎ 56 33 48 80, Ⓦ corneliusrestaurant.no. Smart and expensive seafood restaurant with a splendid location, its huddle of buildings glued to a hilly islet, a 25min boat ride from Bergen harbour. There are actually six different eating areas here, but the main restaurant is *Havsalongen*, which seats eighty and has splendid roll-back windows overlooking the ocean. In the evening, there are several set-menu options, the most affordable of them being the three-course "Meteorological Menu" for 900kr, including the cost of the boat trip, 100kr less at lunchtimes. Boats (2 daily) leave on a set schedule from Bergen harbour, just opposite the *Radisson Blu Royal Hotel*. Advance reservations essential. Mon–Sat noon–10pm.

**Enhjørningen** Bryggen ☎ 55 30 69 50, Ⓦ enhjorningen .no. Smart and fairly formal second-floor restaurant in wonderful premises – all low beams, creaking floors and old oil paintings on the walls. The prices match the decor, with most main courses approaching 340kr, but the seafood is indeed outstanding. Especially popular with tourists. Mid-May to Aug daily 4–11pm; Sept to mid-May Mon–Sat 4–11pm.

**★Lysverket** Rasmus Meyers Allé 9 ☎ 55 60 31 00, Ⓦ lysverket.no. Sharing the same building as the KODE 4 art gallery (see p.196), this superb, ground-floor restaurant, in what can only be described as a semi-industrial space, has a well-conceived menu, whose careful concoctions include a wonderful langoustine soup (195kr) and an immaculate fish-of-the-day (300kr). After the restaurant closes, it turns into one of Bergen's better bars. Restaurant: Mon–Sat 11am–2pm & Tues–Sat 5–10pm; bar: Tues–Sat 10pm–1am.

**Marg & Bein** Fosswinckels gate 18 ☎ 55 32 34 32, Ⓦ marg-bein.no. Sleek and smart restaurant with a period-vintage look and a pleasant outside terrace where the food has garnered all sorts of rave reviews – try, for example, the ox cheek with endives (260kr). Hours vary, but usually Tues–Sat 5–11.30pm, Sun 5–11pm.

**Naboen Restaurant** Sigurdsgate 4 ☎ 55 90 02 90, Ⓦ grannen.no. Easy-going, pleasantly presented restaurant featuring a lively, inventive menu – including Swedish specialities and, on occasion, the likes of kangaroo and ostrich. Offers a good range of fish dishes, including unusual offerings such as sea bass with blood-orange sauce; the cod is especially good. When you've finished eating, you can venture down to the basement bar. Reckon on 250kr for a main course. Restaurant: daily 3–11pm; bar: Mon–Thurs & Sun 8–12pm, Fri & Sat 8pm–1am.

**★Pingvinen** Vaskerelven 14 ☎ 55 60 46 46, Ⓦ pingvinen.no. "The Penguin" is a lively and informal café-restaurant with a long bar, a battery of bar stools and bare-brick walls. The menu concentrates on traditional Norwegian food with such delights as fish pie, reindeer and meatballs costing from as little as 100kr. Kitchen closes down at 10pm, after which the place morphs into a bar. Daily 11am–3am.

## DRINKING AND NIGHTLIFE

As a general rule, Bergen's café-bars – and indeed some of its restaurants – provide the city's more appealing drinking destinations, but there is also a scattering of late-night **bars** and **clubs**, the pick of which attract an arty/boho crew.

**Café Opera** Engen 18 ☎ 55 23 03 15, Ⓦ cafeopera.org. Inside a white wooden building with plant-filled windows, a fashionable crowd gathers to drink beer and good coffee, hunkering down on the terrace when the sun emerges. A DJ rota and live bands get things going at the weekend. Mon 11am–12.30am, Tues–Sat 11am–3am, Sun noon–12.30am.

**Følk & Røvere** Sparebanksgaten 4 ☎ 45 24 34 57. Tucked away among the narrow lanes and alleys near Torget, this boho bar ("People & Robbers") heaves with locals, especially on high days and holidays. Some sample the bar food, but more enjoy the inventive decor and the wide range of ales. As an added pull, it's owned by a local collective – fifty-odd people who wanted to give Bergen a pub to be proud of. Daily 11am–2.30am.

**Garage** Christies gate 14 ☎ 55 32 19 80, Ⓦ garage.no. Busy club catering to a mixed crowd. Two bars on the ground floor, and a live music area in the basement – mostly rock and metal (and lots of hair). Packed at the weekend. At the corner of Nygårdsgaten. Mon–Sat 3pm–3am, Sun 5pm–3am.

**Kippers USF** Georgernes Verft ☎ 55 30 40 80, Ⓦ usf.no. In an intelligently recycled old sardine factory on the Nordnes peninsula, this laidback café-bar is the heart of Bergen's premier contemporary arts complex, USF Verftet (see p.208). The menu is fairly routine (burgers cost 199kr) but, with its sea views and terrace, this is *the* place to come on a sunny evening when the crowds gather, especially when there's some live music or DJ sounds. Daily 11am–11pm.

**Landmark** Rasmus Meyers Allé 5 ☎ 94 01 50 50, Ⓦ kunsthall.no. In one large and plainly decorated room, this café is pretty undistinguished, but, as part of the Bergen Kunsthall gallery (see p.197), it doubles up as a prime events venue for everything from DJ nights through

**4**

## THE BERGEN INTERNATIONAL FESTIVAL

Bergen takes justifiable pride in its **performing arts**, especially during the **Festspillene i Bergen** (Bergen International Festival; ⓦfib.no), held over two weeks at the end of May and the beginning of June, and presenting an extensive programme of music, ballet, folklore and theatre. The principal venue for the festival is the **Grieghallen**, on Edvard Griegs plass (see below), where you can pick up programmes, tickets and information; these are also available from the tourist office. The city's contemporary arts centre, the **USF Verftet**, down on the Nordnes peninsula (ⓦusf.no), contributes to the festival by hosting **Nattjazz** (☎55 30 72 50, ⓦnattjazz.no), a prestigious and long-established international jazz festival held over the same period.

to poetry readings. Mon–Fri 8am–5pm, Sat & Sun 11am–5pm; for events, check the website.

**Logen** Øvre Ole Bulls plass 6 ☎55 23 20 15, ⓦlogen-teater.no. One of the grooviest bars in the city centre: climb the stairs past the entrance to the Logen Teater, and you'll reach this pint-sized bar, all subdued lighting and rickety fittings – plus a great view over Ole Bulls plass from the terrace. Über-cool clientele. Daily 6pm–1am, Sun 8pm–midnight.

**Whisky Bar** Grand Hotel Terminus, Zander Kaaes gate 6 ☎55 21 25 00, ⓦgrandterminus.no. With more whiskies than could possibly be good for you, this discreet bar is a sedate affair ensconced within the really rather fetching 1920s surroundings of the *Grand Hotel Terminus* (see p.205): admire the stained glass, wood panelling and so forth. Mon–Sat 5pm to midnight.

### ENTERTAINMENT

**Bergen Kino** Neumanns gate 3 ☎55 56 90 50, ⓦbergenkino.no. The biggest cinema in town, with no fewer than thirteen screens, showing both mainstream and independent movies. Neumanns gate is a 5min walk from Ole Bulls plass.

**Den Nationale Scene** Engen ☎55 60 70 80, ⓦdns.no. Bergen's main theatre offers a wide range of performances on several stages. Most productions are, as you would expect, in Norwegian, but there are occasional appearances by English-speaking troupes.

**Grieghallen** Edvard Griegs plass; tickets ☎55 21 61 50, ⓦgrieghallen.no. The city's main concert hall offers a wide-ranging programme of performing arts – everything from rock concerts to theatre and dance. The Bergen Filharmoniske Orkester (ⓦharmonien.no)

performs here regularly too.

**Magnus Barfot Kino** Magnus Barfots gate 12 ☎55 56 90 50, ⓦbergenkino.no. This cinema works in tandem with Bergen Kino, just along the street, but it's smaller with just five screens.

**Troldhaugen** Troldhaugveien ☎55 92 29 92, ⓦgrieg museum.no. Throughout the summer, Grieg recitals are performed at the composer's old home (see box, p.202).

**USF Verftet** Georgernes Verft ☎55 30 40 80, ⓦusf.no. The old sardine factory on the Nordnes peninsula is the city's leading contemporary arts complex with a battery of studios and workshops. They showcase a lively programme of concerts, art-house films and contemporary plays with the occasional DJ night thrown in for good measure. There's a café-bar here too (see p.207). Daily 11am–11pm.

### SHOPPING

**Juhls Silver Gallery** Bryggen 39 ☎55 32 47 40, ⓦjuhls.no. In a prime location, this is the Bergen outlet of the celebrated jewellers and silversmiths, who established their first workshop decades ago in remote Kautokeino (see p.356). Many of their glittering designs are Sami-inspired. Mon–Fri 10am–6pm, Sat 10am–4pm, Sun noon–4pm.

**Moods of Norway** Torgalmenningen 12 ☎92 87 22 98, ⓦmoodsofnorway.com. Excellent self-publicists, this small Norwegian chain is noted for its offbeat T-shirts and design logo – the good old Norwegian tractor. Concentrates on clothing for the young – and young at heart. Mon–Fri 10am–8pm, Sat 10am–6pm.

**Norli** Torgalmenningen 8 ☎97 47 82 41, ⓦnorli.no. Easily the best bookshop in town, Norli has a competent range of English titles as well as a wide selection of Norwegian hiking and road maps. Mon–Fri 9am–9pm, Sat 9am–6pm.

**Vinmonopolet** Bergen Storsenter, Strømgarten. There is a large branch of this state-owned liquor store in the city's main shopping mall. Mon–Fri 10am–6pm, Sat 10am–3pm.

### DIRECTORY

**Pharmacy** Vitusapotek Nordstjernen, in the Bergen Storsenter, by the bus station (Mon–Sat 8am–11pm, Sun 1–11pm; ☎55 21 83 84).

**Post office** Bergen's main post office is in the Xhibition shopping centre at the junction of Olav Kyrresgate and Småstrandgaten (Mon–Fri 9am–8pm, Sat 9am–6pm).

# The western fjords

From Bergen, it's a hop, skip and jump over the mountains to the **western fjords**. The most popular initial target is the **Hardangerfjord**, a delightful and comparatively gentle introduction to the wilder terrain that lies beyond, but similarly popular is **Voss**, inland perhaps, but still an outdoor sports centre of some renown. Voss is also a halfway house on the way to the Sognefjord by train, bus or car. By train, it's a short journey from Voss east to **Myrdal**, at the start of a spectacularly dramatic train ride down the Flåmsdal valley to **Flåm**, sitting pretty against the severe shores of the **Aurlandsfjord**, one of the Sognefjord's many subsidiaries; by road, you can head north direct to Flåm along the E16 or stick to Hwy-13 as it careers over the mountains bound for **Vik** and **Vangsnes**. Both of these little towns are on the **Sognefjord** and it's this fjord, perhaps above all others, that captivates visitors, its stirring beauty amplified by its sheer size, stretching inland from the coast for some 200km, and including several magnificent arms, most memorably the **Lustrafjord** and the **Fjærlandsfjord**. Beyond, and running parallel, lies the **Nordfjord**, smaller at 120km long and less intrinsically enticing, though its surroundings are more varied with hunks and chunks of the **Jostedalsbreen glacier** visible and visitable nearby. From here, it's another short journey to the splendid **Geirangerfjord** – narrow, sheer and rugged – as well as the forbidding **Norangsdal** valley, with the wild and beautiful **Hjørundfjord** beyond. Skip over a mountain range or two, via the dramatic **Trollstigen**, and you'll soon reach the town of **Åndalsnes**, which boasts an exquisite setting with rearing peaks behind and the tentacular **Romsdalsfjord** in front. From here, it's another shortish journey west to the region's prettiest town, **Ålesund**, whose centre is liberally sprinkled with charming Art Nouveau buildings, partly paid for by Kaiser Wilhelm II.

A suggested western fjord itinerary is given in the Itineraries section (see pp.22–23), which includes several specific targets: **Ulvik** and **Lofthus** are the most appealing bases in the Hardangerfjord; Sognefjord has Flåm and **Balestrand**; the Fjærlandsfjord has **Mundal**; and further north the cream of the crop are **Loen** and Ålesund. Perhaps above all, this is not a landscape to be hurried – there's little point in dashing from fjord to fjord. Stay put for a while, go for at least one hike or cycle ride, and it's then that you'll really appreciate the western fjords in all their grandeur. The sheer size is breathtaking – but then the **geological movements** that shaped the fjords were on a grand scale. During the Ice Age, around three million years ago, the whole of Scandinavia was covered in ice, the weight of which pushed the existing river valleys deeper and deeper to depths well below that of the ocean floor – the Sognefjord, for example, descends to 1250m, ten times deeper than most of the Norwegian Sea. Later, as the ice retreated, it left huge coastal basins that filled with seawater to become the fjords, which the warm Gulf Stream keeps ice-free.

## ARRIVAL AND GETTING AROUND                                    THE WESTERN FJORDS

The convoluted topography of the **western fjords** has produced a dense and **complex public transport system** that is designed to reach all the larger villages and towns at least once every day, whether by train, bus, car ferry, Hurtigruten coastal boat or Hurtigbåt passenger express boat. Bear in mind, however, that although there may be a transport connection to the town or village you want to go to, many Norwegian **settlements are scattered** and you may be in for a long walk after you've arrived – a particularly dispiriting experience if it's raining. We've covered the western fjords region from south to north – from the Hardangerfjord to Sognefjord, Nordfjord, Geirangerfjord, Åndalsnes and Ålesund. There are certain obvious connections – from Bergen to Flåm, and from Geiranger over the Trollstigen to Åndalsnes, for example – but otherwise routes are really a matter of personal choice; the text details the options.

**By train** The western fjords are not well served by train: NSB (ⓦ www.nsb.no) runs trains to and from Bergen, Finse and Flåm in the south and Åndalsnes in the north, but for everything in between you're confined to buses and ferries.

**By car** Note the main road east from Bergen to the western fjords – the E16 – is prone to congestion and possesses over twenty tunnels, many of which are horribly noxious. Avoid the E16 east of Bergen if you can, and certainly aim to

## NORWAY IN A NUTSHELL

Of all the myriad excursions organized by fjordland tour operators, the most trumpeted is the whistle-stop **Norway in a Nutshell**, which can be booked at any tourist office in the region or online at ⓦnorwaynutshell.com. There are several possible itineraries to choose from, but the classic round-trip from Bergen takes eight and a half hours, and is an exhausting but exhilarating romp that gives you a taste of the fjords in one day. The tour begins with a train ride to Voss and Myrdal, where you change for the dramatic Flåmsbana branch line down to Flåm. Here, a two-hour cruise heads along the Aurlandsfjord and then up the Nærøyfjord to Gudvangen, where you get a bus back to Voss, and the train again to Bergen. You can pick up the tour (and shave an hour and a half off) in Voss for a slightly more affordable 1210kr: the full excursion from Bergen costs 1620kr.

branch off onto the relatively tunnel-free and much more scenic Hwy-7 the first chance you get – about 30km east of the city (see opposite). Bear in mind also that the E39, which cuts an ingenious north–south route across the western edge of the fjords, is potentially useful as a quick way of getting between Bergen, Florø and Ålesund.

**By car ferry** Most car ferries shuttle back and forth every hour or two, if not more often, from around 7am in the morning until 10pm at night every day of the week, all year. There are, however, a confusing number of operators, which can make hunting down timetables difficult, though every tourist office will help or you can consult ⓦrutebok.no for starters. Car ferry fares (*ferjetakster*) are fixed according to a nationally agreed sliding scale, with the shortest crossings (10min or so) currently running at 59kr per car and driver and 27kr per person/passenger – 128kr and 45kr respectively for a 20min trip.

**By Hurtigbåt passenger express boat** Hurtigbåt services are usually fairly infrequent – two a day at most and advance reservations (of at least a couple of hours) are recommended. Hurtigbåt fares are fixed individually and relate to the length of the journey: the 4hr trip from Bergen

to Balestrand, for example, costs 580kr, 795kr for the 5hr 30min trip to Flåm. Return fares are usually double the single, but there are special excursion/return fare deals on some routes – always ask. Several companies operate Hurtigbåt around the western fjords, but the big deal in Bergen is Norled (ⓦnorled.no).

**By Hurtigruten** The Hurtigruten coastal boat (ⓦhurtigruten.co.uk) cuts a handsome route as it sails up along the west coast from Bergen to Trondheim, berthing at Florø and Ålesund throughout the year and detouring via Geiranger from June to August.

**By bus** The curse of competitive tendering is keenly felt on the bus network with routes and companies seemingly in continuous flux. At time of writing, two major companies provide the most useful long-distance routes, Nor-Way Bussekspress (ⓦnor-way.no) and Nettbuss (ⓦnettbuss.no), whose Sognebussen (NX450) links Bergen with Voss, Gudvangen, Flåm and Sogndal. A network of local buses supplements these long-distance routes; again, there are lots of different operators, though Bergen and the Hardangerfjord are pretty much the preserve of Skyss (ⓦskyss.no). For all bus timetables, go to ⓦrutebok.no.

### INFORMATION

Every significant village and all the towns in the western fjords has a tourist office or information centre and each of them concentrates on **local information**, usually including details of **local hikes** and **public transport timetables**. In addition, an extremely useful synopsis of all facilities, including public transport services, is provided in the *Fjord Norway Travel Guide*, an annual publication that is available for free from almost every tourist office and is also online at ⓦfjordnorway.com.

### ACCOMMODATION

**Reservations** At the height of the season, roughly late June to late August, vacant rooms of any description can get very thin on the ground and prices start to climb. Therefore, both for peace of mind and to save money, you're far better making reservations well ahead of time.

At other times of the year, you can pretty much come and go as you please.

**Closing months** Note that many hotels and most hostels close for winter – from October, sometimes November, to March or more likely April.

## TOP 5 FJORDLAND HOTELS

**Brosundet Hotel, Ålesund** See p.258
**Hotel Alexandra, Loen** See p.244
**Hotel Ullensvang, Lofthus** See p.215

**Hotel Union, Gerainger** See p.250
**Walaker Hotell, Solvorn** See p.236

# The Hardangerfjord

To the east of Bergen, the most inviting target is the 180km-long **Hardangerfjord** (whardangerfjord.com), whose wide waters are overlooked by a rough, craggy shoreline and a scattering of tiny settlements. At its eastern end the Hardangerfjord divides into several lesser fjords, and it's here you'll find the district's most appealing villages, **Utne**, **Lofthus** and **Ulvik**, each of which has an attractive fjordside setting and at least one especially good place to stay. To the east of these tributary fjords rises the **Hardangervidda**, a mountain plateau of remarkable, lunar-like beauty and a favourite with Norwegian hikers. The plateau can be reached from almost any direction, but one popular starting point, admittedly for the extremely fit, is from Lofthus, with this approach involving a stiff day-long climb up from the fjord.

## ARRIVAL AND DEPARTURE — THE HARDANGERFJORD

### BY CAR

**From Bergen and the west** From Bergen by bus or car, the fastest approach to the Hardangerfjord is along the E16 via Voss (see p.220), but this is not a particularly enjoyable journey and you're much better off forking onto Hwy-7 after about 30km. This is a rattlingly good trip, with the road twisting over the mountains and down the valleys, gliding past thundering waterfalls and around tight bends before racing down to Norheimsund (see p.212).

**From the north** Arriving from the north, from Voss, Hwy-13 is the quickest route to the Hardangerfjord, though you can enliven the journey by turning off onto the old postal road – Hwy-572 – which cuts a fine course over hill and dale before hairpinning down into Ulvik.

**From the east and south** Even more dramatic are the routes to the Hardangerfjord from the east and south: both Hwy-7 and the E134 thread across the Hardangervidda plateau before sweeping down to the fjord with the latter negotiating the Haukelifjell, one of the region's bleakest and wildest mountain passes.

## GETTING AROUND

**By car ferry & bridge** The main car ferry negotiating the Hardangerfjord shuttles between Kvanndal, Utne and Kinsarvik. The fare between Kvanndal and Utne (car & driver 95kr, passenger 36kr) is a little less than the fare between Utne and Kinsarvik (107kr/39kr). The ferries are operated by Norled (wnorled.no). A stupendous suspension bridge, the Hardangerbrua – a sight in its own right – spans the Hardangerfjord between Brimnes and Bruravik; the toll for cars is 150kr.

**By Hurtigbåt passenger express boat** There is a particularly useful Hurtigbåt service (May to Sept 1 daily) linking Norheimsund, Utne, Lofthus, Kinsarvik, Ulvik and Eidfjord; the operator is Norled (wnorled.no). Sample prices per person are Norheimsund to Eidfjord

**4**

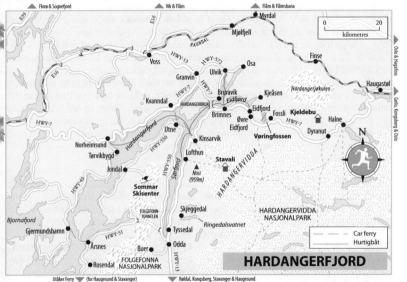

HARDANGERFJORD

311kr, Lofthus to Ulvik 186kr.

**By bus** There are no trains in the Hardangerfjord area, but buses are fairly frequent, allowing you to reach the key villages without too much difficulty. Bus timetables are online at ⓦ rutebok.no and/or ⓦ skyss.no.

## Norheimsund

A small-time port and former furniture-making town, **Norheimsund**, about 80km from Bergen, makes a gallant effort to bill itself as a gateway to the fjords, but in truth it's a modest, middling sort of place and there's precious little reason to hang around: like many fjord settlements, it's the journey to get there that is the main attraction, though to be fair the upgrading of the town's waterfront has been done very nicely.

### ARRIVAL AND DEPARTURE | NORHEIMSUND

**By Hurtigbåt passenger express boat** Hurtigbåt boats dock in the centre of the village.
Destinations Eidfjord (May–Sept 1 daily; 2hr 45min); Kinsarvik (May–Sept 1 daily; 1hr 30min); Lofthus (May–Sept 1 daily; 1hr 15min); Ulvik (May–Sept 1 daily; 2hr 15min); Utne (May–Sept 1 daily; 1hr).

**By bus** Buses pull in beside the boat dock and there are frequent services here from Bergen (every 1–2hr; 1hr 25min) and Voss (every 2hr; 1hr 30min–2hr).

## Utne

The tiny hamlet of **UTNE** occupies a splendid location, its huddle of houses and perky country church overlooking the Hardangerfjord from the tip of the rearing peninsula that divides the Hardangerfjord from the Sørfjord. Utne was long dependent on the orchards that still trail along the Sørfjord's sheltered slopes, its inhabitants making enough of a living to support themselves in some comfort, especially when supplemented by fishing and furniture-making: the brightly painted furniture that once hailed from the district made a popular export.

### Hardanger Folkemuseum

May–Aug daily 10am–5pm; Sept–April Mon–Fri 10am–3pm • 75kr • ⓣ 53 67 00 40, ⓦ hardangerfolkemuseum.no

Utne's heritage is celebrated at the **Hardanger Folkemuseum**, a five-minute walk north along the fjord from the ferry quay. One of the largest and best-appointed folk museums in the region, its collection features a wide range of displays on various aspects of traditional Hardanger life, from fishing and farming through to fruit-growing and trade. A particular highlight is the large display of local **folk costume** – the women's headdresses hereabouts were among the most elaborate in Norway and a popular subject for the Romantic painters of the nineteenth century, notably Adolph Tidemand and Hans Frederik Gude. There are also some fine examples of the Hardanger fiddle, an instrument much loved by both Ole Bull (see p.202) and Grieg. Outside, an assortment of old wooden buildings – farmhouses, cottages, store houses and so forth – rambles over the steep and rocky hillside behind the museum. The logic of this **open-air section** is hard to fathom, but in summertime, when there are demonstrations of farming and craft skills, things make much more sense. One of the more intriguing buildings is a sixteenth-century dwelling, known as an **Uglenesløa**, whose dark and dingy interior is encased by roughly hewn log walls. When the museum is closed, you can still wander round the open-air section as you please.

### ARRIVAL AND DEPARTURE | UTNE

**By car ferry** Utne is the Kvanndal/Kinsarvik ferry's midway point. The ferry dock is in the heart of the village, close to both the hotel and the museum.
Destinations Kinsarvik (1–2 hourly; 30min); Kvanndal (1–2 hourly; 20min).
**By Hurtigbåt passenger express boat** Hurtigbåt boats use the same dock as the car ferry.

Destinations Eidfjord (May–Sept 1 daily; 1hr 45min); Kinsarvik (May–Sept 1 daily; 30min); Lofthus (May–Sept 1 daily; 15min); Norheimsund (May–Sept 1 daily; 1hr); Ulvik (May–Sept 1 daily; 1hr 15min).
**By bus** Buses to and from Utne pull in beside the ferry dock.
Destinations Jondal (1–2 daily; 1hr); Odda (3–5 daily; 50min).

## ACCOMMODATION AND EATING

**Utne Hotel** ☎ 53 66 64 00, ⊕ utnehotel.no. Straight opposite the ferry dock, the *Utne Hotel* is a relaxing spot, its public rooms graced by several fine examples of the painted furniture for which the area was once famous. There are 26 rooms, most in the original building, which dates from 1722, though nine are in the annexe. So far so good, but the walls of the rooms in the main house, which are reached by an unusual spiral staircase, are paper-thin – hard luck if you are billeted next to a champion snorer. The hotel restaurant, a panelled dining room, is first-rate, focusing on local, seasonal ingredients; mains average around 220kr. Restaurant: daily 2–5pm & 7–9pm. **1900kr**

# Jondal and the Folgefonna glacier

Running south of Utne, the jagged peninsula separating the Hardangerfjord from the Sørfjord widens and heightens, its upper reaches holding the **Folgefonna Nasjonalpark**. Remote and mountainous, wild and bleak, the park's 545 square kilometres incorporate Norway's third largest glacier, the tentacular **Folgefonna glacier**. Conditions on the glacier are well-nigh perfect for **summer skiing**, both alpine and telemark, as well as snowboarding, best arranged with Fonna Glacier Ski Resort (see below). There's a narrow mountain road up to the glacier from the fjordside hamlet of **Jondal**, 33km southwest of Utne.

## ARRIVAL AND INFORMATION
## JONDAL AND THE FOLGEFONNA GLACIER

**By bus** There's a daily bus service from Utne to Jondal (1–2 daily; 1hr), where you catch the glacier bus up to the ski resort (1 daily; 45min); check connecting times at your hotel or at the nearest tourist office.

**By car ferry** There are car ferries across the Hardangerfjord between Jondal and Tørvikbygd (every 1–2hr; 20min);

Tørvikbygd is on Hwy-49, 12km south of Norheimsund.

**Tourist office** Jondal tourist office is in the centre of the village beside Hwy-550 (mid-June to late Aug daily 9.30am–4pm; July daily 9.30am–6pm; ☎ 53 66 85 31, ⊕ visitjondal.no).

## ACTIVITIES

**Summer skiing** For summer skiing on the Folgefonna, the place to head for is the Fonna Glacier Ski Resort (early May to mid-Sept daily 9am–4pm; ☎ 46 17 20 11, ⊕ folgefonn.no), some 20km east of Jondal, on the northern edge of the glacier at 1200m above sea level. The resort has ski and snowboard rental, a ski school, a café and a ski lift to the slopes. To get there from Utne, head southwest along Hwy-550 to Jondal, and then turn east up the signposted mountain road for the bumpy 40min ride up to the resort. At the peak of the season,

local bus #982 runs up from Jondal to the resort (late June to mid-Aug 1 daily each way; 45min), giving you just over 5hr up there.

**Glacier hikes and climbs** Flat Earth (☎ 47 60 68 47, ⊕ flatearth.no) runs a programme of guided glacier hikes and climbs (May to late Aug). Day-long excursions begin at 980kr per person including equipment; advance booking – at least the day before – is required. The same company also organizes whitewater-rafting trips (420kr) and guided hikes (from 740kr) in the vicinity of Folgefonna.

# Odda

When the carbide factory opened in **ODDA**, about 55km south of Kinsarvik and 45km from Utne, in 1908 it was great news: fjord Norway was impoverished and locals flocked to the plant to secure a decent industrial wage. Other factories followed, not least a hydroelectric station, and within a decade Odda was something of a boom town. Those heady industrial days are long gone, but although the town still bears some of the scars, a sound attempt has been made to spruce the place up, especially along and around the Sørfjord. Perhaps even better, the nearby, 11km-long **Folgefonntunnelen**, which was opened in 2001, bores west beneath the Folgefonna glacier to connect Odda with the region's star historical turn – the Baroniet Rosendal (see p.214).

## ARRIVAL AND INFORMATION
## ODDA

**By bus** Buses to Odda pull in near the waterfront on the north side of town.

Destinations Bergen (1 daily; 3hr); Kinsarvik (3–5 daily; 1hr); Lofthus (3–5 daily; 40min); Utne (3–5 daily; 50min).

**Tourist office** Odda tourist office is located down by the fjord at Torget 2 (mid-June to Aug daily 9am–7pm; Sept to mid-June Mon–Fri 9am–3pm; ☎ 48 07 07 77, ⊕ hardangerfjord.com).

**4**

## HIKING THE TROLLTUNGA

Much less well known than other, similar vantage points, the **Trolltunga** (troll's tongue) is a narrow ledge of rock that projects out from the mountainside no less than 700m above **Lake Ringedalsvatnet**. Needless to say, the views fair take your breath away. To get there, take Hwy-13 north from Odda to **Tyssedal**, where you follow the signs for the 7km journey up into the mountains to **Skjeggedal**, where you can park. The hike starts here in Skjeggedal beside the (currently defunct) funicular Mågelibanen. The path begins on the right-hand side of the funicular, is marked with painted red Ts, takes between ten and twelve hours there and back, and involves an ascent of around 1000m. This is tough terrain, so you will need to come properly equipped, and you should check weather conditions at Odda tourist office before you set out – the path is closed when the snows come and is usually open from mid-June to early October. There is no mobile phone coverage along the route.

### ACTIVITIES

**Climbing, hiking and kayaking** Odda tourist office has the details of – and makes bookings for – climbing trips, kayaking and guided glacier walking tours on the nearest nodule of the Folgefonna glacier at Buer, 8km or so from town (approximately late June to mid-Aug; advance booking required). The leading local company for outdoor pursuits is Flat Earth (see also p.213; ☎ 47 60 68 47, ⊛ flatearth.no).

### ACCOMMODATION AND EATING

**Tyssedal Hotel** Gamle Oddaveg 3, Tyssedal ☎ 53 64 00 00, ⊛ tyssedalhotel.no. In a distinctive, early twentieth-century, maroon-painted building in Tyssedal, about 6km north of Odda on Hwy-13, this pleasant hotel has 26 large and well-appointed rooms, though some tend towards the spartan. The hotel benefits from the folksy paintings that grace many of its walls – most are by local artists – and its restaurant is the best in town, featuring local, seasonal ingredients: be sure to try the mountain trout if it's on the menu; mains average 240kr. Restaurant: daily noon–2pm & 5–9.30pm. **1400kr**

## The Baroniet Rosendal

Baronivegen, Rosendal • Hourly guided tours: early May to June & late Aug to early Sept daily 11am–5pm, last tour at 4pm; July to mid-Aug daily 10am–6pm, last tour at 5pm • 150kr, gardens only 75kr • ☎ 53 48 29 99, ⊛ baroniet.no • The Baroniet is a 20min walk from Rosendal jetty

From Odda, it's about 50km west via the Folgefonntunnelen to the hamlet of **ROSENDAL**, at the eastern end of which is the **house and estate of the Baroniet Rosendal**, one of Norway's few country houses – the Norwegian landowning aristocracy has always been too thin on the ground to build more than a handful. Dating from the seventeenth century, the Baroniet was in private hands until 1927, when the last owner bequeathed the whole lot to the University of Oslo. By comparison with country houses in other European countries, the house is really quite modest, but it does hold a string of period rooms, among which the Baroque library and the Neoclassical "yellow room" are the most diverting. Afterwards, you can stroll out into the surrounding gardens and **park**, with its ponds, bridges and views out across the fjord. Concerts and art exhibitions are a regular feature here too.

### ARRIVAL AND DEPARTURE          THE BARONIET ROSENDAL

**By car** It takes about an hour to drive west from Odda to Rosendal via the Folgefonntunnelen. If you are pressing on to Bergen from Rosendal, head north along the road back towards Odda as far as Årsnes and catch the car ferry over to Gjermundshamn, on Hwy-48 (every 30min; 20min). From here, it's another 100km or so to Bergen.

**By Hurtigbåt passenger express boat** Rodne (⊛ rodne.no) operates a Hurtigbåt service between Bergen and Rosendal (1–2 daily; 2hr).

**By bus** There are buses to Rosendal from Odda (2–4 daily; 1hr).

### ACCOMMODATION AND EATING

**Rosendal Turisthotell** Skålagato 17 ☎ 53 47 36 66, ⊛ rosendalturisthotell.no. In a handsome old timber building down near the waterfront – and a 20min walk from the Baroniet Rosendal – this country hotel has benefited from a thoroughgoing refit, its public rooms neat, trim and very modern. Many of the fourteen rooms have fjord views and all have shared facilities. The hotel's restaurant is the best in the village, with mains around 250kr. Restaurant: daily 6.30–9pm. **980kr**

## Lofthus

In a handsome location, **LOFTHUS** strings along the Sørfjord for about 1km with the Folgefonna glacier glinting in the distance. The more northerly part of the village – around the *Hotel Ullensvang* – is somewhat routine, but the southern part is an idyllic place of narrow lanes and mellow stone walls, where a scattering of timber houses sits among the orchards, pinky-white with blossom in the springtime, all to the sound of a stream which tumbles down from the escarpment above.

### Ullensvang kirke

Late June to mid-Aug daily 10am–7pm • Free

In the southern part of Lofthus is the village's proudest building, **Ullensvang kirke**, dating from 1250 and named after the district not the village. A good-looking stone structure with immensely thick walls, the church stands just above a pebble beach and a miniature jetty, where the brave propel themselves into the waters of the fjord.

### Hikes on the Hardangervidda plateau

The *Hotel Ullensvang* (see below) gives out simple hiking maps indicating the route to Nosi

Directly behind the *Hotel Ullensvang*, a steep **hiking trail** leads up from Lofthus to the Hardangervidda plateau (see p.217); the upper part of the trail (from 650m above sea level) includes the **Munketreppene**, over six hundred stone steps laid by the monks who farmed this remote spot in medieval times. It takes about two hours to reach the plateau at the **Nosi** (959m) vantage point, and about seven or eight hours to reach the **Stavali** self-service DNT hut.

### ARRIVAL AND DEPARTURE         LOFTHUS

**By Hurtigbåt passenger express boat** Hurtigbåt boats pull in beside the *Hotel Ullensvang*.
Destinations Eidfjord (May to Sept 1 daily; 1hr 30min); Kinsarvik (May to Sept 1 daily; 15min); Norheimsund (May to Sept 1 daily; 1hr 15min); Ulvik (May to Sept 1 daily; 1hr); Utne (May to Sept 1 daily; 15min).
**By bus** Buses stop at the back of the *Hotel Ullensvang*.
Destinations Eidfjord (1–2 daily; 1hr 30min); Kinsarvik (3–5 daily; 20min); Odda (3–5 daily; 40min).
**By car: routes on from Lofthus** Heading south from

Lofthus, it's only a few minutes to Odda (see p.213), but then you're into more rugged terrain with the E134 leading southwest to Haugesund (see p.142) or southeast over the dramatic Haukelifjell to Seljord (see p.181). Driving north, it's just 25km, via Kinsarvik, to the bridge spanning the Hardangerfjord – for Ulvik (see p.218) and Voss (see p.220). If you stay on the coastal road (Hwy-7), it's another 20km or so from the bridge east to Eidfjord (see p.216) with the Hardangervidda (see p.217) just beyond.

### ACCOMMODATION AND EATING

★**Hotel Ullensvang** ☎ 53 67 00 00, ⓦ hotel -ullensvang.no. Spreading out along the Sørfjord, with fine views across to the mountains, this large hotel dates back to the 1840s, when an ambitious young lad rowed across from Utne and built himself a boathouse with a loft for guests. Since then, the great and the good have been visitors, not least Edvard Grieg, whose stay here is recalled by life-size wooden statues of the composer and his entourage; these stand in the hotel grounds, next to the timber hut where Grieg would compose away. The present hotel, which occupies several modern buildings, offers a full basket of facilities, including saunas and a solarium, a swimming pool, a hairdresser, sports facilities, boat rental and several bars. The decor ranges from the subdued to the almost overpowering with the foyer, where there is an open fireplace and lots of Hardanger bygones, being particularly appealing. There are around 170 guest rooms; the better ones have fjord views for which there is a premium of around 600kr. The hotel restaurant offers an all-you-can-eat buffet dinner (daily 7–9pm; 525kr). **2500kr**

**Ullensvang Gjesteheim** Lofthus ☎ 53 66 12 36, ⓦ ullensvang-gjesteheim.no. Appealing guesthouse set within a huddle of antique wooden buildings that roll down towards the fjord from Hwy-13 with a cascading stream immediately behind. Has ten cosy and unassuming rooms with shared facilities – nothing fancy but perfectly OK.

**4**

There's a small premium for weekend stays. They also serve dinner (daily 4–9pm) – try the fried mountain trout with sour cream (190kr). Hotel and restaurant open May to late Sept. **1000kr**

## Kinsarvik

Hugging the Sørfjord, pocket-sized **KINSARVIK**, about 10km from Lofthus, was once an important Viking marketplace. It was just the sort of spot the Vikings liked: the foreshore was gentle, making it easy for them to ground their longships, and it was buried deep in the fjords, making it difficult for any enemy to approach unseen. Today, Kinsarvik is the quietest of villages, though it's a pleasant enough spot and its stone **church** is of passing interest.

### Kinsarvik kirke

Late May to late June Tues–Fri 10am–3pm; late June to mid-Aug daily 10am–7pm • Free

Lurking on the foreshore, Kinsarvik's sturdy, whitewashed **church** dates back as far as the middle of the twelfth century. Those were troubled times, so the church was built with defence in mind – witness the thickness of the walls and the narrowness of the hooped windows – and for several centuries the sails and assorted tackle of the village's *leidangskipet* (defence ship) were stored in its ample loft. Twelfth-century Norwegians knew little of building in stone and it's likely that the church was the work of British masons – though it was clumsily renovated in the 1880s. Inside, the most interesting hints of its medieval past are a series of faint, chalk wall paintings.

### ARRIVAL AND INFORMATION KINSARVIK

**By car ferry** Ferries dock in the centre of the village metres from the church.
Destinations Kvanndal (1–2 hourly; 50min); Utne (1–2 hourly; 30min).
**By Hurtigbåt passenger express boat** Hurtigbåt boats use the same dock as the car ferries.
Destinations Eidfjord (May to Sept 1 daily; 1hr 15min); Lofthus (May to Sept 1 daily; 15min); Norheimsund (May to Sept 1 daily; 1hr 30min); Ulvik (May to Sept 1 daily; 45min); Utne (May to Sept 1 daily; 30min).

**By bus** Buses pull in beside the ferry dock.
Destinations Eidfjord (1–2 daily; 1hr 20min); Lofthus (3–5 daily; 20min); Odda (3–5 daily; 1hr).
**Tourist office** Opposite the ferry dock (April, May & Sept Mon–Fri 9am–3.30pm; June Mon–Fri 9am–5pm & Sat 10am–3.30pm; July to mid-Aug Mon–Fri 9am–5.30pm, Sat 10am–4.30pm & Sun 11.30am–4.30pm; late Aug Mon–Fri 9am–4.30pm, Sat 10am–2pm; ☎53 66 31 12, ⓦvisitullensvang.no).

### ACCOMMODATION AND EATING

**Best Western Kinsarvik Fjord Hotell** Kinsarvik ☎53 66 74 00, ⓦkinsarvikfjordhotel.com. This well-run, seventy-room hotel occupies a straightforward modern block opposite the ferry jetty. The bedrooms are similarly straightforward, with functional furnishings and fittings, and the more appealing among them have fjord views. The hotel restaurant is pretty much the only place to eat in Kinsarvik, but fortunately the food is well cooked and prepared – mains average 200kr. **1500kr**

## Eidfjord and around

Given its dramatic location, with the fjords in front and mountains behind, it's hard not to feel that the village of **EIDFJORD**, 20km east of the Hardangerbrua (bridge), should be a tad more inviting – there's nothing wrong with the place as such, but its modern centre fails to hold the eye. It does, however, boast an unusual attraction in the remote and isolated **Kjeåsen mountain farm**, and it's here also that Hwy-7 starts its remarkable journey up to the **Hardangervidda**, weaving and boring its way in a singularly fine feat of engineering. There's been a settlement here at Eidfjord since prehistoric times and for centuries the village prospered as a trading centre at the end of one of the main routes over the Hardangervidda, though this was very much a two-edged sword: traditionally, the villagers were obliged to build and repair foot and cart tracks up to the plateau, forced labour for which they were not paid.

### Kjeåsen mountain farm

Eidfjord's star turn is **Kjeåsen mountain farm**, a lonely complex of old farm buildings, from where you'll be rewarded with spectacular views over the tapering Simadalsfjord. To get there, head northeast from Eidfjord for 7km along the narrow byroad that hugs the Simadalsfjord to reach the tortuous, 5km-long lane that wriggles up to the farm – it's signed. The lane is much too narrow to take two-way traffic and half the road goes through a tunnel without any lights, but drivers can relax (a little): you can only drive up to the farm on the hour and descend on the half-hour. The byroad is open all the time, but you're asked not to go up after 5pm to respect the privacy of the occupants.

### Hardangervidda Natursenter

Daily: April to mid-June & late Aug to Oct 10am–6pm; mid-June to late Aug 9am–7pm • 130kr • ☎ 53 67 40 00, ⓦ hardangerviddanatursenter.no

The **Hardangervidda Natursenter**, in a glassy modern structure in **Øvre Eidfjord**, 7km from Eidfjord along Hwy-7, tells you all you ever wanted to know about the Hardangervidda, including its natural history and geology by means of a series of dioramas and a short film. The staff also dispense (free) hiking advice and sell hiking maps.

### Vøringfossen waterfalls

Beyond the Hardangervidda Natursenter, 17km from Eidfjord, Hwy-7 passes a large stopping place from where you can view the mighty, 145m-high **Vøringfossen waterfalls**, though the torrent is best viewed from the top at the hamlet/hotel of **Fossli** a little further on: Fossli is signed from – and about 1km off – Hwy-7.

**4**

## ARRIVAL AND INFORMATION                                  EIDFJORD AND AROUND

**By Hurtigbåt passenger express boat** Hurtigbåt boats dock in the centre of the village a few metres from both Hwy-7 and the conspicuous *Quality Hotel & Resort Vøringfoss*. Destinations Kinsarvik (May–Sept 1 daily; 1hr 15min); Lofthus (May–Sept 1 daily; 1hr 30min); Norheimsund (May–Sept 1 daily; 2hr 45min); Ulvik (May–Sept 1 daily; 30min); Utne (May–Sept 1 daily; 2hr).

**By bus** Buses pull in a 4min-walk from the Hurtigbåt dock, beside Hwy-7. Destinations Kinsarvik (1–2 daily; 1hr 20min); Geilo via Hwy-7 (1–2 daily; 1hr 45min); Lofthus (1–2

daily; 1hr 30min).

**Tourist office** Metres from the Hurtigbåt dock at Ostangvegen 1 (May–June Mon–Fri 9am–4pm, Sat & Sun 11.30am–3pm; July to mid-Aug Mon–Fri 9am–7pm, Sat & Sun 11am–6pm; late Aug Mon–Sat 10am–6pm & Sun 11.30am–3pm; Sept Mon–Fri 9am–4pm, Sat & Sun 11.30am–3pm; Oct–April Mon–Fri 9am–4pm; ☎ 53 67 34 00, ⓦ visiteidfjord.no). They can advise on local walks; one popular option is the hour-long haul up to the Hæreid plateau, which has the region's greatest concentration of Viking burial mounds.

## ACCOMMODATION AND EATING

**Quality Hotel & Resort Vøringfoss** Ostangvegen ☎ 53 67 41 00, ⓦ nordicchoicehotels.com. There's been a hotel here at the Eidfjord quayside since the 1880s and the present complex is a large, modern affair built in the general style of its wooden predecessors with mini-towers and decorative gable ends. The eighty-odd rooms are popular with tour groups and decorated in standard chain style, though the pick do have great views over the fjord. 1400kr

**Vik Pensjonat og Hytter** Simadalsvegen 10 ☎ 53 66

51 62, ⓦ vikpensjonat.com. In the centre of the village, a brief walk from the quayside, this pretty wooden house holds seven rooms, half en suite (which cost more at 1200kr), and all tastefully decorated in a bright and cheerful manner. The same family also rents out two neighbouring cabins (*hytter*) – one for up to six people (2800kr), the other for two (900kr) – and operates a café, where they specialize in local dishes – trout and reindeer for example – with mains averaging 200kr. Café and accommodation: May–Sept. Doubles 960kr

## The Hardangervidda plateau

The **Hardangervidda** is Europe's largest mountain plateau, occupying a one-hundred-kilometre-square slab of land east of the Hardangerfjord and broadly south of the Oslo–Bergen railway. The plateau is characterized by rolling fells and wide stretches of level ground, its rocky surfaces strewn with pools, ponds and rivers. The whole plateau is above the tree line, and in places has an almost lunar-like appearance, although even within this elemental landscape there are variations. To the north, in the vicinity of Finse, there are mountains and a glacier, the **Hardangerjøkulen**, while the west is wetter – and the flora somewhat richer – than the barer moorland to the east. The lichen that covers the rocks is savoured by herds of **reindeer**, who leave their winter grazing lands on the east side of the plateau in the spring, chewing their way west to their breeding grounds before returning east again after the autumn rutting season.

Stone Age hunters once followed the reindeer on their migrations, and traces of their presence – arrowheads, pit-traps, etc – have been discovered over much of the plateau. Later, the Hardangervidda became one of the main crossing points between east and west Norway, with horse traders, cattle drivers and Danish dignitaries all cutting across the plateau along cairned paths, many of which are still in use as part of a dense network of **trails** that has been developed – alongside **tourist huts** – by several DNT affiliates. Roughly one-third of the plateau has been incorporated within the **Hardangervidda Nasjonalpark**, but much of the rest is protected too, so hikers won't notice a great deal of difference between the park and its immediate surroundings. The entire plateau is also popular for **winter cross-country, hut-to-hut skiing**. Many hikers and skiers are content with a day on the Hardangervidda, but some find the wide-skied, lichen-dappled scenery particularly enchanting and travel from one end of the plateau to the other, a seven- or eight-day expedition.

## ARRIVAL AND INFORMATION                    THE HARDANGERVIDDA PLATEAU

**By train** Access to the Hardangervidda can be gained from the Oslo–Bergen train line which calls at Finse (see p.222), from where hikers and skiers head off across the plateau in all directions.

**By car** Finse is not reachable by road, so motorists mostly use Hwy-7, which runs across the plateau between Eidfjord (see p.216) and Geilo (see p.175).

**By foot** You can pick up the plateau's hiking trails at several points along Hwy-7, including Dyranut and Halne, respectively 39km and 47km from Eidfjord. Some hikers prefer to walk eastwards onto the Hardangervidda – Lofthus (see p.215) offers the easiest access – while others

plump for Rjukan (see p.176), to the southeast of the plateau, where a cable car eases the uphill part of the trek.

**By boat** There are boat trips (July to late Aug 1–2 daily; 1hr each way; 200kr return) from Halne along the Halnefjord, which cuts south from Hwy-7 across the Hardangervidda for about 15km. For times of departure, consult either Eidfjord tourist office (see p.217) or the operator, Halnekongen (☎ 53 66 57 12, ✆ halne.no).

**Tourist office** Local tourist offices all carry hiking maps and will advise on hiking routes, as will the Hardangervidda Natursenter (see p.217).

## Ulvik

Tucked away in a snug corner of the Hardangerfjord, the village of **ULVIK** strings prettily along the shoreline with orchards dusting the green, forested hills behind. This is one of the gentlest of fjord landscapes, with little of the harsh beauty of many of its neighbours, and although there's nothing specific to see, strolling the waterfront is a pleasant way to pass the time, and there are plenty of hiking trails in the surrounding hills. Ulvik also has one or two claims to fame: this is the spot where potatoes were first grown in Norway (in 1765) and it was one of the few places in the country to take a real pummelling during World War II (see box, p.220).

### Hikes around Ulvik

Ulvik is an excellent place to unwind, and the favourite pastime is walking. **Hiking trails** lattice the rough uplands behind the village and also explore the surrounding coastline. The tourist office sells a map of the Ulvik area describing a dozen, day-long hiking trails, ranging from the easy (2km; 30min) to the more strenuous (8km; 6hr). One of the easiest and most enjoyable is the hour-long, round trip up into the hills to the east of Ulvik, to **Tunheim**, taking in the scant remains of an old Viking burial ground. In the season, from June to August, the tourist office also organizes a daily **cultural walk**

## THE BATTLE OF THE ORANGES

The Germans invaded Norway on April 9, 1940, and during the next couple of weeks, before the Norwegians threw in the towel, there were several naval skirmishes in the Hardangerfjord. In one of them, the so-called **Battle of Ulvik**, the German navy shelled the centre of the village to smithereens after being shot at from the shore. During the battle, the Norwegian navy, seeing the way things were going, scuttled the *Afrika*, a German merchant ship they had previously captured; the wreck remains in Ulvik harbour today. They also scuttled a neutral ship, the *San Miguel*, which had taken refuge here, thereby – in a true *Whisky Galore* moment – releasing the ship's cargo: thousands of **oranges**, which bobbed around the harbour, much to the amazed delight of the locals, for whom fresh fruit was a real treat.

(2hr 30min; 250kr), which includes cider tasting: since a change in the law in 2002, local farmers have been allowed to brew their own **cider** – which is precisely what several of them do.

### ARRIVAL AND INFORMATION ULVIK

**By bus** Buses to Ulvik pull into the centre of the village, metres from the jetty and the waterfront tourist office.
Destinations Eidfjord (1–2 daily; 2hr with one change); Kinsarvik (1–2 daily; 1hr 15min with one change); Voss (3–5 daily; 1hr with one change).
**By Hurtigbåt passenger express boat** Hurtigbåt boats dock next to the tourist office.
Destinations Eidfjord (May–Sept 1 daily; 30min); Kinsarvik (May–Sept 1 daily; 45min); Lofthus (May–Sept 1 daily;

1hr); Norheimsund (May–Sept 1 daily; 2hr 15min); Utne (May–Sept 1 daily; 1hr 15min).
**Tourist office** Located next to the ferry dock at Tyssevikvegen 9, the tourist office (June to mid-Aug Mon–Fri 10am–5pm, Sat 11am–5pm & Sun 11am–4pm; mid-Aug to May Mon–Fri 10am–2pm; ☎56 52 62 80, ⓦ visitulvik.no) issues all the usual information, including bus and ferry timetables, sells detailed hiking maps and rents out bikes.

### ACCOMMODATION AND EATING

**Brakanes Hotel** Promenaden ☎56 52 61 05, ⓦ brakanes-hotel.com. Hogging the waterfront in the centre of the village, this large, four-storey modern hotel with around 140 rooms has all the facilities you might expect, including a fitness centre, and is popular as a conference centre. The rooms are standard-issue chain – wood-laminate floors and so forth – but the better ones do have lovely fjord views and the beds are dead comfy. **2000kr**

★**Ulvik Fjord Hotel & Pensjonat** Eikjeledbakkjen ☎56 52 61 70, ⓦ ulvikfjord.no. This well-maintained and very appealing hotel is situated at the beginning of Ulvik

village, an easy 10min walk west from the centre along the waterfront. It has nineteen guest rooms, some in the main house – an attractive, wooden, two-storey building dating from the 1940s – and some in the modern annexe, where most of the rooms have their own outside area beside a babbling brook. It's not a luxury resort – and makes no claim to be so – but it is very comfortable and the family who own and run the place are the friendliest of hosts. Breakfasts are first-rate and home-made evening meals, which come recommended by several of our readers, are available at their café-bar-cum-restaurant; reckon on 180kr for a main course. **1100kr**

## Voss

With a population of just 14,000, **VOSS**, 100km from Bergen, is a small town with an attractive lakeside setting and a splendid thirteenth-century church. It is, however, best known as an **adventure-sports and winter-skiing centre**, with everything from skiing and snowboarding through to summertime rafting, kayaking and horseriding. Consequently, unless you're here for a sweat, your best bet is to have a quick look round the town's central shops and cafés – it takes just ten minutes to walk from one end of town to the other – and then move on. There is a caveat, however: Voss is the ideal base for a **day-trip by train** east up the Raundal valley, an especially scenic part of the Bergen–Oslo rail line. The most popular target on this stretch of the line is the Myrdal junction, where you change for the dramatic train ride down to Flåm (see box, p.223).

For centuries, Voss was a trading centre of some importance, though you'd barely guess this from the modern appearance of the town centre today. In 1023, King Olav visited to check that the population had all converted to Christianity, and stuck a big stone cross here to ram home his point, and in the 1270s another king, Magnus Lagabøte, built a church in Voss to act as the religious focal point for the whole region – and this church, the **Vangskyrkja**, survives today.

## Vangskyrkja
Vangsgata • June–Aug Mon–Sat 10am–4pm • 15kr • ☎ 56 52 38 80

Guarding the west end of the town centre, the **Vangskyrkja** is Voss's main landmark, its eccentric octagonal spire poking an assertive head high into the sky. Down below, the stone walls of the nave are up to 2m thick, strong enough, as it turned out, to survive the German bombing of the town in 1940. From the outside, the church looks sombre and severe, but the interior is splendid, a surprisingly flamboyant and colourful affair with a Baroque reredos and a folksy rood screen showing a crucified Jesus attended by two cherubs. The ceiling is even more unusual, its timbers painted in 1696 with a cotton-wool cloudy sky inhabited by flying angels – and the closer you get to the high altar, the more angels there are.

## Lake Vangsvatnet
Across the main road from the church, the **Prestegardsalléen** footpath cuts a leafy course along the flat and green shore of **Lake Vangsvatnet**. It's a pleasant stroll that leads past the town's main campsite to a small bathing area that is itself near the point where the River Vosso empties into the lake.

**4**

---

## OUTDOOR ACTIVITIES AROUND VOSS

Every **summer**, hundreds of Norwegians make a beeline for **Voss** on account of its **watersports**. The rivers near the town offer a wide range of conditions, suitable for everything from a quiet paddle to a finger-chewing whitewater ride. In **winter**, **skiing** around Voss starts in mid-December and continues until mid-April – nothing fancy, but good for an enjoyable few days. In January and February some trails are floodlit. There's a choice of red, green and black downhill ski routes, and among the greens is a long and fairly gentle route through the hills above town; cross-country skiing here is limited to around 20km of tracks. Details of all the outdoor activities offered in and around Voss are on the compendious ⓦ visitvoss.no.

### SUMMER SPORTS OPERATORS

**Myrkdalen Hestesenter** ☎ 41 56 68 06, ⓦmyrkdalen-hestesenter.no. Family-friendly horse-back riding school offering everything from a 2hr canter (500kr) to six-day horseback excursions (4000kr). The rolling uplands of the Myrkdalen valley are about 30km north of Voss, on Hwy-13 just to the north of Vinje (see p.224).

**Nordic Ventures** ☎ 56 51 00 17, ⓦnordicventures .com. This company operates from both Voss and Gudvangen (see p.225). They offer all sorts of kayaking excursions with a 5hr trip along the lake flanking

Voss costing 800kr per person; they also do tandem paragliding and parasailing.

**Voss Rafting Senter** ☎ 56 51 05 25, ⓦvossrafting .no. Among several rafting operators, this one sets the benchmark. From May to September, their whitewater-rafting trips venture out onto two rivers – the Strandaelva and Raundalselva – with prices beginning at 1240kr per person for a 4hr excursion, half of which is actually spent on the water. Other options with the same operator include river boarding (4hr; 1240kr) and waterfall rappelling (4hr; 1050kr).

### WINTER SPORTS OPERATORS

**Voss Resort Ski School** ☎ 47 00 47 00, ⓦvossresort .no. Full equipment for both downhill and cross-country skiing can be rented by the day from this ski

school at the upper Hangursbanen station. They also offer lessons in skiing and snowboarding techniques.

## ARRIVAL AND DEPARTURE VOSS

**By train** Voss train station, which is on the Bergen–Oslo line, stands at the western end of – and a 5min walk from – the town centre. Timetables on ⓦ www.nsb.no.

Destinations Bergen (5 daily; 1hr 20min); Finse (3–4 daily; 1hr 20min); Myrdal (3–4 daily; 50min); Oslo (3–4 daily; 5hr 30min). At Myrdal, you change for the world-famous train ride down to Flåm on the Flåmsbåna (4–9 trains daily; 45min; see box opposite). At solitary Finse (see below), you can hike or ski straight from the train station out across the stirring scenery of the Hardangervidda mountain plateau (see p.217).

**By bus** Buses stop outside the train station at the western end of the town centre, a 5min walk or so from the Vangskyrkja (church).

Destinations Nettbuss (ⓦ nettbuss.no) operates the Sognebussen from Voss to Bergen (2–4 daily; 1hr 50min), Gudvangen (2–4 daily; 50min), Flåm (2–4 daily; 1hr 10min) and Sogndal (2–4 daily; 3hr). Local buses (ⓦ skyss .no) link Voss with Ulvik (3–5 daily; 1hr with one change); Vik (1–2 daily except Sat; 1hr 15min) and Vangsnes (1–2 daily except Sat; 1hr 30min). At Vangsnes there are ferries (see p.225) over the Sognefjord to Hella for Sogndal and Dragsvik for Balestrand.

**By car: routes north from Voss** It's a quick and easy 65km northeast from Voss along the E16 to Flåm (see p.226). The E16 is the main road between Bergen and Oslo and you can dodge most of the traffic by forking off the E16 at Vinje (see p.224) to take scenic Hwy-13 down the dales and over the mountains to Vik and Vangsnes (see p.224). From Vangsnes, there are ferries over the Sognefjord.

## INFORMATION

**Tourist office** Voss tourist office is in the town centre – and a 5min walk from the train station along the main drag – at Skulegata 14 (June–Aug Mon–Sat 9am–6pm & Sun 10am–5pm; Sept–May Mon–Fri 9am–4pm; ☎ 40 61 77 00, ⓦ visitvoss.no). They have oodles of information on hiking, rafting, skiing and local touring, the bones of which are detailed in the free *Voss Guide*.

## ACCOMMODATION AND EATING

**Fleischer's Hotel** Evangervegen 13 ☎ 56 52 05 00, ⓦ fleischers.no. Dating from the 1880s, and cheek-by-jowl with the train station, *Fleischer's* high-gabled and towered facade overlooks the lake. Parts of the hotel, which consists of the original building and a modern wing built in the same style, have the whiff of real luxury – as do many of the bedrooms – but others are more mundane. The hotel has two main restaurants and a summer-only terrace restaurant, each of which serves good-quality food, but the best is the *Seckman* (Tues–Sat 6.30–9.30pm), where mains average 320kr. Their all-inclusive food-and-lodging deals can be good value. **2000kr**

**Tre Bør Café og Bar** Vangsgata 28 ☎ 95 10 38 32. Informal, laidback café-restaurant in an old timber house right in the town centre. They serve up filling portions from a down-to-earth menu – burgers and so forth. Good cakes and coffee too. Mains average 155kr. Mon–Wed & Sun 10am–10pm, Thurs–Sat 10am–2.30am.

**Voss Vandrerhjem** Evangervegen 68 ☎ 56 51 20 17, ⓦ hihostels.no. Voss has lots of inexpensive accommodation to cater for all the visiting sportsfolk, but the best budget option is this excellent, all-year HI hostel, in a modern lodge overlooking the water about 800m west of the train station. The hostel serves good breakfasts and inexpensive evening meals – though these need to be pre-booked – and has self-catering facilities; it also has its own laundry and rents out bikes and canoes. Reservations are strongly recommended. To get there, turn right outside the station building and head along the lake away from the town centre – a 10min walk. Dorms **190kr**, doubles **750kr**

# Myrdal and Finse

Heading east from Voss, trains – but not cars as there is no road – scuttle along the **Raundal valley** before climbing up to the bare but eerily beautiful wastes of the Hardangervidda plateau. All trains stop at **Myrdal**, a remote railway junction where you change for the extraordinary train ride down to Flåm (see box opposite), and then proceed onto **Finse**, just half an hour by train from Myrdal and the highest point on the Bergen–Oslo railway line.

## Finse

A solitary lakeside outpost on the northern peripheries of the Hardangervidda plateau, **Finse** comprises nothing more than its station and a few isolated buildings, hunkered down against the howling winds that rip across the plateau in winter. There's snow here from the beginning of November until well into June, and the **cross-country skiing** is

## THE FLÅM RAILWAY – THE FLÅMSBANA

The lonely railway junction of **Myrdal**, just forty minutes or so by train from Voss, is the start of one of Europe's most celebrated branch rail lines, the **Flåmsbana**, a 20km, 900m plummet down the Flåmsdal valley to **Flåm** (see p.226). This 50min train ride should not be missed if at all possible despite the hordes of tourists – it's part of the "Norway in a Nutshell" route (see box, p.210). The track, which took four years to lay in the 1920s, spirals down the mountainside, passing through hand-dug tunnels and, at one point, actually travelling through a hairpin tunnel to drop nearly 300m. The gradient of the line is one of the steepest anywhere in the world, and as the train squeals its way down the mountain, past cascading waterfalls, it's reassuring to know that it has five separate sets of brakes, each capable of bringing it to a stop. The service runs all year round, a local lifeline during the deep winter months. There are nine departures daily from mid-April to early October, and four the rest of the year; Myrdal–Flåm fares are 340kr each way; timetables on Ⓦ www.nsb.no.

The athletic occasionally undertake the **five-hour walk** from the railway junction at Myrdal down the old road into the valley, instead of taking the train, but much the better option is to disembark about halfway down and walk in from there. **Berekvam** station, at an altitude of 345m, is the best place to alight, leaving an enthralling two- to three-hour hike through changing mountain scenery down to Flåm. **Cycling** down the valley road is also perfectly feasible, though it's much too steep to be relaxing.

particularly enthusiastic, with locals skiing off from the station in every direction. You can rent cross-country ski equipment at the *Finse 1222 Hotel* (see below), but you'll need to reserve. After the snow has melted, cycling (see box, p.224) and **hiking** take over.

**4**

### Rallarmuseet
July to mid-Sept daily 9.30am–9.30pm • 40kr • ☏ 90 50 09 40, Ⓦ finse1222.no

Finse may be tiny, but it does have one noteworthy attraction, the **Rallarmuseet** (Navvy Museum), which holds a pictorial record of the planning and construction of the Oslo–Bergen railway, whose final piece of track was laid in 1909. The old black-and-white photos are the most interesting exhibits and a well-earned tribute to the navvies who survived such grim conditions.

### Hikes from Finse
One especially popular **hike** from Finse is the round trip to the northeast edge of the **Hardangerjøkulen glacier** (4hr). Other, longer hiking trails skirt the glacier to traverse the main body of the plateau. Alternatively, it's an eleven-hour haul from Finse to Hwy-7 at **Dyranut** (see p.218), so most hikers overnight after around eight hours at the self-catering **Kjeldebu** DNT hut (March to mid-Oct). Finse has scope for more specialist activities too, most notably **guided glacier walks** on the Hardangerjøkulen. These guided walks take place between July and September and last around seven hours (600kr, including equipment); they are coordinated by *Finse 1222 Hotel* (see below).

### ARRIVAL AND DEPARTURE | MYRDAL AND FINSE

**By train: Myrdal** To all intents and purposes, Myrdal is just a railway junction.
Destinations Bergen (3–4 daily; 2hr); Finse (3–4 daily; 25min); Flåm (4–9 daily; 55min); Oslo (3–4 daily; 4hr 40min); Voss (3–4 daily; 50min).

**By train: Finse** The train station is Finse's focal point and its scattering of buildings flank it.
Destinations Bergen (3–4 daily; 2hr 20min); Geilo (3–4 daily; 40min); Myrdal (3–4 daily; 25min); Oslo (3–4 daily; 4hr 30min); Voss (3–4 daily; 1hr 20min).

### ACCOMMODATION AND EATING

**Finse 1222 Hotel** Finse ☏ 56 52 71 00, Ⓦ finse1222 .no. The smarter of Finse's two places to stay, this hotel occupies a large lodge-style structure beside the train station and its forty-odd modern rooms are all en suite. It's the setting that appeals most – look outside from any window and it's wilderness as far as the eye can see – but

> ## CYCLING FROM FINSE: THE RALLARVEGEN
>
> **Cycling** from Finse is made possible by the **Rallarvegen** ("Navvy Road"; ⓦ rallarvegen.com), which was originally built to allow men and materials to be brought up to the railway during its construction. Now surfaced with gravel and sometimes asphalt, the Rallarvegen begins in **Haugastøl** beside Hwy-7, runs west to Finse and then continues to Myrdal, from where you can cycle or take the Flåmsbana down to Flåm. It's 27km by bicycle from Haugastøl to Finse, 38km from Finse to Myrdal and another 15km to Flåm. The Finse-to-Flåm section, which passes through fine upland scenery before descending the Flåmsdal, is the most popular part of the Rallarvegen. Most cyclists travel east to west as Finse is a good deal higher than Myrdal, and the whole journey from Finse to Flåm takes around twelve hours; the return trip is usually made by train, with NSB railways transporting bikes for 185kr (on spec as advance reservations are not permitted). Locals reckon that the best time to cycle the Rallarvegen is usually from mid-July to late September. However, snow is not cleared from the route and its highest section – between Finse and Myrdal – can be blocked by snow until very late in summer, so check conditions locally before you set out. **Mountain-bike rental** is available from the *Finse 1222 Hotel* (see p.223), but advance reservations are required.

the hotel is comforting and comfortable in equal measure. The hotel also does an excellent sideline in outdoor pursuits, offering expert advice on cycling, hiking and skiing. They rent out bicycles too and coordinate day-long guided glacier hikes (600kr), but note that in both cases advance reservations are required. Prices include full board. Jan to late May & July to mid-Oct. **2600kr**

**Finsehytta** Finse ☏ 56 52 67 32, ⓦ finsehytta.dnt.no. Located a few minutes' walk southeast of the train station, this fully staffed DNT hut offers frugal lodgings for up to 160, with hikers, skiers, climbers and cyclists in mind. Advance reservations are advised and all meals are available. Non-members pay a premium of about 30 percent. Early March to mid-May & July to late Sept. DNT members: dorms **180kr**, doubles **610kr**

# Vik and Vangsnes

From Voss, it's about 20km north along the E16 to **Vinje**, where **Hwy-13** begins its 60-kilometre trek over to **Vik** and **Vangsnes** on the **Sognefjord**. A quintessential fjordland journey, the road begins by clambering up the Myrkdal valley, passing waterfalls and wild ravines before cutting an improbable route across the bleak and icy wastes of **Vikafjell mountain** – so improbable indeed that the highway is closed in winter, usually from November to April, and snow is piled high on either side of the road until at least the end of May.

## Hopperstad stave church

Vik • Daily mid-May to mid-June & mid-Aug to mid-Sept 10am–5pm; mid-June to mid-Aug 9am–5pm • 70kr • ☏ 57 67 88 40, ⓦ stavechurch.com • Signed from – and just off Hwy-13 – about 1500m from the Sognefjord

Sloping back from the Sognefjord, the village of **VIK** is a rather half-hearted affair, its clumps of modern housing stretching out along a wide river valley. Vik's salad days are, however, recalled by **Hopperstad stave church**, whose dark-stained timbers date from the twelfth century, maybe even earlier. The church is well cared for today, but in the 1880s it was about to be knocked down when a visiting architect and his antiquarian chum persuaded the villagers to change their minds. The pair promptly set about repairing the church and they did a good job: Hopperstad is one of the best examples of its type, its angular roofing and dragon finials surmounted by a long and slender tower. The **interior** has its moments too, with a Gothic side-altar canopy, parts of which may have been swiped from France by the Vikings, and a so-called lepers' window through which the afflicted listened to church services.

## Vangsnes

No more than a handful of houses and a ferry dock, **VANGSNES** is about 11km north of Vik along the Sognefjord. Local farmers must have had a real shock when, in 1913,

Kaiser Wilhelm erected a twelve-metre-high statue of the legendary Viking chief Fridtjof the Bold on the hilltop above their jetty. The **Fridtjovstatuen** still stands, an eccentric and vaguely unpleasant monument to the Kaiser's fascination with Nordic mythology – Fridtjof the Bold was in love with Ingebjorg, daughter of King Bele, whose statue, also commissioned by the Kaiser, is across the fjord at Balestrand (see p.231). You can walk the 500m up from the ferry dock to take a closer look at Fridtjof and there's a wide view of the Sognefjord from here too.

## ARRIVAL AND DEPARTURE

### VIK AND VANGSNES

**By bus** There is a limited bus service from Voss to Vik – aka Vikøyri – and Vangsnes (1 daily except Sat; 1hr 15min–1hr 30min; ⑩ skyss.no). In Vangsnes, buses pull in beside the ferry dock.

**By car ferry from Vangsnes** Car ferries across the Sognefjord to either Dragsvik (for Balestrand; every 40min–1hr; 30min) or Hella (for Hwy-55, including Sogndal; every 40min–1hr; 15min).

**By Hurtigbåt passenger express boat from Vik** Hurtigbåt boats (⑩ norled.no) run to Balestrand (1–2 daily; 20min); Bergen (1–2 daily; 3hr 30min); Flåm (1–2 daily; 1hr 40min).

# Stalheim and Gudvangen

At Vinje, about 20km north of Voss, the **E16** veers east for its dramatic defile down to Flåm (see p.226). En route, it passes the scattered hillside hamlet of **STALHEIM**, where you'll find one of the region's most superbly sited hotels (see below), complete with its own folk museum – a platoon of traditional log buildings and a manor house of 1726, all crammed with ancient artefacts. The byroad to the hotel is actually the **old main road** and this continues past the hotel to zigzag over the mountains before rejoining the E16 a little further on – a fine if mildly hair-raising detour with desultory **Gudvangen** lurking beyond.

## Gudvangen

The mini-port of **GUDVANGEN**, 45km from Voss, is a forlorn, shadowy little place at the southern tip of the Nærøyfjord. In the summertime, hundreds of tourists pour through here partly on account of the car-ferry connections to Kaupanger, but mainly because it's on the "Norway in a Nutshell" itinerary (see box, p.210). A modern and singularly unprepossessing complex down by the jetty incorporates souvenir shops, a café and a hotel, whose assorted hut-like structures have turf roofs – an ersatz Vikingarama which you can really do without.

## ARRIVAL AND DEPARTURE

### STALHEIM AND GUDVANGEN

**By boat** Gudvangen's jetty is at the foot of the village and there are car ferries across the Sognefjord to/from Kaupanger (mid-May to mid-Sept 1–4 daily; 2hr 40min; ⑩ fjord2.com). There are also sightseeing cruises to Flåm (see box, p.226).

**By bus** Buses to Gudvangen pull in beside the ferry dock. Nettbuss (⑩ nettbuss.no) operates the Sognebussen

(NX450) from Gudvangen to Bergen (2–4 daily; 2hr 35min), Flåm (2–4 daily; 20min), Sogndal (2–4 daily; 2hr) and Voss (2–4 daily; 50min). Local bus #950 (⑩ skyss.no) links the *Stalheim Hotel* with Voss (May to late Sept; 3 daily except Sun; 1hr) and Gudvangen (May to late Sept; 2–3 daily except Sun; 15min).

## ACCOMMODATION AND EATING

★**Stalheim Hotel** Stalheim ☎ 56 52 01 22, ⑩ stalheim .com. The fourth incarnation of a hotel that was originally built here on this mini-mountain plateau in the late nineteenth century, today's building – dating from the 1960s – is a large and chunky structure short of grace. All is redeemed inside, however, where the large and spacious public rooms have been kitted out in an endearing version of antique Norwegian style, all heirlooms and bygones plus a few landscape paintings and some fine furniture of classic Scandinavian design probably dating to the 1970s. The

*Stalheim*'s bedrooms are large and modern if a tad plain, but really who's bothered when the highlight is the view – a simply breathtaking vista down along the Nærøydal valley; so stunning, in fact, that David Hockney came and painted it. The hotel serves a top-notch breakfast and an excellent buffet dinner – all you can eat for 450kr (daily 6.30–9pm) – and is popular with tour groups. It's located up a twisty byroad, just 1.3km from the E16 on what was once the main road until they tunnelled through the mountain below. May–Sept. **1900kr**

4

## Undredal

Just beyond Gudvangen, the E16 disappears into an 11km tunnel to emerge just 100m or so from the byroad that leads the 6km north along a boulder-strewn valley to tiny **UNDREDAL**. The village perches right on the edge of the **Aurlandsfjord**, its narrow, meandering lanes overshadowed by the severity of the surrounding mountains. There's been a settlement here since Viking times, and for much of its history the village has been reliant on the export of its goat's cheese, now produced in Undredal's two surviving dairies – there were once a dozen. Undredal has just eighty inhabitants (if you discount the five hundred goats) but it is home to a charming **stave church**.

### Undredal stavkirke

Mid-June to July daily 10am–4.30pm · 70kr · ☎ 95 29 76 68, ⊛ undredal-stavkyrkje.com

With its dinky little porch and prim and proper spire, **Undredal stavkirke** is an inordinately pretty country church that dates back as far as the twelfth century, though it was extensively remodelled in the 1720s. A tiny affair – it's one of the smallest churches in the whole of Norway – it's decorated in fine folkloric style, from the floral patterns on the walls through to the crucified Christ above the high altar and the stylized stars and naive figures on the ceiling.

## Flåm

Fringed by meadows and orchards, **FLÅM** sits beside the Aurlandsfjord, a slender branch of the Sognefjord, with the mountains glowering behind. It's a splendid setting, but otherwise first impressions are poor: the fjordside complex adjoining the train station is crass and commercial – souvenir trolls and the like – and on summer days the place heaves with tourists, who pour off the train, have lunch, and then promptly head out by bus and ferry. But a brief stroll is enough to leave the crowds behind at the harbourside, while out of season or in the evenings, when the day-trippers have all moved on, Flåm is a pleasant spot and an eminently agreeable place to spend the night. If you're prepared to risk the weather, late September is perhaps the **best time to visit**: the peaks already have a covering of snow and the vegetation is just turning its autumnal golden brown. Flåm is also an excellent base for further explorations, whether it be the train ride up to Myrdal on the Flåmsbana (see box, p.223), the dramatic ferry trip over to Gudvangen (see box below) or a day-long hike in the surrounding mountains.

### ARRIVAL AND DEPARTURE

FLÅM

**By train** Flåm train station is adjacent to the jetty, with services on the Flamsbåna up to Myrdal (mid-April to early Oct 9 daily; early Oct to mid-April 4 daily; 50min; ⊛ www .nsb.no), on the Bergen–Oslo line.

**By bus** Buses to Flåm pull in beside the ferry dock and train station. Nettbuss (⊛ nettbuss.no) operates the

Sognebussen from Flåm to Gudvangen (2–4 daily; 20min), Voss (2–4 daily; 50min), Bergen (2–4 daily; 3hr), Kaupanger (2–4 daily; 1hr 20min) and Sogndal (2–4 daily; 1hr 30min). There is also a local, seasonal bus (#23-490) to Aurland and up the Aurlandsdal valley (Hwy-50) to Østerbø (see p.229).

---

### FLÅM TO GUDVANGEN: SAILING THE NÆRØYFJORD

Flåm is the starting (or ending) point for one of the most stupendous **sightseeing cruises** in the fjords, the two-hour trip up the **Aurlandsfjord** and down its narrow offshoot, the **Nærøyfjord** (June–Sept 8 daily; Oct–May 2 daily; 2hr 10min; ⊛ visitflam.com), to **Gudvangen** (see p.225). The Nærøyfjord is the narrowest fjord in Europe, its high and broody cliffs keeping out the sun throughout the winter, and its stern beauty makes for a magnificent excursion. Prices depend on the date of travel and which type of boat you choose – they have now added some sleek new ones – but begin at 280kr one-way, 560 return. Incidentally, the cruise forms part of the "Norway in a Nutshell" itinerary (see box, p.210).

**By Hurtigbåt passenger express boat** Hurtigbåt boats pull in at the ever-expanding Flåm jetty at the foot of the village. Timetables on ⓦ norled.no.

**Destinations** Balestrand (1–2 daily; 1hr 30min); Bergen (1–2 daily; 5hr 15min); Vik (1–2 daily; 1hr 40min).

## INFORMATION AND ACTIVITIES

**Tourist office** Flåm's harbourside tourist complex may be modern and ugly, but it is convenient, holding a supermarket, the train station and the tourist office (April–Oct daily 9am–6pm; Oct–March Thurs–Sat 9am–3pm; ☎ 95 43 04 14, ⓦ sognefjord.no), where you can pick up a free and very useful booklet on Aurland, Flåm and Lærdal. They also have details on local hiking routes, sell hiking

maps and rent out mountain bikes.

**Fjord kayaking** Njord (☎ 91 32 66 28, ⓦ njord.as), who operate from the Flåm waterfront, offers an interesting range of tours, the shortest and cheapest of which is their Aurlandsfjord paddle for 650kr per person (3hr); advance reservations are required.

## ACCOMMODATION AND EATING

**Flåm Camping og Vandrerhjem** ☎ 94 03 26 81, ⓦ flaam-camping.no. Handily situated about 300m from the train station towards the back of the village, this well-appointed campsite spreads over a sheltered site beside a stream. Has both tent spaces and dinky little cabins, and also incorporates a small and well-kept HI hostel. March to early Nov. Camping **220kr**, dorms **290kr**, cabins **730kr**, doubles **850kr**

**Flåmsbrygga** ☎ 57 63 20 50, ⓦ flamsbrygga.no. Metres from the train station, this recent addition to the Flåm scene includes a real oddity – a bar (daily 11am–5pm, later in summer) built in the style of a Viking long hall: circular, dark, with heavy wooden beams and an open fire. The architecture may be strange, but the beer of the Ægir microbrewey that's based here certainly is not, ranging from the dark and strong Sumbel Porter to the tangy, but equally strong Bøyla Blonde Ale. To the rear of the bar is a modern accommodation block, though here the Vikingarama has not been duplicated and the rooms are cosy and warm with wood-panelled walls and mini-balconies. **1400kr**

★ **Fretheim Hotel** ☎ 57 63 63 00, ⓦ fretheimhotel.no. Large, rambling hotel with a long pedigree whose attractive older part, with its high-pitched roofs and white-painted clapboard, is now joined to a flashy glass structure that is, in its

turn, attached to a matching modern wing. In the early days of fjord tourism, in the 1890s, the Fretheim family, who were local farmers, took a shine to tourism, welcoming foreign hunters and fishermen for whom they subsequently built a lodge then a hotel. Thereafter, it was full steam ahead and, in deference to this family tradition, the rooms in the hotel's older wing have been restored to an approximation of their original appearance; in this wing also is the immaculately maintained library of Flåm's most notable writer, the poet Per Sivle (1857–1904). The modern rooms in the other wing are more straightforward (and cost around 400kr more), though all are comfortable; the better rooms face the fjord and have mini-balconies. The hotel restaurant is outstanding whether à la carte (mains average 280kr) or at the all-you-can-eat buffet (mid-May to mid-Sept nightly). The restaurant features local, seasonal ingredients, many of which come from the family farm, including the cured meats and smoked fish from the smokery. The hotel is a couple of minutes' walk from the train station. They rent bikes too. Closed mid-Dec to Jan. **1900kr**

**Heimly Pensjonat** ☎ 57 63 23 00, ⓦ heimly.no. Small guesthouse providing simple but perfectly adequate lodgings in a modern block in a quiet location about 450m east of the train station along the shore; it's a friendly place and the views down the fjord are charming. Bike rental too. **900kr**

# The Aurlandsdal valley

The workaday hamlet of **AURLAND**, just 10km from Flåm, strings along the fjord at the foot of the **Aurlandsdal valley** – and near the entrance to the whopping Lærdal tunnel (see p.229). The valley was once the final part of one of Norway's most celebrated **hikes**, a classic two- or three-day expedition that began at Finse train station (see p.223), from where the trail crossed the northern peripheries of the Hardangervidda plateau before descending the Aurlandsdal, with hikers then pushing on to Flåm to get the train back again. The trail incorporated an extravagant range of scenery, from upland plateau to plunging ravines, and parts of it followed an old cattle-drovers' route that once linked eastern and western Norway. The trail lost much of its allure – and some of its beauty – when **Highway 50**, which links Hwy-7 near Geilo (see p.175) with Aurland, was rammed through the Aurlandsdal as part of a hydroelectricity generation scheme in the 1970s, but sections of it still provide some excellent hiking. Perhaps the most scenic

4

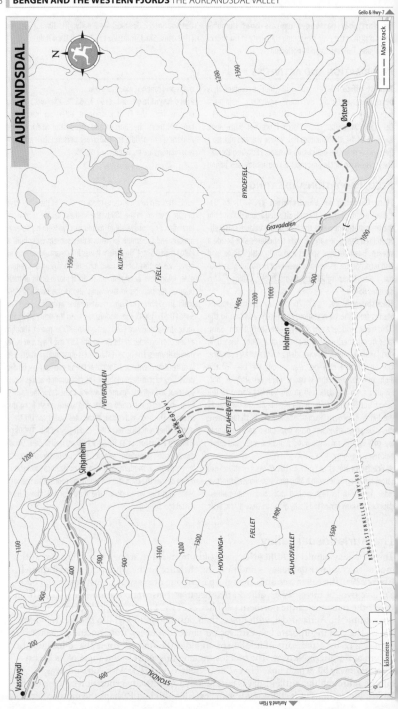

AURLANDSDAL

Geilo & Hwy-7 ▲

– – – Main track

N

Østerbø

BYRDEFJELL

Gravadalen

1000

900

1000

KLUFTA-

FJELL

1500

1460

1200

1000

Holmen

VEIVERDALEN

Bakkegrovi

VETLAHELVETE

Sinjarheim

1200

HOVDUNGA-

FJELLET

SALHUSFJELLET

1400

1500

BERDALSTUNNELLEN (HWY-50)

1100

500

900

1100

1200

1300

400

900

200

STONDAL

600

Vassbygdi

0        1
kilometre

Aurland & Flåm ▲

section today is the 21km stretch between **Østerbø** (820m) and **Vassbygdi** (94m), which takes between six and seven hours to complete (see map opposite). The trail threads its way through the woods and farms of the Aurlandsdal, passing crashing waterfalls and offering handsome valley views as well as one or two tight and steep scrambles. Østerbø, the starting point, comprises a pair of lonely mountain lodges (see below), located about 800m off Hwy-50 about 43km from Flåm; Vassbygdi is a dull hamlet where the trail ends at the car park and bus stop.

## ARRIVAL AND DEPARTURE          THE AURLANDSDAL VALLEY

**By bus** A local seasonal bus (#23-490; late June to late Sept 2–3 daily; ⓦ rutebok.no) travels up the Aurlandsdal valley (Hwy-50). From Flåm, it goes to Aurland (10min), Vassbygdi (30min) and Østerbø (1hr). Timetables are such that it is usually possible to catch the bus from Flåm to Østerbø, make the hike to Vassbygdi then return by bus the same day, but this means you'll be hiking against the clock. To avoid this, either book a taxi for the return leg or overnight in Østerbø at either of its two privately owned mountain lodges.

## ACCOMMODATION

**Østerbø Fjellstove** Østerbø ⓣ 57 63 11 77, ⓦ aurlandsdalen.com. Nestled in a wide and rocky valley beside Hwy-50, this large complex of mountain huts and lodges is a favourite with hikers. On offer are a variety of types of accommodation, from hostel-style beds in some of its lodges through to hotel rooms, which are plain and straightforward but still very comfortable. Full board costs about 300kr on top of the room rate. Late May to Sept.

Dorms 380kr, doubles 1400kr

**Østerbø Turisthytte** Østerbø ⓣ 57 63 11 41, ⓦ www .osterbo-turisthytte.no. As with the *Fjellstove*, this mountain lodge is popular with hikers and offers a range of accommodation – from one- to four-bunk rooms through to cabins. They also offer filling evening meals (320kr). Late May to Sept. Dorms 530kr, cabins 650kr

**4**

# Aurland to Lærdal

Opened in 2000, and linking Aurland with Lærdal, the **Lærdalstunnelen** (Lærdal tunnel) drills its way through the mountains and was the last section of the fast road, the **E16** – from Bergen to Oslo – to be completed. At 24.5km, it's one of the longest road tunnels in the world, but it only took five years to construct, which is, by any standard, a remarkable achievement. Aware that drivers could become bemused and/or disorientated in the tunnel, three **cave-like** areas have been quarried at 6km intervals and whereas the main tunnel has white lights, the caves have blue lighting with yellow lights at the edges, supposedly to give an impression of sunrise, though the end effect is just surreal. Giant fans draw air in from both entrances, with polluted air driven out through ventilation shafts, and the tunnel also employs its own air treatment plant. The Lærdalstunnelen runs northeast from just outside the village of Aurland to the **Lærdal valley**, at a point just 6km south of the fjordside village of Lærdalsøyri. The tunnel is, of course, the fastest route from Aurland to the Lærdal valley – and, even better, there are no tolls – but the 48km mountain road the tunnel replaced, the narrow **Aurlandsvegen**, has survived to provide splendid views and some hair-raising moments; it's open from the beginning of June to around the middle of October.

## Lærdalsøyri

Shadowed by a ring of mountains, **LÆRDALSØYRI** – or simply **LÆRDAL** – is an elongated village that lies sandwiched between Hwy-5 and the River Lærdalselvi as it gurgles into the fjord. In former times, Lærdalsøyri was a busy port and transit centre, but Norway's road building programme put an end to that – witness the almost total lack of harbour facilities. Nowadays, one part of the village is modern and industrial, the other – known as **Gamle Lærdalsøyri** – comprises a batch of old timber buildings that date back to the late nineteenth century. Strolling through this older part of the village is a pleasant way of spending half an hour or so, and afterwards you can have a cup of tea at the *Lindstrøm Hotel* (see p.230).

Norsk Villakssenter

Daily: May & Sept noon–6pm; June–Aug 10am–6pm • 90kr • ☎ 91 55 10 43, ⓦ norsk-villakssenter.no

Lærdalsøyri's showpiece tourist attraction is the **Norsk Villakssenter** (Norwegian Wild Salmon Centre), which occupies a conspicuous – and conspicuously ugly – modern building down by the river on the northern edge of the village, just east of Hwy-5. Inside, a film explains the convoluted life cycle of the salmon, which you then observe swimming around in a large tank, and there are displays on salmon fishing.

### ARRIVAL AND DEPARTURE                                      LÆRDALSØYRI

**By bus** Buses pull into the centre of the village beside the Rådhuset (town hall) on Øyraplassen.

Destinations Nettbuss (ⓦ nettbuss.no) operates the Sognebussen (NX450) from here to Bergen (1–4 daily; 3hr 30min); Flåm (1–4 daily; 50min); Sogndal (1–4 daily; 45min); Voss (1–4 daily; 2hr).

**By car & ferry** From Lærdalsøyri, it's 8km north along Hwy-5 to Fodnes, where a car ferry crosses over the Sognefjord to Mannheller (every 20min, but hourly midnight to 6am; 15min); Mannheller is 18km from Sogndal (see p.234). In the other direction, heading east along the E16, it's about 30km to Borgund stave church (see p.174).

### ACCOMMODATION AND EATING

**Lindstrøm Hotel** Lærdalsøyri ☎ 57 66 69 00, ⓦ lindstroemhotel.com. In the old part of the village, the *Lindstrøm* occupies several buildings, the oldest of which dates back to the late nineteenth century – witness the fancy scrollwork. The hotel's 86 rooms are spread among three of these buildings and are modern and functional. Coffee and snacks are served during the day and there's a self-service buffet at night (daily 7–8.30pm; 400kr). May–Sept. **1400kr**

## The Sognefjord

Profoundly beautiful, the **Sognefjord** (ⓦ sognefjord.no) drills in from the coast for some 200km, its inner recesses splintering into half a dozen subsidiary fjords. Perhaps inevitably, none of the villages and small towns that dot the fjord quite lives up to the splendid setting, but **Balestrand** and **Mundal**, on the Fjærlandsfjord, come mighty close and are easily the best bases. Both are on the north side of the fjord which, given the lack of roads on the south side, is where you want (or pretty much have) to be, Flåm (see p.226) apart. Mundal is also near two southerly tentacles of the Jostedalsbreen glacier – **Flatbreen** and easy-to-reach **Bøyabreen**.

**Highway 55** hugs the Sognefjord's north bank for much of its length, but at **Sogndal** it slices northeast to clip along the lustrous **Lustrafjord**, which boasts a top-notch attraction in **Urnes stave church**, reached via a quick ferry ride from **Solvorn**. Further north, a side road leaves Hwy-55 to clamber up from the Lustrafjord to the east side of the Jostedalsbreen glacier at the **Nigardsbreen nodule**, arguably the glacier's finest vantage point. Thereafter Hwy-55 – as the **Sognefjellsveg** – climbs steeply to run along the western side of the **Jotunheimen mountains**, an extraordinarily beautiful journey even by Norwegian standards and one which culminates with the road thumping down to **Lom** on the flatlands beside Hwy-15.

### GETTING AROUND                                            THE SOGNEFJORD

Public transport to and around the Sognefjord is generally excellent, being a dense combination of car ferries, Hurtigbåt express passenger boats and buses.

**By bus** Nettbuss (ⓦ nettbuss.no) operates the especially useful Sognebussen (NX450), which links Bergen with Gudvangen, Flåm (see p.226), Kaupanger and Sogndal. In addition, local buses run along the northern shore of the Sognefjord between Sogndal and Balestrand and, in the summertime, other buses proceed north from Sogndal to Turtagrø and Lom via the Sognefjellsveg (Hwy-55). For local bus timetables, go to ⓦ rutebok.no.

**By ferry & car ferry** There are two main car ferry services on the Sognefjord: Fodnes to Mannheller (for Sogndal); and Vangsnes to both Hella and Dragsvik (for Balestrand). A third, passenger-only ferry links Balestrand with Mundal on the Fjærlandsfjord (June–Aug only). The last is wonderfully scenic.

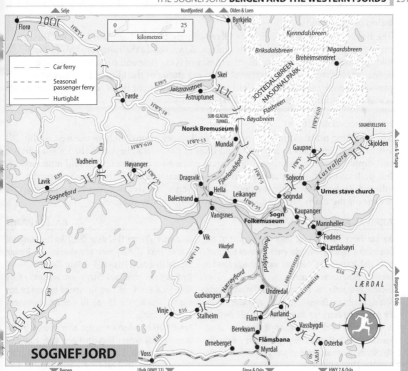

SOGNEFJORD

**By Hurtigbåt passenger express boat** Norled (ⓦ norled.no) currently provides the most useful passenger express boat service to and along the Sognefjord, linking Bergen, Vik, Balestrand, Flåm and Sogndal.

## Balestrand

**BALESTRAND**, an appealing first stop on the Sognefjord, has been a tourist destination since the middle of the nineteenth century, when it was discovered by European travellers in search of cool, clear air and picturesque mountain scenery. One of the visitors was Kaiser Wilhelm II, who became a frequent visitor, sharing his holiday spot with the tweeds and bustles of the British bourgeoisie. These days, the village is used as a touring base for the immediate area, as the battery of small hotels above the quay testifies, but it's all very small-scale, and among the thousand-strong population farming remains the principal livelihood.

An hour or so will suffice to take a peek at Balestrand's several low-profile attractions. Lining up along the **harbour** are the old post office, which features temporary displays on the town and its environs; a brace of art galleries; and an aquarium, the Sognefjord Akvarium.

### English church of St Olav

Kong Belesveg • May–Sept daily 10am–10pm • Free

From the harbour, it's a couple of minutes' walk to the **English church of St Olav**, a spiky, brown and beige, wooden structure dating back to 1897. It was built in the general style of a stave church at the behest of a British émigré, a certain Margaret Kvikne, who moved here after she married a local man, Knut Kvikne, the owner of the *Kviknes Hotel* (see p.232). Poor old Margaret died from tuberculosis three years before the church was opened, but not before she had climbed a string of local mountains, much to her husband's fright/delight.

Viking burial mounds

The British interest is recalled by St Olav's church, but the Germans have left their mark too: about 300m south of the church, down beside the fjord, are two humpy **Viking burial mounds**, supposedly the tombs of King Bele and his wife, who both appear in the Sagas. On the larger of them is a **statue** of the king in heroic pose, plonked there by the Kaiser in 1913 to match the statue of Bele's son-in-law that stands across the fjord in Vangsnes (see p.224).

Hiking around Balestrand

Several **hiking trails** ascend the rocky, forested slopes immediately to the west of the village, clambering up to the peaks and lakes of the plateau beyond. The tourist office will supply a free map of these hiking trails and advise on their length and difficulty, but perhaps the most appealing is the two-hour jaunt through the woods above the village with fine views over the fjord. For an even wider view you can make the short detour off the main path up to **Orrabenken** (370m above sea level).

## ARRIVAL AND INFORMATION                    BALESTRAND

**By car ferry** The main car ferry on this part of the Sognefjord operates a triangular route between Vangsnes, Hella and Dragsvik. The dock you want for Balestrand is Dragsvik, 9km away to the north.
Destinations Hella to Dragsvik (every 40min–hourly; 15min); Vangsnes to Dragsvik (every 40min–hourly; 25min).
**By passenger ferry** The dock in the centre of Balestrand is where you catch the passenger ferry up along Fjærlandsfjord to Mundal (early June to Aug 2 daily; 1hr 40min). This is a tourist route, so prices are above the norm (one-way 270kr, return 450kr).
**By Hurtigbåt passenger express boat** The Hurtigbåt jetty is in the centre of Balestrand.

Destinations Bergen (1–2 daily; 4hr); Flåm (1–2 daily; 1hr 30min); Florø (1 daily with one change; 3hr 30min); Sogndal (1–2 daily; 1hr); Vik (1–2 daily; 20min).
**By bus** Buses arrive and depart from beside the ferry dock. Local buses run from Balestrand to Sogndal bus station (3 daily; 1hr 15min) for onward connections north and south.
**Tourist office** Balestrand tourist office is down by the quayside (May & Sept Mon–Fri 10am–4pm; June–Aug Mon–Fri 9am–4pm, Sat & Sun 10am–4pm; ☎ 94 87 75 01, ✪ sogneford.no). Staff hand out a wide range of fjord leaflets, sell local hiking maps, supply bus and ferry timetables and rent out bicycles.

## ACCOMMODATION AND EATING

### HOTELS

★ **Balestrand Hotell** Kong Belesveg ☎ 57 69 11 38, ✪ balestrand.com. Small and rather comforting family hotel in a three-storey modern block a 5–10min walk from the ferry dock. Has thirty prim-and-proper guest rooms, all en suite, the pick of which overlook the fjord and have mini-balconies (300kr extra). Mid-May to mid-Sept. **1200kr**
**Balestrand Vandrerhjem** Kringsjå Lærargata 9 ☎ 57 69 13 03, ✪ hihostels.no. Just 150m uphill from the ferry dock, this substantial hostel inhabits an attractive timber building with a long veranda overlooking the fjord. There are self-catering facilities, a café-restaurant and a laundry plus a neighbouring activity centre geared up for school parties. Late June to mid-Aug. Dorms **265kr**
**Kviknes Hotel** Kviknevegen 8 ☎ 57 69 42 00, ✪ kviknes .com. The various buildings of this long-established hotel – some old, some new – dominate much of the Balestrand waterfront. Pride of architectural place goes to the original hotel building, an imposing wooden edifice whose balconies and pointy gables look out over the fjord. Inside, its public areas are a treat too, the fittings and furnishings completed in a sort of neo-Viking baronial style, all overseen by a

platoon of fine Norwegian land- and seascape paintings. If you do decide to stay here, however, don't take a room without having a gander first: the rooms in the original building vary enormously – some are lovely and distinctly period, others are really rather dowdy– and you may settle for a room in the modern annexe instead: these are not particularly distinctive, but the best (on the top floors) have wide fjord views and most have mini-balconies. The hotel restaurant serves up a banquet-sized, help-yourself buffet (525kr) every night from 6pm – go early to get the pick and be sure to leave room for the ground-moving, earth-shattering mousse. Late April to Sept. **1800kr**
**Midtnes Hotel** Kong Belesveg 33 ☎ 57 69 42 40, ✪ midtnes.no. About 300m from the ferry dock behind the English church, this low-key, pleasantly sedate hotel has a few workaday but spacious rooms in a modern wing adjoining the original clapboard house; make sure to get a room with a fjord view (200kr extra). Open all year. **1050kr**

### CAMPSITE

**Sjøtun Camping** Sjøtunsvegen ☎ 95 06 72 61, ✪ sjotun .com. The town campsite occupies a treeless field just beyond the Viking burial mounds, 1km or so south of the dock. There are eleven two- to four-person cabins here as well as tent and caravan pitches. **June to late Sept.** Camping **210kr**, two-berth cabins **380kr**

**CAFÉ**

**Pilgrim Restaurant** Down by the quayside ☎ 91 56

28 42, ⓦ detgylnehus.no. The best café in town, an informal, friendly little place with lots of local art and hand-me-downs on the walls. Their menu emphasizes local ingredients and the soups – troll soup (mushrooms, carrots and onions) for one, fish soup another (130kr) – are filling and tasty. Metres from the ferry dock. **Early May to Aug daily 2–9pm.**

## Mundal and the Fjærlandsfjord

Most attractively reached by ferry from Balestrand, the **Fjærlandsfjord** is a wild place, its flanks blanketed by a thick covering of trees that extends down to the water's edge, with a succession of thundering waterfalls tumbling down vast clefts in the rock up above. The village of **MUNDAL** – sometimes referred to as Fjærland – matches its surroundings perfectly, a gentle ribbon of old wooden houses edging the fjord, with the mountains as a louring backcloth. It's one of the region's most picturesque places, saved from the developers by its isolation: it was one of the last settlements on the Sognefjord to be connected to the road system, with Hwy-5 from Sogndal only being completed in 1986. Since then, Mundal has eschewed the crasser forms of commercialism to become the self-styled "**Den Norske Bokbyen**" (Norwegian Book Town; ⓦ bokbyen.no), with a dozen rustic buildings accommodating antiquarian and secondhand **bookshops**. Naturally enough, most of the books are in Norwegian, but there's a liberal sprinkling of English titles too. The main bookselling season runs from May to mid-September and the bookshops are usually open daily from 10am to 6pm, though one or two places do hang on into the winter.

### Mundal kirke

Mundal has two good-looking buildings, the *Hotel Mundal* (see p.234) and the adjacent **church** (free), painted maroon and dating from 1861. The church lacks ornamentation, but it is immaculately maintained and its graveyard hints at the hard but healthy life of the district's farmers – most of them seem to have lived to a ripe old age. One man who didn't make it that far was a German officer, buried here – you'll spot the plinth – after a climbing accident in 1910; his family donated the modest, painted baptismal font.

### Hiking around Mundal

Many locals are still farmers, but in summer precious few of them herd their cattle up to the mountain pastures, as was the custom until the 1960s. The disused tracks to these summer farms (*støls*) now serve as **hiking trails** of varying length and difficulty – the tourist office (see p.234) will advise, but one of the easier routes is the two-hour (each way) hoof west from the village up the country lane that follows **Mundalsdal** to **Fjellstølen**, at 350m. Much easier is the 2.5km stroll north along the quiet byroad that slips prettily along the fjord to link the village with Hwy-5. Just before you get to the main road, you'll spy a large **bird hide** that overlooks the protected wetlands at the tip of the Fjærlandsfjord. These wetlands, **Bøyaøri**, attract over one hundred species of bird with mallard, oystercatcher, heron and lapwing, among many others, all making their appearance.

### Norsk Bremuseum

Mundal • Daily: April, May, Sept & Oct 10am–4pm; June–Aug 9am–7pm • 120kr for exhibits • ☎ 57 69 32 88, ⓦ bre.museum.no

The **Norsk Bremuseum** (Norwegian Glacier Museum), sitting tight against Hwy-5 at the start of the byroad to Mundal, tells you more than you ever wanted to know about glaciers and then some. It features several lavish hands-on displays and screens films about them – and package tourists turn up in their droves. The staff also supply a comprehensive range of information on the **Jostedalsbreen Nasjonalpark**.

## The Jostedalsbreen glacier: Flatbreen

Guided glacier walks: Brekick (☎ 93 23 51 84, ⊛ brekick.no) offers a limited range of stiff and steep guided glacier walks on the Flatbreen nodule. Their two-night excursion (late June to Sept) costs 4200kr, all inclusive • The starting point is the *Rødseter* mountain lodge, northeast of Mundal up a narrow byroad • Advance reservations are essential via the Norsk Bremuseum

If you're after a **guided glacier walk** on the Jostedalsbreen, the usual target from Mundal is the **Supphellebreen**, the Jostedalsbreen's nearest hikeable arm, or, to be precise, that part of it called the **Flatbreen**. Beautiful it may be, but it's also challenging and neither is it easy to get to, requiring an overnight stay way up in the mountains.

## The Jostedalsbreen glacier: Bøyabreen

It's actually possible to get close to the Jostedalsbreen without breaking sweat. Head north from Mundal on Hwy-5 and, after about 10km – just before you enter the tunnel – watch for the signposted, dirt and gravel side-road on the right that leads to the **Bøyabreen**, just 800m away. You can drive the first 600m, to the café and car park, and from here it's an easy stroll to the slender glacial lake that is fed by the sooty shank of the Bøyabreen glacier arm up above.

### ARRIVAL AND DEPARTURE

**By bus** Long-distance buses pull in beside the Norsk Bremuseum, on Hwy-5, about 2.5km from Mundal. Local buses depart from the Mundal ferry dock. A seasonal local bus runs between Mundal and the Norsk Bremuseum (June to mid-Sept 1–2 daily).
Destinations Florø (2–4 daily; 2hr 15min, with one

### MUNDAL AND THE FJÆRLANDSFJORD

change); Skei (3 daily; 1hr 40min); Sogndal (3 daily; 30min).
**By ferry** Mundal's ferry dock is at the south end of the village, the briefest of walks from the tourist office; this is where you catch the passenger boat to Mundal, on the Fjærlandsfjord (early June to Aug 2 daily; 1hr 40min).

### INFORMATION

**Tourist office** Fjaerland tourist office is about 300m from the ferry dock (May to late Sept daily 10am–6pm; ☎ 94 79 80 36, ⊛ sognefjord.no). They will advise on local hiking routes, sell hiking maps and have bus and ferry timetables. They rent out bicycles too.
**Jostedalsbreen Nasjonalpark** Fjærland's Norsk

Bremuseum (⊛ bre.museum.no; see p.233) is one of the Jostedalsbreen Nasjonalpark's three information centres (see box, p.241). The staff supply a comprehensive range of information on the park, including details of Breturar (guided glacier walks) on the nearest negotiable nodule, Flatbreen.

### ACCOMMODATION AND EATING

**Bøyum Camping** ☎ 57 69 32 52, ⊛ boyumcamping .no. Near the Bremuseum, 2km or so from Mundal, this straightforward, family-run campsite occupies a large, grassy field with mountains jagging away in every direction. The service building has self-catering and washing facilities as well as a small bar. There are a handful of turf-roofed modern cabins here too. May–Sept. Camping __210kr__, two-person cabins __850kr__
★ **Fjærland Fjordstue Hotell** ☎ 57 67 57 57, ⊛ fjaerland hotell.no. An immaculately maintained family hotel with fourteen appealing rooms decorated in a cosy, homely manner. Most of the rooms have views over the adjacent fjord, as does the outside terrace and the sitting room. They offer an excellent, three-course evening meal featuring local, seasonal ingredients for hotel guests (450kr) and visitors (490kr); advance reservations are required. May–Sept. __1400kr__

**Hotel Mundal** ☎ 91 90 99 90, ⊛ hotelmundal.no. This is the obvious choice of the two fjordside hotels in Mundal. It's a splendid, somewhat quirky sort of place whose cream-painted, nineteenth-century, high-pitched roofs, turrets and verandas overlook the fjord from among the handful of buildings that amount to the village centre. Inside, the public rooms, which date back to 1891, display many original features, from the parquet floors and fancy wooden scrollwork through to the sliding doors of the expansive dining room. The rooms are perhaps a tad frugal, but somehow it doesn't matter much. If you do stay, look out for the old photos on the walls of men in plus-fours and hobnail boots clambering round the glaciers – only softies bothered with gloves. As usual, the overnight rate includes breakfast and they serve dinner here too, but the food is better at the *Fjærland Fjordstue Hotell* (see above). May–Sept. __1700kr__

## Sogndal and around

**SOGNDAL**, on a narrow arm of the Sognefjord, a short ferry ride and 50km east of Balestrand, is the largest town hereabouts, though, with a population of just over seven thousand, this is hardly a major boast. Neither is Sogndal especially appealing: it has, admittedly, a pleasant fjord setting in a broad valley, sheltered by low, green hills dotted with apple and pear trees, but its straggly centre is a rash of modern concrete and glass. There are, however, a couple of minor attractions within a few kilometres' radius that might detain you.

### De Heibergske Samlinger – Sogn Folkemuseum

Vestreim • May & Sept daily 10am–3pm; June–Aug daily 10am–5pm; Oct–April Mon–Fri 10am–3pm • 80kr • ☎ 57 67 82 06, ⦿ dhs.museum.no • Beside Hwy-5, 8km southeast of Sogndal

The enjoyable **De Heibergske Samlinger – Sogn Folkemuseum** (Heiberg Collections of the Sogn Folk Museum) is named after a certain Mr Heiberg, who was an avid collector of – and expert in – old Norwegian agricultural tools. It's hard to say if Mr Heiberg's special interest made him an entertaining dinner guest, but his legacy, this folk museum, is pleasant enough, its thirty-odd relocated buildings, which mostly date from the nineteenth century, rolling down the bumpy hillside. Together, they give something of the flavour of an older rural Norway, especially when the animals are knocking around in the summer months. Speaking of flavours, the staff bake their own cakes and sell them at the **café** – and very tasty they are, too.

### Kaupanger stave church

Kyrkjegata • June–Aug daily 10am–5pm • 70kr • ☎ 57 67 88 40, ⦿ stavechurch.com • There are regular local buses from Sogndal bus station to the stop near the stave church (every 1–3hr; 25min)

The hamlet of **KAUPANGER**, 13km from Sogndal, spreads up the hill from its miniature harbour, the red and white timber houses of the old part of the village inching up towards **Kaupanger stavkirke** (stave church). A much-modified thirteenth-century structure whose dourness is offset by its situation, the church stands amid buttercup meadows with views of the fjord on one side and forested hills on the other. The interior has several unusual features, most memorably a **musical score** painted on one of the walls. No one is quite sure if the score was meant to be purely decorative or had some musical function, but it does appear to be a (rough) copy of a hymn traditionally sung on Ascension Day. The church also has two sad portraits of Danish bailiffs and their families: one is pictured with three stillborn babies, the other with one young son, who has a tiny red cross (for death) above his head.

## ARRIVAL AND DEPARTURE

## SOGNDAL AND AROUND

**By Hurtigbåt passenger express boat** Hurtigbåt boats dock on the west side of Sogndal's town centre. Destinations Balestrand (1–2 daily; 1hr); Bergen (1–2 daily; 4hr 50min); Vik (1–2 daily; 1hr 10min).

**By car ferry** There are no car ferries to Sogndal. The nearest are between Gudvangen and Kaupanger, 13km from Sogndal (mid-May to mid-Sept 1–4 daily; 2hr 40min; ⦿ fjord2.com); and Mannheller–Fodnes (every 20min, but hourly midnight to 6am; 15min), 18km to the southeast and the fastest route to the E16.

**By bus** Sogndal Skysstasjon (bus station) is on the west side of the town centre near the end of Gravensteinsgata, the long main drag. Nettbuss's Sognebussen (NX450) links Sogndal with Bergen (2–4 daily; 4hr 30min), Flåm (2–4 daily; 1hr 30min), Gudvangen (2–4 daily; 1hr 50min), the Mannheller–Fodnes ferry (2–4 daily; 25min), and Voss (2–4 daily; 2hr 40min). Local buses include services to Balestrand (3 daily; 1hr 15min), Lom (late June to Aug 3 daily; 3hr) and Solvorn (1 direct bus daily; 30min).

## ACCOMMODATION AND EATING

**Quality Hotel Sogndal** Gravensteinsgata 5 ☎ 57 62 77 00, ⦿ nordicchoicehotels.com. A welcome addition to the Sogndal hotel scene, this slick and very glassy modern hotel overlooks the main street at the west end of town. There are over one hundred rooms here – and smart-chain describes them. The hotel restaurant, *La Pergola*, offers Italian food and covers all the classics with mains from 180kr.

Restaurant: Mon–Sat 3–10pm, Sun 1–10pm. <u>1800kr</u>

**Sogndal Vandrerhjem** Helgeheimsvegen 9 ☎ 57 62 75 75, ⦿ hihostels.no. HI hostel which actually manages to feel quite homely despite being housed in a residential rural high school (a Folkehøgskule). Facilities include self-catering and common rooms; some of the double rooms are en suite (755kr). Finding the place is straightforward:

**4**

approaching Sogndal from the southeast on Hwy-5, the hostel is clearly signposted from the main drag, just beyond the bridge at the east end of town; in the opposite direction, coming from the bus station, it's about 400m beyond the roundabout at the east end of Gravensteinsgata. Early June to mid-Aug. Dorms 310kr, doubles 620kr

## Solvorn and around

The bright-white timber houses of **SOLVORN**, about 17km from Sogndal, cluster the sheltered foreshore of the **Lustrafjord** with the craggy mountains louring behind. Solvorn is a lovely little village and, to make things even better, it possesses two great places to stay and is only a quick car ferry ride from one of the region's star attractions – Urnes stave church.

### Urnes stave church

May–Sept daily 10.30am–5.30pm • 90kr • ☎ 57 67 88 40, ⍟ stavechurch.com • From the Ornes car ferry (see below), it's a stiff 15min (1.2km) hike up the hill to the church

Magnificently sited across the Lustrafjord from Solvorn, with the hamlet of **Ornes** down below and the mountains in the distance, **Urnes stave church** is the oldest and most celebrated of its type in Norway. Parts of the building date back to the twelfth century, and its most remarkable feature is its wonderful medieval **carvings**. On the outside, incorporated into the north wall, are several exquisite door panels, alive with a swirling filigree of strange beasts and delicate vegetation. These forceful, superbly crafted panels bear witness to the sophistication of Viking woodcarving – indeed, the church has given its name to this distinctively Nordic art form, found in many countries where Viking influence was felt and now generally known as the "Urnes" style. Most of the interior is seventeenth century – including some splendidly bulbous pomegranates – but there is Viking woodcarving here too, notably the strange-looking figures and beasts carved on the capitals of the staves and the sacred-heart bench-ends. A small display in the neighbouring house-cum-ticket-office fills in all the details and has photographic enlargements of carvings that are hard to decipher inside the (poorly lit) church.

### ARRIVAL AND DEPARTURE                          SOLVORN AND AROUND

**By bus** Buses from Sogndal (1 direct bus daily; 30min) stop beside the ferry dock.

**By car ferry** The jetty is at the foot of Solvorn village and from here a ferry runs across the Lustrafjord to Ornes (for Urnes stave church; May–Sept daily 10am–4.50pm, hourly; Oct–April Mon–Fri 4–6 daily, no Sat & Sun service; 20min; each way: passengers 37kr, car & driver 102kr; ☎ 91 72 17 19, ⍟ urnesferry.com).

### ACCOMMODATION AND EATING

★**Eplet Bed & Apple** Solvorn ☎ 41 64 94 69, ⍟ eplet .net. One of the region's more distinctive places to stay, this combined hostel, hotel and apple juice farm, which inhabits a two-storey modern house, is owned and operated by a one-time long-distance cyclist and traveller who seems to have been just about everywhere. He has created a laidback, easy-going place with dormitory accommodation and a few neat, plain and modern hotel rooms. You can camp in the grounds too (no cars or caravans), while mountain-bike rental is free for guests, and there's a self-catering kitchen. They serve breakfast, but otherwise they refer you to the café down at the harbour. The juice factory is in the basement and the house is surrounded by an orchard, which has its own complement of sheep. *Eplet* is located in the heart of the village about 300m back up the road from the dock – just watch for the sign. No cards – and there are no ATMs in Solvorn. And, by the way, the apple juice is just fantastic. May–Sept. Tents 110kr, dorms 220kr, doubles 690kr

★**Walaker Hotell** Solvorn ☎ 57 68 20 80, ⍟ walaker .com. The *Walaker Hotell* has been in the same family for several generations, as witnessed by the old photographs that decorate the dining-room-cum-lounge. Nowadays, the hotel divides into two distinct halves, beginning with the old house, a comely, pastel-painted, two-storey building whose porch is supported by a pair of columns – a Neoclassical extravagance that must have once amazed the locals. The rooms in the old house (an extra 450kr) have been attractively decorated in several period styles, from the big and beautiful carved wooden beds through to the floral patterns on the curtains. The annexe is something of a contrast, a one-storey, motel-style structure with modern rooms. At the back of the hotel, an old agricultural building is now used for art exhibitions and at the front is a pretty garden and a gazebo, where you can sit and ponder to the light of a silvery moon. The hotel restaurant is outstanding with a limited but well-chosen dinner menu (an extra

700kr) of beautifully prepared dishes that use local ingredients whenever possible; dinner is served at 7.30pm

and advance reservations are required. The hotel is metres from the jetty. May–Sept. **1850kr**

## Jostedalsbreen Nasjonalpark: the Nigardsbreen

A great rumpled and seamed wall of ice that sweeps between high peaks, the **Nigardsbreen** nodule on the eastern flanks of the **Jostedalsbreen Nasjonalpark** is a magnificent spectacle. Most visitors are satisfied with the short hike up the glacier's shaggy flanks from the jetty on the shore of the icy green lake beneath it, but others plump for a **guided glacier walk** (see below): the Nigardsbreen is generally reckoned to have the best glacier walking in the whole of the Jostedalsbreen Nasjonalpark – and it's certainly the easiest arm to reach. The season for glacier walking here on this nodule lasts from mid-May to late September.

### ARRIVAL AND INFORMATION

**By car** Heading northeast from Sogndal on Hwy-55, past the turning to Solvorn (see opposite), it's about 30km to Gaupne, where Hwy-604 forks north for the delightful 33km trip up the wild and forested river valley that leads to the Breheimsenteret (see below), an information centre on the eastern flanks of the Jostedalsbreen Nasjonalpark. From the centre, it's another 3.5km drive or walk along the toll-road (60kr/vehicle) to the lake, where a tiny boat (mid-June to mid-Sept daily 10am–6pm; 60kr return) shuttles across to the bare rock slope beside the Nigardsbreen glacier nodule.

### JOSTEDALSBREEN: THE NIGARDSBREEN

**By bus** The Glacier Bus from Gaupne (late June to late Aug 1–2 daily; 40min) stops outside the Breheimsenteret. For buses from Sogndal to Gaupne, consult ⊚ rutebok.no – but check connections before you set out.

**Tourist information** The Breheimsenteret information and exhibition centre occupies a handsome new building on the approach to the glacier (daily: May to late June & Sept 10am–5pm; late June to Aug 9am–6pm; displays 70kr; ☎ 57 68 32 50, ⊚ jostedal.com). Staff here are experts on all things glacial and will make bookings for guided glacier walks.

### ACTIVITIES

**Guided glacier walks** There is a plethora of guided walks to choose from, beginning with a quick and easy 2–3hr jaunt suitable for children over six (270kr, children 130kr), through to much tougher 6hr 30min excursions (810kr).

Prices include equipment and bookings can be made at the Breheimsenteret up to 1hr before departure, but it's best to plan a few days ahead.

### ACCOMMODATION

**Jostedal Hotell** Gjerde ☎ 57 68 31 19, ⊚ jostedalhotel .no. In a well-maintained mountain lodge, this family-run hotel has around twenty rooms of the simple and straightforward variety. They serve hot and cold meals too,

with much of the food coming from the family farm. The hotel is about 2.5km south of the Breheimsenteret on Hwy-604. **1200kr**

## The Sognefjellsveg

The mountain roads of Norway are some of the most melodramatic in Europe, but the wildest of them all is perhaps the **Sognefjellsveg** (Hwy-55; ⊚ nasjonaleturistveger.no), which runs the 110km from Skjolden, a dull little town at the head of the Lustrafjord, over to Lom (see p.239). Despite the difficulty of the terrain, the Sognefjellsveg – which is closed from late October to May depending on conditions – marks the course of one of the oldest trading routes in Norway, with locals transporting goods by mule or, amazingly enough, on their shoulders: salt and fish went northeast, hides, butter, tar and iron went southwest. That portion of the road that clambers over the highest part of the mountains – no less than 1434m above sea level – was only completed in 1938 under a Great Depression "make-work" scheme, which kept a couple of hundred young men busy for two years. Tourist literature hereabouts refers to the lads' "motivation and drive", but considering the harshness of the conditions and the crudeness of their equipment – pickaxes, spades and wheelbarrows – their purported enthusiasm seems unlikely.

### The route

Beyond **Skjolden**, the Sognefjellsveg weaves its way up the **Bergsdal valley** to a mountain plateau, which it proceeds to traverse, providing absolutely stunning views of the jagged,

---

## HIKES FROM TURTAGRØ INTO THE SKAGASTØLSDAL VALLEY

One tough hike from the *Turtagrø Hotel* (see below) is the six-hour, round-trip haul southeast along the well-worn (but not especially well-signed) path up the **Skagastølsdal valley** to DNT's self-service **Skagastølsbu hut**, though you can of course make the hike shorter by only going some of the way. The valley is divided into a number of steps, each preceded by a short, steep ascent. The hotel is 884m above sea level; the hut, a small stone affair surrounded by a staggering confusion of icecaps, mini-glaciers and craggy ridges, is at 1758m. The terrain is unforgiving and the weather unpredictable, so novice hikers beware – If you'd rather have a guide, the *Turtagrø Hotel* is a base for mountain guides, who offer an extensive programme of **guided mountain walks** as well as **summer cross-country skiing** – the hotel will help to sort things out; the season begins at Easter and extends until October.

---

ice-crusted peaks of the **Jotunheimen Nasjonalpark** (see pp.163–166) to the east. En route, the most obvious stopping point is **TURTAGRØ**, just 15km out from Skjolden, which is no more than a handful of buildings – including a hotel (see below) – but as good a place as any to pick up one of the several **hiking trails** (see box above) that head off into the mountains.

Beyond Turtagrø, the Sognefjellsveg cuts its wild and windy way across a plateau before clipping down through forested **Leirdal**, passing the old farmstead of **ELVESETER**. Here, about 45km from Turtagrø, a complex of old timber buildings has been turned into a hotel-cum-mini-historical-theme-park, its proudest possession being a bizarre 33-metre-high plaster and cyanite column, the **Sagasøyla**. On top of the column is the figure of that redoubtable Viking Harald Hardrada and down below is carved a romantic interpretation of Norwegian history. Dating from the 1830s, the column was brought to this remote place because no one else would have it – not too surprising really. From Elveseter, it's a short hop over the hills to **Bøverdal**, which runs down into the crossroads settlement of Lom. On the way, you'll pass the start of the narrow, 18km-long mountain road that sneaks up the **Visdal valley** to the *Spiterstulen* lodge (see below).

### GETTING AROUND                                   THE SOGNEFJELLSVEG

**By bus** Local bus #23-190 runs the length of the Sognefjellsveg from Sogndal bus station to Lom (late June to Aug 1 daily; 3hr 30min; ⓦ kringom.no).

### ACCOMMODATION AND EATING

**Røisheim** Bøverdal ☎61 21 20 31, ⓦ roisheim.no. In the hamlet of Bøverdal, near the northern end of the Sognefjellsveg – and a 15min drive from Lom – this distinctive hotel occupies fourteen old timber dwellings (outhouses, if you will) that have been sympathetically modernized to a very high spec and with lots of vintage furnishings. In total, there are just twenty rooms, all en suite and some with wooden bathtubs for that ersatz country feel. March–Sept. **1500kr**

**Spiterstulen** Visdalsveien, Spiterstulen ☎61 21 94 00, ⓦ spiterstulen.no. This mountain lodge complex, high up on the tree line at 1100m, offers a variety of accommodation, from the bunk beds of one section to modest double rooms in another, and there's a café-restaurant too (dinners daily 6.30–10pm for 370kr). For part of the season, the lodge becomes an outdoor pursuits centre – the lodge is within a day's hike of no fewer than seventeen peaks. March–April & late May to mid-Oct. Dorms **200kr**, doubles **700kr**

★**Turtagrø Hotel** Fortun ☎57 68 08 00, ⓦturtagro .no. There's been a hotel here beside the Sognefjellsveg since 1888, but the main structure today, a large and attractive red-timber mountain lodge with a sprightly modernist design, was only constructed in 2002, after fire destroyed its predecessor. The interior is very Scandinavian, with spacious public rooms and oodles of pine, and the twenty-odd guest rooms are in similar vein; as well as the rooms in the main lodge, there are also four- to six-bedded bunk rooms in the older "Swiss chalet" next door. The hotel specializes in all things to do with the surrounding Jotunheim mountains: they sell hiking maps, can advise on local hiking conditions, and will arrange guided walks and climbs; they even have their own "mountain library". Considering the hotel's solitary location, the restaurant is very good indeed and is strong on local ingredients – try the reindeer; dinner costs 500kr. Easter till mid-Sept. Dorms **570kr**, main lodge doubles **2000kr**

# Lom

A long-time trading and transport centre, **LOM** benefits – in a modest sort of way – from the farms that dot the surrounding valleys. It also makes a comfortable living from the passing tourist trade, with motorists pausing here before the last thump down Hwy-15 to the Geirangerfjord or the dramatic haul up the Sognefjellsveg mountain road. There are a couple of worthwhile attractions too and one particularly enticing place to stay and eat.

## Lom stavkirke

Daily: mid-May to mid-June & early to late Sept 10am–4pm; mid-June to late Aug 9am–7pm; late Aug to early Sept 9am–5pm • 60kr • ☎ 97 07 53 97, ⓦ lomstavechurch.no

Lom's eighteenth-century salad days are recalled by its **stave church**, a strikingly attractive structure perched on a grassy knoll above the river. The original church was built here in about 1200, but it was remodelled and enlarged after the Reformation, when the spire and transepts were added and the flashy altar and pulpit installed. From the outside, its most attractive features are the dinky, shingle-clad roofs, adorned by dragon finials, and inside it's the Baroque acanthus-vine decoration.

## Norsk Fjellmuseum

Brubakken 2 • Mid-May to late June & mid-Aug to Sept Mon–Fri 9am–4pm, Sat & Sun 10am–3pm; late June to mid-Aug Mon–Fri 9am–7pm, Sat & Sun 9am–5pm • 80kr • ☎ 61 21 16 00, ⓦ norskfjellsenter.no

Museum enthusiasts will want to visit Lom's **Norsk Fjellmuseum** (Norwegian Mountain Museum), a modern place that forms part of the **Norsk Fjellsenter** (Mountain Centre), just a few metres from the stave church. The museum focuses on the Jotunheimen mountains – and it's all here in great detail, from the fauna and the flora to the landscapes, and from the farmers to the past mountaineers, who scaled the peaks in tweeds and hobnail boots. There is a national parks' visitor centre here too.

## Lom Bygdamuseum

Buildings: July to early Aug Tues–Sun 11am–4pm; site: open access • Buildings and site both free • ☎ 47 45 15 23, ⓦ gudbrandsdalsmusea.no

Up behind the Fjellmuseum, in the Skansen area of town, is the town's open-air museum the **Lom Bygdamuseum** (Lom District Museum), a surprisingly enjoyable collection of old log buildings in a forest setting. Norway teems with this type of museum but Lom's is better than most, though you wouldn't think so from the ticket office: it's in what must be the biggest and ugliest late-medieval *storstabburet* (large storehouse) in the country. Persevere, though, as the old wooden buildings in the woods beyond are a delight. One of them, a modest hut known as the **Olavsstugu**, is where St Olav, otherwise King Olav Haraldsson, is said to have spent a night as he beetled his way north to Trondheim. When the museum is closed, you can still wander round the site, though of course all the buildings are locked up.

---

### ARRIVAL AND INFORMATION                                                                LOM

**By bus** Lom bus station is a few metres west along Hwy-55 from the Hwy-55/15 crossroads that marks the centre of town. The church, the museums and several hotels are within easy walking distance of the same crossroads.

Destinations Bergen (1 daily; 8hr 30min); Otta (4 daily; 1hr); Sogndal via the Sognefjellsveg (late June to Aug 1 daily; 3hr 30min; ⓦ kringom.no); Stryn (4 daily; 2hr).

**By car from Lom to the fjords** It's a fine drive west from Lom along Hwy-15 to Stryn (see p.244), 125km away, but at Grotli, you can turn onto the old road, the 27km-long Gamle

Strynefjellsvegen (Hwy-58). This narrow road cuts a dramatic, sometimes nerve-jangling, loop over the mountains to rejoin Hwy-15 – after a few final hairpins – at Videseter.

**Tourist information** Lom's tourist office is in the Co-op building, in the centre of the village, just west of the main crossroads at Sognefjellsvegen 17 (June–Aug Mon–Fri 9am–9pm, Sat 9am–8pm & Sun 10am–6pm; restricted hours rest of year; ☎ 61 21 29 90, ⓦ visitjotunheimen .com). Staff can advise about hiking in the Jotunheimen mountains, issue bus timetables and sell hiking maps.

## ACCOMMODATION AND EATING

**Fossberg Hotel** ☎61 21 22 50, ⓦfossberg.no. In the centre of Lom, a stone's throw from the main crossroads, this large and modern hotel complex is built in the general style of a mountain lodge. They have stolen a march on many of their immediate rivals by having two pools, a sauna, a solarium and a gym. **1600kr**

★**Fossheim Hotell** ☎61 21 95 00, ⓦfossheimhotel .no. There's been a family-owned hotel here on this site for several generations and although the main lodge has been added to on several occasions, it still has a real mountain-rural feel. The public areas are dotted with bygones and the guest rooms, at the back of the hotel, have timber walls,

floors and ceilings. It's all very cosy, and so are the delightful little wooden cabins that trail up the wooded hillside beside the main building; some of them are very old and all are en suite. In the main lodge also is the hotel restaurant, which is outstanding and wherever possible features local ingredients. They serve set meals – three courses 395kr, four courses 650kr – as well as à la carte; try the chicken fricassee in a creamed parmesan sauce. The *Fossheim* is located about 300m east of the village crossroads along Hwy-15. Restaurant: daily 6–10pm. Doubles **1500kr**, cabins **1700kr**

# Nordfjord and the Jostedalsbreen glacier

The inner recesses of the **Nordfjord** (ⓦnordfjord.no), the next great fjord system to the north of the Sognefjord, are readily explored along **Highway 60**, which weaves a pleasant, albeit tortuous, course through a string of little towns. Among them, **Loen** is easily the best base for further explorations, though humdrum **Stryn** is larger and more important. Stryn is also where **Highway 15** begins its long journey west along the length of the Nordfjord, with the road dipping and diving along the northern shore in between deep-green reflective waters and bulging peaks. It's a pleasant enough journey, but the Nordfjord doesn't have quite the allure of its more famous neighbours, at least in part because its roadside hamlets lack much appeal – end-of-the-fjord **Måløy** is unappetizing, though you can loop south to the much more agreeable coastal town of Florø (see p.259). That said – and all in all – you're much better off sticking to Hwy-60.

High up in the mountains, dominating the whole of the inner Nordfjord, lurks the **Jostedalsbreen glacier**, a sprawling ice plateau that creaks, grumbles and moans out towards the Sognefjord and the Jotunheimen mountains. The glacier's myriad arms – or "**nodules**" – nudge down into the nearby valleys, the clay particles of its meltwater giving

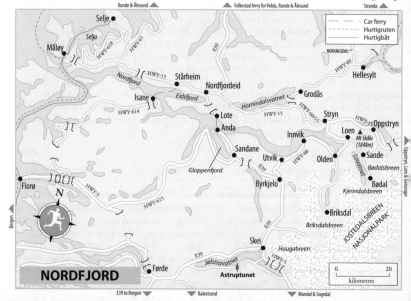

## JOSTEDALSBREEN NASJONALPARK: GUIDED GLACIER WALKS AND INFORMATION CENTRES

Most **guided glacier walks** on the Jostedalsbreen are scheduled between late June and early September, though on some arms of the glacier the season extends from May until October. The walks range from two-hour excursions to five-day expeditions, though all the shorter trips are now confined – with the shrinking of the ice – to the Nigardsbreen, on the east side of the glacier (see p.237). There are currently no guided glacier walks either at the Briksdalsbreen (see p.242) or the Kjenndalsbreen (see p.243), though the movement/melting of the glacier means that nodule accessibility can change from year to year. Day-trip prices for the guided walks are 600–800kr per person for a four- to six-hour gambol, rising to 900–1000kr for six to eight hours. A comprehensive leaflet detailing all the various guided walks on the Jostedalsbreen is widely available across the region and at the national park's three **information centres**, each of which has its own website (see below); all three also have displays on all things glacial and sell books, souvenirs and hiking maps.

**Booking arrangements** for the shorter glacier walks at the Nigardsbreen are straightforward – it's sufficient to turn up at the information centre an hour or two beforehand – but in general it's a good idea to make a reservation at least a day or two ahead. Sometimes this is best done through one of the park's information centres (see below), sometimes direct with the tour operator. In the case of the overnight trips, however, you must reserve at least four weeks beforehand. In all cases, basic **equipment** is provided, though you'll need to take good boots, waterproofs, warm clothes, gloves, hat, sunglasses – and sometimes your own food and drink too.

### THE JOSTEDALSBREEN'S INFORMATION CENTRES

**Breheimsenteret**, on the east side of the glacier at the Nigardsbreen (see p.237).
**Norsk Bremuseum**, on the south side of the glacier near Mundal, Fjærland (see p.233).
**Jostedalsbreen Nasjonalparksenter** Oppstryn, 20km east of Stryn on Hwy-15 (daily: May 10am–4pm; June 10am–5pm; July & early Aug 10am–6pm; late Aug & Sept 11am–3pm; exhibitions on things glacial 60kr; ☎ 48 00 29 97, ⓦ jostedalsbreenadventure.com).

the local rivers and lakes their distinctive light-green colouring. Catching sight of the ice nestling between peaks and ridges can be unnerving – the overwhelming feeling being that somehow it shouldn't really be there. As the poet **Norman Nicholson** had it:

*A malevolent, rock-crystal*
*Precipitate of lava,*
*Corroded with acid,*
*Inch by inch erupting*
*From volcanoes of cold.*

For centuries, the glacier presented an almost impenetrable east–west barrier, crossed only at certain points by determined farmers and adventurers. It's no less daunting today, but access is much freer, a corollary of the creation of the **Jostedalsbreen Nasjonalpark** in 1991. Since then, roads have been driven deep into the glacier's flanks, the comings (but mostly goings) of the ice have been closely monitored and there has been a proliferation of officially licensed **guided glacier walks** (*breturar*) on its various arms (see box above). If that sounds too energetic and all you're after is a close look at the glacier, then this is possible at several places, with the easiest approach being the stroll to the **Bøyabreen** on the south side of the glacier near Mundal (see p.233). On the west side of the glacier, narrow side-roads lead off Hwy-60 to two more vantage points: the **Briksdalsbreen**, the most visited of the glacier's nodules, and the **Kjenndalsbreen**, which is much less crowded, far prettier and a twenty-minute walk from the end of a byroad – a delightful way to spend a morning or afternoon. By contrast, the **Nigardsbreen** (see p.237), on the east side of the glacier, requires more commitment, but the scenery is wilder and, to many tastes, more beautiful – and, with the ebbing of the ice, this is now the best place to come for a guided glacier walk.

| GETTING AROUND | NORDFJORD AND THE JOSTEDALSBREEN GLACIER |
|---|---|

Getting around the Nordfjord by **public transport** is reasonably easy with several long-distance buses supplemented by a patchwork of local buses, though some of these only run in the summer. There are several useful car ferry and Hurtigbåt passenger express boats too.

**By bus** Nettbuss (⦿nettbuss.no) operates the useful NX146 express bus linking Oslo with Otta, Lom, Stryn and ultimately Måloy. Local buses run along the inner recesses of the Nordfjord to link Stryn, Loen and Olden and some of these continue on to Briksdal (for Briksdalsbreen), but there are no buses to the Kjenndalsbreen. For local bus timetables, go to ⦿rutebok.no.

**By car** The most direct way to get from the Sognefjord to the Nordfjord is to travel northwest from Sogndal (see p.234) on Hwy-5 as it tunnels beneath an arm of the Jostedalsbreen glacier. Hwy-5 then presses on to the Kjøsnes junction, where you turn left for the 11km-long detour to Astruptunet, or keep straight for Skei, an important crossroads. Here, you can turn west for the time-consuming, 100km trip to the coast at Florø (see p.259) or head north for the 20km yomp up the valley to the hamlet of Byrkjelo. At Byrkjelo, Hwy-60 forks north, cutting a splendid route over the hills on its way to Loen and ultimately Stryn, both on the Nordfjord. Beyond, Hwy-60 leaves the Nordfjord behind, pressing on north to the Norangsdal valley (see p.245) and Hellesylt on the Geirangerfjord (see p.246).

**By car ferry** There are two main car ferry services across the Nordfjord: Isane to Stårheim (every hour; 15min), about halfway along the fjord, and, on the E39, Anda to Lote (every 30min; 20min). Timetables on ⦿rutebok.no.

### The Astruptunet

Sandalstrand, Sandal i Jølster • Late May to late June Sat & Sun 11am–4pm; late June to mid-Aug daily 10am–5pm; mid-Aug to mid-Sept Sat & Sun 11am–4pm • 50kr • ☎ 47 47 65 81, ⦿astruptunet.com • 11km west of Hwy-5 from the crossroads just south of Skei – follow the signs

The **Astruptunet**, the one-time farmstead-home and studio of the artist **Nikolai Astrup** (1880–1928), sits prettily on the steep slope above the southern shore of Lake Jølstravatnet in the village of **Sandal i Jølster** about 70km from Sogndal. Today's huddle of old turf-roofed timber buildings looks much the same as it did during the artist's lifetime, though the old barn has been replaced by a modern **gallery**, which is used for temporary exhibitions of modern art. A versatile artist, Astrup's work included paintings, sketches, prints and woodcuts, of which a good selection is on display here. However, the bulk of the collection consists of his beautiful landscape paintings, characteristically romanticized rural scenes in bright colours, with soft, flowing forms. Unlike many of his contemporaries, Astrup eschewed Realism in favour of neo-Impressionism and, as such, he bridged the gap between his generation of Norwegian painters and the Matisse-inspired artists who followed.

### Olden and the Briksdalsbreen

From Skei, a small town near the Astruptunet at the junction of Hwy-5 and the E39, it's 60km over the mountains and along the Nordfjord to **OLDEN**, where a light scattering of houses drifts along the foreshore. More importantly, Olden is the starting point for the 24km-long byroad that leads south along a handsome river valley, squeezing between mountains and running along the edge of a glacial lake before arriving at **BRIKSDAL**, where the cluster of mountain chalets is devoted to the tourist industry. Briksdal serves as the starting point for the fairly easy and very popular 45-minute (3km) walk to the **Briksdalsbreen glacier arm**. The path skirts

---

### GUIDED GLACIER WALKS AROUND LOEN AND OLDEN

There are no **guided glacier walks** on either the Briksdalsbreen or the Kjenndalsbreen; the nearest are currently on the **Haugabreen**, on the west side of the glacier, near **SKEI**, 60km from Olden. It's here, from June to August, that Breogfjell (☎41 14 60 70, ⦿breogfjell.no) offers six-hour excursions, including around two hours on the ice, for 800kr per person. Prices include equipment and advance bookings are required – either through one of the Jostedalsbreen's information centres (see box, p.241) or direct with the operator.

waterfalls and weaves up the river until you finally view the glacier, which is surprisingly blue except for streaks of dirt. Alternatively, you can hop on a sort of battery-driven golf cart – known as "troll cars" (groan) – at the café area for the twenty-minute drive up to within 500m or so of the glacier (April–Oct daily 8am–5pm; 210kr).

**ARRIVAL AND DEPARTURE**        **OLDEN AND THE BRIKSDALSBREEN**

**By car** Olden is on Hwy-60 and from here it takes about 30min to drive south along a narrow byroad to Briksdal.
**By bus destinations to/from Olden** Briksdal (Bus

#14-751; 1–3 daily; 30min); Loen (6 daily; 10min); Sogndal (1–2 daily; 2hr 15min); Stryn (6 daily; 20min).

## Loen and the Kjenndalsbreen

**LOEN**, one of Nordfjord's most agreeable villages, straddles the glacial River Loelva as it approaches the fjord with ice-capped mountains breathing down its neck. The village is home to an outstanding hotel, the *Hotel Alexandra* (see p.244), which sits beside the fjord, but the oldest part of Loen is located on slightly higher ground about 500m inland. There's a reason: the old houses that once spread along the foreshore were swept away by floods. In 1905 and again in 1936, a great hunk of the Ramnefjell mountain fell into Lake Lovatnet behind the village and the ensuing **tidal wave** killed many; the second disaster was particularly tragic as the government had only just persuaded many of the locals to return home after the first trauma. The dead are remembered in a pair of **memorial plinths** in the churchyard of **Loen kyrkje** (Loen church), a tidy structure dating from 1837 that perches on top of a gentle ridge. The churchyard also holds a stone Celtic cross that is at least a thousand years old and offers lovely views over the fjord.

### The Kjenndalsbreen

From beside the *Hotel Alexandra*, a 21km-long byroad leads south to the **Kjenndalsbreen** arm of the Jostedalsbreen glacier. The byroad starts by slipping up the river valley past lush meadows, before threading along the shore of **Lovatnet**, a long and thin lake of glacial blue. Thereafter, the road scuttles on to the hamlet of **BØDAL**, whose grassy foreshore marks the sight of the village that bore the brunt of the two tidal waves (see above) – today's houses perch cautiously on the ridge well above the water. After Bødal, it's a further 3km or so to the start of the toll-road (40kr), which culminates in a car park. From here, it's an easy and very pleasant twenty-minute ramble through rocky terrain to the glacier, whose fissured, blancmange-like blue-and-white folds tumble down the rock face, with a furious white-green river, fed by plummeting meltwater, flowing underneath. If the weather holds, it's a lovely spot for a picnic.

### Hiking up Mount Skåla

Loen is also the starting point of a popular five-hour hike east up to the plateau-top of **Mount Skåla** (1848m), from where the fjord and mountain views are simply breathtaking. The path is clearly marked, but you'll have to be in good physical condition and have proper walking gear to undertake the trek; also, check locally for snow and ice conditions at the summit before setting out. The hike back down again takes about three hours, or you can overnight in the circular stone tower at the summit, the **Skålatårnet**, which serves as a self-service DNT hut with twenty beds and a kitchen. Curiously, the tower was built in 1891 at the behest of a local doctor – one Dr Kloumann – as a recuperation centre for tuberculosis sufferers.

**ARRIVAL AND DEPARTURE**        **LOEN AND THE KJENNDALSBREEN**

**By bus** Buses to Loen pull in beside the *Hotel Alexandra*. **Destinations** Olden (6 daily; 10min); Sogndal (1–2 daily;

2hr 25min); Stryn (6 daily; 10min). There are no buses to the Kjenndalsbreen.

**4**

## ACCOMMODATION AND EATING

★**Hotel Alexandra** ☎ 57 87 50 00, ⊚ alexandra.no. Something of a fjordland institution, this long-established, family-owned hotel occupies a capacious and conspicuous modern block looking straight out over the fjord. The expansive foyer sets the tone with its thick carpets, wood panelling and multicoloured, roughly mortared stone walls – very appealing and very 1960s, as if Britt Ekland might appear in a big hat and shiny white boots at any moment. Beyond, the 200-odd rooms are spacious, infinitely comfortable and decorated in pastel shades, the better ones equipped with balconies and wide fjord views. Elsewhere, the hotel clocks up a full battalion of facilities, including a pool, a spa, gardens, a solarium, plus bike and boat rental. Breakfasts are banquet-like, but the evening buffet (from 7pm; 530kr) is perhaps even better, a wonderful selection that lays fair claim to being the best in the fjords. Closed most of Jan. **3000kr**

**Hotel Loenfjord** ☎ 57 87 57 00, ⊚ loenfjord.no. On the water's edge opposite – and owned by – the *Alexandra*, this modern, 140-room hotel is a happy cross between a motel and a lodge, comprising a long and low modern building in a vernacular version of traditional Norwegian style. The rooms are comfortable and kept in prime condition. Depending on demand, closed for periods between Oct and May. **2000kr**

**Sande Camping** ☎ 41 66 91 92, ⊚ sande-camping.no. One of the best of a string of campsites lining up along the road from Loen to Kjenndalsbreen, with a herd of caravans and tents occupying a narrow slice of open ground right next to the lake. They rent out rowboats, canoes, fishing tackle and bikes, and there is a sauna and a café too. Located 4.5km from the *Hotel Alexandra*. Camping **230kr**, cabins **385kr**

## Stryn

**STRYN**, just 12km around the Nordfjord from Loen, is the biggest town hereabouts, though with a population of just seven thousand that's not much of a boast. For the most part, it's a humdrum modern sprawl straggling along beside its elongated main street, but there is a pleasant pocket of antique **timber houses** huddled round the old bridge, down by the river near the tourist office – and just to the south of the main drag; take a few moments to have a look.

**By bus** Stryn bus station is beside the river just to the west of the town centre on Hwy-15/60.

Destinations Ålesund (1–2 daily 3hr 45min); Bergen (1 daily; 6hr 15min); Grodås (3–5 daily; 20min); Hellesylt (2–4 daily; 1hr); Loen (6 daily; 10min); Lom (4 daily; 2hr); Olden (6 daily; 20min); Oslo (3 daily; 8hr 40min); Otta (4 daily; 3hr); Sogndal (2–4 daily; 3hr).

**Tourist office** Stryn tourist office is in the centre at Perhusvegen 24 (June–Aug Mon–Fri 9am–6pm, Sat & Sun 10am–5pm; Sept–May Mon–Fri 9am–4pm; ☎ 57 87 40 54, ⊚ nordfjord.no), just off the main street (Hwy-15) – and about 600m east of the bus station. The staff here issue free town maps, have information on (and will make reservations for) guided glacier walks on the Jostedalsbreen, and sell hiking maps.

## ACCOMMODATION AND EATING

**Stryn Camping** Bøavegen 6 ☎ 57 87 11 36, ⊚ stryn -camping.no. Handily located, just a couple of hundred metres off the main drag on the east side of the centre, this all-year, four-star campsite occupies a large, partly shaded field. There are 24 cabins plus spaces for caravans and tents. Camping **250kr**, two/three-person cabins **850kr**

**Stryn Vertshus** Tonningsgata 19 ☎ 57 87 05 30, ⊚ strynvertshus.no. This pleasant, modern café-restaurant in the centre of Stryn, serves tasty salads, sandwiches, quiches and light meals during the day and traditional Norwegian dishes as well as tapas at night, when mains average around 240kr. Mon–Sat 10am–10pm.

## Grodås

It's hard to warm to Stryn, but its near neighbour, **GRODÅS**, just 20km away to the northwest, is a better bet, a pleasant little town which strings along Hwy-60 with the mountains on one side and a lake on the other. The lake, **Hornindalsvatnet**, is Europe's deepest, at 514m, not that this deterred the Norwegian telecommunications company Telenor from laying an optical fibre cable along the bottom, rather to the surprise of the locals. Apart from its setting, Grodås has one minor attraction, the **Anders Svor Museum** and is also just a half-hour drive from Hellesylt (see p.251), on the scenic Geirangerfjord, and a little less from the turning to the dramatic Norangsdal valley (see opposite).

### Anders Svor Museum

Late May to late June & mid-Aug to mid-Sept Sat & Sun noon–3pm; late June to mid-Aug daily 11am–5pm • 50kr • ☎ 95 10 51 76,
Ⓦ sfk.museum.no

In the centre of Grodås, the **Anders Svor Museum** inhabits a sweet-looking Neoclassical structure built beside the lake in 1953. Hardly a household name today, Svor (1864–1929) was a local lad, who established something of an international reputation as a sculptor of those highly stylized, romantic figures much admired by the European bourgeoisie of the late nineteenth and early twentieth centuries. Some of the more clichéd pieces on display here, such as *Bøn* (Prayer), *Sorg* (Grief) and *Lita jente* (A Small Girl), are typical of his work, though busts of his family and friends, in particular those of his wife, Brit, and his mother, reveal much more originality and talent. Svor's career was typical of his generation: like many other Norwegian artists, he was keen to escape the backwoods, moving to Kristiania (Oslo) in 1881 and four years later to Copenhagen, the start of an extended exile that only ended after Norway won independence in 1905.

### ARRIVAL AND DEPARTURE                                         GRODÅS

**By bus** Buses to Grodås pull into the station just east of the main drag (Hwy-60/E39) on the south side of the centre.

**Destinations** Hellesylt (2–4 daily; 40min); Stryn (3–5 daily; 20min).

### ACCOMMODATION AND EATING

**First Hotel Raftevold** ☎ 57 87 99 99, Ⓦ raftevold.no. There's no strong reason to overnight in Grodås, but the town does possess this agreeable hotel, a modern place, whose well-proportioned concrete and timber lines overlook the lake. The better rooms, all of which are briskly furnished, have mini-balconies with lake views. The hotel also serves up the best food in town, standard Norwegian cuisine with mains averaging 250kr. Restaurant: daily 11am–6pm. **1300kr**

**4**

# The Norangsdal valley

A century ago, pony and trap took cruise-ship tourists from the Geirangerfjord down through the majestic **Norangsdal valley** to what was then the remote hamlet of **Øye**. By car, it's a simple journey today, but one that looks much the same as it did then: steep, snow-tipped peaks rise up on either side of a wide, boulder-strewn and scree-slashed valley, dented by a thousand rockfalls – all in all some of the wildest scenery imaginable. What's more, this wonderful valley is home to one of the region's most original hotels and also abuts the ferocious-looking peaks flanking and fringing the splendid **Hjørundfjord**.

## Highway 655 to Øye

**Highway 655** branches off Hwy-60 to inch its way along the **Norangsdal**, slipping past the *Villa Norangdal* (see p.246) before proceeding through mountain pastures, where local women once spent every summer with their cows. Nobody bothers to herd the cows up here today, but, after about 10km, you'll spy a surviving set of the simple, turf-roofed **cabins** where the cowgirls spent their summers – watch for the roadside plaque, which fleshes out the details of life on these mountain pastures.

Some 3km further along, the road runs besides lake **Lyngstøylvatnet**, created when a large rock-slide dammed the valley's stream in 1908; the lake covers the remains of a group of shacks and the water is so clear that you can still make out their outlines – again, there's a plaque. Thereafter, the road dips down into **ØYE**, whose scattering of farmhouses is flanked by green fields with the glassy-green waters of the Norangsfjord straight ahead.

## Lekneset and the Hjørundfjord

Pressing on along Hwy-655, it's about 8km west from Øye to the minuscule port of **LEKNESET**, no more than a handful of houses and a ferry dock in a magnificent location at the point where the Norangsfjord meets the **Hjørundfjord**, whose blue-black waters stretch away to the north hemmed in by jagged, pyramid-shaped peaks. Only 40km long, the Hjørundfjord is one of the most visually impressive fjords in the whole of the country, a stirringly melancholic place of almost intimidating beauty. Perhaps appropriately, it takes its name from the terrible times when the Black Death swept Norway, leaving the fjord with just one inhabitant, a woman called **Hjørund**, who wandered its peaks crying out at the heavens.

## ARRIVAL AND DEPARTURE

**By car ferry** There's a fairly frequent ferry across the Hjørundfjord from Lekneset to Sæbo (every 1–2hr; 15min), but the best way to see more of the fjord is to leave your car at Lekneset and take a round trip on the ferry that shuttles along the fjord, visiting several of its tiny settlements, including Store Standal (1–3 daily; 1hr); the whole trip takes a couple of hours. Timetables on ⓦ rutebok.no.

**By car** From the Lekneset ferry dock, it's 25km east to Hellesylt on the Geirangerfjord (see below). In the other direction, it's 25km west from Sæbo to Ørsta, on the E39,

### THE NORANGSDAL VALLEY

the main coastal highway, which runs from Bergen to Ålesund. From Ørsta, it's a further 35km to the Festøya–Solevåg ferry (every 30min; 20min) and then 20km on to Ålesund (see p.255). The driving is straightforward, but there is a shorter and more scenic route from Lekneset to Festøya: take the Lekneset ferry to Store Standal (1–3 daily; 40min), from where it's 15km north along the west shore of the Hjørundfjord to the Festøya–Solevåg ferry.

**By bus** There are currently no bus service along the Norangsdal valley.

## ACCOMMODATION AND EATING

★**Hotel Union** Øye, Norangsfjord ☏ 70 06 21 00, ⓦ unionoye.no. Øye's pride and joy is this splendid hotel, whose handsome, high-gabled exterior of 1891 was designed to appeal to touring gentry. Neither is the fineness of the exterior betrayed by what's inside, for every room is crammed with period antiques seemingly hunted down from every corner of the globe. Each of the 27 bedrooms is individually decorated in elaborate, period style and most celebrate the famous people who have stayed here, like King Hakon VII and Kaiser Wilhelm II, not to mention the Danish author Karen "*Out Of Africa*" Blixen. It's a great place to spend the night and the food is first-rate too (set-menu dinners from 500kr). None of the rooms have TVs, which is inducement enough to sit on the terrace and watch the

weather fronts sweeping in off the Norangsfjord, or have a day's fishing – the hotel sells licences and dispenses advice; they also offer bike rental and will arrange guided mountain walks. April to mid-Dec. **2000kr**

**Villa Norangdal** Fivelstadhaugen ☏ 70 26 10 84, ⓦ norangdal.com. Beneath high peaks, up a minor road, this enjoyable hotel occupies a handsome timber building that dates back to the 1880s. There are six guest rooms here – all with views of one sort or another and decorated in a mix of styles, some homely and cosy, others more briskly modern. They serve dinner here too, by prior arrangement, and it's a tasty affair featuring local ingredients with mains averaging 290kr. The hotel is a 15min drive from Hellesylt – 11km along Hwy-60 and then 4km up Hwy-655. **1900kr**

# The Geirangerfjord

The **Geirangerfjord** is one of the region's smallest fjords, but also one of its most breathtaking. A convoluted branch of the Storfjord, it cuts deep inland and is marked by impressive waterfalls, with a village at either end of its snake-like profile – **Hellesylt** in the west and **Geiranger** in the east. Of the two, Geiranger has the smarter hotels as well as the tourist crowds, Hellesylt is tiny and not especially diverting, but it is but a troll's throw from the magnificent **Norangsdal valley** (see p.245).

## ARRIVAL AND DEPARTURE

**By car** There are two roads to the Geirangerfjord. In the west, Hwy-60 passes through Hellesylt on its way between the Nordfjord and Ålesund; in the east, Hwy-63 branches off Hwy-15 to thread its way over the mountains to Geiranger and then continues north to Åndalsnes via the Eidsdal/Linge car ferry and the melodramatic Trollstigen (Trolls' Ladder; see p.252). Note, however, that Hwy-63 between Hwy-15 and Geiranger as well as the Trollstigen north of Geiranger are closed when the snows come.

### THE GERAINGERFJORD

**By car ferry** There are no roads between Hellesyt and Geiranger, but there is a car ferry service (see box, p.250).

**By bus** Hellesylt, at the west end of the Geirangerfjord, is well connected by bus to points north and south, including Stryn and Ålesund. Geiranger, on the other hand, is more difficult to reach by bus except during the high season when a special tourist bus plies the so-called "Golden Route" between Geiranger and Åndalsnes (late June to late Aug 2 daily).

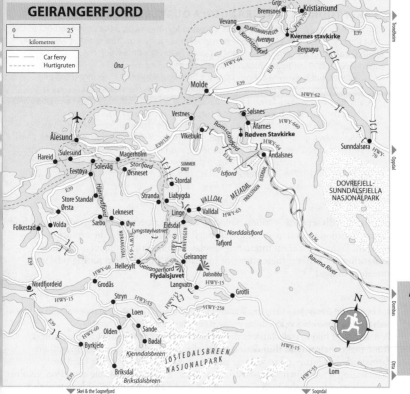

## Geiranger

Any approach to **GEIRANGER** is spectacular. Arriving by ferry reveals the village tucked away in a hollow at the eastern end of the fjord, while approaching from the north by road involves thundering along a fearsome set of switchbacks on the **Ørnevegen** ("Eagle Way"; Hwy-63) for a first view of the village and the fjord glinting in the distance. Similarly, the road in from Hwy-15 to the south squeezes through the mountains before squirming down the zigzags to arrive in Geiranger from behind, passing two celebrated vantage points, **Dalsnibba** and **Flydalsjuvet**, on the way. There can, indeed, be little argument that Geiranger boasts one of the most magnificent settings in western Norway and the **village itself** negotiates the steepest of hillsides, its scattering of houses built on a series of narrow shelves. The only fly in the ointment is the excessive number of tourists at the peak of the season, though, to be fair, the congestion is limited to the centre of the village. It's easy enough to slip away to appreciate the true character of the fjord, hemmed in by sheer rock walls interspersed with hairline waterfalls, with tiny-looking ferries and cruise ships bobbing about on its blue-green waters.

### Norsk Fjordsenter

Daily: May–Sept 10am–6pm; Oct–April 10am–3pm • 115kr • ☏ 70 26 38 10, ⏣ fjordsenter.com

Geiranger's principal man-made attraction is the **Norsk Fjordsenter** (Norwegian Fjord Centre), opposite the *Hotel Union*, a stiff ten-minute walk south up the hill from the waterfront along the main road. The centre follows the usual pattern of purpose-built

## EARLY TOURISM TO GEIRANGER: A QUAKER SURPRISE

No one bats an eyelid when the **cruise ships** nudge their way up the Geirangerfjord today, but the first one to arrive – in 1869 – gave the Norwegians a spiritual shock: it was packed with **Quakers** bearing tracts and bent on saving souls at a time when the locals thought themselves good Lutheran Christians already. The Quakers may not have had much luck as missionaries, but they were certainly taken with the beauty of the Geirangerfjord and spread the word on their return home: within twenty years the village was receiving a regular supply of visitors. Seizing their chance, local farmers mortgaged, sold and borrowed anything they could to buy **ponies and traps**, and by the end of the century tourists were being carted up from the jetty to the mountains by the score. In 1919, the horse was usurped when a group of farmer-cum-trap-owners clubbed together to import **cars**, which they kitted out with a municipal livery – the region's first taxi service. The present owners of the *Hotel Union* (see p.250) have restored a dozen or so of these **classic cars**, including a 1922 Hudson, a 1932 Studebaker and a 1931 Nash, and garaged them at the hotel: hotel guests can sometimes admire them for free – ask at reception.

museums, with separate sections exploring different aspects of the region's history from communications and transportation through to fjord farms and the evolution of tourism. Perhaps the most interesting display examines the problem of fjordland **avalanches** – whenever there's a major rockfall into a fjord, the resulting tidal wave threatens disaster.

### Hiking trails

Boat trip on the M/S *Geirangerfjord* & hike to Skageflå mountain farm: April to mid-Oct 1–2 daily · 245kr single, return price the same as single fare · Advance reservations are advised either in person at the tourist office or online at ⓦ geiranger.no

A network of **hiking trails** lattices the mountains that crimp and crowd Geiranger: some make their way to thundering waterfalls, others visit abandoned mountain farmsteads or venture up to vantage points where the views over the fjord are exhilarating if not downright scary. One popular and very enjoyable excursion involves both a boat ride, on the M/S *Geirangerfjord*, and a four-hour hike. It begins with a short cruise along the fjord to a small jetty, from where it's a very steep, one-hour hike up to the mountain farm of **Skageflå**, followed by either a three-hour trek back to Geiranger or a return by boat.

### Flydalsjuvet and Dalsnibba

Geiranger has two famous viewpoints. There's a short but precarious trail to the nearer of them, the **Flydalsjuvet**, an overhanging rock high above the fjord that features in a thousand leaflets. To get there, drive south from the Geiranger jetty on Hwy-63 and watch for the sign after about 5km; the car park offers extravagant views, but the Flydalsjuvet is about 200m away, out at the end of a slippery and somewhat indistinct track.

A second famous viewpoint, **Dalsnibba** (ⓦdalsnibba.no), at 1476m, is another 12km or so to the south along Hwy-63 and then up a clearly signed, 5km-long, mountain toll-road (120kr/vehicle). There's a large car park at the plateau-summit as well as a café; buses on the so-called "Golden Route" between Åndalsnes and Geiranger (see p.247) detour up here too.

### ARRIVAL AND INFORMATION                                  GEIRANGER

**By car ferry** Car ferries from Hellesylt (see box, p.250) dock at the heart of the village next to the bus stops and the tourist office.

**By bus** Buses arrive and depart from the foot of the village,

a stone's throw from the ferry terminal. The main bus service is the seasonal "Golden Route" bus (late June to late Aug) linking Geiranger and Åndalsnes via both the Linge/Eidsdal car ferry and the Trollstigen (Trolls' Ladder;

THE GEIRANGERFJORD (P.246) >

## GEIRANGER TO HELLESYLT: THE FINEST FERRY TRIP IN THE FJORDS?

With every justification, the seasonal **car ferry** trip between Hellesylt and Geiranger is one of the most celebrated journeys in the whole of Norway. With rearing cliffs to either side, the ferry follows the S-shaped profile of the fjord, whose cold waters are about 300m deep and fed by a series of plunging waterfalls up to 250m in height. The falls are all named, and the multilingual commentary aboard the ferry does its best to ensure that you become familiar with every stream and rivulet. More interesting are the scattered ruins of **abandoned farms**, built along the fjord's 16km length by overly optimistic settlers during the eighteenth and nineteenth centuries. The cliffs backing the fjord are almost uniformly sheer, making farming of any description a short-lived and back-breaking occupation – and not much fun for the children either: when they went out to play, they were roped to the nearest boulder to stop them dropping off.

### PRACTICALITIES

The car ferry between Geiranger and Hellesylt runs throughout the summer (May, Sept & Oct 4 daily; June–Aug 8 daily; 1hr; 505kr for car and driver, passengers 250kr single, 340kr return; timetables on ⓦ visitflam.com).

see p.247); these buses also run up to the Dalsnibba viewpoint. For "Golden Route" timetables, go to ⓦ visitandalsnes.com or drop by Geiranger tourist office. At other times of the year, getting from Åndalsnes to Geiranger takes 4hr, involves three changes and avoids the Trollstigen (ⓦ rutebok.no).

Destinations Åndalsnes (late June to late Aug 2 daily; 3hr); Dalsnibba (late June to Aug 3 daily; 1hr); Trollstigen (late June to late Aug 2 daily; 2hr).

**By Hurtigruten** From June to August only, the Hurtigruten coastal boat (ⓦ hurtigruten.co.uk) calls in at Geiranger as it heads north (but not south). The Hurtigruten is too large a vessel to pull into the village jetty, so it anchors a little offshore and passengers transfer to smaller boats for the last bit of the journey.

**Tourist office** Geiranger tourist office is on the waterfront, beside the ferry dock (June daily 9am–6pm; July & Aug daily 9am–7pm; Sept daily 10am–5pm; ☎ 70 26 30 99, ⓦ geiranger.no). Staff here issue bus and ferry timetables, sell hiking maps and supply free village maps, which usefully outline local hiking routes. They also promote boat tours of the Geirangerfjord, though the car ferry to/from Hellesylt is perfectly adequate.

### ACCOMMODATION AND EATING

Considering its popularity, Geiranger doesn't have many hotels, so vacant rooms are at a premium during the high season, when you should always reserve ahead.

**Geirangerfjorden Feriesenter** ☎ 95 10 75 27, ⓦ geirangerfjorden.net. The better of two neighbouring campsites located by the fjord a couple of kilometres north of the village on the road to Eidsdal – and next to the *Grande Fjordhotell*. The campsite's assorted caravans, cars and tents hunker down on a small field with a batch of modern cabins on the edge. The cabins come in various sizes, housing a maximum of six people. Boat hire is available here too. Camping power connection 40kr. Late April to late Sept. Camping 250kr, cabins 990kr

**Grande Fjordhotell** ☎ 70 26 94 90, ⓦ grandefjordhotel.com. Ultramodern, timber-built hotel in the style of a traditional mountain lodge. The fifty-odd guest rooms have few surprises – they are resolutely modern – but the place does have a handsome fjordside location about 2km north of the centre on the Eidsdal road, adjacent to the *Geirangerfjorden Feriesenter*. 1400kr

★ **Hotel Union** ☎ 70 26 83 00, ⓦ union-hotel.no. Cream of the hotel crop, this large and lavish hotel perches high on the hillside about 500m up the road from the jetty. There's been a hotel here since 1891, and although the present building is firmly modern, it's an attractive structure and the public rooms are spacious and eminently comfortable, plus there is a spa and pool. The bedrooms are pleasantly furnished in modern style and the best have fjord-facing balconies; those on the fourth floor are the pick. The hotel restaurant offers a magnificent, help-yourself buffet dinner during the summer for 525kr, as well as an à la carte menu with mains costing around 290kr; check with the hotel to see when things get started as it's best to get there early before the munching starts in earnest. At both, look out for the fish and meat prepared at the hotel's own smokery. Closed for part of the winter, usually Jan. 2100kr

**Hotell Utsikten** Geirangervegen 348 ☎ 70 26 96 60, ⓦ hotellutsikten.no. On the south side of Geiranger, high up on the hill beside the main approach road, the *Utsikten* offers simply wonderful views across the fjord and its surrounding mountains. The hotel has thirty-odd guest rooms, each decorated in a simple, modern manner with the pick looking out over the fjord. Incidentally, the plinth and the plaque outside the front door commemorates the visit of a youthful Kaiser Wilhelm II. May–Sept. <u>**1500kr**</u>

## Hellesylt

Tiny, inconsequential **HELLESYLT** is now little more than a stop-off on tourist itineraries, with most visitors staying just long enough to catch the car ferry down the fjord to Geiranger (see box opposite) or scuttle off along Hwy-60. For daytime entertainment, there is a tiny **beach** and bathing jetty (*bådehus*) beyond the mini-marina near the ferry quay, the prelude to some very cold swimming, or you can watch the **waterfall** crashing down the cliffs a few metres from the dock. Otherwise, the place seems more than a little down-at-the-mouth: the main dampener has been Mount Åknes, a great chunk of which is eroding away from the rest of the mountain, threatening to collapse into the Storfjord and create a tsunami which will hit Hellesylt in six minutes; experts are monitoring the mountain closely, but of course no one knows if or when it will go, but it's a very real danger – as evidenced at Tafjord (see p.252).

### Peer Gynt Galleriet

May–Aug daily 10am–6pm • 95kr • ☎ 95 01 31 70, ⓦ peergyntgalleriet.no

Occupying a substantial modern building a couple of hundred metres from the ferry dock, the **Peer Gynt Galleriet** (Peer Gynt Gallery) is an idiosyncratic art gallery jam-packed with a set of kitsch-meets-Baroque woodcarvings illustrating Ibsen's *Peer Gynt*. The carvings are the work of a certain Oddvin Parr (1933–2010) from Ålesund and although it's all rather strange, it's good(ish) fun all the same.

**4**

### ARRIVAL AND DEPARTURE                                                 HELLESYLT

**By bus** Buses stop beside the fjordside petrol station, a 5min walk from the ferry dock – walk over the little bridge and turn left.

Destinations Ålesund (2 daily; 3hr); Stryn (4 daily; 1hr).

**By car ferry** Car ferries to/from Geiranger (see box opposite) dock in the centre of the village, a couple of minutes' walk from the tourist office.

### ACCOMMODATION

**Hellesylt Vandrerhjem** ☎ 70 26 51 28, ⓦ hihostels .no. On a miniature plateau just above the harbour, and beside Hwy-60, this HI hostel has a grand location looking out over the fjord. There's a self-catering kitchen and a laundry, but no café per se (though breakfast is included in the overnight rate) and facilities are a little spartan. Most of the bunk beds are in small cabins. En-suite doubles cost 110kr extra. Dorms <u>**260kr**</u>, doubles <u>**640kr**</u>

# Geiranger to Åndalsnes: the Golden Route

Promoted as the **"Golden Route"**, the 90-kilometre journey from **Geiranger to Åndalsnes** along Hwy-63 is famous for its mountain scenery – and no wonder. Even by Norwegian standards, the route is of outstanding beauty, the road bobbing past a whole army of austere peaks whose cold severity is daunting. The journey also incorporates a ferry ride across the **Norddalsfjord**, a shaggy arm of the Storfjord, and can include a couple of brief but enjoyable detours – one west along the Norddalsfjord from Linge to **Stordal**, home to an especially fine church, the other east from Valldal to the intriguing village of **Tafjord**. Yet, the most memorable section is undoubtedly the **Trollstigen** (Troll's Ladder), a mountain road that cuts an improbable course between the Valldal valley and Åndalsnes, the northern terminus of the dramatic Rauma train line (see box, p.166), though be aware that the Trollstigen closes when the snows come.

**By car** Driving the "Golden Route" is straightforward enough, but note that the Trollstigen is generally closed from early Oct to mid-May – earlier/later if the snows have been particularly heavy.

**By bus** There's a seasonal bus service between Geiranger and Åndalsnes (late June to late August 2 daily; 3hr) and this goes over the Trollstigen, at the top of which there is a sightseeing break. Ticket prices are higher than usual for bus travel: Geiranger to Åndalsnes costs a thumping 400kr each way. For timetables, go to ⓦ visitandalsnes.com or pop into the nearest tourist office.

## North from Geiranger: the Ørnevegen and Valldal

Heading north from Geiranger, the first part of the Golden Route is the dramatic 26-kilometre jaunt up and over the **Ørnevegen** ("Eagle Way"; Hwy-63) to **Eidsdal** on the Norddalsfjord. From here, a **car ferry** (every 20–45min; 10min) shuttles over to the **Linge jetty**, from where it's just 4km east to **VALLDAL**, a shadowy, half-hearted village that straggles along the fjord at the foot of the Valldal valley, which marks the start of the Trollstigen (see below).

## Stordal's Rosekyrkja

Stordal • Late June to mid-Aug daily 11am–4pm • 35kr • ☎ 70 27 81 40

West from Linge (see above), it's a 24km detour off the "Golden Route" along Hwy-650 to **STORDAL**, a workaday furniture-making town in a genial valley setting. The town itself may not fire the soul, but it does possess the remarkable **Rosekyrkja** (Rose Church), standing right beside the main road. Dating from the 1780s, the church has a modest exterior, with oodles of whitewashed clapboard, but the interior is awash with beautiful floral decoration, which swirls round the pillars, across the ceiling and down the walls. There's an intensity of religious feeling here that clearly demonstrates the importance of Christianity to Norway's country folk, an effect amplified by a whole series of naive, almost abstract paintings with biblical connotations.

## Tafjord

At Valldal, a narrow byroad branches off Hwy-63 to follow the fjord round to the remote, back-of-beyond village of **TAFJORD**, just 14km away to the east. Ignore the power station at the entrance to the village, but keep going over the river to the pint-sized **harbour**, notable only for its complete lack of old buildings: they were swept away in 1934, when a great slab of mountain dropped into the Norddalsfjord, creating a sixteen-metre tidal wave that smashed into the place, killing 23 locals in the process. Safe just 400m up the slope from the harbour, the upper part of Tafjord did survive and, unlike most of its neighbours, seems to have dodged postwar development almost completely. Here, a string of old houses and barns, with cairn-like chimneys, picket fences and clapboard walls, ramble round twisty lanes demonstrating what these fjord villages looked like as late as the 1950s; it makes for a fascinating hour or so's wander.

## The Trollstigen

The alarming heights of the **Trollstigen** (Troll's Ladder), a trans-mountain route between Valldal and Åndalsnes, are equally compelling in either direction. The road negotiates the mountains by means of eleven hairpins with a maximum gradient of 1:12, but it's still a pretty straightforward drive until, that is, you meet a tour bus coming the other way – followed by a bit of nervous backing up and repositioning. Drivers (and cyclists) should also be particularly careful in wet weather.

From Valldal, the southern end of the Trollstigen starts gently enough with the road rambling up the **Valldal valley**. Thereafter, the road swings north, building up a head of steam as it bowls up the **Meiardal valley** bound for the barren mountains beyond. Now the road starts to climb in earnest, clambering up towards the bleak and icy

## HIKES AROUND THE TROLLSTIGEN

The **Trollstigen** road was completed in 1936 to replace the **Kløvstien**, the original drovers' track that cut an equally improbable course over the mountains. Much of the track has disappeared, but you can pick it up at **Slettvikane**, from where it's a one-hour walk north across a barren mountain plateau to the Trollstigplatået (see below). The Kløvstien then proceeds down the mountains as far as **Bøsetra**, passing the Stigfossen falls on the way; although this stretch only takes an hour or two, it's very steep and exposed, with chains to assist. Both of these hikes are, of course, linear, which is one reason why most hikers prefer to undertake less demanding, circular outings among the peaks and mountain lakes to the west. By contrast, the mountains to the east are part of the **Trollveggen** mountain wall and remain the preserve of climbers. As usual, prospective hikers should come properly equipped and watch for sudden weather changes. It's best to plan your itinerary in advance: hiking maps and advice are available from the tourist offices at both Geiranger and Åndalsnes.

plateau-pass, the **Trollstigplatået** (see below), which marks its high point. Beyond the Trollstigplatået, the sheer audacity of the road becomes apparent, zigzagging across the face of the mountain and somehow managing to wriggle round the tumultuous, 180-metre **Stigfossen falls**. Beyond the hairpins, on the northern part of the Trollstigen, the road resumes its easy ramblings, scuttling along the **Isterdal** to meet the **E136** just 5km short of Åndalsnes (see below).

### Trollstigplatået

Visitor Centre: mid-May to mid-Sept daily 9am–9pm • Free

The clutter of old huts that once patrolled the **Trollstigplatået** have been cleared away and replaced by a slick and sleek **visitor centre**, which incorporates a café and a modest exhibition on the Trollstigen. More importantly, the visitor centre marks the start of an elegantly conceived walkway, which leads over the fast-flowing river that rushes off the plateau to barrel down the mountain below to several vantage points beyond. From the main **Utsikten** (viewing point), there is a simply magnificent panorama over the surrounding mountains and valleys. Clearly visible to the west are some of the region's most famous mountains with Bispen and Kongen (the "Bishop" and the "King") being the nearest two, at 1462m and 1614m respectively.

### ACCOMMODATION                                              THE TROLLSTIGEN

★**Juvet Landscape Hotel** Alstad ☎95 03 20 10, ⊛juvet.com. One of the country's most spellbinding places to stay, this uber-cool and ultramodern hotel stands in the middle of a forested canyon with views of mountain peaks on one side, the Valldøla River on the other. Seven of the guest rooms feature deep, dark woods, playful bathrooms and unique Japanese-Norwegian recliners, each of which is perched so that you can gaze out at the wilderness beyond. There are also a handful of other rooms distributed between a cabin, the old house, a former mill house and two so-called "birdhouses" with notched logs as per traditional Norwegian design. Excellent spa and on-site restaurant, where the three-course set meal will cost you 600kr. The hotel is just off – and signed from – Hwy-63 about 15km from Valldal (before you reach the Trollstigen). Closed Jan & early Feb. **1550kr**

# Åndalsnes and around

At the end of the splendid Rauma train line from Dombås (see box, p.166), the small town of **ÅNDALSNES** is for many travellers their first – and sometimes only – contact with the fjord country, a distinction it finds a little hard to live up to. It's true that Åndalsnes boasts a fine setting between lofty peaks and the chill waters of the Isfjord, but the centre is really rather humdrum – a few modern blocks and that's pretty much it. That said, there is a first-rate HI hostel on the outskirts of town as well as an excellent campsite; plus Åndalsnes is also within easy **hiking** and driving distance of some wonderful mountain scenery and a charming **stave church**.

## Norsk Tindesenter

Havnegata 2 • June to mid-Sept daily 10am–6pm; mid-Sept to June Tues–Sun noon–4pm • 140kr • ☎ 73 60 45 57, ⓦ tindesenteret.no

In a striking building down by the harbour, the **Norsk Tindesenter** (Norwegian Climbing Centre) has a substantial and well-presented exhibition tracing the history of climbing in Norway from the early nineteenth century up to today. There is a specialist climbing library here too as well as a 21m-high **climbing wall**, where you can limber up or watch others going through their paces.

## Rødven stavkirke

Rødven • Late June to late Aug daily 11am–4pm • 60kr • ☎ 91 64 69 69, ⓦ stavechurch.com • To get there from Åndalsnes, take Hwy-64 east round the fjord and, after 24km, take the signed turning that leads, after a further 10km, to the church

In an idyllic setting amid meadows, by a stream and overlooking a slender arm of the Romsdalsfjord, **Rødven stavkirke** (stave church) dates from around 1300, though its distinctive wooden supports may have been added in 1712 during the first of several subsequent remodellings. Every inch a country church, the place's creaky interior holds boxed pews, a painted pulpit and a large medieval crucifix, but it's the bucolic setting that most catches the eye.

## Hiking routes from Åndalsnes

Visit Åndalsnes (see below) carries a wide range of information on local **hikes**, including maps, with some of the most popular being the so-called "**car walks**" (a drive and a walk), like the mildly strenuous, ten-minute stroll from the road to the dramatic **Kylling bru** (bridge) on the Rauma train line (see p.166). There's also a fairly easy 30min hike up from Åndalsnes to the top of **Nebba**, from where the views are predictably fabulous, and you can continue on from here – on a more difficult stretch of trail – to **Mount Nesaksla** and a metal viewing platform that juts out from the mountain into clear air. The most popular hike hereabouts is, however, the longer and much more ambitious trek along the **Romsdalseggen**. This mountain ridge is about 10km long and takes about eight hours to walk; the trail-head is at the Vengedal parking lot, about 12km east then south from town.

### ARRIVAL AND INFORMATION

**By train** Åndalsnes train station is down by the waterfront at the foot of town. Timetables on ⓦ www.nsb.no.
Destinations Dombås (4 daily; 1hr 20min); Oslo (4 daily; 5hr 30min, change at Dombås).
**By bus** Buses to Åndalsnes stop and leave from outside the train station. Timetables on ⓦ rutebok.no.
Destinations Ålesund (2–3 daily; 2hr 10min); Gerainger (late June to late Aug 2 daily; 3hr); Trollstigen (late June to

late Aug 2 daily; 1hr).

**Tourist information** Visit Åndalsnes is at the train station (late May to Aug daily 8am–noon & 4–8pm; Sept daily 8am–noon; ☎ 71 22 16 22, ⓦ visitandalsnes.com). Staff here provide bus and train timetables, issue regional guides and have details of local day-long hikes and guided climbs. They also sell hiking maps.

### ACCOMMODATION AND EATING

**Åndalsnes Camping og Motell** Gryttenveien ☎ 71 22 16 29, ⓦ andalsnes-camping.net. This combined campsite and motel has a fine riverside setting about 3km from the town centre – follow the route to the youth hostel (see below), but take the first left immediately after the river. It's a well-equipped site with cabins and bunk-bedded rooms, from dorms through to doubles. There is bicycle and boat rental too. Camping 190kr, cabins 400kr, doubles 400kr

**Åndalsnes Vandrerhjem** Setnes ☎ 71 22 13 82, ⓦ hihostels.no. This delightful HI hostel has a pleasant semirural setting with open views down to the fjord.

Its simple, spartan rooms, set in a group of antique wooden buildings, are extremely popular, making reservations pretty much essential. The buffet-style breakfast, with its fresh fish, is one of the best hostellers are likely to get in the whole country, but note that the hostel doesn't do evening meals – though there are self-catering facilities, along with cycle storage, common rooms and a laundry. The hostel is located a 2km hike west out of town on the E136. Mid-May to Aug. Dorms 345kr, doubles 860kr

**Grand Hotel Bellevue** Åndalgata 5 ☎ 71 22 75 00, ⓦ grandhotel.no. The *Grand* occupies a large whitewashed block with a distinctive pagoda-like roof on a hillock just up from the train station. It's the third hotel on this site – its predecessor was bombed to bits in World War II – and it has a distinguished pedigree: King Håkon once spoke to the assembled locals from its entranceway and a young and distinctly modish Cliff Richard once stayed here – there is a photo of him skittling down the entrance steps. In more recent times, the hotel has been through its tribulations, but it's on the way up and although it's attached to the ultramodern Rauma Kulturhus, a combined library and theatre, which detracts from the atmosphere, the rooms have been upgraded and are now pleasant and relatively cosy. Those on the top floors have great fjord views. **1400kr**

**Sødahl-Huset** Romsdalsvegen 8 ✆ 40 06 64 01. No-one could say Åndalsnes is a gourmet's paradise, but this friendly little café does something to fill the gap, serving a tasty line in home-made food, from burgers through to cheesecake. In the centre, a 5min walk up and over the bridge from the train station. Mon–Fri 9.30am–5pm & Sat 10am–3pm, but open some evenings in summer till 11pm.

# Ålesund

The fishing and ferry port of **ÅLESUND**, on the coast at the end of the E136, about 110km west of Åndalsnes, is immediately – and distinctively – different from any other Norwegian town. Neither old clapboard houses nor functional concrete and glass is much in evidence in the old centre, but instead there's a proud conglomeration of stone and brick, three-storey buildings, whose pastel-painted facades are lavishly decorated and topped off by a forest of towers and turrets. There are dragons and human faces, Neoclassical and mock-Gothic facades, decorative flowers and even a pharaoh or two, the whole ensemble ambling round the town's several harbours. Ålesund's architectural eccentricities sprang from disaster: in 1904, a dreadful **fire** left ten thousand people homeless and the town centre destroyed, but within three years a hectic reconstruction programme saw almost the entire area rebuilt in an idiosyncratic **Art Nouveau** style, which borrowed heavily from the German *Jugendstil* movement. Many of the Norwegian architects who undertook the work had been trained in Germany, so the *Jugendstil* influence is hardly surprising, but this was no simple act of plagiarism: the Norwegians

**4**

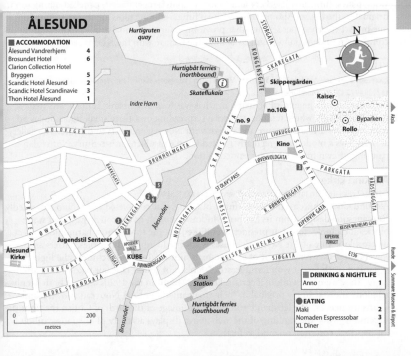

added all sorts of whimsical, often folkloric flourishes to the Ålesund stew. The result was – and remains – an especially engaging stylistic hybrid, and Kaiser Wilhelm II, who footed the bill, was mightily pleased.

Ålesund is a lovely place to spend a couple of days, especially as there are several first-rate hotels, and it bolsters its charms with a couple of other mild attractions – principally the nautical comings and goings of its main **harbour** and the open-air **Sunnmøre Museum**. The town also makes a good base from which to day-trip to the bird cliffs of the island of **Runde** (see box, p.259).

## Jugendstil Senteret

Apotekergata 16 • June–Aug daily 10am–5pm; Sept–May Tues–Sun 11am–4pm • 80kr including KUBE (see below) • ☎ 70 10 49 70, ⓦ jugendstilsenteret.no

To get better acquainted with Ålesund's architectural peccadilloes, you might begin by visiting the **Jugendstil Senteret** (Art Nouveau Centre), bang in the centre of town. The centre occupies one of the town's proudest Art Nouveau buildings, the old **Apothek** (pharmacy), whose spiky tower and heavy-duty stonework lend it a decidedly neo-baronial appearance. Inside, the ground floor is dominated by the ornate wood display cabinets of the former pharmacy and here also is a somewhat gimmicky "Time Machine" in which visitors are "beamed back" to 1904 to watch a short film on the fire that ripped through Ålesund and the reconstruction that followed. As the film explains, the fire happened when Norway's construction industry was in the doldrums, so skilled men turned up here looking for work from all over the country. This pleased the city's burghers no end, but they were frightened half to death when these same men turned out to be unionized, demanding a fair wage for a fair day's work – very different from the more placid country folk who had made up the local workforce beforehand.

Up above the "Time Machine", and approached via a handsome corkscrew staircase, the centre's first floor holds an assortment of Art Nouveau pieces – tapestries, silverware, vases, plates, furniture, jewellery and so forth – plus a magnificent, panelled dining room original to the house. Also on this floor two fifteen-minute films are shown in rotation, one on Art Nouveau per se, the other providing its international and sociopolitical context. An underground passageway links the Centre with the KUBE art gallery.

## KUBE

Apotekergata 16 • June–Aug daily 10am–5pm; Sept–May Tues–Sun 11am–4pm • 80kr, including Jugendstil Senteret (see above) • ☎ 70 10 49 70, ⓦ kunstmuseetkube.no

Next door to the Jugendstil Senteret, in what was formerly a bank, is the town's main art gallery, **KUBE**, whose temporary displays, spreading over three small floors, focus on contemporary art, architecture and design with Norwegian artists to the fore. The gallery also displays a modest and regularly rotated sample of nineteenth-century Norwegian paintings drawn from its permanent collection.

## Ålesund kirke

Kirkegata 2 • Tues–Fri & Sun 10am–3pm, but hours do vary • 30kr • ☎ 70 16 53 00

**Ålesund kirke** (church), the town's finest building, was completed in 1909 to a decidedly Romanesque design, from its hooped windows through to the roughly dressed stone blocks and clunky tower. It presides over **Kirkegata**, the town's most harmonious street, where a long line of Art Nouveau houses is adorned with playful gables, turrets and towers altogether reminiscent of a Ruritanian film set. Inside the church, the high altar is flanked by the most wonderful frescoes, a blaze of colour that fair takes the breath away. They were the work of a certain **Enevold Thømt** in the 1920s and are both keenly religious and startlingly original in their amalgamation of Art Nouveau and Arts and Crafts influences. The left-hand wall carries an image of the birth of Christ, the right the Ascension, while the vaulting of the arch above displays a variety of religious symbols – for baptism, communion, and so forth.

## Kongensgate

Ålesund's main drag, pedestrianized **Kongensgate** is flanked by a string of Art Nouveau buildings. It's the whole ensemble that impresses most, but one or two structures are of special note, beginning with the whimsical medieval tower, hooped windows and geometrical friezes of the **Skippergården**, at no. 18. Nearby, **no. 10b** is the narrowest house in Ålesund, its rough neo-Romanesque stonework contrasting with the smooth tiles, dinky tower and wrought-iron grilles of **no. 9** just across the street. There's more ersatz medievalism round the corner on Løvenvoldgata, where the **Kino** (cinema) is housed in a large and lugubrious stone tower topped by a little cupola.

## Byparken

Lihauggata · Daily dawn to dusk · Free

The town park, **Byparken**, is a pretty slice of greenery at the top of Lihauggata, which runs up from Storgata. It's a surprise to find monkey puzzle and copper beech trees here, as well as a large statue of **Rollo**, a Viking chieftain born and raised in Ålesund, who seized Normandy and became its first duke in 911. Rollo was an ancestor of William the Conqueror, the epitome of the Norman baron and thus evidence of the speed with which the Vikings were absorbed into their host communities. Near to Rollo, up two short flights of steps on top of a mini-hillock, is a rough, stone column whose bronze plaque commemorates the town's benefactor, the **Kaiser**, looking suitably proud and equipped with his trademark moustache. From the park, several hundred steps lead to the top of the **Aksla hill**, where the view out along the coast and its islands is nothing short of delightful.

## Sunnmøre Museum

Museumsvegen, off Borgundvegen · May–Sept Mon–Fri 10am–4pm, Sun noon–4pm & Sat in July 10am–4pm; Oct–April Tues–Fri 10am–3pm, Sun noon–4pm · 80kr · ☎ 70 16 48 70, ⓦ sunnmoremuseum.no

The **Sunnmøre Museum**, about 4km east of the town centre just off the E136, is one of the region's more ambitious heritage museums. It may not be especially large, but everything is well presented and the location is really striking, spreading as it does over the lightly wooded hills of a tiny headland with water to either side. Inside the main building, a series of displays explores various aspects of local life from medieval times onwards, and moored outside is an assortment of old and replica **boats** typical of vessels used hereabouts from the seventh century onwards. From beside the main building, a walking trail heads off over the hills to thread its way past fifty-or-so antique **timber buildings** moved here from other parts of the Sunnmøre district. The buildings include assorted cowsheds, storehouses, stables and dwellings, as well as a row of eighteenth-century *kyrkjebuer* (church shacks), where local country folk once holed up before attending Sunday service. By law, Norwegians had to go to church, and as this involved many of them in long and arduous journeys, *kyrkjebuer* were built next to parish churches so the peasantry could rest and change into their Sunday best. The *kyrkjebuer* also played a romantic role: it was here that many a Norwegian caught the eye of their future wife or husband.

## Atlanterhavsparken

Tuenesvegen · June–Aug Mon–Fri & Sun 10am–6pm, Sat 10am–4pm; Sept–May Mon–Sat 11am–4pm, Sun 11am–6pm · 180kr · ☎ 70 10 70 60, ⓦ atlanterhavsparken.no

In the **Atlanterhavsparken** (Atlantic Sea Park), Ålesund possesses one of those prestige tourist attractions so beloved of development boards and local councillors. It comprises a large-scale re-creation of the Atlantic marine environment, including several enormous fish tanks; there's also an outside area with easy footpaths and bathing sites. The sea park is on a low-lying headland 3km west of the town centre.

**4**

## ARRIVAL AND DEPARTURE

**By air** Ålesund's small, international airport is on the island of Vigra, about 15km north of the town centre. Regular airport buses connect the two (every 1–2hr; 25min; 80kr each way; ⓦframmr.no).

**By car** The drive in from the east, from Åndalsnes, has some attractive fjordside stretches and takes a little under two hours. The main coastal road, the E39, running between Bergen, Ålesund and Trondheim, also offers some fine coastal scenery. Heading south from Ålesund, watch out for one particularly handsome stretch of road between Folkestad and Nordfjordeid. There are four ferry crossings on the E39 between Ålesund and Bergen, so be sure to pick up ferry timetables from Ålesund tourist office before you set out; reckon on 8hr to cover the 420km. Heading north, it's about 300km (6hr) to Trondheim on the E39 with two ferry crossings.

**By bus** Ålesund bus station is beside the waterfront on the southern edge of the town centre, which is about 700m from top to bottom; there are no trains.

Destinations Åndalsnes (2–3 daily; 2hr 10min); Bergen (1 daily; 10hr with 1 change); Hellesylt (2 daily; 3hr); Kristiansund (1–2 daily; 6hr with 2 changes); Molde (4 daily; 2hr); Sæbo for the ferry to Lekneset on the Hjørundfjord (3 daily; 3hr 30min with 2 changes); Stryn (1–2 daily 3hr 45min); Trondheim (1 daily with 2 changes; 10hr).

**By Hurtigbåt passenger express boat** Hurtigbåt boats to the islands off Ålesund arrive and depart from two quays: northbound, on the north side of the harbour; southbound next to the bus station.

**By Hurtigruten** The Hurtigruten (ⓦhurtigruten.co.uk) docks on the northern edge of the town centre. Note that the 13hr cruise south along the coast to Bergen via Florø (see opposite) is a fine way to see this mountainous, fjord-shredded stretch of coastline.

## INFORMATION

**Tourist office** Ålesund's tourist office is located on the north side of the harbour on the Skateflukaia quay (June–Aug daily 8.30am–6pm; Sept–May Mon–Fri 9am–4pm; ☎70 16 34 30, ⓦvisitalesund.com). They supply free town brochures, issue a free if somewhat unrevealing leaflet describing Ålesund's architectural attractions, and coordinate guided walking tours of the centre (mid-June to mid-Aug 1 daily; shoulder seasons 1 weekly; 1hr 30min; 100kr).

## ACTIVITIES

**Birdwatching** The island of Runde (see box opposite) has the region's prime sea-bird nesting cliffs and Ålesund's 62° Nord (☎70 11 44 30, ⓦ62.no) organizes Wildlife Sea Safaris there by boat during the summer (late June to mid-Aug; 2 daily; 2hr; 890kr).

**Sea-kayaking** Ålesund's Kayak More Tomorrow (☎91 11 80 62, ⓦkayakmoretomorrow.com) rents out kayaks for a paddle round the town's harbour (3hr for 700kr) and also organizes a range of day-long sea-kayaking expeditions (from 1400kr).

## ACCOMMODATION

One of Ålesund's real pleasures is the quality of its downtown **hotels** and **guesthouses**. If your wallet is showing signs of strain, however, there are other, less expensive options too, most economically an HI **hostel**.

**Ålesund Vandrerhjem** Parkgata 14 ☎70 11 58 30, ⓦhihostels.no. Small and central HI hostel in a pleasant 1920s building at the top of Rådstugata. Has a laundry and self-catering facilities plus double rooms both with (an extra 100kr) and without en-suite facilities. Open all year. Dorms **300kr**, doubles **750kr**

★**Brosundet Hotel** Apotekergata 5 ☎70 11 45 00, ⓦbrosundet.no. Outstanding hotel, one of fjordland's most delightful, where the staff are extraordinarily efficient and every detail shows finesse, from the Bulgari toiletries and the high-spec showers through to the wonderfully comfortable beds. The hotel has fifty or so rooms – half of which have harbour views – and occupies a tastefully converted, water-side warehouse down by the harbour. The only criticism is that some of the rooms are just a little small. Free bicycles also provided. Advance reservations advised. **1500kr**

**Clarion Collection Hotel Bryggen** Apotekergata 1 ☎70 10 33 00, ⓦnordicchoicehotels.com. Smart chain hotel in a carefully modernized old waterside warehouse, where the public areas are kitted out with all sorts of nautical knick-knacks. The guest rooms are set out around three internal galleries that overlook the public areas in the manner of a cruise ship – and it all works extremely well. **1500kr**

★**Scandic Hotel Ålesund** Molovegen 6 ☎21 61 45 00, ⓦscandichotels.com. It may be one of a chain and occupy a routine modern block, but there's something very appealing about this relaxed and friendly hotel, not least its sea and harbour views. The breakfasts are excellent, served in a breakfast room that overlooks the ocean, and the rooms are bright and cheerful, each comfortably furnished in contemporary style with the pick – once again – offering charming sea views. **1300kr**

**Scandic Hotel Scandinavie** Løvenvoldgata 8 ☎70 15 78 00, ⓦscandichotels.com. Exemplary chain hotel inhabiting a grand Art Nouveau edifice, which has

## BIRDWATCHING ON RUNDE ISLAND

The steep and craggy cliffs on the pocket-sized island of **Runde**, some 80km west along the coast by road and ferry from Ålesund, are the summer haunt of several hundred thousand **sea birds**. Common species include gannet, kittiwake, fulmar, razorbill and guillemot, but the most numerous of all is the **puffin**, whose breeding holes honeycomb the island's higher ground. Most species, including the puffin, congregate here between mid-April and July, though some – like the grey heron and the velvet scoter – are all-year residents. A network of **hiking trails** provides access to a number of birdwatching vantage points, though these invariably involve a fair climb up from the foreshore. One of the more popular hikes is the stiff forty-minute hoof up to the sea cliffs on the island's north shore from the small car park at the end of the road: the island is connected to the mainland by bridge and causeway and this, its one and only road, slips along both the south and east shores. For more detailed advice about hiking routes on Runde, pop into Ålesund tourist office (see opposite), but the easiest way to see the island's bird cliffs is on a **guided tour** (see opposite).

## DRIVING TO RUNDE

It takes about two hours to drive from Ålesund to Runde, mostly via Hwy-61; the journey involves one car ferry ride, from Sulesund to Hareid (every 30min; 25min; passengers 37kr, car & driver 102kr; ⓦ norled.no).

---

been sympathetically modernized, from the handsome wrought-iron work of the main doors through to the intricate friezes and medallion frescoes beyond. Unlike several of its rivals, however, it is not down by the water. **1000kr**

**Thon Hotel Ålesund** Kongensgate 27 ⓣ 70 15 77 00, ⓦ thonhotels.no. Suffers by comparison with its more atmospheric rivals, but this large modern block of a hotel is right in the centre and the rooms are perfectly adequate and competitively priced. **1100kr**

## EATING

For a town of just 45,000 souls, Ålesund does reasonably well for **cafés and restaurants**, with the pick all within a stone's throw of the main harbour.

★**Maki** Brosundet Hotel, Apotekergata 5 ⓣ 70 11 45 00, ⓦ brosundet.no. Immaculate and intimate restaurant, with views out over the harbour and a short but well-chosen menu featuring local, seasonal ingredients – try, for example, the ling in a red wine sauce. Mains average around 330kr. Mon–Sat 6–10pm.

★**Nomaden Espresssobar** Apotekergata 10 ⓣ 90 28 59 01. Tasty sandwiches, light meals, coffees and cakes (including a great cheesecake) in this cosy little café, where the decor is vaguely Edwardian – antique cupboards and

so forth – with prints and paintings on the walls. Smooth, jazzy background music too. Tues–Sat 11am–5pm, Sun noon–4pm.

**XL Diner** Skaregata 1B ⓣ 70 12 42 53, ⓦ xlgruppen.no. Not, perhaps, a very good name for this smart, first-floor restaurant, which serves an outstanding range of seafood from its harbourside premises. This is *the* place to try that old Norwegian favourite, *klippfisk* (salted and dried cod), cooked every which way and costing about 280kr. Reservations are advised. Mon–Sat 5–11pm.

## DRINKING

**Anno** Apotekergata 9 ⓣ 71 70 70 77, ⓦ anno.no. If it's sunny, locals pile down to the harbourside terrace of the Anno, where the restaurant plays second fiddle to the lounge bar – especially on Friday and Saturday

nights – with its moody lighting, wood floors and leather and cloth banquettes. Mon–Thurs 11am–11pm, Fri & Sat 11am–3am, Sun 1–8pm.

# Florø and around

With a population of just nine thousand, **FLORØ**, Norway's westernmost town, midway between Bergen and Ålesund, scores high on west-coast commonalities: it has a blustery island setting, its economy has been boosted by the oil industry, and its tidy centre is wrapped around the traditional focus of coastal life, the harbour. Exploring the town only takes an hour or so and afterwards you can investigate one of the myriad off-shore islets: **Kinn** has a lovely little church and you can overnight in the lighthouse on **Hovden**, a scenic stay if ever there was one. Florø has one major claim to historical fame as the birthplace of that ferocious Viking chieftain **Eric Bloodaxe** (d.954), who raided far and wide, partly – or so the Sagas suggest – to get away from his wife, though judging by his name she might not have been too upset by his roving either. Before the oil, **herrings** were the big economic deal hereabouts, those piscine times recalled by the townsfolk on one day every June when they assemble a 400m-long **herring table** (*sildebord*) on the main street, which groans under the weight of that famous fish served alongside the humble boiled potato.

## The Kystmuseet

Brendøyvegen • Late June to mid-Aug Mon–Fri 11am–6pm, Sat & Sun noon–4pm; mid-Aug to Dec & March to late June Mon–Fri 10am–3pm, Sun noon–3pm • 60kr • ☎ 57 74 22 33, ⓦ kyst.museum.no

Florø's main tourist attraction as such is the mildly diverting **Kystmuseet** (Coastal Museum), a rambling assortment of old boathouses and dwellings set around three modern exhibition buildings, in a tranquil coastal location 2km south of the centre. Here you'll find a ragbag of local artefacts – tools, fishing tackle, kitchen utensils, etc – supplemented by a small armada of local wooden boats.

## Kinn

A passenger ferry runs from Florø to Kinn (Local Route 14-639; 1–4 daily; 30min; 71kr each way); ferry timetables from Florø tourist office (see below) and at ⓦ rutebok.no

Among the confetti of islands and skerries in the vicinity of Florø, the star turn is **Kinn**, a mountainous little lump, whose grassy foreshore holds the stone **Kinnakyrkja** (Kinn church; open access; free), a much-modified Romanesque structure dating from the twelfth century – and located an easy thirty-minute walk from the dock. The church's exterior is plain and unexciting, but the interior is a delight, the slender nave holding an intricately carved gallery, a fancy pulpit and with an ancient model of a sailing ship dangling from the ceiling. Kinn's most famous vicar was a certain Michael Sars (1805–69), who clearly had a lot of time on his hands, churning out theological and biological volumes by the trunk-load; he also squeezed in fathering fourteen children, though what his wife thought of his use of his spare time is not recorded. After the church, you can hike along the foreshore and venture into the hills – and you can even stay the night here (see opposite).

### ARRIVAL AND DEPARTURE

FLORØ AND AROUND

**By car** The fastest road to Florø is Hwy-5 from Skei (100km) and Sogndal (160km). It's also possible to reach Florø via the E39, the main coastal road, from both Bergen (231km with one car ferry) and Ålesund (216km with three car ferries).

**By bus** Florø bus station is about 150m west of the harbour. Bus timetables are on ⓦ rutebok.no and the more local ⓦ kringom.no.

Destinations Ålesund (1–3 daily; 6–8hr with 3 changes); Balestrand (1 daily; 3hr 30min with one change); Bergen (every 3hr; 5hr with one change); Mundal, Fjærland (2–4 daily; 2hr 15min with one change); Skei (every 2hr; 2hr 20min with one change).

**By Hurtigbåt passenger express boat** Norled (ⓦ norled.no) runs Hurtigbåt services to and from Florø's main harbour, abutting the town centre.

Destinations Balestrand (Mon–Fri 1 daily; 3hr 40min); Bergen (1–2 daily; 3hr 30min); Sogndal (Mon–Fri 1 daily; 4hr 30min); Vik (Mon–Fri 1 daily; 3hr 30min).

**By Hurtigruten coastal boat** The Hurtigruten (ⓦ hurtigruten.co.uk) docks on the north side of Florø harbour, a 5min walk from the town centre. From Florø it's 6hr sailing time to Bergen, just under 7hr to Ålesund.

### INFORMATION AND ACTIVITIES

**Tourist office** Florø tourist office is on the ground floor of the town hall, about 50m from the harbourfront at Strandgata 30 (mid-June to mid-Aug Mon–Fri 9am–6pm, Sat 10am–3pm & Sun 11am–2pm; mid-Aug to mid-June Mon–Fri 10am–3pm; ☎ 57 74 30 00, ⓦ fjordkysten.no).

**Sea-kayaking** The sheltered coves, bays and inlets around Florø are great for kayaking – and Florø Rorbu (ⓦ florbu .com), down by the seashore about 2km southeast of town, rents out kayaks (200kr per day) and medium-sized power boats (400kr/day).

## ACCOMMODATION AND EATING

**Kinn** The old schoolhouse on Kinn has been turned into a DNT no-service cabin. There are nine bunk beds, a shared living room, a self-catering kitchen and bathroom. The tap water has to be boiled before you can drink it. The cabin cannot be booked in advance and the key is available from Florø tourist office. Beds 355kr

**Kvanhovden Fyr** Hovden ☎ 90 13 30 23. Perched high above the churning ocean amid bare and rocky cliffs, this 1890s lighthouse comprises a red, 10m-tall wooden beacon attached to the old lighthouse keeper's quarters. The latter has been turned into spartan accommodation – ten bunks in three rooms. You have to bring your own bedding, though there is electricity, a bathroom, hot and cold water and limited self-catering facilities. There

are a couple of ways to get to the lighthouse (the tourist office will advise), which is on the western shore of Hovden island, but the quickest is the 30min trip (350kr) by taxi-boat direct from Florø harbour; Havskyss (☎ 91 34 89 34, ⓦ havskyss.no) provides this service, among others. 400kr

**Quality Hotel Florø** Hamnegata 11 ☎ 57 75 75 75, ⓦ nordicchoicehotels.com. The best place in Florø, this smart, medium-sized chain hotel sits beside the waterfront and occupies a new building in the style of an old warehouse. The rooms are spick, span and very modern – ask for one with a sea view. The hotel restaurant, *Bryggekanten*, specializes in (local) seafood with mains averaging around 250kr. Daily noon–10pm. 1500kr

# Ålesund to Kristiansund

From Ålesund, it's a circuitous yomp over hill and down dale to the southern shore of the Moldefjord, where the **Vestnes car ferry** scuttles over to **Molde**, a workaday sort of town whose main claim to fame is the Molde Jazz festival, held in July (see p.41). From Molde, it's a hop, skip and a nautical jump west to the delightful islet of **Ona** or you can press on north to **Kristiansund**, a middling sort of place with an expansive island setting. There are two main routes from Molde to Kristiansund. The quicker, but less interesting, option is the 72km-long gambol via the **E39** and then **Hwy-70**, which begins with the long, sub-aqua tunnel that links the mainland with the offshore islets prefiguring Kristiansund. The second, slightly longer but far more picturesque route, is along **Highway 64**, which forks north off the E39 just outside Molde. Hwy-64 tunnels through mountains, slips past glassy fjords and barrels over the hills until it reaches the mouth of the **Kornstadfjord**, which marks the start of the much-touted, 8km-long **Atlanterhavsvegen** (Atlantic Highway). A spirited piece of engineering, the Atlanterhavsvegen negotiates the ocean, manoeuvring from islet to islet by a sequence of bridges and causeways. In calm conditions, it's an attractive run, but in blustery weather it's exhilarating with the wind whistling round the car, the surf roaring and pounding but a stone's throw away. On the far side of the Kornstadfjord is the island of **Averøya**, where you'll find **Kvernes stave church** and beyond – approached through a second, sub-aqua tunnel (5.7km) – lies **Kristiansund**.

## Molde

Spreading along the seashore with a ridge of steep and green hills behind, **MOLDE** has an attractive setting, its tidy centre an agreeable combination of modern buildings mostly dating back to the 1950s. Strolling the harbourfront is a pleasant way of spending half an hour or so and there fine views across the fjord to the ice-tipped peaks that jag away towards Åndalsnes. Despite its appearance, Molde is actually one of the region's older towns, but it was razed by the Luftwaffe in 1940, an act of destruction watched by King Håkon from the hills behind town shortly before he was forced into exile in England.

## ARRIVAL AND DEPARTURE                                                      MOLDE

**By bus** Molde's bus station is in the centre of town, down by the fjord on Hamnegata.
Destination Kristiansund (3 daily; 1hr 30min).

**By ferry** The Vestnes car ferry over the Moldefjord (every 30min to 1hr; 35min) docks on the east side of the town centre.

## Ona

Standing on the outermost edge of the multitude of islets that protect the coast, the tiny village of **ONA** is a handsome affair, its handful of brightly painted houses sitting pretty in the lee of a chubby little harbour. It only takes a few minutes to saunter round the village and afterwards you can stroll over to the lighthouse or wander over to a couple of other islets that are attached to Ona by bridge and causeway. Ona village has a resident population of around twenty and this is something of an achievement when most of the neighbouring islands have been abandoned to the birds and the waves.

### ARRIVAL AND DEPARTURE                                                    ONA

**By car & ferry** To get to Ona from Molde, drive west the 19km to Hollingen and take the car ferry over to Aukra (hourly; 10min). From Aukra, it's a 10km drive to Småge, where you catch the ferry to Ona (4 daily; 40min or 1hr 30min). Timetables on ⓦ rutebok.no.

## Kvernes stavkirke

Hwy-247, Averøya island • Late June to late Aug daily 11am–5pm • 50kr • ☎ 92 29 94 38, ⓦ stavechurch.com

On Hwy-64, the scenic **Atlanterhavsvegen** (see p.261) spans the mouth of the Kornstadfjord to reach **Averøya** island, a grizzled hunk, whose coastal flanks were first settled in the Iron Age. Here, tucked away in the southeast corner of the island, about 9km from Hwy-64, is **Kvernes stavkirke** (stave church), which sits pretty beside the fjord. Dating from the fourteenth century, the church was built on what had previously been a pagan ceremonial site, as proved by the discovery of a Viking phallus stone during repair work. Much modified over the centuries, the church is a simple barn-like affair distinguished by its biblical wall paintings, added in the 1630s.

## Kristiansund

Straddling three rocky islets and the enormous channel-cum-harbour that they create, **KRISTIANSUND** has a splendid coastal setting, but it somehow conspires to look and feel quite dull: the Luftwaffe is at least partly to blame as it polished off most of the old town in 1940, and, although Kristiansund dates back to the eighteenth century, precious little remains from prewar days. One minor exception is the handful of antique clapboard houses that string along **Fosnagata**, immediately to the north of the main quay, but otherwise the gridiron of streets that now serves as the **town centre** – just up the slope to the west of the main quay – is resolutely modern. There is, however, a more forceful nod to the past in the **klippfiskkjerring statue** of a woman carrying a fish standing at the south end of the main quay. The statue recalls the days when salted cod was laid out along the seashore to dry, producing the *klippfisk* that was the main source of income in these parts until well into the 1950s.

### Grip

The passenger ferry to Grip leaves from the south end of the main town quay (late May to mid-June & late Aug 5 weekly; late June to early Aug 1–2 daily; 350kr return) • The round trip lasts 3hr 30min, including 1hr 30min on the island • Reservations direct on ☎ 92 60 80 45, ⓦ gripruta.no

Kristiansund's most popular attraction is **Grip**, a tiny, low-lying islet just 14km offshore. Grip is dotted with brightly painted timber homes, has an appealing assortment of antique boathouses, and comes complete with a much-modified medieval **church**, where the islanders once took refuge whenever they were threatened by a storm, as they often were – indeed, when you look at the place, it's amazing anyone ever lived here at all: there's a real touch of claustrophobia on the islet even on a calm day, and when the weather's up the effects can be quite overpowering. There are no permanent residents now – the last ones left in 1964 – but in the summertime fishermen dock in the sliver of a harbour.

## ARRIVAL AND DEPARTURE

**By bus** Buses pull in beside the north end of the main town quay, a few metres from the Hurtigbåt passenger express boat dock. Timetables on ⓦ rutebok.no.

Destinations Ålesund (4–5 daily; 3hr 50min); Molde (3 daily; 1hr 30min); Trondheim (1–3 daily; 4hr 30min–6hr, with a minimum of one change).

**By Hurtigbåt passenger express boat** Hurtigbåt

boats from Trondheim (1–3 daily; 3hr 30min) dock at the north end of the main town quay. Timetables on ⓦ rutebok.no.

**By Hurtigruten coastal boat** The Hurtigruten (ⓦ hurtigruten.co.uk) docks at Holmakaia, also at the north end of the main town quay. The sailing time to Ålesund is 7hr, 4hr to Trondheim.

## GETTING AROUND

**By passenger boat** The three islands that make up Kristiansand are all connected by bridge, but you can still crisscross the harbour by means of a small passenger boat,

the *Sundbåten* (every 20min; 35kr one-way ticket, day-ticket 90kr; ⓦ sundbaten.no), which begins its four-jetty route at the south end of the main town quay.

## ACCOMMODATION AND EATING

**Scandic Hotel Kristiansund** Storgata 41 ☏71 57 12 00, ⓦ scandichotels.com. In a large, grey and white high-rise, this chain hotel has a quiet location a short walk south from the main town quay. The rooms on its upper floors have wide harbour views. **1300kr**

**Smia** Fosnagata 30 ☏71 67 11 70, ⓦ smia.no. Housed

in a converted boat-shed metres from the north end of the town quay, this excellent restaurant stands head and shoulders above its competitors. It serves superb fish dishes and, as you're here in Kristiansund, you should really try the *klippfisk* with bacon and carrots (280kr). Mon–Sat 11am–10pm, Sun 2–9pm.

**KRISTIANSUND**

**4**

# Trondheim to the Lofoten islands

LOFOTEN ISLANDS

# 5

# Trondheim to the Lofoten islands

Marking the transition from the rural south to the blustery north is the 900-kilometre-long stretch of Norway that extends from Trondheim to the island-studded coast near Narvik. Easily the biggest town hereabouts is Trondheim, Norway's third city, a charming place of character and vitality, and a cultural hub for the midriff of the country. The city is readily accessible by train, plane and bus from Oslo, but push on north and you begin to feel far removed from the capital and the more intimate, forested south. Distances between settlements grow greater, travelling becomes a bit more of a slog, and as Trøndelag gives way to the province of Nordland the scenery becomes ever wilder and more forbidding – "Arthurian", thought Evelyn Waugh.

North from the modest little industrial town of **Mosjøen** and **Mo-i-Rana**, is the **Arctic Circle** (see box, p.342) – one of the principal targets for many travellers – at a point where the cruel and barren scenery seems strikingly appropriate. Beyond the Arctic Circle, the mountains of the interior lead down to a fretted, craggy coastline, and even the towns, the largest of which is the port of **Bodø**, have a feral quality about them. The iron-ore port of **Narvik**, in the far north of Nordland, has perhaps the wildest setting of them all, and was the scene of some of the fiercest fighting between the Allied and Axis forces in World War II. To the west lies the offshore archipelago that makes up the **Vesterålen** and **Lofoten islands**. The northerly flanks of the Vesterålen, between **Harstad** and **Andenes**, are mauled by massive fjords, whereas to the south, the Lofoten islands are backboned by the **Lofotenveggen**, a mighty and ravishingly beautiful mountain wall. Among a handful of idyllic Lofoten fishing villages, the pick are the abruptly named **Å**, **Henningsvær**, **Reine** and maybe **Stamsund**.

As for accommodation, the region has a smattering of strategically located **hostels**, and all the major towns have at least a couple of **hotels**, though advance reservations are recommended in the height of the season. In addition, the Lofoten islands offer inexpensive lodgings in scores of atmospheric **rorbuer** (see box, p.317), small huts/cabins once used by fishermen during the fishing season.

## GETTING AROUND

### TRONDHEIM TO THE LOFOTEN ISLANDS

**By plane** There are several local airports, including those at Trondheim, Bodø, Evenes (for Narvik), and Leknes on Lofoten. Internal flights are frequent and often inexpensive with the three main operators being SAS (ⓦ flysas.com), Norwegian (ⓦ norwegian.com) and Widerøe (ⓦ wideroe.no).

REINE

# Highlights

**① Nidaros Domkirke** Trondheim's splendid cathedral makes a stirring focal point for a visit to this delightful city. **See p.270**

**② Ofotbanen railway** A dramatic train ride from Narvik over the Swedish border through ravishing mountain scenery. The adventurous can walk back. **See p.302**

**③ Whale-watching, Andenes** Whale-watching safaris from this remote port are exhilarating – and a sighting is almost guaranteed. **See p.310**

**④ Henningsvær** With brightly painted wooden houses framing the dinkiest of harbours, this is one of Lofoten's most picturesque fishing villages. **See p.322**

**⑤ Reine** Lofoten villages don't get much better than this – and you can catch a ferry to remote Vindstad, as well as the prehistoric cave paintings at Refsvika. **See p.329**

**⑥ Å i Lofoten** Maritime history combines with a stunning fjordside setting at Å, arguably Lofoten's prettiest village. **See p.331**

**HIGHLIGHTS ARE MARKED ON THE MAP ON PP.268–269**

# TRONDHEIM TO THE LOFOTEN ISLANDS

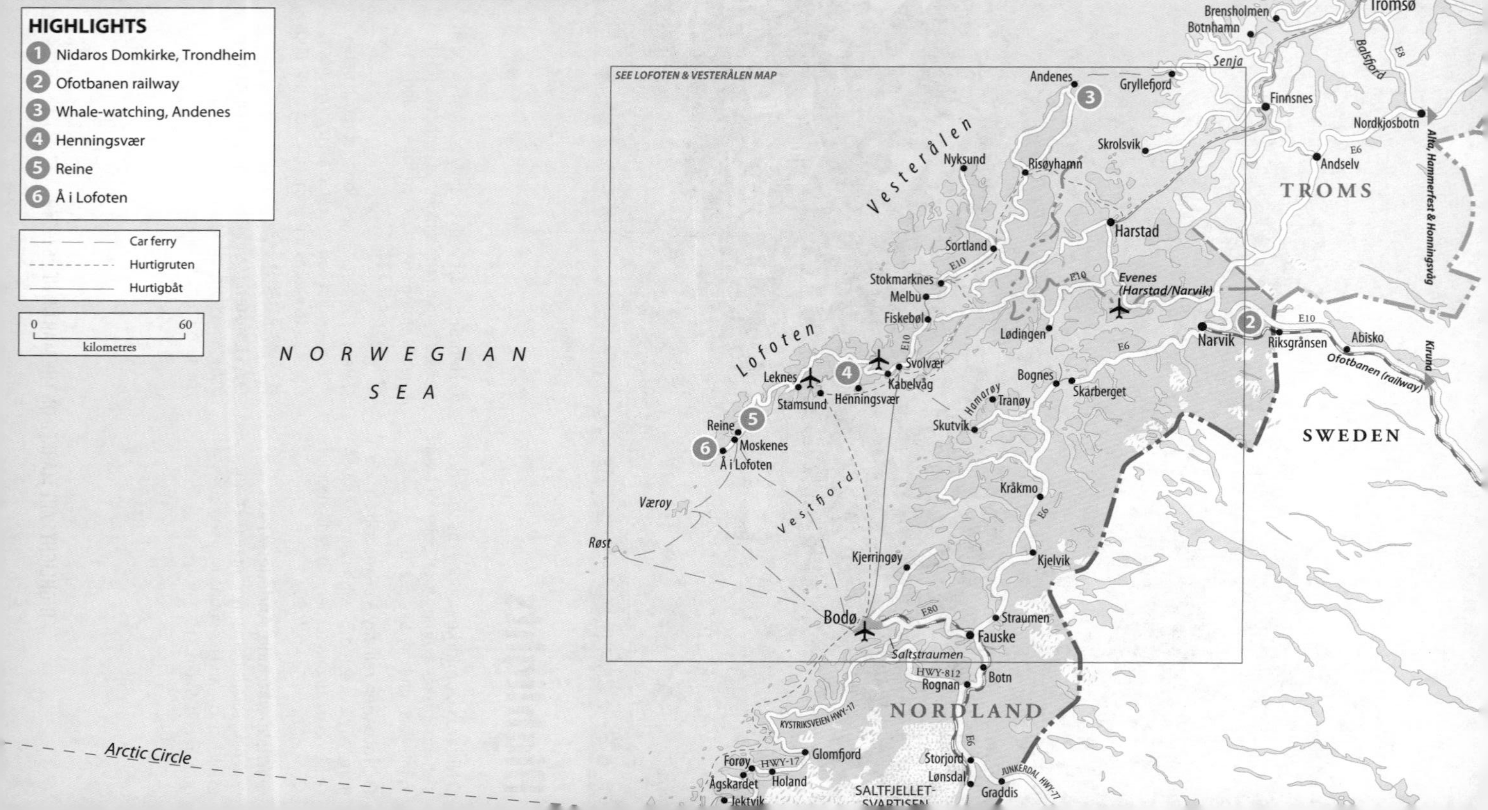

## HIGHLIGHTS

1. Nidaros Domkirke, Trondheim
2. Ofotbanen railway
3. Whale-watching, Andenes
4. Henningsvær
5. Reine
6. Å i Lofoten

- - - Car ferry
-·-·- Hurtigruten
――― Hurtigbåt

0 ――――――― 60
kilometres

SEE LOFOTEN & VESTERÅLEN MAP

Alta, Hammerfest & Honningsvåg

Kiruna

SWEDEN

Hammerfest & Honningsvåg

Tromsø
Balsfjord
E8
Nordkjosbotn
Brensholmen
Botnhamn
Finnsnes
Senja
E6
Andselv
TROMS
Abisko
Otobanen (railway)
Riksgränsen
E10
Narvik
Harstad
Gryllefjord
Skrolsvik
Bjerkvik
Risøyhamn
Evenes
(Harstad/Narvik)
E6
Skårberget
Bognes
Tranøy
Kjelvik
NORDLAND
Straumen
Fauske
Botn
INNERDALEN HWY 77
Gradåis
E6
Storjord
Lønsdal
SALTFJELLET-SVARTISEN
Andenes
Nyksund
Sortland
Stokmarknes
Melbu
Fiskebøl
Ledingen
Hamnøy
Kråkmo
Kjelvik
Rognan
Sulitjelma HWY 830
Vesterålen
Svolvær
Kabelvåg
Skutvik
Saltstraumen
E80
Bodø
Glomfjord
Holand
Inndyr
Jektvik
HWY 17
Lofoten
Leknes
Stamsund
Henningsvær
Kjerringøy
Moskenes
Reine
Å i Lofoten
Vestfjord
Værøy
Røst
Vestfjord

NORWEGIAN SEA

NORWEGIAN SEA

Arctic Circle

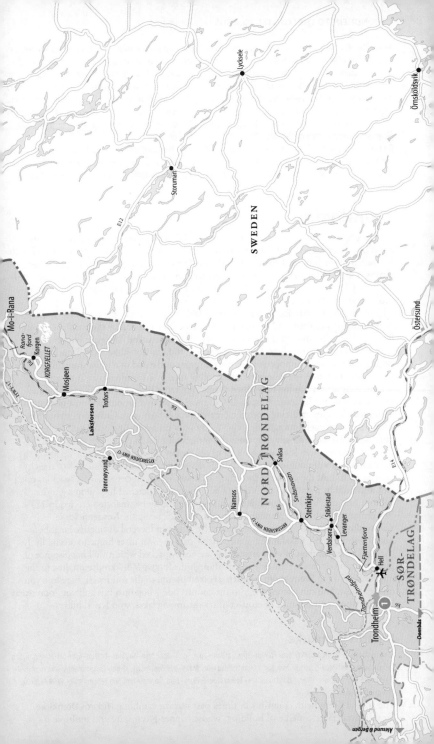

**5**

**By car** The E6, or "Arctic Highway", is the main road north from Trondheim: it's kept in excellent condition, though in summer motorhomes and caravans can make the going frustratingly slow. The obvious alternative is the slower, but stunningly scenic, Kystriksveien coastal road (Hwy-17), which utilizes road, tunnels, bridges and several ferries to run the 650km from Steinkjer up to Bodø, though its most picturesque stretch by far is north of Mo-i-Rana.

**By train** The train network (ⓦ www.nsb.no) reaches as far north as Fauske and nearby Bodø, from both of which buses connect with Narvik, which is the terminal of a separate rail line – the scenic Ofotbanen – that runs the few kilometres to the border and then south through Sweden (see box, p.302).

**By bus** The bus network up here is reasonably good, which is just as well given the isolated nature of many of the region's villages. The only real problem is likely to be time: it's a day or two's journey from Trondheim to Fauske, and another day from there to Narvik and/or the Lofoten.

**By Hurtigruten** The Hurtigruten coastal boat (ⓦ hurtigruten.co.uk) stops at all the major settlements on its way up the Norwegian coast from Bergen to Kirkenes.

# Trondheim

With a population of around 185,000, genial **TRONDHEIM** is Norway's third city, its appealing centre glued to a compact triangle of land within a loop of the River Nid with the sweep of the long and slender Trondheimsfjord stretching out beyond. It's a fine setting and Trondheim's main sights – and excellent restaurants – are best appreciated in a leisurely fashion over a couple of days, a healthy dose of city life before you venture into the wilds of the north.

Until the 1500s, Trondheim was known as **Nidaros** ("mouth of the river Nid"), its importance as a military and economic power base underpinned by the excellence of its harbour and its position at the head of a wide and fertile valley. The early Norse parliament, or Ting, met here, and the cathedral, **Nidaros Domkirke**, now Trondheim's principal sight, was an important pilgrimage centre at the end of a route stretching all the way up from Oslo. A fire destroyed almost all of medieval Trondheim in 1681 and immediately afterwards the far-sighted Danish governor brought in a military engineer from Luxembourg, a certain Caspar de Cicignon, to rebuild Trondheim on a **gridiron plan**, with broad avenues radiating from the centre to act as firebreaks. Cicignon's layout has survived pretty much untouched, giving today's city centre an airy, open feel, though the buildings themselves mostly date from the commercial boom of the late nineteenth century. Among them is a handsome set of old **timber warehouses** that line up along the river and dozens of doughty stone buildings designed to proclaim the success of the city's merchant class. At the centre of the action is **Torvet**, the main city square, a spacious open area anchored by a statue of the Viking Olav Tryggvason perched high atop a granite column, and nearby is the **Stiftsgården**, an extravagant timber mansion erected in 1774. The centre has a clutch of museums too, with the pick being the **Nordenfjeldske Kunstindustrimuseum** (Museum of Decorative Arts), and several distinctive neighbourhoods, most notably **Bakklandet**, a fashionable part of town that's home to several lively bars and cafés. All the city's key attractions are neatly packed within walking distance of each other, on or around the city centre, though the **Ringve Musikkmuseum**, just to the northeast, and the **Sverresborg Trøndelag Folkemuseum** to the southwest, may lure you further afield. You can also escape into the countryside – hop on a bus and you soon reach **Skistua**, where you can hike or cross-country ski among lakes, woods and hills.

## Nidaros Domkirke

Kongsgårdsgata 2 · **Cathedral** May Mon–Fri 9am–3pm, Sat 9am–2pm, Sun 1–4pm; June–Aug Mon–Fri 9am–6pm, Sat 9am–2pm, Sun 1–5pm; Sept–March Mon–Sat 9am–2pm, Sun 1–4pm; guided tours: May to mid-Sept 4 daily; 30min · Cathedral entry 90kr, combined ticket with Erkebispegården 180kr; guided tours free · **Tower** Mon–Fri 9am–6pm, Sat 9am–2pm, Sun 1–5pm · 40kr · ☎ 99 43 60 00, ⓦ nidarosdomen.no

The goal of Trondheim's pilgrims in times past was the rambling **Nidaros Domkirke**, Scandinavia's largest medieval building, whose copper-green spire and multiple roofs lord it over the south end of Munkegata. Gloriously restored following several fires and the upheavals of the Reformation, the cathedral, which is dedicated to St Olav (see box, p.272), remains the focus of any visit to Trondheim and is best explored in the early morning, when it's reasonably free of tour groups. In the summertime, there are free English-language **guided tours** and you can climb the cathedral tower for a panoramic view over the city and its surroundings.

The crowning glory of this magnificent blue- and green-grey soapstone edifice is its **west facade**, a soaring cliff face of finely worked stone sporting a magnificent rose

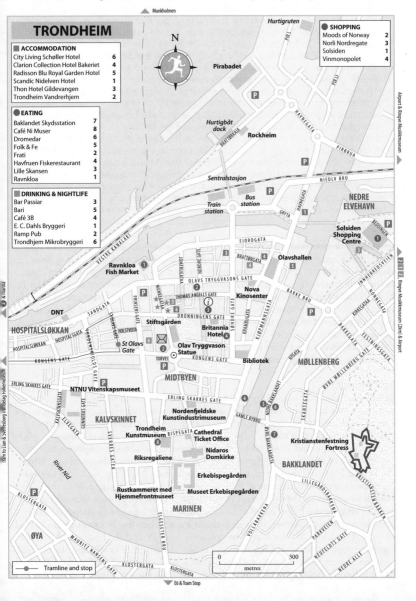

**TRONDHEIM**

| ■ ACCOMMODATION | |
| --- | --- |
| City Living Schøller Hotel | 6 |
| Clarion Collection Hotel Bakeriet | 4 |
| Radisson Blu Royal Garden Hotel | 5 |
| Scandic Nidelven Hotel | 1 |
| Thon Hotel Gildevangen | 3 |
| Trondheim Vandrerhjem | 2 |

| ● EATING | |
| --- | --- |
| Baklandet Skydsstation | 7 |
| Café Ni Muser | 8 |
| Dromedar | 6 |
| Folk & Fe | 5 |
| Frati | 2 |
| Havfruen Fiskerestaurant | 4 |
| Lille Skansen | 3 |
| Ravnkloa | 1 |

| ■ DRINKING & NIGHTLIFE | |
| --- | --- |
| Bar Passiar | 3 |
| Bari | 5 |
| Café 3B | 4 |
| E. C. Dahls Bryggeri | 1 |
| Ramp Pub | 2 |
| Trondhjem Mikrobryggeri | 6 |

| ● SHOPPING | |
| --- | --- |
| Moods of Norway | 2 |
| Norli Nordregate | 3 |
| Solsiden | 1 |
| Vinmonopolet | 4 |

**5**

### TROUBLED TIMES: THE UPS AND DOWNS OF ST OLAV

Born in 995, **Olav Haraldsson** followed the traditional life of a Viking chieftain from the tender age of 12, "rousing the steel-storm" as the saga writers put it, from Finland to Ireland. He also served as a mercenary to both the duke of Normandy and King Ethelred of England, and it was during this time that he was converted to Christianity. In 1015, he invaded Norway, defeated his enemies and became king, his military success built upon the support of the more prosperous farmers of the Trøndelag, an emergent class of yeomen who were less capricious than the coastal chieftains of Viking fame. However, Olav's zealous **imposition of Christianity** – he ordered the desecration of pagan sites and the execution of those who refused baptism – alienated many of his followers and the bribes of Olav's rival Knut (Canute), king of England and Denmark, did the rest: Olav's retainers deserted him, and he was forced into exile in 1028. Two years later, he was back in the Trøndelag, but the army he had raised was far too weak to defeat his enemies, and Olav was killed near Trondheim at the **Battle of Stiklestad** (see p.284).

Olav might have lost his kingdom, but the nationwide **Church** he founded had no intention of losing ground. Needing a local **saint** to consolidate its position, the Church carefully nurtured the myth of Olav, a process of sanctification assisted by the oppressive rule of Olav's successor, the "foreigner" Knut. After the Battle of Stiklestad, Olav's body had been spirited away and buried on the banks of the River Nid at what is today Trondheim. There were rumours of miracles in the vicinity of the grave, and when the bishop arrived to investigate these strange goings-on, he exhumed the body and found it, lo and behold, perfectly uncorrupted. Olav was declared a saint, his body placed in a silver casket and when, in 1066, Olav Kyrre, son of Olav's half-brother Harald the Fair-Haired, became king of Norway, he ordered work to begin on a grand church to house the remains in appropriate style. Over the years the church was altered and enlarged to accommodate the growing bands of medieval pilgrims; it achieved cathedral status in 1152, when Trondheim became the seat of an archbishopric whose authority extended as far as Orkney and the Isle of Man.

window, rank after rank of pointed arches, biblical, religious and royal figures by the dozen and a fancy set of gargoyles. The west facade and the **nave** behind may look medieval, but in fact they date from the nineteenth century: the originals were erected in the early Gothic style of the early thirteenth century, but they were destroyed by fire in 1719 and what you see today is a painstakingly accurate reconstruction. The fire did not, however, raze the Romanesque **transepts**, whose heavy hooped windows and dog-tooth decoration were the work of English stonemasons in the twelfth century. English workmen also lent a hand in the thirteenth-century **choir**, where the arches, flying buttresses and intricate tracery are the epitome of early Gothic – and are reminiscent of contemporaneous churches in England.

### The interior

Inside the cathedral, the gloomy half-light tends to hide much of the lofty decorative work, but you can make out the splendid double row of hooped arches and dog-tooth carving of the **transepts**. It's also possible to examine the strikingly ascetic, early twentieth-century **choir screen**, whose wooden figures are the work of Gustav Vigeland (see p.78). Neither did Vigeland finish there, carving the adjacent soapstone **font**, a superb piece of medievalism sporting four bas-reliefs depicting Adam and Eve, John the Baptist baptizing the Christ, the Resurrection and a beguiling Noah and the Ark: Noah peers apprehensively out of his boat, not realizing that the dove, with the telltale branch, is up above. The other item of particular interest is a famous fourteenth-century **altar frontal** (front panel of an altar painting) displayed in a chapel off the ambulatory, directly behind the high altar. At a time when few Norwegians could read or write, the cult of St Olav had to be promoted visually, and the frontal is the earliest surviving representation of Olav's life and times – or rather an exact copy, the original is in the Museet Erkebispegården (see opposite). In the centre of the frontal, Olav looks suitably beatific holding his axe and orb, while the top left-hand corner shows the

**5**

dream Olav had before the Battle of Stiklestad (see p.284), with Jesus dropping a ladder down to him from heaven. In the next panel down, Olav and his men are shown at prayer before the battle and, in the bottom right-hand corner, Olav meets a sticky end, speared and stabbed by three cruel-looking soldiers. The final panel shows church officials exhuming Olav's uncorrupted body and declaring his sainthood.

What you won't see now is the object of the medieval pilgrims' veneration: St Olav's silver casket-coffin, which was taken to Denmark and unceremoniously melted down to be made into coins in 1537.

# Erkebispegården
Kongsgårdsgata

Behind the cathedral stands the heavily restored **Erkebispegården** (Archbishop's Palace), a courtyard complex that was originally built in the twelfth century for the third archbishop, Øystein, though two stone-and-brick wings are all that survive of the medieval quadrangle – the other two wings were added much later. After the archbishops were kicked out during the Reformation, the palace became the residence of the Danish governors, but today it houses three museums – medieval sculpture in the **Museet Erkebispegården**, military stuff and a good section on World War II in the **Rustkammeret med Hjemmefrontmuseet**, which is free to enter, and Norway's crown jewels in the **Riksregaliene**.

## Museet Erkebispegården
May Mon–Sat 10am–3pm, Sun noon–4pm; June–Aug Mon–Fri 10am–5pm, Sat 10am–3pm, Sun noon–4pm; Sept–April Tues–Fri 10am–1pm, Sat 10am–2pm, Sun noon–4pm • 90kr, combined ticket for cathedral & Erkebispegården 180kr • ☏ 73 89 08 00, ⓦ nidarosdomen.no

The **south wing** of the Archbishop's Palace holds the **Museet Erkebispegården** (Archbishop's Palace Museum), where the prize exhibit is the original version of the altar frontal whose copy is displayed in the cathedral (see p.270). Otherwise, the museum is largely devoted to a few dozen medieval statues retrieved and put away for safekeeping during the nineteenth-century reconstruction of the cathedral's nave and west facade. Many of the statues are too bruised and battered to be especially engaging, but they are well displayed and several are finely carved. In particular, look out for a life-sized sculpture of **St Denis**, his head in his hands (literally) in accordance with the legend that he was beheaded, but then proceeded to irritate his executioners by carrying his head to his grave. Downstairs in the basement, an assortment of artefacts unearthed during a lengthy 1990s archeological investigation of the palace demonstrates the economic power of the archbishops: they employed all manner of skilled artisans – from glaziers and shoemakers to rope-makers, armourers and silversmiths – and even minted their own coins.

## Rustkammeret med Hjemmefrontmuseet
May–Sept Mon–Sat 10am–4pm, Sun noon–4pm • Free • ☏ 73 99 80 81, ⓦ rustkammeret.no

The substantial **Rustkammeret med Hjemmefrontmuseet** (Armoury and Resistance Museum) spreads over three main floors of the Erkebispegården. The **first floor** gives the broad details of Norway's involvement in the interminable **Dano-Swedish Wars** that racked Scandinavia from the fifteenth to the nineteenth centuries. As part of the Danish state, Norway was frequently attacked from the east along the Halden–Oslo corridor, the most memorable incursions being by the warlike Swedish king, Karl XII. Much to the Danish king's surprise, Karl came a cropper in Norway: it was here that he was defeated for the first time and, when he came back for more, he was shot (possibly by one of his own men) while besieging Fredriksten fortress in 1718 (see p.109).

The **second floor** has a section on the union with Sweden (1814–1905) and another dealing with the German invasion of 1940, but it's the **third floor** – the top floor – that is perhaps of most general interest as it chronicles the German occupation of **World War II**, dealing honestly with the sensitive issue of collaboration. In particular, you can

**5**

hear **Vidkun Quisling**'s broadcast announcing his (unsuccessful) coup d'état of April 9, 1940, and see a display on another of Norway's most reviled collaborators, **Henry Oliver Rinnan**. Recruited by the Gestapo in 1940, Rinnan played a leading role in combating the Resistance here in Trondheim, his special skill being the torture (and murder) of his suspects. He was executed after the war along with ten of his accomplices, fellow members of the so-called Rinnanbanden (Rinnan gang).

By contrast, the second floor also has several intriguing displays on the daring antics of the **Norwegian Resistance**, notably an extraordinary – perhaps hare-brained – attempt to sink the battleship *Tirpitz* as it lay moored in an inlet of the Trondheimsfjord in 1942 (see box, p.283). Called Operation Title, this escapade, like so many others, involved **Leif Larsen**, the Resistance hero who is commemorated by a statue on the harbourfront in Bergen. Larsen worked closely with the Royal Navy, organizing covert operations in occupied Norway from the RN base in the Shetlands. Supplies and personnel were transported across the North Sea by Norwegian fishing boats – a lifeline known, in that classically understated British (and Norwegian) way, as the "Shetland bus"; the book of the same name by David Howarth (see p.421) tells the tale of this remarkable enterprise.

### The Riksregaliene

May Mon–Sat 10am–3pm, Sun noon–4pm; June–Aug Mon–Fri 10am–5pm, Sat 10am–3pm, Sun noon–4pm; Sept–April Tues–Fri 10am–1pm, Sat 10am–2pm, Sun noon–4pm • 90kr, combined ticket for cathedral & Erkebispegården 180kr • ☎ 73 89 08 00, ⓦ nidarosdomen.no

Norway's crown jewels, the **Riksregaliene** (Royal Regalia), are displayed in the basement of the first part of the Erkebispegården's west wing. At the end of the Napoleonic Wars, Britain and her allies forced Denmark to cede Norway to Sweden. The Swedish king was himself new to the throne – oddly enough he had previously been one of Napoleon's generals, Jean-Baptiste Bernadotte (see box, p.70) – and although he received Norway as a welcome bonus, he was deemed to be a ruler of two kingdoms rather than one. Sweden already had its own crown jewels, but Norway, which hadn't been independent for centuries, had nothing at all. As a consequence, Bernadotte, now **Karl XIV Johan**, scuttled around Stockholm ordering a new set of crown jewels in preparation for his coronation in Trondheim. The results are on display here, principally a crown, a sceptre, a sword, an orb and a tiny anointing horn, all made in the 1810s. Another set of ceremonial gear was made for the queen, but it's still a very thin collection and the sword – the Sword of State – was actually recycled: it had originally been given to Bernadotte by Napoleon in return for military services rendered. The last Norwegian coronation took place here in Trondheim cathedral in 1906 on the accession of Håkon VII, but his successors – Olav V and Harald V – were elected for benedictions instead, in 1958 and 1991 respectively.

## Trondheim Kunstmuseum

Bispegata 7B • June–Aug daily 10am–4pm; Sept–May Wed noon–8pm, Thurs–Sun noon–4pm • 100kr • ☎ 73 53 81 80, ⓦ trondheimkunstmuseum.no

Metres from the cathedral, the **Trondheim Kunstmuseum** (Trondheim Art Museum) is best known for its temporary exhibitions of contemporary art. The downside is that these exhibitions often leave little space for the museum's permanent collection, which features a particularly enjoyable selection of Norwegian paintings from 1850 onwards. Highlights of the permanent collection include several works by Johan Dahl and Thomas Fearnley, the leading figures of nineteenth-century Norwegian landscape painting, as well as the Romantic canvases of Hans Gude and his friend Adolph Tidemand. The museum also owns the first overtly political work by a Norwegian artist, *The Strike* (*Streik*), painted in 1877 by the radical Theodor Kittelsen (1857–1914), who is better known for his illustrations of the folk tales collected by Jorgen Moe and Peder Asbjørnsen. The museum also possesses a substantial selection of Munch woodcuts, sketches and lithographs, including several of those disturbing, erotically charged personifications of emotions – *Lust, Fear* and *Jealousy* – that are so characteristic of his oeuvre, but these rarely seem to make much of an appearance.

## Nordenfjeldske Kunstindustrimuseum

Munkegata 5 • June to late Aug Mon–Sat 10am–5pm, Sun noon–4pm; late Aug to May Tues–Wed, Fri & Sat 10am–3pm, Thurs noon–8pm, Sun noon–4pm • 90kr • ☎ 73 80 89 50, ⓦ nkim.no

The fascinating **Nordenfjeldske Kunstindustrimuseum** (National Museum of Decorative Arts and Design) has a substantial and diverse permanent collection spanning textiles, furniture, metalwork and the like and also offers an ambitious programme of special exhibitions. Start in the **basement** to the right of the entrance, where the (permanent) historical collection illustrates bourgeois life in Trøndelag from 1500 to 1900 by means of an eclectic assemblage of furniture, faïence, glassware and silver. The modern collection follows on, featuring a small but well-chosen international selection of Arts & Crafts and Art Nouveau pieces, from glass, ceramics and textiles through to furniture – there's even an immaculate William Morris chair. Up above, on the **first floor**, is the museum's prize exhibit, an entire room of simply wonderful **tapestries** by **Hannah Ryggen**. Born in Malmö in 1894, Ryggen moved to the Trondheim area in the early 1920s and stayed until her death in 1970. Her tapestries are classically naive, the forceful colours and absence of perspective emphasizing the feeling behind them. This is committed art at its best, railing in the 1930s and 1940s against Hitler and Fascism, later moving on to more disparate targets such as the atom bomb and social conformism. Yet Ryggen still made time to celebrate the things she cherished: *Yes, we love this country* is as evocative a portrayal of her adopted land as you're likely to find.

Moving on, the rooms to the left of the entrance are mostly given over to temporary exhibitions, but here also are two small period spaces: one is kitted out with early 1950s furnishings and fittings by the Danish designer Finn Juhl (1912–1989); the second does the same with the Art Nouveau work of the Belgian designer and architect **Henri van de Velde** (1863–1957).

## Torvet

At the heart of the city is the main square, **Torvet**, a spacious open area flanked by a so-so mix of old and new buildings and anchored by an imposing statue of **Olav Tryggvason** (c.968–1000), who perches on a tall stone pillar like some medieval Nelson. Tryggvason founded Trondheim in 997, so it's appropriate he has his own column, but the statue, which was raised in 1921, runs the gamut of Viking stereotypes with a stern-looking, muscular Tryggvason kitted out in a full set of chain mail with helmet and sword, one

### TRONDHEIM'S TOP-RANKING VIKING

One of the most fearsome Vikings of his era, **Olav Tryggvason** is surrounded by myth and legend. The most plausible account of his early days has his mother fleeing Norway with her son when he was about three years old, ending up in exile in Sweden and ultimately Russia. Thereafter, Tryggvason cut his Viking spurs in a series of piratical raids, before leading a large fleet in an attack on England in 991. The English bought him off and did so again three years later, the two payments of this "**Danegeld**" making Tryggvason extremely rich. Part of the deal for the second payment was that he become a Christian and, against all expectations, the Viking chieftain seems to have taken his new faith seriously. Tryggvason then hot-footed it back to Norway, where he quickly wrested control of most of the country and founded Trondheim. His brutal imposition of **Christianity**, however, infuriated many of his subjects, especially the Tronders, who were determined to hang onto their pagan gods. Few mourned therefore, when, after just five years as king, Tryggvason was killed in a sea battle – supposedly jumping out of his longship when the battle was lost, never to be seen again.

**5**

arm outstretched presenting an orb, the symbol of monarchical power. Curiously, though it's hard to see without binoculars, the object behind Olav's legs is a representation of one of his victims, a slave by the name of **Tormod Kark**, who made a major miscalculation: Kark killed his master Håkon Sigurdsson, the sworn enemy of Olav, and turned up in Trondheim expecting a reward; Olav surprised him, however, by having him decapitated.

## Stiftsgården

Munkegata 23 • June to late Aug Mon–Sat 10am–4pm, Sun noon–4pm • Guided tours every hour on the hour till 1hr before closing • 90kr • ☎ 73 80 89 50, ⓦ nkim.no/stiftsgarden

One conspicuous remnant of old timber-town Trondheim survives in the city centre – the **Stiftsgården** (Royal Residence), which stretches out along Munkegata just north of Torvet. Built in 1774–78, this handsome mustard-yellow courtyard complex is among the largest wooden structures surviving in northern Europe. These days it serves as an official royal residence with some 140 rooms, a marked ascent of the social ladder from its original function as the home of the provincial governor. Inside, a long string of period rooms illustrates the genteel tastes of the mansion's late eighteenth- to early nineteenth-century occupants. The rooms are decorated in a wide range of styles, from Rococo to Biedermeier, but it's the fanciful Italianate wall paintings that steal the show. The obligatory anecdotal guided tour brings a smile or two – but not perhaps 90kr wide.

## Munkholmen island

**Boats to Munkholmen** Late May 10am–4pm & late Aug to early Sept every day hourly on the hour 11am–4pm; June to mid-Aug daily every 30min 10am–6pm; 15min • 90kr return • ☎ 95 08 21 44

Poking up out of the Trondheimsfjord just 2km offshore, and reached from the Ravnkloa jetty at the foot of Munkegata, the tiny islet of **Munkholmen** has had an eventful history. In Viking times it was used as the city's execution ground, and Olav Tryggvason went to the added trouble of displaying the heads of his enemies on pikes here, which must have made approaching mariners more than a tad nervous. In the eleventh century, the Benedictines founded a monastery on the island – hence its name – but it was not one of their more successful ventures: the archbishop received dozens of complaints about, of all things, the amount of noise the monks made, not to mention alleged heavy drinking and womanizing. After the Reformation, the island was converted into a prison, which doubled as a fortress designed to protect the seaward approaches to the city; later still it became a customs house.

### Munkholmen fortress

Guided tours hourly every day from late May to early Sept; 30min • 50kr

Sturdy stone walls encircle most of Munkholmen, and behind them, sunk in a circular dip, is a set of quaint, almost cottage-like, **prison buildings** that surround a cobbled courtyard. There are guided tours of the central part of the **fortress**, a cheerful romp through its galleries and corridors. The tour includes a visit to the spacious cell occupied by Peder Griffenfeld, and a glimpse of the gun emplacement the Germans installed during World War II. After the tour you can visit the **café**, see some exhibitions of local arts and crafts in the old caretaker's house or scramble along outside the walls and round the rocks beneath to either of a couple of rough, pebbly beaches.

## Rockheim

Brattørkaia 14 • Tues–Sun 10am–6pm • 120kr • ☎ 73 60 50 70, ⓦ rockheim.no

Down on Trondheim's harbourfront, in a recycled warehouse that's been topped off with a dramatic rectangular block, is **Rockheim** (Home of Rock), a gallant attempt to

**CLOCKWISE FROM TOP** GAMLE BYBRO (P.278); OLAV TRYGGVASON STATUE, TORVET (P.275); WINDOW, NIDAROS DOMKIRKE (P.270) >

**5**

make a museum out of popular music. Some exhibits are for listening, others for playing and there's a "wall of sound" too – not the Phil Spector sort, but stand on a dated circle and you can see clips of Norway's most popular bands of yesteryear. It's all really rather enjoyable and you can try to get to grips with one of Norway's specialities too – **Black Metal**: a whole room is devoted to this type of music – insert a tape (yes, a tape) and hear those guitars go, or should it be shriek with the likes of Mayhem, Darkthrone and Gorgoroth leading the charge.

## The east bank of the River Nid

On the northeast edge of the city-centre grid, a slender footbridge spans the **River Nid** to reach **Nedre Elvehavn**, a large leisure and shopping complex that trundles along beside the old quays of what was once Trondheim's docks and shipyard. Original it isn't – dozens of cities have their own modernized docklands – but it's certainly popular. From here, an easy-to-follow walking route leads south. First up is the **Bakke bru** (bridge) and then it's **Nedre Bakklandet**, a gently curving street flanked by old and brightly painted timber houses that proceeds to **Bakklandet**, a pocket-sized neighbourhood with a platoon of cafés and restaurants. Bakklandet abuts the **Gamle Bybro** (Old Town Bridge), a quaint wooden structure offering splendid views over the nineteenth-century gabled and timbered warehouses, now mostly restaurants and offices, that flank one side of **Kjøpmannsgata**.

### Kristianstenfestning fortress
Festningsgata • Open access daylight hours • Free

Narrow Brubakken leads up the hill from Bakklandet to Kristianstensbakken and the **Kristianstenfestning fortress**. Dating from 1681, the fort's earth and stone ramparts remain in reasonably good condition and a surviving artillery tower is of some interest, but the big deal – and the reason to come here – is the views back over Trondheim.

## NTNU Vitenskapsmuseet
Erling Skakkes gate 47 at Gunnerus gate • Tues–Fri 10am–4pm, Sat & Sun 11am–4pm • 60kr • ☎ 73 59 21 45, ⓦ ntnu.no

The **NTNU Vitenskapsmuseet** (Museum of Natural History and Archeology), a few blocks from the cathedral, holds several collections cobbled together by the university. In the large building at the front, you'll find a substantial display of stuffed animals, an extensive section on climate change and another on nature and the environment. Rather more interesting, however, is the **Middelalder i Trondheim** (medieval exhibition), in the old **suhmhuset** (hay storehouse), a low, long building to the rear of the main entrance. This tracks the development of Trondheim from its foundation in the tenth century to the great fire of 1681. The thoroughly researched, multilingual text is supported by an excellent range of archeological finds, and departs from the predictable "Kings and Queens" approach, investigating everything from sanitary towels and reliquary jars to popular games and attitudes to life and death. One of the more remarkable exhibits is the **Kulisteinen** (Kuli stone), which is carved with both a Christian cross and a runic inscription. Found near Trondheim and dating from around 1034, it's a very rare illustration of the transitional period between a pagan and a Christian Norway.

### Kirkekunst
One of the most interesting exhibitions in the NTNU Vitenskapsmuseet is the **Kirkekunst** (church art exhibition) in the building across from the main entrance, though it's normally kept locked and you'll need to ask at reception to gain access. Among the assorted ecclesiastical knick-knacks, there are pulpits and fonts, processional crosses and statues of the saints, plus religious paintings galore. By and large, the workmanship is crude and the painting garish, but there is a raw, naive vitality to many

**5**

of the earlier pieces which is really rather delightful. Highlights include several fancily carved stave-church portals and an idiosyncratic, seventeenth-century *Adam and Eve*, whose belly buttons look like eyes.

# Ringve Musikkmuseum

Lade allé 60 • May daily 11am–4pm; June–Aug daily 11am–5pm; Sept–April Tues–Sun 11am–4pm • 110kr • ☎ 73 87 02 80, ⊛ ringve.no • Bus #3 or #4 from Munkegata to the Ringve Museum stop

The **Ringve Musikkmuseum** (Ringve Music Museum) occupies a delightful eighteenth-century country house and courtyard complex on the hilly Lade peninsula, some 4km northeast of the city centre. Devoted to musical history and to musical instruments from all over the world, the museum is divided into two sections. In the main building, the collection focuses on antique European instruments in period settings, with several demonstrations included in a lengthy – and obligatory – guided tour. The second section, in the old barn, contains an international selection of musical instruments and offers a self-guided zip through some of the key moments and movements of musical history. There are themes like "the invention of the piano" and "pop and rock", as well as the real humdinger, "the marching band movement in Norway". Immaculately maintained, the surrounding **gardens** make the most of the scenic setting.

# Sverresborg Trøndelag Folkemuseum

Sverresborg Allé 13 • June–Aug daily 10am–5pm; 150kr; Sept–May Tues–Fri 10am–3pm, Sat & Sun noon–4pm • June–Aug 150kr; Sept–May 110kr • ☎ 73 89 01 00, ⊛ sverresborg.no • Bus #18 (direction Havstad) from Munkegata

The **Sverresborg Trøndelag Folkemuseum** (Trøndelag Folk Museum), 3km southwest of the city centre, is one of Norway's better folk museums. In a pleasant rural setting, with views over the city, the museum's indoor section kicks off with some well-presented displays tracing everyday life in the Trøndelag from the eighteenth century onwards. Outside, you'll see around sixty relocated Trøndelag timber buildings, including a post office, grocery store, stave church and all sorts of farmhouses and outhouses, built for a variety of purposes from curing meat to drying hay.

## ARRIVAL AND DEPARTURE

## TRONDHEIM

**By plane** Trondheim airport is about 35km east of the city centre at Værnes. From here, there are regular Flybussen to Sentralstasjon and various points in the city centre (45min; 130kr single, 220kr return; ⊛ flybussen.no).

**By car** Trondheim is on the E6, around 500km from Oslo (a 7hr drive). In Trondheim, there's plenty of city-centre, on-street parking, but during restricted periods (Mon–Fri 8am–8pm, Sat 8am–3pm) it's expensive (27kr/hr) with a maximum stay of 3hr. Car parks are plentiful too – and are clearly signed; reckon on 30kr/hr up to a maximum of 250kr for 24hr.

**By train** The city's train station, part of Sentralstasjon, is on the northern edge of the centre, a 10min walk from the main square, Torvet. Timetables on ⊛ www.nsb.no.

Destinations Bodø (2 daily; 9hr 40min); Fauske (2 daily; 9hr); Lønsdal (7hr 40min; request stop only – notify the conductor); Mo-i-Rana (2 daily; 6hr 30min); Mosjøen (2 daily; 4hr 30min); Oslo (4 daily via Dombås, Lillehammer

and Oslo Gardermoen airport; 6hr 30min–7hr 45min); Røros (2–3 daily; 2hr 30min); Steinkjer (hourly; 2hr).

**By bus** Trondheim bus station adjoins the train station (see above); timetables on ⊛ rutebok.no or ⊛ nor-way.no.

Destinations Bergen (1 daily; 14hr); Loen (1 daily; 7hr 40min); Lom (1 daily; 5hr 30min); Otta (1 daily; 5hr); Stryn (1 daily; 7hr 30min).

**By Hurtigbåt passenger express boat** There's an all-year Hurtigbåt express boat between Trondheim and Kristiansund (1–3 daily; 3hr 30min; 632kr). In Trondheim, it docks beside Brattørkaia, a 5min walk from Sentralstasjon – just over the (surprisingly large) stairway.

**By Hurtigruten** The quay for the Hurtigruten coastal boat (⊛ hurtigruten.co.uk) is about 10min walk from Sentralstasjon via Brattørkaia. Northbound, the next major port of call is Bodø (24hr); southbound it's Kristiansund (6hr 30min).

## GETTING AROUND

**By bus and tram** The city's bus network is operated by AtB (⊛ atb.no), who have an enquiry desk in the bus station at

Sentralstasjon (Mon–Fri 10am–1pm & 2–5.30pm). Most buses arrive and depart from the stops around the

**5**

Munkegata/Dronningens gate intersection. Flat-fare, one-way tickets cost 50kr and an unlimited 24hr bus ticket, the *døgnbillet*, costs 100kr; tickets can be bought from the driver – exact change only. The AtB network also includes a tram, which runs out into the countryside to the southwest of the centre; there's a central tram stop on St Olavs gate.

**By bike** Trondheim has a summer public bike scheme with bike racks dotted across the city centre (May–Oct daily 6am–midnight). The bikes are released like supermarket trolleys when you insert your access card, which you can buy at the tourist office for 70kr (plus a deposit of 200kr). This gives you unlimited use of the bikes for 24 hours.

**By taxi** Among several, there are taxi ranks at Sentralstasjon and the *Radisson SAS Royal Garden Hotel*; or call Trønder Taxi (☎ 073 73).

## INFORMATION

**Tourist office** Trondheim tourist office is right in the centre of the city, on the first floor of Nordre gate 11 (mid-June to mid-Aug daily 9am–6pm; reduced hours mid-Aug to mid-June; ☎ 73 80 76 60, ⊛ visittrondheim.no). Staff here issue the free and very useful *Trondheim Guide* as well as a wide range of other tourist literature, including a cycle map of the city and its surroundings.

**DNT** Trondhjems Turistforening is just west of the centre at Sandgata 30 (Mon–Fri 10am–5pm; ☎ 73 92 42 00, ⊛ tt.no). DNT's local branch offers advice on the region's hiking trails and huts, sells hiking maps and outdoor equipment. It also organizes a variety of guided walks and cross-country skiing trips, with activities concentrated in the mountains to the south and east of the city.

## ACTIVITIES

**Walking** The best way to explore the city centre is on foot – it only takes about 10min to walk from one side to the other. For something a little longer, but just as easy, stroll west from the Hurtigbåt ferry terminal along the waterfront to the marina and *Lille Skansen* restaurant (see opposite). This is a pleasant way to spend 20min or so and you can return to the centre via Hospitalsgata, Dronningens gate and Holstveita, which together hold a fine assortment of old timber houses.

**Hiking** The rugged, lightly forested hills to the west of Trondheim are latticed with hiking trails – and the local DNT office (see above) sells hiking maps. An obvious starting point is the Skistua (⊛ skistua.no) lodge at the terminus of the bus #10 route from Munkegata. The journey takes about 20min and the lodge is just 5min walk from Blomstertjønna, a tiny lake that is encircled by an easy footpath. In August and September, the footpath is an excellent place to pick wild blueberries, raspberries and cloudberries.

**River-kayaking** The river that almost encircles the city centre makes for some pleasant kayaking with Trondheim Kajakk (☎ 48 33 83 18, ⊛ trondheimkajakk.no). Their main offering is a 2hr trip for 400kr/person, though the meeting point is a fiddle to get to.

## ACCOMMODATION

Accommodation is plentiful in Trondheim, though the **big chains** very much rule the **hotel** roost. At time of writing, the most distinctive hotel in town, the *Britannia*, an independent at Dronningens gate 5, was having a complete overhaul, though hopefully its Egyptian-style murals and Corinthian columns will survive. Trondheim also has a **youth hostel**.

**City Living Schøller Hotel** Dronningens gate 26 ☎ 73 87 08 00, ⊛ cityliving.no. Independent, economy hotel in the heart of the city. Fifty simple rooms spread over three floors. Competitively priced, but they don't provide breakfast. 800kr

**Clarion Collection Hotel Bakeriet** Brattørgata 2 ☎ 73 99 10 00, ⊛ nordicchoicehotels.com. This competent chain hotel occupies an intelligently revamped former bakery right in the centre of town. The guest rooms, which were once occupied by the bakery workers, are kitted out in standard modern style. 1400kr

**Radisson Blu Royal Garden Hotel** Kjøpmannsgata 73 ☎ 73 80 30 00, ⊛ radissonblu.com/hotel-trondheim. Full marks to the architects here, who have designed this large, modern, riverside hotel in the style of the old timber warehouses that characterize this part of the city. Lots of glass – indeed the interior of the hotel looks a bit like a series of enormous greenhouses – but the rooms do vary in quality. Banquet-like breakfasts. 1500kr

★**Scandic Nidelven Hotel** Havnegata 1–4 ☎ 73 56 80 00, ⊛ scandichotels.com. Large and flashy chain hotel nudging out into and rising up out of the river with lots of glass to maximize views. The public areas are bold and expansive – modernism at its most decisive – though the guest rooms are not perhaps quite as distinctive as they could be. Comes with all mod cons – and has won Best Breakfast awards for the last ten years. 1400kr

**Thon Hotel Gildevangen** Søndre gate 22B ☎ 73 87 01 30, ⊛ thonhotels.no. Substantial chain hotel in two adjoining buildings – an imposing stone structure of 1908 at the front and a routine modern block at the back. The 163 rooms are perfectly adequate if without much distinction, but at least the beds are very comfortable. The rooms at the back on the upper floors are the quietest. Very good breakfasts. 1300kr

**Trondheim Vandrerhjem** Weidemannsveien 41 ☏ 73 87 44 50, ⓦ trondheimvandrerhjem.no. This large, well-equipped hostel offers single, double and four-bed dorm rooms, mostly with shared facilities. It looks more like a hospital from somewhere you'd want to stay from the outside, but the interior is pleasant enough – especially the comfortable, newer rooms. It has self-catering facilities, a laundry and a canteen. A 20min (2km) hike east of the centre: cross the Bakke bru (bridge) onto busy Innherredsveien (the E6) and walk uphill; turn right onto Wessels gate and hang a left at the fourth crossroads. To save your legs, take any bus up Innherredsveien and ask the driver to let you off as close as possible. Open all year. Dorms <u>330kr</u>, doubles <u>625kr</u>

## EATING

Trondheim has a good selection of first-rate **restaurants** serving a variety of cuisines, though the Norwegian places mostly have the gastronomic edge. Also, with one or two notable exceptions, most of the prime spots are handily located in the city centre.

### CAFÉS

★**Café Ni Muser** Bispegata 9 ☏ 73 53 63 11, ⓦ nimuser .no. Metres from the cathedral, this fashionable café occupies an older building that might be glum but for the modern art on the walls (which is for sale) and the terrace out the back. Features a finely judged and creative menu that emphasizes local, seasonal ingredients – try, for example, the simply wonderful creamy cauliflower soup (145kr) or the vegetarian lasagne (165kr). Daily 11am–11pm.

**Dromedar** Nedre Bakklandet 3 ☏ 73 50 25 02, ⓦ dromedar.no. Laidback, cosy-cramped coffee bar in antique wooden premises a few metres north of the Gamle Bybro (the old town bridge). One of a small chain, it serves the best coffee in town plus snacks and light meals – filled bagels, sandwiches, etc – at reasonable prices. Mon–Thurs 7am–7pm, Fri 8am–6pm, Sat & Sun 10am–6pm.

**Ravnkloa** Munkegata 70 ☏ 73 52 55 21, ⓦ ravnkloa .no. The city's fish market has been down here at the foot of Munkegata for decades, but it has recently accumulated a café where they serve – you guessed it – seafood. Sit outside at the sturdy wooden tables overlooking the harbour and munch away at, for example, a large bowl of shrimps with bread for 190kr. Mon–Fri 10am–5pm, Sat 10am–4pm.

### RESTAURANTS

**Baklandet Skydsstation** Øvre Bakklandet 33 ☏ 73 92 10 44, ⓦ skydsstation.no. Friendly, intimate former coaching inn with a warren of homely dining rooms and a small courtyard. The menu features home-cooked staples such as that old Norwegian favourite, *bacalao* (dried and salted cod fish), and an earth-moving cheesecake. Mains

from as little as 200kr. Mon–Fri 11am–1am, Sat & Sun noon–1am.

**Folk & Fe** Nedre Bakklandet 6 ☏ 97 51 81 80, ⓦ folkogfe -bistro.no. Well-regarded, bistro-style restaurant in the Bakklandet area, where the decor – sheepskins draped over the chairs and so forth – reflects the menu: traditional Norwegian with flair and featuring local, seasonal ingredients. Mains average around 220kr. Tues–Sun noon–4pm & 5–10pm.

★**Frati** Kongens gate 20 ☏ 73 52 57 33, ⓦ frati.no. Busy, bustling Italian restaurant in large, neo-industrial premises with a wide-ranging menu covering all the classics and then some. Generous portions, authentic flavours and a great range of draught beers. The pastas are particularly good. Pasta main courses from 150kr, pizzas from 140kr. Mon–Sat 11am–midnight, Sun 1pm–midnight.

★**Havfruen Fiskerestaurant** Kjøpmannsgata 7 ☏ 73 87 40 70, ⓦ havfruen.no. In an old and sympathetically revamped riverside warehouse, this smart and popular restaurant serves the best seafood in town. Caters to an older clientele for the most part with the fish – cod, monkfish, halibut, char and so forth – well presented and prepared. Mains 280–340kr. Mon–Sat 4–11pm.

**Lille Skansen** Nedre Ila 2 ☏ 73 92 11 51, ⓦ lille -skansen.no. Popular waterfront restaurant on the west side of the city centre in a sort of glorified chalet-cabin with an attractive decking terrace and a smart interior. The Norwegian menu is short and inventive – try, for instance, the salmon burger with dill, celery, capers and wasabi sour cream (185kr). May–Sept Mon–Sat 11am–11pm, Sun 11am–9pm; restricted hours the rest of the year.

## DRINKING AND NIGHTLIFE

There are **bars** dotted all over the city centre, but the weekend scene is at its liveliest on and around Brattørgata and in the **Nedre Elvehavn** district, where the former shipyard has been turned into a large leisure complex of shops, bars and restaurants. The favourite local tipple is Dahls Pils (the one with the green, gold and red label).

**Bar Passiar** Dokkparken 4 ☏ 92 60 62 00, ⓦ dokkhuset .no. Just about managing to straddle the fine line between the trendy and pretentious, this is the pick of the bars along the Nedre Elvehavn dockside strip. Showcases house and electro DJs spinning till late, as well as fresh fruit cocktails and outdoor seating on the decking overlooking the old docks. Mon–Thurs 3–11.30pm, Fri 3pm–2.30am, Sat noon–2.30am.

**5**

**Bari** Munkegata 25 ☎73 60 60 24, ⊛bari.no. Smooth and polished bar-restaurant, all dark-stained wood and soft lighting. Attracts an older/smarter crew, who sip wine and cocktails (rather then downing litres of ale). Mon 11am–midnight, Tues–Thurs 11am–1am, Fri & Sat 11am–2am.

**Café 3B** Brattørgata 3B ☎73 51 15 50, ⊛cafe3b.no. Rock'n'roll and indie club-cum-bar, where you can drink into the wee hours. One of the liveliest places in town. Daily 6pm–2.30am.

**E. C. Dahls Bryggeri** Strandveien 71 ☎40 69 74 00, ⊛ecdahls.no. The former Dahls brewery, a 10min walk northeast of the city centre, has just been overhauled by its new owners, Carlsberg. They have revamped the brewing facilities, adding a range of craft ales to the Dahls stable, and turned part of the complex into a bar and restaurant – the bar below and the restaurant up above. The restaurant is especially good for the grilled meats and fish. To get there, walk up Innherredsveien to the traffic island and Strandveien is on the far side. Tues–Sat 4pm–midnight.

★**Ramp Pub** Strandveien 25A ☎73 51 80 20, ⊛lamo ramp.com. This hipster hangout is the coolest place in town. It's decorated in a sort of retro Scandi-diner style, and is made up of just one largish room and a pavement terrace. The bar food is just fine – nothing too fancy, try the lamb burger with the trimmings (175kr) – or just stick to the drinks and enjoy the soundtrack – everything from indie to blues. In the boho/alternative Svart Lamon district, where the (now defunct) "Eat the Rich" community festival used to go down a storm. For directions, see *E. C. Dahls Bryggeri* above. Mon–Thurs 2pm–1am, Fri–Sun noon–1am.

**Trondhjem Mikrobryggeri** Prinsens gate 39 ☎73 51 75 15, ⊛tmb.no. Mainstream bar in a little courtyard just off Prinsens gate. Serves its own microbrewery brews, as well as plates of filling pub food. Mon 5pm–midnight, Tues–Thurs 3pm–2am, Fri & Sat noon–2am.

## ENTERTAINMENT

**Nova Kinosenter** Olav Tryggvasons gate 5 ☎73 80 88 00, ⊛trondheimkino.no. Shows all the movie block-busters on its several screens.

**Olavshallen** Kjøpmannsgata 44 ☎73 99 40 50, ⊛olavshallen.no. The city's main concert hall, offering everything from opera to rock, comedy and musicals. It's also home to the city's symphony orchestra.

## SHOPPING

**Moods of Norway** Olav Tryggvasonsgate 29 ☎92 42 57 22, ⊛moodsofnorway.com. This burgeoning Norwegian chain features (relatively) inexpensive clothing for the young and youthful in bright and cheerful colours. Mon–Sat 10am–6pm.

**Norli Nordregate** Dronningens gate 14 ☎73 88 46 00, ⊛norli.no. The best bookshop in town with a good selection of maps and a competent range of English fiction. Mon–Fri 9am–6pm, Sat 10am–6pm.

**Solsiden** Beddingen 10 ⊛solsidensenter.no. Large and busy shopping mall with lots of shops and boutiques selling clothing and accessories. There's a food hall and supermarket here too. Mon–Fri 9am–9pm, Sat 9am–6pm.

**Vinmonopolet** Søndre gate 8 ☎045 60, ⊛vinmonopolet.no. Large and ultramodern branch of the government-run liquor and wine store. Mon–Fri 10am–6pm, Sat 10am–3pm.

## DIRECTORY

**Pharmacy** Vitusapotek Løven, Olav Tryggvasonsgate 28 (Mon–Fri 9am–6pm, Sat 10am–4pm; ☎73 83 32 83).

**Post office** The main post office is at Munkegata 30 (Mon–Fri 9am–5pm, Sat 10am–3pm).

# North from Trondheim to Bodø

North of Trondheim, it's a long, 710km haul up the coast to the next major place of interest, Bodø, the principal ferry port for the Lofoten. Fortunately, there are several pleasant places to stop en route, beginning with tiny **Stiklestad**, famous among Norwegians as the site of the eponymous battle where Olav Haraldsson, later St Olav, was chopped down – as commemorated today in the lavish Stiklestad National Culture Centre. Stiklestad is in the province of **Trøndelag** as are the next obvious pit stops, **Steinkjer**, a modest little town with one good hotel, and **Snåsa**, a relaxed – and relaxing – village, again with somewhere pleasant to stay. Further north, in **Nordland**, the next province up, both **Mosjøen** and **Mo-i-Rana**, two rejigged and revamped former industrial towns, make enjoyable overnight stays, especially Mo-i-Rana, which serves as a handy starting point for a visit to the mighty **Svartisen glacier**, crowning the coastal peaks close by. The glacier is a major feature of the **Saltfjellet-Svartisen Nasjonalpark**, a wild and windswept mountain plateau that extends west from the E6 on and around the Arctic Circle. The E6 and the railway cut along the edge of the park, giving ready access, but although this is a popular destination for experienced hikers, it's too fierce an environment for the novice or the lightly equipped. Beyond is workaday **Fauske**, where the Norwegian railway network reaches its most northerly point, and **Bodø**, an engaging town and seaport with a scattering of attractions, most notably the charming old trading post at **Kjerringøy**.

## ARRIVAL AND DEPARTURE

**NORTH FROM TRONDHEIM TO BODØ**

**By train** The easiest way to make the bulk of the trip is by train, a rattling good journey on the Nordlandsbanen (Nordland Line) with the scenery becoming wilder and bleaker the further north you go – and you usually get a blast from the whistle as you cross the Arctic Circle; be sure to sit on the left of the carriage going north as the views are much better. The train takes 9hr to get from Trondheim to Fauske, where the line reaches its northern limit and turns west for

the final 55km dash to Bodø. There's precious little to detain you in Fauske, but there are bus connections north to Narvik, a 5hr drive away, and many travellers take an overnight break here, though in fact nearby Bodø makes a far more pleasant stopover; there are buses to Narvik from Bodø too.

**By car** If you're driving, you'll find the main highway, the E6, which runs all the way from Trondheim to Narvik and points north, too slow to cover more than 300–350km

---

## LEIF LARSEN AND THE ATTACK ON THE TIRPITZ

Commissioned in 1941, the German battleship **Tirpitz** spent most of its three-year existence hidden away in the **Fjættenfjord**, a narrow inlet of the **Trondheimsfjord** 20km north of **Hell**, where it was protected from air attack by the mountains and from naval attack by a string of coastal gun emplacements. With the fjord as its base, the *Tirpitz* was able to sally forth to attack Allied convoys bound for Russia and as such was a major irritant to the Royal Navy, who dreamt up a remarkable scheme to sink it. The navy had just perfected a submersible craft called the **Chariot**, which was 6m long, powered by electric motors, and armed with a torpedo. A crew of two volunteer divers manned the craft, sitting astride it at the rear – which must amount to some kind of definition of bravery.

The plan was to transport two of these Chariots across from Shetland to Norway in a Norwegian fishing boat and then, just before the first German checkpoint, to hide them by attaching them to the outside of the boat's hull. Equipped with false papers and a diversionary load of peat, the fishing boat would, it was thought, stand a good chance of slipping through the German defences. Thereafter, as soon as the boat got within reasonable striking distance, the Chariots could be launched towards the *Tirpitz* and, once they got very close to the ship, their torpedoes would be fired.

The boat selected was the *Arthur*, skippered by the redoubtable **Leif Andreas Larsen**, a modest man of extraordinary courage, who, over the course of the war, ran over fifty trips to Norway from the Shetlands. The *Arthur* had a crew of four Norwegian and six British seamen – four to pilot the Chariots and two to help them get into their diving suits. At first the trip went well. As soon as they reached Norway's coastal waters, the crew moved the Chariots from their hiding place in the hold and attached them to the hull. They then fooled the Germans and were allowed into the Trondheimsfjord, but here the weather deteriorated and the Chariots broke loose from the boat, falling to the bottom of the ocean before they could be used. There was, therefore, no choice but to abort the mission, scuttle the *Arthur* and row ashore in the hope that the crew could escape over the mountains to neutral Sweden. They divided into two parties of five, one of which made it without mishap – except for a few lost toes from frostbite – but the other group, led by Larsen, ran into a patrol. In the skirmish that ensued, one of the Englishmen, a certain A.B. Evans, was wounded and had to be left behind; the Germans polished him off.

On September 11, 1944, the *Tirpitz* was caught napping in the **Kåfjord** (see p.351) by Allied bombers, which flew in from a Russian airfield to the east, screened by the mountains edging the fjord. The *Tirpitz* was badly damaged in the attack and although it managed to limp off to Tromsø the warship was finally sunk just outside that city on November 12 by a combined bombing-and-torpedo attack.

comfortably in a day. The main alternative to the E6 is the coastal Hwy-17, the Kystriksveien (ⓦrv17.no), an ingenious and extremely scenic cobbling together of road, tunnel, bridge and car ferry that negotiates the shredded shoreline from Steinkjer, just north of Trondheim, all the way up to Bodø, a distance of nigh on 700km. It's a slow route – there are no fewer than six ferry crossings – but if you can't spare the time or money to do the whole thing, you could join Hwy-17 to the west of Mo-i-Rana, cutting out five ferries and the first 420km, yet still taking in the most dramatic part of the journey, including fabulous views of the Melfjord and the Svartisen glacier.

# Stiklestad

One of Norway's most celebrated villages, **STIKLESTAD**, 100km from Trondheim, was where **Olav Haraldsson**, later St Olav (see box, p.272), was killed in battle in 1030. A descendant of Harald Hårfagre (the Fair-Haired), Haraldsson was one of Norway's most important medieval kings, a Viking warrior turned resolute Christian monarch whose misfortune it was to be the enemy of the powerful and shrewd King Knut of England and Denmark. It was Knut's bribes that did for Olav, persuading all but his most loyal supporters to change allegiance – as a Norse poet commented in the cautionary *Håvamål* (Sayings of Odin), "I have never found a man so generous and hospitable that he would not take a present." Dislodged from the throne, Olav returned from exile in Sweden in 1030 determined to retake power, but was defeated and killed here at the **Battle of Stiklestad**. His role as founder of the Norwegian Church prompted his subsequent canonization, and his cult flourished at Trondheim until the Reformation.

## Stiklestad Nasjonale Kultursenter

Leksdalsveien 1 • Daily: Sept–June 9am–6pm; July–Aug 9am–8pm • ☎ 74 04 42 00, ⓦ stiklestad.no

The Norwegian government has spent millions of kroner developing the **Stiklestad Nasjonale Kultursenter** (Stiklestad National Culture Centre) to commemorate the life, times and most especially the death of Olav Haraldsson. This collection of assorted museums and sights is spread out over a pastoral landscape typical of the Trøndelag.

### The Kulturhus

Daily: Sept–June 9am–6pm; July & Aug 9am–8pm • 180kr

The centre's broad-beamed **Kulturhus** houses a pleasingly melodramatic **museum** that uses shadowy dioramas and a ghoulish soundtrack to chronicle the events leading up to Olav's death. Nonetheless, the dioramas contain few artefacts of note, other than one or two bits of armour and jewellery dating from the period, and neither is the text particularly revealing, which is a pity, since something more could have been made of Olav's position in medieval Christian folklore. One such tale, passed down through the generations, relates how Olav spent the night on a remote Norwegian farm, only to discover the family praying over a pickled horse's penis. Expressing some irritation – but no surprise – at this pagan ceremony, Olav threw the phallus to the family dog and took the opportunity to explain some of the finer tenets of Christianity to his hosts. There's a second display on St Olav upstairs in the museum and this focuses on his cult and how it spread across Western Europe.

### The kirke

Daily: Sept–June 9am–6pm; July & Aug 9am–8pm • Free

The complex's **kirke**, across from the Kulturhus, is a much-modified, twelfth-century stone building, which reputedly marks the spot where Olav was stabbed to death. Claims that the stone on which the body was first laid out had been incorporated into the church's high altar were abandoned during the Reformation in case the Protestants decided to destroy it as blasphemous.

### The amfiteater and folkemuseet

Amphitheatre: open access; Folkemuseet: late June to mid-Aug daily 11am–4pm • Both sights free

The open-air **amfiteater** (amphitheatre) lies just up the hill from the Kulturhus and is where the colourful *Olsokspelet* (St Olav's Play), a costume drama, is performed each year as part of the **St Olav Festival**. This is held over several days either side of the anniversary of the battle, July 29, and thousands of Norwegians make the trek here; tickets need to be booked months in advance via the Kultursenter website. The amphitheatre adjoins an open-air **folkemuseet** (folk museum) containing a few indoor exhibits, and some thirty seventeenth- to nineteenth-century buildings moved here from all over rural Trøndelag.

### Middelaldergården Stiklastadir

Daily: Sept–June 9am–6pm; July & Aug 9am–8pm • Free

Opened in 2009, the **Middelaldergården Stiklastadir**, on the northern side of the Kultursenter, is an imposing, 36m-long replica medieval longhouse comprising a living space and a large banqueting hall, where the resident chieftain would hold feasts and meetings. During the summer, there are plenty of activities and games put on for children, as well as exhibitions, dramatized tours and Viking heritage theatre performances.

#### ARRIVAL AND DEPARTURE                                          STIKLESTAD

**By train & bus** Stiklestad is difficult to reach by public transport. The easiest option is to take the train from Trondheim to Verdal (2–3 daily; 1hr 40min; ⊛ www.nsb .no) and walk the last 6km; there is a local bus from Verdal train station to Stiklestad, but it is infrequent (Mon–Fri

1 daily; 5min; ⊛ rutebok.no). During the St Olav Festival, however, special trains and buses take visitors straight to the site from Trondheim – ask for details from Trondheim tourist office.

#### ACCOMMODATION AND EATING

**Stiklestad Hotel** Leksdalsveien 1 ☎ 74 04 42 00, ⊛ stiklestad.no. Attached to the main building of the cultural centre, this smart, modern hotel is one of the snazziest spots to stay in the area. Despite its focus on business and conference clientele, the rooms here have

oodles of character, with colourful blankets and pillows, lovely hardwood floors and art on the walls. The hotel also has a very decent restaurant where they serve Norwegian dishes with mains averaging 250kr. Restaurant daily 1–8pm. **1500kr**

## Steinkjer

The pleasant, undemanding town of **STEINKJER**, 120km from Trondheim, sits in the shadow of wooded hills, at the point where the river that gave the place its name empties into the fjord. The town was founded in the nineteenth century and achieved some importance as both a trading centre and as the site of a large infantry training camp, but the army base attracted the attention of the Luftwaffe who bombed Steinkjer to bits in 1940. The modern town that has grown up in its stead is a tidy, appealing ensemble that fans out from the long main street, Kongens gate.

#### ARRIVAL AND DEPARTURE                                          STEINKJER

**By train** Steinkjer train station is on Strandvegen in between the E6 and the town centre, which is a 5min walk away. Timetables on ⊛ www.nsb.no.
Destinations Bodø (2 daily; 7hr 45min); Mosjøen (2–3

daily; 3hr 20min); Trondheim (hourly; 2hr).
**By bus** Steinkjer's bus station is next to the train station, with regular services to and from Trondheim (3 daily; 2hr).

#### ACCOMMODATION AND EATING

**Café Madam Brix** Kirkegata 7 ☎ 74 16 74 60, ⊛ madambrix.no. Perhaps the best of Steinkjer's assorted cafés and restaurants, this cosy spot takes its name from

the redoubtable widow who founded an inn here in 1722. In addition to good coffee and cakes, they serve simple meals such as waffles and *smørrebrød* (from 40kr), as well

**5**

as a few wines. Mon–Wed 6–11pm, Thurs 11am–11pm, Fri & Sat 11am–2am.

**Quality Hotel Grand Steinkjer** Kongens gate 37 ☎ 74 16 47 00, ⓦ nordicchoicehotels.com. Right in the centre of town across from the train station, this hotel occupies a clumpy modern block, though the rooms on the upper floors more than redeem matters with their splendid views out along the coast. **1000kr**

## Snåsa

Heading north from Steinkjer along the E6, it's 6km to the point where the **Krystiksveien** (Hwy-17; see p.290) branches off to begin its superbly scenic 650-kilometre journey north to Bodø. Alternatively, the next target on the E6 – or even better along rural **Hwy-763** – is **SNÅSA** a sleepy, scattered hamlet at the top end of long and slender Lake Snåsavatn. It looks as if nothing much has happened here for decades, but Snåsa has one sight of note, a pretty little hilltop **church** of softly hued grey stone, dating from the Middle Ages and very much in the English style. Legend has it that the church marks the spot where St Olav paused to have a drink of water before the battle at Stiklestad; true or not, the church was a pit stop on the pilgrim route to Trondheim right up until the Reformation.

### ACCOMMODATION                                                                   SNÅSA

**Snåsa Hotell** Leiramoen, just off Hwy-763 and 6km from the E6 ☎ 74 15 10 57, ⓦ snasahotell.no. This inviting, modern hotel on Snåsa's western side is in a lovely setting overlooking the lake; its decor is somewhat dated, but the forty-odd guest rooms are comfortable and relaxing. The hotel also operates a small year-round campsite, with nine cabins as well as spaces for tents and caravans. There's a restaurant too, serving workaday but filling Norwegian staples (from 220kr), though if you're likely to arrive after 7pm, you should telephone ahead to check it will still be open. Camping **180kr**, cabins **450kr**, doubles **1250kr**

## Into Nordland: Laksforsen waterfalls

Beyond Snåsa, the **E6** leaves the wooded valleys of the Trøndelag for the wider, harsher landscapes of the province of **Nordland**. The road bobs across bleak plateaux and scuttles along rangy river valleys before reaching, after about 190km, the short (700m), signposted side-road that leads to the **Laksforsen** waterfalls, a well-known beauty spot where the River Vefsna takes a 17-metre tumble. The café here offers a grand view of the falls, which were once much favoured by British aristocrats for their salmon fishing.

## Mosjøen

Wedged between fjord, river and mountain, the town of **MOSJØEN**, 390km north of Trondheim, has a handsome setting, though the sprawling aluminium plant, which hogs the north side of the waterfront, is more than a little off-putting. Persevere, however, for Mosjøen was a small-time trading centre long before the factory arrived, and **Sjøgata**, down by the river just to the south of the plant, is lined by attractive old timber dwellings, warehouses and shops dating from the early nineteenth century. It's an appealing streetscape, especially as the buildings are still in everyday use, apart from the section that is now conserved as a museum.

---

### NORDLAND'S OPEN-AIR SCULPTURES

Dotted across the province of **Nordland** are 36 open-air **sculptures** by some of the world's leading contemporary sculptors, including Dorothy Cross, Anish Kapoor, Antony Gormley and Inge Mahn. Together these works comprise the **Skulpturlandskap** (ⓦ skulpturlandskap.no) and although many of the sculptures are in remote, even obscure locations, others – like Gormley's *Havmannen* in Mo-i-Rana (see opposite) – are very accessible.

**ARRIVAL AND INFORMATION** **MOSJØEN**

**By train** Mosjøen train station is beside the E6 on the north side of town in front of the aluminium plant. From here, it's a well-signed, 1km-long walk to the north end of Sjøgata. Timetables on ⓦ www.nsb.no.
Destinations Bodø (2 daily; 4hr); Fauske (2 daily; 3hr 30min); Mo-i-Rana (2–3 daily; 1hr); Steinkjer (2–3 daily; 3hr 30min); Trondheim (2–3 daily; 4hr 30min).

**By bus** Mosjøen bus station is on Strandgata, about 100m beyond the west end of Sjøgata. Timetables on ⓦ rutebok.no.
Destinations Mo-i-Rana (2 daily; 1hr 40min).

**Tourist office** Mosjøen tourist office is in the centre of town at Sjøgata 2 (late June to late Aug Mon–Fri 9am–6pm, Sat & Sun 11am–4pm; late Aug to late June Mon–Fri 10am–3pm; ☏ 75 01 80 00, ⓦ visithelgeland.com).

**ACCOMMODATION**

**Fru Haugans** Strandgata 39 ☏ 75 11 41 00, ⓦ fru haugans.no. There has been an inn here in the centre of Mosjøen since the eighteenth century – it's one of the oldest hotels in the north of Norway – and the present building comprises a well-judged amalgamation of the old and new. Still family-owned, the hotel has 129 rooms of neat, modern demeanour and the breakfasts are first rate. The River Vefsna flows beside the hotel and is a good place to catch sea-trout – and the hotel will loan you the necessary gubbins. **1400kr**

**De Historiske Gjestehusene** Sjøgata 22 ☏ 75 17 27 60, ⓦ kulturverkstedet.net. An enterprising local heritage association rents out rooms in several pleasantly renovated old wooden houses on and around Sjøgata. The rooms – and in some cases apartments – are simple and very vintage, which is all very appealing, though there is a considerable range in the pricing, with the smarter doubles going for as much as 1800kr. **1200kr**

**EATING**

**Ellenstuen** Fru Haugans hotel, Strandgata 39 ☏ 75 11 41 00, ⓦ fruhaugans.no. Like everywhere else, hotel restaurants in Norway vary enormously, but this one is especially good – smart but informal and offering tasty, mainly Norwegian, dishes from a seasonal menu that makes the most of local ingredients; main courses average 320kr. Daily 6–10pm.

**Kulturverkstedet Kafé** Sjøgata 22 ☏ 75 17 27 60, ⓦ kulturverkstedet.net. Operated by the same heritage association that organizes De Historiske Gjestehusene (see above), this charming – and charmingly old-fashioned – café serves good coffee and tasty Nordland pastries. Mon–Sat 8am–4pm.

# North from Mosjøen to Korgen

Heading north from Mosjøen, the **E6** cuts inland to weave across the mountains of the interior, while the **railway** stays glued to the seashore and the river valleys down below. Either way, it's an enjoyable journey, though the E6 has the scenic edge – despite tunnelling through the flanks of **Korgfjellet** rather than going over the top. The old road is, however, still open, offering panoramic views, its highest point marked by a motel and a **monument** honouring the 550 Yugoslav prisoners of war who built this section of the road during World War II. Just beyond Korgfjellet is the village of **Korgen**, sitting pretty beneath the mountains in the bend of a river. From here, the E6 slips down a river valley and sidles along the fjord to Mo-i-Rana, 90km from Mosjøen.

# Mo-i-Rana and around

Hugging the head of the Ranfjord, **MO-I-RANA**, or more usually "Mo", was known in Old Norse as *Móar*, or grassy lowland. Until World War II, it functioned as a minor port and market town, after which its fortunes – and appearance – were transformed by the construction of a steel plant. The plant dominated proceedings until the 1980s, when there was much economic diversification and the town began to clean itself up: the fjord shore was cleared of its industrial clutter and the E6 was rerouted to create the pleasantly spacious, surprisingly leafy town centre of today. A predominantly modern town, Mo is also home to a large and stern-looking statue, the **Havmannen** (Man of the Sea), which gazes determinedly down the fjord, the work of the British sculptor, **Antony Gormley**. The main reason to come to Mo, however, is as a base for visiting the east side of the **Svartisen glacier** and for exploring the region's caves, principally the **Grønligrotta**.

**5**

E6 to Trondheim

## Mo kirke

Per Hellerviks gate 8 • Late June to late Aug Mon–Fri 9am–6pm; at other times ring ☎ 75 12 33 00 to ask for the church to be opened • Free

On the southeast edge of the centre, **Mo kirke** is the best-looking building in town, its onion dome and ornate, balconied interior dating back to the 1830s. In front of the church is a **bust** commemorating Thomas van Westen (1682–1727), an evangelist-missionary who spearheaded early attempts to convert the Sámi, his efforts – if the surviving portraits are accurate – undoubtedly bolstered by his fantastically frilly ruffs. Next to the church, enclosed by a mossy stone wall, is a well-tended **graveyard**, which contains the graves of six Scots Guards killed hereabouts in May 1940 and a communal tomb for unidentified Soviet prisoners of war. It's actually a wonder that this communal tomb has survived at all. In 1951, in one of the lesser-known episodes in Norway's history, the government decided to dig up the bodies of many of the Soviet POWs who had been buried in Norway and consolidate the burial sites. In Mo-i-Rana feelings ran high over the integrity of the graves and several hundred protestors mobilized to prevent the dig – and the government backed off here if not elsewhere.

## The Grønligrotta

Skonseng • Guided tours mid-June to mid-Aug hourly every day 10am–6pm; late Aug every 2 hours daily 10am–4pm; 35min • 165kr • ☎ 75 13 25 86, ⓦ www.gronligrotta.no • 20km from Mo-i-Rana: head north along the E6 and after about 13km follow the signs to the cave (and Svartisen glacier)

The limestone and marble mountains to the north of Mo-i-Rana are riddled with caves. The most accessible is the limestone **Grønligrotta**, 20km north of Mo-i-Rana, where an easy guided tour follows a subterranean river and takes in a 400-metre-long underground chamber. Grønligrotta is lit by electric lights – it's the only illuminated cave in Scandinavia – and it makes for a pleasant outing on the way to, or back from, Lake Svartisvatnet and the Svartisen glacier (see opposite), which is reached via the same byroad.

## Svartisen glacier

**5**

35km from Mo-i-Rana · **Svartisvatnet lake boats** Mid-June to Aug 2–6 daily; 20min each way · 170kr return · ☎ 75 01 80 00 · **Guided tours** Day-long guided glacier hikes on Svartisen can be arranged through Mo-i-Rana's tourist office (see below); they cost 900kr and must be booked at least three days in advance

Norway's second largest glacier, **Svartisen** – literally "Black Ice" – covers roughly 370 square kilometres of mountain and valley between the E6 and the coast to the northwest of Mo-i-Rana. The glacier is divided into two sections – east and west – by the Vesterdal valley, though this cleft is a recent phenomenon: when it was surveyed in 1905, the glacier was one giant block, about twenty-five percent bigger than it is today, though the reasons for this shrinkage remain obscure. The highest parts of the glacier lie at around 1500m, but its tentacles reach down to about 170m – the lowest-lying glacial arms in mainland Europe.

One of the glacier's **eastern nodules** is within easy reach of Mo-i-Rana: to get there, drive north on the E6 for about 12km and then take the signed byroad to the glacier, a straightforward 23-kilometre trip running past the Grønligrotta caves (see opposite) and ending at the eastern tip of the ice-green, glacial lake **Svartisvatnet**, where you get a boat (see above), though note that services can't begin until the lake ice has melted – usually mid-June – so check with Mo-i-Rana tourist office before setting out. Viewed from the boat, the great convoluted folds of the glacier look rather like bluish-white custard, but close up, after a stiff 3km hike past the rocky detritus left by the retreating ice, the sheer size of the glacier becomes apparent – a mighty grinding and groaning wall of ice edged by a jumble of ice chunks, columns and boulders. The **west side** of the Svartisen glacier can be seen, and accessed from, the "Kystriksveien" Coastal Route along Hwy-17 (see box, p.290); and there are also guided tours to the glacier from Bodø (see p.292).

### ARRIVAL AND DEPARTURE

MO-I-RANA AND AROUND

**By train** Mo's train station, on Ole Tobias Olsens gate, is down by the fjord on the south side of the centre.

Destinations Bodø (2 daily; 3hr); Fauske (2 daily; 2hr 30min); Mosjøen (2–3 daily; 1hr); Steinkjer (2–3 daily; 4hr 30min); Trondheim (2–3 daily; 6hr 30min).

**By bus** Mo's bus station is beside Ole Tobias Olsens gate – and opposite the foot of the main pedestrianized drag, Jernbanegata.

**Car rental** There are a couple of outlets in town, including Hertz, just off the E6 on the south side of the centre at Stigerplatåveien 2 (☎ 98 20 55 99).

### INFORMATION AND ACTIVITIES

**Tourist office** Mo's tourist office is on the south side of the centre at Ole Tobias Olsens gate 3 (May to mid-Sept Mon–Fri 9am–8pm, Sat 9am–4pm & Sun 1–7pm; mid-Sept to April Mon–Fri 10am–3pm; ☎ 75 01 80 00, ⓦ visit helgeland.com). They issue a particularly useful and free booklet detailing the Hwy-17 Coastal Route (see box, p.290). They can also arrange a shared taxi ride to the Svartisen glacier (see above) and will check that the boats that give access to the glacier are running.

**Activities** Staff at the tourist office can make reservations for a wide range of guided excursions, from rafting, kayaking and fishing through to caving, climbing and trekking. The tourist office rents bicycles (advance reservations advised), though you have to be pretty fit to reach most local points of interest – and just forget it altogether if it's raining.

### ACCOMMODATION

**Fjordgården Hotell** Søndre gate 9 ☎ 75 12 10 50, ⓦ fjordgaarden.no. A popular stop with tour groups, this proficient modern hotel is a good budget option, though the rooms hardly fire the soul. It's located in an insipid part of town to the south of the centre and just off the E6. **900kr**

**Mo Hotell & Gjestegaard** Elias Blix gate 5 ☎ 75 15 22 11, ⓦ mo-gjestegaard.no. Tucked away in the back-streets near the church, this family-run guesthouse is a little heavy on the pine, but it's quiet and peaceful and the rooms are pleasant and homely. **900kr**

**Scandic Meyergården Hotell** Fridtjof Nansensgate 28 ☎ 75 13 40 00, ⓦ scandichotels.com. For the most part, this medium-sized chain hotel is a brisk and efficient affair housed in a nicely designed cubic block, but – perhaps rather incongruously – the much older lodge has survived too. Competitively priced and a short walk north of the train station, off Ole Tobias Olsens gate. **1200kr**

**5**

### THE KYSTRIKSVEIEN COASTAL ROUTE (HWY-17)

Branching off the E6 just beyond Steinkjer (see p.285), the tortuous **Kystriksveien** (ⓦrv17.no) – the **coastal route** along Hwy-17 – threads its way up the west coast, linking many villages that could formerly only be reached by sea. This is an obscure and remote corner of the country, but apart from the lovely scenery there's little of special appeal, and the six ferry trips that interrupt the 650-kilometre drive north to Bodø (there are no through buses) make it expensive and time-consuming in equal measure. A **free booklet** describing the route can be obtained at tourist offices throughout the region – including Mo – and it contains all of Hwy-17's car-ferry timetables.

Conveniently, the stretch of Hwy-17 between Mo-i-Rana and Bodø takes in most of the **scenic highlights**, can be negotiated in a day, and cuts out all but two of the ferry trips. To sample this part of the route, drive 35km west from Mo along Hwy-12 to the Hwy-17 crossroads, from where it's some 60km north to the **Kilboghamn–Jektvik** ferry (June–Aug every 1–2hr, Sept–May 3–5 daily; 1hr; driver & car 184kr) and a further 30km to the ferry linking **Ågskardet** with **Forøy** (every 1–2hr; 10min; driver & car 73kr). On the first ferry you cross the Arctic Circle with great views down and along the beautiful **Melfjord**, and on the second, after arriving at Forøy, the road cuts a handsome route along the north side of the slender **Holandsfjord** with a westerly arm of the Svartisen glacier (see p.289) glinting away across the water. From Forøy, it's about 140km to the Saltstraumen (see p.296) and 33km more to Bodø (see p.292).

### EATING

**No.3** Lars Meyersgate 3 ☎73 18 83 33, ⓦno3.no. In one of the town centre's nicest older buildings, this informal café-restaurant offers a tasty range of burgers (165–185kr) and more ambitious dishes such as cod wrapped in chorizo with shrimps and root vegetables (255kr). Mon–Thurs 11am–11pm, Fri & Sat 11am–2am.

**Søilen** Scandic Meyergården Hotell, Fridtjof Nansensgate 28 ☎75 13 40 00, ⓦmeyergarden.no. Quality hotel restaurant serving an excellent range of Norwegian dishes with local ingredients to the fore. Main courses here average around 300kr – less at lunchtimes or for the lighter options, burgers and so forth. A good place to try *bacalao* (295kr). Daily 1–10pm.

## The Arctic Circle: the Polarsirkelsenteret

Saltfjellveien (E6) • Mid-May to mid-Sept daily 8am–10pm • ☎91 85 38 33, ⓦpolarsirkelsenteret.no

Given its appeal as a travellers' totem, and considering the amount of effort it takes to actually get here, crossing the **Arctic Circle**, about 80km north of Mo-i-Rana, comes as a bit of a disappointment. Uninhabited for the most part, the landscape is undeniably bleak, but the gleaming **Polarsirkelsenteret** (Arctic Circle Centre) only serves to disfigure the scene, being a giant lampshade of a building plonked by the roadside and stuffed with every sort of tourist bauble imaginable. You'll whizz by on the bus, the train toots its whistle, and drivers can, of course, shoot past too, though the temptation to brave the crowds is strong. Inside, you should be able to resist the Arctic exhibition, but you'll probably get snared by the "Polarsirkelen" certificate and/or the specially stamped postcards. Less tackily, there are poignant reminders of crueller times back outside, where a couple of simple stone **memorials** pay tribute to the Yugoslav and Soviet POWs who laboured under terrible conditions to build the Arctic railroad – the **Nordlandsbanen** – to Narvik for the Germans in World War II.

## Saltfjellet-Svartisen Nasjonalpark

The louring mountains in the vicinity of the Polarsirkelsenteret are part of the **Saltfjellet**, a vast mountain plateau whose spindly pines, stern snow-tipped peaks and rippling moors extend west from the Swedish border to the Svartisen glacier. The E6 and the railway cut across this range between Mo-i-Rana and Rognan, providing access to the cairned hiking trails that lattice the Saltfjellet, most of which has been protected within the **Saltfjellet-Svartisen Nasjonalpark**. The region is, however, largely the preserve of experienced hikers: the trails are not sufficiently clear to dispense with a compass or equivalent, weather conditions can be treacherous and, although there's a good network of DNT-affiliated huts, none is staffed, nor do any of them supply provisions. Keys to these huts – most of which are owned by BOT, Bodø's hiking association (see p.294) – are available locally at the Nordland Nasjonalparksenter (see below), but clearly you have to arrange this before hiking out.

Among several possible bases for venturing into the national park, two of the more accessible are solitary **LØNSDAL**, on the plateau beside the E6 about 100km north of Mo, and the hamlet of **ROGNAN**, also on the E6 but down beside the Saltdalsfjord, about 150km from Mo; both have train stations.

### ARRIVAL AND INFORMATION

**By train, Lønsdal** The train station at Lønsdal occupies a lonely location on the Saltfjellet plateau, just off the E6 and 200m or so from the *Saltfjellet Hotell Polarsirkelen* (see below). It's a request stop only – so notify the conductor.
Destinations Bodø (2–3 daily; 1hr 30min); Fauske (2–3 daily; 1hr); Rognan (2–3 daily; 40min); Trondheim (2–3 daily; 8hr).
**By train, Rognan** The train station at Rognan is on the south side of the centre, just over 1km from the harbourfront – and the *Rognan Hotell* (see below).

### SALTFJELLET-SVARTISEN NASJONALPARK

Destinations Bodø (2–3 daily; 1hr 10min); Fauske (2–3 daily; 30min); Lønsdal (2–3 daily; 40min; request stop); Trondheim (2–3 daily; 8hr 30min).
**Tourist office** The Nordland Nasjonalparksenter (mid-April to May, Sept & Oct Tues–Sun 10am–3pm; June–Aug daily 10am–5pm; ☎40 06 72 51, ⊚nordlandsnaturen.no) will advise on all things to do with the region's national parks – including hiking. It's located in the tiny village of Storjord at the junction of the E6 and Hwy-77 – 12km north of Lønsdal.

### ACCOMMODATION

**Rognan Hotell** Håndverkeren 14 ☎75 69 00 11, ⊚rognanhotell.no. In a prime waterside setting in the hamlet of Rognan, this medium-sized hotel has attractive public rooms, including a spacious outdoor terrace, and modest guest rooms. **1200kr**
**Saltfjellet Hotell Polarsirkelen** Lønsdal ☎75 69 41 22, ⊚saltfjellethotell.no. Set in a long wooden lodge

in a solitary, wilderness location, and with a cosy modern interior, this appealing hotel has fifty spick-and-span modern rooms – and the only restaurant for miles around with mains costing in the region of 250kr – try the reindeer. It's down a kilometre-long side-road off the E6 on the way to Lønsdal train station. Restaurant: summer daily noon–9pm; rest of year – call ahead for times. **1250kr**

## The Krigskirkegårder

Just after Rognan, a signed 1km-long byroad leads up from **BOTN** to the **Krigskirkegårder**, truly one of Nordland's most mournful and moving places. Buried here, in a wooded glade high above the fjord, are the Yugoslav prisoners of war and their German captors who died in this part of Nordland during World War II. The men are interred in two separate graveyards – both immaculately maintained, though, unlike the plainer Yugoslav cemetery, the German graveyard is entered by a sturdy granite gateway. The Yugoslavs, who were mostly Tito partisans, died in their hundreds from disease, cold and malnutrition, as well as torture and random murder, as they struggled to build the **Arctic railroad** to the iron-ore port of Narvik. When the Germans occupied Norway in 1940, the railway ended at Mosjøen, but they decided to push it north so that their cargo ships might avoid the dangerous voyage along the coast. This line, the **Nordlandsbanen**, involved the labour of 13,000 POWs, but the Germans failed to complete it, and it was not until 1962 that the railway finally reached Bodø.

## Fauske

Aside from a brief stretch of line from Narvik into Sweden (see p.302), **FAUSKE** marks the northernmost point of the Norwegian rail network and is, as a consequence, an important transport hub. Nonetheless, there's no strong reason to linger here – nearby

5

Bodø is a much more palatable place to stay – though it's still a handy place to break your journey. The town's main drag, **Storgata**, doubles as the E6, running parallel to the fjord and holding the handful of shops that passes for the town centre.

## ARRIVAL AND DEPARTURE FAUSKE

**By train** Fauske's train station is on Jernbanegata, a 5–10min walk uphill from the centre of town via Follaveien (E6).

Destinations Bodø (2 daily; 40min); Mo-i-Rana (2 daily; 2hr 30min); Mosjøen (2 daily; 3hr 30min); Steinkjer (2 daily; 7hr); Trondheim (2 daily; 9hr).

**By bus** Long-distance buses stop beside the train station. Bus tickets can be purchased from the driver or in advance online or at any bus station. Timetables on ⓦ rutebuk.no.

Destinations Bodø (1–3 daily; 1hr 15min); Sortland (1–3 daily; 5hr 15min).

**Bus routes north** Fauske bus station is the departure point for the express bus to Narvik (2 daily; 4hr 30min), a gorgeous run with the E6 careering round the mountains and along a series of blue-black fjords. At Narvik, you change for the bus to Tromsø (1–3 daily; 4hr 15min), changing here again for Alta (1 daily; 6hr 30min). It's also possible to go straight from Narvik to Alta, but this involves two changes and takes about 9hr. From Alta, the Nordkappexpressen runs to Honningsvåg (1–3 daily; 4hr), near Nordkapp. From May to September, one Nordkappexpressen bus daily continues on from Honningsvåg to Nordkapp (45min).

## ACCOMMODATION

**Fauske Hotell** Storgata 82 ☏ 75 60 20 00, ⓦ fauske hotell.no. This hotel is a chunky square block whose interior is made slightly sickly by a surfeit of salmon-coloured streaky marble. Quarried locally, the marble is exported all over the world, but is something of an acquired taste. Otherwise, the hotel is a pleasant pit stop with comfortable rooms, and the breakfasts are large and tasty. **1400kr**

**Lundhøgda Camping og Motell** Lundveien 62 ☏ 97 53 98 94, ⓦ lundhogdacamping.no. This small and congenial campsite occupies a splendid location down on a slender peninsula about 3km west of the town centre, overlooking the mountains and the fjord: head out of town along the E80 (the Bodø road), then turn down a signposted country lane, ablaze with wild flowers in the summertime and flanked by old timber buildings. Cabins and motel-style rooms too. Camping **250kr**, motel & cabins **800kr**

## Bodø and around

The bustling port of **BODØ**, some 55km west of Fauske, was founded in 1816, but it wasn't until the herring boom of the 1860s that the place really began to thrive, its harbourfront crowded with the net-menders, coopers, oilskin-makers and canneries that kept the fishing fleet at sea. Later, it accumulated several industrial plants and became an important regional centre, thereby attracting the attentions of the Luftwaffe whose bombs pretty much destroyed all the proud, nineteenth-century buildings that once flanked the waterfront. Nonetheless, Bodø manages a cheerful modernity, a bright and breezy place that rambles over a low-lying peninsula, which pokes out into the Saltfjord, its long and narrow centre concentrated along two parallel streets, Sjøgata and Storgata.

Bodø has long been a regular stop for the Hurtigruten coastal boat route, and is also within comfortable striking distance of two very different attractions – the delightful former trading post of **Kjerringøy**, to the north of Bodø, and the **Saltstraumen** tidal flux, round the fjord to the southeast. Perhaps most important of all, however, is that it is the best place from which to hop over to the choicest parts of the Lofoten islands (see pp.315–335).

### Norsk Luftfartsmuseum

Olav V gate • Mid-June to mid-Aug daily 10am–6pm; mid-Aug to Dec & Feb to mid-June Mon–Fri 10am–4pm, Sat & Sun 11am–5pm • 120kr • ☏ 75 50 78 50, ⓦ luftfartsmuseum.no

Easily Bodø's most popular attraction is the **Norsk Luftfartsmuseum** (Norwegian Aviation Museum), 2km southeast of the centre, which holds a large and imaginative exhibition that tracks through the history of Norwegian aviation. It adopts an imaginative approach to its subject right down to the building itself, which is

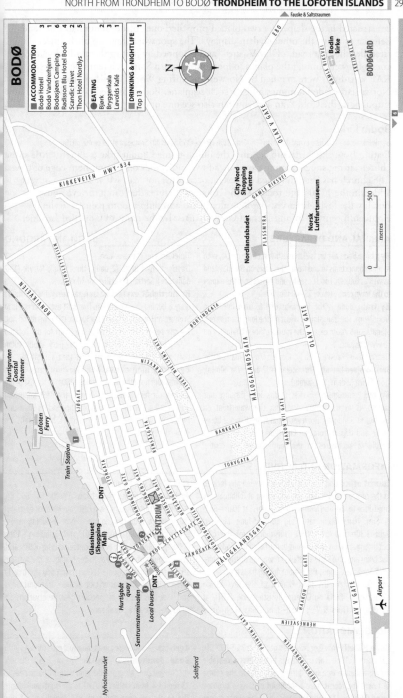

**BODØ**

■ ACCOMMODATION
| Bodø Hotell | 3 |
| Bodø Vandrerhjem | 1 |
| Bodøsjøen Camping | 6 |
| Radisson Blu Hotel Bodø | 4 |
| Scandic Havet | 2 |
| Thon Hotel Nordlys | 5 |

● EATING
| Bjørk | 2 |
| Bryggerikaia | 3 |
| Løvolds Kafé | 1 |

■ DRINKING & NIGHTLIFE
| Top 13 | 1 |

5

**5**

constructed in the shape of a two-bladed propeller: one "blade" houses air force and defence exhibits, the other civilian displays. The spot where the two blades meet straddles the ring road – Olav V gate – and is topped by part of the old Bodø airport control tower. Among the planes to look out for are a Spitfire, a reminder that two RAF squadrons were manned by Norwegians during World War II, and a rare Norwegian-made Hønningstad C-5 Polar seaplane. Bodø was used by the US Air Force throughout the Cold War, and you can also see one of their U2 spy planes.

## Bodin kirke

Gamle Riksvei 68 • Late June to mid-Aug Mon–Fri 10am–3pm • Free • ☎ 75 50 03 00 • Southeast of the centre, off Hwy-80

Dating from the thirteenth century, the onion-domed **Bodin kirke** is a pretty little stone church sitting snugly among clover meadows and woods on the southern edge of town. The church has been modified on several occasions, not least when the transept was added in the 1780s, but today it's the colourful fixtures that catch the eye, most notably the lovingly carved Baroque altarboard and pulpit, both painted in the eighteenth century by an itinerant German artist by the name of Gottfried Ezechiel.

### ARRIVAL AND DEPARTURE

### BODØ AND AROUND

**By plane** Bodø airport is 2km southwest of the centre, with regular connections to and from other cities on the mainland as well as Lofoten. Local buses #1 and #4 run from the airport to the town centre (every 25–40min; 10min).

**By train** Bodø is the terminus of the train line from Trondheim. The train station is just off the long main street, Sjøgata, and 700m east of the tourist office. Timetables on ⓦ www.nsb.no.

Destinations Fauske (2 daily; 40min); Mo-i-Rana (2 daily; 3hr); Mosjøen (2 daily; 4hr); Steinkjer (2 daily; 7hr 40min); Trondheim (2 daily; 9hr 40min).

**By bus** Sentrumsterminalen, Bodø's long-distance bus station, is in the centre down on the waterfront on Sjøgata at Sandgata. However, some long-distance buses arrive and depart from the City Nord shopping centre a couple of kilometres to the southeast of the centre.

Timetables on ⓦ rutebok.no.

Destinations Fauske (2 daily; 1hr 15min); Narvik (1–2 daily; 6hr); Sortland (1 daily; 6hr 30min).

**By Hurtigbåt express passenger ferry** The Hurtigbåt quay is behind the bus station. The most useful service is to Svolvær, on Lofoten (1 daily; 3hr 30min; ⓦ 177nordland.no).

**By car ferry** Bodø is the main ferry port for the Lofoten (see p.316). Ferries depart from the jetty about 400m northeast along the waterfront from the train station.

**By Hurtigruten coastal boat** The Hurtigruten dock is about 600m from the train station – 200m or so east of the Lofoten car ferry jetty. Southbound, the next important port of call is Trondheim (24hr); northbound it's Stamsund (4hr), Svolvær (6hr) and Sortland (12hr). Details on ⓦ hurtigruten.co.uk.

### INFORMATION AND ACTIVITIES

**Tourist office** Bodø tourist office is conveniently located in the centre and down by the waterfront at Tollbugata 13 (mid-June to late Aug Mon–Fri 9am–8pm, Sat 10am–6pm & Sun 10am–6pm; late Aug to mid-June Mon–Fri 9am–3.30pm; ☎ 75 54 80 00, ⓦ visitbodo.com). They give out information on connections to the Lofoten islands, rent out bikes and also issue a detailed town and district guide.

**DNT** For advice about the region's hiking trails and cabins, you can contact the local branch of the DNT hiking organization, Bodø og Omegns Turistforening (BOT), at Sandgata 3 (Tues & Wed noon–3pm, Thurs noon–5pm;

☎ 75 52 14 13, ⓦ bot.no).

**Activities** Nordland Turselskap (☎ 90 63 60 86, ⓦ nordlandturselskap.no) is a first-rate outdoor specialist that offers a wide-ranging programme including moose safaris (June–Aug; 5hr; 800kr), rock climbing (12hr; 3000kr), caving (5–8hr; 800kr), canoeing (5hr; 600kr) and, most popular of all, guided glacier hiking on the western arm of the Svartisen, some 160km from Bodø via Hwy-17 (12hr; 1200kr). The glacier tour includes transport there and back plus the use of specialist gear. Reservations are advised – at least a day ahead.

### ACCOMMODATION

**Bodø Hotell** Professor Schyttes gate 5 ☎ 75 54 77 00, ⓦ bodohotell.no. This mid-range hotel offers acceptable accommodation in a five-storey block right in the centre of town. The rooms have a modicum of class – exposed wood floors and the odd Persian carpet is about as chic as

it gets here – and there are all the usual mod cons. **1300kr**

**Bodø Vandrerhjem** Sjøgata 57 ☎ 75 50 80 48, ⓦ hihostels.no. All-year, HI-hostel with 71 bunk beds in 23 rooms – from singles (695kr) to an eight-bunk dorm. The rooms are neat and trim in a frugal sort of way (depending on who you are sharing with of course), and there are self-catering facilities, a common room and a laundry. Handily located in a three-storey, red-brick block next to the train station. Dorms 325kr, doubles 840kr

**Bodøsjøen Camping** Båtstøveien 1 ☎ 75 56 36 80, ⓦ bodocamp.no. This year-round fjordside campsite is roughly 3km southeast of the centre, not far from the Bodin kirke (see p.294). Flanked by a ridge of evergreens and spread over a somewhat bleak-looking field are a set of cabins of various shapes and sizes, the smallest just a single small room with two beds. Cabins 250kr, camping 260kr

**Radisson Blu Hotel Bodø** Storgata 2 ☎ 75 51 90 00, ⓦ radissonblu.com. The largest hotel in town occupies a modern concrete-and-glass tower: the rooms are comfortable and decorated in a variety of bright and breeezy styles, which makes them feel a little less corporate then many chains. Those on the upper floors have splendid views out to sea. 1300kr

★**Scandic Havet** Tollbugata 5 ☎ 75 50 38 00, ⓦ scandichotels.com. Chain hotel it may be, but the *Havet* has fair claim to be Bodø's best, its commodious, well-appointed rooms occupying a large, bright-white and L-shaped tower block down on the water's edge. The views are better the higher you go. There are around 230 guest rooms here plus a gym and bike hire. 1500kr

**Thon Hotel Nordlys** Moloveien 14 ☎ 75 53 19 00, ⓦ thonhotels.no. This smart and modern chain hotel is right on the harbourfront, and most of the 147 guest rooms have some kind of sea view. The accommodation isn't anything special, and there is little doubt you're in a chain property – it's largely marketed at businesspeople – but the location is about as good as it gets. 1300kr

## EATING

**Bjørk** Glashuset Shopping Centre, Storgata 8 ☎ 75 52 40 40, ⓦ restaurantbjork.no. Pizza, pasta, sandwiches, steaks, catch of the day, even sushi – this is one of those places that tries to do it all. Its reputation as one of northern Norway's best restaurants might seem a bit of a stretch, but they do make tasty seafood dishes, and the place actually pulls off its modern rustic-style interior fairly well. Large dinner mains start at 300kr; lunches cost around 180kr, burgers 200kr. Reservations recommended. Mon–Sat 10am–10pm, Sun 3–10pm.

**Bryggerikaia** Sjøgata 1 ☎ 75 52 58 08, ⓦ bryggerikaia .no. Attractive and modern café/restaurant, where you can pop in for a coffee or a beer or sample some excellent seafood with mains from around 200kr. The veranda offers harbour views and look out for their special buffet deals. Mon–Sat 11am–11pm, Sun noon–11pm.

**Løvolds Kafé** Tollbugata 9 ☎ 75 52 02 61. Long-established, inexpensive, quayside eatery-cum-canteen, where they serve up traditional Norwegian dishes – try the meat balls. Main courses average around 140kr. Mon–Fri 9am–6pm, Sat 9am–3pm.

## DRINKING

**Top 13** Radisson Blu Hotel Bodø, Storgata 2 ☎ 75 51 90 00. Rooftop bar with the best views in town. It only holds about a hundred people, who hover around a few vinyl couches and chairs, so don't be surprised if it's rammed on the weekend. Mon–Thurs 6pm–12.30am, Fri 4pm–2.30am, Sat 11am–2.30am.

## Kjerringøy trading post

Kjerringøy • Mid-May to Aug daily 11am–5pm; guided tours hourly on the hour • 100kr • ☎ 75 50 35 05, ⓦ nordlandsmuseet.no

The **Kjerringøy handelssted** (trading post), 40km north of Bodø, boasts a superbly preserved collection of nineteenth-century timber buildings set beside a slender, islet-sheltered channel. This was once the domain of the **Zahl family**, merchants who supplied the fishermen of Lofoten with everything from manufactured goods and clothes to farmyard foodstuffs in return for fish. It was not, however, an equal relationship: the Zahls, who operated a local monopoly until the 1910s, could dictate the price they paid for the fish, and many of the islanders were permanently indebted to them. This social division is still very much in evidence at the trading post, where there's a marked distinction between the guest rooms of the main house and the fishermen's bunk beds in the boat- and cookhouses. Indeed, the **family house** is remarkably fastidious, with its Italianate busts and embroidered curtains – even the medicine cabinet is well stocked with formidable Victorian remedies like the bottle of "Sicilian Hair Renewer". Also of interest is the old barn, the Zahlfjøsen, where there's a modest display on the life and work of the novelist Knut Hamsun (see p.298).

There are enjoyable, hour-long **guided tours** around the main house throughout the summer, and afterwards you can nose around the reconstructed general store, drop in at the café and stroll the fine sandy beach. Taken altogether, it's an especially peaceful

**5**

and picturesque spot and one that filmgoers may recognize from the movie *I am Dina*, based on *Dina's Book*, by the Norwegian author Herbjørg Wassmo, which was filmed here in the early 2000s.

### ARRIVAL AND DEPARTURE                                KJERRINGØY TRADING POST

**By car and car ferry** Getting from Bodø to Kjerringøy by car is easy enough – a straightforward coastal drive north via Hwy-834 and then Hwy-571 and including a ferry ride from Festvåg to Misten (every 30min–1hr 30min; 10min; car & driver 73kr, passenger 30kr; ☎177, ⓦ177nordland.no).

**By bus** There's one bus daily in each direction between Bodø bus station and Kjerringøy, but the timetable is such that you can't usually get there and back on the same day. Pick up a combined bus-and-ferry timetable at Bodø tourist office.

### ACCOMMODATION AND EATING

**Kjerringøy Havn Bryggehotell** Kaiveien ☎76 30 38 22, ⓦkjerringoybrygge.no. By the fjord just along the coast from the Kjerringøy trading post – and signed from Hwy-571 – is this small, family-owned hotel and conference centre.

It occupies a smart, two-storey timber structure, where the wide-windowed rooms look out over the water. There's a restaurant here too with mains averaging 260kr. Restaurant: daily 3–9pm. <u>**1550kr**</u>

### The Saltstraumen

The maelstrom called **Saltstraumen**, located beside Hwy-17 about 30km from Bodø round the Saltfjord, is a much-publicized phenomenon, whereby billions of gallons of water are forced through a narrow, 150m-wide channel four times a day at speeds of up to 10 knots. It's caused by this part of the ocean having a huge variation in high and low tides and the resulting eddy, one of the world's strongest tidal-current maelstroms, can reach 10m in diameter and 5m in depth with the vibration sometimes producing an uncanny yelping sound. The whirling creamy water is at its most turbulent at high tide, and its most violent when the moon is new or full – a lunar/tidal timetable is available from Bodø tourist office. You can watch the unfurling of the maelstrom from the **bridge** over the channel, though frankly this can be something of an anticlimax as the scenery hereabouts is – by Norwegian standards at least – flat and dull. Fortunately, there are other things to occupy visitors, especially if you're after a bit of **fishing**: the force of the water pulls in all sorts of fish including cod, catfish and coalfish. Bodø tourist office (see p.294) will brief you as to **fishing regulations** and as to where you can rent a rod. The fish also attract significant numbers of sea eagles, which are at their most visible during the colder months.

### ARRIVAL AND DEPARTURE                                     THE SALTSTRAUMEN

**By car** It's a straightforward drive from Bodø to the Saltstraumen – allow 50min.

**By bus** There's a good local bus service direct from Bodø

to the Saltstraumen (5 daily; 1hr; ⓦrutebok.no), though bus times won't necessarily coincide with high tide.

### EATING

**Kafé Kjelen** Saltstraumen ☎75 58 75 29, ⓦkafekjelen .no. Painted red, this cosy little café on the east side of the bridge has a terrace with great views over the maelstrom. It serves soups, salads and substantial fish and meat dishes. Try their *møsbrømlefse*, a traditional,

burrito-like pancake stuffed with a mix of sweet brown-cheese sauce, sour cream and melted butter (70kr). Late June to mid-Aug daily 10am–10pm; early June & late Aug daily noon–8pm; May daily noon–6pm; Sept–April restricted hours – see website.

# North from Fauske to Narvik

The 250-kilometre gambol north from Fauske to Narvik is spectacular, with the **E6** rounding the fjords, twisting and tunnelling through the mountains and rushing over high, pine-dusted plateaux. The scenery is the main event hereabouts, and there's little to merit a stop, with one notable exception – the fascinating old crofter's farmstead at

**FROM TOP** NARVIK (P.300); KJERRINGØY TRADING POST (P.295) >

**5**

Kjelvik, where the hardship of rural life hereabouts is revealed in idyllic surroundings. A further option is to make the short detour west along **Hwy-81** to the island of **Hamarøy**, where the writer **Knut Hamsun** was raised – his controversial life and times now recalled at the lavish **Hamsunsenteret**. Hwy-81 continues onto the Skutvik ferry to the Lofoten (see pp.315–335), but Hamarøy has one more place of interest on another byroad, the remote and relaxing village of **Tranøy**, where you can stay in a lighthouse or at one of the region's best hotels. Back on the E6, the next port of call is **Narvik**, an eminently likeable industrial town that witnessed some especially fierce fighting during the German invasion of 1940. It's a good place for an overnight stop and a useful launching pad for the long haul to the far north, or a visit to the Vesterålen and Lofoten islands.

## ARRIVAL AND DEPARTURE

**By bus** Bodø and Fauske are the most northerly stations on the Norwegian train network, their respective bus stations providing express services onwards north to Narvik: Bodø to Narvik (2 daily; 6hr 10min); Fauske to Narvik (2 daily; 4hr 30min; ⓦ rutebok.no).

**By car and ferry** Between Fauske and Narvik, the E6 is interrupted by the Tysfjord, which you cross on the Bognes-Skarberget car ferry (every 1–2hr; 25min; car & driver 107kr, passengers 39kr; ⓦ ruteinfo.thn.no); Skarberget is 80km from Narvik. These ferries work on a first-come,

first-served basis, and in summer it's worth arriving 2hr before departure to be sure of a space.

**Ferries to Lofoten and Vesterålen** On the E6 between Fauske and Narvik, there are car ferries from Bognes to Lødingen (see p.306), which is handy for onward journeys to both the Vesterålen and the Lofoten. There are also summertime car ferries from Skutvik to Svolvær, on the Lofoten (see p.318); Skutvik is 35km to the west of the E6 along Hwy-81, which forks off the E6 about 140km from Fauske.

## Husmannsplassen Kjelvik

Kjelvik • **Farm** Open access • Free • **Museum** Mid-June to mid-Aug Tues–Sun 11am–5pm • 60kr • ☎ 75 50 35 00 or ☎ 48 20 51 69, ⓦ nordlandsmuseet.no • The signed, 5min-long path up to the farmstead begins beside the E6

The old crofter's farmstead of **Husmannsplassen Kjelvik**, 56km north of Fauske, occupies a beautiful spot with a scattering of old wooden buildings, including a cottage, woodshed, forge and mill, nestling in a green, wooded valley. Tenant farmers worked the land here until 1967, when they finally gave up their battle against the harsh isolation. They had no electricity or running water, the soil was thin, and the only contact with the outside world was by boat – supply vessels would come up the Leirfjord to the Kjelvik jetty, from where it was a steep two-kilometre hike to the farm, 200m above the fjord. Today, the **farm**, which is kept in good condition, is a pleasure to explore and you can follow the old footpath down to the Kjelvik jetty. During **museum** opening hours, volunteers illuminate life on the farm and serve *lefse*, a traditional soft Norwegian flat bread, with butter and sugar. On special occasions, they bake flatbread in the cookhouse – and visitors are welcome to join in the baking.

## Kråkmo

Beyond Kjelvik, the E6 bores through the mountains to reach, after about 40km, the couple of houses that make up **KRÅKMO**, with the lake on one side and the domineering mass of a mighty mountain, **Kråkmotind**, on the other, its distinctive shape reminiscent of a giant anvil. From Kråkmo, it's another 40km or so to the turning for Hamarøy.

## Hamarøy

The large and jigsaw-like island of **Hamarøy**, which begins 15km west of the E6 along Hwy-81, is noteworthy as the boyhood home of the writer **Knut Hamsun** (1859–1952). Long a leading literary light, Hamsun blotted his Norwegian copybook with his admiration for Hitler and the Nazis before, during and after the occupation, though his culpability (as distinct from senility) has been the subject of much debate. Whatever the truth, Hamsun remained something of a hate figure for several decades and only recently has there been a degree of rehabilitation – as witnessed by the opening of several Hamsun-related sites on this, his home island, most notably the **Hamsunsenteret**.

## Hamsunsenteret

Presteid • June to late Aug daily 10am–6pm; late Aug to Dec & Feb–May Tues–Fri 10am to 3.30pm, Sat & Sun 11am–5pm • 120kr • ☎ 75 50 34 50, ⓦ hamsunsenteret.no • The centre is located just beyond the causeway (Hwy-81) linking the mainland with Hamarøy

The most important Hamsun site by a long stretch is the **Hamsunsenteret** (Hamsun Centre), 15km from the E6, not least because of the building itself: opened in 2009, and designed by the American architect Steven Holl, it comprises an auditorium with a telescopic amphitheatre and a six-storey structure, which rises high above the forested shoreline like some sort of medieval siege tower. Inside, a series of extensive displays explore Hamsun's life, works and times, without dodging the man's ferocious politics. In 1945, asked to pen an obituary for Hitler, Hamsun wrote "Hitler was a warrior, a warrior for humankind and a preacher of the gospel of justice for all nations".

## Hamsuns barndomshjem

Hamsund • Mid-June to mid-Aug daily 11am–6pm • 60kr • ☎ 75 50 34 50, ⓦ hamsunsenteret.no

From the Hamsunsenteret, it's another 7km or so along Hwy-81 to tiny **HAMSUND**, where the writer's boyhood home, a substantial, turf-roofed, ochre-painted house sitting in a wide valley, has been preserved as the **Hamsuns barndomshjem** (Hamsun's Boyhood Home). From here, it's 16km to the Skutvik ferry over to Lofoten (see pp.315–335), or you can retrace your steps and then proceed north up to Tranøy.

## Tranøy

In between Hamsund and the Hamsunsenteret, **Hwy-665** branches north for the 14km-long journey to the northern tip of Hamarøy, where a wide and mostly flat headland is fretted and shredded by fjords and inlets. On the eastern side of the headland lies the sprawling hamlet of **TRANØY** – peaceful and quiet and with two good places to stay, but the pick of the lodgings is at the **Tranøy Fyr** (lighthouse) on the western side of the headland.

### Hamsungalleriet

Tranøy • June–Aug daily 11am–6pm • Free • ☎ 48 22 71 51, ⓦ www.tranoy-galleri.com

Located in the old general store where Hamsun worked as a youth, the **Hamsungalleriet** (Hamsun Gallery) features paintings influenced by the local landscape and Hamsun's writings. More impressive, however, is the permanent open-air exhibition out on the rocks just a short stroll from the gallery, showing nature-related pictures in a stunning setting.

---

**ACCOMMODATION AND EATING**                                      **TRANØY**

**Edvardas hus** Tranøy, beside Hwy-665 ☎ 75 77 21 82, ⓦ edvardashus.no. A family-run hotel occupying two old buildings set a couple of hundred metres apart – one is a merchant's house dating back to the 1910s, the other a former bank built a decade later. There are nine, impeccably stylish, extremely comfortable bedrooms here and the food is outstanding – both at breakfast and in the evening, when a three-course set dinner is served at 7pm (515kr); reservations are essential. **1400kr**

**Svolværing** Tranøy ☎ 95 04 22 82. The best spot for a drink hereabouts is in this old whaling-boat-turned-pub down beside the harbour. They also serve tasty fish dishes (250kr), with seating both outside and in. Mid-June to mid-Aug daily 11am–1am.

★ **Tranøy Fyr** Tranøy ☎ 99 70 44 99, ⓦ tranoyfyr.no. About 3km from Tranøy, this red-and-white-striped, nineteenth-century lighthouse stands on a tiny islet, which is connected to the mainland by a dinky little pedestrian

**5**

bridge. The coast here is rocky and bare, seabirds abound and the views are magnificent, making this one of the region's most atmospheric places to stay. There are a dozen or so pleasantly and simply decorated rooms in the old lighthousemens' quarters, as well as a newer annexe, and there's a good small café-restaurant too, with seafood the house speciality (mains average 260kr). May–Sept. <u>1300kr</u>

## Narvik

A relatively modern town, **NARVIK** was established just over a century ago as an ice-free port to handle the iron ore brought here by train from the mines in northern Sweden, its first wave of settlers the navvies who built the connecting railway line, the **Ofotbanen** (see box, p.302). Even today, the town makes no bones about what is still its main function with the **iron-ore docks** immediately conspicuous, slap-bang in the centre, the rust-coloured machinery overwhelming much of the waterfront. Yet, for all the mess, the industrial complex is strangely impressive, its cat's cradle of walkways, conveyor belts, cranes and funnels oddly beguiling and giving the town a frontier, very Arctic, feel. In similar vein, the **town centre** may lack grace, but it still musters a certain breezy northern charm, though many of its brick and concrete buildings are replacements for the wooden houses that were destroyed during World War II, when Narvik witnessed fierce fighting for control of the harbour and its iron-ore terminal. Of late, Narvik has also had a fair old stab at reinventing itself: its main street has been freshened up by the addition of several prestige buildings and its wild surroundings have made it something of an **adventure sports** centre. Many extreme sports enthusiasts – hang- and paragliders, for example – come here under their own steam,

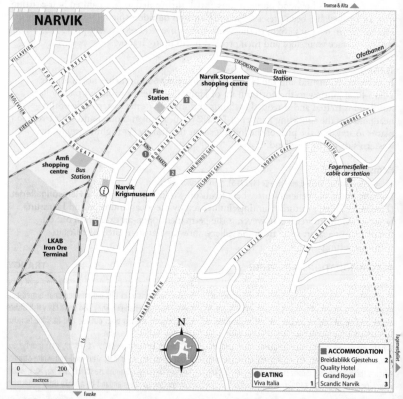

but Narvik does have a number of adventure tour companies, who mostly stick to hiking, mountain biking, climbing and skiing.

**5**

## Narvik Krigsmuseum

Kongens gate 39 • June–Aug Mon–Fri 10am–8pm, Sat 10am–6pm, Sun noon–6pm; Sept–May Mon–Sat 10am–4pm, Sun noon–4pm, but check website for times as they may vary • 100kr • ☎ 76 94 44 26, ⓦ warmuseum.no

The fascinating **Narvik Krigsmuseum** (Narvik War Museum), in the same building as the tourist office (see below), tracks through the general course of World War II as it affected Norway and zeroes in on Narvik, from the German saturation bombing of the town through to the bitter and bloody sea and air battles in which hundreds of foreign servicemen died alongside a swathe of the local population. It was a complicated campaign, with the German invasion of April 1940 followed by an Allied counterattack spearheaded by the Royal Navy. The Allies actually recaptured Narvik, driving the Germans into the mountains, but were hurriedly evacuated when Hitler launched his invasion of France. The fight for Narvik lasted two months and the German commander wrote of the sea change among his Norwegian adversaries, who became much more determined soldiers, and skilled ones at that: many were crack shots from their hunting days and all could ski. In the short term, this change of attitude prefigured the formation of the Resistance; in the long term it pretty much put paid to Norway's traditional isolationism. Several sections of the museum are especially moving, notably the one dealing with punishment and genocide, the other featuring live recordings of some of the participants.

## Fagernesfjellet cable car

Skistua • Mid-June to late July daily 1pm–1am; late July to Aug daily 1–8pm; Dec–April Mon–Fri 5–8pm, Sat & Sun 10am–5pm • 160kr return • ☎ 90 54 00 88, ⓦ narvikfjellet.no • A stiff 15min walk from the town centre, up behind the train station

Narvik's **Fagernesfjellet cable car** is the easiest way to reach the town's mountainous environs, whisking passengers up the first 656m of the mighty **Fagernesfjellet**. There's a café and viewing point at the top of the cable car, and from here, on a clear day, you can experience the midnight sun in all its glory (end of May to mid-July). In addition, **hiking trails** delve further into the mountains, and in the winter season, from late November to early May, the cable car provides a shuttle service for **skiers** and **snowboarders**. The network of skiing facilities includes several ski lifts, prepared slopes and unlimited off-piste skiing, with some floodlit areas; for further details contact the tourist office or check the website. The cable car stops running in windy or foggy conditions, so you might want to check it's operating before setting out.

**By train** Narvik train station is at the north end of the town centre, just off the main drag (the E6) on Stasjonsveien; it's the terminus of the Ofotbanen line from Sweden (see box, p.302).

**By bus** The bus station abuts the Amfi shopping centre, just off the main street on the south side of the town

centre. Timetables on ⓦ rutebok.no.

Destinations Å (1–2 daily; 8hr); Bodø (2 daily; 6hr); Evenes airport (every 30min–1hr; 1hr 15min); Fauske (2 daily; 4hr 30min); Reine (1–2 daily; 7hr 50min); Svolvær (2 daily; 4hr 20min); Tromsø (1–3 daily; 4hr 15min).

## INFORMATION

**Tourist office** Narvik tourist office is in the same building as the Narvik Krigsmuseum (see above), in the centre on the main drag at Kongens gate 39 (late June to late Aug Mon–Fri 10am–7pm, Sat & Sun 10am–6pm; late Aug to late June Mon–Fri 10am–3pm; ☎ 76 96 56 00,

ⓦ visitnarvik.com). The staff here issue free town maps, provide lots of information on outdoor pursuits and have the full range of bus and ferry timetables; they will also assist with ferry and activity reservations.

## ACTIVITIES

**Climbing and skiing** Narvik Mountain Guides (☎ 45 25 41 04, ⓦ narvikguides.no) offers a variety of guided

mountain-climbing excursions and skiing trips – Narvik has some of Nordland's best ski slopes on the

**5**

## THE OFOTBANEN

One of the real treats of a visit to Narvik is the **train ride** into the mountains that rear up behind the town and spread east across the Swedish border. Completed in 1903, this railway line – the **Ofotbanen** – was, by any standard, a remarkable achievement and the hundreds of navvies that made up the workforce endured astounding hardships during its construction. The line passes through some visually stunning scenery, slipping in between hostile peaks before reaching the rocky, barren and loch-studded mountain plateaux beyond. Even better, the timings of the trains mean that a short day-trip into the mountains is easy enough, and the obvious target is **Riksgränsen**, a pleasant hiking and skiing centre just over the border in Sweden – so take your passport. The journey from Narvik to Riksgränsen takes 50min and costs anywhere between 60kr and 100kr each way. Most train travellers nose around Riksgränsen for a few hours before returning to Narvik, but the more adventurous can **hike** at least a part of the way back on the **Rallarveien**, the refurbished trail originally built for the railway workers. This extends west for 15km from Riksgränsen to **Rombaksbotn**, a deep and narrow inlet where the navvies once started their strenuous haul up into the mountains. A favourite option is to walk from Riksgränsen back towards the coast, picking up the return train at one of the several Norwegian stations on the way.

The area around the Ofotbanen isn't nearly as remote now that the **E10** crosses the mountains to the north of the railway, but the terrain is difficult and the weather unpredictable, so hikers will need to be well equipped. For hiking maps, visit Narvik tourist office (see p.301).

### OFOTBANEN TIMETABLES

SJ, the Swedish national rail service (ⓦ sj.se/en/), operates the Ofotbanen. From Narvik, services are as follows: Kiruna, Sweden (3–4 daily; 3hr); Luleå, Sweden (2 daily; 7hr); Riksgränsen, Sweden (3–4 daily; 50min); Rombak, Norway (3–4 daily; 20min).

---

Narvikfjellet (ⓦ narvikfjellet.no). One of the company's more distinctive offerings is a 3hr evening avalanche course for 350kr.

**Diving** World War II shipwrecks are dotted around Narvik and are a real pull for divers. Dive Narvik (ⓣ 99 51 22 05, ⓦ divenarvik.com) are the recognized specialists and should be your first port of call. Their start-off package of ten dives costs around 6500kr.

**Wilderness adventures** Fjellguiden Altevatn (ⓣ 90 21 30 00, ⓦ fjellguiden.net) have a varied programme of wilderness adventures, including snowmobiling, dog-sledding, camping and cabins in the great outdoors.

### ACCOMMODATION

**Breidablikk Gjestehus** Tore Hunds gate 41 ⓣ 76 94 14 18, ⓦ breidablikk.no. The tidy and trim rooms in this pleasant, unassuming guesthouse have a certain modern charm. Those on the upper floors also have attractive views over town, and the breakfasts are good and hearty. Located at the top of the steps at the end of Kinobakken, a side road leading east off Kongens gate, just up from the main town square. 1195kr

**Quality Hotel Grand Royal** Kongens gate 64 ⓣ 76 97 70 00, ⓦ nordicchoicehotels.com. Well kept and well maintained, the *Grand*'s public areas are really rather swish – think gleaming floors and ceiling lighting – while the bedrooms are perfectly adequate albeit in standard chain style. As a break from the modernism, the hotel's *Rallarn Pub* is all wood panelling with sepia photos of Narvik's pioneer days. 1300kr

**Scandic Narvik** Kongens gate 33 ⓣ 76 96 14 00, ⓦ scandichotels.com. Well, whatever else you might say about this chain hotel, you certainly can't miss it – the hotel occupies a slender, and glassy, fifteen-storey high-rise that soars above its surroundings. The interior is noticeably bright, cheerful and modern as are the guest rooms, which offer panoramic views on the upper floors. 1300kr

### EATING

**Viva Italia** Dronningensgate 53 ⓣ 76 95 29 00. Narvik is short of good restaurants – it is, after all, only a small town – but this cosy Italian restaurant does something to fill the gap. Serves tasty pizzas and pastas as well as dishes not usually on an Italian menu – beef stroganoff being a case in point. Mains from 200kr. Daily 2–11pm.

# The Vesterålen islands

**5**

A raggle-taggle archipelago nudging out into the Norwegian Sea, the **Vesterålen islands**, and their southerly neighbours the Lofoten, are like western Norway in miniature: the terrain is hard and unyielding, the sea boisterous and fretful, and the main – often the only – industry is fishing. The weather is temperate but wet, and the islanders' historic isolation has bred a distinctive culture based, in equal measure, on Protestantism, the extended family and respect for the ocean.

Somewhat confusingly, the Vesterålen archipelago is shared between the counties of **Troms** and **Nordland**: the northern Vesterålen islands are in Troms, while the southern half of the Vesterålen and all the Lofoten islands are in Nordland. The Vesterålen islands are the less rugged of the two groups – greener, gentler and less mountainous, with more of the land devoted to agriculture, though this gives way to tracts of peaty moorland in the far north. The villages are less immediately appealing too, often no more than narrow ribbons straggling along the coast and across any available stretch of fertile land. Consequently, many travellers simply slide past en route to the better-known Lofoten, a mistake as the Vesterålen have their own particular charm, not least in the small fishing port of Andenes, which beckons with its strange but enthralling back-of-beyond charm and its litany of whale-watching tours. Other Vesterålen highlights include the magnificent but extremely narrow Trollfjord, where vessels – and the Hurtigruten – perform some nifty manoeuvres and the solitary hamlet of **Nyksund**, set amid a gaggle of grassy peaks and ridges. Towns are few and far between, but both **Sortland**, the capital of Vesterålen, and **Harstad**, the archipelago's near neighbour and a comparative giant with a population of 25,000, offer a degree of urban comfort.

## Brief history

The Vesterålen was first settled by seminomadic hunter-agriculturalists some 6000 years ago, and it was they and their Iron Age successors who chopped down the birch and pine forests that once covered these coasts. It was **boatbuilding**, however, which brought prosperity: by the seventh century, the islanders were able to build ocean-going vessels, a skill that enabled them to join in the Viking bonanza. Local clan leaders became important warlords, none more so than the eleventh-century chieftain **Tore Hund**, one-time liegeman of Olav Haraldsson, and one of the men selected to finish Olav off at the Battle of Stiklestad (see p.284) – the fulfilment of a blood debt incurred by Olav's execution of his nephew. In the early fourteenth century, the islanders both here and on the Lofoten **lost their independence** and were placed under the control of Bergen: by royal decree, all the fish the islanders caught had to be shipped to Bergen for export. This may have suited the economic interests of the Norwegian monarchy and the Danish governors who succeeded them, but it put the islanders at a terrible disadvantage. With their monopoly guaranteed, Bergen's merchants controlled both the price they paid for the fish and the prices of the goods they sold to the islanders – a **truck system** that was to survive, increasingly under the auspices of local merchants, until the early years of the twentieth century. Since World War II, improvements in fishing techniques and, more latterly, the growth in tourism and the improvement and extension of the road network have all combined to transform and improve island life.

## ARRIVAL AND DEPARTURE

**THE VESTERÅLEN ISLANDS**

### BY PLANE

**Harstad/Narvik, Evenes airport** The main airport for the Vesterålen is located at Evenes, in between Harstad and Narvik on the E10. There are regular flights to Evenes from the likes of Oslo, Trondheim, Bodø and Tromsø with the main carriers being SAS, Norwegian and Widerøe airlines. A regular airport bus service (⦿flybussen.no) runs to Harstad, Narvik and Sortland.

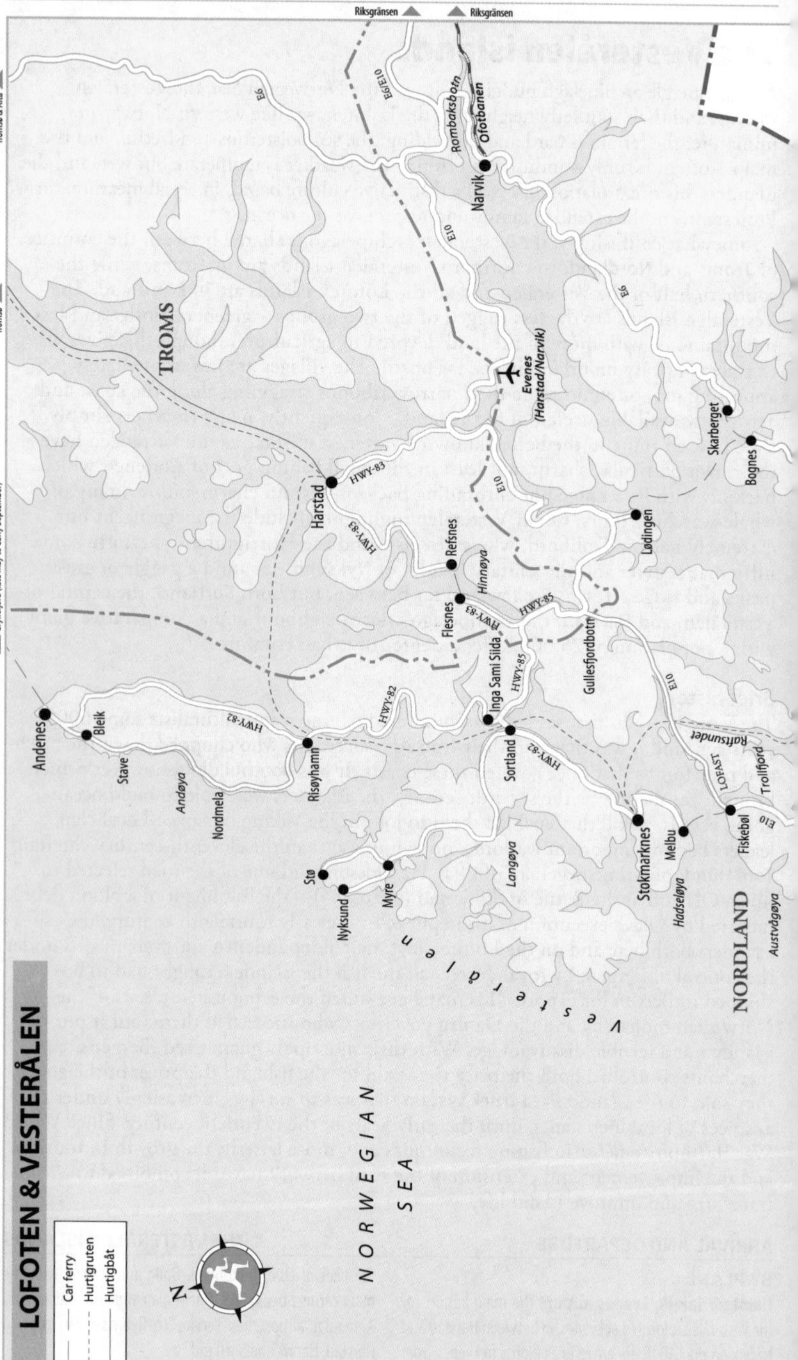

LOFOTEN & VESTERÅLEN

— Car ferry
--- Hurtigruten
— Hurtigbåt

Riksgränsen

Tromsø & Alta

Tromsø

Gryllefjord (late May to early September)

TROMS

NORDLAND

E6

E6/E10

E10

Rombaksbotn

Ofotbanen

Narvik

Evenes (Harstad/Narvik)

E10

E6

Skarberget

Bognes

Lødingen

Harstad

HWY-83

E8/HWY-83

Refsnes

Flesnes

Hinnøya

HWY-83

HWY-85

Gullesfjordbotn

E10

Raftsundet

Trollfjord

LOFAST

Andenes

Bleik

Stave

Andøya

Nordmela

Risøyhamn

HWY-82

HWY-82

HWY-82

Inga Sami Siida

HWY-85

Sortland

HWY-85

Langøya

Stokmarknes

Melbu

Hadseløya

Fiskebøl

Austvågøya

Vesterålen

Stø

Nyksund

Myre

NORWEGIAN SEA

N

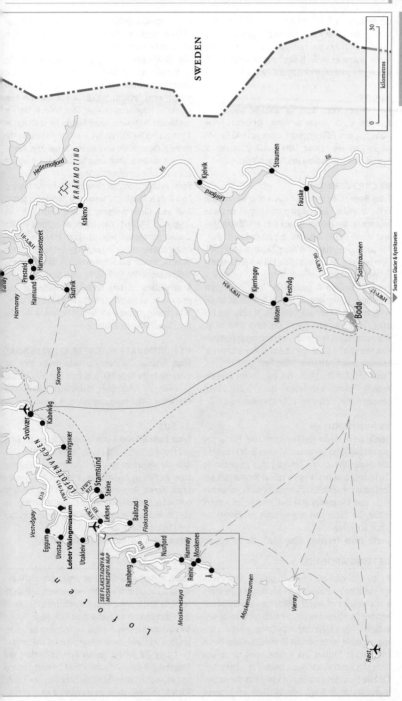

**5**

**Car rental** From Evenes airport, it's a good hour's drive to either Harstad or Narvik. Car rental is available at the airport – both Avis and Hertz have outlets here. If you reserve in advance (which is pretty much essential in high season), the price can drop to around 700kr a day.

### BY CAR

The E10 runs direct from the mainland towards the Vesterålen islands, passing the turning for Harstad before proceeding onto Gullesfjordbotn, where you take Hwy-85 for Sortland and beyond. From Narvik, it's 120km to Harstad, 200km to Sortland and 290km to Andenes.

### BY CAR FERRY

**From Bognes** The principal car ferry from the mainland to the Vesterålen islands departs from Bognes, on the E6 between Fauske and Narvik, and sails to Lødingen (late June to mid-Aug 16 daily; mid-Aug to late June 13 daily; 1hr; passengers 70kr, car & driver 220kr; ⓦ rutebok.no). From Lødingen, it's just 4km to the E10 at a point midway between Harstad and Sortland.

**From Gryllefjord** A seasonal car ferry links remote Gryllefjord, 110km west of the E6, to Andenes at the northern tip of the Vesterålen (late May to early Sept 2–3 daily; 1hr 40 min; passengers 220kr, car & driver 571kr; ⓦ tromskortet.no). Reservations are not currently permitted – so turn up a couple of hours before sailing to be sure of boarding; Gryllefjord is about 240km from Narvik.

**From Fiskebøl** The Melbu–Fiskebøl car ferry links the Vesterålen islands with Lofoten (every 1–2hr; 30min; passengers 40kr, car & driver 115kr; ⓦ rutebok.no).

### BY HURTIGRUTEN

**North from Bodø** Heading north, the Hurtigruten coastal boat (ⓦ hurtigruten.co.uk) leaves Bodø to thread a scenic route through the Lofoten before proceeding to the Vesterålen islands, where it calls at Stokmarknes and Sortland in the south, Risøyhamn in the north and Harstad in the east. The journey time from Bodø to Stokmarknes is 10hr, 3hr 30min more to Risøyhamn and another 2hr 30min to Harstad.

**South from Tromsø** Sailing south, the Hurtigruten

departs Tromsø to follow the same itinerary, but in reverse (Harstad, Risøyhamn, Sortland, Stokmarknes); the sailing time from Tromsø to Harstad is just under 7hr.

**The Raftsundet** Scenically, the highlight of the Hurtigruten cruise through the Lofoten and Vesterålen islands is the cruise along the Raftsundet, a long and narrow sound between Svolvær and Stokmarknes that adjoins the magnificent Trollfjord. Note, however, that the northbound Hurtigruten leaves Svolvær for Vesterålen at 10pm and so the Raftsundet is only visible during the period of the midnight sun (late May to mid-July); southbound, boats leave Stokmarknes for the 3hr trip to Svolvær at a much more convenient 3.15pm.

**Fares** As illustrations, the passenger fare for the 14hr trip from Bodø to Risøyhamn, the nearest Hurtigruten port to Andenes, is 1040kr in summer, 825kr in winter; a car with driver costs 1925kr/1705kr. Cabins are optional on this shortish journey, but begin at about 2300kr in winter, double that in summer. The passenger fare for the 3hr trip between Svolvær and Stokmarknes is 470kr in summer, 390kr in winter (1050kr/970kr for driver & car).

**Reservations** For both cabins and vehicles, advance reservations are essential, and can be made either online or by phoning the ship – ask down at the harbour or at the port's tourist office for assistance.

### BY HURTIGBÅT PASSENGER EXPRESS BOAT

**From Tromsø** The main Hurtigbåt service from the mainland to the Vesterålen runs from Tromsø to Harstad (2–4 daily; 2hr 30min; 600kr; ⓦ tromskortet.no). Advance reservation – most easily done online – is a good idea.

### BY BUS

**From Bodø & Fauske** There are direct buses from Bodø and Fauske to Sortland, the capital of the Vesterålen (1–3 daily; 6hr 30min from Bodø/5hr 15min from Fauske). These buses use the Bognes–Lødingen car ferry.

**From Narvik** There are no direct buses from Narvik to Sortland or Harstad – you have to change at bus stops on the E10. Reckon on 4hr to get from Narvik to Sortland, two and a bit to get to Harstad.

**Information** Bus timetables on ⓦ rutebok.no.

## GETTING AROUND

**By car** With your own vehicle, it's possible to drive from one end of the Vesterålen/Lofoten island chain to the other, a total distance of around 340km from the Gryllefjord/Andenes ferry (see above) in the north to the Moskenes/Bodø ferry (see p.316) in the south. Drivers intent on a less epic trip might opt to take the E6 and E10 in from Narvik with Harstad, Sortland and Andenes being the obvious route, plus Stokmarknes if you're heading on to Lofoten.

**Car hire** If you intend to rent a car locally, note that advance reservations are well-nigh essential. There are car rental

outlets at Harstad/Narvik, Evenes airport (see p.303) and several in Harstad itself, including Rent-a-Wreck, Storgata 79 (ⓣ 77 00 10 44, ⓦ rent-a-wreck-scandinavia.com). Special short-term deals can work out at about 700kr a day.

**By bus** Local bus services across the Vesterålen are patchy, but there is a useful service between Harstad and Sortland (1–2 daily; 2hr 10min), another between Sortland and Andenes (2–4 daily; 2hr), and a third between Sortland and Stokmarknes (Mon–Fri 9 daily, Sat 2 daily, Sun 3 daily; 40min). Timetables are online at ⓦ rutebok.no.

# Harstad

Home to much of northern Norway's engineering industry, **HARSTAD**, just 120km from Narvik, is easily the largest town in the Vesterålen region, its sprawling docks a tangle of supply ships, repair yards and cold-storage plants, which spread out along the gentle slopes of the Vågsfjord. This may not sound too enticing, and it's true that Harstad wins few beauty contests, but the town and its immediate environs do have the occasional attraction and if you're tired of sleepy Norwegian villages, Harstad does rustle up something of a bustling interlude. Downtown, the comings and goings of the ferryboats are a mild diversion and almost everything you need is conveniently clustered around the harbour, with the bus station, and the jetties for the Hurtigbåt and Hurtigruten boats within a few metres of each other. The other spark of interest takes place in late June, when the eight-day **North Norway Arts Festival** (Festspillene i Nord-Norge; ⓦfestspillnn.no) provides concerts, drama and dance performances; note, however, that the town's hotels are full to bursting throughout the proceedings.

## The Trondenes peninsula

Local Trondenes bus #12 from Harstad bus station (Mon–Sat hourly; 10min) runs past Trondenes kirke; or take a taxi from the town centre (ⓣ 77 04 10 00, ⓦ harstadtaxi.no)

Harstad's three main sights are clustered together on the **Trondenes peninsula**, 3km north of the town centre. The medieval **Trondenes kirke** is perhaps of most general

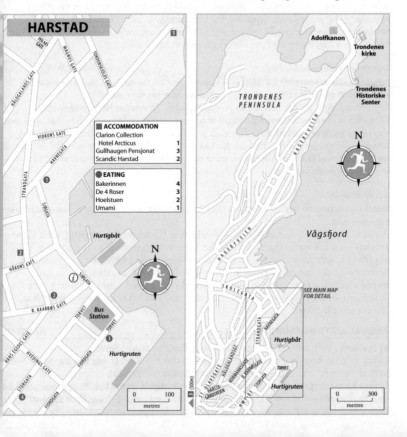

**5**

appeal with the vintage military hardware of the **Adolfkanonen** the runner-up. To get there by car, follow Hwy-83 north and watch for the signposted turning on the right.

## Trondenes kirke

Trondenesveien • Opening times vary, but always include late June to July Mon–Fri 10am–2pm • Free • ☎ 77 01 89 89, ⓦ kirkesok.no /kirker/Trondenes-kirke

Harstad's historical pride and joy is **Trondenes kirke** (Trondenes church) in a lovely leafy location beside the fjord. The original wooden church was built at the behest of King Øystein at the beginning of the twelfth century and had the distinction of being the northernmost church in Christendom for several centuries. Øystein (c.1088–1123) was one of the more constructive rulers of the period, spending time and effort developing the local economy, building a number of churches like this one in Harstad and, perhaps most unusual of all, refusing to plot against his brother and co-ruler, Sigurd, when the latter joined the First Crusade. The stone church that survives today was erected in the 1300s, its thick walls and the remains of its surrounding ramparts reflecting its dual function as a church and stronghold, for these were troubled, violent times. The **churchyard**, which is bordered by a dry-stone wall, holds a Soviet memorial to the eight hundred prisoners of war who died hereabouts in World War II.

After the stern exterior, the church's warm and homely **interior** comes as a surprise. Here, the dainty arches of the rood screen lead into the choir, where a late medieval, bas-relief wooden triptych surmounts each of the three altars. Of the trio, all of which were imported from northern Germany, the middle triptych is the most visually appealing: the main panel, depicting the holy family, is fairly predictable, but down below is a curiously cheerful sequence of biblical figures, each of whom wears a turban and sports a big, bushy and exquisitely carved beard.

## Trondenes Historiske Senter

Trondenesveien 122 • Mid-June to mid-Aug daily 11am–5pm; mid-Aug to mid-June Mon–Sat 10am–2pm, Sun 11am–4pm • 90kr • ☎ 77 01 83 80, ⓦ stmu.no • About 500m south along the fjord from the church, back towards Harstad

The second sight on the Trondenes peninsula is the **Trondenes Historiske Senter** (Trondenes Historical Centre), a plush modern complex holding exhibits that span two thousand years of local history. The museum itself is a low-rise structure, half buried beneath the ground, with a turf-covered roof. Inside, the bulk of the material focuses on the medieval era, with dioramas, paintings, statues and mood music, as well as incidental Viking artefacts.

## Adolfkanonen

Trondenes • Guided tours: June–Aug 1–3 daily • 80kr • ☎ 77 01 89 89, ⓦ adolfkanonen.com • You must have your own vehicle and be on a guided tour to visit

A massive artillery piece and relic of World War II, the **Adolfkanonen** (Adolf Gun) perches on a hilltop in the middle of the Trondenes peninsula to the north of the church. Manufactured by Krupp for a battleship in the 1930s, the gun ended up here, one of the largest in Hitler's Atlantic Wall. The Adolfkanonen is located inside a military zone and can only be visited on a guided tour. The tour begins at the gate of the compound, 1km from the gun, and takes in the gun itself plus the adjacent **bunkers**.

### ARRIVAL AND INFORMATION

**HARSTAD**

**By bus** Harstad bus station is in the centre of town on Sjøgata at Torvet, down by the waterfront and just south of the tourist office. There is a direct bus to Sortland, but to pick up the region's main long-distance bus, the Lofotenekspressen (see p.317), you have to catch a local bus to the E10, where you change.

Timetables on ⓦ rutebok.no.
Destinations Narvik (2 daily with one change; 2–3hr); Sortland (1–2 daily; 2hr).
**By Hurtigbåt express boat** Hurtigbåt express boats link Harstad and Tromsø (2–4 daily; 3hr; ⓦ tromskortet.no).
**By Hurtigruten** Southbound, the Hurtigruten

(⊛ hurtigruten.co.uk) sails for ports in the Vesterålen and Lofoten islands; northbound, the next major port is Tromsø (6hr 30min).

**Tourist office** Harstad tourist office is handily located at Sjøgata 1B (mid-June to mid-Aug daily 10am–6pm; mid-Aug to mid-June Mon–Fri 8am–3.30pm; ☎77 01 89 89, ⊛ visitharstad.com).

## ACCOMMODATION

**Clarion Collection Hotel Arcticus** Havnegata 3 ☎77 04 08 00, ⊛ nordicchoicehotels.com. Located to the northeast of the city centre next to the Kulturhus, this is the pick of Harstad's several chain hotels, primarily because of its engaging waterfront location with views across to the mountains. The rooms are large, comfortable and decorated in a bright and breezy modern style. **1000kr**

**Gullhaugen Pensjonat** St Olavsgata 83 ☎77 06 64 66, ⊛ gullhaugenkp.no. Small pension in tidy premises offering simple, clean and unpretentious accommodation.

Bathroom facilities are shared and there is self-catering. About 15min walk west of the centre, opposite the hospital. **600kr**

**Scandic Harstad** Strandgata 9 ☎77 00 30 00, ⊛ scandichotels.com. Since they bought this long-established city-centre hotel, Scandic have revitalized the place, modernizing the public areas in crisp modern style and making the bedrooms cheerful, if hardly exhilarating. The hotel is located a few metres from the port. **1350kr**

## EATING

**Bakerinnen** Storgata 17 ☎41 58 78 20, ⊛ bakerinnen .no. Something of a local institution, this old-style coffee, cake and sandwich shop does what it does very well. Everything is freshly baked on the premises, including the bread, and you can eat in or take out. It's located just up the hill from the harbour. Mon–Fri 10am–5pm, Sat 10am–3pm.

**De 4 Roser** Torvet 7A ☎77 01 27 50, ⊛ de4roser.com /harstad. In a handsome yellow wooden building on the main square, this well-established restaurant has an excellent reputation for the quality of its French and Italian cuisine, served formally upstairs and informally – and more affordably – downstairs. Daily specials are chalked up on a blackboard and due prominence is given to local ingredients. Salads and pasta dishes from 160kr downstairs, a three-course set meal 600kr upstairs. Mon–Sat 10am–11pm.

**Hoelstuen** Rikard Kaarbøs Plass 4 ☎77 06 55 00, ⊛ hoelstuen.com. Housed within a three-storey, late nineteenth-century building in the centre of town, this pastel-painted restaurant prepares its food in the classic French manner, but with Norwegian ingredients. The lamb is especially tasty. A four-course set menu costs 650kr. Mon–Sat 5–11pm.

★ **Umami** Havnegata 23 ☎95 09 09 11, ⊛ umami harstad.no. Harstad's top restaurant, in an imposing building just west of the port, gives a showing to the New Nordic food tradition in Harstad, using time-honoured Norwegian food traditions as the starting point for imaginative fusions with other cuisines, like tapas and sushi. The food looks splendid and tastes even better. Try, for example, the braised beef-flank (*okseculotte*). Advance reservations essential. A four-course set menu costs 745kr. Tues–Sat 6–11pm.

# Andenes

At the very tip of Andøya island, **ANDENES** strains northwards, its solid breakwaters protecting a central lagoon like the pincers of a stag beetle. In 1944, the writer Poul Alm dropped by, proclaiming "It is the fish, and that alone, that draws people to

## A SCENIC DRIVE: HARSTAD TO ANDENES

The three- to four-hour drive between **Harstad and Andenes** is one of northern Norway's most appealing, the wild coastline an exercise in bleak and rugged desolation. The first part of the journey is to Sortland (see p.312), either south via Hwy-83 and then west along the E10, or – and this is the more scenic choice – southwest via Hwy-83 and the Refsnes–Flesnes car ferry (hourly; 30min; passenger 40kr, car & driver 100kr). At **Sortland**, Hwy-82 strikes north, threading along the craggy coastline on its way to humdrum **Risøyhamn**, the only Hurtigruten port on Andøya, the most northerly of the Vesterålen islands. Here at Risøyhamn, the main road – Hwy-82 – scuttles past the rolling hills and peaty moorland of **Andøya's east coast** en route to Andenes, while the much more enticing Hwy-974/976 inches along **Andøya's west coast** with its white-sand beaches, lagoons, churning surf and rippling peaks.

**5**

Andenes – the place itself has no other temptations" and still today the emphasis remains firmly nautical if not exactly piscine: the port's low-slung buildings lead straight to the clutter of wooden warehouses and mini boat-repair yards that edge the harbour. There's no denying that Andenes feels rather like the end of the world, but the combined effects of the Gulf Stream and the proximity of the Eggakanten continental shelf make the waters off Andenes especially rich in wildlife – enough to spawn a small tourist industry built on **whale-watching** and **wildlife safaris**. The marine high point is in late winter, when the Arctic cod migrate south from the Barents Sea to spawn in the waters around Andenes, a migration that attracts millions of sea birds and scores of whales, especially sperm whales.

## Hvalsenter

Hamnegata • Daily: late May to mid-June & mid-Aug to mid-Sept 8.30am–4pm; mid-June to mid-Aug 8.30am–7pm • 110kr • ☎ 76 11 56 00, ⊛ whalesafari.no

A visit to Andenes **Hvalsenter** (Whale Centre), in an old warehouse metres from the harbour, is included at the beginning of all whale safaris (see opposite) and, indeed, it does provide a good explanation of the whale's biological life and times. One particular highlight is the enormous 16m-long sperm-whale skeleton, which was washed up on an Andenes beach. That said, the centre's incidental displays hardly fire the imagination, and neither does the massive – and deliberately dark and gloomy – display of a whale munching its way though a herd of squid.

## Andenes fyr

Hamnegata • Late June to Aug; key from the tourist office • 50kr

Dating from 1859, the strikingly red **Andenes fyr** (lighthouse) is an imposing 40m-high structure that offers sweeping views of the town and ocean from the top, though you'll have to clamber up 148 steep steps to get there. The lighthouse was recently sold to a private buyer and is still in use for much of the year – although it has been unmanned since 1978.

## Polarmuseet

Hamnegata • Daily: mid-June to mid-Aug 10am–5pm; early June & late Aug 10am–3pm • 50kr • ☎ 76 11 54 32, ⊛ museumnord.no

In a modest little building with a pretty wooden porch, the low-key **Polarmuseet** (Polar Museum) is situated a few metres south of the lighthouse. Inside, its main exhibit is a giant stuffed polar bear that gazes at you from a frightening height; it was allegedly shot by accident on an expedition to Spitsbergen. The rest of the interior is mostly dedicated to the Arctic knick-knacks accumulated by a certain Hilmar Nøis, an Andøy man who wintered on Svalbard no fewer than 38 times. Unfortunately all the labelling is in Norwegian, but helpful staff are willing to translate.

## Whale-watching safaris

Andenes is famous for its **whale-watching safaris**, with a marine biologist on board to point out whales, including pilots, minkes, humpbacks and sperm, as well other sea creatures like dolphins and porpoise – all drawn here by the nutrient-rich waters that lie just offshore. With every justification, operators claim a ninety-five percent chance of a whale sighting, and most will reimburse the price of your ticket if you don't see any. The safaris, which help support the research and protection of offshore whale colonies, take place aboard small vessels and use hydrophone technology to pick up the sounds of the whales – essential for locating the mammals without disturbing them. Taking an evening safari during the period of the midnight sun can be especially rewarding, as the eerie light often makes it easier to spot the surfacing sperm whales. Details of who to contact for a whale-watching safari are given in the activities section (see opposite).

## NORWEGIAN WHALING

To many foreigners at least, Norway has a shabby reputation as one of the few countries in the world that's still **hunting whales** for commercial purposes. In doing so, the Norwegians ignore the worldwide **ban** on commercial whaling adopted by the International Whaling Commission in 1986. Neither does Norway disguise its main reason for whaling as "scientific research", but is upfront that the hunting is for human consumption, though its whalers are restricted to the killing of minke whales. Norway's fisheries department works out its own quota. In 2012, this was 1286 minke, though only 464 were actually killed, and in 2015 the quota was the same, but the kill rose to 660. **Whale meat** (*hval*) is considered a delicacy by many Norwegians and can still be found on many Norwegian menus, though opinion polls indicate that about one in four Norwegians under thirty oppose the hunt. The method of killing the animals is also subject to bitter dispute. Norwegian whalers invented the exploding harpoon and they still use it today. Activists claim there's no humane way to kill a whale, but many abhor this particular method: one in five whales suffer a long and painful death. Ironically enough, the waters where thousands of tourists venture out on whale-watching safaris are often the same as those used by the whale hunters.

## ARRIVAL AND DEPARTURE
## ANDENES

**By bus** Andenes bus station is just back from the harbour, a few metres east of Storgata. For bus timetables, consult ⓦ rutebok.no.

Destinations Sortland (2–4 daily; 2hr).

**By car ferry** There's a seasonal car ferry between Gryllefjord and Andenes (see p.306). Gryllefjord is about 230km from Narvik (see p.300) and 220km from Tromsø (see pp.342–350).

## INFORMATION

**Tourist office** Kong Hansgate 8 (mid-June to Aug daily 9am–6pm; Sept to mid-June daily 8am–3pm; ☎ 41 60 58 52, ⓦ visitandoy.info). Centrally located, the tourist office can make reservations for bird and whale safaris; has details of local bicycle rental; and can provide information on local hiking trails.

## TOURS AND ACTIVITIES

**Birdwatching trips** Sea Safari Andenes at Hamnegata 9 (☎ 91 67 49 60, ⓦ seasafariandenes.no) is a well-regarded operator that offers a range of birdwatching expeditions in RIB boats. The standard tour (495kr) is a 2hr outing over to the islet of Bleiksøya for sightings of gannets, sea eagles, auks, puffins and the like. The quay at Hamnegata 9 is a few metres west of the foot of Storgata. Tours run daily from May till September.

**Whale-watching trips** Whalesafari Andenes (☎ 76 11 56 00, ⓦ whalesafari.no), is an excellent company that offers whale-watching trips throughout the year (1–4 daily depending on demand; 4–5hr). Vessels depart from their base, a few metres from the lighthouse – just follow the signs. Prices, including a guided tour of the Whale Centre (see opposite), are 945kr for adults, children (5–13 years) 595kr, children (1–4 years), 210kr. Warm clothing and sensible shoes are essential as are reservations, which should be made at least a day in advance.

## ACCOMMODATION

Andenes has a fair sprinkling of inexpensive accommodation and several households offer **private rooms** – just look for the signs – but, considering how isolated a spot this is, you'd be well advised to make a reservation before you actually get here.

**Andenes Rorbu Hotel** Hamnegate 31 ☎ 76 14 64 00, ⓦ andrikkenhotell.no. Right down on the harbourfront, this stylish hotel offers ultramodern rooms plus two handsomely converted, green-painted timber *sjøhus*, which have been divided into apartments. Almost all have great views. Booking via the *Andrikken Hotel* (see below). Doubles 1200kr, apartments 1400kr

**Andrikken Hotel** Storgata 53 ☎ 76 14 12 22, ⓦ andrikkenhotell.no. About 500m back from the harbour along the main drag, this 1960s block may look a tad Stalinist from the outside, but the forty-odd rooms have been refurbished in an attractive modern style. The buffet breakfast is generous. 1200kr

★ **Fargeklatten Veita** Sjøgata 38A ☎ 97 76 00 20, ⓦ fargeklatten.no. Just near the harbour, this stylishly decorated guesthouse is the nicest place to stay in town, an inviting little place with all sorts of bygones and the cosiest of bedrooms. It's housed in a cluster of eighteenth- and nineteenth-century buildings that includes a small museum and an art gallery. 950kr

**Havhusene** Bleik ☎ 76 14 12 22, ⓦ andrikkenhotell .no. The *Havhusene* comprises a cluster of sympathetically renovated *sjøhus* offering a number of smart and modern apartments for up to six guests. Most have three bedrooms, a spacious living room, a dining area and a small kitchenette. They are in Bleik, a pretty little village with a sandy beach and ringed by craggy hills about 10km southwest along the coast from Andenes. There's a pub and a shop a short walk away. Booking via the *Andrikken Hotel* (see p.311). May–Sept. **1500kr**

### EATING

**Jul. Nilsens Bakeri & Konditori** Kong Hansgate 1 ☎ 76 14 10 18. A small bakery-café by the bus station that is a good place for cakes and freshly baked snacks. Mon–Wed 8am–1pm, Thurs 10am–3pm & 7–8pm, Fri 7am–3pm & 8–9pm, Sun 2–6pm.

**Lysthuset** Storgata 51 ☎ 76 14 14 99. Next to the *Andrikken Hotel*, this is Andenes' longest-established eatery, with a cosy wood-clad interior. Fish, whale and reindeer feature prominently on the menu, but the star turn is the local salt-marsh lamb. Mains from 220kr. Tues–Sat 5.30–11pm.

## Sortland and around

**SORTLAND**, the capital of the Vesterålen, is a modest sort of place, its centre tucked away on the eastern shore of Langøya, about 200km from Narvik and half that from Andenes. In the 1990s, a local artist by the name of Bjørn Elvenes determined to cheer the place up, hatching a plan to paint the town's buildings a particular shade of blue. The scheme took off and today much of the town is indeed blue, earning it the nickname "Blåbyen" (Blue Town). The success of the project is best viewed from Sortland's steeply bowed bridge, from where the town looks almost iridescent, especially on a sunny day. Blueness aside, Sortland is short of specific attractions, but it is a handy launching pad for the 50km drive north to the remote former fishing village of **Nyksund** and a convenient pit stop on the route south to Stokmarknes (see p.314) and the Melbu car ferry over to the Lofoten.

### Inga Sámi Siida

Kvalsauken • Daily mid-June to Aug 10am–3pm • 150kr • ☎ 90 87 75 58, ⓦ inga-sami-siida.no • 4km north of Sortland, over the bridge on Hwy-82

A living museum of Sámi heritage and culture, **Inga Sámi Siida** is operated by a family of reindeer herders, who offer the opportunity not only to see but also to engage and participate in aspects of Sámi life. Food, singing and animal husbandry feature strongly on the agenda, but there is no shrinking from the political issues that continue to plague the Sámi – and there's certainly nothing mawkish about the place.

### Nyksund

At the exposed tip of Langøya, about 50km north of Sortland, **NYKSUND** is one of the most interesting villages in the Vesterålen, its huddle of wooden houses sitting pretty on either side of a stumpy harbour. In the 1970s, after a horrendous storm, the last locals decided they had had enough and abandoned the place, but in the last decade or so an intrepid band of outsiders have brought the village back to life. A road connection has helped – it's a narrow but easily driveable road – and there are now a dozen or so all-year inhabitants and a small seasonal tourist industry sustains a couple of places to eat and drink.

#### The Dronningruta – The Queen's Route

In 1994, Norway's Queen Sonja put on her walking shoes to undertake the challenging hike between Nyksund and **Stø**, another small fishing village situated a few kilometres northeast along the Langøya coast. The superb 15km-long **Dronningruta** commemorates her efforts, a well-signposted, circular route – marked with splodges of red paint on stones and trees – that takes about eight hours to complete. The trail skirts mountain lakes, clambers along narrow ridges, negotiates steep gullies and offers wonderous views over the rocky coast. Parts of the hike are challenging – some sections are fitted with safety ropes – and you do have to have a

**5**

head for heights. Neither should you attempt the hike without being properly equipped, and you need to take food and water.

### ARRIVAL AND INFORMATION
### SORTLAND AND AROUND

**By bus** Sortland bus station is located just a block back from the waterfront, off Strandgate. For bus timetable details, go to ⓦ rutebok.no.

Destinations Andenes (2–4 daily; 2hr); Harstad (1–2 daily; 2hr); Nyksund (1–3 daily; 1hr); Stø (1–3 daily; 1hr 30min); Stokmarknes (Mon–Fri 9 daily, Sat 2 daily, Sun 3 daily; 40min); Svolvær (1–4 daily; 2hr 30min).

**By Hurtigruten** The Hurtigruten (ⓦ hurtigruten.co.uk)

docks on the north edge of the town centre, 300m or so from the tourist office. Northbound, it's just under 4hr to Harstad; southbound, it's 1hr 30min to Stokmarknes.

**Tourist office** Sortland tourist office is on the north side of the town centre at Kjøpmannsgate 2 (mid-June to late Aug daily 9am–6pm; Sept to mid-June Mon–Sat 8am–3pm; ☎ 76 11 14 80, ⓦ visitvesteralen.no).

### ACCOMMODATION AND EATING

#### SORTLAND

**Ekspedisjonen Lunsjbar og Restaurant** Rådhusgata 26, Sortland ☎ 76 20 10 40, ⓦ ekspedisjonen .wordpress.com. Right by the Hurtigrut quay, the *Ekspedisjonen* offers affordable lunches and dinners based on a standard Norwegian repertoire and in stylish surroundings. It does a good line in vegetarian dishes too. Mains from 220kr. Times vary, but normally Mon–Tues 10am–6pm, Wed–Fri 10am–10pm, Sat 11am–11pm.

**Kulturfabrikken** Strandgata ☎ 79 10 91 10, ⓦ kulturfabrikkensortland.no. The cultural heart of Sortland, *Kulturfabrikken* showcases a varied programme of films, exhibitions, performing arts and live music. The place comes complete with an attractively airy snack bar with changing daily specials – from pastas and soups to pizzas – at around 140kr. Mon–Sat 10am–5pm.

**Sortland Hotel** Vesterålsgaten 59 ☎ 76 10 84 00, ⓦ sortlandhotell.no. Just off the main road in the middle of town, this well-maintained, modern hotel has

spacious comfortable rooms, some of which have fjord views. **1500kr**

**Vesterålen Sjøhus Senteret** Ånstadsjøen ☎ 76 12 37 40, ⓦ lofoten-info.no/vesteralen-sjohus. On the road to Myre, about 2km north of town, this collection of seven, brightly painted wooden houses occupies an attractive waterside setting. There is a restaurant and sauna facilities too. **800kr**

#### NYKSUND

**Holmvik Brygge** ☎ 76 13 47 96 or ☎ 95 86 38 66. In a substantial and sympathetically restored quayside warehouse, this combined guesthouse and restaurant is owned and operated by the German couple who have led the way in revitalizing Nyksund. The rooms are plain and simple and the restaurant features local ingredients, especially fish; they have their own smokehouse, too. Restaurant: June–Aug daily 11am–10pm; otherwise by prior arrangement. **850kr**

## Stokmarknes

Despite its pleasant coastal setting, pocket-sized **STOKMARKNES**, some 30km south of Sortland, conspires to be really rather humdrum, its workaday, modern buildings sidling along the waters of the Langøysundet. Perhaps surprisingly, it is, however, a Hurtigruten port and its one and only attraction – the **Hurtigrutemuseet** – celebrates this maritime connection.

### Hurtigrutemuseet

Markedsgata 1 • Daily: mid-May to mid-June & mid-Aug to mid-Sept noon–4pm; mid-June to mid-Aug 10am–6pm; mid-Sept to mid-May 2–4pm • 90kr • ☎ 76 11 81 90, ⓦ hurtigrutemuseet.no

The **Hurtigrutemuseet** tracks through the history of Norway's most famous coastal ferry service, which was once the economic and social lifeline of a string of isolated ports stretching round the Norwegian coast as far as Kirkenes. The collection is supplemented by a disused 1950s ferry, the M/S *Finnmarken*, which is parked outside on the quayside rather like a beached whale, but one – frankly – that has been beached here for too long. Also on the quayside is a statue of **Richard With** (1846–1930), the politician, businessman and one-time skipper, who was responsible for streamlining and regularizing the route of the Hurtigruten in the 1890s. Before Richard With, long-distance coastal boats did not stick to a rigorous timetable and anchored whenever they arrived; With changed all that and became something of a folk hero hereabouts as a result, though some of his more religious neighbours did disapprove of his personal life: his first wife died in 1878 and he promptly married her sister.

### The Trollfjord

The Hurtigruten (ⓦ hurtigruten.co.uk) visits the Trollfjord on its 3hr cruise between Stokmarknes and Svolvær • Southbound, it leaves Stokmarknes daily at 3.15pm; northbound, it departs Svolvær daily at 10pm • The passenger fare is 470kr in summer, 390kr in winter (1050kr/970kr for driver and car) • There are also special boat trips to the Trollfjord from Svolvær (see p.320)

The main reason to stop in **Stokmarknes** is to catch the **Hurtigruten** south to Svolvær via the **Trollfjord**, a majestic tear in the landscape just 2km long. The boats first tackle the **Raftsundet**, the narrow sound separating the harsh, rocky cliffs of Hinnøya and Austvågøya. Towards the southern end of the sound, the ship usually slows to a gentle chug, inching up the narrow Trollfjord with the smooth, stone shanks of the surrounding mountains towering high above. At the head of the **Trollfjord**, it then effects a nautical three-point turn and crawls back to rejoin the main waterway. It's very atmospheric, and the effect is perhaps even more extraordinary when the weather is up. Note that the Hurtigruten will not enter the Trollfjord when there's the danger of a rockfall, but pauses at the fjord's mouth instead. Check locally before embarkation, though you're only likely to miss out, if at all, in spring.

#### ARRIVAL AND DEPARTURE                                    STOKMARKNES

**By bus** Buses to Stokmarknes pull in on Havnegata between the Hurtigrutemuseet and the bridge. Timetables on ⓦ rutebok.no.
Destinations Sortland (Mon–Fri 9 daily, Sat 2 daily, Sun

3 daily; 40min); Svolvær (1–4 daily; 1hr 45min).
**By car ferry** From Stokmarknes, it's 15km south along Hwy-82 to the Melbu–Fiskebøl car ferry (see p.316).

#### ACCOMMODATION AND EATING

**Vesterålen Kysthotell** Børøya ❼76 15 29 99, ⓦ vesteralenkysthotell.no. On a humpy little island just off Stokmarknes – and beside Hwy-82 – this appealing modern hotel offers a range of smart rooms, apartments and cabins in a string of wooden buildings built in

traditional style. The beds are exceptionally comfortable and there are all mod cons. The in-house restaurant, *Bølgen*, is similarly smart and serves a good line in both seafood and meat dishes with mains from 280kr. Mon–Sat 11am–10pm, Sun 11am–5pm. **1100kr**

# The Lofoten islands

A skeletal curve of mountainous rock stretched out across the Norwegian Sea, the **Lofoten islands** have been the focal point of northern Norway's winter fishing from time immemorial. At the turn of the year, cod migrate from the Barents Sea to spawn here, where the coldness of the water is tempered by the Gulf Stream. The season only lasts from February to April, but fishing impinges on all aspects of island life and is impossible to ignore at any time of the year. At almost every harbour stand the massed ranks of wooden racks used for drying the cod, burgeoning and odiferous in winter, empty in summer like so many abandoned climbing frames.

Sharing the same history, but better known and more beautiful than their neighbours the Vesterålen, the Lofoten islands have everything from sea-bird colonies in the south to beaches and fjords in the north. The traditional approach is by boat from Bodø and this brings visitors face to face with the islands' most striking feature, the towering peaks of the **Lofotenveggen** (Lofoten Wall), a 160-kilometre stretch of mountains, whose jagged teeth bite into the skyline, trapping a string of tiny fishing villages tight against the shore. The mountains are set so close together that on first inspection there seems to be no way through, but in fact the islands are riddled with straits, sounds and fjords and possess a string of exceptionally charming villages, most memorably **Henningsvær, Stamsund, Nusfjord, Reine** and **Å**.

**5**

The Lofoten have their own relaxed pace, and are perfect for a simple, uncluttered few days. For somewhere so far north, the weather can be exceptionally mild: summer days can be spent sunbathing on the rocks or hiking and biking around the superb coastline, and when it rains – as it frequently does – life focuses on the *rorbuer* (fishermen's huts), where freshly caught fish are cooked over wood-burning stoves and time is gently wasted. It's rare to find anyone who isn't completely enthralled by it all.

## ARRIVAL AND GETTING AROUND

### THE LOFOTEN ISLANDS

### BY PLANE

**Svolvær & Leknes airports** There are two airports on the Lofoten islands, Leknes and Svolvær, and there are regular direct flights to both from several Norwegian airports, including Bodø, though flights are much more frequent (and usually less expensive) to Leknes. The main operator is Widerøe (ⓦ wideroe.no). Fares vary enormously, but a standard summer return ticket to Leknes should cost in the region of 1250kr.

**Car rental** Car rental is available at either airport – Avis and Hertz have outlets at both. Good-value short-term deals abound – from around 650kr/day – though you may find better prices at one of the locally-run rental companies – try Rent a Car Lofoten in Svolvær (ⓣ 47 64 35 60, ⓦ rentacar-lofoten.com); they also rent out scooters and motorcycles. Advance reservation is well-nigh essential, especially during high season.

### BY CAR

The E10 runs direct to the Lofoten from the mainland to weave a scenic route across the archipelago, hopping from island to island by bridge and causeway and by occasionally tunnelling through the mountains and under the sea. The highway passes through or within a few kilometres of all the islands' most interesting villages and towns, but it's only when you leave the car and head off into the landscape that the real character of Lofoten begins to reveal itself; allow time for at least one walk or sea trip. Conversely, if you don't have a vehicle and want to reach the islands' remoter spots, it's worth considering renting a car, an inexpensive option if a few people share the cost (see above). Distances are manageable – Narvik to Svolvær is 240km, Narvik to Å is 365km.

### BY CAR FERRY

**From Bodø** The traditional approach to the Lofoten from the mainland is by car ferry from Bodø. There are three destinations to choose from, all on the southern peripheries of the archipelago: Moskenes, a tiny port in between Reine and Å – and just a few kilometres from the end of the E10 – and the isolated islets of Værøy and Røst. Ferry routes vary, but there's almost always one ferry a day (and often more) to Moskenes throughout the year, with marginally less frequent services to the two islets; Moskenes is often the first port of call. The trip from Bodø to Moskenes takes about 4hr; allow a further 2hr to Værøy, and two more for Røst, and be prepared for a rough crossing. Out of season,

the ferries work on a first-come, first-served basis, so it's a good idea to turn up a couple of hours before departure, whereas in the summer you are advised to make an advance reservation with the operator, Torghatten Nord (ⓣ 177, ⓦ torghatten-nord.no). The fare from Bodø to Moskenes is 705kr for car and driver, 196kr for passengers. Timetables on ⓦ 177nordland.no.

**From Skutvik** The shortest car ferry route from the mainland to Lofoten links Skutvik with Svolvær (June–Aug 2–3 daily; 2hr 15min; car & driver 355kr, passengers 103kr); Skutvik is 35km west of the E6 midway between Fauske and Narvik. Given the infrequency of the service, advance reservations are strongly recommended. Timetables on ⓦ 177nordland.no.

**From the Vesterålen** The Melbu to Fiskebøl car ferry (every 1–2hr; 30min; passengers 40kr, car & driver 115kr; ⓦ 177nordland.no) links the Vesterålen islands with Lofoten; Fiskebøl is on the E10, 40km from Svolvær.

### BY HURTIGRUTEN

**North from Bodø** Northbound, the Hurtigruten coastal boat (ⓦ hurtigruten.co.uk) leaves Bodø daily to call at two ports in the Lofoten – Stamsund and Svolvær – before nudging through the dramatic Raftsundet (see p.306) en route to Vesterålen's Stokmarknes. Approximate sailing times are Bodø to Stamsund 4hr, 6hr to Svolvær and 9hr to Stokmarknes.

**South from Harstad** Southbound, the Hurtigruten departs Harstad to follow the same itinerary as northbound, but in reverse. Approximate sailing times: Harstad to Sortland is 4hr, Stokmarknes 5hr 30min, Svolvær 9hr, Stamsund 12hr and Bodø 17hr.

**Fares** As illustrations, the passenger fare for the cruise from Bodø to Stamsund is 630kr in summer, 510kr in winter; car & driver costs 1100kr all year; the 3hr trip from Svolvær to Stokmarknes is 470kr in summer, 390kr in winter (1050kr/970kr for driver and car). Cabins are optional on these shortish journeys.

**Reservations** For both cabins and vehicles, advance reservations are essential, and can be made either online or by phoning the ship – ask down at the harbour or at the port's tourist office for assistance.

### BY HURTIGBÅT

**From Bodø** An especially useful Hurtigbåt boat links Bodø with Svolvær (1 daily; 3hr 30min; 450kr; ⓦ 177nordland.no).

## BY BUS

**The Lofotenekspressen and local buses** The long-distance Lofotenekspressen provides the main bus service from the mainland to the Lofoten islands. There are three or four buses a day on the first section of the route from Narvik to Svolvær; and one or two buses a day on the second leg, from Svolvær to Å. As examples of journey times, Narvik to Svolvær takes just over 4hr and it's 8hr from Narvik to Å.

This long-distance bus service is supported by a reasonably good network of local buses to the more isolated villages. Timetables on ⓦ rutebok.no or ⓦ 177nordland.no.

## BY BIKE

Bike rental is available at many hostels, hotels and guesthouses, and the detailed *Cycling in Lofoten* booklet, which includes route maps, is sold at all tourist offices.

## INFORMATION

**Tourist offices & websites** Almost all the major settlements have a tourist office and there's comprehensive information online at ⓦ lofoten.info, though ⓦ lofoten -info.no covers two of the more southerly islands, Moskenesøya and Flakstadøya, in greater detail. There's also lots of useful information at ⓦ nordnorge.com.

## ACTIVITIES

**Fishing and boat trips** The breathtakingly beautiful towns of Henningsvær, Stamsund, Reine and Å all make great bases for further explorations by boat. There are lots of options, from island cruises, sea-rafting and fishing excursions through to birdwatching trips. Scores of places also rent out fishing boats and tackle, although, because of the strong currents, you should always seek advice about local conditions.

**Hiking** Although the islands don't have a well-developed network of huts and hiking trails, the byroads, where you'll rarely see a car, provide mile after mile of excellent walking as they delve deep into the heart of the landscape.

**Mountaineering** There's plenty of scope for mountaineering on the Lofoten: Austvågøya has the finest climbing, with some of the best ascents in Norway, and there's a prestigious climbing school at Henningsvær (see p.325).

## ACCOMMODATION

The Lofoten islands have a sprinkling of **hotels**, a few of which are first-rate, though some are blandly modern, as well as four HI **hostels** (Kabelvåg, Stamsund, Ballstad and Å), numerous **campsites** and the local speciality, the *rorbuer* and *sjøhus* (see box below).

---

### LOFOTEN: STAYING IN A RORBU OR SJØHUS

All across Lofoten, **rorbuer** (fishermen's shacks) are rented out to tourists for both overnight stays and longer periods. The name *rorbu* is derived from *ror*, "to row" and *bu*, literally "dwelling" – and some older islanders still ask "Will you row this winter?", meaning "Will you go fishing this winter?" *Rorbuer* date back to the twelfth century, when King Øystein ordered the first of them to be built round the Lofoten coastline to provide shelter for visiting fishermen who had previously been obliged to sleep under their upturned boats. Traditionally, *rorbuer* were built on the shore, often on poles sticking out of the sea, and usually coloured with a red paint based on cod-liver oil. They consisted of two sections, a sleeping and eating room and a smaller storage area.

At the peak of the fisheries in the 1930s, some 30,000 men were accommodated in *rorbuer*, but during the 1960s fishing boats became more comfortable and since then many fishermen have preferred to sleep aboard. Most of the original *rorbuer* disappeared years ago, and, although a few have survived, visitors today are much more likely to stay in a modern version, mostly prefabricated units churned out by the dozen with the tourist trade in mind. At their best, they are comfortable and cosy seashore cabins, sometimes a well-planned conversion of an original *rorbu* with bunk beds and wood-fired stoves; at their worst, they are little better than prefabricated hutches in the middle of nowhere. Most have space for between four and six guests and the charge for a hut averages around 1500kr per night – though some can cost as little as 1000kr, while others rise to around 3500kr. Similar rates are charged for the islands' **sjøhus** (literally sea-houses), originally the large quayside halls where the catch was processed and the workers slept. Many of the original *sjøhus* have been cleverly converted into attractive apartments with self-catering facilities, a few into dormitory-style accommodation – and again, as with the *rorbuer*, the quality varies enormously. A full list of *rorbuer* and *sjøhus* is given in the *Lofoten Info-Guide*, a free booklet that you can pick up at any local tourist office and on ⓦ lofoten.info.

**5**

# Svolvær

Hugging and hogging the serrated shore of a long peninsula, **SVOLVÆR** rambles over and around several headlands and bays on the southeast coast of **Austvågøya**, the largest of the Lofoten islands. The town is the region's administrative and transport centre and although it's certainly not the most attractive of the archipelago's settlements, the harbour's red-painted wooden buildings do have a certain breezy charm. The town also boasts more accommodation and better restaurants than its neighbours – and its surroundings are perfect for a range of activities, from fishing and boat-trips through to hiking and climbing (see box, p.320).

## Lofoten Krigsminnemuseum

On Fiskergata, just off Torget • June–Sept Mon–Sat 10am–10pm, Sun noon–3pm; rest of year by appointment • 80kr • ☎ 91 73 03 28, ⓦ lofotenkrigmus.no

One of the region's more engaging museums, the **Lofoten Krigsminnemuseum** (War Museum) holds a wide range of artefacts from documents, uniforms and photographs through to weapons and personal mementoes, all relating to World War II as it unfolded in Norway. Most chilling is the reconstruction of the SS's interrogation facility in Svolvær.

## Nordnorsk Kunstnersenter

Torget 20 • Tues–Sun 10am–4pm • Free • ☎ 40 08 95 95, ⓦ nnks.no

Right in the centre of town, the **Nordnorsk Kunstnersenter** (North Norwegian Art Centre) concentrates on temporary exhibitions that feature the work of modern Norwegian artists in a range of media – oil painting, ceramics, sculpture and so forth. Earlier paintings in the collection are mostly naturalistic, but later pieces are often more adventurous/obscure. Among the former, look out for the work of **Gunnar Berg** (1863–93), who was born in Svolvær, but trained in Germany. On display here is his most celebrated painting, the *Battle of the Trollfjord*, a stirring canvas of snow-tipped mountains rising high above the fjord, where – depicting a real event of 1890 – fishermen in traditional open boats try to block the path of the new kid on the nautical block, a steam-driven fishing ship.

### ARRIVAL AND DEPARTURE · SVOLVÆR

**By bus** Svolvær bus station is down in the centre and around the corner from the tourist office on Fiskergata. Bus timetables on ⓦ 177nordland.no or ⓦ rutebok.no.
Destinations Å (4 daily; 3hr 30min, change at Leknes); Henningsvær (2–6 daily; 30min); Kabelvåg (5 daily; 15min); Narvik (2 daily; 4hr 20min); Sortland (1–4 daily, 2hr 30min).

**By car ferry** Car ferries to Svolvær from Skutvik (June–Aug 2–3 daily; 2hr 15min; car & driver 355kr, passengers 103kr) dock about 1km west of the town centre.
**By Hurtigbåt express boat** Hurtigbåt boats dock in the centre, a short walk from the bus station. The most useful service is to Bodø (1 daily; 3hr 30min; 450kr).

---

### THE BRITISH COMMANDO RAIDS OF 1941

The **Germans occupied Norway** in April 1940 with such speed and efficiency that the British were stumped as to how best to respond. Eventually, in 1941, the Brits decided on a **commando raid** on Lofoten with three main aims: firstly, it was hoped that a successful attack would boost British morale; secondly, it was a way of getting the Germans to commit more troops to garrison duty in Norway; and thirdly, most important of all, the British wanted to destroy as much of Lofoten's plentiful supply of herring oil as they could: the Germans used the oil in the manufacture of explosives.

In April 1941, the **first commando raid** hit Svolvær, Stamsund and Henningsvær, while a second, a few months later, attacked Reine and nearby Sørvangen at the southern end of Lofoten. The first was the more successful, bagging two thousand prisoners and destroying hundreds of barrels of oil, but the Germans extracted a bitter revenge by burning down the houses of all those Norwegians deemed to have been sympathetic to the attackers.

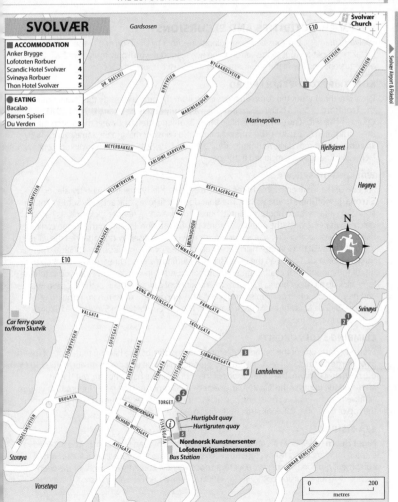

By Hurtigruten The Hurtigruten (⊕hurtigruten.co.uk) docks in the town centre near the Hurtigbåt jetty.

Northbound, it's 3hr to Stokmarknes; southbound, it's a little under 2hr to Stamsund.

## INFORMATION

**Tourist office** On Torget, the main square, near the harbour (March to mid-Oct Mon–Fri 9am–3.30pm; mid-Oct to Feb Mon–Fri 8.15–11.15am & 12.15–3.30pm; plus Sat mid-May to early Sept 10am–2pm & Sun early June to early Aug 10am–9pm; ☎76 07 05 75, ⊕lofoten.info).

## ACCOMMODATION

Svolvær has a reasonably good supply of accommodation, but nevertheless finding a room in high season can be a real challenge – so reserve ahead. The nicest places to stay are in **rorbuer**.

★**Anker Brygge** Lamholmen ☎76 06 64 80, ⊕anker -brygge.no. Easily the town's smartest and most desirable

accommodation, in a prime location on the tiny islet of Lamholmen, at the end of a causeway in the middle of the

**5**

## SVOLVÆR: ACTIVITIES AND EXCURSIONS

Svolvær's dramatic environs deserve exploration, either by climbing one of the local peaks, or by taking a boat trip out to the surrounding fjords, though you'll only really find the full range of excursions on offer in the summertime: out of season, tours go out once a week, at best.

### BOAT TRIPS TO THE TROLLFJORD

Every day throughout the summer, boats leave from the quay alongside the Torget bound for the **Trollfjord** (2 times daily; return trip 3hr; 490kr; buy tickets on board; ☎91 61 79 41, ⓦlofotencharterbat.no), an impossibly narrow, 2km-long stretch of water that's also visited by the Hurtigruten (see p.306). The intrepid might also consider making the same excursion by **speedboat** (3 times daily; return trip 2hr; 700kr; ☎97 15 22 48, ⓦlofoten-explorer.no; heavy jackets and goggles are included in the price).

### WALKING ON SKROVA

For one of the more enjoyable **hikes** in the area, take a ferry over to the pretty islet of **Skrova**, just offshore from Svolvær. The boat docks at Skrova's one and only settlement, an appealing affair, whose brightly painted houses track along a slender rocky spit, its harbour holding what was once the country's largest whaling station. Exploring the village can take half an hour or so and afterwards you can stroll over the causeway that attaches the village to the main body of the island, which is itself dominated by Mount Høgskrova (258m). There are three colour-coded hikes on the main island, including a steep (1hr each way) hoof up to the top of the mountain or a rather gentler gambol round its lower slopes. Before you catch the ferry, pick up a proper hiking map plus the makings of a picnic at one of the shops in Svolvær and prepare to munch away in splendid isolation. **Ferries** to Skrova run from the quay in Svolvær (3–5 daily; 30min; 45kr each way) and the car ferry between Svolvær and Skutvik often calls in here too.

### CLIMBING SVOLVÆRGEITA

Svolvær boasts one of the archipelago's most famous **climbs**, the haul up to the top of the **Svolværgeita** (the "Svolvær Goat"), a two-pronged pinnacle that rises high above the E10 to the northeast of town. The lower slopes of the mountain are hard enough, but the last 40m – up the horns of the "Goat" – require nerve and expertise. The rashly intrepid crown the achievement by jumping from one pinnacle to the other. It's worth remembering that, from the top of the horns, you look straight down on Svolvær's cemetery….

### SEA-FISHING

**Nigel Hearn** (☎99 75 93 42, ⓦnoproblemsportfishing.com), an Englishman who has lived in Lofoten for years, offers fishing trips from Svolvær tailor-made to your specification, with all equipment provided. There's not a lot Nigel doesn't know about the denizens of the deep – pick his brains. A 4hr excursion costs 2500kr, 3500kr for 6hr, based on a party of six.

---

harbour. It consists of twenty-two spacious and gorgeously decorated *rorbuer* (all with full kitchen): number 228 is the swankiest, a two-bedroom suite with dual balconies. Great sea views; great atmosphere. **1990kr**

**Lofototen Rorbuer** Jektveien 10 ☎91 59 54 50, ⓦlofoten-rorbuer.no. There are eighteen modest rooms, some with bunk beds, at this long-established place on the Marinepollen lagoon. A few of the rooms share a kitchen and/or a bathroom, while others have self-contained kitchenettes. About 1km north of town along the E10. **800kr**

**Scandic Hotel Svolvær** Lamholmen ☎76 07 22 22, ⓦscandichotels.com. This top-ranking chain hotel has an attractive modern design with acres of glass on top of

timber piles. The rooms are compact but comfortable, and most have a balcony, many with sea views. In the middle of the harbour on the islet of Lamholmen. **1390kr**

**Svinøya Rorbuer** Gunnar Bergsvei 2, Svinøya ☎76 06 99 30, ⓦsvinoya.no. At the northeast end of town, a causeway crosses over to the long and slender island of Svinøya, which is home to this well-appointed set of *rorbuer*. They range from the plain and simple to the deluxe. **1400kr**

**Thon Hotel Svolvær** Torget ☎76 04 90 00, ⓦthonhotels.no. Smart and slick chain hotel in a high-rise block that looms over downtown Svolvær. About 190 neat and comfortable bedrooms presented in contemporary style. **1800kr**

**5**

## EATING

**Bacalao** Havnepromenaden 2 ☎ 76 07 94 00, ⓦ bacalaobar.no. Down on the harbour, this spacious café-restaurant offers an imaginative international menu, burgers, wraps, salads as well as a cracking fish-soup and tasty *bacalao*. Lunches and evening main courses average around 180kr. Excellent coffee too. At night it turns into the town's liveliest bar, which is rammed at the weekend. Mon–Thurs 10.30am–1am, Fri & Sat 10.30am–2.30am, Sun noon–1am.

★ **Børsen Spiseri** Svinøya Rorbuer, Gunnar Bergsvei 2, Svinøya ☎ 76 06 99 30, ⓦ svinoya.no. Across the water on Svinøya, this must be Lofoten's most atmospheric restaurant, in a gorgeous old waterfront building dating from 1828, adorned with maritime paraphernalia such as skin kayaks and primitive fishing gear. Its speciality is stockfish (*bacalao*) but whatever you order will be skilfully and delicately prepared with mains averaging 300kr. Also look out for the "krambua", or general store, a museum of sorts, with old wares and shop equipment from days of yore. Reservations recommended. March–Oct daily 6pm–10pm; Nov–Feb Thurs–Sun 6pm–10pm.

★ **Du Verden** Torget 15 ☎ 76 07 09 75, ⓦ duverden .no. On the central square, this place aspires to cover a lot of bases – seafood, pizza, pasta, sushi – and just about succeeds. The food is always attractively presented and the place is generally heaving. It's fairly expensive though – even the pizzas start at 155kr. After the kitchen closes, at 10pm, it turns into a bar (Mon–Fri till 11pm, Fri & Sat till 2.30am). Mon–Sat 11am–10pm & Sun 1pm–10pm.

# Kabelvåg

Its handsome centre draped around the shore of a narrow and knobbly inlet, **KABELVÅG** is smaller but more appealing than neighbouring Svolvær, just 6km away. From Viking times until the early twentieth century, this was the most important village on Lofoten, the centre of the coastal fishery and home to the country's first *rorbuer*, built in 1120, as well as one of its first inns, dating back to 1792. Kabelvåg is quiet today, but its high times are recalled by an especially delightful medley of brightly painted timber houses, a charming ensemble at their prettiest down by the water's edge.

## Vågan kirke

Villaveien 9 • May–Aug Mon–Fri 10am–6pm, Sun noon–6pm • 40kr • ☎ 76 06 71 90, ⓦ lofotkatedralen.no

The late nineteenth-century **Vågan kirke**, also known as the Lofotkatedralen, is a big, breezy and somewhat garish, wooden church that overlooks the E10 on the northeastern edge of the village. A reminder of Kabelvåg's more populous days, the church's hangar-like interior was built to hold a congregation of over a thousand, its cobweb of supporting timbers now its most appealing feature.

## Lofotmuseet

Storvåganveien 25 • May & late Aug daily 11am–3pm; June to mid-Aug daily 10am–6pm; Sept–April Mon–Fri 11am–3pm • 80kr or 200k for a Storvågan multi-ticket, including the gallery & aquarium • ☎ 76 15 40 00, ⓦ museumnord.no/lofotmuseet

The **Lofotmuseet** (Lofoten Museum), by the seashore in Storvågan about 1.5km west of Kabelvåg, is one of Lofoten's more diverting museums. In an old house and country store dating from the 1800s, it traces the history of the islands' fisheries, boats and *rorbuer*, and displays the definitive collection of maritime equipment and other cultural paraphernalia. It also houses a great little gift shop.

## Galleri Espolin

Storvåganveien • May & late Aug daily 11am–3pm; June to mid-Aug daily 10am–6pm; Sept–April Mon–Fri 11am–3pm • 80kr, or 200k for a Storvågan multi-ticket, including the museum & aquarium • ☎ 76 07 84 05, ⓦ galleri-espolin.no

Cleverly shoehorned into a hillside near the Lofotmuseet, the **Galleri Espolin** (Espolin Gallery) features Norway's largest collection of paintings and sketches by **Kaare Espolin Johnson** (1907–94), a renowned Norwegian artist of Romantic inclination, who specialized in Arctic images and imagery. The artist's haunting, almost three-dimensional style is distinguished by its use of watercolour, oil, lead and soot – he was forced to experiment with techniques partly because of his poor eyesight. Two of the gallery's halls exhibit Johnson's works, while a third is used for temporary exhibitions.

**5**

## Lofotakvariet

Storvåganveien 28 • Feb–April & Sept–Nov Mon–Fri & Sun 11am–3pm; May daily 11am–3pm; June–Aug daily 10am–6pm • 120kr, or 200k for a Storvågan multi-ticket, including the museum & gallery • ☎ 76 07 86 65, ⓦ lofotakvariet.no

Displaying a wide variety of Atlantic species, the indoor and outdoor **Lofotakvariet** (Lofoten aquarium) has a number of exhibits on the fauna of the Norwegian coast. The most engaging part of the visit, however, is watching the regular feeding times of various sea creatures, including otters and seals.

### ARRIVAL AND DEPARTURE                                              KABELVÅG

**By bus** Local buses drop passengers right in the centre of Kabelvåg, just off the main drag, Torggata. Timetables on ⓦ rutebok.no.

Destinations Henningsvær (5 daily; 30min); Svolvær (5 daily; 15min).

### ACTIVITIES

**Sea-kayaking** Lofoten Aktiv at Rødmyrveien 24 (☎ 99 23 11 00, ⓦ lofoten-aktiv.no) specializes in sea-kayaking with day-long tours costing 1450kr per person. Also runs biking, hiking and rowing trips.
**Skiing, hiking & climbing** Northern Alpine Guides at

Kalleveien 23 (☎ 94 24 91 10, ⓦ alpineguides.no) is the best operator hereabouts for most outdoor pursuits. They organize a range of challenging, year-round activities, including day-hikes, ski outings and rock- and ice-climbing courses. Prices for most activities start at 1200kr/day.

### ACCOMMODATION AND EATING

**Lofoten Sommerhotell & Kabelvåg Vandrerhjem** Finnesveien 24 ☎ 76 06 98 80, ⓦ www.lofoten sommerhotell.no. Sited in a folk high school on the eastern edge of the village, Kabelvåg's youth hostel is a tad frugal, but perfectly adequate – and inexpensive. The *Sommerhotell* is in the same complex and offers a degree more comfort. The breakfasts are particularly generous. Finnesveien is a turning off the E10 just south of Vågan kirke. Both the hostel and the hotel are open June to mid-Aug. Dorms **290kr**, hostel doubles **730kr**, hotel doubles **1250kr**
**Nyvågar Rorbuhotell** Storvåganveien 26 ☎ 76 06 97 00, ⓦ nyvagar.no. This is by far the most luxurious choice hereabouts, comprising an assortment of smart four-bedded *rorbuer*. The rooms/apartments are kitted out in bright, modern style and the nicest are right on the

waterfront with secluded terraces. A large wooden hot tub outside hosts some lively get-togethers, and there is bicycle (55kr/day) and boat rental (200kr/hr). The on-site restaurant, *Lorchstua*, is similarly smart and does a tasty line in seafood; mains from 200kr. Restaurant: daily noon–10pm. **1330kr**
★ **Præstengbrygga Pub** Torget 9 ☎ 41 51 58 69. On the square overlooking the dock, this lively spot with its varnished wood interior is the heart of the Kabelvåg social scene. They serve enormous, excellent-value sandwiches, salads, and pizzas from 150kr, have a popular bottomless-cup-of-coffee deal, and feature a locally famous fish soup in autumn and winter plus the best *bacalao* you'll taste in summer. June–Aug Sun–Thurs 11am–1am, Fri & Sat 10am–2.30am; Sept–May Mon–Thurs 11am–4pm, Fri & Sat 11am–2.30am, Sun noon–3pm.

## Henningsvær

Approached from the E10 along a spectacular, 10km-long byroad that skips from islet to islet, **HENNINGSVÆR** is one of Lofoten's most picturesque and beguiling seaports, its lattice of cramped and twisting lanes lined with brightly painted wooden houses. In turn, these frame a tiny inlet that literally cuts the place in half, forming a sheltered, postcard-pretty harbour that was long Henningsvær's economic mainstay. Tourism is the big deal here today and consequently the town is well supplied with places to eat, drink and sleep – and there's even some congestion as tour parties are bussed in and out; but nonetheless it's a lovely spot that well deserves an overnight stay at the very least.

### Kaviar Factory

Henningsværveien 13 • Times & admission depend on exhibitions • ☎ 90 73 47 43, ⓦ kaviarfactory.com

The long and white cuboid building at the entrance to Henningsvær was built in the 1950s for the manufacture of caviar paste. The caviar is long defunct, but the

### COD FISHING

For hundreds of years fishermen have gathered in the waters off Lofoten to catch the **cod** that have migrated here from the Barents Sea to spawn. The fish arrive in late January or early February and the season lasts until April. There are tremendous fluctuations in the number of cod making the journey and although the reasons for this variation are not fully understood, relative water temperatures and, more recently, over-fishing are two key components. Sometimes the cod arrive packed together, at other times they are thinly spread, their distribution dictated by water temperature. The fish prefer a water temperature of about 5°C, which occurs here off Lofoten between the warm and salty bottom current and the colder surface waters: sometimes this band of water is thick, sometimes thin; sometimes it's close to the shore, sometimes it's way out to sea, all of which affect the fishing. If you fancy going **fishing**, one good place to try your hand is **Henningsvær** (see p.322).

building now houses the **Kaviar Factory**, a particularly well-lit exhibition space, which offers an excellent programme of temporary exhibitions of both modern and contemporary art and design.

### Galleri Lofotens Hus

Hjellskjæret • Daily: March, April & late Sept 10am–4pm; May to early Sept 10am–7pm • 85kr • ☎ 91 59 50 83, ⓦ galleri-lofoten.no

Set in a former fish-processing plant, the **Galleri Lofotens Hus** is one of the town's main draws, featuring a prime collection of north Norwegian paintings. Most of the paintings date from the late nineteenth and early twentieth centuries when Realism dominated the artistic roost, its prime practitioners including Einar Berger, Adelsteen Normann, Gunnar Berg and Otto Sinding, whose whopping *Funeral in Lofoten* of 1886 is impossible to miss. There is more contemporary stuff too, including a battery of photos and the more Impressionistic work of **Karl Erik Harr**, who was born in Troms in 1940.

### Engelskmannsbrygga

Dreyersgate 1 • Mid-Jan to mid-March Sat & Sun 11am–4pm; mid-March to May & Sept–Dec Wed–Sun 11am–4pm; early June Wed–Sun 10am–6pm; mid-June to mid-Aug daily 10am–9pm; late Aug daily 10am–6pm • Free • ☎ 48 12 98 70, ⓦ engelskmannsbrygga.no

Henningsvær's Arctic light, combined with the severity of the surrounding mountains, has long attracted Norwegian painters, making it something of an arts-centre-cum-colony. Right in the centre of town, **Engelskmannsbrygga** (Englishman's Wharf) is a gallery run by a collective of artists, who you can watch at work. It's a good place to purchase, or simply admire, the art, plus a selection of ceramics, photography and glassware.

### Galleri Vidars Lyse Verden

Dreyersgate 54 • June–Aug daily 10am–8pm; telephone for opening hours out of season, reduced hours Sept–May • Free • ☎ 95 90 03 91, ⓦ vidars-lyse-verden.origo.no

Just up from the main square, the pint-sized **Galleri Vidars Lyse Verden** showcases the photographs of Vidar Lysvold. The subject matter is the familiar imagery of Lofoten – the northern lights, birdlife, the cod fishery and the mountains – but it's all to a very high standard and although Lysvold's work is his living, he is happy just to chat and there's no pressure to buy.

### ARRIVAL AND DEPARTURE · HENNINGSVÆR

**By bus** The Lofotenekspressen (see p.317) does not detour off the E10 to Henningsvær, but there are local bus services between Henningsvær and its nearest neighbours. In Henningsvær, buses pull into the centre of the village at the junction of Henningsværveien and Dreyersgate. Timetables on ⓦ rutebok.no.

Destinations Kabelvåg (5 daily; 30min); Svolvær (2–6 daily; 30min).

## ACTIVITIES

**Mountaineering** Henningsvær is home to one of Lofoten's foremost mountaineering schools, Nord Norsk Klatreskole, Misværveien 10 (☎ 90 57 42 08, ⓦ nordnorskklatreskole .no), who offer a range of all-inclusive climbing holidays in the mountains nearby, catering for various degrees of fitness and experience. Prices vary depending on the trip, but summer climbing tends to run in the region of 2000kr per person per day, including equipment and food.

**Sea adventures** Lofoten Opplevelser (☎ 90 58 14 75, ⓦ lofoten-opplevelser.no) runs a range of marine activities. During the summer season, they offer fishing trips (3hr; 850kr), sea-eagle safaris (2hr; 600kr) and snorkelling trips (2hr; 850kr). In the colder months, they arrange orca safaris (3hr; 1250kr), snorkelling with orcas (3hr; 1950kr) and trips to view the northern lights (2hr; 600kr).

## ACCOMMODATION

★ **Henningsvær Bryggehotell** Misværveien 18 ☎ 76 07 47 50, ⓦ henningsvaer.no. This attractive modern building right on the quayside is the town's smartest hotel, with thirty rooms kitted out in spick-and-span modern style. It can be popular with large groups; the use of the sauna is included in the price. **1200kr**

**Henningsvær Rorbuer** Banhammaren 53 ☎ 76 06 60 00, ⓦ henningsvar-rorbuer.no. This stylish, well-kept complex consists of twenty-odd, well-equipped *rorbuer* at the outer end of the Henningsvær promontory, each accommodating from two to six guests. Some have outdoor

seating and loft beds and you can use a giant wooden hot tub and sauna. There's boat rental too. Minimum two nights' stay during most of the season. **1500kr**

**Nord Norsk Klatreskole** Misværveien 10 ☎ 90 57 42 08, ⓦ nordnorskklatreskole.no. Henningsvær's mountaineering school (see above) offers basic but adequate lodgings, located right in the centre. One of the rooms is where author Johan Bojer (1872–1959) penned his popular *The Last of the Vikings* – though the room retains little of its nineteenth-century charm. Dorms **300kr**, singles **500kr**, doubles **600kr**

## EATING AND DRINKING

**Climbers Café** Misværveien 10 ☎ 90 57 42 08, ⓦ nordnorskklatreskole.no. Described as a cross between a French bistro, Everest base-camp and a Nepali teahouse, this friendly place offers lunches, full meals, snacks and great coffee. There's regular live music too. Climbing paraphernalia and candlelight provide atmosphere, and, surprise, surprise, much of the conversation is to do with mountaineering. Feb–May & Oct–Dec Wed, Fri & Sat 7–11.30pm; June–Sept daily noon–11.30pm.

★ **Fiskekrogen** Dreyersgate 29 ☎ 76 07 46 52, ⓦ www .fiskekrogen.no. This smart and classy, waterside

restaurant has a great location and fine views. The seafood dishes in general, and the fish soup (185kr) in particular, are simply superb. Mains such as cod, monkfish and mussels cost around 270kr. Mid-May to mid-Aug daily noon–11pm; mid-Aug to mid-May Tues–Sun noon–6pm.

**Lysstøperi** Gammelveien 2 ☎ 90 55 18 77, ⓦ henningsvarlys.no. Inside a colourful candle shop, this is the town's best cake and tea shop – delicious cinnamon buns, chocolate cake, cheese cake and all manner of home-baked delights. June–Sept daily 10am–6pm; Oct–May Wed–Sat 11am–4pm.

# Vestvågøy

A jagged hunk of rock perforated by scores of coves and inlets, the island of **Vestvågøy**, to the southwest of Austvågøya, is quite simply captivating. For starters, the island's south coast possesses, in **Stamsund** and **Ballstad**, a pair of charming, easygoing ports, while the wild beauty of its northern coast frames a series of hardy fishing villages – **Unstad**, **Eggum** and **Utakleiv** – which sit on the edge of the ocean with severe peaks rising to their rear. The E10 weaves a pretty route across the island, skirting its largest settlement and transport hub, humdrum **Leknes**.

## Lofotr Vikingmuseum

Prestegårdsveien 59, Bøstad • Nov–Jan Wed & Sat noon–5pm; Feb–April & mid-Sept to Oct Wed–Sat noon–5pm; May to mid-Sept daily 10am–5pm • 140kr, 160kr in high season • ☎ 76 15 40 00, ⓦ lofotr.no • Beside the E10, 55km southwest of Svolvær and 14km northeast of Leknes

In 1981, a local farmer accidentally discovered the remains of a Viking chieftain's house here on Vestvågøy, prompting – after a lot of huffing and puffing – the construction of the **Lofotr Vikingmuseum**. The exhibits, including a scattering of archeological finds, are now displayed within a reconstructed 83-metre Viking hall, with flickering lights,

**5**

wood-tar smells and so forth all adding to the atmosphere. Afterwards, you can have a look at the museum's pair of replica Viking longships, which are taken out on the water during the summer.

## Unstad

Hidden away on the north coast, at the end of a byroad that branches off the E10 just west of the Lofotr Vikingmuseum, the hamlet of **Unstad** sits in a diminutive river valley beneath stern mountains and with wide views out to sea. Apart from the sheer isolation of the place, the main draw is the ocean: this is by far the best **surfing** spot on the island with a great and stable swell, quite enough to attract a steady stream of surfers, who make a beeline for **Unstad Arctic Surf** (see below).

### ACCOMMODATION AND ACTIVITIES                                            UNSTAD

**Unstad Arctic Surf** Unstadveien 105 ☎ 97 06 12 01, ⓦ unstadarcticsurf.com. Making the most of the surfing, this enterprising business offers, among much else, introductory tuition sessions (1200kr for 4hr) and weekend surf packages (2500kr for 3 days), including equipment,

food and accommodation. Advance booking is strongly recommended. Accommodation is in a set of wooden cabins (twelve-, eight-, three- and two-person) and there is a campground here as well. Two-bunk cabin **990kr**

## Utakleiv

Tiny **UTAKLEIV** has a handsome, north-coast setting, its flat grazing land dotted with far-flung sheep and cows and surrounded on three sides by austere cliffs and jagged peaks. On the fourth side is the white-sand **beach**, a wild and lonely strand nominated – perhaps surprisingly – as one of Europe's most romantic by the *Sunday Times* in 2010. To get to Utakleiv, take the signed turning off the E10 in between the Lofotr Vikingmuseum (see p.325) and Leknes. The turning leads over the hills for 10km before running past a sandy beach, at **Haukland**, and then reaches the village by means of a narrow tunnel.

## Stamsund

Rambling **STAMSUND**, just 60km from Henningsvær, has a certain laidback charm, its older buildings strung out along the rocky, fretted seashore in an amiable jumble of crusty port buildings, wooden houses and *rorbuer*. Stamsund is a Hurtigruten port, has the largest trawler fleet on the Lofoten and was one of the targets for the British commando raids of 1941 (see box, p.318). The British captured 230 German soldiers and Quisling collaborators, were joined by 300 Norwegian volunteers and took possession of the wheels and code books of an enigma machine. Tongue in cheek, the commandos also sent a telegram to Berlin saying how unprepared the German garrison had been – which irritated the German generals no end. Today, it's the general flavour of the place that appeals, rather than any specific sight, though you might want to pop into a local art gallery, **Galleri 2**.

### Galleri 2

J. M. Johansens vei 18 • June–Aug daily noon–6pm; rest of year by appointment • 20kr • ☎ 90 95 65 46, ⓦ galleri2.no

Stamsund is home to **Galleri 2**, a pleasant little art gallery 100m from the Hurtigruten dock, which features the work of modern Norwegian artists in several different media.

---

### A HIKE FROM UNSTAD TO EGGUM

A popular, 9km-long **hiking trail** with mountains and lakes on one side and the surging ocean on the other, runs northeast from the village of **UNSTAD** to the tiny hamlet of **EGGUM** on Vestvågøy's northern coast. The trail passes the remains of a radar station built by the Germans during World War II. Eggum is itself an especially pretty spot, its handful of houses clinging onto a precarious headland dwarfed by the mountains behind and with a whopping pebble beach in front. You can also reach Eggum by car from the E10: the signed byroad begins just to the northeast of the Lofotr Vikingmuseum (see p.325).

The gallery was founded by an American, Scott Thoe, and his Norwegian partner, Vebørg Hagene Thoe, whose works are displayed here as well.

## ARRIVAL AND DEPARTURE
## STAMSUND

**By bus** The Lofotenekspressen (see p.317) runs along the E10 from Svolvær to Å via Leknes, where you change for Stamsund. In Stamsund, buses pull in near the Hurtigruten jetty. Timetables on ⓦ 177nordland.no or ⓦ rutebok.no. Destinations Leknes (6 daily; 30min).

**By Hurtigruten** The Hurtigruten (ⓦ hurtigruten.co.uk) docks in what amounts to the centre of Stamsund. Northbound, the Hurtigruten takes a little under 2hr to reach Svolvær; southbound it's 4hr to Bodø.

## ACCOMMODATION

**Stamsund Rørbuer** J. M. Johansens vei 47 ☎ 95 23 80 72, ⓦ www.stamsundrorbuer.no. Just a few seconds' walk from the Hurtigruten quay, this complex of pleasantly refurbished and comfortable *rorbuer*, each with a full kitchen, mainly deals with weekly rentals (8000kr), but if space permits, double rooms are available per night for 1500kr

★ **Stamsund Vandrerhjem** Hartvågen 13 ☎ 76 08 93 34, ⓦ hihostels.no. This popular and relaxing hostel comprises several *rorbuer* and a bright yellow *sjøhus*, all perched on the edge of a bonny little bay. You can rent bikes here (100kr/day) and there are self-catering facilities. It's located about 1.2km north of the port. March to mid-Oct. Dorms 160kr, doubles 460kr

## EATING

**Mannfallet** Steineveien 16 ☎ 91 38 54 65. This tiny and modern café-bar offers surprisingly good food, pizzas, fish soup and the like. Usually crowded, often boisterous, it's a great place to watch football on TV. April–Sept daily 6pm–midnight; Oct–March Wed–Sun 6pm–midnight.

**Skjærbrygga** Hjellskjæret ☎ 76 05 46 00, ⓦ skjaerbrygga.no. This restaurant and bar is located right by the harbour in an old and attractively renovated *sjøhus*. The menu is strong on seafood with mains going for around 250kr. June–Sept daily noon–midnight; check website for hours at other times of the year.

## Ballstad

One of Lofoten's largest cod-fishing ports and a centre for boat repairs and refits, **BALLSTAD**, about 25km from Stamsund and 8km south of the E10, is a bustling little place with a handsome coastal setting and two harbours – an inner harbour for the fishery, an outer one for leisure craft. Look out in particular for the massive blue and white seafaring murals painted on the side of the main boatyard by American artist Scott Thoe, a long-standing local resident (see above).

## ARRIVAL AND DEPARTURE
## BALLSTAD

**By bus** The Lofotenekspressen (see p.317) runs along the E10 from Svolvær to Å via Leknes, where you change for Ballstad. In Ballstad, buses pull in beside the Joker

Supermarket, close to the boatyard. Bus timetables on ⓦ rutebok.no.
Destinations Leknes (6 daily; 30min).

## ACTIVITIES

**Sea-fishing** Several operators offer sea-fishing trips from Ballstad. The pick is Sjøstrand Fisk, whose seasoned fishermen ply from the inner harbour, Ballstadlandet 86 (☎ 48 11 35 65, ⓦ rorbuer.info). The cost is 550kr for a 3hr trip to the best inshore fishing spots.
**Sea safaris and diving** Lofoten Diving at Skarsjyveien

67 (☎ 40 04 85 54, ⓦ lofoten-diving.com) offers sea safaris in an RIB craft, exploring the area's mammal and birdlife (3hr; 790kr). Diving trips are available for those with considerable experience or none at all, and include scuba training, wildlife diving and exploring wrecks (3hr; 590kr).

## ACCOMMODATION AND EATING

**Ballstad Vandrerhjem & Rorbuer** Kræmmervikveien 3 ☎ 76 06 09 20, ⓦ kremmervika.no. A first-rate hostel, with both reception and dorm accommodation set in an old fisherman's mission from the late nineteenth century. The single and double rooms are housed in original *rorbuer*.

Breakfast (110kr) is generous and sustaining and so is the weekly Sunday dinner buffet (served 3–8pm). Dorms 230kr, singles 350kr, doubles 450kr
**Kræmmervikahavn Rorbuer** Kræmmervikveien 36 ☎ 91 66 13 30, ⓦ kremmervikahavn.no. This new *rorbu*

5

complex near the outer edge of the leisure harbour features twelve self-catering units for between two and seven guests and a cosy pub/restaurant whose forte is fish and lamb. The waterside terrace offers wonderful coastal and mountain views. Mains start at 220kr. Restaurant: daily 11am–11pm. <u>**950kr**</u>

## Flakstadøya and Moskenesøya

By any standard, the next two islands of the Lofoten archipelago, **Flakstadøya** and **Moskenesøya**, are extraordinarily beautiful. As Lofoten tapers towards its southerly conclusion, so the rearing peaks of the **Lofotenveggen** crimp the sea-shredded coastline, providing a thunderously scenic backdrop to a necklace of tiny fishing villages, primarily **Nusfjord**, **Reine** and **Å**. The **E10** travels along almost all of this

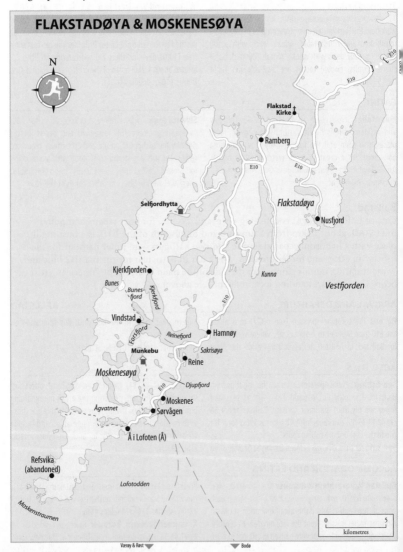

### FLAKSTADØYA & MOSKENESØYA

N

E10

E10

Flakstad Kirke †

● Ramberg

E10    E10

Selfjordhytta ◫

*Flakstadøya*

● Nusfjord

Kjerkfjorden ●

*Bunes*   Bunes-   fjord

*Kjerkfjord*

*Kunna*

*Vestfjorden*

Vindstad ●

*Fotsfjord*

*Reinefjord*   ● Hamnøy

*Sakrisøya*

Munkebu ◫

● Reine

*Moskenesøya*

E10   *Djupfjord*

*Ågvatnet*

● Moskenes

● Sørvågen

Å i Lofoten (Å) ●

Refsvika (abandoned) ●

*Lofotodden*

*Moskenstraumen*

0    5
kilometres

**5**

shoreline in what is, quite simply, one of the most stunning drives in the whole of Europe. It's a steely harsh terrain, but people have been eking out a living here for centuries – indeed Flakstadøya was known to the Vikings as "Vargfot", or wolf's paw, on account of its shape.

## Nusfjord

Pocket-sized **NUSFJORD**, an extravagantly picturesque fishing village in a tight and forbidding cove, is located about 40km from Stamsund, down an improbable byroad that runs south through the mountains from the E10. Unlike many *rorbuer* elsewhere in Lofoten, the ones here are the genuine nineteenth-century article, and the general store, with its wooden floors and antique appearance, fits in nicely too. Perhaps inevitably, it's tourism that keeps the local economy afloat and coachloads of day-trippers zip in and out, paying an 80kr entrance fee per person for the privilege during the summer. Don't let that deter you – some of the buildings, like the cod-liver refinery, the smithy and the sawmill, have been attractively restored and in the evening, when the crowds have disappeared, Nusfjord is truly beguiling.

**ARRIVAL AND DEPARTURE**                                **NUSFJORD**

**By bus** The Lofotekspressen (see p.317) does not detour off the E10 to Nusfjord, but there is a limited bus service from Leknes (Mon–Fri 2 daily; 1hr). Timetables ⓦ 177 nordland.no or ⓦ rutebok.no.

### ACCOMMODATION

**Nusfjord Rorbuer** Nusfjord ☎ 76 09 30 20, ⓦ nusfjord .no. On offer here are various types of comfortably refurbished *rorbuer*, ranging from simple, standard versions sleeping up to four people, to luxurious two-bedroom affairs that cost an arm and a leg; advance reservations are strongly advised. They also rent out bicycles (200kr/day), kayaks (580kr/day) and boats (550kr/day), as well as fishing gear (no charge). **1300kr**

## Ramberg's Flakstad kirke

Beside the E10, on the outskirts of Ramberg • June–Aug Tues–Sun 11am–3pm • Free • ☎ 76 05 22 01, ⓦ kirkesok.no

Sitting pretty in sight of the main road, the red-timbered **Flakstad kirke**, with its distinctive onion dome, dates from 1780, replacing an earlier structure that was blown down by a storm a few years before. Inside, the church's ornate pulpit was retrieved from the earlier church and is the work of Gottfried Ezechiel, an itinerant German artist, who made a living hereabouts from a series of ecclesiastical commissions. By necessity a versatile artist, Ezechiel also did Flakstad's altar painting, a folksy affair whose main motif is the Last Supper. Incidentally, the plaque by the main door commemorates the church's use as a polling station in the 1814 referendum on independence from Denmark. Alas, transport difficulties and inclement weather meant that the votes from Flakstad arrived at the National Assembly, in Eidsvoll, too late to be counted.

The church lies on the eastern approach to **RAMBERG**, Flakstadøya's administrative centre, which strings the seashore with a smattering of services (garage, supermarket and suchlike).

## Reine

Beyond Ramberg, the **E10** slips along the coast with rearing peaks on one side, the ocean on the other, a beautiful journey that takes you over to **Moskenesøya**, the next island along. About 25km from Ramberg, you reach delightful **REINE**, an old fishing port which occupies the northern half of a pint-sized promontory, its spindly jetties inching out into the water flanked by a scattering of red-painted cabins with sheer dog-toothed mountains rising all around. What sets Reine apart is the extraordinary quality of the light, a crystal clarity that has attracted artists and photographers from far and wide. Reine is also the departure point for a variety of **boat trips**, including those to **Vindstad** (see box, p.330), the **Moskenstraumen** (see box, p.332), and the **Refsvika cave paintings** (see box, p.331); the last two are usually seen on the same trip.

**5**

## A FERRY AND A HIKE FROM REINE TO VINDSTAD AND BUNES

**VINDSTAD**, an eerily deserted village with just one permanent inhabitant and a few holiday homes, is an excellent starting point for the 90min hike over to Moskenesøya's northwest coast. The first 30min of the hike, along an old dirt trail, are not especially enjoyable, but things improve thereafter as you proceed along the west shore of the narrow and very steep Bunesfjord with jagged mountains rearing up in every direction. The dirt trail ends abruptly just past the cemetery and you have to make a sharp left, continuing up a steep grass path that takes you over a ridge between the mountains. An hour or so on from here, you'll reach the sandy cove of **Bunes**, the epitome of isolation and a smashing place to watch the midnight sun. It isn't a difficult hike, but given that this last section can get very slippery and the weather can change in minutes, you'll need to be properly equipped.

### BY BOAT

To get from Reine to Vindstad, catch the M/S *Fjordskyss*, a small passenger ferry that runs up the Reinefjord (1–2 daily; 55kr each way; ☎ 99 49 18 05, ⦿ reinefjorden.no).

Eva Harr Gallery

Reine Kultursenter, beside the tourist office on the waterfront • May–Sept daily 11am–6pm • 70kr • ☎ 76 09 10 10, ⦿ evaharr.no

Reine is home to the **Eva Harr Gallery**, which is devoted to this Harstad-born contemporary artist's work. Her expressive paintings of Lofoten are displayed alongside a selection of her graphic work.

### ARRIVAL AND INFORMATION                                                    REINE

**By bus** Local buses stop in the centre of Reine by the kiosk and petrol station, while the Lofotenekspressen (see p.317) stops by the bridge on the E10 at the edge of the village. Bus timetables on ⦿ 177nordland.no or ⦿ rutebok.no. Destinations Å (6 daily; 25min); Evenes airport (1–2 daily; 6hr); Moskenes (6 daily; 10min); Narvik (1–2 daily; 8hr); Svolvær (1–2 daily; 3hr 30min).

**Tourist office** The Moskenesøya tourist information office is in the Reine Kultursenter, the square white building on the left as you reach the centre of the village (May to mid-June & mid-Aug to mid-Sept daily 10am–2pm; mid-June to mid-Aug daily 10am–7.30pm; ☎ 98 01 75 64, ⦿ lofoten-info.no/turkont.htm).

### ACTIVITIES

**Fishing, diving and boat trips** Aqua Lofoten Coast Adventure (☎ 99 01 90 42, ⦿ aqualofoten.no) is a well-regarded adventure specialist that offers a range of sea trips, fishing expeditions and diving excursions. They are among the few outfits licensed to take people to the ancient cave paintings at Refsvika, at the outer tip of Lofoten (see box opposite). The Refsvika excursion, which takes 6hr and includes the Moskenstraumen (Maelstrom), costs 995kr; the Moskenstraumen trip lasts just over 2hr and costs 800kr. There is also a 4hr fishing trip for 700kr and assorted diving trips for 650–1100kr.

**Hiking, cycling and kayaking** Reine Adventure (☎ 93 21 45 96 ⦿ reineadventure.com) is an environmentally conscious operator that provides a wide range of (nonmotorized) outdoor activities with hiking, biking and kayaking as their stock in trade. All their hire equipment is first-rate and reasonably priced; for instance mountain bike and helmet for 185kr/day, and a double-kayak 700kr/day. Their guided hikes are popular too, particularly the ascent of Reinebringen right behind the village (400kr) ending up at the top with one of Lofoten's most superlative views.

### ACCOMMODATION AND EATING

**Det Gamle Hotellet** Reine ☎ 99 03 80 68, ⦿ guesthouse lofoten.com. This charming little guesthouse, in an old building near the main harbour, offers a clutch of basic but very comfortable single and double rooms with shared facilities. Free coffee, but no meals. Good breakfasts are available next door at the *Bringen* café. Mid-May to mid-Sept. **800kr**

**Reine Rorbuer** Reine ☎ 76 09 22 22, ⦿ reinerorbuer

.com. Trailing back from the harbour, these 22 renovated *rorbuer* (and three apartments) are a great place to stay in Reine. An on-site restaurant, *Gammelbua*, occupies the old general store and offers top-notch seafood risottos, local lamb, fresh cod and marinated whale with a terrace overlooking the harbour. Mains cost from 180kr and reservations are advised. Daily 5–10pm, closed Nov. **1300kr**

**5**

★**Sakrisøy Rorbuer** Sakrisøya (E10) ☎ 90 03 54 19, ⓦ sakrisoyrorbuer.no. On Sakrisøya, a rocky islet at the mouth of the Reinefjord, some 4km north of Reine, these cosy, ochre-coloured and attractively restored *rorbuer* are located in a collection of original 1870 cabins; they come with kitchenettes and wood stoves. There's a restaurant on-site, too. They rent out bikes for a small charge and will lend out rowboats for free. The owners, two sisters, also run the fishmongers opposite, where they sell delicious home-made fish burgers as well as freshly caught fish. **1200kr**

## Moskenes

Humdrum **MOSKENES**, 5km south of Reine, is the archipelago's main port to and from Bodø. There's not much to the place, however – just a handful of houses dotted round a horseshoe-shaped bay – and most visitors make a prompt exit.

### ARRIVAL AND DEPARTURE                                                       MOSKENES

**By bus** The long-distance Lofotenekspressen (see p.317), linking Narvik and Å, pauses at the Moskenes ferry terminal. There are also local buses between Moskenes and both Reine and Å. Note, however, that bus times do not usually coincide with ferry arrivals or departures, meaning that you'll either have to walk to or from Reine or Å – both about 5km away – or take a taxi. For bus timetables, consult ⓦ 177nordland.no or ⓦ rutebok.no.
Destinations Å (6 daily; 10min); Evenes airport (1–2 daily; 6hr); Fiskebøl ferry quay (1–2 daily; 4hr 15min); Narvik (1–2 daily; 8hr); Reine (6 daily; 10min); Svolvær (1–2 daily; 3hr 30min).

**By ferry** Moskenes is connected by car ferry with Bodø and Værøy. Out of season, the ferries work on a first-come, first-served basis, so it's a good idea to turn up a couple of hours before departure, whereas in summer you are advised to make an advance reservation. The passenger fare is 196kr from Bodø, 705kr for a car and driver; from Værøy it's 87kr/294kr. Torghatten Nord (ⓦ torghatten -nord.no) currently operates these ferries and timetable details are available on ☎ 177 or ⓦ 177nordland.no.
Destinations Bodø (Mon–Sat 1–2daily; 4hr); Værøy (Mon–Sat 1–2daily; 1hr 30min).

## Å i Lofoten (Å)

Tersely named **Å**, 10km south of Reine at the end of the E10, is one of Lofoten's most charming villages, its huddle of antiquated buildings rambling along a foreshore that's wedged in tight between the grey-green mountains and the surging sea. No one knows for sure when the village was founded, but it first appears in parish records in 1567 and, at least until the recent tourist boom, it has always relied on cod fishing – as witnessed by the two **museums**, which are its main attractions today.

### Norsk Fiskeværsmuseum

June to late Aug daily 9am–7pm; late Aug to May Mon–Fri 10am–5pm • 80kr • ☎ 76 09 14 88, ⓦ museumnord.no

Pretty much left to its own devices for many decades, Å is something of a late nineteenth-century museum piece, where the pride of historic place goes to the engaging **Norsk Fiskerværsmuseum** (Norwegian Fishing Village Museum). There are

---

### CAVE PAINTINGS AT REFSVIKA

Near the southern tip of Moskenesøya, the remote fishing village of **REFSVIKA** was abandoned in the 1950s. There is no road leading there and the footpath from the rest of the island is arduous to say the least, but you can get to Refsvika by boat on **guided tours** from either Reine (see p.329) or Å (see above). It's not, however, the remains of the village which are the main draw, but rather the prehistoric **cave paintings** that decorate a huge cavern called the **Refsvikhula**. The cavern had long been used as a cattle shelter, but in the 1980s a group of archeology students stumbled across three groups of figures painted on the walls. There are 21 in total, each around 35cm tall, and tests have indicated that the figures, which date back some 3000 years, were created with a red-iron oxide found nearby. The significance of the figures has been the subject of much debate, but it seems likely that they had a religious or cult significance – especially as the midnight sun bathes the cavern's interior with an iridescent yellow light during midsummer.

about fifteen buildings to explore here, including a boathouse, forge, cod-liver-oil processing plant, *rorbuer*, and the houses of both the traders who dominated things hereabouts and the fishermen who did their bidding. According to the census of 1900, Å had 91 inhabitants, of whom ten were traders and their relatives, 18 servants, and 63 fishermen and their dependants. It was a rigidly hierarchical society underpinned by terms and conditions akin to serfdom: the fishermen did not own any land and had to pay rent for the ground on which their houses stood. Payment was made in the form of unpaid labour on the merchants' farmland during the summer harvest and, to rub salt into the wounds, the fishermen couldn't control the price of the fish upon which they were reliant – no wonder Norwegians emigrated in their thousands. The museum has a series of **displays** detailing every aspect of village life – and very well presented it is too.

### Tørrfiskmuseum

June to late Aug daily 9am–7pm; late Aug to May Mon–Fri 10am–5pm • 50kr • ☎ 76 09 12 11, ⓦ lofoten-info.no/stockfish.htm

To extend your knowledge of all things fishy, head for the **Tørrfiskmuseum** (Stockfish Museum) down at the harbour – the fish concerned being the air-dried cod that served as the staple diet of most Norwegians well into the twentieth century. The museum details the laborious process by which fresh cod becomes dried stockfish, from the lifting baskets traditionally used to unload the boats to the way the cod were tied in pairs and racked up to dry.

### ARRIVAL AND DEPARTURE
### Å I LOFOTEN (Å)

**By bus** The Lofotekspressen (see p.317), linking Narvik and Å, is the main long-distance bus; its services are supplemented by a couple of local buses. The nearest ferry port is Moskenes, just 5km away to the north (see p.331). For timetable details, consult ⓦ 177nordland.no or ⓦ rutebok.no.

Destinations Evenes airport (1–2 daily; 6hr 15min); Fiskebøl ferry quay (1–2 daily; 4hr 30min); Lødingen ferry quay (1–2 daily; 5hr 45min); Moskenes (6 daily; 10min); Narvik (1–2 daily; 8hr 15min); Reine (6 daily; 25min); Svolvær (1–2 daily; 3hr 45min).

### ACTIVITIES

**Fishing and boat trips** Daily between May and September, boats depart Å for 4hr fishing trips (600kr/person); coastal cruises (3hr; 600kr); and, weather and tides permitting, excursions to both Refsvika (see box, p.331) and the Moskenstraumen (5hr; 900kr), the dramatic maelstrom at the southern tip of Moskenesøya (see box below). Many of these trips start in Reine with Aqua Lofoten Coast Adventure (see p.330).

**Hikes** Å does not offer too much in the way of hiking trails, but there is an enjoyable route leading west from the village to the other side of Moskenesøya island. This begins by skirting the south shore of Lake Ågvatnet, before climbing over a steep ridge and then pushing on to the sea cliffs of the exposed west coast. The hike takes a whole day, and shouldn't be attempted in bad weather.

---

### THE MOSKENSTRAUMEN

The churning currents off the southern tip of Moskenesøya combine to create the **Moskenstraumen**, easily the most dramatic of Norway's several maelstroms. The intensity of the maelstrom varies enormously, but at its most ferocious it can strike fear into the hardiest of seafarers, though local fishermen have long been drawn here – weighing profit against danger – by the shoals of fish it attracts. Depending on conditions, excursions to the caves of Refsvika (see p.331) usually include passage of the Moskenstraumen in some form or another. The maelstrom fascinated Jules Verne, but it was **Edgar Allan Poe** who wrote most compellingly about it in his short story *A Descent into the Maelstrom*, though he never actually witnessed the Moskenstraumen himself:

*Even while I gazed, this current acquired a monstrous velocity. Each moment added to its speed – to its headlong impetuosity. In five minutes the whole sea … was lashed into ungovernable fury… Here the vast bed of the waters seamed and scarred into a thousand conflicting channels, burst suddenly into frenzied convulsion – heaving, boiling, hissing…*

**5**

## ACCOMMODATION

**Å-Hamna Rorbuer & Vandrerhjem Å i Lofoten** Å ☎ 76 09 12 11, ⓦ hihostels.no. In the centre of Å, by the waterside, this appealing HI-hostel has an assortment of smart one- to eight-bedded *rorbuer*. Also offers equally smart, hotel-standard rooms in the adjacent *sjøhus*. Open year-round. Dorms <u>260kr</u>, doubles <u>540kr</u>

**Hotel Smaken av Lofoten** ☎ 76 09 21 00, ⓦ smaken avlofoten.no. In the centre of Å, down by the harbour, this collection of buildings feature *rorbuer* of various shapes and sizes. Some of the nicest are extremely comfortable and the pick have period furnishings; others have shared facilities. <u>1200kr</u>

## EATING

**Gammelgården Bakery** Å ☎ 76 09 14 88. Built in the 1880s, this good-looking, late nineteenth-century building, with its gabled slate roof, started out as a lodging house for seasonal fishermen. Today, it's Lofoten's best bakery, cooking excellent cinnamon buns in a vintage oven. Mid-June to mid-Aug daily 9am–5pm.

**Smaken av Lofoten** Å ☎ 76 09 21 00, ⓦ smakenav lofoten.no. In the centre of the village, down by the harbour, this is Å's best restaurant, serving up top-ranking seafood dishes – like stockfish with a bacon and pesto sauce – in a great location; mains hover around 150kr. There's a cosy bar here too, which runs till midnight. June–Aug daily noon–10pm.

# Værøy

The second most southerly of the Lofoten islands, **VÆRØY** is just 8km long, with a slender, lightly populated, grassy-green coastal strip that shunts up towards the steep, bare mountains that form its backbone. The weather out here in Lofoten's remoter isles is uncommonly mild throughout the year, potential **hiking routes** are ubiquitous, and the occasional **beach** glorious and deserted. Værøy's few kilometres of road primarily connect the farmsteads of the plain, including the scattering of houses that make up **SØRLAND**, the main village, but one squeezes round the mountains to snake along a portion of the northwest coast. Here you'll find a handful of **Viking burial sites** and the oldest church in Lofoten, the onion-domed **Værøy Gamle Kirke** with its alabaster altarpiece from 1430, originally crafted in Nottingham and moved here in 1799 from its earlier location in Kabelvåg.

The island is well known for its **bird colonies: Måstadfjell** (at 435m) hosts well over a million puffins, eiders and gulls that breed in the summer months, as well as cormorants, terns, kittiwakes, guillemots, sea eagles and more recent migrants like the fulmar and gannet. Værøy's most important **bird cliffs** occupy the southwest corner of the island, but they are much too steep and slippery to approach on foot, so the best bet is to take a **boat trip** (see p.334). The best walking is elsewhere on the island, along the easier and clearer paths that lead out along the **Nupsneset** promontory, which hooks out into the ocean on the south coast.

## ARRIVAL AND DEPARTURE                                                                        VÆRØY

**By helicopter** Værøy can be reached from Bodø by helicopter with Lufttransport (1–2 daily; 25min; ☎ 77 60 83 00, ⓦ lufttransport.no); the single fare is currently 890kr.

**By car ferry** Værøy is one of the most time-consuming of the Lofoten islands to reach: indeed, unless you're careful, the irregular ferry schedules – between Bodø, Røst and Moskenes – can leave you stranded here for a couple of days. Out of season, the ferries work on a first-come, first-served basis, so it's a good idea to turn up a couple

of hours before departure, whereas in the summer you are advised to make an advance reservation. From Bodø to Værøy, the fare is 182kr per person and 651kr for car and driver, 87kr/294kr from Moskenes. Torghatten Nord (ⓦ torghatten-nord.no) currently operates these ferries and timetable details are available on ⓦ 177nordland.no. On Værøy, the ferry docks at the island's southeastern tip, about 800m from the tourist office.

Destinations Bodø (1–3daily; 5hr); Moskenes (1–3 daily; 1hr 15min); Røst (1–3 daily; 2hr).

## INFORMATION

**Tourist office** In the summer (late June to mid-Aug), a tourist information kiosk opens down by the jetty when

the ferries come in. Otherwise, there's a tourist office inside the Husfliden craft shop in the centre of Sørland,

### THE PUFFIN DOGS OF MÅSTAD

The inhabitants of the abandoned hamlet of **Måstad**, on the southwest shore of Værøy, varied their fishy diet by catching **puffins** from the neighbouring sea cliffs, then curing the bird meat in salt. They were assisted in this arduous task by specially bred dogs known as puffin dogs, or **Lundehund**. In order to improve their stability and traction on the steep cliffs, these small (32–38cm high) dogs developed several distinctive features, including six-toed paws (as opposed to the usual four), which helped them to grip on slippery skerries and wriggle themselves through small spaces. They were extremely flexible, with legs that bent outwards to the extent that the dog can lie completely prone on its chest (reindeer can perform similar manoeuvres). They could also close their ears against dust and moisture and could bend their heads right round onto their backs. Once reduced to only five remaining dogs, the breed was brought back from near-extinction in the 1960s and now numbers well over a thousand, a quarter of whom bark away in the United States.

about 2km from the ferry dock (Mon–Sat 9.45am–noon & Mon–Fri 1–2.30pm; ☏ 75 42 06 14, ⊛ bit.ly/varoy tourism). Both offices can advise on boat tours and accommodation – though you would be foolhardy not to arrange this beforehand.

### ACTIVITIES

**Bike rental** Bicycles can be rented next to the supermarket in the centre of Sørland.

**Boat trips** Several island operators run birdwatching boat trips: for a 3hr excursion expect to pay between 350kr and 450kr. You can book at the tourist office, or just ask around to see which boats are going out.

### ACCOMMODATION AND EATING

**Gamle Prestegård** Værøy ☏ 76 09 54 11, ⊛ prestegaarden.no. Set on the northern side of the island, this well-maintained guesthouse ("The Old Vicarage") has eleven rooms, several of which have shared facilities – en suite costs an extra 100kr. The nicest rooms are in the "Hønsehuset" building, done out from top to bottom in pine. The restaurant, which features fish and whale dishes, sports exposed beams and the original nineteenth-century decor. **830k**

**Lofoten Værøy Brygge** Værøy ☏ 76 09 50 10, ⊛ lvb .no. Choose from spacious, modern but rather soulless rooms or more rustic accommodation in half a dozen large red cabins. The suite-type cabins are big, but with small bathrooms, or go for the "Barbecue cabin", which can sleep an extended family and features a wood-fired seawater hot tub (3600kr). There's a seafood restaurant on site that offers an evening buffet for 300kr. Restaurant daily 5–11pm. Cabins **1350kr**, doubles **1450k**

## Røst

With a population of 600 and falling, the island of **RØST** is even smaller than neighbouring Værøy, its smattering of lonely farmsteads dotted over a pancake-flat landscape interrupted by dozens of tiny lakes. This is the most southerly inhabited island in the Lofoten archipelago and just about as remote as you can get along the Norwegian coast. It was here in 1431 that the lifeboat of a shipwrecked Italian nobleman, Pietro Querini, was washed up after weeks at sea. Querini, and his fellow Venetians, stayed the winter and his written account is one of the few surviving records of everyday life in Nordland in the Middle Ages – and a hard life it was too. The Venetian connection might partly explain why today over ninety percent of the island's air-dried cod is exported to Italy – and Røst is said to produce the best stockfish in Lofoten. The **church** on the north side of the island, consecrated in 1900, features one of the five altar triptychs – restored several times over – which was given to Norway by Princess Elizabeth of the Netherlands in 1520.

### ARRIVAL AND INFORMATION

**By plane** Røst has a tiny airstrip with regular Widerøe (⊛ wideroe.no) flights from Bodø (1–2 daily; 30min) costing around 650kr each way. A taxi into the village from the airport will cost around 140kr (Røst taxi ☏ 93 03 73 00).

**By ferry** Ferries from Bodø and Værøy dock on the island's southwest corner, 3km from the main village. Out of season, the ferries work on a first-come, first-served basis – but it's still a good idea to turn up a couple of hours before departure – whereas in the summer you are advised to make an advance reservation. The passenger fare is 221kr from Bodø, 803kr for car and driver; from Værøy it's 102kr/350kr. Timetables and info on ⓦ 177nordland.no.

Destinations Bodø (1–3daily; 4hr); Værøy (3daily; 2hr).

## INFORMATION AND ACTIVITIES

**Tourist office** The tourist office is located by the jetty (late June to late Aug Mon–Sat 10am–1.30pm & usually when the boat arrives; ☎ 76 05 05 15).

**Cycling, boating & kayaking** The *Røst Bryggehotell* (see below) rents out boats (650kr/day), kayaks (450kr/day) and bicycles (102kr/day), and also organizes boat trips to the sea-bird colonies on the islets to the southwest of Røst.

## ACCOMMODATION

**Kårøy Rorbucamping** Kårøy ☎ 76 09 62 38, ⓦ karoy.no. Originally built as *rorbu* for the fishermen of a stockfish factory, these plain and inexpensive lodgings have two-, four- and six-bedded rooms, all with shared showers, toilets and kitchens. There's also a small campsite. Located on Kårøy island, a few minutes' boat ride from Røst ferry dock; the campsite will organize transport over. May–Aug.

Tents 170kr, doubles 550kr

**Røst Bryggehotell** Riksveg 80 ☎ 76 05 08 00, ⓦ rostbryggehotell.no. Not far from the ferry at the Kårøysundet pier, this small hotel has sixteen frugal rooms with the ocean and the mountains as your closest neighbours. There's also an outdoor wood-heated jacuzzi on the quayside, which you can book for several hours for 750kr. 1220kr

# North Norway

MIDNIGHT SUN, SVALBARD

# North Norway

Karl Baedeker, writing a hundred years ago about Norway's remote northern provinces of Troms and Finnmark, observed that they "possess attractions for the scientific traveller and the sportsman, but can hardly be recommended for the ordinary tourist" – a comment that isn't too wide of the mark even today. These are enticing lands, no question: the natural environment they offer is stunning in its extremes, with the midnight sun and polar night further emphasizing the strangeness of the terrain, but the travelling can be hard going, the individual sights geographically disparate and, once you do reach them, rather subdued in their appeal.

The intricate, fretted coastline of **Troms** has shaped its history since the days when powerful Viking lords operated a trading empire from the region's islands. And while half the population still lives offshore in dozens of tiny fishing villages, the place to aim for first is **Tromsø**, the so-called "Capital of the North" and a lively university town where King Håkon and his government proclaimed a "Free Norway" in 1940, before fleeing into exile. Beyond Tromsø, the long trek north and east begins in earnest as you enter **Finnmark**, a vast wilderness covering 48,000 square kilometres, but home to just two percent of the Norwegian population. Much of this land was laid to waste during World War II, the combined effect of the Russian advance and the retreating German army's scorched-earth policy, and it's now possible to drive for hours without coming across a building much more than sixty years old. The first obvious target in Finnmark is **Alta**, a sprawling settlement – relatively speaking, of course – and an important crossroads famous for its splendid prehistoric rock carvings. From here, most visitors make straight for the steely cliffs of **Nordkapp** (the North Cape), ostensibly but not actually Europe's northernmost point, with or without a detour to the likeable port of **Hammerfest**, and leave it at that; but some doggedly press on to **Kirkenes**, the last town before the Russian border, where you feel as if you're about to drop off the end of the world. The main alternative from Alta is to travel inland across the eerily endless scrubland of the **Finnmarksvidda**, where winter temperatures can plummet to -35°C. This high plateau is the last stronghold of the **Sámi**, northern Norway's indigenous people, some of whom still live a seminomadic life tied to the movement of their reindeer herds. You'll spot Sámi in their brightly coloured traditional gear all across the region, but most notably in the remote towns of **Kautokeino** and **Karasjok**, strange, disconsolate places in the middle of the plain.

Finally, and even more adventurously, there is the **Svalbard archipelago**, whose icy mountains rise out of the Arctic Ocean over 800km north of mainland Norway. Once

ZODIAC EXCURSION ON ISFJORD, SVALBARD

# Highlights

**❶ Emmas Drømmekjøkken, Tromsø** Try the Arctic specialities – reindeer and char for instance – at this exquisite Tromsø restaurant. **See p.348**

**❷ Alta's prehistoric rock carvings** Admire northern Europe's most extensive assemblage of prehistoric rock carvings. **See p.352**

**❸ Juhls' Silver Gallery, Kautokeino** The first and foremost of Finnmark's Sámi-influenced jewellery-makers and designers. **See p.356**

**❹ Engholm's Husky Lodge, Karasjok** Snow and huskies, sledding across the Arctic tundra – what could be better. **See p.358**

**❺ The Hurtigruten** Cruise around the tippity top of the European continent and across the Barents Sea – the most remote and spectacular section of this long-distance coastal voyage. **See p.368**

**❻ Wildlife safaris on the Svalbard archipelago** Take a snowmobile or Zodiac boat out across this remote archipelago to find over one hundred species of migratory bird as well as seals, walruses, whales, arctic foxes, reindeer and, most famous of all, polar bears. **See p.375**

**HIGHLIGHTS ARE MARKED ON THE MAP ON P.340**

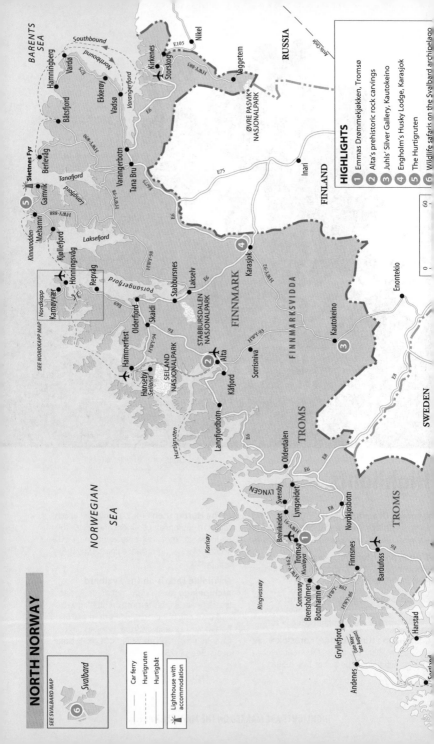

# NORTH NORWAY

### SEE SVALBARD MAP

**6** Svalbard

— — — Car ferry
· · · · · Hurtigruten
– – – Hurtigbåt
✸ Lighthouse with accommodation

## HIGHLIGHTS

**1** Emmas Drømmekjøkken, Tromsø
**2** Alta's prehistoric rock carvings
**3** Juhls' Silver Gallery, Kautokeino
**4** Engholm's Husky Lodge, Karasjok
**5** The Hurtigruten
**6** Wildlife safaris on the Svalbard archipelago

BARENTS SEA

NORWEGIAN SEA

RUSSIA

FINLAND

SWEDEN

FINNMARK

TROMS

TROMS

FINNMARKSVIDDA

ØVRE PASVIK NASJONALPARK

SEILAND NASJONALPARK

STABBURSDALEN NASJONALPARK

Nikel
Kirkenes
Storskog
E105
Vaggetem
HWY-885
Varangerbotn
Tana Bru
E6
E75
Inari
Enontekio
Kautokeino
HWY-93
Karasjok
HWY-92
Sorrisniva
Kåfjord
Alta
Langfjordbotn
E6
E8
Olderdalen
Nordkjosbotn
Lyngseidet
Svensby
Breivikeidet
HWY-91
Tromsø
Finnsnes
Bardufoss
E8
E6
Kautokeino

Hamningberg
Varda
Båtsfjord
Berlevåg
Ekkerøy
Vadsø
Slettnes Fyr
Gamvik
Mehamn
Kjøllefjord
Honningsvåg
Repvåg
Kamøyvær
Nordkapp

Vardø
Tanafjord
Langfjord
Laksefjord
Porsangerfjord

HWY-890
HWY-98
HWY-888

Kinnarodden
SEE NORDKAPP MAP

Skaidi
Olderfjord
Stabbursnes
Lakselv
E6
HWY-94
Hammerfest
Hanseby
Seiland

Sommarøy
Brensholmen
Botnhamn
HWY-862
HWY-866
Gryllefjord
Andenes
Harstad
HWY-82

Karlsøy
Ringvassøya
Kvaløya

LYNGEN

Hurtigruten

Southbound
Northbound
Varangerfjord

Arctic Circle

0        60

the exclusive haunt of trappers, fishermen and coal miners, Svalbard now makes a tidy income from adventure tourism, offering everything from guided glacier walks to hard-core snowmobile excursions and husky sledding – excursions that will take you out to places as wild as anywhere on earth. What's more, you can fly to Svalbard independently from Tromsø and Oslo – and even the UK – at surprisingly bearable prices, though most people opt for a package tour.

As for **accommodation**, all the major settlements have at least a couple of hotels/ guesthouses and the main roads are sprinkled with campsites. If you have a tent and a well-insulated sleeping bag, you can, in theory, bed down more or less where you like, but the hostility of the climate and the ferocity of the summer mosquitoes, especially in the marshy areas of the Finnmarksvidda, make most people think (at least) twice.

**6**

## GETTING AROUND                                                    NORTH NORWAY

Public transport in north Norway is by **plane**, **bus**, the Hurtigruten coastal **boat** and the occasional Hurtigbåt passenger express boat; there are **no trains**. For all but the most truncated of tours, the best idea is to pick and mix these different forms of transport – for example by flying from Tromsø to Kirkenes and then taking the Hurtigruten back, or vice versa. What you should try to avoid is endless doubling-back on the E6, though this is often difficult as it is the only road to run right across the region. To give an idea of the distances involved, from Tromsø it's 400km to Alta, 640km to Nordkapp and 800km to Kirkenes.

### BY PLANE

**Airports** North Norway has a number of small airports, including those at Alta, Hammerfest, Honningsvåg, Kirkenes, Mehamn, Tromsø, and Longyearbyen, on Svalbard.

**Airlines** SAS (w flysas.com) and Widerøe (w wideroe.no) have the widest range of flights to northern Norway, including Longyearbyen, on Svalbard, but Norwegian Airlines (w norwegian.com) chips in too, flying regularly from Tromsø to the likes of Alta and Kirkenes and from Oslo to Longyearbyen, on Svalbard.

**Fares** The expansion of Norwegian Airlines has made the market for internal flights much more competitive and in recent years prices have dropped dramatically – for example Tromsø to Alta can now cost as little as 570kr. In addition, Widerøe has a couple of multi-flight passes and deals (see p.28).

### BY CAR

The main roads in north Norway are kept in an excellent state of repair and sterling efforts are made to keep them open in winter, though at this time of the year ice and snow can make the roads treacherous, if not temporarily impassable, at any time. In the summer, you can expect to cover 250/300km in a day without any problem, half that in winter, but much more and it all becomes rather wearisome. Keep an eye on the fuel indicator too, as petrol stations are largely confined to the larger settlements and they may be 100km to 200km apart. Car repairs can take time since workshops are scarce and parts often have to be ordered from the south. Note also that if you are renting a car, one-way drop-off charges in Norway are invariably excessive – pick up in Tromsø and drop off in Kirkenes and you'll be looking at an extra 6000kr.

**Summer** Be warned that in July and August the E6 north

of Alta can get congested with caravans and motorhomes on their way to Nordkapp. You can avoid the crush by starting early or, for that matter, by driving overnight – an eerie experience when there's bright sunlight in the wee hours of the morning.

**Winter** If you're not used to driving in winter conditions, don't start here – especially during the polar night (late Nov to late Jan), which can be extremely disorientating. If you intend to use the region's minor, unpaved roads, be prepared for the worst and take food and drink, warm clothes and a mobile phone.

### BY BOAT

**Hurtigruten coastal boat** A leisurely way to explore the region is on the daily Hurtigruten coastal boat (w hurtigruten.co.uk), which takes about 40hr to round the northern reaches of Norway between Tromsø and Kirkenes. En route, it calls at eleven ports, mostly remote fishing villages but also Hammerfest and Honningsvåg, where northbound ferries pause for just over 3hr so that special buses can cart passengers off to Nordkapp and back.

**Car and boat travel** One especially appealing option, though this has more to do with comfort than speed, is to travel by land and sea. Special deals on the Hurtigruten can make this surprisingly affordable and tourist offices at the Hurtigruten's ports of call will make bookings – or you can do it online. If you are renting a car, taking your vehicle onto the Hurtigruten will almost certainly work out a lot cheaper than leaving it at your port of embarkation.

**Hurtigbåt passenger express boats** North Norway has various Hurtigbåt services between a string of its smaller settlements as well as two especially useful routes, one between Tromsø and Harstad (2–5 daily; 3hr), the other between Alta and Hammerfest (1–2 daily; 1hr 40min).

**6**

## ARCTIC PHENOMENA

On and above the **Arctic Circle**, an imaginary line drawn round the Earth at latitude 66.5 degrees north, there is a period around midsummer during which the sun never makes it below the horizon, even at midnight – hence the **midnight sun**. On the Arctic Circle itself, this only happens on one night of the year – at the summer solstice – but the further north you go, the greater the number of nights without darkness: in Bodø, it's from the first week of June to early July; in Tromsø from late May to late July; in Alta, from the third week in May to the end of July; in Hammerfest, mid-May to late July; and in Nordkapp, early May to the end of July. Obviously, the midnight sun is best experienced on a clear night, but fog or cloud can turn the sun into a glowing, red ball – a spectacle that can be wonderful but also strangely uncanny. All the region's tourist offices have the exact dates of the midnight sun, though note that these are calculated at sea level; climb up a hill and you can extend the dates by a day or two. The converse of all this is the **polar night**, a period of constant darkness either side of the winter solstice; again, the further north of the Arctic Circle you are, the longer this lasts.

The Arctic Circle also marks the typical southern limit of the **northern lights**, or **aurora borealis**, though this extraordinary phenomenon has been seen as far south as latitude 40 degrees north – roughly the position of New York or Ankara. Caused by the bombardment of the atmosphere by electrons, carried away from the sun by the solar wind, the northern lights take various forms and are highly mobile – either flickering in one spot or travelling across the sky. At relatively low latitudes hereabouts, the aurora is tilted at an angle and is often coloured red – the sagas tell of Vikings being half scared to death by them – but nearer the pole, they hang like gigantic luminous curtains, often tinted greenish blue. Naturally enough, there's no predicting when the northern lights will occur. They are most likely to appear during the darkest period (between November and February) – though they can be seen as early as late August and as late as mid-April. On a clear night the fiery ribbons can be strangely humbling.

### BY BUS

**Routes** The Norwegian rail network does not stretch as far as north Norway and the nearest you'll get is Bodø/Fauske (see p.298). From here, you can reach Tromsø in two segments, Alta in three: Bodø to Narvik via Fauske (2 daily; 6hr 30min) and Narvik to Tromsø (1–3 daily; 5hr) and then Tromsø to Alta (1 daily; 6hr 30min). It's also possible to go straight from Narvik to Alta (without having to head west via Tromsø), but this involves two changes and takes about 9hr. From Alta, the Nordkappexpressen runs to Honningsvåg (1–3 daily; 4hr), near Nordkapp. From May to September, one Nordkappexpressen bus daily continues on from Honningsvåg to Nordkapp (45min) and there are several daily local buses covering this route too. Alta is also where you can pick up buses to Hammerfest (1 daily; 2hr 20min), Kautokeino (Mon–Fri 2 daily; 2hr), Karasjok (2 weekly; 3hr 30min), and Kirkenes (2 weekly; 7hr 30min).

**Timetables and tickets** The bus network is operated by a bewildering variety of companies, but timetables are usually available at most tourist offices and are online at ⓦ rutebok.no and/or ⓦ 177finnmark.no. On longer rides, it's a good idea to buy tickets in advance, or turn up early – especially in the summer when buses fill up fast.

# Tromsø

Likeable **TROMSØ**, located about 250km from Narvik, has been referred to, rather farcically, as the "Paris of the North", and while even the tourist office doesn't make any explicit pretence to such grandiose titles today, the city is without question the de facto social and cultural capital of northern Norway. Easily the region's most populous town, its credentials hark back to the Middle Ages and beyond, when seafarers made use of its sheltered harbour, and there's been a church here at least since the thirteenth century. Tromsø received its municipal charter in 1794, when it was primarily a **fishing port** and trading station, and flourished in the middle of the nineteenth century when its seamen ventured north to Svalbard to reap rich rewards hunting arctic fox, polar bear, reindeer, walrus and, most profitable of all, seal. Subsequently, Tromsø became famous as the jumping-off point for a string of Arctic expeditions, its celebrity status assured when the explorer **Roald Amundsen** (see box, p.345) flew from here to his death somewhere on the Arctic icecap in 1928. Since those headline days, Tromsø has grown into an urbane and engaging city with a population of 72,000 employed in a wide range of industries and at the university, though its harbour is still important: the city is maybe some 360km north of the Arctic Circle, but its climate is moderated by the Gulf Stream, which sweeps up the Norwegian coast and keeps its waterways ice-free. Give or take the odd **museum**, the city may fall somewhat short on top-ranking **sights**, but its amiable atmosphere, fine mountain-and-fjord setting, and clutch of lively **restaurants** and **bars** more than compensate. It's easy to get your bearings, too: the compact **centre**, just a few

**6**

**TROMSØ**

Skansen

Polarmuseet

Perspektivet Museum
Verdensteatret

Kystens Hus

STORTORGET

Rådhus

Kulturhuset

Tromsø
Biblioteket

Tromsø
Outdoor

Domkirke

Nordnorsk
Kunstmuseum

Troms Turlag
(DNT)

Buses  PROSTNESET

Hurtigruten
Quay

Hurtigbåt Quay

STRAND-
TORGET

Mack
Bryggeri

Tromsø
Kunstforening

0      200
metres

N

▼ Polaria (100m) & Tromsø Museum (3km)

| ACCOMMODATION | |
| --- | --- |
| Ami | 4 |
| Clarion Collection Hotel With | 2 |
| Clarion Hotel The Edge | 6 |
| Radisson Blu Hotel Tromsø | 5 |
| Scandic Ishavshotel Tromsø | 3 |
| Tromsø Camping | 1 |
| Viking Hotel | 7 |

| EATING | |
| --- | --- |
| Emmas Drømmekjøkken | 2 |
| Fiskekompaniet | 1 |
| Thai House | 4 |
| Vertshuset Skarven | 3 |

| DRINKING & NIGHTLIFE | |
| --- | --- |
| Blå Rock Café | 2 |
| Ølhallen Pub | 4 |
| Rorbua Pub | 1 |
| Studentsamfunnet Driv | 3 |

| SHOPPING | |
| --- | --- |
| Bokhuset Libris | 1 |
| Vinmonopolet | 2 |

minutes' walk from one side to the other, slopes along the eastern shores of the hilly island of Tromsøya and is connected to the mainland by bridge and tunnel. The busiest part of town spreads south from **Stortorget**, the main square, along Storgata, the main street and north–south axis, as far as Kirkegata and the harbourfront.

## Stortorget

You would be hard pressed to say that Tromsø's main square, **Stortorget**, was charming – it's flanked by a platoon of routine office blocks – but it does have an airy and relaxed atmosphere. It's also the site of a daily flower and knick-knack market and it nudges down towards the waterfront, where fresh fish and prawns are sold direct from inshore fishing boats throughout the summer.

## Domkirke

Kirkegata • Mon–Sat 1–3pm, plus concerts during the summer daily at 5pm • Free • ☎ 77 60 50 90, ⓦ kirken.tromso.no

Dating from the 1860s, the pastel-painted **Domkirke** (Cathedral) bears witness to the prosperity of the town's former merchants, who became rich on the back of the barter trade with Russia. They part-funded the cathedral's construction, the result being the large and handsome structure of today, whose dinky little tower and slender spire poke high into the sky above the neo-Gothic pointed windows of the nave.

## Nordnorsk Kunstmuseum

Sjøgata 1 • Daily 10am–4pm • Free • ☎ 77 64 70 20, ⓦ nnkm.no

Located in a grand and good-looking, nineteenth-century building metres from the cathedral, the **Nordnorsk Kunstmuseum** (Northern Norway Art Museum) offers an enterprising programme of temporary exhibitions with special attention given to contemporary Norwegian artists. The **permanent collection** is not particularly large, but it does cover all of Norway's artistic bases, beginning in the nineteenth century with the ingenious landscapes of Thomas Fearnley and Johan Dahl (see p.66). There are lots of north Norway landscapes and seascapes here too, including several delightful paintings by Kongsberg-born Otto Sinding (1842–1909) – look out for his *Spring Day in Lofoten* – as well as a whole battery of paintings by the talented and prolific Axel Revold (1887–1962), whose work typically maintains a gentle, heart-warming lyricism. By contrast, Willi Midelfart (1904–75) was clearly enraged when he painted his bloody *Assault on the House of Karl Liebknecht*, a reference to the murder of one of Germany's leading Marxists in 1919. The museum also owns a handful of minor works by Edvard Munch, including a handsome portrait entitled *Parisian Model*.

## Tromsø Kunstforening

Muségata 2 • Wed–Sun noon–5pm • Free • ☎ 77 65 58 27, ⓦ tromsokunstforening.no

Just to the south of the town centre, at the upper end of Muségata, the **Tromsø Kunstforening** (Tromsø Art Society) occupies part of a large and attractive Neoclassical building dating from the 1890s. This cultural organization puts on imaginative temporary exhibitions of contemporary art with the emphasis on the work of northern Norwegian artists.

## Polaria

Hjalmar Johansens gate 12 • **Polaria** Daily: mid-May to Aug 10am–7pm; Sept to mid-May 10am–5pm • 125kr • ☎ 77 75 01 00, ⓦ polaria.no • **Polstjerna** Mid-June to mid-Aug daily 11am–5pm • 40kr

A lavish waterfront complex, in a good-looking modern structure built to resemble stacked ice floes, **Polaria** deals with all things Arctic. There's an aquarium stocked with

Arctic species, a 180-degree cinema showing a film on Svalbard shot from a helicopter, a display on the effects of global warming and several exhibitions on polar research. Parked outside in a glass greenhouse is a 1940s sealing ship, the **M/S Polstjerna**.

## Perspektivet Museum

Storgata 95 • June–Aug Tues–Fri 10am–4pm, Sat & Sun 11am–5pm; reduced hours rest of year • Free • ☎ 77 60 19 10, ⓦ perspektivet.no

The enterprising **Perspektivet Museum** features temporary exhibitions on contemporary issues usually illustrated by means of still photographs, but for the visitor it is perhaps the local stuff that is of most interest: the museum holds an extensive **photographic collection** – some 400,000 images and counting – and commissions new works from local photographers to document the changing face of the modern city. The building itself, dating from 1838, is also of interest as the one-time home of the local writer **Cora Sandel** (1880–1974), who was born Sara Fabricius and lived in Tromsø from 1893 to 1905, before moving to Paris. Sandel's important works include the *Alberte Trilogy*, a set of semiautobiographical novels following the trials and tribulations of a young woman as she attempts to establish her own identity. The museum has a small section on Sandel on the first floor, but it's confined to a few of her knick-knacks and several photos of her on a Tromsø walkabout.

## Polarmuseet

Søndre Tollbodgate 11 • Daily: mid-June to mid-Aug 9am–6pm; mid-Aug to mid-June 11am–5pm • 60kr • ☎ 77 62 33 60, ⓦ polarmuseum.no

Down by the water, an old wooden warehouse holds the city's most intriguing museum, the **Polarmuseet** (Polar Museum). The collection begins with a less-than-stimulating series of displays on trapping in the Arctic, but beyond is an outstanding section on Svalbard, including archeological finds retrieved in the 1980s from an eighteenth-century **Russian whaling station**. Most of the artefacts come from graves preserved by permafrost and, among many items, there are combs, leather boots, parts of a sledge, slippers and even – just to prove illicit puffing is not a recent phenomenon – a clay pipe from a period when the Russian company in charge of affairs forbade trappers from smoking. Two other sections on the first floor focus on **seal hunting**, an important part of the local economy until the 1950s.

---

### DERRING-DO: THE ADVENTURES OF ROALD AMUNDSEN

One of Norway's most celebrated personalities, **Roald Amundsen** (1872–1928) was intent on becoming a polar explorer from his early teens. He read everything there was to read on the subject, even training as a sea captain in preparation, and, in 1897, he embarked with a Belgian expedition on his first trip to Antarctica. Undeterred by a winter on the ice after the ship broke up, he was soon planning his own expedition. In 1901, he purchased a sealer, the *Gjøa*, in Tromsø, leaving in June 1903 to spend three years sailing and charting the **Northwest Passage** between the Atlantic and the Pacific. The *Gjøa* (now on display in Oslo; see p.87) was the first vessel to complete this extraordinary voyage, which tested Amundsen and his crew to the very limits. Long searched for, the Passage had for centuries been something of a nautical Holy Grail and the voyage's progress – and at times the lack of it – was headline news right across the world. Amundsen's next target was the **North Pole**, but during his preparations, in 1909, the American explorer Robert Peary got there first. Amundsen immediately switched his attention to the **South Pole** and, in 1910, he headed south in a new ship, the *Fram* (also exhibited in Oslo; see p.86), famously reaching the pole on December 14, 1911, just a couple of weeks ahead of the British expedition led by Captain Scott.

Neither did Amundsen's ambitions end there: in 1926, he became one of the first men to fly over the North Pole in the **airship** of the Italian Umberto Nobile, though it was this last expedition that did for Amundsen: in 1928, the Norwegian flew north out of Tromsø in a bid to rescue the stranded Nobile and was never seen again.

Upstairs, on the second floor, a further section is devoted to the exploits of one **Henry Rudi** (1889–1970), the so-called "**Isbjørnkongen**" (Polar Bear King), who spent 27 winters on Svalbard and Greenland, bludgeoning his way through the local wildlife, killing 713 polar bears in the process. Rather more edifying is the extensive display on the polar explorer **Roald Amundsen** (1872–1928), who spent thirty years searching out the secrets of the polar regions (see box, p.345). The museum exhibits all sorts of oddments used by Amundsen and his men – from long johns and pipes through to boots and ice picks – but it is the photos that steal the show, providing a fascinating insight into the way Amundsen's polar expeditions were organized and the hardships he and his men endured. Amundsen clearly liked having his picture taken, judging from the heroic poses he struck, his derring-do emphasized by the finest set of eyebrows north of Oslo.

Finally, there's another extensive section on Amundsen's contemporary **Fridtjof Nansen** (1861–1930), a polar explorer of similar renown who, in his later years, became a leading figure in international famine relief. In 1895, Nansen and his colleague Hjalmar Johansen made an abortive effort to reach the North Pole by dog sledge after their ship was trapped by pack ice. It took them a full fifteen months to get back to safety, a journey of such epic proportions that tales of it captivated all of Scandinavia.

## Ishavskatedralen

Hans Nilsens vei 41 • Mid- to late May daily 3–6pm; June to mid-Aug Mon–Sat 9am–7pm, Sun 1–7pm; mid-Aug to mid-May daily 3–6pm • 40kr • ☎ 41 00 84 70, ⓦ ishavskatedralen.no

A few minutes' walk east from the centre, across the spindly Tromsøbrua bridge, rises the desperately modern **Ishavskatedralen** (Arctic Cathedral). Completed in 1965, the church has a strikingly white, glacier-like appearance, achieved by means of eleven immense triangular concrete sections, representing the eleven Apostles that were left after the betrayal. The entire east wall is formed by a huge stained-glass window, one of the largest in Europe, and the organ is unusual too, built to represent a ship when viewed from beneath – recalling the tradition, still seen in many a Nordic church, of suspending a ship from the ceiling as a good-luck talisman for seafarers.

## Fjellheisen funicular

Sollivegen • Daily: mid-May to mid-Aug 10am–1am; mid-Aug to mid-May 10am–10pm; every 30min • 170kr return • ☎ 92 61 78 37, ⓦ fjellheisen.no • Bus #26 from the city centre

The **Fjellheisen funicular**, on the far side of the bridge 3km southeast from the city centre, whisks passengers up **Mount Storsteinen**. From the upper station, at 420m, the views of the city and its surroundings are extensive and it's a smashing spot to catch the midnight sun; there's a café at the top too. Note that funicular services are suspended during inclement weather.

## Tromsø Museum

Lars Thørings veg 10 • June–Aug daily 9am–6pm; Sept–May Mon–Fri 10am–4.30pm, Sat noon–3pm, Sun 11am–4pm • 60kr • ☎ 77 64 50 00, ⓦ uit.no/tmu • Bus #37 from the centre (every 30min)

The **Tromsø Museum**, about 3km south of the centre, near the southern tip of Tromsøya, is a historical and ethnographic museum run by the university. It's a varied collection, featuring nature and the sciences downstairs, and culture and history above. Pride of place goes to the **medieval religious carvings**, naive but evocative pieces retrieved from various northern Norwegian churches. There's also an enjoyable section on the **Sámi** featuring displays on every aspect of Sámi life – from dwellings, tools and equipment through to traditional costume and hunting techniques. In addition, the aurora borealis exhibit gives a particularly good explanation of exactly why and how the phenomenon exists.

## ARRIVAL AND DEPARTURE

TROMSØ

**By plane** Tromsø airport is 5km northwest of the centre on the other side of Tromsøya island. Frequent Flybussen (🖥 flybussen.no; 90kr, 140kr return) link the airport with the city, stopping at several downtown locations, including the *Rica Ishavshotel* on Sjøgata. A taxi to the centre will cost about 200kr, more in the evenings and at night.

**By bus** Long-distance buses pull in at the stops on Prostneset, near the Hurtigruten quay. Timetables on 🖥 rutebok.no.

Destinations Alta (1 daily; 6hr 30min); Honningsvåg (1–3 daily; 3hr 20min); Narvik (1–3 daily; 4hr 15min).

**By Hurtigruten** The Hurtigruten coastal boat (🖥 hurtigruten.com) docks in the town centre beside the Prostneset quay. Northbound, it's about 11hr to Hammerfest (see p.358); southbound it's just over 6hr to Harstad (see p.307).

**By Hurtigbåt** Hurtigbåt ferries arrive and depart from the jetty about 150m to the south of the Hurtigruten dock. For Lofoten (see pp.315–335), it's quickest and easiest if you take the Hurtigbåt to Harstad, then the bus.

Destinations Harstad (2–5 daily; 3hr).

**By car** Among several car hire companies at the airport are Europcar (☎ 77 67 56 00) and Hertz (☎ 48 26 20 00). There's also a Hertz in the centre at Fridtjof Nansenplass 3C (☎ 40 43 64 81).

## GETTING AROUND

**By bus** For Tromsø's outlying attractions you'll need to catch a municipal bus (🖥 tromskortet.no); the standard, flat-rate fare is currently 36kr.

**By bike** Bikes, including electric bikes, can be rented from Tromsø Outdoor, in the centre at Sjøgata 14 (☎ 97 57 58 75, 🖥 tromsooutdoor.no).

## INFORMATION AND ACTIVITIES

**Tourist office** Tromsø tourist office is conveniently located down at the harbour at Kirkegata 2 (Jan–March & mid-May to Aug Mon–Fri 9am–7pm, Sat & Sun 10am–6pm; April to mid-May, Sept & Oct Mon–Fri 9am–4pm, Sat 10am–4pm; Nov & Dec Mon–Fri 9am–4pm, Sat & Sun 10am–4pm; ☎ 77 61 00 00, 🖥 visittromso.no). They issue free town maps and provide oodles of local information, including details of bus and boat sightseeing trips around neighbouring islands.

**Hiking** Troms Turlag, next door to the tourist office at Kirkegata 2 (Wed & Fri noon–4pm, Thurs noon–6pm; ☎ 77 68 51 75, 🖥 troms.dnt.no), is a DNT affiliate with bags of information on local hiking trails and DNT huts.

**Wilderness tours** Among several wilderness-tour specialists, Tromsø Villmarkssenter at Straumsvegen 603 (Tromsø Wilderness Centre; ☎ 77 69 60 02, 🖥 villmarks senter.no), offers a wide range of activities from guided glacier walks, kayak paddling and mountain climbing in summer through to ski trips and dog-sled rides in winter. Overnight trips staying in a *lavvo* (a Sámi tent) can also be arranged. The owner-operators are two of Norway's most experienced dog-sled racers. The centre is located about 8km from downtown Tromsø, beyond the airport and over the bridge on the island of Kvaløya. Advance reservations are required and they have a seasonal downtown booking office in the Kystens Hus, Stortorget 1A. As a sample price, a day in a kayak costs 1200kr.

## ACCOMMODATION

Tromsø has a good supply of modern, central **hotels**, though the majority occupy chunky concrete high-rises whose exterior may or may not be indicative of what lies inside. Less expensive – and sometimes more distinctive – are the town's **guesthouses** and there's a fairly handy **campsite** too.

### HOTELS AND GUESTHOUSES

**Ami** Skolegata 24 ☎ 77 62 10 00, 🖥 amihotel.no. Few-frills guesthouse-cum-hotel with twenty-odd simple rooms both en suite and with shared facilities. In an old wooden villa on the hillside behind the town centre. One bonus is the wide views over the city centre. **1100kr**

**Clarion Collection Hotel With** Sjøgata 35 ☎ 77 66 42 00, 🖥 nordicchoicehotels.com. In an attractive setting, down by the harbour, this is one of Tromsø's several Nordic Choice hotels. Each is individually branded – and here the public areas hold a variety of nautical objects. The main facade is a pleasing modern version of a traditional ware-house, but the rooms beyond are standard chain; that is, spick-and-span, and without much distinction. Price includes a light, early evening meal. **1200kr**

**Clarion Hotel The Edge** Kaigata 6 ☎ 77 66 84 00, 🖥 nordicchoicehotels.com. Opened in 2014, and occupying a large modern block with a striking modernist interior, this chain hotel has a grand waterside setting and is a popular venue for conferences. The rooms are standard-issue chain – wooden floors and so forth – but are very comfortable and the pick have exquisite coastal views. **1200kr**

**Radisson Blu Hotel Tromsø** Sjøgata 7 ☎ 77 60 00 00, 🖥 radissonblu.com. Large and popular chain hotel occupying two clumpy towers down at the harbour. The rooms have been kitted out in two styles – Arctic (calming white, orange and green finishes) and Chilli (somewhat warmer red tones); the Superior ones (as well as the gym and sauna) have cracking views over the harbour.

**6**

**6**

Ultra-efficient service too. Downstairs is the lively and well-known (to Norwegians, at least) *Rorbua Pub*, which occasionally features live music. 1300kr

★ **Scandic Ishavshotel Tromsø** Fredrik Langes gate 2 ☎ 77 66 64 00, ⓦ scandichotels.com. Perched on the harbourfront a few metres from the Hurtigruten dock, this imaginatively designed hotel is partly built in the style of a ship, complete with a sort of crow's-nest bar. Well-appointed rooms decorated in crisp Scandi style and unbeatable views over the harbour with the mountains glinting behind. 1300kr

**Tromsø Camping** Elvestrandvegen 10 ☎ 77 63 80 37, ⓦ tromsocamping.no. Reasonably convenient riverside site about 2km east of the Arctic Cathedral (Ishavskatedralen), on the mainland side of the main bridge, with several dozen modern and rustic cabins. Open year-round. Camping 300kr, cabins 700kr

**Viking Hotel** Grønnegata 18 ☎ 77 64 77 30, ⓦ viking hotell.no. The 24 bright and modern rooms at this breezy guesthouse are considerably more appealing than most other places in town. They also have several contemporary apartment-style rooms with kitchenettes and large living spaces. Centrally located near the Mack brewery. 1000kr

## EATING

Tromsø boasts a clutch of first-rate **restaurants** and several enjoyable **cafés**, the pick of which are handily concentrated in the vicinity of the Domkirke.

★ **Emmas Drømmekjøkken** Kirkegata 8 ☎ 77 63 77 30, ⓦ emmasdrommekjokken.no. Much praised in the national press as a gourmet treat, "Emma's Dream Kitchen" lives up to its name, with an imaginative and wide-ranging menu focused on Norwegian produce. The grilled arctic char with Gorgonzola sauce and cowberries is a treat as is the delicious Tana reindeer fillet with port sauce and roasted garlic. Excellent service in a smart environment – both downstairs and upstairs. Main courses upstairs are 300–365kr, less down below. Upstairs dining starts at 6pm. Reservations recommended. Mon–Fri 11am–10pm, Sat noon–10pm.

**Fiskekompaniet** Killengreens gate 29 ☎ 77 68 76 00, ⓦ fiskekompani.no. Down by the harbour in the centre of town, this neat and trim modern restaurant specializes in seafood, almost entirely caught in local waters. The catch of the day costs around 315kr, while dishes such as cod in a creamy sauce cost 345kr. Daily 4–10pm.

**Thai House** Storgata 22 ☎ 77 67 05 26, ⓦ thaihouse .no. Decent Thai cooking – if a little hit and miss – with the welcome inclusion of some excellent fish and vegetable dishes; the spicy salads are especially good, as are the soups, though prices aren't cheap, with mains from around 220kr. Daily 3–11pm.

**Vertshuset Skarven** Strandtorget 1 ☎ 77 60 07 20, ⓦ skarven.no. This substantial, older building, down by the harbour, is divided into several different sections, most notably the *Arctandria Sjømatrestaurant*, an upstairs restaurant where they offer a superb range of fish with the emphasis on Arctic species. There's also reindeer, whale and seal and main courses start at around 315kr. Here also is the *Skarven Kro* café-bar, whose tasty snacks and light meals cost much less – and are served in an equally convivial setting. Skarven Kro: daily 11am–11.30pm; Arctandria Sjømatrestaurant: Mon–Sat 4pm–11pm.

## DRINKING AND NIGHTLIFE

Tromsø may be comparatively small, but it punches way above its weight when it comes to **late-night bars**. Even better, the best of these bars – as well as its **clubs** – are concentrated in the city centre. The favourite local tipple is the **Mack** beers and lagers brewed here in town.

**Blå Rock Café** Strandgata 14 ☎ 77 61 00 20. Definitely the place to go for loud – that's very loud – rock music. Also features regular live acts, plus the best burgers in town (try the amazing blue-cheese Astroburger). They serve several dozen beers, most priced at around 70kr. Mon–Thurs 11.30am–2am, Fri & Sat 11.30am–3.30am, Sun 1pm–2am.

**Ølhallen Pub** Storgata 4 ☎ 77 62 45 80, ⓦ olhallen.no. Solid (some might say stolid) basement pub adjoining the Mack brewery, whose various ales are its speciality. It's the first pub in town to start serving – so expect to rub shoulders with some serious drinkers. Mon–Wed 10am–

7.30pm, Thurs–Sat 10am–12.30am.

**Rorbua Pub** Sjøgata 7 ☎ 77 75 90 86, ⓦ rorbuapub.no. Known all over the country thanks to being the long-time home of a popular weekly talk show, *Du skal høre mye* ("You'll Hear a Lot"), this popular bar is hardly cutting edge, but it's good fun all the same – recalling a fisherman's cabin where a fair number of the crew are sozzled. The proceedings are presided over by a large stuffed polar bear. Mon & Tues noon–12.30am, Wed–Sat noon–1.30am, Sun noon–midnight.

**Studentsamfunnet Driv** Storgata 6 ☎ 77 60 07 76, ⓦ driv.no. Run on a voluntary basis by local students, this

large, ambitious and artsy hangout never wants for its share of barflies. In part of the Mack brewery, it holds four bars and three stages, which together cater for every

known musical taste, including DJ nights, live concerts and disco. Come early to snag a seat. Mon–Thurs noon–1.30am, Fri & Sat noon–3am.

## ENTERTAINMENT

**Kulturhuset** Erling Bangsunds plass 1 ☎ 77 79 16 66, ⓦ kulturhuset.tr.no. The principal venue for cultural events of all kinds, this large space beside Grønnegata tends to focus on live Nordic music bands, though there are also touring dance troupes and the occasional musical revue as well.

**Verdensteatret** Storgata 93B ☎ 77 75 30 90,

ⓦ verdensteatret.no. In a good-looking older building, dating from 1915, Tromsø's main art-house cinema features an enterprising range of films with Norwegian flicks getting some prime coverage. Open two or three evenings a week, but daily during film festivals. There are concerts and literary readings too.

## SHOPPING

**Bokhuset Libris** Storgata 86 ☎ 77 68 30 36, ⓦ libris.no. Hardly the biggest bookshop in Norway, but this family-owned franchise of the big chain is Tromsø's best, with a very good selection of English-language publications. Mon–Thurs 9am–6pm, Fri 9am–4.30pm, Sat 10am–4pm.

**Vinmonopolet** Nerstranda 9 ☎ 04560, ⓦ vinmonopolet .no. Tromsø and its environs have several Vinmonopolet stores and this is the most central option. The store has a monopoly on strong ales, most wines and spirits. Mon–Fri 10am–6pm, Sat 10am–3pm.

## DIRECTORY

**Pharmacy** Among many pharmacies, Vitusapotek Svanen is located in the town centre near the *Scandic Ishavshotel Tromsø* at Killengrens gate 5 (Mon–Fri 8.30am–4.30pm, Sat 10am–2pm & Sun 6–8pm; ☎ 77 21

26 00, ⓦ vitusapotek.no).
**Post office** Main office at Sjøgata 7 (Mon–Fri 8am–6pm, Sat 10am–3pm).

---

## WEST FROM TROMSØ: THE BYROAD TO ANDENES

There are several potential routes **west from Tromsø to Andenes** on the Vesterålen islands (see p.309), but the most scenic is the 150km (3hr 30min) journey via **Highway 862** to the Gryllefjord car ferry (see below). Hwy-862 begins by heading north out of Tromsø to cross the Sandnessundet straits over to the mountainous island of **Kvaløya**, whose three distinct parts are joined by a couple of narrow strips of land. On the far side of the straits, the highway meanders west offering lovely fjord and mountain views on the way to the **Brensholmen–Botnhamn car ferry** (see below), about 60km from Tromsø. From Botnhamn, it's a further 80km to Gryllefjord, where a second car ferry (see below) takes you across the wide and deep Andfjord to Andenes. This is an exceptionally pretty drive in itself and you can also break the journey at the enjoyable *Sommarøy Arctic Hotel*, on the tiny islet of **Sommarøy**, which is linked to Kvaløya by a causeway that forks off Hwy-862 a few kilometres short of Brensholmen.

### CAR FERRIES

Both **car ferries** on the Hwy-862 route between Tromsø and Andenes are seasonal: Brensholmen–Botnhamn (May–Aug 5–7 daily; 35min; car & driver 260kr); Gryllefjord–Andenes (late May to early Sept 2–3 daily; 2hr 15min; car and driver 570kr). Timetable details on ⓦ tromskortet.no. Advance booking is recommended on the Gryllefjord–Andenes ferry; the Tromsø tourist office (see p.347) will assist.

### ACCOMMODATION AND EATING

**Sommarøy Arctic Hotel** Skipsholmvegen, Sommarøy ☎ 77 66 40 00, ⓦ sommaroy.no. This relaxing hotel and conference centre has an easy-on-the-eye rural location down by the seashore. The guest rooms in the main building are neat, crisp and modern, and there are

high-quality, well-equipped seashore cabins too. There's a sauna and spa plus a restaurant, where the speciality is local seafood with mains averaging 250kr. Restaurant: daily noon–8pm. Doubles 1090kr, six-berth cabins 3000kr

# The road to Finnmark: Tromsø to Alta

**Beyond Tromsø**, the vast sweep of the northern landscape slowly unfolds, with silent fjords cutting deep into the coastline beneath ice-tipped peaks, which bump away towards the high plateau of the interior. The next obvious target north from Tromsø is **Alta** (see below), over the provincial border in **Finnmark** and a long day's drive away. For the first part of the journey, to **OLDERDALEN**, there are **two routes** to choose from. The more scenic – and the more straightforward – is along the **E8/E6**, a wonderful drive of 185km through the mountains and along the fjords that takes a little less than three hours to complete. The alternative, marginally duller route, using the **E8 and then Hwy-91**, is 100km shorter, but you won't save time (or money) as it includes two car ferries – Breivikeidet/Svensby and Lyngseidet/Olderdalen (see below). On both routes, grassy valleys interrupt this forbidding, elemental terrain and it's here that a few hardy souls struggle on, often by dairy farming. Curiously enough, one particular problem for local farmers is the abundance of Siberian garlic (*Allium sibiricum*): the cows love the stuff – it tastes much more like chive than garlic – but if they eat a lot of it, the milk they produce tastes of onions.

**6**

## ARRIVAL AND DEPARTURE      THE ROAD TO FINNMARK: TROMSØ TO ALTA

**By car ferry** If you choose to drive the E8/Hwy-91 route from Tromsø to Olderdalen (for Alta), there are two car ferries to negotiate: Breivikeidet–Svensby (hourly; Mon–Fri 6.30am–10.30pm, Sat 8am–8pm, Sun 8am–9.30pm; 25min; 110kr car & driver); Lyngseidet–Olderdalen (hourly; Mon–Fri 7.20am–9.05pm, Sat 9.05am–7.20pm, Sun 9.05am–9.05pm; 40min; 150kr car and driver). Timetables on ⓦ tromskortet.no).

## Kåfjord

Beyond Olderdalen, the E6 eventually enters the province of **Finnmark** as it approaches the hamlet of **LANGFJORDBOTN**, at the head of the long and slender Langfjord. Thereafter, the road sticks tight against the water as it wends its way to the tiny village of **KÅFJORD**, whose sympathetically restored nineteenth-century church was built by the English company who operated the area's copper mines until they were abandoned as uneconomic in the 1870s. The Kåfjord itself is a narrow and sheltered arm of the Altafjord, which was used as an Arctic hideaway by the *Tirpitz* (see p.283) and other German battleships during World War II. From Kåfjord, it's 15km to Alta.

## Alta

First impressions of **ALTA**, some 400km from Tromsø, are not encouraging with the town's 15,000 inhabitants hunkering down in a string of humdrum, modern settlements that spread out along the E6 for several kilometres. The least appealing part is **Alta Sentrum**, now befuddled by a platoon of soulless concrete blocks, and even Alta's oldest district, **Bossekop**, where Dutch whalers settled in the seventeenth century, does little to cheer the soul. Alta was much more interesting once – for a couple of centuries not Norwegian at all, but Finnish and Sámi, and host to an ancient and much-visited Sámi fair. World War II polished off the fair and destroyed Alta's old wooden buildings, but the town does have one star attraction, the **Alta Museum**, where you'll find the most extensive area of **prehistoric rock carvings** in northern Europe. Alta also makes an excellent base for explorations out into the **Finnmarksvidda plateau**, whether it be hiking, riverboat safaris, dog-sledding, snowmobiling or cross-country skiing. Indeed, Europe's largest dog-sled race, the **Finnmarksløpet** (ⓦfinnmarkslopet.no), takes place here in mid-March, complemented by a big week-long cultural celebration, the **Borealis Winter Festival**.

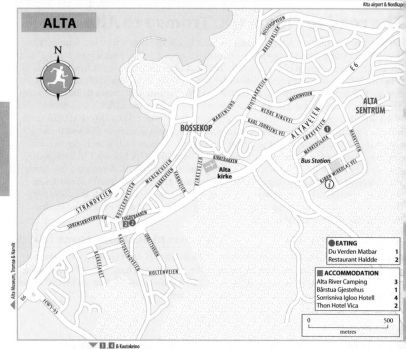

## Alta Museum and the rock carvings

Altaveien 19 • **Museum** Mid-May to mid-June daily 8am–5pm; mid-June to mid-Aug daily 8am–8pm; mid-Aug to mid-Sept daily 8am–5pm; mid-Sept to mid-May Mon–Fri 9am–3pm, Sat & Sun 11am–4pm • **Rock carvings** Same hours, but only when the snow has gone (usually May–Sept) • May–Sept 105kr, Oct–April 70kr • ☎ 41 75 63 30, ⓦ alta.museum.no • Beside the E6, on the western edge of town, 5km from Alta Sentrum. A local bus (*bybussen*) runs from the bus station to the museum (Mon–Fri every 15–30min, Sat & Sun hourly; 7min); or call Alta Taxi ☎ 08125

In a neat modern building, the first part of **Alta Museum** provides an excellent introduction to prehistoric Finnmark in general and the rock carvings in particular. It also offers a potted history of the Alta area, with exhibitions on the salmon-fishing industry, copper mining and so forth. The **rock carvings** themselves – the **Helleristningene i Hjemmeluft** – extend down the hill from the museum to the fjordside along an easy-to-follow 3km-long footpath and boardwalk. On the trail, which takes at least an hour to explore thoroughly, there are a dozen or so vantage points offering close-up views of the carvings, recognizable though highly stylized representations of boats, animals and people picked out in red pigment (the colours have been retouched by researchers). They make up an extraordinarily complex tableau, whose minor variations in subject matter and design – there are **four identifiable bands** – represent successive historical periods from 6000 to 2500 years old. The carvings are indisputably impressive – clear, stylish, and touching in their simplicity. They provide an insight into a prehistoric culture that was essentially settled and largely reliant on the hunting of land animals, who were killed with flint and bone implements; sealing and fishing were of lesser importance. Many experts think it probable that the carvings had a spiritual significance if for no other reason than the sheer effort involved in their creation, but this is the stuff of conjecture.

### ARRIVAL AND INFORMATION                                     ALTA

**By bus** Alta is reasonably well connected by long-distance bus to Tromsø and points to the immediate north and south along the E6, but services onto the Finnmarksvidda plateau are patchy. Alta bus station is just off the E6 in Alta Sentrum, on Bjorn Wirkolas vei, a few metres from the conspicuous *Thon Hotel Alta*. For bus timetables, consult ⓦ rutebok.no.

Destinations Hammerfest (1 daily; 2hr 20min); Honningsvåg (1–2 daily; 4hr); Karasjok (2 weekly; 3hr 30min); Kautokeino (Mon–Fri 2 daily; 2hr); Kirkenes (2 weekly; 7hr 30min); Nordkapp (May–Sept 1–2 daily; 4hr 20min); Tromsø (1 daily 6hr 30min).

**By Hurtigbåt passenger express boat** The VargsundXpressen links Alta with Hammerfest (1–2 daily; 1hr 40min). Alta's Hurtigbåt quay is just off the E6 at the north end of town.

**By car: north to Honningsvåg and Nordkapp** From

Alta, it's 110km along the E6 to Olderfjord, where the E69 forks north to slip along the western shore of the Porsangerfjord, a deep and wide inlet flanked by bare, low-lying hills whose flaky stone has been fractured by the biting cold of winter. It's an agreeable journey and in an hour or so you'll spy the island of Magerøya, a hunk of brown rock looking something like an inverted blancmange. The straits between the mainland and Honningsvåg are negotiated by an ambitious series of bridges and tunnels and you emerge on the western edge of Honningsvåg, just 34km from Nordkapp.

**6**

## INFORMATION AND ACTIVITIES

**Tourist office** Bjorn Wirkolas vei 11, Alta Sentrum (mid-June to mid-Aug Mon–Sat 9am–8pm; mid-Aug to mid-June Mon–Fri 8.30am–4pm ☎ 99 10 00 22, ⓦ visitalta .no). Alta tourist office issues free town maps, will advise on hiking the Finnmarksvidda and help with finding accommodation. The latter is a particularly useful service if you're dependent on public transport – the town's hotels and motels are widely dispersed and occasionally

jam-packed at the height of the season.

**Tours** Apart from operating the *Igloo Hotell* (see below), Sorrisniva (Sorrisniva ☎ 78 43 33 78, ⓦ sorrisniva.no) organizes a comprehensive range of outdoor sports – from ice-fishing and snowmobile tours (from 1400kr) to dog-sled trips and summer boat trips partway along the 400m-deep Sautso canyon (from 750kr).

## ACCOMMODATION

**Alta River Camping** ☎ 78 43 43 53, ⓦ alta-river -camping.no. The pick of the campsites around Alta, this well-equipped, three-star site is set on a large green plot beside the Alta River. They have tent spaces here as well as hotel-style rooms and cabins with refrigerators, though showers and self-catering facilities are shared; there's also a sauna right on the water. Located about 5km out of town along Hwy-93, which branches off the E6 in between Bossekop and the rock carvings. Open year-round. Camping 320kr, cabins 500kr, doubles 600kr

**Bårstua Gjestehus** Kongleveien 2A ☎ 78 43 33 33, ⓦ baarstua.no. Of Alta's several guesthouses, this is the most appealing, located just off the E6 on the north side of town. The eight rooms here are large and pleasant enough and all of them have kitchenettes. 800kr

**Sorrisniva Igloo Hotell** Sorrisniva ☎ 78 43 33 78,

ⓦ sorrisniva.no. Sorrisniva boasts a substantial, 2,500-square-metre hotel built entirely out of ice and snow, including the beds and the glasses in the bar. It's out in the sticks, down by the riverside, a 25min-drive south from Alta via Hwy-93, and while staying in an ice hotel seems gimmicky, it's a (erm) cool – and memorable – way of avoiding the bland Ikea-style decor of most chain hotels. It's fantastically popular, so advance reservations are essential. Rates include transport to and from Alta. Mid-Dec to March. 4500kr

**Thon Hotel Vica** Fogdebakken 6 ☎ 78 48 22 22, ⓦ thon hotels.com. Alta has a platoon of chain hotels, among which this is the most distinctive and attractive. In the Bossekop district, it occupies several buildings that have evolved from the original farmhouse. The rooms are noticeably cosy, smart and brightly decorated. Also has a suntrap of a terrace. 1200kr

## EATING

**Du Verden Matbar** Markedsgata 21 ☎ 45 90 82 13, ⓦ duverden.no/alta. In the centre of Alta, this friendly and intimate restaurant is kitted out in imaginative modern style. The menu covers all the Norwegian basics and then some – the king crab (460kr) and the grilled stock fish (375kr) come especially recommended. Mon–Sat 10am– 11.30pm, Sun 1–10.30pm.

**Restaurant Haldde** Thon Hotel Vica, Fogdebakken 6 ☎ 78 48 22 22, ⓦ thonhotels.com. Large and smart hotel restaurant that specializes in regional delicacies – cloudberries, arctic char, reindeer and the like – all perfectly prepared and well presented. Mains in the region of 280kr. Mon–Sat 6–10pm, Sun 1–10pm.

# The Finnmarksvidda

Venture far inland from Alta and you enter the **Finnmarksvidda**, a vast mountain plateau which spreads southeast up to and beyond the Finnish border. Rivers, lakes and marshes lattice the region, but there's nary a tree, let alone a mountain, to break

> ## EASTER FESTIVALS IN THE FINNMARKSVIDDA
>
> **Easter** is without question the best time to visit the Finnmarksvidda for it's then that the inhabitants celebrate the end of the polar night and the arrival of spring. There are folk-music concerts, church services and traditional sports, including the famed **reindeer races** – not, thank goodness, reindeers racing each other (they would never cooperate), but reindeer pulling passenger-laden sleds. Details of the Easter festivals are available at any Finnmark tourist office.

the contours of a landscape whose wide skies and deep horizons are eerily beautiful. Distances are hard to gauge – a dot of a storm can soon be upon you, breaking with alarming ferocity – and the air is crystal-clear, giving a whitish lustre to the sunshine. A handful of roads cross this expanse, but for the most part it remains the preserve of the few thousand seminomadic **Sámi** (see box opposite), who make up the majority of the local population. Many still wear traditional dress, a brightly coloured, wool-and-felt affair of red bonnets and blue jerkins or dresses, all trimmed with red, white and yellow embroidery. You'll see permutations on this traditional costume all over Finnmark, but especially at roadside souvenir stalls and, on Sundays, outside Sámi churches.

Despite the encroachments of the tourist industry, lifestyles on the Finnmarksvidda have remained remarkably constant. The main occupation is **reindeer herding**, supplemented by hunting and fishing, and the pattern of Sámi life is still largely dictated by the biology of these animals. During the winter, the reindeer graze the flat plains and shallow valleys of the interior, migrating towards the coast in early May as the snow begins to melt, and temperatures inland begin to climb, even reaching 30°C on occasion. By October, both people and reindeer are journeying back from their temporary summer quarters on the coast. The long, dark winter is spent in preparation for the great **Easter festivals** (see box above), when weddings and baptisms are celebrated in the region's two principal settlements, **Karasjok** and **Kautokeino**. Summer visits, on the other hand, can be rather disappointing, culturally speaking at least, since many families and their reindeer are kicking back at coastal pastures and there is precious little activity in either town – and your best bet for spotting small herds are along the road to Hammerfest and around Nordkapp.

The best time to **hike** the Finnmarksvidda is in late August and early September, after the peak mosquito season and before the weather turns cold. For the most part the plateau vegetation is scrub and open birch forest, which makes the going fairly easy, though the many marshes, rivers and lakes often impede progress. There are a handful of clearly demarcated **hiking trails** as well as a smattering of appropriately sited but unstaffed huts; for detailed information, ask at Alta tourist office (see p.353).

### ARRIVAL AND DEPARTURE                                    THE FINNMARKSVIDDA

**By car** From Alta, the only direct route into the Finnmarksvidda is south along Hwy-93 to Kautokeino, a distance of 130km. Just short of Kautokeino, about 100km from Alta, Hwy-93 connects with Hwy-92, which travels the 100km or so northeast to Karasjok, where you can rejoin the E6 (but well beyond the turning to Nordkapp).

**By bus** Bus services across the Finnmarksvidda are patchy with a regular service between Alta and Kautokeino (4–5 daily; 2hr) and between Kautokeino and Karasjok (1–2 daily; 1hr 30min), but a poor service between Alta and Karasjok (2 weekly; 3hr 30min). A further service links Hammerfest with Karasjok (1–2 daily; 4hr). For bus timetables, consult ⓦ rutebok.no.

## Kautokeino

It's a two-hour drive or bus ride from Alta across the Finnmarksvidda to **KAUTOKEINO** (Guovdageaidnu in Sámi), the principal winter camp of the Norwegian Sámi and their reindeer, who are kept on the surrounding plains. The Sámi are not, however, easy town dwellers and although Kautokeino is very useful to them as a supply base, it's still a desultory, desolate-looking place that straggles along Hwy-93 for a couple of kilometres. The handful of buildings that pass for the town centre are gathered at the point where the road crosses the Kautokeinoelva River.

## THE SÁMI

The northernmost reaches of Norway, Sweden and Finland, plus the Kola peninsula of northwest Russia, are collectively known as **Lapland**. Traditionally, the indigenous population were called "Lapps", but in recent years this name has fallen out of favour and been replaced by the term **Sámi**, although the change is by no means universal. This more commonly used term comes from the Sámi word *sámpi* referring to both the land and its people, who now number – though the statistics are the subject of much debate – 110,000 scattered across the whole of the region, though some estimates put the total as low as 65,000. Among the oldest peoples in Europe, the Sámi most likely descended from prehistoric clans who migrated here from Siberia by way of the Baltic. Their **language** is closely related to Finnish and Estonian, though it's somewhat misleading to speak of a "Sámi language" as there are, in fact, three distinct versions, each of which breaks down into a number of markedly different regional dialects. All share many common features, however, including a superabundance of words and phrases to express variations in snow and ice conditions.

Originally, the Sámi were a seminomadic people, living in **small communities** (*siidas*), each of which had a degree of control over the surrounding hunting grounds. They lived from hunting, fishing and trapping, preying on all the edible creatures of the North, but it was the wild reindeer that supplied most of their needs. This changed in the sixteenth century when the Sámi moved over to **reindeer herding**, with communities following the seasonal movements of the animals.

### COLONIZATION

The contact the Sámi have had with other Scandinavians has almost always been to their disadvantage. In the ninth century, they paid significant fur, feather and hide taxes to Norse chieftains. Later, in the seventeenth century, they faced **colonization** and moves to **dislocate their culture** from the various rulers of Sweden, Russia and Norway. The frontiers of Sámiland were only agreed in 1826, by which point hundreds of farmers had already settled in "Lapland", to the consternation of its native population. By that point, Norway's Sámi had kowtowed to Protestant missionaries and accepted the **religion** of their colonizers – though the more progressive among the evangelicals did support the use of Sámi languages and even translated hundreds of books into their language. In Norway in the nineteenth century, the government's aggressive Social Darwinist policy of **"Norwegianization"** banned the use of indigenous languages in schools, and only allowed Sámi to buy land if they could speak Norwegian. Only in the 1950s were these policies abandoned and slowly replaced by a more considered, progressive approach.

### CHERNOBYL AND AFTER

Nineteen eighty-six was a catastrophic year for the Sámi: the **Chernobyl nuclear disaster** contaminated much of the region's flora and fauna, which effectively meant the collapse of the reindeer export market. As a result, reindeer herding is now the main occupation of just one-fifth of the Sámi population, but nonetheless expressions of Sámi **culture** have expanded. Traditional arts and crafts are now widely available in all of Scandinavia's major cities and a number of Sámi films – including the critically acclaimed *Veiviseren* (The Pathfinder) – have been released. Sámi music (*joik*) has also been given a hearing by world-music, jazz and even electronica buffs. Although their provenance is uncertain, the rhythmic song-poems that constitute *joik* were probably devised to soothe anxious reindeer; the words are subordinated to the unaccompanied singing and at times are replaced altogether by meaningless, sung syllables.

In recent years, the Norwegians have been obliged to thoroughly re-evaluate their relationship with the Sámi – initially, in 1988, by amending the national constitution to include Sámi social, cultural and linguistic rights, then a year later establishing a Sámi Parliament, the **Sameting**, in Karasjok. Certain deep-seated problems do remain – issues such as land and mineral rights and the identity of Sámi both as an indigenous, partly autonomous people and as citizens of a particular country – but at least Oslo is asking the right questions.

## Juhls' Silver Gallery

Galaniitoluodda • June to early Aug daily 9am–8pm; early Aug to May daily 9am–6pm, but ring in winter to confirm hours • Regular guided tours (30min; free) • ☎ 78 48 43 30, ⓦ juhls.no • On a ridge above the west bank of the Kautokeinoelva River, 2.5km south of the town centre – follow the signs

Though it lacks obvious appeal, Kautokeino has become something of a tourist draw on account of the **jewellers Frank and Regine Juhls**, who braved all sorts of difficulties to set up their workshop here in 1959. It was a bold move at a time when the Sámi were very much a neglected minority, but the Juhls had a keen interest in nomadic cultures and, although the Sámi had no tradition of jewellery-making, they did adorn themselves with all sorts of unusual items traded in from the outside world. The couple were much influenced by this Sámi style of self-adornment, repeating and developing it in their own work, and their business prospered – perhaps beyond their wildest dreams. As testimony to the Juhls' commercial success, the plain and simple workshop they first built has been replaced by an extensive complex of low-lying **showrooms and workshops** – the **Juhl's Silver Gallery** (Juhls' Sølvsmie). Exquisitely beautiful, high-quality silver work is made and sold here alongside a much broader range of classy craftwork. The complex's interior is intriguing in its own right, with some rooms decorated in crisp, modern pan-Scandinavian style, others done out in an elaborate version of Sámi design.

## Kautokeino kirke

Goahtedievva 2 • June to mid-Aug daily 9am–8pm • Free • ⓦ kirkesok.no • Located just south of the centre on the east bank of the Kautokeinoelva River

Visible from pretty much everywhere in town, **Kautokeino kirke** (Kautokeino church) is a folksy-looking affair, painted red on the outside and with an interior that is decorated in bright, typically Sámi colours. The best time to visit is a Sunday morning, when the Sámi turn up here in their Sunday best. The church, which seats three hundred, was originally built by the Swedes in 1701, and then rebuilt following a German torching in 1944. It sports a ridged turret over the entrance – typical of churches built in the 1950s.

## Kautokeino Bygdetun og Museum

Boarinjárga 23 • Early June to mid-Aug Mon–Sat 9am–6pm, Sun noon–6pm; late Aug Mon–Fri 9am–3pm, Sat & Sun 10am–4pm; Sept to early June Wed & Thurs 9am–5pm • 40kr • ☎ 40 61 31 83, ⓦ rdm.no • On the southern side of the centre, signed from the E6

The small and mildly diverting **Kautokeino Bygdetun og Museum** (Guovdageaidnu Gilisillju; Kautokeino Parish Museum) displays a history of the town inside and a number of draughty-looking Sámi dwellings outside. You'll spot the same little turf huts and tents (known as *lavvo*) all over Finnmark, sometimes housing souvenir stalls.

### ARRIVAL AND DEPARTURE                                    KAUTOKEINO

**By bus** Buses stop at both the *Thon Hotel* and the Statoil petrol station. For bus timetables, consult ⓦ rutebok.no.

Destinations Alta (4–5 daily; 2hr); Karasjok (1–2 daily; 1hr 30min).

### INFORMATION AND TOURS

**Tourist office** Kautokeino tourist office (late June to mid-Aug daily 9am–4pm, July till 8pm; ☎ 78 48 70 00) is something of a moveable feast, but it is currently inside the *Thon Hotel* (see below). It provides town maps and has details of local events and activities, from fishing and

hiking through to "Sámi adventures", which typically include a boat trip and a visit to a *lavvo* ("tent"), where you can sample traditional Sámi food and listen to *joik* (rhythmic song-poems); reckon on 400kr.

### ACCOMMODATION AND EATING

**Thon Hotel Kautokeino** Biedjovaggeluodda 2 ☎ 78 48 70 00, ⓦ thonhotels.no. The largest hotel in Kautokeino, this fortress-like modern structure north of the river just off Hwy-93 is set on a small hillside overlooking town. The 65 guest rooms are furnished in a bright and

breezy style, with walls decorated by photos shot by a local artist. The hotel's passable restaurant, *Duottar*, specializes in local dishes with a modern twist – reindeer soup, baked salmon and sea crab, for example – with mains that range between 150kr and 350kr. Daily 5–10pm. **1000kr**

## ENTERTAINMENT

**Kautokeino Kulturhus** Bredbuktnesveien 50 ☎ 78 48 44 60, ⓦ beaivvas.no. Winner of various architectural awards, the Kautokeino Kulturhus (Guovdageaidnu Kulturviessu or Cultural Centre) houses the only state-sponsored Sámi theatre in Norway. If there's anything going on in town entertainment-wise, this is where you'll find it.

# Karasjok

Norway's Sámi capital, **KARASJOK** (Kárásjohka in Sámi), on the Finnmarksvidda 130km from Kautokeino, straddles the E6 on the main route from Finland to Nordkapp – and consequently sees plenty of tourists. Spread across a wooded river valley, the town has none of the desolation of Kautokeino, yet it still conspires to be fairly humdrum despite the presence of the **Sámi Parliament** and the country's most ambitious Sámi attraction, **Sápmi Park**.

## Sápmi Park

Leavnnjageaidnu 1, 100m from the main town crossroads on the E6 • Early June & late Aug daily 9am–4pm; mid-June to mid-Aug daily 9am–7pm; Sept–May Mon–Fri 9am–4pm & Sat 11am–3pm • 150kr • ☎ 78 46 88 00, ⓦ visitsapmi.no • The souvenir shop here doubles as tourist information (see p.358)

To all intents and purposes a miniature Sámi theme park, **Sápmi Park** offers a super-duper multimedia introduction to the Sámi in the Stálubákti ("Magic Theatre"), comprising a multilingual exploration of their traditional beliefs and customs. Included is a performance of the *joik*, the Samis' yodel-like singing. Here also are examples of traditional Sámi dwellings, Sámi shops plus displays of various ancient Sámi skills with the obligatory reindeer brought along as decoration or to be roped and corralled.

## De Samiske Samlinger

Mari Boine Geaidnu 17 • Early June to mid-Aug Mon–Sat 9am–6pm, Sun noon–6pm; late Aug Mon–Fri 9am–3pm, Sat & Sun 10am–4pm; Sept to early June Wed & Thurs 9am–5pm • 75kr • ☎ 78 46 99 50, ⓦ rdm.no • 400m from Sápmi Park: walk north along the Nordkapp road (the E6) and look out for the sign

The small collection here at **De Samiske Samlinger** (Sámiid vourká dávvirat; Sámi Collections) does a good job of providing an overview of Sámi culture and history. The outdoor exhibits consist of an assortment of old dwellings that illustrate the frugality of Sámi life. Inside, a large and clearly presented collection of incidental bygones includes a colourful sample of Sámi costumes.

## Samisk Kunstnersenter

Suomageaidnu 14 • Tues–Fri 10am–4pm, Sat & Sun 11am–4pm • Free • ☎ 90 24 40 62, ⓦ samidg.no • Just off Hwy-92, on the north side of the river

This unassuming gallery, the **Samisk Kunstnersenter** (Sámi daiddaguovddás; Sámi Artists' Centre), showcases the work of contemporary Sámi artists, mostly in a series of temporary exhibitions. Don't expect folksy canvases, however – Sámi artists are a diverse bunch and are as likely to be influenced by postmodernism as reindeer herding.

---

### HIKING THE FINNMARKSVIDDA

**Karasjok** is an excellent departure point for further explorations of the Finnmarksvidda. The region's most popular long-distance **hike** is the five-day haul across the heart of the Finnmarksvidda, from Karasjok to Alta via a string of strategically located huts – gorgeous and invigorating but not for the faint-hearted or inexperienced. A more gentle trek is the 3.5km **Ássebákti nature trail**, which passes more than a hundred Sámi cultural monuments on the way. Clearly signed, the trail begins some 14km west of Karasjok along Hwy-92 towards Kautokeino. For information on walks in the region, enquire at either the Karasjok or Alta tourist offices.

## Gamle kirke

Bieskkangeaidnu • June–Aug daily 8am–9pm • Free • ☎ 78 46 97 30 • Just off Hwy-92, on the south side of the river

Dating from 1807, Karasjok's **Gamle kirke** (Old Church) was pretty much the only building left standing here at the end of World War II. Of simple and unfussy design, it's the oldest-surviving church in Finnmark and it has an attractive, leafy location.

### ARRIVAL AND DEPARTURE                                       KARASJOK

**By car** Both the E6 and Hwy-92 dog-leg through Karasjok and share a small stretch of road between the town's two roundabouts. The E6 comes in from the north and turns east; Hwy-92 comes in from the west and also turns east. East of Karasjok, the E6 and Hwy-92 run parallel to each other on their way to Finland.

**By bus** There are several bus stops in Karasjok, but the handiest is on the E6, outside Sámpi Park – and a 5min-walk from the *Scandic Karasjok*. For bus timetables, consult ⓦ rutebok.no or ⓦ 177finnmark.no.
Destinations Alta (2 weekly; 3hr 30min); Hammerfest (1–2 daily; 4hr); Kautokeino (1–2 daily; 1hr 30min).

### INFORMATION

**Tourist office** The souvenir shop at Sápmi Park (see p.357) provides tourist information (mid-June to mid-Aug daily 9am–7pm; early June & late Aug daily 9am–4pm; Sept–May Mon–Fri 9am–4pm & Sat 11am–3pm; ☎ 78 46 88 00,

ⓦ visitsapmi.no). Staff here issue free town maps, organize authentic(ish) Sámi expeditions, and have details of local tour operators – though excursions run by *Engholm Husky Lodge* (see below) are the pick of the bunch.

### ACCOMMODATION AND EATING

★**Engholm Husky Lodge** 6km west of Karasjok on Hwy-92 ☎ 91 58 66 25, ⓦ engholm.no. This fantastic, all-year lodge features a number of home-made cabins of various shapes and sizes. They offer self-catering facilities, a sauna and Arctic dinners, where guests sit on reindeer skins around an open fire. The owner, the illustrious Sven, is an expert dog-sled racer and keeps about forty huskies; he uses them on a variety of guided winter tours and in summer organizes everything from fishing trips and guided wilderness hikes to horseback riding. Day-long adventure tours average around 1200kr. Pick-up from

Karasjok costs 200kr. Full board from 1300kr per person per night. Cabins from **1100kr**

**Scandic Karasjok** Leavnnjageaidnu 49 ☎ 78 46 88 60, ⓦ scandichotels.com. Though much less atmospheric than *Engholm*'s, this breezy modern establishment is the best option for staying in the town centre and is set in a large, appealing chalet-like building beside the E6 – and about 300m from Sápmi Park. The hotel also has a more than competent restaurant, where they feature local ingredients such as reindeer and cloudberries; reckon on 250kr for a main course. Restaurant: daily 6–10pm. **700kr**

# Hammerfest

Engaging **HAMMERFEST**, on the western shore of the rugged island of Kvaløya some 140km north of Alta, often claims to be the world's northernmost town. In truth, this prize goes to Longyearbyen on Svalbard, but nevertheless the locals, who number about 8000, do take pride in making the most of what is an inhospitable, northerly location – Hammerfest was, for example, the first town in Europe to be kitted out with electric street-lighting. It's a wonder the town has survived at all: a hurricane flattened the place in 1856; it was burnt to the ground in 1890; and the retreating Germans mauled it at the end of World War II. Yet, instead of being abandoned, Hammerfest was stubbornly rebuilt each time, and the resulting town is not the grim industrial place you might expect from the proximity of the offshore oil wells and gas terminals, but rather a bright and cheerful port, which drapes around a horseshoe-shaped **harbour** sheltered from the elements by a steep, rocky hill.

Hammerfest has a couple of good **museums**, is within comfortable striking distance of the wilderness **Seiland Nasjonalpark** and also benefits from the occasional dignified **wooden building** that recalls its nineteenth-century heyday as the centre of the Pomor trade in which Norwegian fish were exchanged for boatloads of Russian flour. But don't get too carried away: Bill Bryson, in *Neither Here Nor There*, hit the nail on the head

with his description of Hammerfest as "an agreeable enough town in a thank-you-God-for-not-making-me-live-here sort of way".

## The town quay

The busiest part of Hammerfest is down by the **town quay** with tourists emerging from the liners to beetle round the harbourfront, eat shellfish from the stalls along the wharf or buy souvenirs in the small, summertime Sámi market. The modest, modern

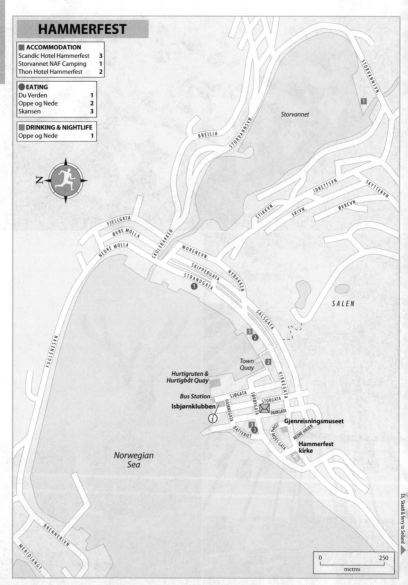

**HAMMERFEST**

**ACCOMMODATION**
| | |
|---|---|
| Scandic Hotel Hammerfest | 3 |
| Storvannet NAF Camping | 1 |
| Thon Hotel Hammerfest | 2 |

**EATING**
| | |
|---|---|
| Du Verden | 1 |
| Oppe og Nede | 2 |
| Skansen | 3 |

**DRINKING & NIGHTLIFE**
| | |
|---|---|
| Oppe og Nede | 1 |

Storvannet

BREILIA

STORVANNSVN.

STORVANNSVN.

IDRETTSVN.

SKYTTERVN.

STIKKVN.

SKIVN.

ØVREVN.

FJELLGATA

ØVRE MOLLA

NEDRE MOLLA

SKOLEBAKKEN

MORENEVN.

SKIPPERGATA

NYBAKKEN

STRANDGATA

SALSGATA

SALEN

KIRKEGATA

Town Quay

Hurtigruten & Hurtigbåt Quay

Bus Station

Isbjørnklubben

SJØGATA

HAMMERGATA

SØRØYGATA

STORGATA

PARKGATA

Gjenreisningsmuseet

BATTERIET

MYRS GATA

NEDRE HAUEN

SJØ

Hammerfest kirke

FUGLENESVN.

Norwegian Sea

BRENNERIVN.

MERIDIANGT.

N

0        250
metres

E6, Skaidi & Ferry to Seiland

buildings abutting the quay nudge up towards **Sjøgata** and then **Strandgata**, the town's principal street, where a run of shops and stores is partly fuelled by the town's role as a stop-off point for cruise ships en route to Nordkapp.

# Isbjørnklubben

Hamnegata 3 • June–Aug Mon–Fri 8am–7pm, Sat & Sun 9am–4pm; May & Sept Mon–Fri 9am–4pm, Sat & Sun 10am–2pm; Oct–April Mon–Fri 9am–4pm, Sat & Sun 10am–1pm • Free; membership 200kr • ☎ 78 41 31 00, Ⓦ isbjornklubben.no

One of Hammerfest's renowned attractions is the quayside **Isbjørnklubben** (Royal and Ancient Polar Bear Society). The society's pint-sized museum – filled with stuffed polar bears and seal-skin-covered furniture – tells the story of Hammerfest's heyday as a supply centre for Arctic expeditions and explorations, and gives the background to the creation of the society itself in 1963. You can also join thousands of others by becoming a lifetime member of the society, whose proceeds are put towards preserving local history and culture. The membership fee is 200kr and for an extra 100kr you can enjoy the dubious pleasure of being ceremonially "knighted" with a walrus's penis bone – an experience which may make you cringe with embarrassment for weeks on end.

# Gjenreisningsmuseet

Kirkegata 21 • June to mid-Aug daily 10am–4pm; mid-Aug to May Mon–Fri 9am–3pm, Sat & Sun 11am–2pm • 50kr • ☎ 78 40 29 40, Ⓦ gjenreisningsmuseet.no

The first-rate **Gjenreisningsmuseet** (Museum of Reconstruction), a five-minute walk west of the old town quay up Kirkegata, begins with a fascinating section on the hardships endured by the inhabitants of Finnmark during the **German retreat** in the face of the advancing Soviets in late 1944. The Germans ordered a general evacuation and then applied a scorched-earth policy, which left almost all of the region's towns and villages in ruins. Just in case any of his soldiers got the wrong idea, Hitler's orders stipulated that "Compassion for the population is out of place." Refugees in their own country, the Norwegians found shelter wherever they could and several thousand hid out in caves until liberation in May 1945, though many died from cold and malnutrition.

Subsequent sections of the museum deal with **postwar reconstruction**, giving a sharply critical account of the central government bureaucracy initially put in charge. Under the weight of complaints, it was disbanded in 1948 and control was passed back to the municipalities and many locals gave a huge sigh of relief: the left-of-centre Labour Party, who coordinated the initial reconstruction programme, adopted an almost evangelical stance, crusading against dirtiness, inequality and drunkenness in equal measure.

# Salen

To stretch your legs, take the **footpath** that zigzags up **Salen**, the hill behind town. It takes about fifteen minutes to reach the plateau at the top, from where there are panoramic views out across the town and over to the nearby islands. The footpath begins a couple of minutes' walk from the old town quay on **Salsgata**, one block south of Strandgata.

**ARRIVAL AND INFORMATION** **HAMMERFEST**

**By bus** Buses to Hammerfest pull into the bus terminal at the foot of Sjøgata, near the Hurtigruten quay. Hammerfest is 55km from Skaidi, on the E6, via Hwy-94. For bus timetables, go to Ⓦ rutebok.no.

Destinations Alta (1 daily; 2hr 20min); Honningsvåg (2–3 daily; change at Skaidi; 3hr 30min or 5hr 30min); Karasjok (1–2 daily; 4hr); Kirkenes (1 daily except Sat; 8hr).

**By Hurtigbåt passenger express boat** The VargsundXpressen, departing from the quay just east of the main harbour, links Hammerfest with Alta (1–2 daily; 1hr 40min).

**By Hurtigruten** The Hurtigruten (ⓦhurtigruten.no) quay is located close to the foot of Sjøgata. From Hammerfest, it's 5hr to Honningsvåg (for excursions to Nordkapp, see p.364) and 12hr to Tromsø.

**Tourist office** The tourist office is in the same building as the Isbjørnklubben at Hamnegata 3 (June–Aug Mon–Fri 8am–7pm, Sat & Sun 9am–4pm; May & Sept Mon–Fri 9am–4pm, Sat & Sun 10am–2pm; Oct–April Mon–Fri 9am–4pm, Sat & Sun 10am–1pm; ☎78 41 21 85, ⓦhammerfest-turist.no).

## ACTIVITIES

**Seiland Nasjonalpark** A mountainous chunk of pristine wilderness, Seiland, a large island to the southwest of Hammerfest, is mostly protected within the Seiland Nasjonalpark. Here, on the north side of the island, in tiny Hønseby, Seiland Explore (☎78 41 96 40, ⓦseiland -explore.com) offers a wide range of outdoor pursuits, including hiking, guided glacier tours, deep-sea fishing, snowmobiling and hunting. They offer simple overnight accommodation too, but it only takes an hour or so to drive from Hammerfest to Hønseby with one short ferry ride on the way. Prices run the gamut – from deep-sea fishing for 1000kr per person per day to a two-day guided glacier tour at around 7000kr per group.

## ACCOMMODATION

**Scandic Hotel Hammerfest** Sørøygata 15 ☎78 42 57 00, ⓦscandichotels.com. In an ungainly modern building a couple of minutes' walk west of the old town quay, this well-maintained Scandic hotel sits on a grassy knoll, which provides the best of its rooms with wide sea views. The rooms are kitted out in standard chain style – functional and comfortable, but nothing more. There's a sprawling breakfast buffet. **1000kr**

**Storvannet NAF Camping** Storvannsveien 103 ☎78 41 10 10, ⓦnafcamp.com. Your best camping option in town, this quiet lakeside site is located a couple of kilometres southeast of the town centre. Also offers a handful of cabins, simple affairs that often get booked up well in advance. Late May to Aug. Camping **280kr**, cabins **450kr**

**Thon Hotel Hammerfest** Strandgata 2–4 ☎78 42 96 00, ⓦthonhotels.com. Occupying a prime spot just metres from the town quay, this bright and breezy hotel is housed in a routine modern block, but the rooms are spick and very span and mostly decorated in bright colours. Those facing the street can get noisy. **1200kr**

## EATING

**Du Verden** Strandgata 32 ☎45 25 07 00, ⓦduverden .no. Smart and airy restaurant with a well-considered menu featuring the likes of reindeer with fried mushrooms and chestnuts, potato tart and glazed beets. Main courses start at around 220kr. Mon–Sat 11am–midnight, Sun 3–9pm.

**Oppe og Nede** Strandgata 22 ☎90 59 29 30, ⓦonhammerfest.blogspot.co.uk. Also known as *ON*, this popular restaurant serves salads, soups, pasta and larger mains like sirloin with stir-fried vegetables (165kr), though it is perhaps better known as the town's "hottest" nightspot (see below). Mon 10.30am–3pm, Tues–Thurs 10.30am–1am, Fri & Sat 11am–3am, Sun 3–10pm.

**Skansen** Scandic Hotel Hammerfest, Sørøygata 15 ☎78 42 57 00, ⓦscandichotels.com. Hotel restaurants rarely hit the heights, but this one is really very good, covering all the Norwegian basics with an especially good line in seafood. The coastal views are an added bonus. Mains average 220kr. Mon–Sat 5–10pm.

## DRINKING AND NIGHTLIFE

**Oppe og Nede** Strandgata 22 ☎90 59 29 30, ⓦonhammerfest.blogspot.co.uk. Few visitors come to Hammerfest for the nightlife, but this popular spot – usually known as *ON* – holds both a restaurant (see above) and a nightclub with multiple dancefloors – downstairs for teens (weekends only), upstairs for everyone else. Tues–Thurs 10pm–1am, Fri & Sat 10pm–3am.

# Nordkapp and around

At the northern tip of Norway, the treeless and windswept island of **Magerøya** is mainly of interest to travellers as the location of **NORDKAPP** (North Cape), generally regarded as Europe's northernmost point – though, in fact it isn't: that distinction belongs to neighbouring **Knivskjellodden**, a slender peninsula that pips Nordkapp by about 1500m. Somehow, almost everyone seems to have conspired to ignore this simple latitudinal fact and now, while Nordkapp has become one of the more popular tourist destinations in the country, there isn't even a road to Knivskjellodden, though you can hike there. Neither has the development of the Nordkapp as a tourist spot been without its critics, who argue that the cape's large and lavish visitor centre, the **Nordkapphallen**, is crass and grossly overpriced; their opponents simply point to the number of people who visit. Whichever side you're on, pretty much everyone who comes this far north does so to visit the cape and there's back-up with Magerøya possessing a bleak and rugged beauty, which is readily appreciated from the **E69** as it threads across the island. Magerøya also holds three appealing fishing villages – **Honningsvåg**, the main settlement, tiny **Kamøyvær**, nestling beside a narrow fjord just off the main road, and remote **Gjesvær** with its offshore seabird islets. Honningsvåg may be the obvious base for a visit to Nordkapp, just 34km away, but the cape is

also within striking distance of other places back on the mainland, including Hammerfest (see p.358) and Alta (see p.351), respectively 210km and 240km away.

**ARRIVAL AND DEPARTURE**                                  **NORDKAPP AND AROUND**

If you are aiming for **Nordkapp**, you can get there by **bus** either direct from the mainland or by changing at Honningsvåg. The nearest **airport** to Nordkapp is at Honningsvåg and the **Hurtigruten** docks here as well. Short-term **car rental** is also available at Honningsvåg.

# Honningsvåg

**HONNINGSVÅG**, a minor fishing and sea port about 100km from the E6, straggles along the seashore for about 1km, its jumble of well-worn modern buildings sheltered from the blizzards of winter by the surrounding crags – though, given the conditions, sheltered is a comparative term. Honningsvåg is at its prettiest in the vicinity of its main **harbour**, where an assortment of timber warehouses, dating back to the days when the village was entirely reliant on fish, makes an attractive ensemble. Draped with fishing nets and tackle, these buildings have wide eaves to protect against the snow and perch on crusty timber stilts that jut out of the water; each has its own jetty where fishing smacks are roped in tight against the wind.

> ### OUT NORTHING NORTH ON THE NORDKAPP
>
> When it comes to the out-northing game, **Knivskjellodden** may beat **Nordkapp**, but Norway's most northerly extreme is far away in Svalbard (see p.374). These two capes are, however, on the island of Magerøya, leaving **Kinnarodden**, a remote headland about 80km east of Nordkapp, as mainland Europe's northernmost point. If you thought it was hard work getting to Knivskjellodden (see p.365), then Kinnarodden is even more daunting – via a long and very difficult 25km hike from **Mehamn** (see p.368).

**6**

## ARRIVAL AND DEPARTURE

**By air** Honningsvåg's tiny airport, the nearest airport to Nordkapp, is located a 5min drive due north of town. There are regular flights to and from several destinations including Hammerfest and Tromsø with Widerøe (ⓦwideroe.no). A taxi on into town costs around 120kr.

**By bus** Buses to and from Honningsvåg pull in beside the Nordkapphuset (North Cape Museum), just metres from the harbour in the centre of the village; the tourist office is here too (see below). The most useful long-distance bus is the Nordkappexpressen running from Alta to Honningsvåg; from May to September, one Nordkappexpressen bus daily continues on to Nordkapp. In the same period, there are also four local buses daily between Honningsvåg and Nordkapp. You don't really want to get stuck at Nordkapp for more than a couple of hours – so check times before you set out. The last bus from Honningsvåg to Nordkapp is at 9.30pm with a return service at 12.15am, which means, of course, that you can view the midnight sun. For bus timetables, consult ⓦrutebok.no.

Destinations Alta (1–3 daily; 4hr); Hammerfest (1–2

daily; change at Olderfjord; 3hr or 5hr); Nordkapp (May–Sept 4–6 daily; 45min); Tromsø (1–3 daily; 3hr 20min).

**By boat** The Hurtigruten docks at the main jetty at the centre of Honningsvåg. Northbound boats arrive in the morning and depart just over 3hr later; southbound, the boats don't overlay here, arriving early in the morning and departing 15min later. The northbound service is met by special Nordkapp excursion buses – details on board.

**By car** The easiest way to get from Honningsvåg to Nordkapp is by car. Car rental is available in Honningsvåg from Nordkapp Bilservice, Nordkappveien 80 (☎78 47 60 60, ⓦwww.nordkappbilservice.no). Reckon on about 950kr/day, slightly less for half a day, which is more than enough time to head up to Nordkapp and back; reserve in advance if possible. Bear in mind that the last stretch of the Honningsvåg–Nordkapp road is closed by snow in winter, roughly from November to late April.

**By taxi** Honningsvåg's Nordkapp Taxisentral (☎78 47 22 34) run excursions up to Nordkapp, including an hour's waiting time once you get there.

## INFORMATION AND ACTIVITIES

**Tourist office** Honningsvåg tourist information office shares premises with the Nordkapphuset (North Cape Museum), in the centre near the harbour on Fiskeriveien (mid-June to mid-Aug Mon–Fri 9am–8pm, Sat & Sun noon–7pm; mid-Aug to mid-June Mon–Fri 10am–2pm; ☎78 47 70 30, ⓦwww.nordkapp.no).

**Destinasjon 71° Nord** Sjøgata 2 (☎47 28 93 20, ⓦ71-nord.no). This excellent company offers enjoyable king crab safaris throughout the summer (late May to Sept

1 daily; 3hr 30min; 1500kr). The Zodiac-based excursions begin by emptying the crab traps in the Sarnesfjord and then proceed to land to cook them; the crabs are ugly brutes, which can measure up to 2m in length and weigh some 10kg, but they do taste good. Among other activity tours and excursions, the same operator also offers ice-fishing and snowmobile safaris in winter, ocean rafting and sea-fishing in summer.

## ACCOMMODATION

**Nordkapp Camping** Skipsfjord ☎78 47 33 77, ⓦnordkappcamping.no. Out in the sticks on the road to Nordkapp, about 9km from Honningsvåg, there's a substantial grassy and treeless campground here, as well as double rooms (May–Sept), bungalows (May–Sept) and prefabricated cabins (June–Aug) for a maximum of four guests; all the doubles, bungalows and cabins have self-catering facilities, but only some are en suite. Camping 260kr, cabins 600kr, doubles 700kr, bungalows 1200kr

**Scandic Bryggen** Vågen 1 ☎78 47 72 50, ⓦscandic hotels.com. This boxy but smart modern hotel has a good location at the head of the harbour. Offers bright, modern

and comfortable rooms, mostly decorated in browns and creams. 1800kr

**Scandic Nordkapp** Skipsfjord ☎78 47 72 60, ⓦscandic hotels.com. With nearly three hundred rooms, this is the largest hotel on Magerøya, occupying a low-slung, modern complex, painted in a pleasant shade of red. The hotel has a solitary location on a grassy plateau just off the E69 about 9km from Honningsvåg, and is popular with groups heading to and from Nordkapp. The rooms are fine, if a little frugal, and there is a canteen-style restaurant. June–Sept. 1300kr

## EATING AND DRINKING

**Arctico Icebar** Sjøgata 1A ☎78 47 15 00, ⓦartico icebar.com. You might think that people up here would have quite enough of the cold to be getting on with, but curiously enough this ice bar, in a large storage freezer, offers a wintertime Arctic experience in the spring- and summertime. Odd – and oddly popular. Entrance 140kr,

which includes two (nonalcoholic) drinks. May–Sept open daily, but hours vary as per website; core hours: May & Sept daily 11am–4pm; June–Aug daily 10am–7pm.

**Corner** Fiskeriveien 2 ☎78 47 63 40, ⓦcorner.no. Close to the harbour, this modern bistro serves the freshest of seafood – try the sautéed cod tongue with remoulade and chilli sauce or the herb-baked king crab symphony, served on a bed of salad with bread; also does burgers and stews. Occasionally puts on theme evenings, such as the well-attended crab nights. Mains average 220kr. After the kitchen closes, the place morphs into a pub. Kitchen: daily 10am–9pm; pub: Tues–Sat 8pm–2am.

# Kamøyvær

Gallery – East of the Sun: Duksfjordveien 4 • Mid-May to Aug daily noon–9pm • ☎ 78 47 51 37

**KAMØYVÆR**, a pretty little place just off the E69 about 11km from Honningsvåg, strings along the seashore before coalescing around its hoop-shaped harbour. It's all very low-key and relaxing – there's a resident population of only about seventy inhabitants – and the village guesthouse (see below) is a handy launchpad for Nordkapp. Here also is the **Gallery – East of the Sun**, a small harbourside gallery, where resident German artist Eva Schmutterer exhibits a collection of intriguing, Arctic-inspired paintings and handicrafts; originals of her multicoloured canvases start at around 1500kr.

## ACCOMMODATION · KAMØYVÆR

**Hotel Árran Nordkapp** Kamøyvær ☎ 75 40 20 85 or ☎ 78 47 51 29, ⦿ arran.as. Pleasantly informal, family-run hotel, with strong Sámi connections, where the fifty-odd guest rooms are distributed among several brightly painted and well-tended houses down by the harbour. They serve seafood dinners here too, though it's best to reserve ahead. Mid-May to Aug. **1100kr**

# Gjesvær

About 14km north of Honningsvåg on the E69, a 21km-long byroad begins its looping route west across Magerøya to reach the remote hamlet of **GJESVÆR**, where a scattering of brightly painted houses nudges up against the water. Until the byroad was completed in the 1970s, this was one of the most isolated villages hereabouts, but one with a recorded history that dates back to Viking times. The Vikings came here for the fishing and to harvest the sea birds, especially puffins and kittiwakes, who congregate in their thousands on the offshore islets that today comprise the **Gjesværstappan Nature Reserve**.

## ACTIVITIES

**Bird safaris to Gjesværstappan** Bird Safari, Nygårdsveien 38, Gjesvær (☎ 41 61 39 83, ⦿ birdsafari.no), offers two-hour tours to the nature reserve during the nesting season (early April to early Sept 1–3 daily; 650kr), when the cliffs seethe and squawk with guillemots, puffins, gannets and kittiwakes, among many other types of sea bird.

## ACCOMMODATION · GJESVÆR

**Barents Cabin** Walsøenesvegen 34 ☎ 48 17 41 56, ⦿ barentscabincruise.com. Stuck on stilts right on the harbour, this comfortable little cabin is almost entirely made of wood – including the furnishings and fittings. The cabin has self-catering facilities and comes with use of a small boat. The same company also does larger, more modern "sea cabins" at a higher price. Cabin (price for two guests) **800kr**, sea cabins **1200kr**

# The hike to Knivskjellodden

North of the Gjesvær turning, the **E69** cuts a solitary route across a high-tundra plateau with the mountains stretching away on either side. It's a fine run, with snow and ice lingering well into the summer and impressive views over the treeless and elemental Arctic terrain. From June to October this is pastureland for herds of reindeer, who graze right up to the road, paying little heed to passing vehicles. The Sámi, who still bring them here by boat, combine herding with souvenir selling, setting up camp at the roadside in full costume to peddle clothes, jewellery and sets of antlers – which some motorists are daft enough to attach to the front of their vehicles. About 29km from Honningsvåg (and 6km from Nordkapp), the E69 passes the start of the well-marked **hiking trail** that leads to the headland of **Knivskjellodden**, stretching about 1500m further north than its famous neighbour. The 18km hike – there and back – takes between three and three and a half hours each way, but though the terrain isn't too severe, the climate is too unpredictable for the novice or poorly equipped hiker.

# 6 Nordkapp

When they finally reach **Nordkapp** (North Cape), many visitors feel desperately disappointed – it is, after all, only a cliff and, at 307m, it isn't even all that high. But for others there's something about this greyish-black hunk of slate, stuck at the end of a bare, wind-battered promontory, that exhilarates the senses. Some such feeling must have inspired the prehistoric Sámi to establish a sacrificial site here – and Nordkapp certainly stirred the romantic notions of earlier generations of tourists, often inspiring them to metaphysical ruminations. In 1802, the Italian naturalist, Giuseppe Acerbi, author of *Travels through Sweden, Finland and Lapland*, exclaimed: "The northern sun, creeping at midnight along the horizon, and the immeasurable ocean in apparent contact with the skies, form the grand outlines in the sublime picture presented to the astonished spectator." Quite – though the seventeenth-century traveller Francesco Negri wasn't far behind: "Here, where the world comes to an end, my curiosity does as well, and now I can return home content."

## Nordkapphallen

Daily: mid-May to mid-Aug 11am–1am; late Aug 11am–10pm; Sept to mid-May 11am–3pm • 260kr for 24hr, including parking, but free if you walk or cycle here • ☎ 78 47 68 60, ⚙ visitnordkapp.net

Cut into the rock of the Cape, the lavish **Nordkapphallen** (North Cape Hall) entertains hundreds of visitors every day. Fronted by a plinth honouring King Oscar II, who visited in 1873, the main building contains a restaurant, a café, a souvenir shop, a post office where you can get your letters specially stamped, and a panoramic cinema showing – you guessed it – films about the Cape and its surroundings. There's a viewing area too, but there's not much to see except the sea – and, weather permitting, the midnight sun from May 12 to July 29. A **tunnel** runs from the main building to the cliff face. It's flanked by a couple of little side-chambers, in one of which is a **chapel** where

---

### NORTHERN NAVIGATIONS

The first known tourist to visit **North Cape** was a Franciscan friar by the name of Francesco Negri, who arrived here in 1664, but it was the English explorer **Richard Chancellor** who named the cape in 1553, as he drifted along the Norwegian coast in an attempt to find the Northeast Passage from the Atlantic to the Pacific. Chancellor failed, but managed to reach the White Sea, from where he and his crew travelled overland to Moscow, thereby opening a new, northern trade route to Russia. Chancellor's account, published in the geographer Richard Hakluyt's *Navigations*, brought his exploits to the attention of seamen across Europe, but it was to be another three hundred years before the Northeast Passage was finally negotiated by the Swede, Nils Nordenskjøld, in 1879. In the meantime, just a trickle of visitors ventured to the Nordkapp. Among them, in 1795, was the exiled Louis Philippe of Orleans (subsequently king of France), and King Chulalongkorn of Thailand, who had his name carved into a nearby rock. But it was the visit of the Norwegian king **Oscar II** in 1873 that opened the tourist floodgates – and **Thomas Cook** sent a tour group of 24 people here just two years later. There were no island roads to the plateau, so the tourists had to be ferried by rowing boat from Gjesvær to Hornvika, at the base of the cliffs, before being instructed to climb the steep crags up to the top. The globe monument that now stands in for the actual cape – famous in postcards all over the country – was erected in 1978.

you can get married should you have the inclination, and by a series of displays detailing past events and visitors, including the unlikely appearance of the king of Siam in 1907, who was so ill that he had to be carried up here from his boat on a stretcher. At the far end, a cavernous **bar** offers caviar and champagne and long views out to sea through a massive glass wall. Alternatively, to escape the hurly-burly, you may decide to walk out on to the surrounding headland, though this is too bleak a spot to be much fun.

# Overland east from Nordkapp to Kirkenes

**Southeast of Nordkapp**, the landscape is a vast and relentless expanse of barren plateaux, mountains and ocean. Occasionally a determined village relieves the monotony with commanding views over the fjords that slice deep into the mainland, but generally there is little for the eyes of a tourist. Nor is there much of anything to actually do in what are predominantly fishing and industrial settlements – and, indeed, there are few tangible attractions beyond the sheer impossibility of the chill wilderness.

The **E6** weaves a circuitous course across this enormous territory, hugging the Finnish border for much of its length, with the only obvious targets being the rough landscapes of **Stabbursdalen Nasjonalpark** and the Sámi centre of Karasjok (see p.357). Frankly, there's not much reason to push on further east unless you're intent on picking up the **Hurtigruten coastal boat** at Kirkenes (see p.373), 320km to the east of Karasjok at the end of the E6 and near the Russian frontier: if any European town comes close to defining remoteness then this must be it.

## Stabbursnes

Beyond its junction with the E69 Nordkapp road, the **E6** bangs along the western shore of the **Porsangerfjord**, a wide inlet that slowly shelves up into the sticky marshes and mud flats at its head. After about 45km, the road slides past **STABBURSNES**, a scattered hamlet some 180km south of Nordkapp, whose redeeming features are its museum and its proximity to the **Stabbursdalen Nasjonalpark**.

### Stabbursnes Naturhus og Museum

Early June daily 11am–6pm; mid-June to mid-Aug daily 9am–8pm; late Aug daily 11am–6pm; Sept–May Tues & Thurs noon–3pm, Wed noon–6pm • 80kr • ☎ 78 46 47 65, ⓦ stabbursnes.no

The small but enjoyable **Stabbursnes Naturhus og Museum** (Stabbursnes Nature House and Museum) provides an overview of the region's flora and fauna. There are diagrams of the elaborate heat-exchanger in the reindeer's nose that helps stop the animal from freezing to death in winter, for example, and magnified images of the warble fly which torments it in summer. There are also examples of traditional Sámi handicrafts and a good section on Finnmark's topography, examining, for example, how and why some of the region's rivers are slow and sluggish, while others have cut deep gashes in the landscape. The museum stands on the eastern periphery of Stabbursdalen Nasjonalpark.

### Stabbursdalen Nasjonalpark

The Stabbursnes Naturhus og Museum (see above) serves as the park's information centre, and sells guides with details on local hiking

A large slab of wilderness that holds the world's most northerly pine forest, the **Stabbursdalen Nasjonalpark** covers the slopes of the Stabbursdalen river valley, which runs down from the Finnmarksvidda plateau to the Porsangerfjord. The lower end of the park's valley is broad and marshy, but beyond lie precipitous canyons and chasms – challenging terrain, with a couple of marked **hiking trails**. If that sounds too much like hard work, opt instead for the easy 2.8km stroll east from the museum along the nature trail that traverses the thick gravel banks of the Stabbursdalen River where it trickles into the Porsangerfjord. It's an eerily bare and barren landscape and there's a good chance of spotting several species of **wetland bird** in spring and summer: ducks, geese and waders like the lapwing, the curlew and the arctic knot are common. Indeed, these salt marshes and mud flats are such an important resting and feeding area for migratory wetland birds that they have been protected as a **nature reserve**.

### ARRIVAL AND DEPARTURE                                                    STABBURSNES

**By bus** Most of the long-distance buses linking Alta and Hammerfest with Kirkenes pass through Stabbursnes as they travel along the E6. Timetable details on ⓦ rutebok.no.

Destinations Hammerfest (4–6 daily except Sat; 2hr 15min); Karasjok (4–6 daily except Sat; 1hr 30min); Kirkenes (3 daily except Sat; 7hr); Tana Bru (3 daily except Sat; 4hr 30min).

### ACCOMMODATION

**Stabbursdalen Resort** ☏ 78 46 47 60, ⓦ stabbursdalen .no. Within shouting distance of the E6, this sprawling complex has tent pitches and thirty cabins of various sizes and degrees of luxury/frugality. Most, but not all, of the

cabins have hot water, showers and self-catering facilities. Especially popular with fishermen. Mid-May to mid-Sept. Camping 200kr, two-bed cabins 550kr

## Tana Bru

From Stabbursnes, it's 90km south to Karasjok (see p.357) and a further 180km northeast along the Finnish border to **TANA BRU**, a Sámi settlement clustered around a grand suspension bridge over the River Tana. Some 300km in length, the river rattles down to the Tanafjord, an inlet of the Barents Sea and on the way it provides some of Europe's finest **salmon fishing**, though the fishing here is hedged with restrictions about what you can catch and when. Tana Bru is 140km from Kirkenes (see p.372).

### ARRIVAL AND DEPARTURE                                                         TANA BRU

**By bus** Most of the long-distance buses from Alta and Hammerfest to Kirkenes travel the E6, passing through Tana Bru, though some shortcut through Finland. Timetables on ⓦ rutebok.no.

Destinations Hammerfest (3 daily except Sat; 6hr 30min); Kirkenes (3 daily except Sat; 2hr 30min); Stabbursnes (3 daily except Sat; 4hr 30min).

# By sea: east from Nordkapp to Kirkenes

Beyond Nordkapp the **Hurtigruten** steers a fine route round the very top of the country, nudging its way past craggy bluffs, wind-blasted plateaux and deep inlets to stop at a string of remote towns and fishing villages. The Hurtigruten takes around eighteen hours to sail from Honningsvåg to Kirkenes and, among the ports it visits, the most interesting is **Vardø**, though both **Mehamn** and **Berlevåg** are more typical of the solitary fishing villages that lie dotted over this northern wilderness. Almost remarkably, all these settlements are now connected to the road network, but the distances involved are verging on the epic – stick to the Hurtigruten.

## Mehamn and Gamvik

Northbound from Honningsvåg (see p.363), the Hurtigruten's first port of call is **Kjøllefjord**, where a scattering of brightly painted houses skirts the edge of a pronged inlet with grey-green hills all around. Next up is the flat-lining town of **MEHAMN**, where you should skip whatever little life you find here for the 20km drive east to the more agreeable hamlet of **GAMVIK**, whose scattering of cheerful timber houses spread out along a low and grassy foreshore. This really does feel like the end of the world and, to hammer home the point, this is where you'll find mainland Europe's most northerly **lighthouse**.

## Gamvik Museum

Strandveien 93, Gamvik • Mid-June to mid-Aug daily 10am–4pm; late Aug to mid-June Mon–Fri 10am–4pm • 50kr • ☎ 78 49 79 49, ⓦ kystmuseene.no

Perched on the edge of the harbour in a former fish factory, **Gamvik Museum** tracks through the history of the village and its people with a particularly good section on the economic clout of the local merchant. Other sections cover, for example, the role of women in local daily life, hunting, trapping, whaling and the Pomor trade with Russia.

## Slettnes Fyr

Gamvik • Guided tours of the tower: mid-June to mid-Aug daily every hour • ☎ 78 49 76 02, ⓦ slettneslighthouse.com

The Gamvik Museum (see above) is in charge of mainland Europe's northernmost lighthouse, the red-and-white-striped, cast-iron **Slettnes Fyr** (Slettnes lighthouse), which is located 4km to the north of the village at the end of a treeless, pancake-flat headland. Dating from the 1940s, the lighthouse is fully automated, but in the summertime you can clamber the tower and eat and sleep here (see below). The Slettnes headland also holds a small nature reserve, where in the warmer months you can find sizeable populations of breeding arctic terns, skuas and white-billed divers.

**6**

### ARRIVAL AND GETTING AROUND                MEHAMN AND GAMVIK

**By Hurtigruten** Northbound, the Hurtigruten (ⓦ hurtigruten.no) docks in Mehamn in the early evening; southbound it's after midnight. The sailing time to and from Honningsvåg is 4hr 30min; Berlevåg, the next port northbound, 2hr 30min.

**By taxi** Mehamn taxi is on ☎ 99 49 75 40.

### ACCOMMODATION

**Red Tree Guesthouse** Vaerveien 88, Mehamn ☎ 41 57 55 38, ⓦ redtree.no. Welcoming and extremely cosy guesthouse in the centre of Mehamn, where the hosts brim with ideas as to how to fill your time. The pleasantly decorated, unfussy rooms are wood-panelled with shared bathrooms and kitchen. **880kr**

**Slettnes Fyr** 4km north of Gamvik ☎ 78 49 76 02, ⓦ slettneslighthouse.com. You really have reached the back of beyond here at this lighthouse, which guards the headland just 4km north of Gamvik. The old lighthouse keeper's quarters have been upgraded to hold five guest rooms – nothing fancy, but comfortable and well-maintained. There's a café here too – and that's where you get breakfast. Mid-June to mid-Aug. **750kr**

# Berlevåg

Spread out over the coastal plain with bare hills swelling in the background, parts of **BERLEVÅG** manage to look almost suburban – quite an achievement given the village's location – with splashes of colour in a land otherwise stripped by the elements. Berlevåg has a population of just 1000 and its cultural traditions and tight community spirit were deftly explored in Knut Jensen's documentary *Heftig og Begeistret* (Cool & Crazy), released in 2001. The film received rave reviews both in Norway and across Europe, a welcome fillip to Berlevåg in general and the subject matter of the film – the local men's choir, the **Berlevåg Mannsangforening** – in particular.

## Berlevåg Havnemuseum

Havnegata • Mid-June to mid-Aug Mon–Fri 10am–6pm, Sat & Sun 1–6pm; mid-Aug to mid-June Mon–Fri 10am–3pm • Free • ☎ 78 98 13 66, ⓦ kystmuseene.no

Set within a 1950s retrofitted stockhouse, the **Berlevåg Havnemuseum** (Harbour Museum) is the village's main attraction. Exhibits here include an old ferryboat and a less-than-scintillating display on Berlevåg's concrete breakwaters, used to dissipate the force of coastal waves. The museum also focuses on the history and lives of local fishermen.

### ARRIVAL AND DEPARTURE                BERLEVÅG

**By Hurtigruten** Both northbound and southbound, the Hurtigruten (ⓦ hurtigruten.no) arrives in Berlevåg late in the evening; the boat stays here for just 15min. From Berlevåg, it's 2hr 30min to Mehamn, just over 5hr to Vardø.

**6**

## ACCOMMODATION

**Berlevåg Pensjonat og Camping** Havnegata 8 ☎ 41 54 42 55, ⓦ berlevag-pensjonat.no. This straightforward place offers tent pitches and a handful of simple guest rooms in a cabin-like building. Reservations recommended; breakfast 135kr per person extra. Camping **195kr**, doubles **820kr**

# Vardø and around

VARDØ, just over five hours on the Hurtigruten from Berlevåg, is Norway's most easterly town and a busy fishing port with a population of around two thousand. Like everywhere else in Finnmark, it was savaged in World War II and although the modern town that grew up in the 1950s could hardly be described as beautiful, it does rustle up a couple of enjoyable attractions, principally a pocket-sized fortress, the **Vardøhus Festning**, and the modern **Steilneset monument**, built in memory of those local women who were killed as witches here in the seventeenth century. Vardø's geography is unusual, too: the town spreads out over two little islets that are connected by a short and stumpy causeway, which in turn forms the apex of the town's harbour; a tunnel connects Vardø with the mainland, just a couple of kilometres away. Vardø is also useful as a base for exploring the offshore bird island of **Hornøya**.

## Vardøhus Festning

Festningsgata • Daily: mid-April to mid-Sept 10am–9pm; mid-Sept to mid-April 10am–6pm • 50kr • ☎ 91 68 85 58

Vardø's star turn is the **Vardøhus Festning** (Vardø fortress), a tiny but inordinately pretty star-shaped fort located just to the west of the main harbour – and about 600m from the Hurtigruten quay. The site was first fortified in the early fourteenth century, but the present structure dates from the 1730s, built at the behest of King Christian VI. When this singularly unprepossessing monarch toured Finnmark he was greeted, according to one of his courtiers, with "expressions of abject flattery in atrocious verse" – and the king loved it. Christian had the stronghold built to guard the northeastern approaches to his kingdom, but it has never seen much in the way of active service – though the Germans did use it during World War II.

## Steilneset

Andreas Lies gate • Open access • Free • By the seashore, about 800m west of the main harbour

Inaugurated by Queen Sonja in 2011, the **Steilneset monument** commemorates those women who were put to death as witches in the Vardø region in the seventeenth century (see box below). Designed by the Swiss architect Peter Zumthor and the artist Louise Bourgeois, the monument consists of two structures: a long and narrow building lined with windows – one for each victim of the witch hunts – and a glass building holding a chair with an eternal gas flame rising out of it. The memorial is located on the isolated and sea-battered spot thought to have been the witches' place of execution. During the summer months, an on-site guide gives the historical lowdown.

---

### THE DEVIL'S BREW: WITCHFINDING IN FINNMARK

In medieval Christendom, the far north – sometimes "**Ultima Thule**" – was a land of mystery and conjecture, nowhere more so than in **Finnmark**, where, as one popular legend had it, the road to hell began as a small, unpaved lane presided over by devils and dark knights. For many centuries, no-one bothered too much about such neo-pagan folklore, but the Christian screw began to tighten in the early 1500s with an increased emphasis on the need for doctrinal orthodoxy. When a dollop of misogyny was added to the stew, these religious tensions helped fuel a **witchfinding** fever that convulsed Finnmark in the 1620s – half a century or so later than in the rest of Europe. In Vardø, it was widely believed that a coven had set up shop in a local cave and, over the next sixty years, magistrates indicted 135 "witches" and burned 91 of them at the stake – a huge number considering the size of the population.

## Hornøya

Boats depart from Vardø harbour • April to Sept 4–5 daily • 2hr, including 10min boat ride each way • 400kr • Advance bookings essential • ☏ 78 98 72 75, ⓦ vardohavn.no

Among Vardø's outdoor attractions, the pick is a visit to **Hornøya**, a rocky, offshore islet that is the country's easternmost protected nature reserve. It's here that thousands of Atlantic puffins, European shags, razorbills, guillemots and great black-backed gulls nest each spring and summer – and a marked footpath on the island gets you close to them.

## Hamningberg

**6**

A narrow, albeit paved, byroad leads northwest along the coast from Vardø, threading its way through a bare and bleak, lunar-like landscape en route to the scattered fishing village of **Hamningberg**. It's a picturesque spot and scores of locals walk here from Vardø during the town's main festival – Pomordagene (Pomor Days), in early July.

### ARRIVAL AND INFORMATION

### VARDØ AND AROUND

**By Hurtigruten** The northbound Hurtigruten (ⓦ hurtigruten.no) reaches Vardø early in the morning and leaves just 15min later; southbound it docks in the afternoon and leaves 1hr later. Boats dock on the west side of the harbour.

**By bus** There is a reasonable bus service connecting Vadsø and Vardø with Varangerbotn, on the E6, where you pick up connections to/from Kirkenes and points west. Check

connection times before you depart on ⓦ rutebok.no.

**Destinations** Vadsø (4–6 daily; 1hr); Varangerbotn (4–6 daily except Sat; 2hr).

**Tourist office** The tourist office is located on the harbourfront near the Hurtigruten quay (mid-June to mid-Aug Mon–Fri 9am–5.30pm, Sat & Sun 11am–5.30pm; ☏ 78 98 69 07, ⓦ vardo.kommune.no).

### ACCOMMODATION AND EATING

**Vardo Hotell** Kaigata 8 ☏ 78 98 77 61, ⓦ vardohotel.no. Housed in a low-slung, modern block near the harbour, Vardø's only hotel hardly sets the pulse racing – from either outside or in. The rooms are functional and adequate but

nothing more. The hotel restaurant, on the other hand, is really rather good, with due prominence given to local ingredients (mains around 250kr). Daily 6–10pm. 1200kr

# Vadsø and around

To the south of Vardø, the coastline begins to turn west as it approaches the **Varangerfjord**, a wide and singularly bleak inlet, seemingly drained of almost all of its colour except for a light sprinkling of cold-bleached farm houses and rusting fishing boats. The only settlement to speak of hereabouts is **VADSØ**, once a Finnish-speaking town, where over half the population of five thousand still claim Finnish descent – hence the **Innvandrermonumentet** (Immigration Monument), which commemorates the many Finns who migrated here in the eighteenth and nineteenth centuries. The **centre** of Vadsø occupies a stumpy little headland, which pokes out from the mainland, and a bridge attaches it to the islet of **Vadsøya**, where the Hurtigruten docks. It's not a bad-looking town, but its main claim to fame and fortune is as the administrative centre of Finnmark, which – to be blunt – isn't a heck of a lot to get excited about. Both the Russians and the Germans did some damage here in World War II, but a surprisingly large number of fetching nineteenth-century houses have survived and the town holds several local history sites and museums, each of which is part of the **Varanger Museum**. It's most unlikely you will want to visit all of them, but the most interesting are the **Kjeldsenbruket**, a former fish processing plant, in Ekkerøy, about 15km east of Vadsø via the E75, and the **Vadsøya Kulturpark**, on Vadsøya, a couple of kilometres from the Hurtigruten dock.

## Vadsøya Kulturpark

Brugata • Open access daylight hours • Free • ☏ 78 94 28 90, ⓦ varangermuseum.no • The nature trail begins beside the *Vadsø Fjordhotell*

The small, flat and grassy headland at the east end of Vadsøya has been turned into the **Vadsøya Kulturpark**. A 2km-long nature trail winds its way around the park and on the way it passes a few, incidental historical remains, including reminders of the medieval settlement that prefigured Vadsø, a few bits and pieces from World War II, and the **airship mast** used by Roald Amundsen and Umberto Nobile during their North Pole expedition in 1926. Nonetheless, it's the birdlife which is perhaps more enjoyable with ducks and waders gathering here by the flock load.

### Kjeldsenbruket

Ekkerøy • Mid-June to mid-Aug daily 11am–5pm • 40kr • ☏ 78 94 28 90, ⓦ varangermuseum.no

The hamlet of **EKKERØY**, 15km from Vadsø, spreads along the shore of a tiny islet as well as the slender causeway that connects it to the mainland. It's here you'll find the intriguing **Kjeldsenbruket**, a former fish processing plant and shrimp factory, whose assorted buildings include the quay, a shop, a warehouse, a fish-processing hall, a cod-liver-oil plant and several small baiting sheds. Unusually, the complex survived World War II intact, but it has been restored to its 1950s appearance – the plant closed in 1969. You can also stay the night in Ekkerøy too (see below).

#### ARRIVAL AND DEPARTURE
#### VADSØ AND AROUND

**By boat** In Vadsø, the Hurtigruten docks on Vadsøya island, about 1km from the town centre on the far side of the bridge. The northbound Hurtigruten reaches Vadsø early in the morning and leaves 30min later; the southbound boat does not dock here at all. Northbound from Vadsø, the ship takes nearly 2hr to cross the blue-black waters of the Varangerfjord on the last stage of its journey to Kirkenes (see p.372).

**By bus** A reasonably good bus service links Vadsø and Vardø with Varangerbotn, on the E6, where you pick up long-distance connections. Vadsø bus station is in the centre of town on Strandgata – and about 1km from the Hurtigruten dock. Timetable details on ⓦ rutebok.no.
Destinations Varangerbotn (4–6 daily except Sat; 1hr); Vardø (4–6 daily; 1hr).

#### ACCOMMODATION AND EATING

**Ekkerøy Feriehus** Ekkerøy ☏ 90 89 15 58, ⓦ ekkeroy .net. Run by an ecotourism company, these pleasantly refurbished, freestanding homes have self-catering facilities, washing machines and DVD players, as well as access to a wood sauna. Beside the seashore, on the causeway connecting Ekkerøy with the mainland, they also offer excellent views over the Varangerfjord and are especially popular with birders. Ekkerøy is about 15km from Vadsø and 60km from Vardø; the Kjeldsenbruket museum (see above) is here too. **1500kr**

**Scandic Vadsø** Oscars gate 4 ☏ 78 95 52 50, ⓦ scandichotels.com. A large, modern and really rather pleasant hotel in the town centre with rooms kitted out in standard style – wood floors and so forth. The rooms on the upper floors at the front have reasonably good views over the town. Definitely Vadsø's best place to stay, and also holds the town's best restaurant with mains upwards of 230kr – try the king crab. Daily 5–10.30pm. **1200kr**

## Kirkenes and around

During World War II, the iron-ore mining town and ice-free port of **KIRKENES**, 170km from Vadsø, was bombed more heavily than any other place in Europe apart from Malta. The retreating German army torched what was left as they fled in the face of liberating Soviet soldiers, who found 3500 locals hiding in the mines. As a consequence, Kirkenes is now almost entirely modern, with long rows of uniform houses spreading out along the Bøkfjord, a narrow arm of the Barents Sea. If that sounds dull, it's not to slight the town, which makes the most of its inhospitable surroundings with some pleasant public gardens, lakes and residential areas – it's just that it seems an awfully long way to come for not very much. The stirring part Kirkenes played in the war is recalled in the **Grenselandmuseet** and also by a couple of **monuments** – one dedicated to the town's wartime women in the main square, and a second to the Red Army, plonked on Roald Amundsens gate, just to the east.

From Kirkenes, it's just 15km along the E105 to **Storskog**, Norway's only official border crossing point with **Russia**. Yet, apart from the achievement of actually getting there – you are further east than Istanbul and as far north as Alaska – there's nothing much to see or do, unless, that is, you're heading for the *Sollia Guesthouse* (see p.374). The crossing is busy, but access restrictions apply and, in any case, the only convenient settlement over the border is the incredibly grim mining town of **Nikel**.

## Grenselandmuseet

Førstevannslia • Daily: late June to late Aug 9.30am–5pm; late Aug to late June 9.30am–3pm • 50kr • ☎ 78 94 28 90,
Ⓦ varangermuseum.no • The museum is about 1.5km south of the main harbourfront, back along the E6 and on the east side of one of
the town's several little lakes

The **Grenselandmuseet** (Frontier Museum), one branch of the multifarious Sør-Varanger museum, focuses on the history of Kirkenes and its people, and includes a detailed account of the events of World War II, illustrated by some fascinating old photos. In the same building is a display of the work of **John Savio** (1902–38), a local Sámi artist whose life was brief and tragic. Orphaned at the age of three, when his father drowned on the way to Vadsø to buy a coffin for his wife, Savio was ill from childhood onwards and died in poverty of tuberculosis at the age of 36. This lends poignancy to his woodcuts and paintings, with their lonely evocations of the Sámi way of life.

## Andersgrotta

Haganesveien, off Presteveien • Mid-June to mid-Aug guided tours only, daily at 10.30am, 11am & 3pm • 120kr • ☎ 78 97 05 40

In the face of successive waves of Soviet bombing, the **Andersgrotta air-raid shelter** was commissioned by the occupying Germans and blasted out of the ground in 1941. After the war, the bunker was strengthened with concrete and continued to be used as a nuclear shelter throughout the Cold War. Stairs lead down to the extensive (but rather cold) space, where you can amble the corridors and catch a short English-language film about Kirkenes's role during the war.

## ARRIVAL AND DEPARTURE
### KIRKENES AND AROUND

**By plane** Widerøe (Ⓦ wideroe.no) flies to Kirkenes direct from several north Norwegian towns, including Alta, Hammerfest and Tromsø; a one-way ticket from Tromsø can go for as little as 955kr, though 2000kr is a more usual fare. SAS (Ⓦ flysas.com) and Norwegian (Ⓦ norwegian.com) also offer direct flights. The airport is located 13km west of town just off the E6; Flybussen (2–4 daily; 30min) connect the airport with the centre. A taxi (☎ 78 99 13 17) will run in excess of 350kr.

**By bus** Buses stop at the west end of the main harbourfront;

bus timetables on Ⓦ rutebok.no.
**Destinations** Alta (2 weekly; 7hr 30min); Hammerfest (1 daily except Sat; 8hr); Tana Bru (3 daily except Sat; 2hr 30min).

**By Hurtigruten** Kirkenes is the northern terminus of the Hurtigruten (Ⓦ hurtigruten.no). Taking the boat means that you can avoid the long haul back the way you came – and by the time you reach Kirkenes you'll certainly be heartily sick of the E6. The Hurtigruten uses the quay just over 1km east of the town centre.

## ACTIVITIES

**Pasvikturist** Dr. Wesselsgate 9 ☎ 78 99 50 80, Ⓦ pasvikturist.no. Well-established outdoor pursuits specialist offering a wide programme of guided tours and excursions. Options include 3hr king crab safaris (1800kr in winter, 1500kr in summer); 3hr riverboat tours (June to

mid-Sept; 1200kr); and 9hr guided hikes to the point where Norway, Russia and Finland intersect (mid-June to Sept; 2900kr), south of Kirkenes in the midst of the Siberian taiga of the remote Øvre Pasvik Nasjonalpark.

## ACCOMMODATION AND EATING

**Kirkenes Snowhotel** Sandnesdalen 14, Bjørnevatn ☎ 78 97 05 40, Ⓦ kirkenessnowhotel.com. The adventurous will jump at the chance to experience a night in this unique – and remarkably cosy – hotel. Rooms, built out of ice and snow, are kept at -5°C and for shut-eye, guests hop into expedition-strength, subzero Ajungilak sleeping bags, then lie down on a furry blanket of reindeer hide. Set near

the Gabba Reindeer Park, 10km south of Kirkenes via the E6 and Hwy-885. Also a fine spot to catch the northern lights. Price includes transfer from Kirkenes and half-board. Open mid-Dec to mid-April. **2650kr**

**Scandic Kirkenes** Kongensgate 1 ☎ 78 99 59 00, Ⓦ scandichotels.com. It's a chain hotel all right, but the ninety rooms are well-appointed and occupy a smart modern block in the centre near the town square. Swimming pool and sauna to boot. **1400kr**

**Sollia Gjestegård & Gapahuken Restaurant** ☎ 78 99 08 20, ⓦ storskog.no. Set about 15km from Kirkenes close to the Russian border, this excellent rustic Norwegian guesthouse and restaurant actually looks right into Mother Russia. They rent out simple, unassuming cabins and double rooms. In the restaurant, the whale steak and king crab are excellent – and main courses average 320kr. Advance booking is recommended and they offer minibus transport here from Kirkenes for about 130kr/person.

Mid-June to mid-Aug Tues–Sat 4–10pm, Sun 3–7pm. Doubles **1450kr**, cabins **1850kr**

**Thon Hotel Kirkenes** Johan Knudtzens gate 11 ☎ 78 97 10 50, ⓦ thonhotels.com. In a brisk, modern block down by the fjord in the centre of town, this medium-sized chain hotel has bright and cheerful rooms, the pick of which have sea views. The hotel restaurant does a more than competent take on Nordic cuisine with local ingredients – from both land and sea – to the fore. Mains at around 200k. In the warmer months, get a seat on the waterfront terrace. Bar menu: daily 11am–11pm; restaurant: daily 6–10pm. **1200kr**

# Svalbard

The mammoth **Svalbard archipelago**, some 400km wide and 500km long, is one of the most hostile places on earth, its southern tip around 830km north of the Norwegian mainland, its northern extremity not much more than 1000km from the North Pole. Glaciers cover two-thirds of its surface and its soils are frozen to a depth

## SVALBARD ADVENTURE TOURS

**Guided tours** are big business on Svalbard and you can choose anything from hiking and snowmobiling through to kayaking, ice-caving, dog-sledding and Zodiac boat trips. There are also wildlife safaris either by Zodiac boat or snowmobile with the polar bear providing the most prized sightings, though there are all manner of other Arctic fauna too, as well as trips to a former coal mine and to glaciers – and glacier tunnels. The winter season runs from December to late May, while June to November is the season for "summer" activities. For details of what's on offer, begin by consulting **Visit Svalbard's website** (ⓦvisitsvalbard.com), which presents a fairly thorough overview of everything you can do and when, and then select a **tour operator** – some of the best are listed below. Note that almost all the operators run day-trips from Longyearbyen to neighbouring **Barentsburg** (see p.380) by snowmobile or Zodiac, and some do overnight trips as well, including a stay in Barentsburg's one and only (basic) hotel. Nearly all of Svalbard's tour companies provide the necessary equipment and will pick you up at your hotel. Whatever you choose, you'd be well advised to **reserve** your excursions well before you get here – you could trust to luck and try on spec, but many outback trips are fully booked weeks in advance. Finally, if you are determined and competent enough to strike out into the wilderness **independently**, you first have to seek permission from, and log your itinerary with the governor's office, Sysselmannen på Svalbard, Postboks 633, N-9171 Longyearbyen (ⓣ79 02 43 00, ⓦsysselmannen.no); they will certainly require you to carry some form of weapon (see box, p.379).

### LOCAL TOUR OPERATORS

**Basecamp Spitsbergen** ⓣ79 02 46 00, ⓦbasecamp explorer.com. Arguably Svalbard's most innovative adventure company, whose offerings include a day's mountain scrambling (1190kr); 4hr at a former mine (500kr); a day's dog-sledding and glacier exploration (2000kr); an adventure week (17,000kr); and a three-day dog-sledding trip that includes accommodation in Nordenskiöld, a remote lodge that the company has recently refitted (15,000kr). They also own the *Basecamp Hotel* (see p.378) and the outlying, boutique *Isfjord Radio* guesthouse (see box, p.380).

**Poli Arctici** ⓣ91 38 34 67, ⓦpoliarctici.com. Run by an affable Italian outdoorsman, this small specialist operator is one of the best in town, offering snow-mobiling, boating and hiking tours, both short and long, from 950kr. They also rent out small apartments in Longyearbyen (500kr–800kr/person), and have a cabin out at Van Mijenfjord, some 65km away, that's available for stays during the winter (650kr/person). The wilderness cabin is a rarity – there are only a couple for rent across the whole of the archipelago – but obviously you have to be something of a survivalist to stay there safely.

**Spitsbergen Travel** ⓣ79 02 61 00, ⓦspitsbergen travel.no. One of Svalbard's largest outfitters, they run hotels, restaurants, safaris and can even rent out weapons and clothing. Their enjoyable 4hr dog-sledding trip, for example, costs just 950kr, while their 10hr combined hiking and kayaking trip costs 1325kr.

**Svalbard Husky** ⓣ78 40 30 78, ⓦsvalbardhusky .no. A first-rate dog-sledding specialist with a platoon of huskies based about 10min outside of Longyearbyen. A 4hr-long winter husky tour costs 1290kr, 1390kr when the snow has partly melted and you have to start at higher elevations.

**Terra Polaris** ⓣ79 02 10 68, ⓦwww.terrapolaris .com. One of the most hard-core of Svalbard's adventure companies, this company specializes in extended journeys out to some of the archipelago's more remote spots. Pick from, for instance, a skiing expedition to Newtontoppen and Atomfjella (fifteen days), a tour of Spitsbergen and eastern Greenland (thirteen days), or a visit to Franz Josef Land and Novaya Zemlya by Russian ice breaker (twelve days). Needless to say, it's pricey – 25,000kr and up.

of up to 500m, but despite the hardships such topography engenders, there are convincing reasons to make a trip. For one, Svalbard's hinterland makes it a devastatingly gorgeous place to visit whether in summer, autumn or spring when a magical light engulfs a Bergmanesque landscape and the Arctic opens itself up to the curious. Experiences up here can be other-worldly: hiking a permafrost landscape strewn with antlers and whalebones; donning a massive orange drysuit to float around in icy waters; and dining at a snowy beach on campfire-cooked ox gruel and fjord-chilled champagne. It's not your average place to visit – this is a land where there are twice as many polar bears as people – it is a once-in-a-lifetime destination if ever there was one.

**Weather**-wise, things are actually much better than you might expect. The warming Gulf Stream helps keep the coastal waters of this Arctic wilderness largely ice-free and navigable for much of the year – though the main fjords do tend to freeze over for several months of the winter – and the land is oddly fertile. Between late April and late August there's continuous daylight and, with temperatures bobbing up into the high teens, the snow has all but disappeared by July, leaving the valleys covered in wild flowers. And then there's the **wildlife** – an abundance of Arctic fauna – including over a hundred species of migratory bird, arctic foxes, polar bears and reindeer on land, and seals, walruses and whales offshore. In winter, it's a very different story: the polar night, during which the sun remains a full 8° below the horizon, lasts from late October to mid-February. The average temperature in February, Svalbard's coldest month, is -16.2°C, though this has plummeted to a staggering record low of -46°C – and that's not counting wind-chill.

## Brief history

The **Vikings** almost certainly made it up to Svalbard, whose name derives from the Old Norse for "land with the cold coast", but the first recorded discovery of the archipelago was by Dutch explorer **Willem Barentsz** on June 17, 1596. It was the third year in a row that the Dutchman had come in search of the Northeast Passage, and when his crew saw the icy peaks of Svalbard, they actually believed they had reached Greenland. After a protracted maritime battle with a polar bear, Barentsz was forced to winter at Bjørnøya just south of the main island, and shortly afterwards died after his ship was trapped in sea ice off the Russian Arctic island of Novaya Zemlya. A decade later, an English ship landed to hunt walrus, followed by French and Danish whalers, and then Russian and Norwegian polar bear and fox trappers. These European adventures and adventurers are recalled today by place names that read like an encyclopedia of Arctic exploration: aside from the Barents Sea, there is Taylorfjellet, a mountain recalling the Victorian editor of *The Scottish Geographical Magazine*, W.A. Taylor; Murraypynten, a cape named after Scottish oceanographer Sir John Murray; and a group of islands named after sixteenth-century merchant and adventurer Thomas Smythe.

The discovery of **coal deposits** in 1899 transformed Svalbard. At first, it seemed unlikely that the coal – the geological residue of a prehistoric tropical forest – was in sufficient quantities to make it worth exploiting, but in fact the deposits were rich and the first **coal mine** was opened by an American in 1908, passing into Norwegian hands eight years later. Meanwhile, other countries, particularly Russia and Sweden, were getting into the coal-mining act, and when, in 1920, **Norway's sovereignty** over the archipelago was ratified by international treaty, it was on condition that those other countries who were operating mines could continue to do so. It was also agreed that the islands would be a demilitarized zone, which made them, incidentally, sitting ducks for a German squadron, which arrived here to bombard the Norwegian coal mines during World War II. Today, only two of the collieries are still in operation – and they look doomed – and Svalbard's role is now primarily as an outpost for **Arctic research** and a place where tourists come to experience the remote and the extreme.

### ARRIVAL AND DEPARTURE

SVALBARD

**By plane** The simplest way to reach Svalbard is to fly to the archipelago's one and only airport at the main settlement, Longyearbyen, on the main island, Spitsbergen. In terms of prices, the budget airline Norwegian Air (W norwegian.com) have now opened things up, flying here direct from Oslo (3hr) with returns starting at around 3000kr (4500kr from London Gatwick via Oslo). SAS (W flysas.com) have more frequent flights to Longyearbyen from Oslo at comparable prices and

they also fly here direct from Tromsø (1hr 40min) three or four times a week with return fares from 2300kr. The airport is 4km from Longyearbyen and an airport bus (W svalbard buss.no; 75kr each way) links the two, stopping at most of the settlement's hotels. Before you book your flight, you'll need to reserve accommodation (see p.378) and, unless you're happy to be stuck in your lodgings, you'd be well advised to pre-book any guided excursions you fancy too.

## GETTING AROUND

There are **four inhabited settlements** on the main island, Spitsbergen, but all the other islands are uninhabited. Of the four, two are Norwegian (Longyearbyen and Ny Ålesund), one is Polish (Hornsund), and one is Russian (Barentsburg); there is also a recently abandoned Russian mining settlement at Pyramiden.

**By car** Longyearbyen has around 40km of road, but there are no roads to the other settlements and anyway you have to be armed to leave Longyearbyen (except by air) because of the danger presented by polar bears (see box, p.379).

**By public transport** Public transport is limited to the airport bus, occasional cargo ships from Longyearbyen to both Barentsburg and Ny Ålesund, and a light-aircraft service from Longyearbyen to Ny Ålesund, though government employees and researchers take priority on these flights.

**On a tour** Tour operators (see box, p.379) present the one real chance of getting out of Longyearbyen to visit the other places, principally by boat or snowmobile, but it is Svalbard's natural attractions that are the main draw rather than the other settlements.

**6**

# Spitsbergen

Looking something like a giant's jigsaw piece, **Spitsbergen** ("pointed mountains"), the main island of the Svalbard archipelago, is speared by fjords and dominated by mighty mountains. It was named by the Dutch explorer Willem Barentsz in 1596, though the appellation was first applied to both the main island and the archipelago as a whole – and in fact Svalbard continues to be known as Spitsbergen in most countries around the world. Spitsbergen is the archipelago's only inhabited island, its scant population distributed between **Longyearbyen**, the capital, two small research stations – **Hornsund** and **Ny Ålesund** – and **Barentsburg**, a Russian coal-mining settlement. Longyearbyen is the obvious and easily the best base for a visit: it holds almost all of Svalbard's accommodation; has a good selection of bars and restaurants; and is the starting point for a wide range of guided tours out into the wilderness – and, for most, it's the wilderness that they are after exploring.

## Longyearbyen

With a resident population of around two thousand, the only Norwegian settlement of any size up here is **LONGYEARBYEN**, a comparatively desolate spot that huddles on the narrow coastal plain below the mountains and beside the Adventfjord, a small bay on the southern side of the Isfjord, which jags deep into the middle of Spitsbergen. The settlement was founded in 1906, when John Munroe Longyear, an American mine-owner, established the Arctic Coal Company here. From most angles, Longyearbyen is an altogether ramshackle sort of place hunkered down against the blast of winter. Strewn about with large containers, transport vehicles and building machinery, it resembles something of a junkyard construction site, the few buildings that pass for the town centre located about 500m in from the waterfront. Longyearbyen is, however,

## GLOBAL SEED VAULT

Longyearbyen is home to the **Global Seed Vault**, a "doomsday" bank built in 2008 that stores seeds from thousands of crop varieties and their botanical wild relatives from all over the world. The current total number of seed samples numbers some 250 million (representing 500,000 different varieties), including members of one-third of the world's most important varieties of food crops. The vault is most commonly used in the event that any of the world's thousand-plus collections of diverse crops accidentally lose or destroy samples – not an infrequent occurrence. The structure is about as impervious to an end-of-the-world catastrophe as possible, constructed some 120m inside a sandstone mountain and 130m above sea level, which ensures the site will stay dry even in the event that all the icecaps melt. Seeds are kept in specially constructed four-ply packets and heat-sealed to exclude moisture. For obvious reasons, the vault is closed to visitors unable to prove some specific scientific purpose.

well equipped with services, including shops, cafés, a post office, bank, swimming pool, a platoon of tour companies, a campsite, a couple of guesthouses and half a dozen hotels, though advance reservations are essential for all accommodation.

### Svalbard Museum

Longyearbyen • Daily: Feb–Sept 10am–5pm; Oct–Jan noon–5pm • 90kr • ☎ 79 02 64 90, ⓦ svalbardmuseum.no

Sitting near the water's edge at the centre of Longyearbyen, the large and ambitious **Svalbard Museum** is the town's main tourist attraction. A massive polar bear looms over displays of ethnographic artefacts, documents and dioramas, while there are several multimedia presentations on the history of the region – and some of the issues it is currently facing. It's definitely worth at least an hour of your time before or after exploring the back of beyond outside of town, and has a great gift shop too, selling maps and a large selection of Arctic-related books.

## INFORMATION

**Tourist office** Visit Svalbard's office is in the town centre (daily: May–Sept 10am–4pm; Oct–April noon–4pm; ☎ 79 02 55 50, ⓦ visitsvalbard.com). They have information on a wide range of excursions and will give the lowdown on upcoming cultural events such as concerts, art exhibitions and films. Their website has comprehensive details on all Svalbard's outdoor activities.

**Listings** *Icepeople* (ⓦ icepeople.net) is a weekly printed and online English-language publication covering every aspect of Svalbard life; it's produced in Longyearbyen.

## ACCOMMODATION

★ **Basecamp Hotel** ☎ 79 02 46 00, ⓦ basecampexplorer .com. Possibly the most classically "Arctic" of Longyearbyen's places to stay is this sort of enlarged mock-up of a trapper's cabin, centrally located and complete with sealskins and a sauna; mostly made from old, recycled lumber, it all feels vaguely kitsch and put-on but great fun all the same – and very convivial. Be sure to visit the upstairs "Cognac attic", where you can sip on an ultra-pricey drink as you gaze out to the mountains from the glass roof. **1700kr**

**Longyearbyen Camping** ☎ 79 02 14 44, ⓦ longyearbyen-camping.com. For obvious climatic reasons, camping in Svalbard is not for the faint-hearted but this large site – about an hour's walk from town by the airport on the tundra coastal plain – is certainly likely to be the most remote spot you've ever pitched a tent. March–Sept. Tent pitch per person **120kr**

**Mary Ann's Polarrigg** ☎ 79 02 37 02, ⓦ polarriggen .com. Set a few minutes' drive from town and looking right onto the Hjorthfjellet mountain face, "The Rig" opened its doors several decades ago as a small wooden barracks for local labourers. The three buildings have since been converted and kitted out with Arctic ephemera vaguely evocative of what Svalbard was probably like for the miners and trappers who came here a century ago – give or take the restorative on-site spa. The forty-odd atmospheric rooms feature exposed beams and rustic amenities, there's a comfy lounge filled with books

and curiosities, and a great Thai-inspired restaurant (daily noon–2am, kitchen 4–10.30pm) serving the likes of cod tongue, whale tartare and steak of seal – though the beef stew is a real winner too. **1275kr**

**Radisson Blu Polar Hotel** Vei 500 ☎ 79 02 34 50, ⓦ radissonblu.com. This centrally located, modern chalet-like affair has nearly a hundred rooms decorated in fairly standard Nordic chain style, the pick of which have views over to the Isfjord. There are discounts for advanced bookings. **2000kr**

★ **Spitsbergen Hotel** ☎ 79 02 62 00, ⓦ scandichotels .com. Once housing the CEOs and technical engineers of local mining companies – and also known as "Funken" – this is the settlement's most appealing mid-level hotel, occupying a wooden chalet complex on a low ridge. The eighty-odd rooms are, for the most part, pretty standard, but the public areas and some of the guest rooms retain a scattering of older features – rich exposed wood floors, gold-plated fixtures and so forth. There's a small library and a sauna too. Located a 10min walk from the town centre. **2500kr**

**Svalbard Hotell** ☎ 79 02 50 01, ⓦ svalbardbooking.com. Opened in 2011, this sleek and surprisingly soulful hotel stands at the top of the town's main road. The twenty-or-so rooms are bright, cheerful and stylish with strong colours and lots of wood panelling, and many feature wall-sized Arctic photographs (of polar bears, for instance). **1900kr**

## EATING

**Fruene Kaffe & Vinbar** Lompensentret ☎ 79 02 76 40. This buzzy, centrally located café has friendly staff and is especially popular at lunchtimes. Sells soups, sandwiches (around 150kr) and great cinnamon buns (25kr), plus

twelve flavours of ice cream – in case you happen to need an extra shot of cold. Daily 10am–5pm.

★ **Huset** ☎ 79 02 50 02, ⓦ huset.com. Situated on the west side of the river at the southern end of town, this outstanding and notably smart restaurant specializes in Arctic dishes; for example local reindeer and Barents Sea crab. They serve à la carte and set meals (five courses for 800kr), but prices are much less if you eat at the attached bistro. Here also is the "Herring and Aquavit bar", Svalbard's closest approximation to a cocktail bar. Restaurant Tues–Sun 7–10pm; bistro daily 4–10pm; bar daily 10pm–3am.

**Kroa** Hilmar Rekstens vei ☎79 02 13 00, ⓦkroa -svalbard.no. Built out of the remains of a former Russian coal mine, this rivals *Huset* in terms of gastronomic quality and choice, and the decor is unbeatable for its end-of-the-world rustic charm. The sizeable dishes tend towards the "continental" – the seal and whale being two of the few exceptions. Mains average 250kr. Daily 11am–11pm.

**Nansen** Radisson Blu Polar Hotel Vei 500 ☎79 02 34 57, ⓦradissonblu.com. A good bet for a proper sit-down meal, serving all manner of Arctic specialities from char to reindeer, seal and (like it or not) whale. Burgers and salads start at 140kr, though more local dishes such as Barents Sea catfish with garlic bok choy, cassava root and king crab wonton with shellfish sauce (280kr), are better. Go for a window table, with great views out to the fjord. Attached, is the sometimes rowdy bar, *Barentz*. Restaurant daily 6–10pm; bar daily 4pm–2am.

## DRINKING

**★Karlsberger Pub** Lompensentret ☎79 02 25 11, ⓦkarlsbergerpub.no. Set into a cosy (and often cramped) wooden room, this is Longyearbyen's most atmospheric place to get sauced. While they don't serve draught beers, what they do offer is an astounding thousand bottles of different whiskies and other top- and bottom-shelf spirits – a 1908 Armagnac, for example, or a Cognac from 1802 (you don't even want to know how much). Six shots of whatever the drink of the day is – more often Jägermeister or something of equal shelf weight – will cost you

about 250kr. Mon–Fri & Sun 5pm–2am, Sat 3pm–2am.

**Svalbar** ☎79 02 50 03, ⓦsvalbar.no. With a Les Paul electric guitar signed by four members of Mötley Crüe and enough Drakkar Noir-wearing Norwegians to film a school reunion reality show, this spacious, modern bar, filled with large vinyl couches, is your best bet for authentic after-hours local colour. Also the place to play pool or darts, or catch the football. Carlsberg on draught, and good burgers too. Mon–Thurs 11am–2am, Fri–Sun noon–2am; Nov–Jan daily 3pm–2am.

## SHOPPING

**Lompensentret** ⓦamfi.no. The local indoor mall features a dozen-or-so shops and cafés, including Gullgruva Arctic Design (☎79 02 18 16), which sells gold and silver jewellery, silverware and souvenirs. You'll also find a pharmacy and the local library here, the latter offering a good selection of polar-related titles. Mon–Fri 10am–6pm, Sat 10am–3pm;

Library: Mon–Thurs 9am–9pm, Fri 9am–6.30pm, Sat 9.45am–5.30pm.

**Svalbardbutikken** ☎79 02 25 20, ⓦsvalbardbutikken .no. Also known as Coop Svalbard, this large modern supermarket in the centre of town sells almost any food product you'd find elsewhere in Norway – including freshly

---

### VENTURING OUT OF LONGYEARBYEN – AND BEARING ARMS

Longyearbyen lends itself to notching up all sorts of **geographic superlatives** – most northerly kebab, most northerly naff souvenir shop, most northerly egg and spoon race, and most northerly place in the world where you can walk around with a **gun** without ever getting a second look from your neighbour. Svalbard law requires everyone of age to carry a firearm to ward off polar bears anywhere outside of Longyearbyen: most residents travel with a Ruger .30 rifle as well as a "shocking device", a signal pistol or suchlike. Firearms can be rented from, among other places, Longyearbyen's **Ingeniør G. Paulsen** (☎79 02 32 00), though you'll need to either show documentation that you have permission to possess a firearm in your home country or apply for a licence with the governor (see box, p.375).

These regulations are a constant reminder that somewhere out there lurks *Ursus maritimus*, the common, hungry **polar bear**. Polar bear attacks are far from commonplace – there have only been fifty major incidents (and five human deaths) since 1973 – but they usually get plenty of attention in the international media, which temporarily tarnishes Svalbard's good name and results in a few cancelled holidays. The root cause of all these incidents isn't carelessness, but **global warming**. As the sea ice retreats – or the patterns of icing change – the bears, who more commonly hunt seals, are forced to look inland for sustenance, even targeting such unlikely food sources as the eggs of barnacle geese. As food and hunting grounds dwindle, interactions between polar bears and humans are likely to increase, particularly as the number of polar bears in and around Spitsbergen is on the increase – they currently number around three thousand.

baked goods – as well as a good selection of souvenirs. More crucially, though, it contains the only liquor store in town – a popular stop given Svalbard's exemption from Norway's exceedingly high taxes on alcohol. Be sure to bring your airline ticket to prove that you're a visitor. Supermarket Mon–Fri 10am–8pm, Sat 10am–6pm, Sun 3–6pm; liquor store Mon–Fri 10am–6pm, Sat 10am–3pm.

## Isfjord

Extending west from Longyearbyen into the Arctic Sea, the **Isfjord** is Svalbard's second longest fjord, and is one of the most popular places to head out on an organized overland (or water-based) excursion not least as a large chunk is preserved in the **Nordre Isfjord Nasjonalpark**. Visits include trips to the Russian settlement of **Barentsburg** (see below), and crossings to **Trygghamna**, a quiet, snowy pocket of the fjord that attracted Basque and English whalers during the sixteenth century. Another option is out to the bird cliffs of **Alkhornet**, where the umber land undulates in tussocky patches of arctic poppy, polar willow and saxifrage – flora that take advantage of the long periods of midnight sun to compensate for the polar nights. Here you'll encounter thousands of squawking Brünnich guillemots, fulmars and petrels breaking the Arctic silence. The best spot to base yourself for any of these excursions is Basecamp Spitsbergen's *Isfjord Radio* (see box below).

## Barentsburg

At the mouth of the Isfjord, around 50km west of Longyearbyen, the coal-mining township of **BARENTSBURG** sprawls along the foreshore, its grim and foreboding industrial (and postindustrial) buildings home to around four hundred Russians and Ukrainians. If you want harsh and bleak, this is it, with street lamps lit by coal fire, rusty scrap iron littered here and there and the odd sauced miner staggering down the street at midday. There isn't a heck of a lot to do in town, beyond visiting the ageing Soviet **sports hall** and taking a peek at the statue of Lenin, but – rather surprisingly – there is a hotel here, the *Barentsburg*, a Soviet-era block whose basic, wood-panelled interior holds a few rooms where you can stay if you are on a guided tour (see box, p.375). Indeed, for logistical and safety reasons, visits to Barentsburg should always be arranged as part of a tour. Note that Norwegian kroner, US dollars and euros are accepted for payment in Barentsburg, but not UK pounds sterling.

## Pyramiden

To the north of Longyearbyen, on the other side of the fjord, is the abandoned Russian mining settlement of **PYRAMIDEN**, whose rotting and rusting buildings edge along the foreshore beneath the long coal chutes, which stretch up the mountain behind. Pyramiden was abandoned in 1998 when the coal seams ran out and today it has the feel of a ghost town, where everyone just up and left mid-sentence. Since its abandonment, there have been lengthy debates as to what to do with the place – the

---

### ARCTIC POSH: ISFJORD RADIO

**Isfjord Radio Station**, the huddle of houses that inhabit **Cape Linné**, on the Isfjord's southwest tip, has been turned into one of Svalbard's premier **adventure destinations**. The radio station was established in 1933 as the sole telecommunications link between Svalbard and the Norwegian mainland, but in the early 2000s the laying of underwater fibre optics made the station obsolete overnight. The radio tower and giant satellite dish have survived, but down below the Norwegian adventure company **Basecamp Spitsbergen** (☎ 79 02 46 00, ⓦ basecampexplorer.com; inclusive stays from 7000kr per person) have turned the settlement's half-dozen buildings into a remote, rustic-chic base for wilderness explorations. The 23 swish, blue-grey rooms are kitted out with exposed wood, large comfy beds, goatskin blankets and driftwood sculptures, while high-powered binoculars await you at the window sills (the station looks out onto a protected bird area).

establishment of an international science station seems the most popular option – and a handful of Russians are still resident here, supposedly to keep an eye on things, but more so that the Russian state avoids forfeiting its claim on the land. Few visitors to Svalbard make a beeline for Pyramiden, which is best visited as part of an excursion to the neighbouring **Nordenskiöld glacier**, where a wide sheet of growling ice dips down to the fjord framed by brown and barren hills.

## Spitsbergen's other settlements

Of Spitsbergen's other settlements, Norway's **NY ÅLESUND** (25–120 inhabitants, depending on the season), located well to the northwest of Longyearbyen, functioned as a colliery town until an explosion in 1962 forced the closure of the mine; since then, it has become a polar research centre staffed by scientists. To the southeast of Longyearbyen is another Norwegian outpost, **SVEAGRUVA** (or simply "Svea"), where the coal mine is worked by three hundred nonresident shift workers, though the future of the mine is currently under review. Finally, there's **HORNSUND**, on the southwest corner of Spitsbergen, where a small research station is staffed by a dozen or so Polish scientists.

# Contexts

# History

For much of its early history, Norway punched well above its international weight. By the tenth century its people had explored – and conquered – much of northern Europe, and roamed the Atlantic as far as the North American mainland. Yet these heady days came to an end when Norway lost its independence in the fourteenth century, coming under the sway of first Denmark and then Sweden – and thereafter, as something of a colony, the country became isolated and poor in equal measure. Independent again from 1905, Norway was propelled into World War II by the German invasion of 1940, an act of aggression that transformed the Norwegians' attitude to the outside world. Gone was the old insularity, replaced by a liberal internationalism exemplified by Norway's leading role in the environmental movement. And then came the money – or rather the oil: since its discovery in the late 1960s, Norway's North Sea oil has made it one of the wealthiest countries in Europe, a bonanza that fair took older Norwegians' breath away.

## Early civilizations

The earliest signs of human habitation in Norway date from the end of the last Ice Age, around 10,000 BC. In the Finnmark region of north Norway, the **Komsa culture** was reliant upon sealing, whereas the peoples of the **Fosna culture**, further south near present-day Kristiansund, hunted both seals and reindeer. Both these societies were essentially static, dependent upon flint and bone implements. At Alta, the Komsa people left behind hundreds of **rock carvings and drawings** (see p.352), naturalistic representations of their way of life dating from the seventh to the third millennium BC.

As the edges of the icecap retreated from the western coastline, so new migrants slowly filtered north. These new peoples, of the **Nøstvet-økser culture**, were also hunters and fishers, but they were able to manufacture stone axes, examples of which were first unearthed at Nøstvet, near Oslo. Beginning around 2700 BC, immigrants from the east, principally the seminomadic **Boat Axe** and **Battle-Axe peoples** – so named because of the distinctive shape of their stone weapons/tools – introduced animal husbandry and agriculture. The new arrivals did not, however, overwhelm their predecessors; the two groups coexisted, each picking up hints from the other – a reflection of the harsh infertility of the land.

| 10,000 BC | 4000 BC | 3000 BC | 2700 BC |
| --- | --- | --- | --- |
| As the icecap retreats, so hunters and gatherers spread across most of Norway | Job creation? Locals begin work on the Alta rock carvings | Norwegians start farming, eking out a living from the country's thin soils | Animal husbandry gets off to a slow start – chickens yet to arrive |

---

**RANDOM THOUGHTS FROM NORWAY**

"Welcome tourists – don't leave us alone with the Danes." Popular T–shirt logo, Oslo 2009

*"Adventure is just bad planning."* Roald Amundsen

*"Hollywood is loneliness beside the swimming pool."* Liv Ullmann

*"The burden of disease falls on the poor."* ex-Norwegian PM Gro Harlem Brundtland

*"We do not regard Englishmen as foreigners. We look on them only as rather mad Norwegians."*
Halvard Lange, Norwegian politician and diplomat

*"I have no fear of photography as long as it cannot be used in heaven and in hell."* Edvard Munch

*"For many years, it seemed as if nothing changed in Norway. You could leave the country for three months, travel the world… and come home to find that the only new thing in the newspapers was the crossword puzzle."* Jo Nesbø

---

## Into the Bronze Age

These **late Stone Age** cultures flourished at a time when other, more southerly countries were already using metal. Norway was poor and had little to trade, but the Danes and Swedes exchanged amber for copper and tin from the bronze-making countries of central Europe. A fraction of the imported bronze subsequently passed into Norway, mostly to the Battle-Axe people, who appear to have had a comparatively prosperous aristocracy. This was the beginning of the Norwegian **Bronze Age** (1500–500 BC), which also saw a change in burial customs. In the Stone Age, the Battle-Axe peoples had dug shallow earth graves, but these were now supplanted by **burial mounds** enclosing coffins in which supplies were placed in readiness for the afterlife. Building the mounds involved a substantial amount of effort, suggesting the existence of powerful chieftains who could organize the work, and who may also have been priests. **Rock carvings** became prevalent in southern Norway during this period too – workaday images of men ploughing with oxen, riding horses, carrying arms and using boats to navigate the coastal waters, which were supplemented by drawings of religious or symbolic significance. In general terms, however, the Bronze Age was characterized more by the development of agriculture than by the use of metal, and stone implements remained the norm.

## 500 BC to 200 AD

Around **500 BC** Norway was affected by two adverse changes: the climate deteriorated and the westward movement of the Celts across central Europe disrupted trade with the Mediterranean. The former encouraged the development of settled, communal farming in an attempt to improve winter shelter and storage, with each clan resident in a large stone, turf and timber dwelling; the latter cut the supply of tin and copper and subsequently isolated Norway from the early Iron Age. The country's isolation continued through much of the Classical period. The Greek geographer Pytheas of Marseille, who went far enough north to note the short summer nights, probably visited southern Norway, but the regions beyond remained the subject of vague speculation. Pliny the Elder mentions "Nerigon" as the great island south of the legendary "**Ultima Thule**", the outermost region of the earth; while Tacitus, in his *Germania*, demonstrated knowledge only of the Danes and Swedes.

| 1500 BC | 500 BC | 200 AD | 3rd century AD |
|---|---|---|---|
| The Norwegian Bronze Age begins – better tools mean bigger harvests | Norway gets colder; Norwegians club together to gather winter feed | Norwegians take up rune carving – patient, time-consuming work with a complicated alphabet | Roman goods filter their way north to Norway – coins, vessels, glass beakers and buckles are the most common items |

The expansion of the Roman Empire in the first and second centuries AD revived Norway's **trading links with the Mediterranean**. Evidence of these renewed contacts is provided across Scandinavia by **runes**, carved inscriptions dating from around 200 AD, whose 24-letter alphabet – the *futhark* – was clearly influenced by Greek and Latin capitals. Initially, runes were seen as having magical powers and it was to gain their knowledge that the god Odin hung for nine nights on *Yggdrasill*, the tree of life, with a spear in his side; they also turn up in the sagas with Egil, in *Egil's Saga* for instance, destroying a whale bone carved with runes because they contained "Ten secret characters, [which] gave the young girl [the daughter of his friend] her grinding pain." But gradually rune carving became more prosaic, and most of the eight hundred or so runic inscriptions extant across southern Norway commemorate events and individuals: mothers and fathers, sons and slain comrades.

## The Norwegian Iron Age and early medieval Norway

The renewal of trade with the Mediterranean also spread the use of **iron**. Norway's agriculture was transformed by the use of iron tools, and the pace of change accelerated in the fifth century AD, when the Norwegians learned how to smelt the brown iron ore, limonite, that lay in their bogs and lakes – hence its common name, **bog-iron**. Clearing the forests with iron axes was relatively easy and, with more land available, the pattern of settlement became less concentrated. Family homesteads leapfrogged up the valleys, and a class of wealthy farmers emerged, their prosperity based on fields and flocks. Above them in the pecking order were **local chieftains**, the nature of whose authority varied considerably. Inland, the chieftains' power was based on landed wealth and constrained by feudal responsibilities, whereas the coastal lords, who had often accumulated influence from trade, piracy and military prowess, were less encumbered. Like the farmers, these seafarers had also benefited from the **iron axe**, which made boat building much easier. An early seventh-century longship found at Kvalsund, near Hammerfest, was 18m long, its skilfully crafted oak hull equipped with a high prow and stern, prefiguring the vessels of the Vikings.

By the **middle of the eighth century**, Norway had become a country of small, independent kingships, its geography impeding the development of any central authority. In the event, it was the **Yngling chieftains** of southeast Norway who attempted to assert some sort of wider control. Their first leaders are listed in the *Ynglinga Tal*, a paean compiled by the Norwegian *skald* (court poet) Thjodolf in the ninth century. According to Thjodolf, early royal life had its ups and downs: King Domaldi was sacrificed to ensure the fertility of his land; Dag was killed by an accidental blow from a pitchfork; and Fjolnir got up in the night to take a leak, fell into a vat of mead and drowned.

## The Vikings

Overpopulation, clan discord, commerce and the lure of plunder all contributed to the sudden explosion that launched the **Vikings** (from the Norse word *vik*, meaning creek, and *-ing*, frequenter of), upon an unsuspecting Europe in the ninth century. The patterns of attack and eventual settlement were dictated by the geographical

| **5th century AD** | **583** | **8th century** |
| --- | --- | --- |
| Norwegians enter the Iron Age: even better tools mean even bigger harvests | Norwegians start using drinking horns; practice makes perfect; teetotallers concerned | King Fjolnir drowns in a vat of mead; teetotallers even more concerned |

position of the various Scandinavian countries. The Swedish Vikings turned eastwards, the Danes headed south and southwest, while the **Norwegians sailed west**, their longships landing on the Hebrides, Shetland, Orkney, the Scottish mainland and western Ireland. The Pictish population they encountered was unable to muster much resistance and the islands were quickly overrun, becoming, together with the Isle of Man, the nucleus of a new Norse kingdom that provided a base for further attacks on Scotland and Ireland.

The Norwegians founded Dublin in 836, and from Ireland turned their attention eastward to northern Britain. Elsewhere, Norwegian Vikings settled the Faroe Islands and Iceland, and even raided as far south as Moorish Spain, attacking Seville in 844. The raiders soon became settlers, sometimes colonizing the entire country – as in Iceland and the Faroes – but mostly intermingling with the local population. The speed of their assimilation is, in fact, one of the Vikings' most striking features: **William the Conqueror** (1027–87) was the epitome of the Norman baron, yet he was also the descendant of Rollo, the Viking warrior whose army had overrun Normandy just a century before.

The whole of Norway felt the **stimulating effects** of the Viking expeditions. The economy was boosted by the spoils of war and the population grew in physical stature as health and nutrition improved. Farmland was no longer in such short supply; cereal and dairy farming were extended into new areas in eastern Norway; new vegetables, such as cabbages and turnips, were introduced from Britain; and farming methods were improved by overseas contact – the Celts, for instance, taught the Norwegians how to thresh grain with flails.

### Alfred the Great and Ottar

The Vikings also rigorously exploited the hunting and fishing peoples who roamed the far north of Norway. Detailed information on Finnmark in the late ninth century comes from a surprising source, the court of **Alfred the Great**, which was visited by a Norwegian chieftain named **Ottar** in about 890. Ottar dwelt, so he claimed, "northernmost of all Norsemen", and he regaled Alfred with tales of his native land, which the king promptly incorporated within his translation of a fifth-century Latin text, the *History of the World* by Paulus Orosius. Ottar, who boasted that he owed political allegiance to no one, had a few cows, sheep and pigs and a tiny slice of arable land, which he ploughed with horses, but his real wealth came from other sources. Fishing, whaling and walrus hunting provided both food for his retinue and exportable commodities. He also possessed a herd of six hundred tame reindeer – plus six decoy animals used to snare wild reindeer – and extracted a heavy tribute from the Sámi (see box, p.355), payable in furs and hides.

### Viking religion and art

The Vikings' brand of **paganism** (see p.407), with its wayward, unscrupulous deities, underpinned their inclination to vendetta and clan warfare. Nevertheless, institutions slowly developed which helped regulate the blood-letting. Western Norway adopted the Germanic *wergeld* system of cash-for-injury compensation; every free man was entitled to attend the local *Thing* (*Ting*) or parliament, while a regional *Allthing* made laws and settled disputes. Justice was class-based, however, with society divided into

| **9th century AD** | 836 | 871 | 900 |
|---|---|---|---|
| Vikings are propelled out of Scandinavia, falling on an unsuspecting Europe borne hither and thither by their remarkably seaworthy longships; they do not, however, wear horned helmets | Norwegian Vikings found Dublin | Alfred the Great becomes king of Wessex | Harald Hårfagre becomes Norway's first widely recognized king |

### VIKING JEWELLERY

The Vikings were particularly keen on **jewellery**, both as a form of adornment and as a way of showing their wealth. Silver was the primary metal of value, as gold was in desperately short supply and only used by the most privileged. The early Vikings were quite content to wear imported – or indeed looted – jewellery of pretty much any description, but by the tenth century it was the silver- and goldsmiths back home who produced the most valued pieces, decorated with a densely wrought filigree of abstract patterns. Viking gold- and silver-work is categorized into several different periods, beginning with the intricate **Oseberg** and **Borre** styles of the ninth century and culminating in the more sophisticated **Jellinge** and **Urnes** styles of the tenth. However, only the wealthier Vikings could afford gold and silver and most had to make do with bronze jewellery, which was mass-produced in clay moulds. The most common items were bracelets and brooches, armlets and buckles, neck rings and pendants; earrings were unknown and finger rings rare. The two finest collections of surviving Viking silver-work are in Oslo – at the Kulturhistorisk Museum (see p.69), and at the Vikingskipshuset (see p.84).

three main categories: the lord, the freeman, and the thrall or slave, who was worth about eight cows. The Vikings were industrious slavers, opening slave markets wherever they went, sending hundreds to work on their land back home and supplying the needs of other potential buyers.

Viking **decorative art** was also pan-Scandinavian, with the most distinguished work being the elaborate and often grotesque animal motifs that adorned their longships, sledges, buildings and furniture. This craftsmanship is seen to good advantage in the **longship burials** of Oseberg and Gokstad, the retrieved artefacts which are on display in Oslo's Vikingskipshuset (Viking Ship Museum; see p.84). The Oseberg longship is thought to be the burial longship of Åse, wife of the early ninth-century **Yngling** king, Gudrød Storlatnes. She was also the mother of Halfdan the Black, whose body had a very different fate from her own – it was chopped up, and the bits were buried across his kingdom to ensure the fertility of the land.

## Norway's first kings

It was from the **Ynglings of Vestfold** that Norway's first widely recognized king, **Harald Hårfagre** (Fair-Hair; c.850–930), claimed descent. Shortly before 900 (the exact date is unclear), Harald won a decisive victory at Hafrsfjord (near modern Stavanger), which gave him control of the coastal region as far north as Trøndelag, though it sparked an exodus of minor rulers, most of whom left to settle in Iceland. The thirteenth-century *Laxdaela Saga* records the departure of one such family, the Ketils of Romsdal, who would not be "forced to become Harald's vassals or be denied compensation for fallen kinsmen". Harald's long rule was based on personal pledges of fealty and, with the notable exception of the regional *Allthings*, there were no institutions to sustain it; consequently, when he died, Harald's kingdom broke up into its component parts. Harald did, however, leave a less tangible but extremely important legacy: from now on every ambitious chieftain was not content to be a local lord, but strove to be ruler of a kingdom stretching from the Trøndelag to Vestfold.

| 900–1300 | 954 | 980s | 985 |
|---|---|---|---|
| Viking boom and population explosion – from 150,000 to 400,000 | Eric Bloodaxe driven out of York by the English | The Gothi, the priests of pagan Norway, start to worry about Christianity – with good reason | Erik the Red colonizes Greenland |

Harald's son, **Erik Bloodaxe** (d.954), struggled to hold his father's kingdom together, but was outmanoeuvred by his youngest brother, **Håkon the Good** (920–60), who secured the allegiance of the major chieftains before returning home from England where he had been raised (and Christianized) at the court of King Athelstan of Wessex. Erik fled to Northumbria and became, albeit temporarily, the king of Viking York. Initially, Håkon was well received, and, although his attempts to introduce Christianity failed, he did carry out a number of far-ranging reforms. He established a common legal code for the whole of Vestfold and Trøndelag, and also introduced the system of *Leidangr*, the division of the coastal districts into areas, each of which was responsible for maintaining and manning a warship.

### Harald Greycloak Eriksson and Håkon Sigurdsson

Yet, Håkon's rule was punctuated by struggles against Erik's heirs, who – with the backing of the Danish king **Harald Bluetooth** – defeated and killed Håkon in battle in 960. Håkon's kingdom then passed to one of Erik's sons, **Harald Greycloak Eriksson** (935–70). This forceful man set about extending his territories with vim and gusto. Indeed, he was, in Bluetooth's opinion, much too successful and so, keen to keep Norway within his sphere of influence, the Dane killed Greycloak on the battlefield in 970 and replaced him with a Danish appointee, **Håkon Sigurdsson** (d.995), the last genuine heathen to rule Norway. But again Bluetooth seems to have got more than he bargained for. Sigurdsson based himself in Trøndelag, a decent distance from his overlord, and it's believed he soon refused to recognize Danish suzerainty: certainly the Christian Bluetooth would not have sanctioned Sigurdsson's restitution of pagan sacred sites.

### Olav Tryggvason

In 995 the redoubtable **Olav Tryggvason** (c.968–1000), another Viking chieftain who had been baptized in England, sailed to Norway to challenge Sigurdsson, who was conveniently dispatched by one of his own servants before the fighting started. Olav quickly asserted control over the Trøndelag and parts of southern and western Norway. He founded Nidaros (now Trondheim), from where he launched a sustained and brutal campaign against his pagan compatriots – which incidentally secured him the adulation of later saga-writers. Despite his evangelical zeal, Olav's religious beliefs are something of an enigma: he had pagan magicians in his personal retinue, and was so good at predicting the future from bird bones that he was called *Craccaben* (Crowbone). Olav's real problem remained the enmity of the Danish-controlled southeastern regions of Norway, and of Bluetooth's son **Svein Forkbeard** (d.1014), who regarded Norway as his rightful inheritance. In alliance with the Swedish king, Svein defeated Olav at a sea battle in the Skaggerak in 1000, and Norway was divided up among the victors.

## West across the Atlantic

Meanwhile, amid all these dynastic shenanigans, Norwegian settlers were laying the foundations of independent Norse communities in the **Faroes and Iceland**, where they established a parliament, the *Allthing*, in 930. The Norwegian Vikings went on to make further discoveries: Erik the Red, exiled from Norway and then banished from Iceland for three years for murder, set out in 985 with 25 longships, fourteen of which arrived

| 990s | 995 | 1000 | 1020s |
| --- | --- | --- | --- |
| Olav Tryggvason attacks his pagan enemies with Christian zeal | Birth of Knut (Canute), the future king of Denmark, England and Norway | Leif Eriksson reaches the North American mainland (Vinland); native Americans object (violently) | Olav Haraldsson turns Norway Christian; worship of pickled horses' penises banned |

in **Greenland**. The new colony prospered, and by the start of the eleventh century there were about three thousand settlers. This created a shortage of good farmland, making another push west inevitable. The two **Vinland Sagas** (see p.422) provide the only surviving account of these further explorations, recounting the exploits of Leif Eriksson the Lucky, who founded a colony he called Vinland on the **shores of North America** around 1000 AD.

Norse settlers continued to secure resources from Vinland for the next few decades, until the native population drove them out. The Viking site discovered at L'Anse aux Meadows in Newfoundland, Canada, may have been either Vinland itself or the result of one of these further foragings. The Greenland colonists carried on collecting timber from Labrador up until the fourteenth century, when the climate is known to have cooled and deteriorated, making the sea trip too dangerous. Attacks by the Inuit and the difficulties of maintaining trading links with Norway then took their toll on the main Greenland colonies. All contact with the outside world was lost in around 1410, and the last of the half-starved, disease-ridden survivors died out towards the end of the fifteenth century, just as **Christopher Columbus** was eyeing up his "New World".

## The arrival of Christianity

In 1015, **Olav Haraldsson** (995–1030), a prominent Viking chieftain, sailed for Norway from England, intent upon conquering his homeland. Significantly, he arrived by merchant ship with just one hundred men, rather than with a fleet of longships and an army, a clear sign of the passing of the Viking heyday. He gained the support of the yeoman farmers of the interior – a new force in Norway that was rapidly supplanting the old warrior aristocracy – and with Svein Forkbeard's son and successor Knut (King Canute of England) otherwise engaged, Haraldsson soon assumed the mantle of king of much of the country.

For twelve years Olav ruled in peace, founding Norway's first national government. His authority was based on the regional *Things* – consultative and broadly democratic bodies, which administered local law – and on his willingness to deliver justice without fear or favour. The king's most enduring achievement, however, was to make Norway **Christian**. Olav had been converted during his days as a Viking, and vigorously imposed his new faith on his countrymen. Wherever necessary he executed persistent heathens and destroyed their sacred places. The dominant position of the new religion was ensured by the foundation of the Norwegian Church, whose first priests were consecrated in Bremen in Germany.

### Olav's death and Magnus the Good

It was foreign policy rather than pagan enmity that brought about Olav's downfall. By scheming with the Swedish king against **Knut** (d.1035), who had now consolidated his position as king of Denmark and England, Olav provoked a Danish invasion, whose course was smoothed by massive bribes. The Norwegian chieftains, who had suffered at the hands of Olav, could be expected to help Knut, but even the yeomen failed to rally to Olav's cause, possibly alienated by his imperious ways. In 1028, Olav was forced to flee, first to Sweden and then to Russia, while Knut's young son **Svein** and his mother, the English queen Aelfgifu, took the Norwegian Crown. Two years later, Olav made a

| 1030 | 1035 | 1047 | 1066 |
|---|---|---|---|
| Olav Haraldsson killed at the Battle of Stiklestad | Death of Knut; Norway independent again | Harald Hardrada, the last of the great Viking chieftains, becomes king of Norway | Hardrada is killed at the battle of Stamford Bridge in England |

sensational return at the head of a scratch army, only to be defeated and killed by an alliance of wealthy landowners and chieftains at **Stiklestad**, the first major Norwegian land battle (see p.284).

The petty chieftains and yeoman farmers who had opposed Olav soon fell out with their new king: Svein had no intention of relaxing the royal grip and his rule was at least as arbitrary as that of his predecessor. The rebellion that ensued seems also to have had nationalistic undertones – many Norwegians had no wish to be ruled by a Dane. Svein fled the country, and Olav's former enemies popped over to Sweden to bring back Olav's young son, **Magnus the Good** (1024–47), who became king in 1035. The chastening experience of Svein's short rule transformed the popular memory of Olav. With surprising speed, he came to be regarded as a heroic champion, and there was talk of miracles brought about by the dead king's body (see p.272).

### Harald Hardrada

On Magnus's death in 1047, **Harald Hardrada** (1015–66), Olav Haraldsson's half-brother, became king, and soon consolidated his grip on the whole of Norway from the Trøndelag to the Oslofjord. The last of the legendary Vikings, Hardrada was a giant of a man, reputedly almost seven feet tall with a sweeping moustache and eccentric eyebrows. He had fought alongside Olav at Stiklestad and, after the battle, he and his men had fled east, fighting as mercenaries in Russia and ultimately Byzantium, where Hardrada was appointed the commander of the Varangians, the Norse bodyguard of the Byzantine emperor.

Back in Norway, Harald dominated the country by force of arms for over twenty years, earning the soubriquet "Hardrada" (the Hard) for his ruthless treatment of his enemies, many of whom he made "kiss the thin lips of the axe" as the saga writers put it. Neither was Hardrada satisfied with being king of just Norway. At first he tried to batter Denmark into submission through regular raiding, but the stratagem failed and he finally made peace with the Danish king, Svein, in 1064.

In 1066, the death of Edward the Confessor presented Harald with an opportunity to press his claim to the English throne. The Norwegian promptly sailed on England, landing near York with a massive fleet, but just outside the city, at **Stamford Bridge**, his army was surprised and trounced by Harold Godwinson, the new Saxon king of England. It was a battle of crucial importance, and one that gave rise to all sorts of legends, penned by both Norse and English writers. The two kings are supposed to have eyed each other up like prize fighters, with Hardrada proclaiming his rival "a small king, but one that stood well in his stirrups", and Harold promising the Norwegian "seven feet of English ground, or as much more as he is taller than other men". Hardrada was defeated and killed, and the threat of a Norwegian conquest of England had – though no one realized it at the time – gone forever. Not that the victory did much good for Godwinson, whose weakened army trudged back south to be defeated by William of Normandy at the **Battle of Hastings**.

## Medieval consolidation

After the Battle of Stamford Bridge, the life of Harald Hardrada's son, **Olav Kyrre** (the Peaceful; d.1093), was spared on condition that he never attacked England

| 1217 | 1263 | 1266 | 1316 |
|---|---|---|---|
| Håkon IV becomes king; Norway's "Period of Greatness" follows | Magnus the Lawmender, Norway's wisest ruler, becomes king; Norwegians are happy | Magnus sells the Hebrides and the Isle of Man to Scotland | Norway loses its independence; Norwegians dispirited |

again. He kept his promise and went on to reign as king of Norway for the next 25 years. Peace engendered economic prosperity, and treaties with Denmark ensured Norwegian independence. Three native bishoprics were established, and cathedrals built at Nidaros, Bergen and Oslo. It's from this period, too, that Norway's surviving **stave churches** (see box, p.174) date, each lavishly decorated with dragon heads and scenes from Norse mythology, proof that the traditions of the pagan world were slow to evaporate.

The first decades of the twelfth century witnessed the further consolidation of Norway's position as an independent power, despite internal disorder as the descendants of Olav Kyrre competed for influence. Civil war ceased only when **Håkon IV** (1204–63) took the throne in 1217, ushering in what is often called "**The Period of Greatness**". Secure at home, Håkon strengthened the Norwegian hold on the Faroe and Shetland islands, and in 1262 both Iceland and Greenland accepted Norwegian sovereignty. A year later, however, the king died in the Orkneys during a campaign to assert his control over the Hebrides, and three years later the Hebrides and the Isle of Man (always the weakest links in the Norwegian empire) were sold to the Scottish Crown by Håkon's successor, **Magnus the Lawmender** (1238–80).

Under Magnus, Norway prospered. Law and order were maintained, trade flourished and, in striking contrast to the rough-and-ready ways of Hardrada, the king's court even followed a code of etiquette compiled in what became known as the *Konungs skuggsja* or "King's Mirror". Neither was the power of the monarchy threatened by feudal barons as elsewhere in thirteenth-century Europe: Norway's scattered farms were not susceptible to feudal tutelage and, as a consequence, the nobility lacked both local autonomy and resources. Castles remained few and far between and instead the energies of the nobility were drawn into the centralized administration of the state, a process that only happened several centuries later in the rest of western Europe. Norwegian **Gothic art** reached its full maturity in this period, as construction began on the nave at Nidaros Cathedral and on Håkon's Hall in Bergen.

Magnus was succeeded by his sons, first the undistinguished Erik and then **Håkon V** (1270–1319), the last of medieval Norway's talented kings. Håkon continued the policy of his predecessors, making further improvements to central government and asserting royal control of Finnmark through the construction of a fortress at Vardø. His achievements, however, were soon to be swept away along with the independence of Norway itself.

## Loss of sovereignty

Norway's independence was threatened from two quarters. With strongholds in Bergen and Oslo, the merchants of the **Hanseatic League** had steadily increased their influence, exerting a virtual monopoly on the region's imports and controlling inland trade. They also came to exercise undue influence on the royal household, which grew dependent on the taxes the merchants paid. The second threat was **dynastic**. When Håkon died in 1319 he left no male heir and was succeeded by his grandson, the 3-year-old son of a Swedish duke. The boy, **Magnus Eriksson** (1316–74), was elected Swedish king two months later, marking the virtual end of Norway as an independent country until 1905.

| 1349 | 1397 | 1410 | 1430s |
|---|---|---|---|
| Black Death ravages Norway, killing around 60 percent of the population | Sweden, Denmark and Norway united by the Kalmar Union | Norway loses contact with Greenland, where the Viking colonists slowly starve to death | A full-scale peasants' rebellion breaks out in Telemark – the revolt is only suppressed with great difficulty |

Magnus assumed full power over both countries in 1332, but his reign was a difficult one. When the Norwegian nobility rebelled he agreed that the monarchy should again be split: his 3-year-old son, Håkon, would become Norwegian king (as Håkon VI) when he came of age, while the Swedes agreed to elect his eldest son Erik to the Swedish throne. It was then, in 1349, that the **Black Death** struck, spreading quickly along the coast and up the valleys, killing almost two-thirds of the Norwegian population. It was a catastrophe of unimaginable proportions, its effects compounded by the way the country's agriculture was structured: animal husbandry was easily the most important part of Norwegian farming, and harvesting and drying winter fodder was labour-intensive. Without the labourers, the animals died in their hundreds and famine conditions prevailed for several generations.

Many farms were abandoned and, deprived of their rents, the petty chieftains who had once dominated rural Norway were, as a class, almost entirely swept away. The vacuum was filled by royal officials, the **syslemenn**, each of whom exercised control over a large chunk of territory on behalf of a Royal Council. The collapse of local governance was compounded by dynastic toing and froing at the top of the social ladder. In 1380, Håkon VI died and Norway passed into Danish control with **Olav**, the son of Håkon and the Danish princess **Margaret**, becoming ruler of the two kingdoms.

## The Kalmar Union

Despite Olav's early death in 1387, the resourceful **Margaret** persevered with the union. Proclaimed regent by both the Danish and (what remained of the) Norwegian nobility, she engineered a treaty with the Swedish nobles that not only recognized her as regent of Sweden but also agreed to accept any king she should nominate. Her chosen heir, **Erik of Pomerania** (1382–1459), was foisted on the Norwegians in 1389. When he reached the age of majority in 1397, Margaret organized a grand coronation with Erik crowned king of all three countries at Kalmar in Sweden – hence the **Kalmar Union**.

After Margaret's death in 1412, all power was concentrated in Denmark. In Norway, foreigners were preferred in both State and Church, and the country became impoverished by the taxes levied to pay for Erik's various wars. Incompetent and brutal in equal measure, Erik managed to get himself deposed in all three countries at the same time, ending his days as a Baltic pirate.

## Union with Denmark

The Kalmar Union was to struggle on until 1523, but long before that it was wracked by dynastic conflict with one or other of Sweden and Denmark trying to break out. The big turning point for Norway came in 1450, when a Danish count, **Christian of Oldenburg**, was crowned king of Norway and Denmark (but not Sweden) after lengthy negotiations between the Swedes and the Danes, neither of whom bothered to consult the Norwegians. Thereafter, Norway simply ceased to take any meaningful part in Scandinavian affairs. Successive monarchs continued to appoint foreigners to important positions, appropriating Norwegian funds for Danish purposes and even mortgaging Orkney and Shetland to the Scots in 1469. Danish became the official tongue, replacing **Old Norse**, which came to be regarded as the language of the ignorant and

| 1448 | 1523 | 1536 | 1596 |
| --- | --- | --- | --- |
| War between Sweden and Denmark – one of many | Final break-up of the Kalmar Union; Norway in thrall to Denmark | Denmark breaks with Rome; Lutheran Church of Norway founded | Willem Barents becomes the first known European to land on Svalbard |

inconsequential. Of local institutions, only the **Norwegian Church** retained any power, though this was soon to be undermined and then transformed by the Reformation, and only once did it look as if Norway might break the Danish stranglehold. This was in 1501, when a Swedish-Norwegian nobleman, **Knut Alvsson**, crossed the border and overran southern Norway, but the Danes rallied and Alvsson was treacherously murdered as he sued for peace.

The Danish victor, King **Christian II** (1481–1559), imposed a crash programme of "Danicization" on the Norwegians and mercilessly hunted down his opponents, but his attempts to dominate the Swedes led to his enforced abdication in 1523. The leaders of the Norwegian opposition coalesced under the archbishop of Nidaros, Olav Engelbrektsson, but their attempt to gain terms from the new king **Frederik I** failed. The Danish civil war that followed the death of Frederik resulted in the victory of the Protestant **Christian III** (1503–59) and the loss of Norway's last independent national institution, the Catholic Church. In 1536 Christian III declared that Norway should cease to be a separate country and that the Lutheran creed should be established there. Christian even carted the silver casket that had contained the bones of St Olav back to Copenhagen, where he promptly melted it down and turned it into coins.

Thereafter, Norway became, to all intents and purposes, simply a source of raw materials – fish, timber and iron ore – whose proceeds lined the Danish royal purse. Naturally enough, the Swedes coveted these materials too, the upshot being a long and inconclusive war (1563–70), which saw much of Norway ravaged by competing bands of mercenaries. Ironically, the Swedish attempt to capture Norway induced a change of attitude in Copenhagen: keen to keep their subjects happy, a degree of decentralization became the order of the day, and the Danes appointed a **Governor-General** (*Stattholder*) to administer justice with some reference to traditional Norwegian law.

### Reformation, Renaissance and after

Slow to take root among the Norwegian peasantry, **Lutheranism** served as a powerful instrument in establishing Danish control. The Bible, catechism and hymnal were all in Danish and the bishops were all Danes too. Thus, the Norwegian **Reformation** was very much an instrument of Danish colonization rather than a reflection of widespread intellectual ferment: the urban apprentices and craftsmen who fired the movement elsewhere in Europe simply didn't exist in significant numbers here in rustic Norway. Neither had the **Renaissance** made much impact: the first printing press wasn't established in Norway until 1643, and the reading public remained minuscule. However, the country did manage to produce a surprising number of humanist writers and something of the Renaissance spirit arrived in the form of **Christian IV** (1588–1648). Among the Danish kings of the period, he proved the most sympathetic to Norway. He visited the country often, improving the quality of its administration and founding new towns – including Kongsberg, Kristiansand and Christiania (later Oslo) – whose buildings were laid out on a spacious gridiron plan.

At last, in the **late sixteenth century**, the Norwegian economy began to pick up. The population grew, trade increased and, benefiting from the decline of the Hanseatic League, a native bourgeoisie began to take control of certain parts of the economy, most notably the herring industry. But Norwegian cultural self-esteem remained at a low ebb: the country's merchants spoke Danish, mimicked Danish manners and read

| **1620s** | **1643** | **1660** | **1700s** |
|---|---|---|---|
| Finnmark falls prey to a bout of savage witch-hunting | Norway enters the literary age with the founding of its first printing press | Frederik III establishes an absolute monarchy over Denmark and Norway | Copper in Røros, silver in Kongsberg – Norway experiences an early mining boom |

Danish literature. What's more, Norway was a constant bone of contention between Sweden and Denmark, the result being a long series of **wars** in which competing armies regularly overran its more easterly provinces.

## The beginnings of Danish absolutism

The year **1660** marked a turning point in the constitutional arrangements governing Norway. For centuries, the Danish Council of State had had the power to elect the monarch and impose limitations on his or her rule. Now, a powerful alliance of merchants and clergy swept these powers away to make **Frederik III** (1609–70) absolute ruler. This was, however, not a reactionary coup, but an attempt to limit the power of the conservative-minded nobility. In addition, the development of a centralized state machine would, many calculated, provide all sorts of job opportunities for the low-born but adept. As a result, Norway was incorporated into the administrative structure of Denmark with royal authority delegated to the beefed-up office of *Stattholder*, who governed through what soon became a veritable army of professional bureaucrats. In the event, these changes provided several advantages for Norway – the country acquired better defences, simpler taxes, a separate High Court and further doses of Norwegian law – but once again power was exercised almost exclusively by Danes. The functionaries were allowed to charge for their services, and there was no fixed tariff – a swindler's charter for which the peasantry paid heavily.

# The eighteenth century

The **absolute monarchy** established by **Frederik III** soon came to concern itself with every aspect of Norwegian life. The ranks and duties of a host of minor officials were carefully delineated, religious observances tightly regulated and restrictions were imposed on everything from begging and dress through to the food and drink that could be consumed at weddings and funerals. This extraordinary superstructure placed a leaden hand on imagination and invention. Neither was it impartial: there were some benefits for the country's farmers and fishermen, but by and large the system worked **in favour of the middle class**. The merchants of every small town were allocated exclusive rights to trade in a particular area and competition between towns was forbidden. These local monopolies placed the peasantry at a dreadful disadvantage, nowhere more iniquitously than in the Lofoten islands, where fishermen not only had to buy supplies and equipment at the price set by the merchant, but had to sell their fish at the price set by him too.

The Dano-Norwegian functionaries who controlled Norway also set the **cultural agenda**, patronizing an insipid and imitative art and literature. Only the writings of **Petter Dass** (1647–1707) stand out from the dross – heartfelt verses and descriptions of life in the Nordland where he worked as a pastor. There were liberal, vaguely nationalist stirrings too, in the foundation of a "Norwegian Society" in Copenhagen twelve years later.

## Missionaries into the north

There was also renewed missionary interest in Norway's old colony of **Greenland**. In part, this was down to the eccentric ethnic obsessions of the clergyman concerned, one **Hans Egede** (1686–1758), who was looking for Inuit with Viking features, but Bergen's

| 1707 | 1720 | 1727 | 1750 |
|------|------|------|------|
| Death of Petter Dass, Lutheran clergyman, hymn-writer and poet | The naval hero Peter Tordenskiold dies in a duel, four years after inflicting a crushing defeat on the Swedes | Death of Thomas von Westen, Lutheran clergyman and evangelist to the Sámi | Bergen has a population of 14,000 – and is twice the size of Christiania (Oslo) |

merchants went along with Egede on condition that he build them a Greenland fur-trading station. As it happened, this was a poor investment, as the trading monopoly was given to a Dane. There was also missionary work in **Finnmark**, where a determined effort was made to Christianize the Sámi (see box, p.355). This was a very different undertaking from Egede's, and one that reflected the changing temperament of the Lutheran Church of Norway, which had been reinvigorated by **Pietism**. One of their number, **Thomas von Westen** (1682–1727), learned the Sámi language and led an extraordinarily successful mission to the far north. He was certainly a good deal more popular than many of his fellow Pietists down south who persuaded **Christian VI** (1730–46) to impose draconian penalties for such crimes as not observing the Sabbath and not going to church regularly.

## War and peace

In the meantime, there were more wars between Denmark and Sweden. In 1700, **Frederik IV** (1699–1730) made the rash decision to attack the Swedes at the time when their king, **Karl XII** (1682–1718), was generally reckoned to be one of Europe's most brilliant military strategists. Predictably, the Danes were defeated and only the intervention of the British saved Copenhagen from falling into Swedish hands. Undeterred, Frederik tried again, and this time Karl retaliated by launching a full-scale invasion of Norway. The Swedes rapidly occupied southern Norway, but then, much to everyone's amazement, things began to go wrong. The Norwegians successfully held out in the Akershus fortress in Christiania (Oslo) and added insult to injury by holding on to Halden too. Furthermore, a naval commander, one **Peter Tordenskiold** (1691–1720), became a national hero in Norway when he caught the Swedish fleet napping and ripped it to pieces off Strømstad. Karl was forced to retreat, but returned with a new army two years later. He promptly besieged the fortress at Halden for a second time, but while he was inspecting his troops someone shot him in the head – whether it was one of his own soldiers or a Norwegian has been the subject of heated debate (in Scandinavia) ever since. Whatever the truth, Karl's death enabled the protagonists to agree the **Peace of Frederiksborg** (1720), which ended hostilities for the rest of the eighteenth century. Tordenskiold, however, did not benefit from the peace: he was killed in a duel after an argument at the gaming table.

## Trade and religious revival

Peace favoured the growth of **trade**, but although Norway's economy prospered it was hampered by the increasing **centralization** of the Dano-Norwegian state. Regulations pushed more and more trade through Copenhagen, much to the irritation of the majority of Norwegian merchants who were accustomed to trading direct with their customers. Increasingly, they wanted the same privileges as the Danes, and especially, given the chronic shortage of capital and credit, their own national bank. In the 1760s, Copenhagen did a dramatic U-turn, abolishing monopolies, removing trade barriers and even permitting a free press – and the Norwegian economy boomed. Nonetheless, the bulk of the population remained impoverished and prey to famine whenever the harvest or fishing was poor. The number of **landless agricultural labourers** rose dramatically, partly because more prosperous farmers were buying up large slices of land, and for the first time Norway had something akin to a proletariat.

| 1814 | 1828 | 1843 | 1852 |
|------|------|------|------|
| Treaty of Kiel compels the Danes to give Norway to Sweden at the end of the Napoleonic Wars | Henrik Ibsen born in Skien | Edvard Grieg born in Bergen | Sámi uprising against the Norwegians breaks out in Kautokeino |

Nonetheless, proletariat or not, Norway was one of the few European countries little affected by the French Revolution. Instead of political action, there was a **religious revival**, with a carpenter by the name of **Hans Nielson Hauge** (1771–1824) emerging as the leading evangelist. The movement's characteristic hostility to officialdom caused concern, and Hauge was imprisoned, but in reality it posed little threat to the status quo. Rather, the end result was the foundation of a **Christian fundamentalist movement** that is still a force to be reckoned with in parts of west Norway.

## Into the nineteenth century: the end of union with Denmark

Denmark and its satellite, Norway, had remained neutral throughout the Seven Years' War (1756–63) between England and France, and renewed that neutrality in 1792, during the period leading up to the **Napoleonic Wars**. Neutrality was good for Norway: overseas trade, especially with England, flourished, and demand for Norwegian timber, iron and cargo-space heralded a period of unparalleled prosperity – for the bourgeoisie, at least. However, when Napoleon implemented a trade blockade – the **Continental System** – against Britain, he roped in the Danes. As a result, the British fleet bombarded Copenhagen in 1807 and forced the surrender of the entire Dano-Norwegian fleet. Denmark, in retaliation, declared war on England and Sweden. The move was disastrous for the Norwegian economy, which had also suffered bad harvests in 1807 and 1808, and the English blockade of its seaports ruined trade.

By 1811 it was obvious to many Norwegians that the Danes had backed the wrong side, and the idea of a union of equals with Sweden, which had supported Britain, became increasingly attractive. By attaching their coat-tails to the victors, they hoped to restore the commercially vital trade with England. They also thought that the new Swedish king would be able to deal with the Danes if it came to a fight – just as the Swedes had themselves calculated when they appointed him in 1810. The man concerned, **Karl XIV Johan** (1763–1844) was, curiously enough, none other than Jean-Baptiste Bernadotte, formerly one of Napoleon's marshals (see box, p.70). With perfect timing, he had helped the British defeat Napoleon at Leipzig in 1813 and his reward came in the **Treaty of Kiel** the following year, when the great powers instructed the Danes to cede to Sweden all rights in Norway (although they did keep the dependencies of Iceland, Greenland and the Faroes). Four hundred years of union were ended at a stroke.

## Union with Sweden (1814–1905)

The high-handed transfer of Norway from Denmark to Sweden did little to assuage the demand for greater Norwegian independence. Furthermore, the Danish Crown Prince Christian Frederik roamed Norway stirring up fears of Swedish intentions. The prince and his supporters then convened a **Constituent Assembly**, which met in a country house outside Eidsvoll (see p.150) in April 1814 and produced a **constitution** in the teeth of the Swedes. Issued on May 17, 1814 (still a national holiday), this declared Norway to be a "free, independent and indivisible realm" with Christian Frederik as its king. Not surprisingly, Karl Johan would have none of this and – with the support of the great powers – he promptly invaded Norway. Completely outgunned, Christian

| 1863 | 1867 | 1898 | 1901 |
|------|------|------|------|
| Edvard Munch born in a farmhouse in Hedmark | Alfred Nobel patents his new invention – dynamite | Universal male suffrage introduced | First Nobel Peace Prize award. Jean Henry Dunant and Frédéric Passy are the recipients |

Frederik barely mounted any resistance. In exchange for Swedish promises to recognize the Norwegian constitution and the *Storting* (parliament), he abdicated as soon as he had signed a peace treaty – the so-called **Convention of Moss** – in August 1814.

The ensuing period was marred by struggles between the *Storting* and **Karl XIV Johan** over the nature of the union. Although the constitution emphasized Norway's independence, Johan had a suspensive veto over the *Storting*'s actions, the post of *Stattholder* in Norway could only be held by a Swede, and foreign and diplomatic matters concerning Norway remained entirely in Swedish hands. Despite this, Karl Johan proved popular in Norway, and during his reign the country enjoyed a degree of independence. The Swedes allowed many of the highest offices in Norway to be filled by Norwegians and democratic local councils were established, in part due to the rise of the peasant farmers as a political force.

## Pan-Scandinavianism
Under both Oscar I (1844–59) and Karl XV (1859–72), however, it was **pan-Scandinavianism** that ruled the intellectual roost. This belief in the natural solidarity of Denmark, Norway and Sweden was espoused by the leading artists of the period, but died a toothless death in 1864 when the Norwegians and the Swedes refused to help Denmark when it was attacked by Austria and Prussia. Some of the loudest cries of treachery came from a young writer by the name of Henrik Ibsen, whose poetic drama, *Brand*, was a spirited indictment of Norwegian perfidy.

## The end of the union with Sweden
In the 1850s, domestic politics were transformed by the rise to power of **Johan Sverdrup** (1816–92), who started a long and ultimately successful campaign to wrest executive power from the king and transfer it to the *Storting*. By the mid-1880s, Sverdrup and his political allies had pretty much won the day, though a further bout of sabre-rattling between the supporters of Norwegian independence and the Swedish king **Oscar II** (1872–1907) was necessary before both sides would accept a plebiscite. This took place in August 1905, when there was an overwhelming vote in favour of the **dissolution of the union**, which was duly confirmed by the Treaty of Karlstad. A second **plebiscite** determined that independent Norway should be a monarchy rather than a republic, and, in November 1905, Prince Karl of Denmark (Edward VII of England's son-in-law) was elected to the throne as **Håkon VII** (1872–1957).

## Norway's National Romantic movement
In the meantime, Norway's increasing prosperity was having important social and cultural effects. The layout and buildings of modern Oslo – the Royal Palace, Karl Johans gate, the university – date from this period, while **Johan Christian Dahl** (1788–1857), the most distinguished Scandinavian landscape painter of his day, was instrumental in the foundation of Oslo's Nasjonalgalleriet (National Gallery; see p.66) in 1836. More importantly, Dahl and other prominent members of the middle class formed the nucleus of a **National Romantic movement**, which championed all things Norwegian. The movement's serious intent was flagged up by Jens Kraft, who produced a massive six-volume topographical survey of the country, and the poet, prose writer and propagandist **Henrik Wergeland** (1808–45), who decried the civil-servant culture

| 1902 | 1905 | 1911 | 1913 |
|---|---|---|---|
| Criminal law amended to abolish the death penalty in peacetime | Norway breaks from Sweden to become independent | Roald Amundsen reaches the South Pole, but complains about the weather | Universal suffrage introduced |

## FRIDTJOF NANSEN

One of Norway's most celebrated sons, **Fridtjof Nansen** (1861–1930), was something of a Renaissance man – in fact, his skills and abilities were so wide-ranging that it almost seems unfair. As a teenager, he was a champion skier and ice skater and in his twenties he moved on to **exploration**: in 1888, he led the first expedition across the interior of Greenland and in the 1890s he made a gallant, if ultimately unsuccessful, attempt to reach the North Pole. He then went on to study zoology, becoming an influential figure in the field of neurology, and, after supporting Norway's break with Sweden in 1905, he was appointed the Norwegian representative in London. The last years of his life were devoted to the **League of Nations**, where he became the High Commissioner for Refugees. Among much else, Nansen struggled manfully to mitigate the effects of the famine in the Soviet Union in 1921 and pioneered the use of the so-called "Nansen passport" for the stateless and dispossessed at the end of World War I. In 1922, he was awarded the Nobel Peace Prize.

that had dominated Norway for so long in favour of the more sincere qualities of the peasant farmer. Indeed, the movement endowed the Norwegian peasantry with all sorts of previously unidentified qualities, while the **temperance movement** sought to bring them up to these lofty ideals by promoting laws to prohibit the use of small stills, once found on every farm. The government obliged by formally banning these stills in 1844, and by the mid-nineteenth century, consumption of spirits had dropped drastically and coffee rivalled beer as the national drink.

Similarly, the **Norwegian language** and its folklore was rediscovered by a number of academics, helping to restore the country's cultural self-respect. Following on were authors like Alexander Kielland, whose key works were published between 1880 and 1891, and **Knut Hamsun** (1859–1952), whose most characteristic novel, *Hunger*, was published in 1890. In music, **Edvard Grieg** (1843–1907) was inspired by old Norwegian folk melodies, composing some of his most famous music for Ibsen's *Peer Gynt*, while the artist **Edvard Munch** (1863–1944) completed many of his major works in the 1880s and 1890s. Finally, the internationally acclaimed dramatist **Henrik Ibsen** (1828–1906) returned to Oslo in 1891 after a prolonged self-imposed exile.

## Early independence: 1905–39

Norway's **independence** came at a time of further economic advance, engendered by the introduction of hydroelectric power and underpinned by a burgeoning merchant navy, the third-largest after the US and Britain. Social reforms, largely prompted by the emergence of a strong trade-union movement, also saw funds being made available for unemployment relief, accident insurance schemes and a Factory Act (1909), governing safety in the workplace. An extension to the franchise gave the **vote** to all men over 25, and, in 1913, to women too. The education system was reorganized, and substantial sums were spent on new arms and defence.

Since 1814, Norway had had little to do with European affairs, and at the outbreak of **World War I** it declared itself neutral, though its sympathies lay largely with the Western Allies. Initially, the war boosted the Norwegian economy as its ships and timber were in great demand, but, by 1916, the country had begun to feel the pinch as

| 1914 | 1919 | 1922 | 1926 |
| --- | --- | --- | --- |
| Norway neutral in World War I, and initially its merchants make a packet from trading with both Britain and Germany | A referendum sanctions Prohibition | Vinmonopolet, which still operates a state monopoly of liquor, wine and strong beer, founded in preparation for a relaxation of Prohibition (which comes in 1923) | Prohibition fully repealed |

German submarines took to sinking both enemy and neutral shipping, and by the end of the war Norway had lost half its chartered tonnage and two thousand crew. Indeed, the overall price of neutrality turned out to be very high: the cost of living soared and, at the end of the war, with no seat at the conference table, Norway received neither compensation nor a share of confiscated German shipping. The only windfall was in the far north, where it gained sovereignty over **Spitsbergen** and its coal deposits – the first extension of Norwegian frontiers for five hundred years. In 1920 Norway also entered the new League of Nations.

### The late 1920s

In the **late 1920s**, the decline in world trade led to decreased demand for Norwegian shipping and raw materials. This led to a prolonged period of economic disarray during which there was a string of bank failures, wild currency fluctuations and bitter industrial strife, with wage cuts and burgeoning unemployment as the backdrop. A strengthening, left-wing Norwegian **Labour Party** took advantage of the situation, breaking out of its urban heartlands in the election of 1927 to become the largest party within the *Storting*, but it could not muster an overall majority and the old Liberal-Conservative elite manoeuvred them out of office within a fortnight. Many Norwegians felt cheated and trade disputes and lockouts continued with troops often used to protect strike-breakers.

### The early 1930s

During World War I, **Prohibition** had been introduced as a temporary measure and a referendum of 1919 showed a clear majority in favour of its continuation. Yet the ban did little to quell – and even exacerbated – drunkenness, and it was completely abandoned in 1926, replaced by the government monopoly on the sale of wines and spirits that remains in force today. The **1933 election** gave the Labour Party more seats than ever, reflecting the growing popular conviction that state control and a centrally planned economy were the only answer to Norway's economic problems. In 1935 the Labour Party, in alliance with the Agrarian Party, took power – an unlikely combination since the Agrarians were profoundly nationalist in outlook, so much so that one of their defence spokesmen had been the rabid anti-Semite **Vidkun Quisling** (1887–1945). Frustrated by the democratic process, Quisling had left the Agrarians in 1933 to found **Nasjonal Samling** (National Unification), a fascist movement that garnered little support in Norway – in 1937 party membership was just 1500.

The Labour government under **Johan Nygaardsvold** (1879–1952) presided over an improving economy. By 1938 industrial production was 75 percent higher than it had been in 1914 and unemployment dropped as expenditure on roads, railways and public works increased. When war broke out in 1939, Norway was lacking only one thing – **adequate defence**. A vigorous member of the League of Nations, the country had pursued disarmament and peace-oriented policies since the end of World War I and was determined to remain **neutral** in any future European conflict.

## World War II

Strange as it may seem with hindsight, in **early 1940** the Norwegian government was more preoccupied with Allied mine-laying off the Norwegian coast than the threat posed

| 1928 | 1940 | 1941 |
| --- | --- | --- |
| Amundsen disappears in the Arctic while undertaking a rescue mission; his body is never found | Germans occupy Norway; Norwegians taken completely by surprise | Norway's government-in-exile reinstates the death penalty for torture, treason and murder – and applies the new law (sparingly) after the liberation |

by Hitler. The Allies mined Norwegian waters in an attempt to prevent Swedish iron ore being shipped from Narvik to Germany, but the Norwegians felt this compromised their neutrality. Indeed, such was Norwegian naivety that they made a formal protest to Britain on the day of the **German invasion**, April 9, 1940. Caught napping, the Norwegian army offered little initial resistance and the south and central regions of the country were quickly overrun. King Håkon and the *Storting* were forced into a hasty evacuation of Oslo and headed north to Elverum, evading capture by just a couple of hours. At the government's temporary headquarters in Elverum, the executive was granted full powers to take whatever decisions were necessary in the interests of Norway – a mandate which later formed the basis of the Norwegian government-in-exile in Britain.

The Germans contacted the king and his government in Elverum, demanding, among other things, that Quisling be accepted as prime minister as a condition of surrender. Though their situation was desperate, the Norwegians rejected this outright and instead chose resistance. The ensuing **campaign** lasted for two months, but the Norwegians were simply no match for the German army. In June 1940, both king and government saw the end was nigh and fled to Britain from Tromsø.

### Civil resistance

After the invasion, the Germans soon consolidated their position and Hitler dispatched one of his fellow Nazis, **Josef Terboven**, to take charge of Norwegian affairs. Norway's own fascist party, the **Nasjonal Samling**, was declared the only legal party and the media, civil servants and teachers were brought under its control. The backlash was quick to arrive and, as **civil resistance** grew, so a state of emergency was declared and punishment administered – two trade-union leaders were shot, arrests increased and a concentration camp was set up outside Oslo. In February 1942 Quisling was installed as "Minister President", but it soon became clear that his government didn't have the support of the Norwegian people. The Church refused to cooperate, schoolteachers protested and trade-union members and officials resigned en masse. In response, deportations increased, death sentences were announced and a compulsory labour scheme was introduced.

### Military resistance

**Military resistance** escalated as the German occupation hardened. A military organization (**MILORG**) was established as a branch of the armed forces under the control of the High Command in London. By May 1941 it had enlisted 20,000 Norwegians (32,000 by 1944) in clandestine groups all over the country. Arms and instructors came from Britain, radio stations were set up and a continuous flow of intelligence about German movements was sent back. Sabotage operations were legion, the most notable being the destruction of the heavy-water plant at **Rjukan** (see p.176), foiling a German attempt to produce an atomic bomb. Reprisals against the Resistance were severe – all the men of **Telavåg**, a village near Bergen, were, for example, either executed or sent to a concentration camp in 1942 after the murder of two members of the Gestapo; some of these reprisals were carried out by Norwegian **collaborators**, around 15,000 of whom enlisted in the German army.

The **government-in-exile** in London continued to represent free Norway to the world, mobilizing support on behalf of the Allies. Most of the Norwegian merchant fleet was

| 1942 | 1945 | Late 1940s | 1949 |
| --- | --- | --- | --- |
| The pogrom. The Jewish population of Norway is 2100; the Germans deport 774 (34 survive) and the remainder seek refuge in Sweden | The traitor Vidkun Quisling is executed; few grieve | Musk oxen reintroduced into Norway; local wildlife confused | Air crash near Trondheim: nonsmokers at the front are killed, the smokers at the back survive; the philosopher Bertrand Russell is saved by his pipe |

abroad when the Nazis invaded, and by 1943 the Norwegian navy had seventy ships helping the Allied convoys. With the German position deteriorating, neutral Sweden adopted a more sympathetic policy to the Resistance, allowing the creation of thinly disguised training grounds for its fighters. These camps also served to produce the police detachments that were to secure law and order after liberation; nevertheless, many Norwegians felt bitter that the Swedes did not do much more.

### German surrender

When the Allies landed in Normandy in June 1944, overt action against the occupying Germans in Norway was temporarily discouraged as the US and Britain could not guarantee military supplies. Help was at hand, however, in the form of the **Soviets** who crossed into the far north of Norway in late October, driving back the Germans at double-quick speed. Cruelly, the Germans chose to burn everything in their path as they retreated, a scorched-earth policy that inflicted untold suffering on the local population, many of whom hid in the forests and caves. To prevent the Germans reinforcing their beleaguered Finnmark battalions, the Resistance organized a campaign of mass railway sabotage, stopping three-quarters of troop movements overnight.

With their control of Norway crumbling, the Germans finally **surrendered** on May 7, 1945, and the day after Terboven blew himself up with 50kg of dynamite. King Håkon returned to Norway on June 7, five years to the day since he'd left for exile. A caretaker government took office, staffed by Resistance leaders, and this was replaced in October 1945 by a majority **Labour government**. The Communists won eleven seats, reflecting the efforts of Communist saboteurs in the war and the prestige that the Soviet Union enjoyed in Norway after the liberation. Meanwhile, several thousand **collaborators** were rounded up and there were heated debates as to how to proceed, with opinion divided between the "ice front" (who proposed the application of the death penalty) and the "silk front" (who didn't). In the event, several hundred collaborators were punished with varying degrees of severity and 25 high-ranking traitors were executed, including **Quisling**.

## Postwar reconstruction

At the end of the war, Norway was on its knees: the far north – Finnmark – had been laid waste, half the mercantile fleet lost, and production was at a standstill. Nevertheless, a palpable sense of national unity fostered a speedy recovery and within three years GNP had returned to its prewar level. In addition, Norway's part in the war had increased her international prestige. The country became one of the founding members of the **United Nations** in 1945, and the first UN Secretary-General, Trygve Lie, was, at the time of his appointment, Norwegian Foreign Minister. With the failure of discussions to promote a Scandinavian defence union, the *Storting* also voted to enter **NATO** in 1949.

Domestically, there was general agreement about the form that **social reconstruction** should take with the government taking the lead role and, in 1948, the *Storting* passed the platoon of laws that introduced the Welfare State. The 1949 election saw the Labour government returned with a larger majority, and Labour continued to be elected throughout the following decade, with the dominant political figure being **Einar Gerhardsen** (1897–1987). A confident Labour Party set itself a progressive course,

| 1949 | 1960 | 1969 | 1972 |
|---|---|---|---|
| Norway joins NATO – a controversial move among many Norwegians, who want to remain neutral | Laws on abortion relaxed – but married women still need the consent of their husbands | Oil and gas discovered beneath the Norwegian Sea | Referendum 1: Norwegians decide not to join the EEC |

determined to create a more egalitarian society, levelling up rather than down as national prosperity increased. Subsidies were paid to the agricultural and fishing industries, wages increased, and a comprehensive social security system helped reduce poverty. The state ran the important mining industry, was the largest shareholder in the national hydroelectric company and built an enormous steelworks at Mo-i-Rana to develop the economy of the devastated northern counties. Rationing ended in 1952 and, as the demand for higher education grew, so new universities were created in Bergen, Trondheim and Tromsø.

## Beyond consensus: the 1960s and early 1970s

The political consensus began to fragment in the early 1960s. Following the restructuring of rural constituencies in the 1950s, there was a realignment in centre-right politics with the outmoded Agrarian Party becoming the **Centre Party**. There was change on the left too, where defence squabbles within the Labour Party led to the formation of the **Socialist People's Party (SF)**, which wanted Norway out of NATO (it had joined in 1949) and sought a renunciation of nuclear weapons. The Labour Party's 1961 declaration that no nuclear weapons would be stationed in Norway except under an immediate threat of war did not placate the SF, who unexpectedly took two seats at the election that year and thereby held the balance of parliamentary power. The SF voted with the Labour Party until 1963, when it helped bring down the government over mismanagement of state industries. A replacement coalition collapsed after only one month, but the writing was on the wall. Rising prices, grumblings over high taxation and a continuing housing shortage meant that the 1965 election put a **non-socialist coalition** in power for the first time in twenty years under the leadership of the Centre Party's **Per Borten** (1913–2005). More significantly, it was in 1969 that **oil and gas** were discovered beneath the North Sea and, as the vast extent of the reserves became clear, it became obvious that the Norwegians were to enjoy a magnificent bonanza – one that was to make Norway one of the world's richest countries in the space of thirty years.

### Norway and the EEC

As a member of the European Free Trade Association (EFTA), Norway applied to join the **European Economic Community (EEC)** in 1962 and 1967, but on both occasions France's General de Gaulle cast a veto. Negotiations were restarted in 1970 after the resignation of de Gaulle, but a year later Per Borten was forced to resign following his indiscreet handling of the negotiations and the Labour Party then formed a minority administration. The majority of Labour's representatives were in favour of EEC membership, but when the issue was put to the vote in the **1972 referendum**, a majority of Norwegians (53.5 percent) said "No" to joining the EEC. The reasons for the rejection have been the subject of much debate and are certainly complex, but had much to do with fears as to how EEC membership would affect Norwegian agriculture and fisheries.

## The late 1970s to the early 1990s

The Labour Party remained in power for the most of the 1970s, but the old confidence in state control and management had begun to evaporate and, when they returned to office in 1986, led by the remarkable **Dr Gro Harlem Brundtland** (b.1939), Norway's first woman

| 1978 | 1981 | 1985 | 1989 |
|------|------|------|------|
| The Norwegian Labour Party pushes through a law legalizing abortion on demand in the first twelve weeks of pregnancy | Gro Harlem Brundtland becomes Norway's first woman prime minister | Norway's a-ha release their debut album; audio delight | Sámi Parliament established in Karasjok, bringing some degree of political independence to the indigenous population of the Arctic north |

prime minister, they were a very different party. Brundtland made sweeping changes to the way the country was run, introducing eight women into her eighteen-member cabinet, and pursued an internationalist agenda, albeit within a neoliberal framework. In power for a total of ten years, in three different administrations (1981, 1986–1989 & 1990–1996), Brundtland was the dominant political figure of the period – and indeed cartoonists were wont to draw just her shoes and ankles with other politicians scurrying around at her feet. The late 1980s also saw the rise of the **Progress Party**, an avowedly anti-immigration, law-and-order party, who made spectacular gains in the 1989 election, securing 13 percent of the popular vote; subsequently, the Progress Party's electoral fortunes were something of a rollercoaster ride, ranging from 6.3 percent in 1993 to 16.3 percent in 2013.

### Norway and the EU

Brundtland and the Labour Party won the **1993 election** at a canter with double the votes of their nearest rival, but thereafter the country tumbled into a long and fiercely conducted campaign over **membership of the EU**. Brundtland and her main political opponents wanted in, but the Norwegians – despite the near-unanimity of their political class – narrowly rejected the EU in a **1994 referendum**. It was a close call (52.5 percent versus 47.5 percent), but in the end farmers and fishermen afraid of the economic results of joining, as well as women's groups and environmentalists, who felt that Norway's high standards of social care and "green" controls would suffer, came together to swing opinion against joining.

## The late 1990s: political argy-bargy

After the 1994 referendum, the Brundtland administration soldiered on, wisely soothing ruffled feathers by promising to shelve the whole EU membership issue until at least 2000, though in the event the issue has never been put to the vote again. Nevertheless, the **1997 election** saw a move to the right, the main beneficiaries being the Christian Democratic Party and the ultra-conservative Progress Party. In itself, this was not enough to remove the Labour-led coalition from office – indeed Labour remained comfortably the largest party – but the right was dealt a trump card by the new Labour leader, **Thorbjørn Jagland** (b.1950). During the campaign Jagland had promised that the Labour Party would step down from office if it failed to elicit more than the 36.9 percent of the vote it had secured in 1993. Much to the chagrin of his colleagues, Jagland's political chickens came home to roost when Labour only received 35 percent of the vote – and they had to go, leaving power in the hands of an unwieldy right-of-centre, minority coalition. Bargaining with its rivals from a position of parliamentary weakness, the new government found it difficult to cut a clear path – or at least one very different from its predecessor – apart from managing to antagonize the women's movement by some reactionary social legislation whose none-too-hidden subtext seemed to read "A woman's place is in the home". In the spring of 2000, the government resigned and the Labour Party resumed command.

## The early 2000s

To the surprise of many pundits, the Labour Party lost the **election of 2001** and was replaced by an ungainly centre-right coalition. This coalition battled on until

| 1991 | 1993 | 1994 | 2000 |
|------|------|------|------|
| Harald V of Norway ascends the throne upon the death of his popular father, Olav V | Norway resumes commercial hunting of the minke whale | Referendum 2: Norwegians decide not to join the EU | Opening of the Lærdal–Aurland road tunnel, at 24.5km one of the longest in the world |

**late 2005** when the Labour Party, along with its allies the Socialist Left Party and the Centre Party, won the election, with the politically experienced **Jens Stoltenberg** (b.1959) becoming Prime Minister. Stoltenberg proceeded to bolt together one of Norway's more secure coalitions with a standard-issue, centre-left political agenda: for instance, a flexible retirement from the age of 62 (it was 67) was introduced in 2010; a careful incomes policy was geared to the needs of both employer and employee; and there were detailed promises on tackling climate change and global warming. As Stoltenberg put it himself at the time of his election victory "Our gains are due to a clear political message about jobs, education, and giving people security in their old age. Our aim is to give this country a stable and predictable government." Perhaps so, but Stoltenberg was certainly not averse to some political shimmying, conspicuously tightening **immigration** rules to undercut criticism coming from the Progress Party to his political right. And neither was he committed to the leading role of the state, privatizing a basket of government assets in the manner of neoliberals all over the western world.

### The banking crisis

In the summer of 2008, the wheels began to come off the Stoltenberg wagon with arguments about the killing of wolves, corruption, and the state of the health-care system. Stoltenberg's popularity sank, but then came the worldwide **banking crisis** during which Stoltenberg started to look more like a prime minister who could take care of business – and the opinion polls gave him and his Labour Party greatly improved ratings. He was helped by the relative soundness of the Norwegian banking system, which had learnt some harsh lessons about capitalization during the country's own banking crisis, which had run from 1988 to 1993. Even so, Stoltenberg was obliged to dip into the country's oil wealth in 2009 to set up two funds totalling 100 billion kroner to bolster the country's banks and bond market.

## 2010 to the present day

Further proof of Stoltenberg's political skill came in the electoral pudding of **2009**, when the Labour Party-led coalition won another parliamentary majority, albeit with less of the popular vote than its rivals (47.9 percent versus 49.5 percent). Stoltenberg had now emerged as the country's standout politician and aspects of his private life attracted much sympathetic attention, not least the heroin addiction of his sister Nini. More importantly, Stoltenberg was equal to the task of speaking to the nation's grief at a memorial service held in Oslo cathedral after the dreadful events of July 22, 2011, when the right-wing extremist **Anders Behring Breivik** killed 77 innocent people by detonating a bomb in Oslo and then went on a shooting spree at a Labour Party summer camp on the island of Utøya.

Yet, some of the gloss came off the government the following year when the **Gjørv report** into the Breivik massacre proved highly critical of the police; for example, the Oslo police were unable to use their one and only helicopter because the crew was on holiday. There were also rumblings and grumblings about high taxation, government inefficiency, health-care queues and immigration – with recent immigrants accounting for around 13 percent of the population. In the **election of 2013**, there was a dip in

| 2004 | 2009 | 2009 |
|------|------|------|
| Munch's *The Scream* stolen from the Munchmuseet in Oslo. Much Norwegian embarrassment | Same-sex marriages become legal | Norway wins the Eurovision Song Contest; country euphoric |

Labour Party support (from 35.4 percent to 30.8 percent) and this was enough to unseat Stoltenberg, who was replaced as Prime Minister by **Erna Solberg** (b.1961), the leader of the Conservative Party, who formed a right-wing administration with the Progress Party; Solberg remains in power at time of writing. Curiously, the **Progress Party** had actually experienced something of a collapse in the 2013 election (23 percent to 16.3 percent), possibly because Breivik had once been a member.

In the event, the 2013 election may well have been a good one to lose: in August 2014, the price of a barrel of crude was US$97, but by January 2016 it had fallen to US$28 – and the results for the Norwegian oil industry were calamitous with the loss of 30,000 jobs. Inevitably, attention turned to the vast financial reserves accumulated in Norway's Government Pension Fund – or **Oil Fund** (*Oljefondet*): how much of the 7 trillion Norwegian kroner in the fund should be diverted to support government spending, including the maintenance of a splendid welfare system, against how much will the country need in the future when the oil runs out. No-one really knows, but the whole issue is a matter of great national anxiety – temporarily at least, the unexpected bonanza turned into incubus.

## Into the future

In the long term, assuming the oil market stabilizes, Norway's prospects look distinctly rosy. They have, after all, a superabundance of natural resources – primarily 0.6 percent of the world's proven oil reserves and 1.6 percent of the gas – and arguably the most educated workforce in the world with unemployment at consistently low levels (4 percent or so). But that doesn't mean the country doesn't collectively **fret**: Norway's Lutheran roots run deep and, if an old joke is to be believed, the low point of the average Norwegian's year is the summer vacation. There's also a vague feeling of (Lutheran) unease about the country's prosperity with no less a figure than Jo Nesbø declaring, in no uncertain terms, that "money has corrupted us".

The Norwegians also fret (and argue) about quite what sort of relationship Norway should have with the **EU**; how **immigration** should be dealt with; and over **environmental** issues, with one hot potato being the country's **road building** programme. A curse afflicting prewar Norway had always been rural isolation and the Norwegians of 1945 were determined to connect (almost) all of the country's villages to the road system. Give or take the occasional hamlet, this has now been achieved and a second phase is underway, involving the upgrading of roads and the construction of innumerable tunnels. Wherever this makes conditions safer, the popular consensus for the programme survives, but there is increasing opposition to the prestige projects so beloved by politicians – the enormous tunnel near Flåm (see p.229) being a case in point. There is, however, precious little internal argument when it comes to **whaling and sealing**, with the majority continuing to support the hunting of these animals as has been the custom for centuries; indeed, for some Norwegians whaling and sealing go some way to defining what they consider to be the national identity. This is inexplicable to many Western Europeans, who point to Norway's eminently liberal approach to most other matters, but the Norwegians see things very differently: why, many of them ask, is the culling of seals and minke seen in a different light from the mass slaughter of farmed animals?

| 2012 | 2016 |
|---|---|
| After a two-week strike over pensions, the government uses emergency powers to force oil and gas workers back to work | Life expectancy at birth of the average Norwegian approaches 81 years – but it's still behind Sweden |

# Legends and folklore

Norway has an exceptionally rich body of historical legend and folk tradition – and it plays an important part in the national consciousness even today. Most famous are the sagas, mainly written in Iceland between the twelfth and fourteenth centuries and constituting a vast collection of part-historical, part-fictionalized stories covering several centuries of Norse history. Thanks to the survival of one of these sagas, the *Poetic Edda* (see below), our knowledge of Norse mythology is also far from conjectural. In addition, much that was not recorded in the sagas survived in the country's oral tradition and this was revived from the 1830s onwards by the artists and writers of the National Romantic movement. Some members of this movement also set about collecting the folk tales and legends of the rural regions. The difficulties they experienced in rendering the Norwegian dialects into written form – there was no written Norwegian language per se – fuelled the language movement, and sent the academic Ivar Aasen (1813–96) roaming the countryside to assemble the material from which he formulated *Landsmål* (see p.426).

## Sagas

The Norwegian Vikings settled in **Iceland** in the ninth century and throughout the medieval period the Icelanders had a deep attachment to, and interest in, their original homeland. The result was a body of work that remains one of the richest sources of European medieval literature. That so much of it has survived is due to Iceland's isolation – most Norwegian sources disappeared centuries ago.

All the **sagas** feature real people and tell of events that are usually known to have happened, though the plots are embroidered to suit the tales' heroic style. They reveal much about a Norse culture in which arguments between individuals might spring from comparatively trivial disputes over horses or sheep, but where a strict code of honour and revenge meant that every insult, whether real or imagined, had to be avenged. Thus personal disputes soon turned into clan vendettas. Plots are complex, the dialogue laconic, and the pared-down prose omits unnecessary detail. New characters are often introduced by means of tedious genealogies, necessary to explain the motivation behind their later actions (though the more adept translations render these explanations as footnotes). Personality is only revealed through speech, facial expressions and general demeanour, or the comments and gossip of others.

The earliest Icelandic work, the **Elder** or **Poetic Edda**, comprises 34 lays dating from as early as the eighth century, and they combine to give a detailed insight into early Norse culture as well as pagan cosmogony and belief. It's not to be confused with the **Younger** or **Prose Edda**, written centuries later by Snorri Sturluson, the most distinguished of the saga writers. Also noteworthy are *The Vinland Saga*, *Njal's Saga* and the *Laxdaela Saga*, tales of ninth- and tenth-century Icelandic derring-do; and *Harald's Saga*, a rattling good yarn celebrating the life and times of Harald Hardrada. English translations of all the above are readily available.

# Norse mythology

The Vikings shared a common **pagan faith**, whose polytheistic tenets were upheld right across Scandinavia. The deities were worshipped at a thousand village shrines, usually by means of sacrifices in which animals, weapons, boats and other artefacts, even humans, were gifted to the gods. There was very little theology to sanctify these rituals; instead the principal gods – Odin, Thor and Frey – were surrounded by **mythical tales** attributing to them a bewildering variety of strengths, weaknesses and powers.

## Odin and Frigga

The god of war, wisdom, poetry and magic, **Odin** was untrustworthy, violent and wise in equal measure. The most powerful of the twelve Viking deities, the Aesir, who lived at Asgard, he was also lord of the **Valkyries**, women warrior-servants who tended his needs while he held court at **Valhalla**, the hall of dead heroes. As with many of the other pagan gods, he had the power to change into any form he desired. Odin's wife, **Frigga**, was the goddess protecting the home and the family. Among the Anglo-Saxons, the equivalent of Odin was Woden, hence "Wednesday".

## Yggdrasil

At the beginning of time, it was Odin who made heaven and earth from the body of the giant **Ymir**, and created man from an ash tree, woman from an alder. However, **Yggdrasil**, the tree of life that supported the whole universe, was beyond his control; the Vikings believed that eventually the tree would die and both gods and mortals would perish in the **Ragnarok**, the twilight of the gods.

## Thor

One of Odin's sons, **Thor** appears to have been the most worshipped of the Norse gods. A giant with superhuman strength, he was the short-tempered god of thunder, fire and lightning. He regularly fought with the evil Frost Giants in the Jotunheim mountains, his favourite weapon being the hammer, Mjolnir, which the trolls (see p.408) had fashioned for him. His chariot was drawn by two goats – Cracktooth and Gaptooth – who could be killed and eaten at night, but would be fully recovered the next morning, providing none of their bones were broken. It's from Thor that we get "Thursday".

## Loki and Sigyn

A negative force, **Loki** personified cunning and trickery. His treachery turned the other deities against him, and he was chained up beneath a serpent that dripped venom onto his face. His wife, **Sigyn**, remained loyal and held a bowl over his head to catch the venom, but when the bowl was full she had to turn away to empty it, and in those moments his squirmings would cause earthquakes.

## Frey and Freya

The god of fertility was **Frey**, whose pride and joy was *Skidbladnir*, a longship that was large enough to carry all the gods, but could still be folded up and put into his bag. He often lived with the elves (see p.408) in Elfheim. **Freya** was the goddess of love, healing and fertility – and "Friday" was named after her.

## Hel and the Norns

The goddess of the dead, **Hel** lived on brains and bone marrow. She presided over "Hel", where those who died of illness or old age went, living a miserable existence under the roots of Yggdrasil, the tree of life. Representing the past, the present and the future, the **Norns** were the three goddesses of fate, casting lots over the cradle of every newborn child.

## Folk tales and legends

Norway's extensive oral folklore was first written down in the early nineteenth century, most famously by **Peter Christen Asbjørnsen** and **Jørgen Moe**, the first of whose compilations appeared to great popular acclaim in 1842. These tales succoured the country's emergent nationalism, but in fact many of them were far from uniquely Norwegian, sharing characteristics with – and having the same roots as – folk tales across the whole of northern Europe. They were, however, populated by stock characters who were recognizably Norwegian; the king, for example, was always pictured as a wealthy farmer.

There are three types of Norwegian **folk tale**: comical tales; animal yarns, in which the beasts concerned – most frequently the wolf, fox and bear – talk and behave like human beings; and most common of all, magical stories populated by a host of supernatural creatures. The folk tale is always written matter-of-factly, no matter how fantastic the events it retells. In this respect it has much in common with the **folk legend**, though the latter purports to be factual. Norwegian legends "explain" scores of unusual natural phenomena – the location of boulders, holes in cliffs, etc – and are crammed with supernatural beings, again as is broadly familiar right across northern Europe.

The assorted **supernatural creatures** of folk tale and legend hark back to the pagan myths of the pre-Christian era, but whereas the Vikings held them of secondary importance to their gods, in Norwegian folk tales they take centre stage. In post-pagan Norwegian folk tradition, these creatures were regarded as the descendants of children that Eve hid from God. When they were discovered by him, they were assigned particular realms in which to dwell, but their illicit wanderings were legion. Towards the end of the nineteenth century, book illustrations by **Erik Werenskiold** and **Theodor Kittelsen** effectively defined what the various supernatural creatures looked like in the Norwegian public's imagination. As mythologized in Norway, the creatures of the folk tales possess a confusing range of virtues and vices. Here's a brief round-up of some of the more important.

### Giants

Enormous in size and strength, the **giants** of Norwegian folklore were reputed to be rather stupid and capable both of kindly actions and great cruelty towards humans. They usually had a human appearance, but some were monsters with many heads. They were fond of carrying parts of the landscape from one place to another, dropping boulders and even islands as they went. According to the Eddic cosmogony, the first giant, Ymir, was killed by Odin and the world made from his body – his blood formed the sea, his bones the mountains and so on. Ymir was the ancestor of the evil **Frost Giants**, who lived in Jotunheim, and who regularly fought with Thor.

### Trolls

Spirits of the underground, **trolls** were ambivalent figures, able both to hinder and help humans – and were arguably a folkloric expression of the id. The first trolls were depicted as giants, but later versions were small, strong, misshapen and of pale countenance from living underground; sunlight would turn them into stone. They worked in metals and wood and were fabulous craftsmen. They made Odin's spear and Thor's hammer, though Thor's inclination to throw the weapon at them made them hate noise; as late as the eighteenth century, Norwegian villagers would ring church bells for hours on end to drive them away. If the trolls were forced to make something for a human, they would put a secret curse on it; this would render it dangerous to the owner. Some trolls had a penchant for stealing children and others carried off women to be their wives.

### Elves

Akin to fairies, **elves** were usually divided between good-hearted but mischievous white elves, and nasty black elves, who brought injury and sickness. Both lived underground in a world, Elfheim, that echoed that of humans – with farms, animals and the like – but made excursions into the glades and groves of the forests up above. At night, the white elves liked singing and dancing to the accompaniment of the harp. They were normally invisible, though you could spot their dancing places wherever the grass grew more luxuriantly in circular patterns than elsewhere. The black elves were also invisible, a good job considering they were extremely ugly and had long, filthy noses. If struck by a sunbeam, they would turn to stone. Both types of elf were prone to entice humans into their kingdom, usually for a short period – but sometimes forever.

## Wights

In pre-Christian times, the Vikings believed their lands to be populated with invisible guardian spirits, the **wights** (*vetter*), who needed to be treated with respect. One result was that when a longship was approaching the shore, the fearsome figurehead at its prow was removed so as not to frighten the *vetter* away. Bad luck would follow if a *vetter* left the locality.

## Witches

As with **witches** across much of the rest of Europe, the Scandinavian version was typically an old woman who had made a pact with the Devil, swapping her soul in return for special powers. The witch could inflict injury and illness, especially if she was in possession of something her victim had touched or owned – anything from a lock of hair to an item of clothing. She could disguise herself as an animal, and had familiars – usually insects or cats – which assisted her in foul deeds. Most witches travelled through the air on broomsticks, but some rode on wolves bridled with snakes.

## Water spirits

Personifying all those who have died at sea, the **draugen** was a ghostly apparition who appeared as a headless fisherman in oilskins. He sailed the seas in half a boat and wailed when someone was about to drown. Other water spirits included the malicious river sprite, the **nixie**, who could assume different forms to lure the unsuspecting to a watery grave. There were also the shy and benign **mermaids** and **mermen**, half-fish and half-human, who dived into the water whenever they spied a human. However, they also liked to dress up as humans to go to market.

# Viking customs and rituals

The Vikings have long been the subject of historical discussion and debate
with accurate and unbiased contemporary accounts being few and far
between. A remarkable exception is the annals of Ibn Fadlan, a member of a
diplomatic delegation sent from the Baghdad Caliphate to Bulgar on the Volga
in 921–922 AD. In the following extracts Fadlan details the habits and rituals of
a tribe of Swedish Vikings, the Rus, who dealt in furs and slaves. The first piece
notes with disgust the finer points of Viking personal hygiene, the second
provides a sober eyewitness account of the rituals of a Viking longship burial.

## Habits and rituals

I saw the Rus when they arrived on their trading mission and anchored at the River Atul
(Volga). Never had I seen people of more perfect physique; they are tall as date-palms,
and reddish in colour. They wear neither mantle nor coat, but each man carries a cape,
which covers one half of his body, leaving one hand free. Their swords are Frankish in
pattern, broad, flat and fluted. Each man has (tattooed upon him) trees, figures and the
like from the finger-nails to the neck. Each woman carries on her bosom a container
made of iron, silver, copper or gold – its size and substance depending on her man's
wealth. Attached to the container is a ring carrying her knife, which is also tied to her
bosom. Round her neck she wears gold or silver rings; when a man amasses 10,000
*dirhems* he makes his wife one gold ring; when he has 20,000 he makes two; and so the
woman gets a new ring for every 10,000 *dirhems* her husband acquires, and often a
woman has many of these rings. Their finest ornaments are green beads made from clay.
They will go to any length to get hold of these; for one *dirhem* they procure one such
bead and they string these into necklaces for their women.

They are the filthiest of god's creatures. They do not wash after discharging their
natural functions, neither do they wash their hands after meals. They are as stray
donkeys. They arrive from their distant lands and lay their ships alongside the banks of
the Atul, which is a great river, and there they build big wooden houses on its shores.
Ten or twenty of them may live together in one house, and each of them has a couch
of his own where he sits and diverts himself with the pretty slave-girls whom he has
brought along to offer for sale. He will make love with one of them in the presence of
his comrades, sometimes this develops into a communal orgy and, if a customer should
turn up to buy a girl, the Rus will not let her go till he has finished with her.

Every day they wash their faces and heads, all using the same water, which is as filthy
as can be imagined. This is how it is done. Every morning a girl brings her master a large
bowl of water in which he washes his face and hands and hair, combing it also over the
bowl, then blows his nose and spits into the water. No dirt is left on him which doesn't
go into the water. When he has finished the girl takes the same bowl to his neighbour –
who repeats the performance – until the bowl has gone round the entire household. All
have blown their noses, spat and washed their faces and hair in the water.

On anchoring their vessels, each man goes ashore carrying bread, meat, onions, milk,
and *nabid* [wine], and these he takes to a large wooden stake with a face like that of a
human being, surrounded by smaller figures, and behind them tall poles in the ground.
Each man prostrates himself before the large post and recites: "O Lord, I have come
from distant parts with so many girls, so many furs (and whatever other commodities
he is carrying). I now bring you this offering." He then presents his gift and continues
"Please send me a merchant who has many dinars and *dirhems*, and who will trade

favourably with me without too much bartering." Then he retires. If, after this, business does not pick up quickly and go well, he returns to the statue to present further gifts. If results continue slow, he then presents gifts to the minor figures and begs their intercession, saying, "These are our Lord's wives, daughters and sons." Then he pleads before each figure in turn, begging them to intercede for him and humbling himself before them. Often trade picks up, and he says "My Lord has required my needs, and now it is my duty to repay him." Whereupon he sacrifices goats or cattle, some of which he distributes as alms. The rest he lays before the statues, large and small, and the heads of the beasts he plants upon the poles. After dark, of course, the dogs come and devour the lot – and the successful trader says, "My Lord is pleased with me, and has eaten my offerings."

If one of the Rus falls sick they put him in a tent by himself and leave bread and water for him. They do not visit him, however, or speak to him, especially if he is a serf. Should he recover he rejoins the others; if he dies they burn him. If he happens to be a serf, however, they leave him for the dogs and vultures to devour. If they catch a robber they hang him in a tree until he is torn to shreds by wind and weather…

## The burial

… I had been told that when their chieftains died cremation was the least part of their whole funeral procedure, and I was, therefore, very much interested to find out more about this. One day I heard that one of their leaders had died. They laid him forthwith in a grave, which they covered up for ten days till they had finished cutting-out and sewing his costume. If the dead man is poor they make a little ship, put him in it, and burn it. If he is wealthy, however, they divide his property and goods into three parts: one for his family, one to pay for his costume, and one to make *nabid*. This they drink on the day when the slave woman of the dead man is killed and burnt together with her master. They are deeply addicted to *nabid*, drinking it day and night; and often one of them has been found dead with a beaker in his hand. When a chieftain among them has died, his family demands of his slave women and servants: "Which of you wishes to die with him?" Then one of them says "I do" – and having said that the person concerned is forced to do so, and no backing out is possible. Those who are willing are mostly the slave women.

So when this man died they said to his slave women "Which of you wants to die with him?" One of them answered "I do." From that moment she was put in the constant care of two other women servants who took care of her to the extent of washing her feet with their own hands. They began to get things ready for the dead man, to cut his costume and so on, while every day the doomed woman drank and sang as though in anticipation of a joyous event.

When the day arrived on which the chieftain and his slave woman were going to be burnt, I went to the river where his ship was moored. It had been hauled ashore and four posts were made for it of birch and other wood. Further there was arranged around it what looked like a big store of wood. Then the ship was hauled near and placed on the wood. People now began to walk about talking in a language I could not understand, and the corpse still lay in the grave; they had not taken it out. They then produced a wooden bench, placed it on the ship, and covered it with carpets of Byzantine *dibag* (painted silk) and with cushions of Byzantine *dibag*. Then came an old woman whom they called "the Angel of Death", and she spread these cushions out over the bench. She was in charge of the whole affair from dressing the corpse to the killing of the slave woman. I noticed that she was an old giant-woman, a massive and grim figure. When they came to his grave they removed the earth from the wooden frame and they also took the frame away. They then divested the corpse of the clothes in which he had died. The body, I noticed, had turned black because of the intense frost. When they first put him in the grave, they had also given him beer, fruit, and a lute, all of which they now removed. Strangely enough the corpse did not smell, nor had anything about him changed save the colour of his flesh. They now proceeded to dress him in hose, and trousers, boots, coat, and a mantle of *dibag* adorned with gold buttons; put on his head a cap of *dibag* and sable fur; and carried him to the tent on the ship, where they put him on the blanket and supported him with cushions. They then produced *nabid*, fruit, and aromatic plants, and put these round his body; and they also brought bread, meat, and onions which they flung before him. Next they took a dog, cut it in half, and flung the pieces into the ship, and after this they took all his weapons and placed them beside him.

Next they brought two horses and ran them about until they were in a sweat, after which they cut them to pieces with swords and flung their meat into the ship; this also happened to two cows. Then they produced a cock and a hen, killed them, and threw them in. Meanwhile the slave woman who wished to be killed walked up and down, going into one tent after the other, and the owner of each tent had sexual intercourse with her, saying "Tell your master I did this out of love for him."

It was now Friday afternoon and they took the slave woman away to something which they had made resembling a doorframe. Then she placed her legs on the palms of the men and reached high enough to look over the frame, and she said something in a foreign language, after which they took her down. And they lifted her again and she did the same as the first time. Then they took her down and lifted her a third time and she did the same as the first and second times. Then they gave her a chicken and she cut its head off and threw it away; they took the hen and threw it into the ship. Then I asked the interpreter what she had done. He answered: "The first time they lifted her she said: 'Look! I see my mother and father.' The second time she said: 'Look! I see all my dead relatives sitting around.' The third time she said: 'Look! I see my master in Paradise, and Paradise is beautiful and green and together with him are men and young boys. He calls me. Let me join him then.'"

They now led her towards the ship. Then she took off two bracelets she was wearing and gave them to the old woman, "the Angel of Death", the one who was going to kill her. She next took off two anklets she was wearing and gave them to the daughters of that same woman. They then led her to the ship but did not allow her inside the tent. Then a number of men carrying wooden shields and sticks arrived, and gave her a beaker with *nabid*. She sang over it and emptied it. The interpreter then said to me, "Now with that she is bidding farewell to all her women friends." Then she was given another beaker. She took it and sang a lengthy song; but the old woman told her to hurry and drink up and enter the tent where her master was. When I looked at her she seemed completely bewildered. She wanted to enter the tent and she put her head between it and the ship. Then the woman took her head and managed to get it inside the tent, and the woman herself followed. Then the men began to beat the shields with the wooden sticks, to deaden her shouts so that the other girls would not become afraid and shrink from dying with their masters. Six men entered the tent and all of them had intercourse with her. Thereafter they laid her by the side of her dead master. Two held her hands and two her feet, and the woman called "the Angel of Death" put a cord round the girl's neck, doubled with an end at each side, and gave it to two men to pull. Then she advanced holding a small dagger with a broad blade and began to plunge it between the girl's ribs to and fro while the two men choked her with the cord till she died.

The dead man's nearest kinsman now appeared. He took a piece of wood and ignited it. Then he walked backwards, his back towards the ship and his face towards the crowd, holding the piece of wood in one hand and the other hand on his buttock; and he was naked. In this way the wood was ignited which they had placed under the ship after they had laid the slave woman, whom they had killed, beside her master. Then people came with branches and wood; each brought a burning brand and threw it on the pyre, so that the fire took hold of the wood, then the ship, then the tent and the man and the slave woman and all. Thereafter a strong and terrible wind rose so that the flame stirred and the fire blazed still more.

I heard one of the Rus folk, standing by, say something to my interpreter, and when I inquired what he had said, my interpreter answered: "He said: 'You Arabs are foolish'". "Why?" I asked. "Well, because you throw those you love and honour to the ground where the earth and the maggots and fields devour them, whereas we, on the other hand, burn them up quickly and they go to Paradise that very moment." The man burst out laughing, and on being asked why, he said: "His Lord, out of love for him, has sent this wind to take him away within the hour!" And so it proved, for within that time the ship and the pyre, the girl and the corpse had all become ashes and then dust. On the spot where the ship stood after having been hauled ashore, they built something like a round mould. In the middle of it they raised a large post of birch-wood on which they wrote the names of the dead man and the king of the Rus, and then the crowd dispersed.

*The above extract, translated by Karre Stov, was taken from* The Vikings *by Johanes Brøndsted, and is reprinted by permission of Penguin Books.*

# Flora and fauna

There are significant differences in climate between the west coast of Norway, which is warmed by the Gulf Stream, and the interior of the country, but these variations prove much less significant for the country's flora than altitude and latitude. With regard to Norway's fauna, wild animals survive in significant numbers in the more inaccessible regions, but have been hunted extensively elsewhere, while the west coast is home to dozens of extensive sea-bird colonies.

## Flora

Much of the Norwegian landscape is dominated by vast **forests of spruce**, though these are, in fact, a relatively recent feature: the original forest cover was mainly of pine, birch and oak, and only in the last two thousand years has spruce spread across the whole of southeast and central Norway. That said, a rich variety of **deciduous trees** – notably oak, ash, lime, hazel, rowan, elm and maple – still flourishes in a wide belt along the south coast, up through the fjord country and as far north as Trondheim, but only at relatively low altitudes. For their part, **conifers** thin out at around 900m above sea level in the south, 450m in Finnmark, to be replaced by a birch zone, where there are also aspen and mountain ash. Norway's deciduous trees contrive to ripen their seeds despite a short, cool summer, and can consequently be found at low altitudes almost as far north as Nordkapp (North Cape) – as can the pine, the most robust of the conifers. At around 1100m/650m, the birch fizzle out to be replaced by willow and dwarf birch, while above the timber line are bare mountain peaks and huge plateaux, the latter usually dotted with hundreds of lakes.

### Berries

Norway accommodates in the region of two thousand plant species, but few of these are native. The most sought-after are the **berrying** species that grow wild all over Norway, mainly cranberries, blueberries and yellow **cloudberries**. Common in the country's peat bogs, and now also extensively cultivated, the cloudberry is a small herbaceous bramble whose fruits have a tangy flavour that is much prized in Norway – and very fashionable today in some of the country's best restaurants. In drier situations and on the mountain plateaux, **lichens** – the favourite food of the reindeer – predominate, while in all but the thickest of spruce forests, the ground is thickly carpeted with **moss** and **heather**.

### Wild flowers

Everywhere, spring brings **wild flowers**; these splashes of brilliant colour are at their most intense on the west coast, where a wide range of mountain plants is nourished by the wet conditions and a geology that varies from limestone to acidic granites. Most of these species can also be found in the Alps, but there are several rarities, notably the **alpine clematis** (*Clematis alpina*) found in the Gudbrandsdal valley, hundreds of miles from its normal homes in eastern Finland and the Carpathian mountains. Another, larger group comprises about thirty **Canadian mountain plants**, found in Europe only in the Dovre and Jotunheim mountains; quite how they come to be there has long baffled botanists.

The mildness of the west-coast winter has allowed certain species to prosper beyond their usual northerly latitudes. Among species that can tolerate very little frost or snow are the star hyacinth (*Scilla verna*) and the purple heather (*Erica purpurea*), while a short distance inland come varieties that can withstand only short icy spells, including the foxglove (*Digitalis purpurea*) and the holly (*Ilex aquifolium*). In the southeastern part of the country, where the winters are harder and the summers hotter, the conditions support species that can lie dormant under the snow for several months a year; for example, the blue anemone (*Anemone hepatica*) and the aconite (*Aconitum septentrionale*).

In the far north, certain Siberian species have migrated west down the rivers and along the coasts to the fjords of Finnmark and Troms. The most significant is the **Siberian garlic** (*Allium sibiricum*), which grows in such abundance that farmers have to make sure their cows don't eat too much of it or else the milk becomes garlic-flavoured. Other Siberian species to look out for are the fringed pink (*Dianthus superbus*) and a large, lily-like plant, the sneezewort (*Veratrum album*).

## Fauna

The larger Arctic **predators** of Norway, principally the lynx, wolf, wolverine and bear, are virtually extinct, and where they have survived they are mainly confined to the more inaccessible regions of the north. To a degree this has been caused by the timber industry, which has logged out great chunks of forest. The smaller predators – the arctic fox, otter, badger and marten – have fared rather better and remain comparatively common.

In the 1930s, the **beaver** population had dropped to just five hundred animals in southern Norway. A total ban on hunting has, however, led to a dramatic increase in their numbers, and beavers have begun to recolonize their old hunting grounds right across Scandinavia. The elk has benefited from the rolling back of the forests, grazing the newly treeless areas and breeding in sufficient numbers to allow an annual cull of around 40,000 animals; the red deer of the west coast are flourishing too. Otherwise, the Norwegians own about two million sheep and around 200,000 domesticated **reindeer**, most of whom are herded by the Sámi. The last wild reindeer in Europe, some 25,000 beasts, wander the Northern plateau and mountainous provinces; the largest group – some 7000 animals – can be found on Hardangervidda. There is also a herd of **musk oxen** in the Dovrefjell-Sunndalsfjella Nasjonalpark (see p.168), though these prodigious beasts are not native – they were imported from Greenland in the late 1940s.

### Lemmings

Among Norway's rodents, the most interesting is the **lemming**, whose numbers vary over a four-year cycle. In the first three to four years there is a gradual increase, which is followed, in the course of a few months, by a sudden fall. The cause of these variations is not known, though theories are plentiful. In addition to this four-year fluctuation, the lemming population goes through a violent explosion every eleven to twelve years. Competition for food is so ferocious that many animals start to range over wide areas. In these so-called lemming years the mountains and surrounding areas teem with countless thousands of lemmings, and hundreds swarm to their deaths by falling off cliff edges and the like in a stampede of migration (though there is no truth in the idea that they commit mass suicide). In lemming years, predators and birds of prey have an abundant source of food and frequently give birth to twice as many young as normal – not surprising considering the lemmings are extremely easy to catch. More inexplicably, the snowy owl leaves its polar habitat in lemming years, flying south to join in the feast: quite how they know when to turn up is a mystery. The Vikings were particularly fascinated by lemmings, believing that they dropped from the sky during thunderstorms.

## THE PUFFIN

Some 30cm tall, with a triangular, red, blue and yellow striped bill, the **puffin** (*Fratercula arctica*) is the most distinctive of the many sea birds that congregate along the **Norwegian coast**. It feeds on small fish, and breeds in holes it excavates in turf on cliffs or grassy flatlands, sometimes even adapting former rabbit burrows. When hunting, puffins use their wings to propel themselves underwater and, indeed, are much better at swimming than flying, finding it difficult both to get airborne and to land – collisions of one sort or another are commonplace. Their nesting habits and repetitive flight paths make them easy to catch, and puffin has long been a west-coast delicacy, though hunting them is now severely restricted. In the summer, puffins nest along the whole of the Atlantic coast from Stavanger to Nordkapp, with Værøy (see p.333) and Runde (see p.258) being two of the most likely places for a sighting. In the autumn the puffins move south, though residual winter populations remain on the southerly part of the west coast between Stavanger and Ålesund.

## Birds

With the exception of the raven, the partridge and the grouse, all the **mountain birds** of Norway are **migratory**, reflecting the harshness of winter conditions. Most fly back and forth from the Mediterranean and Africa, but some winter down on the coast. **Woodland** species include the wood grouse, the black grouse, several different sorts of owl, woodpecker and birds of prey, while the country's **lakes and marshes** are inhabited by cranes, swans, grebes, geese, ducks and many types of wader. Most dramatic of all are the coastal nesting cliffs, where millions of **sea birds**, such as kittiwake, guillemots, puffin, cormorant and gull, congregate. What you won't see is the great auk, a flightless, 50cm-high bird resembling a penguin that once nested in its millions along the Atlantic seaboard but is now extinct: the last Norwegian great auk was killed in the eighteenth century and the last one of all was shot near Iceland a century later.

## Fish

The waters off Norway once teemed with **seals** and **whales**, but indiscriminate hunting has drastically reduced their numbers, prompting several late-in-the-day conservation measures. The commonest species of **fish** – cod, haddock, coalfish and halibut – have been overexploited too, and whereas there were once gigantic shoals of them right along the coast up to the Arctic Sea, they are now much less common. The cod, like several other species, live far out in the Barents Sea, only coming to the coast to spawn, a favourite destination being the waters round the Lofoten islands.

The only fish along Norway's coast that can survive in both salt and fresh water is the **salmon**, which grows to maturity in the sea and only swims upriver to spawn and die. In the following spring the young salmon return to the sea on the spring flood. Trout and char populate the rivers and lakes of western Norway, living on a diet of crustacea, which tints their meat pink, like the salmon. Eastern Norway and Finnmark are the domain of **whitefish**, so-called because they feed on plant remains, insects and animals, which keep their flesh white. In prehistoric times, these species migrated here from the east via what was then the freshwater Baltic; the most important of them are the perch, powan, pike and grayling.

# Cinema

For most of its short history, Norwegian cinema has been overshadowed by its Nordic neighbours and has struggled to make any sort of impact on the international scene. In the last decade or so, however, a group of talented film-makers has emerged and they have been responsible for a string of stylish, honest and refreshingly lucid films, often assisted by healthy government subsidies. For the latest news on Norwegian cinema, consult the Norwegian Film Institute website (ⓦnfi.no).

## 1950s to the mid-1980s

Early Norwegian cinematic successes were few and far between, but in 1957, *Nine Lives* (*Ni Liv*), produced and directed by the Norwegian **Arne Skouen** (1913–2003), was widely acclaimed for its tale of a betrayed Resistance fighter, who managed to drag himself across northern Norway in winter to safety in neutral Sweden. Two years later **Erik Løchen**'s *The Hunt* (*Jakten*) was much influenced by the French New Wave in its mixture of time and space, dream and reality, as was the early work of **Anja Breien** (b.1940), whose *Growing Up* (*Jostedalsrypa*) relates the story of a young girl who is the sole survivor from the Black Death in a remote fjordland village. Breien followed this up in 1975 with a successful improvised comedy *Wives* (*Hustruer*), in which three former classmates meet at a school reunion and subsequently share their life experiences. Breien developed this into a trilogy with *Wives Ten Years Later* (*Hustruer ti år etter*) in 1985 and *Wives III* in 1996. She also garnered critical success at Cannes with *Next of Kin* (*Arven*; 1979), and won prizes at the Venice Film Festival with *Witch Hunt* (*Forfølgelsen*; 1982), an exploration of the persecution of women in the Middle Ages.

## Mid-1980s to 2000

**Liv Ullmann** (b.1939) is easily the most famous Norwegian actor, but in Scandinavia she has worked chiefly with Swedish and Danish producers and directors, most famously Ingmar Bergman (with whom she also had a daughter). In 1995, Ullmann brought the popular Norwegian writer Sigrid Undset's medieval epic *Kristin Lavransdatter* to the screen in a three-hour film that attracted mixed reviews. Another Norwegian writer to have had his work made into films is Knut Hamsun (see p.298, p.398, p.423 & p.424): in the mid-1990s, the Swedish director Jan Troell filmed the superb biographical *Trial against Hamsun* (*Prosessen mot Hamsun*), while in 1993 Oslo's **Erik Gustavson** (b.1955) directed *The Telegraphist* (*Telegrafisten*), based on a Hamsun story. The success of *The Telegraphist* led to Gustavson being offered the job of bringing Jostein Gaarder's extraordinarily popular novel *Sophie's World* (*Sofies Verden*; 1999) to the screen.

**Nils Gaup**'s (b.1955) debut film *The Pathfinder* (*Veiviseren*; 1987), an epic adventure based on a medieval Sámi legend, was widely acclaimed, not least because the dialogue was in the Sámi language. Gaup followed it up with a nautical adventure, *Shipwrecked* (*Håkon Håkonsen*; 1990), and then a thriller *Head Above Water* (*Hodet over vannet*; 1993). Among other Norwegian successes in the 1990s was **Pål Sletaune**'s *Junk Mail* (*Budbringeren*; 1997), a darkly humorous tale of an Oslo postman who opens the mail himself, and **Erik Skjoldbjaerg**'s *Insomnia* (1997), a film noir set in the permanent summer daylight of northern Norway. Much praised, too, were **Berit Nesheim**'s *The Other Side of Sunday* (*Søndagsengler*; 1996), the story of a vicar's daughter desperate to escape from her father's oppressive control, and **Eva Isaksen**'s *Death at Oslo Central*

(*Døden på Oslo S*; 1990), a moving story of drug abuse and family conflict among the capital's young down-and-outs.

## 2000 to 2005

In 2001, **Knut Erik Jensen**'s surprise hit *Cool and Crazy* (*Heftig og Begeistret*) was a gentle, lyrical documentary about the male voice choir of Berlevåg (see p.369), a remote community in the far north of the country. Similarly successful was **Peter Næss**'s *Elling* (2001), a sort of tragicomedy that relates the heart-warming/-rending story of Elling, a fastidious and obsessive ex-mental patient who moves into an Oslo flat with one of the other former patients – an odd coupling if ever there was one. Equally idiosyncratic was **Bent Hamer**'s *Kitchen Stories* (*Salmer fra kjøkkenet*; 2003), a comic tale in which a tester for a Swedish kitchen-design company is dispatched to Norway to study the culinary goings-on of Isak, a farmer who lives a solitary life deep in the countryside. The two become friends, but it's a bumpy business.

Cinematic highlights of 2005 included **Sara Johnsen**'s *Kissed by Winter* (*Vinterkyss*), a harrowing tale of death, racism and murder in rural Norway, and an ambitious reworking of an Ibsen play, *An Enemy of the People* (*En folkefiende*), by **Erik Skjoldbjaerg**, in which the contamination of the medicinal baths in a small coastal town becomes a moral barometer about who wants to admit the disaster and who wants to cover it up.

## 2006 to 2010

In 2006, *The Bothersome Man* (*Den brysomme mannen*), directed by **Jens Lien**, was a hard-edged parable of a man who suddenly finds himself in an outwardly perfect, but entirely soulless world – no points for comparing this dystopia with Norway; whereas **Joachim Trier**'s *Reprise* was a playful, subtle film about love and sorrow, success and failure, creativity and friendship. The same year also saw a cracking Norwegian horror film, **Roar Uthaug**'s *Cold Prey* (*Fritt Vilt*), with Uthaug producing a second offering, *Cold Prey 2* (*Fritt Vilt II*), two years later. The year 2008 also saw several rather more interesting productions, including *Man of War* (*Max Manus*), based on the wartime exploits of the Resistance fighter Max Manus: something of an epic, it had 1800 extras and a budget that dwarfed any other previous Norwegian film. Even more intriguing perhaps was *The Kautokeino Rebellion* (*Kautokeino-opprøret*) marking a return to cinematic form by Nils Gaup and focusing on the oppression of the Sámi by a deliciously evil Norwegian priest and merchant in Kautokeino in 1852.

The high point of 2010 was certainly **André Øvredal**'s *The Troll Hunter* (*Trolljegeren*), a mockumentary in which the Norwegian government hides the existence of trolls from the population. The film "claims", for example, that the musk oxen of the Dovrefjell were imported to feed the mountain trolls – a troll larder if you will.

## 2011 to the present

The standout film of 2011 was *Headhunters*, based on a searingly brutal yarn by Jo Nesbø (see p.425) and directed by **Morten Tyldum**. In 2012, there was **Joachim Rønning**'s *Kon-Tiki*, an entertaining retelling of Thor Heyerdahl's epic trip across the Pacific by raft (see p.87), and **Nils Gaup**'s classic fairy tale *The Journey to the Christmas Star* (*Reisen til julestjernen*). In 2013, there was more Norwegian angst in **Ole Gjaever**'s *Out of Nature*, while one of the best Norwegian films of the following year was **Bent Hamer**'s *10001 Gram*, in which a woman scientist goes to a conference in Paris, only to end up (you guessed it) confronted by grief and a sense of disappointment. In 2015, a tsunami sweeps the Geirangerfjord in **Roar Uthaug**'s *The Wave* (*Bølgen*) and in 2016 **Erik Poppe** tackles King Håkon's decision of 1940 not to surrender to the Germans in *The King's Choice* (*Kongens nei*). The best Scandinavian film of these years was, however, Swedish – 2014's *Force Majeure*, a tantalizing family breakdown after a spilt-second show of cowardice.

# Books

Perhaps surprisingly, precious few travellers have written in English about the joys of journeying around Norway, though you might want to dig out a copy of a vintage *Baedeker's Norway and Sweden*, if only for the phrasebook, from which you can learn such gems as the Norwegian for "Do you want to cheat me?". Neither has Norwegian history been a major preoccupation – with the notable exception of the Vikings, who have attracted the attention of a veritable raft of historians and translators, whose works have often focused on the sagas, a rich body of work mostly written in Iceland between the twelfth and fourteenth centuries (see p.406). Scandinavian fiction is, however, an entirely different matter, with a flood of translations appearing on the market, a literary charge led by the immaculate crime novels of the Swede, Henning Mankell, with the Norwegians following in his slipstream.

Most of the books listed below are **in print and in paperback**, and those that are **out of print** should be easy to track down either in secondhand bookshops or online. Look out also for the books published by the Scandinavian specialist, Norvik Press (ⓦnorvikpress.com). Finally, while we recommend all the books we've listed below, we have marked our particular favourites with ★.

## TRAVEL AND GENERAL

**Thor Heyerdahl** *Kon-Tiki: Across the Pacific by Raft*. You may want to read this after visiting Oslo's Kon-Tiki Museum (see p.87). Heyerdahl's account of the *Kon-Tiki* expedition aroused huge interest when it was first published, and it remains a ripping yarn – though surprisingly few people care to read it today. Heyerdahl's further exploits are related in *The Ra Expeditions* and *The Tigris Expedition* as is his long research trip to Easter Island in *Aku-Aku: The Secret of Easter Island*. These last three titles are out of print, but are still easy to get hold of.

**Roland Huntford** *Scott and Amundsen: The Last Place on Earth*. There are dozens of books on the polar explorers Scott, Amundsen and Nansen, but this is one of the most lucid, describing with flair and panache the race to the South Pole between Scott and Amundsen. Also worth a read is the same author's *Nansen* (o/p), a doorstep-sized biography of the noble explorer, academic and statesman Fridtjof Nansen. Huntford (b.1927) is a polar writer of ability and renown.

**Lucy Jago** *The Northern Lights: How One Man Sacrificed Love, Happiness and Sanity to Solve the Mystery of the Aurora Borealis*. Intriguing biography of Kristian Birkeland (1867–1917), who spent years ferreting around northern Norway bent on understanding the northern lights – a quest for which he paid a heavy personal price.

★**Mark Kurlansky** *Cod: A Biography of the Fish that Changed the World*. This wonderful book tracks the life and times of the cod and the generations of fishermen who have lived off it. There are sections on overfishing and the fish's breeding habits, and recipes are provided too. Norwegians figure frequently – after all, cod was the staple diet of much of the country for centuries. Published in 1998.

**Raymond Strait** *Queen of Ice, Queen of Shadows: The Unsuspected Life of Sonja Henie* (o/p). In-depth biography of the ice-skating gold medallist, film star and conspicuous consumer Sonja Henie, whose art collection was bequeathed to the Oslo museum that bears her name (see p.90). An unpleasant woman by (almost) all accounts, whose alleged obsessions were money and sex, supposedly including affairs with Joe Louis and Tyrone Power.

**Roger Took** *Running with Reindeer*. A thoughtful account of Took's extended visit to – and explorations of – Russia's Kola peninsula in the 1990s, with much to say about the Sámi and their current predicament.

**Paul Watkins** *The Fellowship of Ghosts*. Modern-day musings as Watkins travels through the mountains and fjords of southern Norway. Easy reading, but sometimes over-written – and if that doesn't get you, the barrage of jokes probably will. There again, to be fair, there are lots of useful bits and pieces about Norway and its people.

**Mary Wollstonecraft** *Letters written during a Short Residence in Sweden, Norway and Denmark*. For reasons that have never been entirely clear, Wollstonecraft, the author of *A Vindication of the Rights of Women*, and mother of Mary Shelley, travelled Scandinavia for several months in 1795. Her letters home represent a real historical curiosity, though her trenchant comments on Norway often get sidelined by her intense melancholia.

## CULTURE AND SOCIETY

**Leo Abbott** *Norway: History, Culture and Tourism: Early History, Government, Politics, Economy, People and Lifestyle.* Interesting attempt to get to grips with the Norwegian psyche – and its many manifestations from government and folklore through to etiquette. Jerkily written, but an excellent introduction all the same.

★**Michael Booth** *The Almost Nearly Perfect People: the Truth about the Nordic Miracle.* Relaxed and light-hearted romp through Scandinavia examining exactly why the Nordics attract such international envy (Norwegian oil is an easy one) – and the truth behind the image. The answers aren't clear, but the details are intriguing: let's begin with the Swedish army ordering 50,000 hairnets in 1971 when long hair for men was the vogue.

**Neil Kent** *The Soul of the North: A Social, Architectural and Cultural History of the Nordic Countries 1700–1940* (o/p). Immaculately illustrated, erudite chronicle of Scandinavian art and architecture during its most influential periods. Published in 2001.

★**Sven Lindqvist** *Bench Press.* Delightful little book delving into the nature of weight-training – and the Swedish/Scandinavian attitude to it. Wry and perceptive cultural commentary by one of Sweden's wittiest and most impassioned cultural commentators. Published in 2003.

**Eva Maagerø and Birte Simonsen** (eds) *Norway: Society and Culture.* Published in 2008, this ambitious collection of essays attempts to summarize where Norway is sociologically and culturally – and where it has come from. Among much else, there are essays on the welfare state, religion, literature, art, music and language. Some are very good, but others are really rather pedestrian.

**Trygve Mathiesen** *Sex Pistols: Exiled to Trondheim 1977.* The curious tale of the Sex Pistols' two-day stay in Trondheim and Sid's tingles and tangles with a Norwegian. If you like it, try the same author's *Sex Pistols Exiled to Oslo 1977.*

**Åsne Seierstad** *One of Us.* Norwegians were desperately keen to know the what and whys of Anders Breivik, the right-wing fantasist who murdered 77 of his compatriots in 2011 – and this detailed book filled the gap, from Breivik's childhood onwards. It is, however, a deeply depressing read.

## HIKING AND CLIMBING

**James Baxter** *Scandinavian Mountains and Peaks over 2000 Metres in the Hurrungane* (Jotunheim). Published in 2005, this specialist text details a series of walks and climbs in the Jotunheim mountains. Detailed text with maps, but you'll still need to invest in a proper hiking map. By the same author, and published in 2012, there's also *Norway: the Outdoor Paradise – A Ski and Kayak Odyssey in Europe's Great Wilderness.* An energetic chap, this James Baxter.

**Runar Carlsen** *Climb Norway National Climbing Guide.* Comprehensive guide to sport climbing across Norway with a particular concentration of climbs in the south. Published in 2014.

**Anthony Dyer** *Walks and Scrambles in Norway.* English-language books on Norway's hiking trails are thin on the ground. This one describes over fifty hikes from one end of the country to the other, though the majority are in the western fjords (as in our Chapter 4). Lots of photographs, and the text is detailed and thoroughly researched, but the maps are only general and you'll need to buy specialist hiking ones to supplement them. Published in 2006.

**Tony Howard** *Climbs, Scrambles and Walks in Romsdal.* Originally published in 1970, but thoroughly updated and revised in 2005, this book – easily the best on its subject – explores the mighty mountains near Åndalsnes (see p.254). Tips, hints and details of three hundred climbs and walks with some maps and diagrams.

**Tony Howard** *Troll Wall.* It's 1965 and a group of climbers from the north of England are encamped at the foot of the Troll Wall near Åndalsnes (see p.254). The Wall has never been climbed before – but it is now and Howard tells the tale with vim and gusto.

**Bernhard Pollmann** *Norway – South.* This Rother Walking Guide describes fifty suggested hikes in southern Norway. The descriptions are clear and concise, the photos helpful and the maps useful for preparation. The walks themselves range from the short and easy to the long and very strenuous. New, revised edition published in 2009.

## GENERAL HISTORY

**Martin Conway** *No Man's Land.* Anecdotal and entertaining account of the history of Spitsbergen (Svalbard) from 1596 to modern times. Full of intriguing detail, such as Admiral Nelson's near-death experience (aged 14), when he set out on the ice at night to kill a polar bear. Written in 1906 and last published in 2012 by London's Forgotten Books (ⓦ forgottenbooks.com).

**Thomas Kingston Derry** *A History of Scandinavia* (o/p). This is a scholarly history of Scandinavia, a detailed and thorough account of the region from prehistoric times onwards and including Iceland and Finland. It's rather better as a reference source than as a read, however, and having been originally published in 1980, parts are out of date.

**Tony Griffiths** *Scandinavia: At War with Trolls – A Modern History from the Napoleonic Era to the Third Millennium.* Engaging title for an engaging, well-written and well-researched book covering its subject in a very manageable 320 pages. First published in 2004.

**Knut Helle et al** *The Cambridge History of Scandinavia* (o/p). Comprehensive history, from the Stone Age onwards, in three whopping (and expensive) volumes. No stone is left unturned, no rune unread. Published in 2003.

**Alan Palmer** *Bernadotte* (o/p). Biography of Napoleon's marshal, later King Karl Johan of Norway and Sweden, a fascinating if enigmatic figure whom this lively and comprehensive book presents to good effect.

**Geoffrey Parker** *The Thirty Years' War.* First published in the 1980s, this book provides the authoritative account of the pan-European war that so deeply affected Scandinavia in general and Sweden in particular. It's superbly written and researched.

**Birgit Sawyer** *Medieval Scandinavia: From Conversion to Reformation (800–1500).* Precious few books link the Viking period with what came after, but this academic text does that – and does it very well. Published by the University of Minnesota in 1993.

## WORLD WAR II

**Jack Adams** *The Doomed Expedition* (o/p). Well-researched account of the 1940 Allied campaign in Norway in all its brave but incompetent detail. Published in 1989.

**Patrick Bishop** *Target Tirpitz.* Bishop's fascination with the life, times and sinking of the *Tirpitz* off Norway in 1944 enlivens this thoroughly researched and very detailed account (at 448 pages). Inevitably, there's a plethora of military stuff here, but some historical nuggets, too – like a description of the Barnes Wallis-designed "Tallboy" bombs that did for the *Tirpitz*, painted bright green and flying like darts.

**Fredrik Dahl** *Quisling: A Study in Treachery.* A comprehensive biography of the world's most famous traitor, Vidkun Quisling, who got his just deserts at the end of World War II. Well-written and incisive exploration of Quisling's complex character – and one that also sheds a grim light on the nature and extent of Norwegian collaboration. Published by Cambridge University Press in 1999.

**Geirr Haarr** *The Battle for Norway, April to June 1940.* Thorough, lucid and thought-provoking account of the German invasion of Norway and the ensuing campaign. At 480 pages, it is perhaps a little too detailed, but the pages do skip by. Haarr is a Norwegian, who lives in Stavanger.

★**David Howarth** *Shetland Bus.* Entertaining and fascinating in equal measure, this excellent book, written by one of the British naval officers involved, details the clandestine wartime missions that shuttled between the Shetlands and occupied Norway in World War II. Howarth died in 1991; this book was first published in 1974.

**Chris Mann** *Hitler's Arctic War.* An account (2002) of the war that raged across the Arctic wastes of Norway, Finland and the USSR from 1940–45, both on sea and land.

**Kathleen Stokker** *Folklore Fights the Nazis: Humor in Occupied Norway 1940–1945.* A book that can't help but make you laugh – and one that also provides a real insight into Norwegian society and its subtle mores. The only problem is that Stokker adopts an encyclopedic approach, which means you have to plough through the poor jokes to get to the good ones. Stokker adopted a similar approach in her comparable *Remedies and Rituals: Folk Medicine in Norway and the New Land.*

## THE VIKINGS

**Johannes Brøndsted** *The Vikings* (o/p). Extremely readable account with fascinating sections on social and cultural life, art, religious beliefs and customs: see pp.410–413 for an extract from this book. Published in 1976.

**Robert Ferguson** *The Hammer and the Cross: A New History of the Vikings.* There are scores of books on the Vikings, but this is one of the best and the most recent, published in 2010. The author is a well-regarded Scandinavia expert – see also *Enigma: the Life of Knut Hamsun* (see p.423). Thoroughly researched and lucidly written.

**Paddy Griffith** *The Viking Art of War.* This detailed text examines its chosen subject in detail. Excellently researched with considered if sometimes surprising conclusions.

**John Haywood** *The Penguin Historical Atlas of the Vikings.* Accessible and attractive sequence of maps charting the Vikings' various wanderings as explorers, settlers, raiders, conquerors, traders and mercenaries. Also *The Encyclopaedia of the Viking Age,* an easy-to-use who's who and what's what of the Viking era. Published in 1996 and 2000 respectively.

★**Gwyn Jones** *A History of the Vikings.* Superbly crafted, erudite and very detailed account of the Vikings, with excellent sections on every aspect of their history and culture. First published in 2001. The same author wrote *Scandinavian Legends and Folk Tales* (see p.422).

**Philip Parker** *The Northmen's Fury: A History of the Viking World.* You wouldn't think there was much more to say about the Vikings, but in this recently published book Parker ploughs along, providing all the historical details.

**Else Roesdahl** *The Vikings.* A clearly presented, 384-page exploration of Viking history and culture, including sections on art, burial customs, class divisions, jewellery, kingship, kinship and poetry. An excellent introduction to its subject; an updated version was reprinted by Penguin in 2016.

**Peter Sawyer** (ed) *The Oxford Illustrated History of the Vikings.* First published in 2001, this book brought together what was then the latest historical research on the Vikings in a series of well-considered essays by leading experts. Includes sections on religion, shipbuilding and diet. And the illustrations are a diversionary treat, too.

## NORSE MYTHOLOGY, SAGAS AND FOLK TALES

**Peter Christen Asbjørnsen and Jørgen Moe** *Norwegian Folk Tales*. Of all the many books on Norwegian folk tales, this is the edition you want – the illustrations by Erik Werenskiold and Theodor Kittelsen are superb. A Pantheon book published in 1991, but is currently out of print.

**Nancy Marie Brown** *Song of the Vikings*. The sagas have become something of a publishing mini-industry, but Brown goes one better by examining the life and times of their key creator, the "crafty and ambitious", thirteenth-century Icelander Snorri Sturluson, the "Homer of the North". Informative, but can be heavy going.

**H.R. Ellis Davidson** *The Gods and Myths of Northern Europe*. This classic text, first published over forty years ago, gives a who's who and who did what of Norse mythology, including some useful summaries of the more obscure gods. Importantly, it displaced the classical deities and their world as the most relevant mythological framework for northern and western Europeans.

**Gwyn Jones** *Scandinavian Legends and Folk Tales* (o/p). The Oxford University Press commissioned this anthology, whose stories are drawn from every part of Scandinavia and cover many themes – from the heroic to the tragic – and are populated by a mixed crew of trolls, wolves, bears and princelings.

**Magnus Magnusson and Hermann Palsson** (translators) *The Vinland Sagas: The Norse Discovery of America*. These two sagas tell of the Vikings' settlement of Greenland and of the "discovery" of North America in the tenth century. The introduction of this particular edition,

which was first published in the 1960s, is an especially interesting and acute analysis of these two colonial outposts. There's also a newer edition in the Penguin Classics series by Leifur Ericksson (2008). See also Snorri Sturluson (see below).

**Heather O'Donoghue** *From Asgard to Valhalla: the Remarkable History of the Norse Myths*. Well, the "remarkable" in the title may well have been dreamed up by someone in PR, as what you get here is a well-researched and detailed investigation/exploration of its subject matter. The chapters are arranged by theme – "Creation and Cosmos" and "Heroes and Humans" for example.

★**Jane Smiley** *The Sagas of the Icelanders*. Easy-to-read translations of all the main sagas – galloping, rip-roaring tales from medieval Iceland. The index makes it an excellent reference book too.

**Snorri Sturluson** *Egil's Saga, Laxdaela Saga, Njal's Saga, and King Harald's Saga*. These Icelandic sagas (for more on which, see p.406) were written in the early years of the thirteenth century, but relate tales of ninth- and tenth-century derring-do. There's clan warfare in the *Laxdaela* and *Njal* sagas, more bloodthirstiness in *Egil's*, and a bit more biography in *King Harald's*, penned to celebrate one of the last and most ferocious Viking chieftains – Harald Hardrada (see p.390). Among those who have worked on translating these sagas was the former UK TV celebrity Magnus Magnusson, long a leading light in the effort to popularize them; see also the *Vinland Sagas* and *The Sagas of Icelanders* above.

## ART AND FILM

**Ketil Bjørnstad** *The Story of Edvard Munch* (o/p). Precise and detailed biography of the great artist that makes liberal use of Munch's own letters and diaries as well as contemporary newspapers and periodicals. A vivid tale indeed, just a shame that Munch isn't more likeable. Published in 2005.

**Angela Cheroux** *Edvard Munch: The Modern Eye*. Published by Tate in 2012, this scholarly work fills something of an artistic hole – and benefits from an especially lavish set of illustrations. Munch revealed in all his enigmatic/unpleasant detail.

**J.P. Hodin** *Edvard Munch* (o/p). A good general introduction to Munch's life and work, with much interesting historical detail. Beautifully illustrated, as you would expect from a Thames & Hudson publication. Reprinted in 1991.

**David Jackson** *Nordic Art: The Modern Breakthrough (1860–1920)*. Well-regarded and well-reviewed book that describes this key period in the evolution of Nordic art. Finely illustrated, but expensive; published in 2012.

**Marion Nelson** (ed) *Norwegian Folk Art: The Migration of*

*a Tradition* (o/p). Lavishly illustrated, specialist book discussing the whole range of folk art, from woodcarvings through to bedspreads and traditional dress. It's particularly strong on the influence of Norwegian folk art in the US, but the text sometimes lacks focus. It's earth-shatteringly expensive too.

**Sue Prideaux** *Edvard Munch: Behind the Scream*. Not a classic biography perhaps, but it's a thorough (520 pages) and well-researched trawl through the life of a man who fulfilled most of the stereotypes of the alienated and tormented (drunken) artist. Published by Yale University Press.

★**Tytti Soila et al** *Nordic National Cinemas* and *The Cinema of Scandinavia*. These two books are the best there is on Scandinavian cinema in general and Norwegian cinema in particular. Published in 1998, the first of the two has separate chapters on each of the Nordic countries and each chapter provides a chronological overview. The second book, published in 2005, adopts a more cinematic approach with 24 extended essays on key Scandinavian films – and an intriguing bunch they are too.

## MUSIC, DRAMA AND LITERARY CRITICISM

**Paul Binding** *With Vine-Leaves in His Hair: The Role of the Artist in Ibsen's Plays*. Academic title ideal for Ibsen lovers and students.

**Robert Ferguson** *Enigma: the Life of Knut Hamsun*. Detailed and well-considered biography of Norway's most controversial writer (see p.424). The same author also wrote *Ibsen*, an in-depth biography of the playwright.

★**Barry Forshaw** *Death in a Cold Climate: A Guide to Scandinavian Crime Fiction (o/p); Nordic Noir*. Right across Europe, Scandinavian crime writing has never been more popular and these outstanding books, published in 2012/13, summarize and analyse the nature of the genre and the reasons for its success. Includes extensive – and very apposite – quotes from the likes of Karin Fossum and Jo Nesbø.

**Einar Haugen and Camilla Cai** *Ole Bull: Norway's Romantic Musician and Cosmopolitan Patriot* (o/p). A neglected figure, Ole Bull (see p.202), the nineteenth-century virtuoso violinist and utopian socialist, deserves a better

historical fate. This biography attempts to rectify matters by delving into every facet of his life, but it's ponderously written and over-detailed. For Bull lovers only.

★**Henrik Ibsen** *Four Major Plays*. The key figure of Norwegian literature, Ibsen (see p.71) was a social dramatist with a keen eye for hypocrisy, repression and alienation. Ibsen's most popular plays – primarily *A Doll's House* and *Hedda Gabler* – pop up in all sorts of editions, but this particular collection, in the Oxford World Classics series, contains both these favourites as well as *Ghosts* and *The Master Builder*. What's more, it's inexpensive and translated by one of the leading Ibsen experts, James McFarlane. In print also are several editions of Ibsen's whole oeuvre.

**Robert Layton** *Grieg* (o/p). Clear, concise and attractively illustrated book on Norway's greatest composer. Essential reading if you want to get to grips with the man and his times. Published in 1998.

## LITERATURE

**Kjell Askildsen** *A Sudden Liberating Thought* (o/p). Short stories, in the Kafkaesque tradition, from one of Norway's most uncompromisingly modernist writers (b. 1929).

**Jens Bjørneboe** *The Sharks*. Set at the end of the last century, this is a thrilling tale of shipwreck and mutiny by a well-known Norwegian writer (1920–76), who had an enviable reputation for challenging authoritarianism of any description. Also recommended is his darker trilogy – *Moment of Freedom*, *The Powderhouse* and *The Silence* – exploring the nature of cruelty and injustice. All of these titles are, however, out of print.

**Johan Bojer** *The Emigrants* (o/p). One of the leading Norwegian novelists of his day, Bojer (1872–1959) wrote extensively about the hardships of rural life. *The Emigrants*, perhaps his most finely crafted work, deals with a group of young Norwegians who emigrate to North Dakota in the 1880s – and the difficulties they experience. In Norway, Bojer is better known for *Last of the Vikings* (o/p), a heart-rending tale of fishermen from the tiny village of Rissa in Nordland, who are forced to row out to the Lofoten winter fishery, no matter what the conditions, to keep from starving; it was first published in 1921.

**Lars Saabye Christensen** *Herman* (o/p). Christensen (b.1953) made a real literary splash with *The Half Brother*, an intense tale focused on four generations of an Oslo family in the years following World War II, with the narrator being Barnum, a midget, alcoholic screenplay-writer. It is, however, a real doorstopper of a book and before you embark on such a long read you might want to sample Christensen's *Herman* (o/p), a lighter (and much shorter) tale of adolescence with an Oslo backdrop.

**Camilla Collett** *The District Governor's Daughters*. First published in 1854, this heartfelt demand for the emotional

and intellectual emancipation of women is set within a bourgeois Norwegian milieu. The central character, Sophie, struggles against her conditioning and the expectations of those around her. An important, early feminist novel.

**Kjell Ola Dahl** *Lethal Investments*. Dahl's first novel is a fast-paced and particularly well-written tale of murder and mystery, seediness and unwholesomeness, all set in Oslo. Smart observations and clever dialogue plus an à la mode jaded detective, Inspector Frolich. There's more Frolich in *The Fourth Man*, which has the feel of a classic American noir thriller/chiller.

**Thomas Enger** *Burned*. Enger's debut novel where the protagonist – Henning Juul – returns to work as a journalist after a domestic fire which has killed his son. Vulnerable and newly sensitive to death and loss, Juul is put to work on a crime case – with unexpected results. There are more trials and tribulations for poor old Henning in the more recent *Scarred*.

★**Per Olov Enquist** *The Visit of the Royal Physician*. Wonderfully entertaining and beautifully written novel, set in the Danish court in Copenhagen at the end of the eighteenth century – a time when Denmark governed Norway.

**Knut Faldbakken** *Adam's Diary* (o/p). Three former lovers describe their relationships with the same woman – an absorbing and spirited novel by one of Norway's more talented writers, born in Hamar in 1941.

★**Karin Fossum** *Don't Look Back; Calling out for You; Black Seconds; The Caller; The Water's Edge; The Murder of Harriet Krohn*. Arguably Norway's finest crime writer, Fossum has written a string of superb thrillers in the Inspector Sejer series – and each gives the real flavour of contemporary Norway. These six novels are the best place to get started – but avoid *When the Devil Holds the Candle*, which is a bit of

## NORWEGIAN LITERATURE

It was **Jostein Gaarder**'s *Sophie's World* that brought **Norwegian literature** to a worldwide audience in the 1990s, though in fact the Norwegians have been mining a deep, if somewhat idiosyncratic, literary seam since the middle of the nineteenth century. From Ibsen onwards, the country's authors – and playwrights – have been deeply influenced by Norway's unyielding geography and stern pietism, their preoccupations often focused on anxiety and alienation. These themes also underpin many of the Norwegian **crime novels** that have proved so internationally popular in the last decade or so – with Karin Fossum and Jo Nesbø two of the big authorial names. There is a caveat: Norwegian crime has – though it may not always want to admit it – followed in the slipstream of Henning Mankell (1948–2015), a Swede who is undoubtedly Scandinavia's leading crime writer, never mind what fans of his fellow Swede, Stieg Larsson, may say.

a dud. Born in Sandefjord, on the south coast of Norway, in 1954, Fossum began her literary career with the publication of a collection of poetry, but it was the sharp brilliance of her crime writing which has made her famous, her taut and tight tales gripping and unpredictable in equal measure. Refreshingly, these are compassionate thrillers examining the motives and emotions of the murderer and the murdered, and how some individuals become outcasts.

**Jostein Gaarder** *Sophie's World*. Hugely popular novel (of 1991) that deserves all the critical praise it has garnered. Beautifully and gently written, with the puff of whimsy, it bears comparison with Hawking's *A Brief History of Time*, though the subject matter here is philosophy, and there's an engaging mystery story tucked in too. Also try Gaarder's comparable *Through A Glass Darkly* and his *The Castle in the Pyrenees*, an elaborate love story, which is – despite the title – set in Norway.

**Janet Garton** (ed) *Contemporary Norwegian Women's Writing*. Wide-ranging anthology, beginning with the directly political works of the 1970s and culminating in the more fantastical tales typical of the 2000s. Fiction, drama and poetry all make an appearance and there are lots of issues too – from prostitution and abuse through to women's empowerment. Published by Norvik Press in 2008 (ⓦ norvikpress.com).

**Knut Hamsun** *Hunger*. Norway's leading literary light in the 1920s and early 1930s, Knut Hamsun (1859–1952) was a writer of international acclaim until he disgraced himself by supporting Hitler – for which many Norwegians never forgave him. Of Hamsun's many novels, it was *Hunger* (1890) that made his name, a trip into the psyche of an alienated and angst-ridden young writer, which shocked contemporary readers. The book was to have a seminal influence on the development of the modern novel. In the latter part of his career, Hamsun advocated a return to the soil and basic rural values. He won the Nobel Prize for Literature for one of his works from this period, *Growth of the Soil* (1917), but you have to be pretty determined to plough through its metaphysical claptrap. In recent years, Hamsun has been tentatively accepted back into the Norwegian literary fold and there has been some

resurgence of interest in his works; there's also been a biographical film, *Hamsun*, starring Max von Sydow.

**William Heinesen** *The Black Cauldron*. It would be churlish to omit the Faroe-islander William Heinesen (1900–91), whose evocative novels delve into the subtleties of Faroese life – and thereby shed light on the related culture of western Norway. This particular book, arguably his best, is rigorously modernistic in approach and style – an intriguing, challenging read, with the circling forces of Faroese society set against the British occupation of the Faroes in World War II. If this whets your appetite, carry on with the same author's *The Tower at the Edge of the World*.

**Sigbjørn Holmebakk** *The Carriage Stone* (o/p). Evil and innocence, suffering and redemption, with death lurking in the background, make this a serious and powerful novel. These themes are explored through the character of Eilif Grotteland, a Lutheran priest who loses his faith and resigns his ministry. Holmebakk (1922–81), who was a leading light in the Ban the Bomb movement, wrote several other excellent novels, but no other has ever appeared in translation.

**Anne Holt** *1222*. Anne Holt is one of Norway's most popular crime writers, making her debut in 1993 with the first of a series of books that starred a female cop, Hanne Wilhelmsen. *1222* is one of Wilhelmsen's later outings.

★**Jan Kjærstad** *The Seducer*. This remarkable novel weaves and wanders, rambles and roams around the life of its protagonist, Jonas Wergeland, in a series of digressions as our hero/anti-hero sits in his flat with his murdered wife lying in an adjoining room. Mysterious and convoluted, pensive and whimsical, it's a truly extraordinary work that won the Nordic Prize for Literature in 2001.

★**Jan Kjærstad** (ed) *Leopard VI: The Norwegian Feeling for Real*. Promoted by the queen of Norway no less, this first-rate anthology of modern Norwegian writers hits all the literary buttons – from boozy nights out in Oslo to the loneliness of rural Norway and small-town envy. Contains 28 short stories plus potted biographies of all the featured writers. Published in 2005.

**Karl Ove Knausgaard** *A Death in the Family*; *A Man in Love*; *Boyhood Island*; *Dancing in the Dark*; *Some Rain Must*

*Fall*. They reckon that at least half a million Norwegians have read at least one of Knausgaard's six-volume memoir, collectively known as *Min Kamp* (*My Struggle*), some achievement considering its harrowing content and sheer length – the first volume alone weighs in at 496 pages. Every aspect of Knausgaard's life is examined in minute detail and, if you can wade through the banal, there are some exquisite sections – *A Death in the Family* (the death concerned is his father's) begins, for example, with a section on post-mortem microbes. Published in 2009–2011 to superb reviews.

**Jonas Lie** *The Seer & Other Norwegian Stories* (o/p). Part of the Norwegian literary and cultural revival of the late nineteenth century, Jonas Lie is largely forgotten today, but this collection of mystical folk tales makes for intriguing reading. It is printed alongside his first great success, the novella *The Seer*, in which a teacher is saved from insanity, born of ancient (pagan) superstitions, by the power of Christianity. Also *Weird Tales from Northern Seas: Norwegian Legends*, a collection much enjoyed by no less than Roald Dahl.

**Erlend Loe** *Doppler*. Trondheim's Loe has built up something of a cult following for his novels, which seem to get darker as the years slip by. This particular novel, from 2004, has our disenchanted protagonist wandering off to live in the woods – to consort with the elks.

★**Henning Mankell** *Faceless Killers*; *Sidetracked*; *The Troubled Man*. Cracking yarns from Scandinavia's most famous crime writer featuring Inspector Kurt Wallander, a shambolic and melancholic middle-aged police officer struggling to make sense of all the evils washed up into small-town southern Sweden. Hard to beat. A leftist of profound convictions, Mankell (1948–2015) was diagnosed with throat and lung cancer in 2014 and wrote movingly about his illness and its effects before his death.

**Jo Nesbø** *The Devil's Star*; *The Redbreast*; *The Redeemer*; *Cockroaches*; *The Bat*. No-holds-barred crime fiction in the sardonic (American) style from Norway's answer to Stieg Larsson – as Nesbø is often billed. Nesbø's star detective, Inspector Harry Hole, is on the case. Grim/scintillating reading, depending on your tastes.

**Per Petterson** *Out Stealing Horses*. Doom and gloom, guilt and isolation deep in the Norwegian woods. Hardly cheerful fare perhaps, but stirring, unsettling stuff all the same. If you like it, try Petterson's *It's Fine by Me*, a tale of troubled adolescence set in 1970s Oslo.

**Cora Sandel** *Alberta and Freedom*; *Alberta Alone*; *Alberta and Jacob*. Set in a small town in early twentieth-century Norway, the Alberta trilogy follows the attempts of a young woman to establish an independent life/identity. Characterized by sharp insights and a wealth of contemporary detail. For more on Sandel (1880–1974), who lived in Tromsø as a young woman, see p.345.

**Kjersti Scheen** *Final Curtain* (o/p). Fast-paced detective story from one of the country's more popular crime writers.

Refreshingly, the detective isn't a middle-aged man, but an Oslo-based woman.

**Amalie Skram** *Under Observation* and *Lucie*. Bergen's Amalie Skram (1846–1905) married young and went through the marital mangle before turning her experiences into several novels and a commitment to women's emancipation, including attempts to regulate prostitution. Published in 1888, *Lucie* was a coruscating attack on bourgeois morality in general, and male sexual hypocrisy in particular, with the eponymous heroine gradually ground down into submission. Inevitably, the novel created a huge furore.

**Dag Solstad** *Shyness & Dignity*. One of the big names of Norwegian literature, Solstad's (b.1941) sombre tale of a middle-aged teacher's psychological collapse is set in a dour Oslo. "What shall become of me?" he complains – yes, what indeed. Solstad's latest novel, *Professor Andersen's Night*, reprises the theme of a mid-life crisis brought on when the eponymous protagonist witnesses a murder on Christmas Eve. Isolation and alienation are given another good Norwegian airing.

**Sven Somme** *Another Man's Shoes*. In World War II, the redoubtable Sven Somme managed to escape the Germans and flee over the mountains into neutral Sweden. Sixty years later, his two daughters, now resident in England, retraced his steps as described in his memoirs – and this is the result, a combination of the original text and their comments on their own journey. The title comes from the pair of shoes left behind by Sven and (touchingly) kept by one of the families who helped him.

**Sigrid Undset** *Kristin Lavransdatter: The Cross*; *The Bridal Wreath*; *The Garland*; *The Mistress of Husaby*. Whatever else you could say about Undset (1882–1949), one of Norway's leading literary lights, she could certainly churn it out. This historical series – arguably encapsulating her best work – is set in medieval Norway and has all the excitement of a pulp thriller, along with subtle plots and deft(ish) characterizations.

**Helene Uri** *Honey Tongues*. A former doctor of linguistics at Oslo University, the prolific Uri is one of Norway's most popular contemporary writers, producing everything from novels to children's books. This particular novel exposes malevolent rivalry and manipulation between the (all-female) members of a sewing group when they go on a trip to Copenhagen.

**Herbjørg Wassmo** *Dina's Book: A Novel*. Set in rural northern Norway in the middle of the nineteenth century, this strange but engaging tale (published in 1989) has a plot centred on a powerful but tormented heroine. Dina is wilful to the point of ruthlessness: she eliminates her husband and takes a new lover, while the funeral is in progress elsewhere. Yet beneath her toughness is a deep sense of betrayal: rejected as a child by her father after she accidentally caused her mother's death, Dina has grown up expecting betrayal. Also *Dina's Son* (o/p), again with a nineteenth-century setting, but with intriguing sections focused on the protagonist's move from rural Norway to the city.

# Norwegian

There are two official Norwegian languages: *Bokmål* (book language) or *Riksmål*, a modification of the old Dano-Norwegian tongue left over from the days of Danish dominance; and *Nynorsk* (new Norwegian) or *Landsmål*, which was codified during the nineteenth-century upsurge of Norwegian nationalism and is based on rural dialects of Old Norse provenance. Roughly ninety percent of schoolchildren have *Bokmål* as their primary language, and the remaining ten percent are *Nynorsk* dialect speakers, concentrated in the fjord country of the west coast and the mountain districts of central Norway. Despite the best efforts of the government, *Nynorsk* as an official language is in decline – in 1944 fully one-third of the population used it. As the more common of the two languages, *Bokmål* is what we use here in this guide.

You don't really need to know any Norwegian to get by in Norway. Nearly everyone speaks some English, and in any case many words are not too far removed from their English equivalents; there's also plenty of English (or American) on billboards, the TV and at the cinema. Mastering "hello" or "thank you" will, however, be greatly appreciated, while if you speak either Danish or Swedish you should have few problems being understood. Incidentally, Norwegians find Danish easier to read than Swedish, but verbally it's the other way round.

   **Phrasebooks** are fairly thin on the ground, but Berlitz's *Norwegian Phrasebook with Dictionary* has – as you would expect from the title – a mini-dictionary, not to mention a useful grammar section and a menu reader; Dorling Kindersley's *Norwegian Phrasebook* is comparable. There are several **dictionaries** to choose from, all of which include pronunciation tips and so forth. The best is generally considered to be the Collins *English–Norwegian Dictionary*, though this is currently out of print so you might decide to opt for the Berlitz *Norwegian Pocket Dictionary* instead.

## Pronunciation

Pronunciation can be tricky. A **vowel** is usually long when it's the final syllable or followed by only one consonant; followed by two it's generally short. Unfamiliar ones are:

| | |
|---|---|
| **æ** before an r, as in **bad**; otherwise as in **say** | **øy** between the ø sound and **boy** |
| **ø** as in **fur** but without pronouncing the r | **ei** as in **say** |
| **å** usually as in **saw** | |

**Consonants** are pronounced as in English except:

| | |
|---|---|
| **c, q, w, z** found only in foreign words and pronounced as in the original language | **j, gj, hj, lj** as in **yet** |
| | **rs** almost always as in **shut** |
| **g** before i, **y** or ei, as in **yet**; otherwise hard | **k** before i, y or j, like the Scottish lo**ch**; otherwise hard |
| **hv** as in **view** | **sj, sk** before i, y, ø or øy, as in **shut** |

### WORDS AND PHRASES

| BASIC PHRASES | | | |
|---|---|---|---|
| **do you speak English?** | snakker du engelsk? | **no** | nei |
| **yes** | ja | **do you understand?** | forstår du? |
| | | **I don't understand** | jeg forstår ikke |

| | | | |
|---|---|---|---|
| I understand | jeg forstår | near/far | i nærheten/langt borte |
| please (is near enough, though there's no direct equivalent) | vær så god | good/bad | god/dårlig |
| | | vacant/occupied | ledig/opptatt |
| | | a little/a lot | litt/mye |
| thank you (very much) | takk (tusen takk) | more/less | mer/mindre |
| you're welcome | vær så god | can we camp here? | kan vi campe her? |
| excuse me | unnskyld | is there a youth hostel near here? | er det et vandrerhjem i nærheten? |
| good morning | god morgen | | |
| good afternoon | god dag | how do I get to …? | hvordan kommer jeg til …? |
| good night | god natt | | |
| goodbye | adjø | how far is it to …? | hvor langt er det til …? |
| today | i dag | ticket | billett |
| tomorrow | i morgen | one-way/return | en vei/tur-retur |
| day after tomorrow | i overmorgen | can you give me a lift to …? | kan jeg få sitte på til …? |
| in the morning | om morgenen | | |
| in the afternoon | om ettermiddagen | left/right | venstre/høyre |
| in the evening | om kvelden | go straight ahead | kjør rett frem |

## SOME SIGNS

## NUMBERS

| | | | |
|---|---|---|---|
| entrance | inngang | 0 | null |
| exit | utgang | 1 | en |
| gentlemen | herrer/menn | 2 | to |
| ladies | damer/kvinner | 3 | tre |
| open | åpen | 4 | fire |
| closed | stengt | 5 | fem |
| arrival | ankomst | 6 | seks |
| police | politi | 7 | sju |
| hospital | sykehus | 8 | åtte |
| cycle path | sykkelsti | 9 | ni |
| no smoking | røyking forbudt | 10 | ti |
| no camping | camping forbudt | 11 | elleve |
| no trespassing | uvedkommende forbudt | 12 | tolv |
| no entry | ingen adgang | 13 | tretten |
| pull/push | trekk/trykk | 14 | fjorten |
| departure | avgang | 15 | femten |
| parking fees | avgift | 16 | seksten |
| | | 17 | sytten |
| | | 18 | atten |

## QUESTIONS AND DIRECTIONS

| | | | |
|---|---|---|---|
| where? (where is/are?) | hvor? (hvor er?) | 19 | nitten |
| when? | når? | 20 | tjue |
| what? | hva? | 21 | tjueen |
| how much/many? | hvor mye/hvor mange? | 22 | tjueto |
| why? | hvorfor? | 30 | tretti |
| which? | hvilken/hvilket? | 40 | førti |
| what's that called in Norwegian? | hva kaller man det på norsk? | 50 | femti |
| | | 60 | seksti |
| can you direct me to …? | kan du vise meg veien til …? | 70 | sytti |
| | | 80 | åtti |
| it is/there is (is it/is there?) | det er (er det?) | 90 | nitti |
| what time is it? | hva er klokken? | 100 | hundre |
| big/small | stor/liten | 101 | hundreogen |
| cheap/expensive | billig/dyrt | 200 | to hundre |
| early/late | tidlig/sent | 1000 | tusen |
| hot/cold | varm/kald | | |

## DAYS

| | | | |
|---|---|---|---|
| **Monday** | mandag | **March** | mars |
| **Tuesday** | tirsdag | **April** | april |
| **Wednesday** | onsdag | **May** | mai |
| **Thursday** | torsdag | **June** | juni |
| **Friday** | fredag | **July** | juli |
| **Saturday** | lørdag | **August** | august |
| **Sunday** | søndag | **September** | september |
| | | **October** | oktober |
| | | **November** | november |

## MONTHS

| | | | |
|---|---|---|---|
| **January** | januar | **December** | desember |
| **February** | februar | | |

(Note: days and months are never capitalized)

## MENU READER

### BASICS AND SNACKS

| | |
|---|---|
| **brød** | bread |
| **eddik** | vinegar |
| **egg** | egg |
| **eggerøre** | scrambled eggs |
| **flatbrød** | crispbread |
| **fløte** | cream |
| **grønsaker** | vegetables |
| **grøt** | porridge |
| **iskrem** | ice cream |
| **kaffefløte** | single cream for coffee |
| **kake** | cake |
| **kaviar** | caviar |
| **kjeks** | biscuits |
| **krem** | whipped cream |
| **marmelade** | marmalade |
| **melk** | milk |
| **nøtter** | nuts |
| **olje** | oil |
| **omelett** | omelette |
| **ost** | cheese |
| **pannekake** | pancakes |
| **pepper** | pepper |
| **pommes-frites** | chips (French fries) |
| **potetchips** | crisps (potato chips) |
| **ris** | rice |
| **rundstykker** | bread roll |
| **salat** | salad |
| **salt** | salt |
| **sennep** | mustard |
| **smør** | butter |
| **smørbrød** | open sandwich |
| **sukker** | sugar |
| **suppe** | soup |
| **syltetøy** | jam |
| **varm pølse** | hot dog |
| **yoghurt** | yoghurt |

### MEAT (KJØTT) AND GAME (VILT)

| | |
|---|---|
| **dyrestek** | venison |
| **elg** | elk |
| **kalkun** | turkey |
| **kjøttboller** | meatballs |
| **kjøttkaker** | rissoles |
| **kylling** | chicken |
| **lammekjøtt** | lamb |
| **lever** | liver |
| **oksekjøtt** | beef |
| **pølser** | sausages |
| **postei** | pâté |
| **reinsdyr** | reindeer |
| **ribbe** | pork rib |
| **skinke** | ham |
| **spekemat** | dried meat |
| **stek** | steak |
| **svinekjøtt** | pork |
| **varm pølse** | frankfurter/hot dog |

### FISH (FISK) AND SHELLFISH (SKALLDYR)

| | |
|---|---|
| **ål** | eel |
| **ansjos** | anchovies (brisling) |
| **blåskjell** | mussels |
| **brisling** | sprats |
| **hummer** | lobster |
| **hvitting** | whiting |
| **kaviar** | caviar |
| **klippfisk** | salted whitefish, usually cod |
| **krabbe** | crab |
| **kreps** | crayfish |
| **laks** | salmon |
| **makrell** | mackerel |
| **ørret** | trout |
| **piggvar** | turbot |
| **reker** | shrimps |
| **rødspette** | plaice |
| **røkelaks** | smoked salmon |
| **sardiner** | sardines (brisling) |
| **sei** | coalfish |
| **sild** | herring |
| **sjøtunge** | sole |

| | |
|---|---|
| småfisk | whitebait |
| steinbit | catfish |
| torsk | cod |
| tunfisk | tuna |

## VEGETABLES (GRØNSAKER)

| | |
|---|---|
| agurk | cucumber/gherkin/pickle |
| blomkål | cauliflower |
| bønner | beans |
| erter | peas |
| gulrøtter | carrots |
| hodesalat | lettuce |
| hvitløk | garlic |
| kål | cabbage |
| linser | lentils |
| løk | onion |
| mais | sweetcorn |
| nepe | turnip |
| paprika | peppers |
| poteter | potatoes |
| rosenkål | Brussels sprouts |
| selleri | celery |
| sopp | mushrooms |
| spinat | spinach |
| tomater | tomatoes |

## FRUIT (FRUKT)

| | |
|---|---|
| ananas | pineapple |
| appelsin | orange |
| aprikos | apricot |
| banan | banana |
| blåbær | blueberries |
| druer | grapes |
| eple | apple |
| fersken | peach |
| fruktsalat | fruit salad |
| grapefrukt | grapefruit |
| jordbær | strawberries |
| multer | cloudberries |
| pærer | pears |
| plommer | plums |

| | |
|---|---|
| sitron | lemon |
| solbær | blackcurrants |
| tyttbær | cranberries |

## COOKING TERMS

| | |
|---|---|
| blodig | rare, underdone |
| godt stekt | well done |
| grillet | grilled |
| grytestekt | braised |
| kokt | boiled |
| marinert | marinated |
| ovnstekt | baked/roasted |
| røkt | smoked |
| saltet | cured |
| stekt | fried |
| stuet | stewed |
| sur | sour, pickled |
| syltet | pickled |

## DRINKS

| | |
|---|---|
| akevitt | aquavit (strong spirit) |
| appelsin | orange juice |
| brus | fizzy soft drink |
| eplesider | cider |
| fruktsaft | sweetened fruit juice |
| kaffe | coffee |
| melk | milk |
| mineralvann | mineral water |
| øl | beer |
| saft/juice | juice |
| sitronbrus | lemonade |
| te med melk/sitron | tea with milk/lemon |
| vann | water |
| varm sjokolade | hot chocolate |
| vin | wine |
| søt | sweet |
| tørr | dry |
| rød | red |
| hvit | white |
| rosé | rosé |
| skål | cheers |

## GLOSSARY OF NORWEGIAN TERMS

**allting** parliament or public gathering

**apotek** chemist

**bakke** hill

**bokhandel** bookshop

**bre** glacier

**bro/bru** bridge

**brygge** quay or wharf

**dal** valley/dale

**DNT (Den Norske Turistforening)** nationwide hiking organization whose local affiliates maintain hiking paths across almost the entire country

**Domkirke** cathedral

**drosje** taxi

**E.kr** AD

**elv/bekk** river/stream

**ferje/ferge** ferry

**fjell/berg** mountain

**F.kr** BC

**Flybussen** airport bus (literally "plane bus")

**foss** waterfall

**gågate** urban pedestrianized area

**gate (gt.)** street

**Gamlebyen** literally "Old Town"; used wherever the old part of town has remained distinct from the rest (eg Fredrikstad). Also spelt as Gamle byen.

**hav** ocean

**havn** harbour

**Hurtigbåt** passenger express boat; usually a catamaran

**Hurtigruten** literally "quick route", but familiar as the name of the boat service along the west coast from Bergen to Kirkenes

**hytte** cottage, cabin

**innsjø** lake

**jernbanestasjon** train station

**Kfum/kfuk** Norwegian YMCA/YWCA

**kirke/kjerke** church

**klippfisk** salted whitefish, usually cod

**klokken/kl.** o'clock

**moderasjon** discount or price reduction

**Moms or mva** sales tax – applied to almost all consumables

## NORWEGIAN SPECIALITIES

**brun saus** gravy served with most meats, rissoles, fishcakes and sausages.

**fenalår** marinated mutton that is smoked, sliced, salted, dried and served with crispbread, scrambled egg and beer.

**fiskeboller** fish balls, served under a white sauce or on open sandwiches.

**fiskekabaret** shrimps, fish and vegetables in aspic.

**fiskesuppe** fish soup.

**flatbrød** a flat unleavened cracker, half barley, half wheat.

**gammelost** a hard, strong-smelling, yellow-brown cheese with veins.

**geitost/gjetost** goat's cheese, slightly sweet and fudge-coloured. Similar cheeses have different ratios of goat's milk to cow's milk.

**gravetlaks** salmon marinated in salt, sugar, dill and brandy.

**juleskinke** marinated boiled ham, served at Christmas.

**kjøttkaker med** home-made burgers with surkål cabbage and a sweet and sour sauce.

**koldtbord** a midday buffet with cold meats, herrings, salads, bread and perhaps soup, eggs or hot meats.

**lapskaus** pork, venison (or other meats) and vegetable stew, common in the south and east, using salted or fresh meat, or leftovers, in a thick brown gravy.

**lutefisk** fish (usually cod) preserved in an alkali solution and seasoned. It's an acquired taste (see box, p.39).

**multer** cloudberries – wild berries mostly found north of the Arctic Circle and served with cream (*med krem*).

**mysost** brown whey cheese, made from cow's milk.

**nedlagtsild** marinated herring.

**pinnekjøtt** western Norwegian Christmas dish of smoked mutton steamed over shredded birch bark, served with cabbage; or accompanied by boiled potatoes and mashed swedes (*kålrabistappe*).

**reinsdyrstek** reindeer steak, usually served with boiled potatoes and cranberry sauce.

**rekesalat** shrimp salad in mayonnaise.

**ribbe, julepølse** eastern Norwegian Christmas dish of pork ribs, sausage and dumplings.

**spekemat** various types of smoked, dried meat.

### BREAD, CAKE AND DESSERTS

**bløtkake** cream cake with fruit.

**fløtelapper** pancakes made with cream, served with sugar and jam.

**havrekjeks** oatmeal biscuits, eaten with goat's cheese.

**knekkebrød** crispbread.

**kransekake** cake made from almonds, sugar and eggs, served at celebrations.

**lomper** potato scones-cum-tortillas.

**riskrem** rice pudding with whipped cream and sugar, usually served with *frukt saus*, a slightly thickened fruit sauce.

**tilslørtbondepiker** stewed apples and breadcrumbs, served with cream.

**Trondhjemsuppea** kind of milk broth with raisins, rice, cinnamon and sugar.

**trollkrem** beaten egg whites (or whipped cream) and sugar mixed with cloudberries (or cranberries).

**vafle** waffles.

**museet** museum

**NAF** nationwide Norwegian automobile association; membership covers rescue and repair

**øy/øya** islet

**rabatt** discount or price reduction

**rådhus** town hall

**rorbu** originally a simple wooden cabin built near the fishing grounds for incoming (ie non-local) fishermen. Many cabins are now used as tourist accommodation, especially in the Lofoten (see box, p.317).

**Sámi** formerly called Lapps, the Sámi inhabit the northern reaches of Norway, Finland and Sweden – aka Lapland

**sentrum** city or town centre

**sjø** sea

**sjøhus** harbourside building where the catch was sorted, salted, filleted and iced. Many are now redundant and some have been turned into tourist accommodation (see box, p.317).

**skog** forest

**slott** castle, palace

**Stavkirke** stave church

**Storting** parliament

**tilbud** special offer

**torget** main town square, often home to an outdoor market; sometimes spelt torvet

**Vandrerhjem** youth hostel

**vann/vatn** water or lake

**vei/veg/vn.** road

## GLOSSARY OF NORWEGIAN MOTORING TERMINOLOGY

**avgiftsvei** toll-road

**bensinstasjon** petrol station

**bilutleie firma** car rental agency

**blyfri bensin** unleaded petrol

**bomstasjon** toll

**innkjorsel** entrance

**motorolje** motor oil

**motorvei** highway

**omkjonng** detour

**parkering** parking

**politi** police

**politistasjon** police station

**sykehus** hospital

**utkjorsel** exit

## GLOSSARY OF ENGLISH ART AND ARCHITECTURAL TERMS

**Ambulatory** Covered passage around the outer edge of the choir in the chancel of a church.

**Art Deco** Geometrical style of art and architecture popular in the 1930s.

**Art Nouveau** Style of art, architecture and design based on highly stylized vegetal forms. Particularly popular in the early part of the twentieth century.

**Baroque** The art and architecture of the Counter-Reformation, dating from around 1600 onwards, and distinguished by extreme ornateness, exuberance and the complex but harmonious spatial arrangement of interiors.

**Classical** Architectural style incorporating Greek and Roman elements – pillars, domes, colonnades, etc – at its height in the seventeenth century and revived, as Neoclassical, in the nineteenth century.

**Diptych** Carved or painted work on two panels. Often used as an altarpiece.

**Fresco** Wall painting – made durable through applying paint to wet plaster.

**Gothic** Architectural style of the thirteenth to sixteenth centuries, characterized by pointed arches, rib vaulting, flying buttresses and a general emphasis on verticality.

**Misericord** Ledge on a choir stall on which the occupant can be supported while standing; often carved with secular subjects (bottoms were not thought worthy of religious ones).

**Nave** Main body of a church.

**Neoclassical** Architectural style derived from Greek and Roman elements – pillars, domes, colonnades, etc – that was popular in Norway throughout the nineteenth century.

**Renaissance** Movement in art and architecture developed in fifteenth-century Italy.

**Rococo** Highly florid, light and graceful eighteenth-century style of architecture, painting and interior design, forming the last phase of Baroque.

**Rood screen** Decorative screen separating the nave from the chancel.

**Romanesque** Early medieval architecture distinguished by squat forms, rounded arches and naive sculpture.

**Stucco** Marble-based plaster used to embellish ceilings, etc.

**Transept** Arms of a cross-shaped church, placed at ninety degrees to nave and chancel.

**Triptych** Carved or painted work on three panels. Often used as an altarpiece.

**Vault** An arched ceiling or roof.

# Small print and index

## A ROUGH GUIDE TO ROUGH GUIDES

Published in 1982, the first Rough Guide – to Greece – was a student scheme that became a publishing phenomenon. Mark Ellingham, a recent graduate in English from Bristol University, had been travelling in Greece the previous summer and couldn't find the right guidebook. With a small group of friends he wrote his own guide, combining a contemporary, journalistic style with a thoroughly practical approach to travellers' needs.

The immediate success of the book spawned a series that rapidly covered dozens of destinations. And, in addition to impecunious backpackers, Rough Guides soon acquired a much broader readership that relished the guides' wit and inquisitiveness as much as their enthusiastic, critical approach and value-for-money ethos. These days, Rough Guides include recommendations from budget to luxury and cover more than 120 destinations around the globe, from Amsterdam to Zanzibar, all regularly updated by our team of roaming writers.

Browse all our latest guides, read inspirational features and book your trip at **roughguides.com**.

## Rough Guide credits

**Editor**: Olivia Rawes
**Layout**: Nikhil Agarwal
**Cartography**: Richard Marchi, Ed Wright
**Picture editor**: Phoebe Lowndes
**Proofreader**: Diane Margolis
**Managing editor**: Keith Drew
**Assistant editor**: Divya Grace Mathew

**Production**: Jimmy Lao
**Cover photo research**: Sarah Stewart-Richardson
**Photographer**: Roger Norum
**Editorial assistant**: Aimee White
**Senior DTP coordinator**: Dan May
**Programme manager**: Gareth Lowe
**Publishing director**: Georgina Dee

## Publishing information

This seventh edition published March 2017 by
**Rough Guides Ltd**,
80 Strand, London WC2R 0RL
11, Community Centre, Panchsheel Park,
New Delhi 110017, India
**Distributed by Penguin Random House**
Penguin Books Ltd, 80 Strand, London WC2R 0RL
Penguin Group (USA), 345 Hudson Street, NY 10014, USA
Penguin Group (Australia), 250 Camberwell Road,
Camberwell, Victoria 3124, Australia
Penguin Group (NZ), 67 Apollo Drive, Mairangi Bay,
Auckland 1310, New Zealand
Penguin Group (South Africa), Block D, Rosebank Office
Park, 181 Jan Smuts Avenue, Parktown North, Gauteng,
South Africa 2193
Rough Guides is represented in Canada by DK Canada, 320
Front Street West, Suite 1400, Toronto, Ontario M5V 3B6
Printed in Singapore
© Phil Lee, 2017
Maps © Rough Guides

448pp includes index
A catalogue record for this book is available from the
British Library
ISBN: 978-0-24124-318-3
The publishers and authors have done their best to
ensure the accuracy and currency of all the information in
**The Rough Guide to Norway**, however, they can accept
no responsibility for any loss, injury, or inconvenience
sustained by any traveller as a result of information or
advice contained in the guide.
1 3 5 7 9 8 6 4 2

## Help us update

We've gone to a lot of effort to ensure that the seventh
edition of **The Rough Guide to Norway** is accurate
and up-to-date. However, things change – places get
"discovered", opening hours are notoriously fickle,
restaurants and rooms raise prices or lower standards.
If you feel we've got it wrong or left something out,
we'd like to know, and if you can remember the
address, the price, the hours, the phone number, so much
the better.

Please send your comments with the subject line
**"Rough Guide Norway Update"** to mail@uk.roughguides
.com. We'll credit all contributions and send a copy of the
next edition (or any other Rough Guide if you prefer) for
the very best emails.

## ABOUT THE AUTHOR

**Phil Lee** A one-time deckhand in the Danish merchant navy, Phil Lee has been writing for Rough Guides for well over twenty years. His other books in the series include Amsterdam, Norfolk & Suffolk, Mallorca & Menorca and Belgium & Luxembourg. He lives in Nottingham, where he was born and raised.

## Acknowledgements

**Phil Lee** would like to thank his editor, Olivia Rawes, for all her hard work and attention to detail in the preparation of this new edition of *The Rough Guide to Norway*. Special thanks also to Juliette Berry for all her tips and hints; Dave Robson for his excellent contributions; Annett Brohmann of Visit Oslo; Linn Kjos Falkenberg of Visit Bergen; Helen Siverstøl of Fjord Norway; Nils Henrik Geitle of De Historiske – historic hotels and restaurants; Lisbeth Fallan of Visit Trondheim; Nicole Richards and Stuart Buss of Norwegian Airlines; Anne Line Kaxrud of Innovation Norway; and Johanne Meyer of NSB railways.

## Readers' updates

Thanks to all the readers who have taken the time to write in with comments and suggestions (and apologies if we've inadvertently omitted or misspelt anyone's name):

Tommy Andreasen; Richard Ault; Katy Ball; Simon Barton; Tim Baxter; Gavin Bell; Natalie Birk; Solga Bogdan; Angela Bohlke; Dr Lisa Bradley-Klemko; Ross Brown; Yuraisha Chavan; Noel Cooper; Stephen Dodd; Andrew Eccles; Monika Filasiewicz; Simon Frayers; Per Goller; Colin Hamilton; Tony Howard; Sarah Huesmann; Trine Grønn Iversen; Lindsay Jack; Sam Joffe; Alan Kraus; Anthony Lunn; Niall and Jenny Martin; Raymond Maxwell; Greg Minshall; Bob Morris; Birgit Myrie; Gijsbert Ooms; David Paul; Daniel Payne; Siri Pedersen; Per Persson; Bill Pike; Michael Plunkett; Ian Robins; Viv Robins; Peter Rollason; Stacey Ross; Peter Roth; Bogdan Solga; Joyce Space; Anthony Stern; Marianne Supphellen; Alan Tait; Alan and Sally Thornber; Ingrid Tønneberg; Yanni Vikan

## Photo credits

All photos © Rough Guides, except the following:
(Key: t-top; c-centre; b-bottom; l-left; r-right)

**1 Alamy Stock Photo:** Radius Images
**2 Alamy Stock Photo:** Rowan Romeyn
**4 Dreamstime.com:** Noracarol
**5 www.visitnorway.com:** Casper Tybjerg
**9 Corbis:** Jon Hicks (t). **www.visitnorway.com:** Christopher Hagelund (c, b)
**10 www.visitnorway.com:** CH
**11 Corbis:** Douglas Pearson
**12 Corbis:** Robert Harding World Imagery/Jochen Schlenker
**13 www.visitnorway.com:** Terje Borud (t); Pal Bugge (c); Johan Wildhagen (b)
**14 www.visitnorway.com:** Nordic life/Terje Rakke
**15 Corbis:** Tim Davis (c); Jose Fuste Raga (tr). **www.visitnorway.com:** Frithjof Fure (b)
**16 www.visitnorway.com:** Sónia Arrepia Photography (b); Nancy Bundt (tl); Per Eide (tr)
**17 Flåm Railway:** www.rakke.no/Morten Rakke (b). **www.visitnorway.com:** Terje Borud (t)
**18 Dreamstime.com:** Nikolai Sorokin (c). **Getty Images:** Jens Kuhfs (tr). **www.visitnorway.com:** Anders Gjengedal (b)
**19 Alamy Stock Photo:** imageBROKER (bl). **www.visitnorway.com:** Andrea Giubelli (tr); Jens Henrik (tl)
**20 Juvet Landscape Hotel:** Jan Olav (t). **www.visitnorway.com:** Bård Løken (br)
**21 Munch museum:** (tl). **www.visitnorway.com:** CH (b); Anders Gjengedal (c); Johan Wildhagen (tr)
**24 www.visitnorway.com:** Kurt Hamann
**57 Corbis:** Reuters/Scanpix Norway
**97 Alamy Stock Photo:** Kim Kaminski (br). **Tom Sivesinde** (tr)
**115 Alamy Images:** Robert Harding Picture Library/ Amanda Hall
**131 Corbis:** Christian Kober (b)
**144–145 Corbis:** Marco Cristofori
**147 Heidal Rafting:** Outdoor Photo (t)
**167 www.visitnorway.com:** Morten Helgesen
**184–185 Getty Images:** Age Fotostock RM
**187 www.visitnorway.com:** Per Eide
**199 Alamy Stock Photo:** Luis Dafos (br). **www.visitnorway.com:** CH (t)
**219 Corbis:** Douglas Pearson (t). **Getty Images:** ullstein bild (b)
**249 Corbis:** Arctic-Images
**264–265 www.visitnorway.com:** Sonia Arrepia Photography
**267 Alamy Images:** Egil Korsnes
**277 Alamy Stock Photo:** parkerphotography (t). **www.visitnorway.com:** CH (bl)
**297 Getty Images:** Johner (t). **www.visitnorway.com:** Avani (b)
**313 www.visitnorway.com:** CH (t); Nordic life/Terje Rakke (b)
**323 www.visitnorway.com:** CH
**349 www.visitnorway.com:** CH (c); Johan Wildhagen (t). **Dreamstime.com:** Jirka13 (b)
**359 www.visitnorway.com:** Nordic Life/Terje Rakke (t, bl)
**382 Corbis:** Werner Forman

**Front cover, spine and back:** *Rorbuer in the Lofoten Islands* **4Corners:** Luigi Vaccarella

# Index

Maps are marked in grey

# W

# Map symbols

The symbols below are used on maps throughout the book

 International boundary

County boundary

Chapter division boundary

Road

Pedestrianized road

Tunnel

Unpaved road/track

Footpath

Steps

Railway

Railway tunnel

Castle/fortress wall

Cable car

Ferry route

Bridge

Airport

Bus stop/taxi stand

T-Bane

Parking

Post office

Tourist office/information

Hospital

Place of interest

Statue

Lighthouse

Country house

Viewpoint

Waterfall

Mountain range

Mountain peak

Mountain lodge/hut

Church (regional map)

Ski resort/ski centre

Building

Market

Church (town map)

Stadium

Park/gardens

Beach

Cemetery

Glacier

## Listings key

Accommodation

Eating

Drinking and nightlife

Shopping

# A ROUGH GUIDE TO
# ROUGH GUIDES

Published in 1982, the first Rough Guide – to Greece – was a student scheme that became a publishing phenomenon. Mark Ellingham, a recent graduate in English from Bristol University, had been travelling in Greece the previous summer and couldn't find the right guidebook. With a small group of friends he wrote his own guide, combining a highly contemporary, journalistic style with a thoroughly practical approach to travellers' needs.

The immediate success of the book spawned a series that rapidly covered dozens of destinations. And, in addition to impecunious backpackers, Rough Guides soon acquired a much broader readership that relished the guides' wit and inquisitiveness as much as their enthusiastic, critical approach and value-for-money ethos.

These days, Rough Guides include recommendations from budget to luxury and cover more than 120 destinations around the globe. Visit Ⓦ roughguides .com for travel tips and inspiring features, to buy our latest ebooks and plan your next trip.